HISTORY OF
LATIN AMERICAN CIVILIZATION

sources and interpretations

HISTORY OF
LATIN AMERICAN
CIVILIZATION

edited by LEWIS HANKE

Methuen & Co Ltd

sources and interpretations

volume two
The Modern Age

11 New Fetter Lane
London EC4

First published in the USA by Little, Brown and
Company (Inc.)
© 1967 by Little, Brown and Company (Inc.)

First published in Great Britain 1969
by Methuen & Co Ltd
11 New Fetter Lane London EC4

Printed in Great Britain by
Redwood Press Limited, Trowbridge, Wiltshire

SBN 416 12330 9

Preface

The contents of this volume and of the companion work on the colonial period published earlier this year have been drawn from the rich store of material that has appeared in widely scattered publications. But as the historian comes closer to contemporary Latin America, his difficulties in discovering fundamental sources and sound interpretations become more severe; moreover, the modern age of Latin American history raises some questions not encountered in the first volume. The colonial period is fairly easy to define. But when did Latin America begin to be "modern"? The historian finds it convenient to divide up the past into fairly neat chronological packages but he well knows that history flows tumultuously onward, tossing aside or swirling around the man-made barriers set up to contain it. The independence movements erupting about 1810 have long been recognized as a watershed between the colonial period and the modern. But in certain respects there was no sharp break with the past for, despite the clash of arms and the many pronunciamentos, many economic activities and administrative arrangements persisted which reflected important continuities during the dynamic hundred years from about 1750 to the mid-nineteenth century.

But the revolutionary epoch 1810 to 1830 deserves to be marked off and should not be downgraded, writes Charles C. Griffin, for the political break from the mother countries made possible choices that would not have been open had Latin America remained a bloc of colonial dependencies. Yet independence was not an isolated wave of events, artificially breaking the period; it was, rather, a manifestation of forces of "earlier origin opening the way for the continuing evolution of the following generation."[1]

[1] Personal communication from Professor Griffin. For a report on the discussion at the 1966 meeting of the American Historical Association on "New Approaches to Latin American Periodization: The Case for an Eighteenth-Century Watershed," see *The Hispanic American Historical Review*, XLVII (1967), pp. 318–319.

The later years of the nineteenth century also present problems of periodization. Gilberto Freyre has maintained that the majority of Brazilians in the 1850's were living in the middle ages, and he considered that even the elite were eighteenth century in habits and outlook.[2] One of the great advantages of the historian of Brazil today is that he can still observe different layers of civilization, representing profoundly different ways of thought and action, merely by considering one part of that vast country or another.

The variety of peoples in Latin America also helps to explain why it is difficult to fit its modern history into clear-cut periods. Even the history of such a country as Argentina, with its relatively homogeneous population, does not lend itself to confident generalization. How could Argentina be defined, after a century of independence?

Was it the educated, progressive elite who administered the nation, as their patrimony, from the floor of congress or the stock exchange or over an after-dinner brandy at the Jockey Club, the Club del Progreso, or the Círculo de Armas? Or was it the burgeoning middle class so evident as grocers, clerks, office managers, and foremen in the coastal cities? Or was it the Indian working in the cane fields of Tucumán or the quebracho forests of the Chaco, the Italian sharecropper in his hovel on the pampas, the Irish sheepherder in Patagonia, or the native peon in the province of Buenos Aires? Or was it the rapidly expanding urban proletariat in the ports — the mestizo cook from Santiago del Estero, the Basque laborer in the slaughter house or packing plant, the porter from Galicia, or the Italian peddler? Little wonder was it that, after a century of independence, Argentines were still searching for identity and that the nation presented simultaneously all shades of prosperity and poverty, progress and reaction, learning and illiteracy.[3]

Emphases change in the interpretation of past events, often as the result of contemporary pressures and developments. Orlando Fals Borda, the Colombian scholar who has done so much to lay bare the reasons for the continuing violence in his country, now looks back on Colombian history as a tale of repeated frustration and subversion.[4] The veteran Peruvian historian Jorge Basadre, who has completed a many-tomed work on nineteenth-century Peru, con-

[2] Gilberto Freyre, "Social Life in Brazil in the Middle of the Nineteenth Century," *The Hispanic American Historical Review*, V (1922), p. 599.

[3] James R. Scobie, *Argentina: A City and a Nation* (New York: Oxford University Press, 1964), p. 135.

[4] Orlando Fals Borda, "El cambio social en la historia. Dinámica de la subversión en Colombia" (Unpublished ms., 1966).

siders this period "a history of lost opportunities."[5] A "generation gap" also exists. Some half century ago Percy Alvin Martin scarcely mentioned economic changes in explaining the causes for the collapse of the Brazilian Empire in 1889;[6] today probably the majority of Brazilianists give special emphasis to the economic factors.

Whatever may be the particular orientation of a historian analyzing modern Latin America, most historians agree that colonial ideas and institutions still powerfully influence the present and are sure to affect the future. At times this influence has been almost overwhelming, as under the dictatorship of Porfirio Díaz in Mexico:

> The Díaz dictatorship presents an extraordinarily close analogy to the colonial regime. Except for the superficial differences that time brings, little really essential had changed since the viceroys. Mexico continued a quasi-feudal state, which, beneath the exotic hum of twentieth-century industrialism, maintained a sixteenth-century social structure and a corresponding psychology.[7]

The face of Mexico has radically altered since the Revolution of 1910. Yet throughout Latin America the mass of people remain in a precarious position. Gunnar Mendoza, in one of the most challenging interpretations in this volume, looks upon the history of Latin America since 1492 as one characterized principally by social injustice.[8] A North American sociologist has described the situation in a different but equally devastating way: "In Brazil, Haiti, and the eighteen Spanish American countries taken as a whole at least one half of the agriculturalists are dependent upon methods of extracting a living from the soil that are more primitive, less efficient, and more wasteful of human energy than those the Egyptians were using at the dawn of history."[9]

This sweeping judgment may be too dogmatic. Yet one experienced Venezuelan writer has stated: "characteristic of Venezuela, as of almost all the Latin American countries in the nineteenth century, is the tragic contrast between the social reality and the false

---

[5] Jorge Basadre, *Meditaciones sobre el destino histórico del Perú* (Lima: Ediciones Huascarán, 1947), p. 130.

[6] Percy Alvin Martin, "Causes of the Collapse of the Brazilian Empire," *The Hispanic American Historical Review*, IV (1921), pp. 4–48.

[7] Ernest Gruening, *Mexico and Its Heritage* (New York: The Century Co., 1928), p. 64.

[8] See pp. 516–523.

[9] T. Lynn Smith, ed., *Agrarian Reform in Latin America* (New York: Knopf, 1965), p. 40.

coating of laws, customs, and institutions imported or translated from Europe, by which our backwardness and neglect are hidden rather than remedied."[10] Thus this volume of readings offers no bland or comforting view of the past.

Students of modern Latin American history labor under some special difficulties because the records they need do not exist, or are likely to be poorly organized. Even more distressing is the prohibitory attitude to be found in many countries. One scholar has remarked that "'history is too important to be left to historians' appears to be the motto of diplomats and officials of foreign offices who jealously guard the fundamental records."[11] Some of the deficiencies of documentation may be partially overcome by intelligent use of questionnaires and personal consultations, methods that were successfully employed by the Scottish historian William Robertson in the eighteenth century while he was preparing his classic work on the Spanish conquest of America.[12] But much will remain unknown because of the inaccessibility of many sources, which constitutes a major handicap. Some progress may be seen, however. A younger generation of historians is growing which will help to overcome these obstacles. For example, two of the selections in this volume are taken from recently completed doctoral dissertations.

Though we have much to learn about modern Latin America, the importance of the years since 1810 is obvious and historians are determined to make it better known. Some of them look to the colonial experience to help illuminate both the modern period and the contemporary scene: "It is only if one perceives what this [Latin] America conserves of its colonial nature that one can understand the kinship of its problems with those of the underdeveloped nations of the world."[13]

History and historians have therefore become a part of the great

---

[10] Mariano Picón Salas, in *Venezuela independiente, 1810–1960* (Caracas: Fundación Eugenio Mendoza, 1962), p. 12.

[11] Bryce Wood, *The United States and Latin American Wars, 1932–1945* (New York: Columbia University Press, 1966), p. 394.

[12] On Robertson's methods, see R. A. Humphreys' "William Robertson and His History of America," as reprinted in Volume I of *History of Latin American Civilization: Sources and Interpretations* (Boston: Little, Brown and Company, 1967), p. 530.

[13] Marcel Bataillon, "The Pizarrist Rebellion. The Birth of Latin America," *Diogenes* (Montreal, 1963), no. 43, p. 62. For a valuable discussion on this topic, see the remarks by Woodrow Borah, Charles Gibson, and Robert A. Potash, "Colonial Institutions and Contemporary Latin America," *The Hispanic American Historical Review*, XLIII (1963), pp. 371–394.

debate on the future of Latin America, which is struggling to enter the society of developed nations. The tone sometimes becomes bitter, the range of topics is large: "What is under debate is the whole heritage of the archaic society — the economic, political, and intellectual heritage — as well as the archaic society itself — its structure, its values, its prospects."[14] One inescapable element in the discussion is the doubt expressed inside and outside Latin America on the actions of the United States in this struggle as the forces representing tradition and revolt confront each other south of the Rio Grande.

Citizens of the United States need to know about this debate, and the purpose of these "Sources and Interpretations" is to help them to understand it by providing a selection of significant material on Latin American civilization.

Acknowledgments

Though I take full responsibility for the planning and execution of this volume, I have received much help from colleagues and students. Helen Delpar provided excellent editorial assistance throughout the preparation of this work, and gave valuable advice on historical matters as well. Others who contributed with their insights and experience were Germán Carrera Damas, Robert Conrad, Tom Davis, Ricardo Donoso, Georgette M. Dorn, Ceferino Garzón Maceda, Charles C. Griffin, Michael M. Hall, Kate Gilbert Hanke, Fritz L. Hoffmann, Clifton R. Kroeber, Robert Levine, Joseph E. Love, Gunnar Mendoza, Magnus Mörner, Fredrick B. Pike, Frank Safford, Peter H. Smith, Fredrick C. Turner, Donald F. Wisdom.

For a memorable discussion in New York City last December, I am indebted to Dauril Alden, C. Richard Arena, Marvin Bernstein, David Bushnell, Richard Graham, Charles A. Hale, Hugh M. Hamill, Jr., John Te Paske, Rollie Poppino, and Ronald C. Turner.

I owe a special debt to David W. Lynch of the Little, Brown editorial staff who supervised the manuscript through the press with unusual despatch and competence.

To all who helped to prepare this volume I offer my grateful thanks.

Lewis Hanke

[14] Luiz Aguiar Costa Pinto, as quoted in Charles Wagley, ed., *Social Science Research on Latin America* (New York: Columbia University Press, 1964), p. 244.

Table of Contents

Section I

What Kind of Revolution Occurred
in Latin America
Between 1810 and 1830?

The Liberator Simón Bolívar and other military figures have until recently dominated the story of how the new world dominions of Portugal and Spain won their independence. Historians in and outside of Latin America have emphasized most often the political, biographical, and diplomatic aspects of the struggle, and have paid relatively scant attention to cultural, economic, and social developments. And since Bolívar himself proclaimed on his deathbed that he "had ploughed the sea," later writers have sometimes concluded that no basic changes in the fabric of society took place.

New approaches, fortunately, are now being made.[1] Charles C. Griffin, of Vassar College, surveys the present state of knowledge on "the profound shock" which the revolutionary wars caused in the social and economic life of the colonies, and describes the "accelerated tempo of evolutionary transformation" which took place (Reading I.1).

To document these changes, a copious literature is available in travel accounts and official reports by representatives of Great Britain and the United States (Reading I.2). Latin America aroused enormous interest, particularly among British merchants and manu-

[1] For an informed view of past and recent literature, see R. A. Humphreys, "The Historiography of the Spanish American Revolutions," *Hispanic American Historical Review*, XXXVI (1956), pp. 81–93.

facturers who hoped to win great profits through joint stock companies (mines, gas, railways, insurance, docks, and canals). Cornish miners were to bring new techniques; another project aimed at joining the Pacific and the Atlantic by a ship canal. There was capital enough to organize a company for almost any project:

> There were companies and plans to navigate the rivers of South America by steamboats, to fish for pearls in Colombia, to establish the "unemployed poor" of Great Britain and Ireland as agricultural colonists in the United Provinces of the Río de la Plata. There were companies to promote emigration to Chile and Colombia. There was a company which proposed to export milkmaids to Buenos Aires in order to make butter.[2]

Cultural changes were involved too, particularly attempts to prepare the citizens of the new nations for the life of independence. The history of education in Latin America has long been neglected, but enough is known to establish that some of the revolutionary leaders understood the need to improve and enlarge the school system, as David Bushnell of the University of Florida explains (Reading I.3). Another basic but little-studied topic is race relations, which Magnus Mörner of Queens College has investigated (Reading I.4).

What fundamental changes in society resulted from all the bloodshed and turmoil of the revolutionary period? We do not know precisely, for detailed studies based on the scattered and sometimes inaccessible source materials are still lacking. R. A. Humphreys of the University of London provides an educated guess (Reading I.6), and Professor Griffin gives some further refinements and reflections (Reading I.7).

Brazil, as in most other matters, was different from Spanish America. It preserved its monarchy and achieved its independence from Portugal by peaceful means, which the late Clarence H. Haring of Harvard University described (Reading I.8). Brazilian and Portuguese historians still dispute the nature of Dom João's rule, 1808–1821. Was the monarchy a positive force that saved national unity and set Brazil on a peaceful road to independence, or was it a neocolonial instrument of repressive centralism and elitist control, an alien regime that isolated the country from the revolutionary destinies of the New World?[3] Though much more study

---

[2] R. A. Humphreys, *Liberation in South America, 1806–1827: The Career of James Paroissien* (London: The Athlone Press, 1952), p. 140.

[3] Arnold Clayton, "Interpretations of the Rule of Dom João VI in Brazil, 1808–1821" (Master's Thesis, Columbia University, 1967), p. 75.

will be needed to bring the economic and social developments into clearer view, no one questions that the period leading to the declaration of independence in September, 1822, was indeed a decisive one in the history of Brazil.

A. General

1. Only the Beginnings of a Basic Transformation Took Place

CHARLES C. GRIFFIN

The revolutions which brought about the establishment of independent governments in America differed in marked degree from the classic revolutions of modern Europe — the French and the Russian — in that their primary effect was to throw off the authority of a transatlantic empire rather than to bring about a drastic reconstruction of society. In the case of the United States, however, it has long been recognized that the revolutionary struggle did not confine itself to the political sphere, i.e., to independence and the establishment of a new federal government. Almost a generation ago the late J. Franklin Jameson published his essays on *The American Revolution Considered as a Social Movement* in which he suggested relations between the revolution and the manifold changes of the era, some already recognized, and others destined to be more fully charted by a subsequent generation of scholars. Because many of these changes were not the result of conscious revolutionary planning, but came about under the stimulus of new conditions created during and after the revolution, they had not earlier been sufficiently closely related to the revolution and to each other.

It is possible that the time may be ripe for a similar shift in em-

From "Economic and Social Aspects of the Era of Spanish-American Independence" by Charles C. Griffin, *Hispanic American Historical Review*, XXIX, 1949, pp. 170–187, *passim*. Reprinted by permission.

phasis in the interpretation of the revolutions for independence in Spanish America. It was natural that these movements, as starting points for new national traditions, should have been regarded at first as epic conflicts. Heroism and leadership were the main themes. When this was not enough, diplomatic and constitutional history were emphasized, in consonance with the popularity of such studies in nineteenth-century European historiography. Interest in political change led eventually to the study of political theories in relation to the revolutions and hence to the broader field of the history of thought. On the one hand, the background of the revolutions has been clarified by studies of the impact of the Enlightenment on Latin America; on the other, changes closely related to the triumph of new ideologies have been charted. Of these, the new status of church-state relations and the abolition of slavery can be mentioned as examples. Until fairly recently, however, the study of economic and social history has been directed primarily to the antecedents of the revolutions rather than to the developments of the era itself. . . .

The presentation of a general view, however exploratory, is complicated by regional diversity in the character and course of the independence movement in its various centers. Differences in geography, in population, in tradition, as well as in the duration and intensity of military operations must be considered, together with variations in the extent of contact with Europe and the United States. These differentiating factors modified certain general tendencies: the destructive force of war, and the stimulation produced by free intercourse with foreign countries.

The immediate economic consequence of revolution, except in a few favored areas, was disaster. The prosperity of the later colonial economy of Spanish America was shattered by warfare which was everywhere waged with little regard for the rights of private property and the lives of non-combatants. It is only possible to suggest here the terrible destruction suffered by many regions. This reached its maximum in Venezuela, where both the human and the livestock population declined, the latter by more than one-half between 1810 and 1830. Almost as severe were the losses in the Banda Oriental and in certain parts of the Viceroyalty of New Spain. New Granada and Chile represent areas which were less continuously theatres of military action, and with a consequently lighter incidence of destruction. The extreme horrors of the *guerra a muerte* in Venezuela and the slaughter in Mexico during the early stages of revolution were not often matched in scale elsewhere, but, even where loss of life was less severe, interruption of normal economic life was serious. People were uprooted from their homes in various ways. Men were recruited, often by force, for the rival armies. Even when they escaped death they frequently never returned, taking up life again elsewhere. There were also many examples of emigration on a substantial scale. These dislocations of population had unfavorable results for agriculture and mining, removing the necessary labor force, and on business in general owing to the flight of capital along with its owners.

The interruption of normal lines of trade and communication also had serious adverse effects. Northwest Argentina suffered from the halting of trade with Peru. Montevideo, while in hands hostile to Buenos Aires, lost part of its commercial function. Guerrilla warfare in New Spain at times disrupted internal communications except by armed convoys. Wartime financial exactions, ranging from confiscation to forced loans, appropriation of goods for the use of the rival armies, forced acceptance of depreciated currency, and high and arbitrary taxation brought ruin to many. Cattle-raising countries like the Banda Oriental and the Venezuelan hinterland suffered from wholesale robbery and expropriation of the livestock on which the economy of these regions was based. Mining regions were paralyzed by flooding of the workings and destruction of equipment.

It is impossible to measure exactly the total effect of these varied consequences of war, but it is probably safe to say that from 1810 to 1820 Buenos Aires and Peru, the strongholds of the rival forces in South America, were least affected. Regions like Paraguay and, to a lesser extent, Central America suffered from isolation but were little damaged. Chile, New Granada, and Mexico underwent severe destruction at times, but were not equally affected throughout the decade. On the other hand, Venezuela and Uruguay saw no real peace during the period and their normal economic activities were totally upset.

In the second decade of revolution theatres of military operations shifted. Warfare on a large scale was over in Mexico by 1821, and in Colombia after 1822. Fighting in Chile ceased, except for guerrilla warfare in the far south. On the other hand, Peru, which had previously escaped, became the center of the fighting. Though devastation here was not so widespread nor long continued as in some other areas, the burden of supporting large armies (patriot and royalist) in the field for several years was a heavy one. The duration of military activity in what is now Ecuador was briefer, but this region gave a good deal of support to the later Peruvian campaigns. For the war as a whole, therefore, only the province of Buenos Aires and its immediate neighbors to the north and west were able to escape the direct scourge of war. Even here there were intermittent skirmishes between patriot factions especially after the year 1820.

The upheaval caused by war was not limited to destruction of life and property and the disorganization of business; it also brought changes in society which were not envisaged by the creole aristocrats and intellectuals who headed the revolts of the *cabildos* in 1809 and 1810. Except in Mexico, the revolutions had begun with efforts to dislodge the peninsular bureaucracy without otherwise changing relations among classes, but war unleashed forces that these early revolutionists were unable to harness. Race and class antagonisms flared up which could only be brought under control by the exaltation of nationalism and a parallel minimizing of class distinctions. Without any general upset in these relations, there was a blurring of lines. None of the new independent governments recognized legal disabilities for *pardos* or *mestizos*. In Mexico, the clergy no longer kept the elaborate records of caste as a part of their parochial registers.

The "career open to talents" seems to have been the rule. A mestizo general might rise to the presidency of his country; a *mulato* colonel might become a large landowner. This does not mean that an equalitarian society grew out of the wars, but it does indicate that the wars brought new blood into the ruling class and simplified the social distinctions in lower strata of the population.

The annals of revolution in Mexico and Colombia are well sprinkled with the names of prominent military officers with Indian or Negro blood in their veins, or both. Piar and Padilla in Colombia were conspicuous examples. In Mexico, Guerrero and Morelos reached even higher renown. In the lower ranks officers with similar racial antecedents were numerous. In Peru and Bolivia mestizos also held high military rank. Santa Cruz, who became president of the latter republic, was the son of an Indian woman and a Spaniard. In the naval service of Colombia a number of mulatos held commissions. The large percentage of color in the ranks of Bolívar's officers was frequently commented on by the race-conscious European officers who served in Colombia.

The tendency toward greater racial tolerance was not unchecked. White creole fear accounts in part for the severe treatment meted out to such officers as Piar and Padilla. Their insubordination might well have been condoned if it had not been for their race. If there had not been great gains for the mixed bloods, such severity as that which led to the execution of both, in spite of the brilliant military services they had rendered to the cause of independence, might not have been considered necessary.

In Río de la Plata and in Chile there do not seem to have been instances of high military commanders of recognized mixed blood. We can cite, however, the cases of politicians and journalists like Vicente Kanki Pazos (an Indian from upper Peru) and the meteoric career of Bernardo Monteagudo (a mulato from Tucumán). The strength of the creole element in the population in the Viceroyalty of Buenos Aires, except in the north, and the fact that it was not heavily depleted by the wars may be one explanation for the less conspicuous place of the mestizo in military leadership. The relatively stable agrarian economy of Chile with its strong personal ties between landowner and *inquilino* provided fewer opportunities for social change than the more elaborately stratified population of Peru, Colombia, and Mexico. In these southern regions, however, the revolution brought increasing fluidity among economic groups. "Self-made men," among them many foreigners, began to make themselves increasingly evident, beginning the process which was to ease their way into the upper social ranks of *estancieros* and merchants. This tendency was stimulated by the procedure followed by many governments in paying off officers and men with land confiscated from royalists or from the public domain. Land had been for so long a badge of social position that it proved impossible to discriminate for more than a generation against the owner of a large estate.

Another series of important social and economic changes grew out of the increasing contact with foreign lands during the course of the wars of independence. In this respect local differences are also notable. Buenos Aires, without question, developed a new economy based on foreign trade earlier than any other Spanish-American country. The accumulated demand for free trade during the later years of the viceroyalty had paved the way and the absence of Spanish power to interfere, after 1810, gave the development free rein. This ushered in the cattle boom which was to fix the character of the Argentine economy for generations. It led to expansion on the Indian frontier and to the rapid growth of the city of Buenos Aires, as population flowed in to serve the needs of an expanded commerce. Small shops and factories on a handicraft basis multiplied and the accumulation of wealth created new luxury trades. On the other hand, as Burgin has shown, free trade brought depression to

Cuyo and to the northern provinces from Tucumán to Jujuy, which lost much of their market for home manufactures to foreign competition.

In Chile, with interruptions due to the wars, similar changes can be seen. Free trade meant a larger market for the grain and other food surpluses which before the revolution had been shipped almost exclusively to Peru. Valparaíso became a port of call for ships bound to the Orient and for the northwest coast of America. The export of Chilean silver and copper increased under the pressure of need to balance imported manufactures. By 1825 a number of English mining experts were planning developments in the Coquimbo region. Chilean naval activity stimulated the work of shipyards and attracted both businessmen and laborers to the port city, which soon lost its sleepy colonial aspect. Free trade, however, had a less violently stimulating effect on the economy of Chile than in Río de la Plata. The immediately available resources of Chile were less vast, and depended, for expanded exploitation, on growth of population and on a long-range development of mining equipment and transportation which could not be carried through at once.

The ports of Peru and Colombia were opened to world trade at a later time and these republics were less favorably situated than those of the far south from a commercial point of view. Trade did not develop here on a healthy basis. . . .

In Mexico free trade did not actually begin until 1823. Until that time, all but a trickle of irregular trade had continued to follow traditional colonial channels to Spain and Cuba. When commerce with Spain was suspended, great difficulty arose owing to the disappearance of Spanish commercial capital at Veracruz. It was to take time to build up a new system of credit depending on agents of European manufacturers established at Mexico City. In spite of English interest in Mexican mining, production of the precious metals, which accounted for most of Mexico's surplus, did not wholly recover in the period before 1830.

The foregoing would appear to indicate some correlation between commercial progress and a lesser degree of severity in military operations in the different regions mentioned. This factor, however, cannot have been decisive. The extent to which free trade brought economic revolution also depended on the existence of resources in demand in the world markets and on adequate transportation facilities for bringing these to the seaports. Obviously, Buenos Aires, with its easily traversed *pampa*, and Chile, with production located never very far from the sea, had a great advantage over Peru, Colombia, and Mexico. . . .

The rate and extent of trade expansion varied considerably from region to region, but the direction of change was the same. All the new republics headed toward a broader production of resources demanded by the world market and became increasingly intimately linked with the expanding economy of the nineteenth century, centered on and directed by Great Britain. This trade expansion brought other economic developments in its wake. Taxation shifted from the complex system of colonial days, with its multiple excises, monopoly franchises, and sales taxes, toward reliance on the customs duties on imports as the all-important source of revenue. Consumption of imported goods tended to outrun the ability of exports to balance them, leading to the negotiation of foreign loans on highly disadvantageous terms. Buenos Aires, Chile, Peru, Mexico, and Colombia all experienced the beginnings of their troubles with foreign creditors during this epoch. The too rapid expansion of imports may have been one cause of the financial crises which contributed to widespread political instability after the establishment of independence.

Along with the economic liberalism, of which the removal of trade barriers was concrete evidence, there developed a broader liberalism which also influenced society. The story of the abolition of slavery has often been told and need not be repeated here. It should be remembered, however, that outright abolition in some countries and gradual emancipation in others had reduced slavery to insignificant proportions in republican Spanish America before 1830. This was, of course, preceded by the manumission of slaves on a considerable scale in the course of the revolutionary wars. Freedmen formed part of San Martín's liberating forces that fought at Chacabuco and of the army of Sucre that completed the liberation of Peru at Ayacucho.

The Indian fared less well in this era. In spite of frequent references to their ancient woes in propaganda directed against the Spanish regime, the achievement of independence meant little to the native race. Though frequently involved in revolutionary fighting, Indians never wholeheartedly sided with either party in the struggle. In southern Chile they were active as royalist guerrillas. In Mexico they fought and bled with Hidalgo. In Peru and Colombia they fought on both sides, either because they were forced to do so, or because they followed some leader who had a personal reason for taking sides. The lapse of colonial protective legislation exposed them to exploitation under the increasingly individualistic republican legal codes and the war of independence ruined many of the missions which had preserved their existence, even if they did not succeed in fitting them for the competitive society they now had to face.

Perhaps the most marked social change of the era was the growth of the rift between the society of the seaports and capitals, on the one hand, and rural and provincial society, on the other. At the seats of government and in the ports upper and middle classes began to be affected by the streams of foreigners (diplomats, visiting scholars, pedagogues, merchants, soldiers, and sailors) which began to appear on the scene. Fashions began to ape the styles of London and Paris; new sports and pastimes replaced colonial recreations; even habits of food and drink changed. Provincial cities were but little affected by these newfangled notions and the countryside was largely unconscious of them. Thus, the wider, European outlook of the elite in almost every country began to show itself in minor ways long before it was enshrined in law, educational institutions, and in the arts.

The hypothesis suggested by the foregoing remarks may be summarized as follows: the revolutionary wars which led to independence were a profound shock to the society and to the economic life of the Spanish colonies. Wartime destruction left many countries less able to maintain traditional ways and opened the way for new developments. Ensuing changes were brought about, first of all, by the expansion of foreign trade, which, in turn, had repercussions on the whole economic and social structure. Nevertheless, only the beginnings of a basic transformation took place and there were many ways in which colonial attitudes and institutions carried over into the life of republican Spanish America. Liberal ideas, however, used at first to buttress the rising power of landowners and businessmen, weakened paternalistic aspects of colonialism.

The Río de la Plata region was most deeply changed by the revolution. Throughout the continent, too, the greater cities and the ports were more affected by the new than were the provinces and the countryside. There emerged, therefore, no single clearly identifiable pattern of change, and developments noted were not so much revolutionary as they were examples of an accelerated tempo of evolutionary transformation.

B. Contemporary Descriptions of Conditions

2. Reports by British and United States Officials

a. CAESAR A. RODNEY on Argentina (1818)

The effects of the revolution are visible in the changes produced in the state of society. The difference in the freedom of acting and thinking which preceded the revolution must necessarily be great. The freedom of commerce must have given a spring to exertions of native enterprise and intelligence; while the active scenes of war and politics, for the last ten years, have awakened the genius of the country which had so long slumbered. The generation now on the stage may almost be said to have been reared under a new order of things. The common stock of ideas among the people has been greatly augmented, the natural consequence of the important political events which daily transpire, and in which every man, like the citizen of Athens, feels an interest. The newspapers are everywhere circulated, together with the manifestoes of the Government, which is obliged to court the approbation of public opinion on all measures of moment. It is not very unusual for the same countryman, who, a few years ago, never troubled himself about any thing beyond the narrow circle of his domestic concerns, to purchase a newspaper on coming to town, as a matter of course, and, if unable to read, to request the first one he meets to do him that favor. The country curates are, moreover, enjoined to read the newspapers and manifestoes regularly to their flocks. The spirit of improvement may be seen in every thing. Even some of those who are under the influence of strong prejudices against the revolution frequently remark the changes for better which have taken place. Their habits, manners, dress, and mode of living, have been improved by intercourse with strangers, and the

From *Diplomatic Correspondence of the United States Concerning the Independence of the Latin-American Nations*, William R. Manning, ed. (New York: Oxford University Press, 1925), I, pp. 510–513. Reprinted by permission of the Carnegie Endowment for International Peace.

free introduction of foreign customs, particularly English, American, and French. Great prejudices prevail against whatever is Spanish. It is even offensive to them to be called by this name; they prefer to be identified with the aborigines of the country. The appellation which they have assumed, and in which they take a pride, is that of South Americans.

A powerful stimulus must necessarily have been given to their industry by two important circumstances — the diminution in prices of foreign merchandise, and the great increase in value of the products of the country, with the consequent rise of property. Though the grounds in the neighborhood of cities are highly improved, as I have already stated, agriculture, comparatively speaking, is in a low condition. In general, the lands are badly tilled; the plough is rarely used, and the substitute is a very different one. But, notwithstanding the disadvantages of the present method of culture, I was informed by reputable persons that the average crop of wheat is not less than fifty bushels per acre in good seasons.

On the subject of religion, especially, the change in the public mind has been very great. The Catholic faith is established as that of the state; but there are many advocates, both in conversation and in writing, of universal toleration. Some members of Congress are said to be strongly in favor of it; but the ignorant and superstitious part of the people, together with the regular clergy, would not be satisfied with such a measure, while the liberality prevailing among the better informed classes is such as to secure a virtual toleration for the present. Besides, from the circumstances of there being no sects in the country, such a provision may wait the progress of liberality in public opinion. In fact, the human mind has been set free on all matters of a general abstract nature, although the liberty of the press is circumscribed, in some degree, with respect to strictures on public measures and men, and the established religion; but there is neither inquisition nor previous license. They acknowledge the Pope as a spiritual head merely, and do not think him entitled to any authority to interfere in their temporal concerns. His bull in favor of the King of Spain against the colonists, which may be almost regarded as an excommunication, produced little or no sensation.

The number of monks and nuns never was very great in Buenos Ayres, when compared with other portions of the Spanish dominions. They have diminished since the revolution. There was at one time a positive law passed forbidding anyone to become a monk or a nun; but they were obliged to repeal it, and it was afterwards passed with some modifications. The restrictions substituted, aided by public opinion, have nearly produced the desired effect. Few of the youth of the country apply themselves to the study of theology, since other occupations much more tempting to their ambition have been opened to their choice. Formerly, the priesthood was the chief aim of young men of the best families who were desirous of distinction, as, in fact, it constituted almost the only profession to which those who had received a liberal education could devote themselves; which will readily account for the circumstance of so many of the secular clergy directing their attention at present almost exclusively to politics. The regular clergy, who are not permitted by the nature of their profession to take part in the business of the world, or to hold secular offices, are many of them Europeans; but those of them who are natives take the same lively interest in passing events with the other classes of the community.

They have gone cautiously to work in reforms in the different branches of their municipal laws and the administration of them. The number of offices has been considerably diminished, and responsibility rendered more direct and severe. The judiciary system has undergone many improvements, and nearly all the leading features of the law which did not harmonize with the principles of free government have been expunged, though some of the former evils still remain. The barbarous impositions on the aborigines have been abolished; the odious alcavala and other obnoxious taxes modified so as no longer to be vexatious; slavery and the slave trade forbidden in future; and all titles of nobility prohibited under the pain of the loss of citizenship. The law of primogeniture is also expunged from their system. In the provisional statute, as has already been stated, nearly all the principles of free representative government are recognised, accompanied, it is true, with certain drawbacks, for which they plead the necessity of the times, but which they profess their intention to do away with on the final settlement of the Government — a consummation anxiously desired by all classes of inhabitants. The example of France has warned them not to attempt too much at first. They have followed the plan of the United States in the introduction of gradual reforms, instead of resorting to violent and sudden innovations and revolutions.

Next to the establishment of their independence by arms, the education of their youth appears to be the subject of the most anxious interest. They complain that every possible impediment was thrown in the way of education previous to the revolution; that, so far from fostering public institutions for this purpose, several schools were actually prohibited in the capital, and the young men were not without restraint permitted to go abroad for their education. There was a college at Cordova, at which those destined for the bar or the priesthood completed their studies upon the ancient monkish principles. Another, called San Carlos (now the Union of the South), had been opened at Buenos Ayres, but was afterwards converted into barracks for soldiers. It is an immense building, more extensive, perhaps, than any which has been dedicated to learning in this country, and it has lately been fitted up at very great expense. The school was to have been opened in May or June last on a more modern and liberal plan of discipline and instruction. The library of the state is kept in an adjoining building; it occupies a suite of six rooms, and contains nearly twenty thousand volumes, the greater part rare and valuable. It is formed out of the library of the Jesuits, the books collected in the different monasteries, donations from individuals, and an annual appropriation by the Government, and contains works on all subjects and in all the languages of the polished nations of Europe. A very valuable addition has been lately made of several thousand volumes, brought to Buenos Ayres by M. Bonpland, the companion of the celebrated Humboldt.

Besides the University of Cordova, at which there are about one hundred and fifty students, there are public schools in all the principal towns, supported by their respective corporations. In Buenos Ayres, besides an academy, in which are taught the higher branches, and the college before mentioned, there are eight public schools, for whose support the corporation contributes about seven thousand dollars annually; and, according to the returns of last year, the number of scholars amounted to eight hundred and sixty-four. There are five other schools, exclusively for the benefit of the poor, and under the charge of the different monasteries; these are supplied with books and stationery at the public expense. There are also parish schools in the country, for the support of which a portion of the tithes has been lately set apart. It is rare to meet with a boy ten or twelve years of age, in the city of Buenos Ayres, who cannot read and write. Besides the scholars thus instructed, many have private tutors. In addition to all this, I must not omit to mention the military academies, supported by the Government, at Buenos Ayres and Tucumán, at which there are a considerable number of cadets.

There are no prohibited books of any kind; all are permitted to circulate freely, or to be openly sold in the bookstores; among them is the New Testament in Spanish. This alone is a prodigious step towards the emancipation of their minds from prejudices. There are several bookstores, whose profits have rapidly increased; a proof that the number of readers has augmented in the same proportion. There had been a large importation of English books, a language becoming daily more familiar to them. Eight years ago the mechanic art of printing was scarcely known in Buenos Ayres; at present, there are three printing offices, one of them very extensive, containing four presses. The price of printing is, notwithstanding, at least three times higher than in the United States; but as there is no trade or intercourse with Spain, all school books used in the country, some of them original, are published at Buenos Ayres; the business is therefore profitable, and rapidly extending. There are many political essays, which, instead of being inserted in the newspapers, are published in loose sheets; there are also original pamphlets, as well as republications of foreign works. The constitutions of the United States and of the different States together with a very good history of our country, and many of our most important state papers, are widely circulated. The work of Dean Funes, the venerable historian of the country, comprised in three large octavo volumes, considering the infancy of the typographic art in this part of the world, may be regarded as an undertaking of some magnitude.

There are three weekly journals, or newspapers, published in the city, which have an extensive circulation through the United Provinces. They all advocate the principles of liberty and republican forms of government, as none other would suit the public taste. The year before last, it is true, one of the papers ventured to advocate the restoration of the Incas of Peru, with a limited monarchy; but it was badly received. No proposition for the restoration of hereditary power, of any kind, as far as I could learn, will be seriously listened to for a moment by the people. Even the ordinary language has changed. They speak of "the state," "the people," "the public," "country," and use other terms, as in the United States, implying the interest that each man takes in what appertains to the community. The first principle constantly inculcated is, "that all power rightfully emanates from the people." This, and similar dogmas, form a part of the education of children, taught at the same time with their catechism. It is natural that the passion for free government should be continually increasing.

b. CHARLES MILNER RICKETTS *on Peru* (1826)

It is just here to observe, considering the late cry which has been raised against the mother country, that during the period adverted to, Peru was not only in a flourishing state both in respect to her mines and to her commerce, but also as referable to the capitals possessed by individuals, to the comparative extent of her manufactures, and to her navigation. Between the years 1790 and 1800 there existed in Lima a *commercial* capital of above 15 millions of dollars; whereas in the present year it is under one million, and of this the greater part is unavailable. In 1800 were manufactured to the extent of 187,500 dollars of tocuyos (coarse cotton cloths) at 1½ reals the vara; 150,000 of coarse woolens at 4 reals; and 137,500 of fine woolens at 5½ reals; in preparing the last of which articles 500 to 600 serons of Guatemala indigo were consumed. The sugar estates in the vicinity of Lima yielded 200,000 arrobas, of which 120 to 125,000 were exported to Chile at the price of 18 to 20 reals the arroba, 180 to 200,000 fanegas of wheat being received in return, which were sold to the bakers at 16 to 20 reals the fanega of 135 pounds. The merchants possessed 42 vessels, 12 of which were from 400 to 800 tons burthen; and it is asserted as a well known fact that good faith was so prevalent that although large sales were effected on credit, no instance of failure occurred during 30 years, nor even any kind of dispute between buyer and seller.

Unfortunately this favorable picture can no longer be drawn, as the horrors which have attended the struggle for independence have so obscured the horizon that a glimmering only is seen of the bright prospect which may await Peru. At present on whatever point it may be viewed the scene is dismal, and the appearance such as if the country had just suffered from one of those dreadful earthquakes which lay all in ruin and devastation. The lands are waste, edifices to be rebuilt, the population diminished, the government unstable, just laws to be established, new capitals to be raised, and tranquility to be secured. The ground plan of improvement is not yet traced,

From *British Consular Reports on the Trade and Politics of Latin America, 1824–1826*, R. A. Humphreys, ed. (London: Royal Historical Society, 1940), pp. 114–158, *passim*. Reprinted by permission.

and I lament to add that in the train of evils pressed on the country, Great Britain is exposed to become a sharer.

The several difficulties which oppose the commercial prosperity of South America, as so frequently brought to your notice in the reports from the several States, exist in an equal if not in a stronger degree in Peru. A want of population necessarily causes an excessive scarcity and dearness of labor; the disposition of the people is feeble and inert; they are most ignorant; and the comforts and even the decencies of life are generally unknown. The independence of Mexico was followed by the liberal and judicious polity of retaining the Spanish capitalists in the country, and many therefore remained; whereas in Peru they were all persecuted, and ultimately banished, and the consequence has been that the capital which existed has disappeared with its possessors, the European Spaniards. The narrow views of the revolutionary governments have opposed the fundamental principle of its boasted freedom of trade. In their desire to obtain resources they conceived that the readiest mode of acquiring them was by the imposition of heavy duties; old prejudices prevented their believing that the income of a state will be progressively augmented by leaving merchants to derive the advantages which they expect from low profits on extensive dealings; and contemplating the mines as yielding an inexhaustible supply of wealth, they saw not that the results of a liberal commercial system would prove the only sure means of securing an increase of trade, industry, capital, and population. Prohibitions and absurd enactments met the fair trader at every step; he was obliged to abandon his speculations unless he became a party to the contraband system which others pursued; and he found that he could resort to it with impunity, as in case of detection a bribe ensured connivance.

At the breaking out of the revolution the success of the first British traders was very great; the goods imported were all in demand, and there was a pressure for remitting the wealth which had been accumulated by those who sought to leave the country; the gold and silver money and ornaments were taken from the places of their concealment; the British captain was astonished at the riches he received; and the most exaggerated notions were entertained of the wealth of the country. . . .

The leaders of the Spanish and revolutionary armies were also alert in stripping the capitalists; confiscations were made on frivolous pretexts; and churches were robbed of their ornaments to pay the expenses of the troops. The riches of Peru thus gradually disappeared; part has been drawn to Spain, part has been received by England, and the remainder has been dispersed by payments to the naval armaments and to the troops of Buenos Aires, Chile, and Colombia, which assembled to aid Peru in the cause of liberty.

The late disastrous wars have further diminished the already scanty population; and mining, which displayed some advancement to industry, and formed the productive wealth of the country, has been checked in its operations . . . by the want of capital, by the destruction of machinery, and by the enlistment of the miners in the army. The ruin of many rich families, the emigration of others, and the long suffering of the people from the late continual wars, have occasioned so much poverty and such extensive desolation to the country, that commerce was only likely to thrive by the creation and prudent application of new capital. Hence the obvious course for the British merchants to have adopted was to supply the market by degrees; but instead of this, the spirit of speculation and the exaggerated accounts of the wealth of Peru, induced the consignment of numerous ships hither with cargoes far exceeding the wants of the people and their ability to pay for them. The consequence is that the British commodities generally have been reduced in price, and that many will not yield their prime cost. . . .

The returns from Peru for cargoes imported from Europe, the United States, India, and China, may be said to be limited to the precious metals, since the few other productions are in such inconsiderable quantities as to form no object at present to foreign interests. A cargo or two of bark, value about 148,000 dollars; cotton 97,000; vicuña wool 28,750; sheep's wool 43,750; and hides 50,000; add to these an estimated increase of bark and cotton, 132,500, will give an estimated total of 500,000 dollars. The exports of the precious metals to Europe have, as already stated, been very considerable since the breaking out of the revolution, but the amount forms no criterion of the future returns for foreign imports. In my despatch No. 19, I have explained my reasons for considering that for the next three or four years the annual produce of the mines will not exceed four millions of dollars, and that no more than two millions or £400,000 sterling should be estimated as a remittance from Peru to England, in payment of British imports and of the interest on the loans; but I have shewn also that Peru and Bolivia abound in metallic riches, and that under prudent management, British capital, skill, and industry, cannot fail to bring the mines into active operation. . . .

It is desirable here to consider also what products Peru yields for exportation to Chile and Guayaquil, in return for articles of consumption for which she is dependent on them, so that a notion may be formed whether or not the natural productions of her soil balance those which she draws from these States. Sugar, cotton, salt, Pisco brandies, and rice, constitute the articles supplied by Peru; and she receives cacao, hemp, leather, and wood from Guayaquil, and chiefly wheat, wood, and some tallow and dried fruits from Chile. In 1789 when the trade was flourishing under the Spaniards, the exports to Guayaquil amounted to 128,295 dollars, and the imports thence to 284,460, so that the balance against Lima was 156,164. The amount of the exports to Chile was 458,317 dollars, and of the imports 629,800, leaving a balance in favor of Chile of 171,483. A deduction, however, should be made from this as a part consisted of foreign productions, but the quantity of wheat alone was 218,000 bushels, valuing 275,000 dollars.

During the revolutionary times the slaves who were the cultivators of the sugar cane, etc., were dispersed from the several estates; many were engaged in the different armies, and others fled into the interior, whilst their places have not been and cannot be supplied, as slavery is abolished, and as all efforts have hitherto failed to induce the Peruvians to hire themselves as agriculturists, owing to their disinclination to the labor, and to their belief that they cannot live in the lowlands. The consequence is that the quantity formerly produced of the articles mentioned is now considerably diminished, and that any material increase is unlikely. The price of sugar imported into Chile during the time of the Spaniards was 2 dollars and 2 reals the arroba of 25 pounds. This is now the price obtained by the planter at his estate. It can be sold in Lima by him or by the purchaser at wholesale for 4½ to 5 dollars, which leaves the importer a fair profit taking the average of the charges whether by sea or land; and the retail price in Lima is 7 to 7½ dollars. The amount estimated to be sent to Chile calculated its cost on board at 3½ dollars per arroba is 175,000 dollars; but to Guayaquil none is now exported owing to a prohibitory duty there on it. . . .

The foregoing explanations will shew, unfortunately, that the commerce of Peru is in a deplorable condition; a government pursuing the mistaken notion of augmenting its resources by heavy exactions on all commodities; the exports of the country almost confined to a diminished amount of the precious metals; the necessary articles of consumption bearing exorbitant prices; every difficulty thrown in the way of the fair trader; no means of arresting under the existing system the demoralizing efforts of contraband trade; a lamentable want of all stimulus to exertion; a scanty population without industry, capital, or knowledge; and the trade conducted on a most erroneous if not deceptious plan, which not only the late but the present peculiar circumstances of the country, perhaps necessitate. The commerce was too hazardous for regular established British houses to embark in it; the country was in a state of convulsion; and even now the Government is not fixed; the British resident here is consequently insecure, and information is wanting in England regarding the articles best suited to the market and the amount of the returns. The fate hovering over the existing trade is that which attends most gambling speculations; and a serious duty devolves on your public functionaries to devise measures for diminishing the portended evils, and for guarding against their recurrence. On the first point every endeavour on my part shall be exerted; and on the second, a clear understanding of the errors is the first advance towards remedying them, and in this respect the insight which I have attempted to convey will perhaps be found sufficient. An anxiety among the parties interested to amend the system is the second step; and the means of placing the commerce on a just and solid basis is the third. In justice to the British mercantile body in these countries, I have much satisfaction in stating that I have found every disposition to promote wholesome reforms, whilst hopes of improvement are opening in the respective governments. In Peru, though old jealousies and prejudices against foreigners are not eradicated, the government is aware that the State suffers from the ignorance and indolence of the people, and that the example of British industry is essential for the public welfare. My suggestions to it to commence on those measures which are calculated to secure the objects of revenue and internal improvement have heretofore been received with a kind feeling, but accompanied by the declaration that the proper period for their consideration is when Great Britain will authorize a commercial treaty to be entered into with Peru. Indeed an earlier agitation of the question of commercial reforms might hazard the establishment by this government of all the proposed checks, and the refusal of any reduction of duties, which should be the forerunner of them. His Excellency General Bolivar has certainly shewn that he is sensible the income of a State will progressively augment by promoting foreign intercourse, since just and liberal principles are exhibited in the commercial regulations of Bolivia, and important commercial changes have been adopted in

Colombia. If corresponding measures be observed in Peru and Chile, if these Governments and Bolivia be acknowledged, and security and protection consequently be obtained for British subjects, a trade will be established along the Pacific on a fixed and proper footing; branches from regular British houses will be sent hither; supplies of articles of necessity and convenience will be proportioned to the demand; instead of a monopolizing principle, profits will be derived from extensive sales at low prices, to the benefit of the community; any temporary stagnation of commerce will be unfelt; and money, the commodity most needed in these countries at present, will be imported for the purpose of assisting on moderate terms the pressing exigencies of these States and of individuals, and above all for advances to the miners. The Peruvians have certainly acquired a taste for the commodities of Great Britain and prefer them to those imported from France and other parts of Europe. The diversity of climate causes among all classes of people a want of most of the manufactured goods of England; the principal houses are supplied with English glass, brass ornaments, chintz and other hangings, plate, earthenware, kitchen utensils, knives, forks, etc.; the better class of females though still using in the daytime the saya and manto, adopt in evening parties the English dress; English mechanics, carpenters, cabinet makers, blacksmiths, watchmakers, etc., meet with ready employment; and many establishments, such as a pottery or manufactory of common earthenware, would prove very advantageous. But supposing that a treaty with Peru is effected, that a preference continues to be given to British manufactures, and that the British merchant is enabled to defeat his immediate competitor, the North American, still the commerce to this port can be of little importance to Great Britain, until new capitals are raised in the country; since on their creation will depend the means of effecting an extension of the produce of the mines . . . and I am quite sure that without the aid of British capital and industry, the expectation of improvement here to any extent is visionary.

Contemplating, however, this favourable change in the aspect of affairs in Peru, and taking in the meantime the benefit, though small, to our commercial interests from the present returns of the precious metals, the further advantages are to be added of the trade to ports along the eastern coast of the Pacific. This commerce in the aggregate merits the attention of Great Britain, since the British merchant who trades to the Pacific becomes more or less connected with each port; even in the present unsettled state of the countries,

the accumulated exports form an object of consideration; the resources of the republics of Chile and Bolivia are improving; both are
receiving large supplies of British goods; and the policy of the latter
is to have a port on the Pacific in order to facilitate her imports and
exports. A review of this subject brings me to the second part of my
report.

Many of the evils and disadvantages which I have described in
respect to the state of Peru, will unfortunately be found applicable
to most parts of South America; idleness, ignorance, and vice, too
commonly prevail; the inhabitants are scanty in number; and
prejudicies against foreigners exist founded on the bigotry of the
people, and their supposition that strangers rob them of their gold
and silver; but the higher class of the community feel the importance
of cementing the friendship and forming an extensive intercourse
with Great Britain. In many parts the climate is salubrious and the
land fertile; the natural productions are various and valuable; and
many of the harbours safe and commodious; every prospect therefore offers for the employment of European arts and industry.

c. JOEL ROBERTS POINSETT *on Mexico* (1829)

The character of this people cannot be understood, nor the causes
of their present condition be fully developed without recurring to
the oppression under which they formerly laboured. It would lead
you into error to compare them with the free and civilized nations of
America and Europe in the Nineteenth Century. They started from a
period nearer to the age of Charles the fifth, and it is even a matter
of some doubt whether this Nation had advanced one step in knowledge and civilization, from the time of the conquest to the moment of
declaring themselves Independent. No portion of the Spanish dominions in America was watched over by the Mother Country with
such jealous care as Mexico. Its comparatively dense population, its
extensive and fertile territory, its rich and varied productions, and
especially its mineral wealth, rendered it a source of great profit to

From *Diplomatic Correspondence of the United States Concerning the Independence of the Latin-American Nations,* William R. Manning, ed. (New York:
Oxford University Press, 1925), III, pp. 1673–1676. Reprinted by permission of
the Carnegie Endowment for International Peace.

Spain; while the history of the ancient splendour of Mexico, and the glory of its conquest could not fail to enhance the value of its possession in the eyes of that chivalrous people. In order to preserve that possession every precaution was taken that human prudence could devise to prevent the access of strangers to Mexico and to keep the people in profound ignorance of their own strength and resources as well as of their relative position with regard to other Nations. Until the publication of the voyage of Baron Humboldt, the Nations of Europe and even their immediate neighbours were ignorant of the very names of many of the fertile districts and populous Cities which he first described. In the permission granted to this gentleman to explore these Countries the pride of the Court of Spain appears to have overcome its habitual caution, and the Baron seems to have in view the gratification of that pride in the highly coloured and exaggerated accounts he put forth of the institutions, the wealth, the resources and the growing prosperity of the Spanish Colonies. It is true that Baron Humbolt saw these Countries before they were desolated by the wars of the Revolution, still to judge from what remains, his accounts of the number and excellence of the public Institutions, of the very advanced state of the arts and sciences in Mexico, and of the splendour and magnificence of the style of living of the nobles, altho they may not have been altogether creations of his own imagination, are very highly exaggerated pictures.

The nobility and gentry then as now, inhabited spacious hotels, built after the fashion of those of the mother Country, solid and substantial; but still more destitute of all comfort or convenience. Their style of living was not generous or hospitable, altho they sometimes gave costly and ostentatious entertainments. From their absurd pretentions to rank and from their unmeaning jealousy of each other, there never did exist that social intercourse among the higher orders, which in every other Country forms the chief charm of life. Here every man of distinction considered it beneath his dignity to visit his friends or neighbours, and remained in his own house, where in a large gloomy apartment dimly lighted and miserably furnished he received a few visitors of inferior rank who formed his tertulia of every night. It is not to be wondered at therefore that the sons of these men equally uneducated with themselves, fled from the gloomy mansions of their fathers to the Theatre, the coffee houses or the gambling table; and this circumstance united to the absence of all excitement to industry, from the preference given by the Council of the Indies to Europeans for all appointments, rendered the Aristocracy of Mexico an ignorant and immoral race. The same state of society existed among the higher orders of the clergy and marked their character in the same unfavorable manner. The regular clergy formed from the very dregs of the people, was then and is now disgustingly debauched and ignorant. They have lost the influence they formerly possessed over the common people, and so sensible are they of the universal contempt which they have brought upon themselves by their unworthy conduct, that they would not oppose a thorough reform of their orders if the Government had courage to attempt it.

But what more particularly distinguishes the condition of the people in the Spanish Colonies is the character of the labouring classes. That portion of America conquered by Spain was inhabited by a people in a high state of civilization for the age in which they lived. The higher classes fell a sacrifice to the cruelty and rapacity of their Conquerors, and the common people were reduced to a state of the most abject slavery. The existence of this degraded race had a singular effect upon the character of the Spanish Settler. The poorest white man scorned to be placed on a level with the unfortunate Indian. His colour ennobled him, and Spaniards and their descendants would have perished rather than degrade their caste in America by working in the field, or by following any other laborious occupation in which the Indians are habitually employed. Here therefore is wanting that portion of a community which forms the strength of every nation, but especially of a Republic, a free and virtuous peasantry. The Indians cannot as yet be regarded in that light. They are laborious, patient and submissive, but are lamentably ignorant. They are emerging slowly from the wretched state to which they had been reduced; but they must be educated and released from the gross superstition under which they now labour before they can be expected to feel an interest in public affairs. The only political feeling which these people now possess is a bitter hatred of the Spaniards or *Gachupínes* as they call them, a hatred which has never ceased to exist, and which has been kept alive both by tradition and by constantly recurring instances of cruelty and oppression. Less attention has been paid by this Government to the establishment of primary schools than in any other part of Spanish America. This has been a lamentable oversight, for not only do the great mass of the population require to be educated in order that the real principles of a representative Government may be carried fully into operation; but to inspire them with a decent pride and to induce them to more constant labour and to employ their earnings in rendering their habitations comfortable and in purchasing clothing for themselves and families. At present seven eighths of the population live in wretched hovels destitute of the most ordinary conveniences. Their only furniture a few coarse mats to sit and sleep on, their food indian corn, pepper and pulse, and their clothing miserably coarse and scanty. It is not that the low price of labor prevents them from earning a more comfortable subsistance in spite of the numerous festivals in each year, but they either gamble away their money, or employ it in pageants of the catholic church, in which pagan and christian rites are strangely mingled. All these evils if not cured entirely, would be greatly mitigated by education.

The colleges and other academic Institutions were liberally endowed; but their administration has always been defective and the education the Méxican youth receive at them is very superficial. Previous to the Revolution the Creoles were discouraged from the attainment of knowledge. An acquaintance with foreign languages and general science rendered them dangerous in the eyes of their superiors and operated against their success in life. Since that event they are much changed for the better. The improvement in the condition of the lower orders of the people is very remarkable, altho they are still far behind all other civilized Nations.

It appears then that the successful precautions taken by Spain to prevent all intercourse between Mexico and other Countries prevented the light of knowledge from penetrating into this Country. Not only were the Mexicans deprived of the means of keeping pace with the rapid progress of knowledge in other Countries during the seventeenth and eighteenth centuries; but the peculiar circumstances in which they were placed scarcely allowed them to retain the station they occupied at the time of the conquest. The emigrants from Spain who alone were permitted to settle in the Country were among the most ignorant and vicious of that people, who are notoriously a century behind the rest of Christian Europe. They were for the most part the favorites of great men, and came to lord over the creole, to occupy all the offices of honor and emolument and to keep the natives in subjection. As has been already remarked one mode of effecting this object was to keep them even more ignorant than they were themselves. They were assisted in their efforts to this effect by a variety of causes. The want of means of acquiring knowledge, the absence of all excitement to exertion, the facility of procuring the means of subsistence almost without labour, a mild and enervating climate and their constant intercourse with the aborigines, who were and still are degraded to the very lowest class of human beings, all contributed to render the Mexicans a more ignorant and debauched people than their ancestors had been. Another cause operated still more strongly to produce this effect. The puerile ceremonies of their worship, and the excessive ignorance and shocking profligacy of the clergy. The creoles were taught from their infancy to reverence their pastors as Superior beings and it is not therefore surprising that their pernicious example should have produced such melancholy results. When therefore we examine the actual condition of this people, we ought always to bear in mind the point from which they set out. They were in every respect, far behind the mother Country which is notoriously very inferior in moral improvement to all other Nations. They were not even equal to the other Spanish colonies in America, because their comparative importance and their vicinity to the United States rendered Spain more vigilant in preventing all intercourse with foreigners as well as the introduction of all works, which could enlighten their minds and inspire them with liberal ideas.

C. Special Topics

3. Education in Colombia

DAVID BUSHNELL

Bolívar had been in Bogotá scarcely a month after the victory of Boyacá when he ordered the convent abandoned by the royalist Capuchins, together with all its revenues, to be set aside for a free school to train orphans, the poor, and the sons of patriot martyrs. As it turned out, this particular school was never opened, but it set a pattern for future efforts to expand educational facilities, and in particular to expand them at the expense of the Church. Slightly later, while still serving as Vice-President of Cundinamarca, San-

From *The Santander Regime in Gran Colombia* by David Bushnell (Newark: University of Delaware Press, 1954), pp. 183–194, *passim*. Reprinted by permission.

tander issued orders for every village and every convent or monastery to set up a school of its own. In 1821, finally, the Congress of Cúcuta set out to organize the educational system on a more or less permanent footing. First it announced that without knowing how to read "Citizens cannot basically know the sacred obligations which religion and Christian morality impose upon them, or the rights and duties of man in society"; then it decreed the establishment of a primary school for boys in every town of 100 or more families, made attendance compulsory from six to twelve years of age except when a legitimate excuse was offered, and provided for support of the school system by assessments against all who could afford to pay, the children of the poor being educated free of charge. The curriculum was to consist of the "three R's" plus religion, morality, and "the rights and duties of man in society." The same subjects, plus sewing and embroidery, were to be taught to young girls, save that there was no pretense of founding schools for all of them. With regard to higher education, the Founding Fathers called for a *colegio* (or *casa de educación*) in each province, teaching not less than grammar, rhetoric, philosophy, and "the branches of mathematics which are most important to the residents of the province" — and teaching as much more as the province could afford. Assorted revenues were assigned for the secondary schools, including general tax funds as a last resort; but their chief source of income was to be the capital holdings of the smaller Colombian convents, which were suppressed forthwith.

The work of the Cúcuta Congress remained a model for all educational planning during the years of the Santander regime. Its main principles were reaffirmed by subsequent legislation and were given more concrete application in the Plan of Studies which was issued by Santander in 1826 as a detailed guide for Colombian educators to follow. As far as organization is concerned, the only important changes were made by the Congress of 1826 and were designed simply to round out the existing structure, remedying any major omissions, and applying to education the ideal symmetry already in use, at least on paper, for political, judicial, and military organization. There was now to be a primary school in each ward or parish, apparently whether it had 100 families or not, and also in each army corps; a rudimentary grammar school at the center of each canton; a colegio in each province; and, as a fitting climax to it all, a university for every department. With undue optimism Santander's Plan of Studies added that each parish school should be open by Christmas,

1827, and that its main room should be 36 feet wide "at the least and wherever possible."

Needless to say, the legal provisions on width of floors were not the only parts of the official scheme of education that remained in practice a dead letter. And yet within a short time a surprisingly good start had been made. In primary education the most spectacular progress was to be found in the rapid extension of schools using the Lancasterian method of "mutual teaching," which was currently the rage in Europe and was specifically approved for use in Colombia by the Congress of Cúcuta. The method had already been introduced in Colombia by Fray Sebastián Mora of the Franciscan order, who learned it when deported to Spain in punishment for his patriot activities. On his return in 1820 Mora promptly established a small school in the miserable town of Capacho in western Venezuela. However, he was rescued from obscurity when he was brought to Bogotá by Santander the following year in order to found the first Lancasterian school in New Granada and thereby prepare the way for the general expansion of primary education under the dictates of the Constituent Congress. Mora's school in Bogotá was thus to serve as the first of three central "normal schools" of the Lancasterian method which Santander ordered set up in Bogotá, Caracas, and Quito; each of these was supposed to receive at least one student from every surrounding province, who would learn the new technique and then carry it to the people at home when the course was over. The Vice-President hoped that in this way it would soon be known throughout Colombia.

Probably even more important for the spread of the Lancasterian method was the work done by a variety of traveling educational missions, of which the most successful was one entrusted to Mora himself. Once Mora had his Bogotá school running smoothly, he moved on to Popayán and ultimately to Ecuador, founding schools and training teachers as he went. His mission consumed several years, and was not complete until he had personally established the Lancasterian method in Loja and Cuenca, the southernmost provinces of the republic. Mora's work was paralleled in the North by the mission of a French educator, Pierre Comettant, whose services were especially contracted in Europe by the Colombian agent José Rafael Revenga. Comettant's first assignment was to relieve Fray Sebastián at Bogotá; afterwards he moved to Caracas and then traveled along the Caribbean coast organizing Lancasterian schools as he went and engaging prominently in Masonic activities on the side. Comettant had constant difficulties in obtaining funds for his work, and not all his achievements were permanent; but meanwhile the *Gaceta del Istmo de Panamá* seriously affirmed that in his schools one could learn in a year what normally took five or six. A still more famous traveling educator was Joseph Lancaster himself, the originator of the new system, who came from England to Caracas at the express invitation of Bolívar. Unfortunately, Lancaster accomplished less than either Mora or Comettant. He took over the management of the Lancasterian school already established in the Venezuelan capital, but he was soon embroiled in a dispute over finances with the Caracas municipality. As he himself loudly complained, he was "obliged *to borrow money to buy bread.*" Since Bolívar's personal offer of funds could not be very promptly turned into cash, he finally went home in disgust.

Despite the unhappy fate of Mr. Lancaster personally, his teaching method had won remarkable acceptance. The openings and public exercises of Lancasterian schools were everywhere a major attraction, commemorated by masses and bullfights and attended by such dignitaries as the intendants in the provinces and the Vice-President in Bogotá. Their numbers increased rapidly, and so did the number of non-Lancasterian schools, which benefited somewhat less directly from the same primary education craze. In 1823 the province of Bogotá alone boasted fifteen Lancasterian primary schools; by 1827 the Secretary of Interior reported that the country as a whole had 52 Lancasterian and 434 old-style primary schools for boys, with a total enrollment of about 20,000. In a population of between two and three millions the latter figure is not high, but it was better than nothing.

Statistics, however, are not very instructive, for none are wholly reliable and there are few colonial totals to compare them with. Where comparative figures do exist, they are highly favorable to the republic: thus the province of Pamplona had one public primary school in 1810, 30 in 1822. The main thing is that a real effort was being made to found new schools, and some of them were distinctly praised even by foreign observers. Not only the government but also the clergy and private citizens had their hand in the good work, and the numerous cases of failure serve merely to emphasize the obstacles that were being gradually overcome. Thus even with the Lancasterian "normal schools" there was an obvious shortage of teachers, especially in such isolated spots as Río Hacha, which had to plead for a schoolmaster in the Cartagena press. Equally or more serious was the lack of money, for the assessment system enacted by the Congress of Cúcuta was quite inadequate, and even a town the size of Maracaibo had trouble paying for any primary education at all. It was also necessary to contend with the laxity and indifference of many provincial officials who did not share the zeal of the national government; at Cúcuta no school was set up despite the fact that both teacher and funds were available. These obstacles were doubly severe when it came to founding schools for girls: even the nuns, who were ordered by law to open schools for them, alleged lack of funds to do the job. All things considered, one can only marvel that the number of children who received an education of some sort was no smaller.

The very same obstacles hampered the growth of secondary education. The supply of funds and teachers was insufficient, and such teachers as there were preferred the delights of Caracas and Bogotá to the quiet of Cumaná and Angostura. There were also special difficulties to overcome, such as the rivalry of Socorro and San Gil to be the seat of the same provincial colegio. This dispute was solved first by placing the colegio proper in San Gil while allowing Socorro to possess its own separate chair of philosophy, and finally by establishing a true colegio in each city; but this is not the only case in which the planned symmetry and centralization collided with the demand for at least a little secondary education in several different towns of a province. Nevertheless, the five colegios existing in 1821 had grown to 21 colegios and one casa de educación — which was almost the same thing — by the start of 1827. Seven of the new institutions were schools that had existed before the War of Independence and were now simply revived, generally in expanded form, but there were ten that had been organized where nothing existed before, and in such places as Ibagué and the city of Antioquia this was no mean accomplishment.

The increase in the number of universities was much less striking. The colonial regime had founded universities only in Bogotá, Caracas, and Quito, so that there were nine more to be created before every department could have its own as provided in the legislation of 1826. For the present, however, Santander decreed the establishment of new universities only at Tunja and Popayán, and as these were due to be organized just when the country was floundering in the political crisis set off by the Venezuelan revolt of 1826, only the University of the Cauca in Popayán became a functioning institution. A rector was named for the one at Tunja in the Department of

Boyacá, but apparently that is as far as it got. This suited the people of Socorro and San Gil very nicely, for the departmental university was meant to absorb the more advanced courses of instruction given in their local colegios, and they had therefore been campaigning vigorously against the project for its creation.

In any case, the most important institutional change at the university level was simply the reorganization of the three colonial universities so that they might take their place in the new educational system. In Bogotá, accordingly, the Dominican fathers' *Universidad de Santo Tomás* was now replaced by the official *Universidad Central de Bogotá*. The former had been little more than a central clearing-house for the granting of degrees, while the real work of teaching was done in the two colegios of San Bartolomé and Rosario. In 1826, by decree of Santander, all the courses given in the two colegios save Castilian and Latin grammar were transferred to the Universidad Central, and the Dominican university was superseded altogether. The result was a formal protest by the Rector of the *Colegio del Rosario* and a considerable struggle with the Dominican fathers, who denied that their university was legally suppressed and resisted the demand to surrender its archives to the Universidad Central. The Rector and the Dominicans were unsuccessful in all their pretensions, however; and though Santander was inclined to be lenient on the archives question, Bolívar turned out to be adamant. At most the Dominicans had some revenge by giving out degrees hand over fist in the last days of their university's existence, thus creating, as the saying went, *doctores al vapor*.

The authorities also sought to encourage institutions of learning and culture outside the regular school and university system. First of all there had to be a national library, which was formed out of the public library of colonial Bogotá plus a few significant additions such as the collection of the *sabio* José Celestino Mutis. The library originally contained an estimated 10,000 to 12,000 books, which was not many, but it grew steadily: when jailed in the library building after the attempt on Bolívar's life in September, 1828, Santander personally counted 14,847. Similarly, an *Academia Literaria Nacional* was organized in 1826 under a law which directed Santander himself to select the 21 original members. . . .

Finally, there were certain state institutions designed to give instruction of a specialized nature. Bogotá in 1820 had possessed a short-lived military academy. Three years later, under a contract made by Francisco Antonio Zea with a group of foreign scholars in

Paris, the Colombian capital acquired a *Museo Nacional* with a mining school attached to it. According to the decree of Congress which approved the contract, the mining school was to receive at least one youth from each department, and the museum staff was to give instruction in sciences ranging from entomology to astronomy. This ambitious program was not fully carried out. Yet a few of the less exotic courses were actually given, and the mining school did formally open even though it never accomplished much. . . .

The museum and mining school were really part of a general reform-movement which affected the quality and content as well as the quantity of Colombian education, and of which one aspect was a post-war revival of the scientific movement fostered by Mutis and Caldas in the late colonial regime. Thus the teaching of mineralogy had been ordered at the provincial colegios of Cali and Medellín even before a special school for mining was set up in Bogotá. Some progress was also made in the field of medical education, where in truth progress was badly needed. There were whole provinces without a doctor: as one investigating committee lamented, "the people of Colombia absolutely lack surgeons and even mere blood-letters, with notable prejudice to health." Even in the latter part of 1822 the University of Caracas had exactly one medical student, and the situation of Bogotá was only slightly better. There medical instruction had been an unremunerated public service before the Revolution, and so it continued for a time under the republic. In due course, however, volunteer teaching was supplemented by that of two French doctors who gave formal classes in anatomy and physiology in return for a government stipend, and a part of this program was incorporated in the Universidad Central when it was set up, for the new university boasted a regular medical curriculum. In provincial centers as well, medical instruction was encouraged by the administration; at one point there were actually more medical students in the provincial colegio of Tunja than in Caracas. Not only this, but Santander's Plan of Studies for the first time required a doctor's degree for the practice of medicine in Colombia. This measure was not made retroactive to cover all current practitioners, and there is ample evidence of official laxity in enforcing medical standards even at Bogotá, but at least the ruling illustrates a growing awareness of the importance of formal training.

A more important change in the nature of Colombian education was the steady decline of clerical influence. During the colonial regime most schools had been managed directly by the Church, and clerical influence was by no means eliminated under the republic. However, even though Colombian leaders were at first hesitant about asserting official control over the Church as a whole by means of the *patronato*, they never wavered in their claim that education of all varieties must be under the immediate guidance of the state. One of the measures taken by Santander as Vice-President of Cundinamarca was to bring the colegio of San Bartolomé back under public control after twenty years of episcopal management; and Bolívar not only gave prompt endorsement to this move but ordered that the same control should be exercised over all colegios whatsoever. Even ecclesiastical seminaries were placed under direct government regulation. When exceptions were made to the general rule, as in permitting the Bishop of Mérida himself to name the rector of a colegio which he founded and supported at Pamplona, it was only through a special delegation of authority on the part of Santander.

The mere tightening of state control did not, of course, prevent the liberal use of individual clergymen as teachers. The decrees of Santander often required that particular teaching posts be filled by members of the clergy, and the archbishop-designate of Bogotá, Dr. Fernando Caicedo, was named first rector of the Universidad Central. Likewise, Church funds were extensively used for educational purposes, whether they consisted of the capital holdings confiscated from suppressed convents, the income from special clerical endowments traditionally assigned for use in education, or the voluntary contributions of individual clergymen. Gifts for education were made with particular lavishness by the exroyalist Bishop of Popayán, Salvador Jiménez de Enciso, but they were also made by humble curates, and in every case the money was eagerly welcomed. Nor was there any attempt to exclude religious education from the official school system. Church attendance on stated occasions was made compulsory for school children, although in 1826 the children of non-Roman Catholics were implicitly exempted. The principal change was simply a shift of emphasis: with the decline of ecclesiastical control religion was to become a subordinate rather than the central element in Colombian education.

The new emphasis, needless to say, was to be placed on whatever doctrines were being expounded at the moment by the most popular liberal writers of western Europe. The respect shown for scientific studies is really one aspect of this development, but even more significant was the reform of the curriculum in such fields as political science, law, and liberal arts. For one thing, there were particular aspects of the social sciences that had been taught very little if at all during the colonial regime, and which had to be firmly established in Colombian schools before the nation could consider itself really up-to-date. Francisco Soto thus began a new course in political economy at San Bartolomé, using the text of the French liberal economist Jean Baptiste Say, and this moved the official *Gaceta* to remark gleefully that "from the conquest until now the words political economy, values, productive and unproductive capitals . . . had not resounded in our colleges." For the moment political economy as a separate course was apparently taught nowhere else, but the government hoped that ultimately it might become a standard element in the Colombian curriculum. San Bartolomé also led the way in the formal teaching of French and English, although both subjects were to be offered at other institutions as soon as possible. Santander's Plan of Studies in 1826 required that they be taught at every colegio and university in Colombia. Neither language in itself had any ideological significance, but they were included in the curriculum not only for their commercial and diplomatic usefulness but also as a way of helping Colombians to familiarize themselves with the writings of the best modern authorities on the social and natural sciences. The encouragement of French and English thus went hand in hand with a campaign to limit the use of· Latin, which was by contrast the language of the traditional and orthodox authorities. Latin also was too closely associated with "the syllogistic form of teaching used by the peripatetics," which was now formally banished from Colombian schools. The decline of Latin was profoundly lamented by such clerical conservatives, as the Bishop of Mérida, Lasso de la Vega, but the trend could not be halted: the Congress of 1826 decreed that only certain legal studies, theology, and Scripture might be taught from Latin texts, while at the same time everything possible was done to eliminate the oral use of Latin in Colombian classrooms.

The most controversial innovation of all, however, was the introduction of new textbooks of doubtful religious orthodoxy. This concerned both new courses like political economy and old ones like jurisprudence, and heading the list of controversial authors was the English philosopher Jeremy Bentham, undoubtedly the favorite writer of Santander and his liberal circle. From the outset Bentham had been cited with the most laudatory epithets by *La Gaceta de Colombia,* and his writings were placed on the curriculum at San Bartolomé and possibly elsewhere at an early date. Finally, in

November, 1825, a decree of Santander made Bentham's text on principles of legislation compulsory for law students throughout the republic. This step unleashed a storm of criticism, for Bentham was a confessed materialist whose works were full of statements directly contrary to Roman Catholic orthodoxy. The clergy was almost unanimously indignant, and so were the more conservative laymen. Santander thus referred the problem for further study to the national *Dirección de Estudios* established by decree of Congress in 1826 in order to supervise all branches of Colombian education. One of the three Directors, Dr. Félix Restrepo, was opposed to Bentham altogether; the other two, Vicente Azuero and Estanislao Vergara, conceived the idea that as long as no entirely satisfactory alternative was available teachers might simply point out the "mistaken" passages in Bentham as they went along, thus warning their students not to be misled. This suggestion was incorporated in the definitive Plan of Studies issued in October of 1826, but it still did not quiet the opposition. It would not suffice to delete a few passages from Bentham when his central doctrine of utilitarianism and everything that stemmed from it was basically in conflict with the Roman Catholic religion. In the end Santander had to authorize the Dirección de Estudios to import a different text if it saw fit, but there was no time to act on this suggestion before the end of the Santander regime.

Bentham was only the most prominent of the authors who were under attack. Santander's decree of November, 1825, was also criticized for including the Protestant Wattel as a prescribed authority on international law, and the Plan of Studies a year later greatly extended the list of heretical or at least mildly unorthodox writers whose works were placed on the school curriculum. The Plan ordered children in primary school to learn good behaviour from the "moral catechism" of an author who was not a Roman Catholic in good standing. Even the required texts on canon law left a good bit to be desired from the orthodox viewpoint. . . .

Although it was not always expressly stated at the time . . . conservative elements often objected quite as strongly to the teachers as to the textbooks they used. Many instructors, it was felt, were leading the young to think of religion as a stupid waste of time and in general were undermining sound moral principles. Nor could this charge be denied entirely, at least from the viewpoint of orthodox Roman Catholicism. Thus the teaching of legislation according to the textbook of Bentham was entrusted at Bogotá to Dr. Vicente

Azuero, a freethinker who was quite frankly sympathetic toward the basic doctrines of the English philosopher. Whether Azuero's private character was good or bad, he could hardly be expected to point out as erroneous all the passages that were deemed contrary to good religion and morals by the fully or even moderately orthodox. Similar objections could be made against many other eminent liberals who assumed teaching assignments as a part-time occupation. Francisco Soto is one more obvious example, although in his special field of economics he was not so directly concerned with religious dogma. Even the clergymen who were named to high places in the field of education were usually chosen from the radical wing of the Colombian priesthood.

At the lower levels of instruction, and especially in the provinces, the atmosphere was not quite so liberal. José Manuel Restrepo complained that there were far too many teachers who still found it "painful to confess that very little that is useful can be learned from our ancestors" and who believed "that nothing should be taught but in Latin, condemning the contrary opinion as endangering the religion of Jesus Christ." As a matter of fact, there were not enough qualified doctrinaire liberals to fill all the teaching positions in the country even if the government wanted them to, which it probably did not. Quite apart from all ideological considerations, moreover, there is no doubt that the teaching profession had come to include a high number of unusually gifted citizens. Among the liberals there were not only Soto and Azuero but also the brilliant young Rufino Cuervo and the future President José Ignacio de Márquez, who took time out from his duties as Intendant of Boyacá in order to teach at the provincial colegio in Tunja. The moderates were represented above all by Dr. Félix Restrepo, who taught philosophy at Bogotá. The men chosen for the principal supervisory posts in the educational system both in Bogotá and in the departments were equally capable for the most part, including a good selection of clergymen and the conservative aristocrat Joaquín Mosquera as well as the inevitable Dr. Vicente Azuero. The great difficulty in Colombian education was simply that the capable men at the top were always hindered both by the scarcity of human and material resources at their command and by the partisan controversies that so much of their work necessarily entailed.

4. The Ethnic Factor

Magnus Mörner

The enormous extent of historiography devoted to the Wars of Emancipation notwithstanding, much remains to be done on the social aspects of these wars. There can be no doubt that these conflicts had the character of civil wars, thus making the social aspects particularly important. Nevertheless, the pioneering articles and preliminary conclusions of Charles Griffin are supplemented only in a limited way by the results of more recent research. Although they imply some useful revision of traditionalist, patriotically biased historiography, recent Marxist interpretations seem to convey somewhat anachronistic ideas about the socioeconomic structure of the revolutionary era. Thus they tend to disregard interethnic conflict; instead they stress the struggle of economic classes. The Marxist view of Latin American colonial history also discerns, of course, similar class exploitation and conflict within the so-called "Caste Society." Other students (including the present author) prefer to interpret Latin American colonial society mainly by comparing it with the hierarchic estate-based society that in part persisted in Europe until the French Revolution. It was, in fact, the result of transferring the latter kind of society to a multiracial colonial situation. Without denying that a system of social classes was gradually taking shape even before the Emancipation, particularly in the rural sector, we maintain that the misnamed "Caste Society" continued to exist as the basis of social attitudes, legal and social discrimination, and social status until the very end of the colonial era. That is to say, the struggle between the different strata of the population that occurred in the Wars of Emancipation may not necessarily be explained only as class exploitation and conflict. It may also derive from frustration engendered by the ethnic discrimination imposed by the "Caste Society."

The most dramatic examples of social conflict with ethnic over-

From "Report on the State of Research in History" by Magnus Mörner, pp. 3–6. Paper delivered at the Conference on Race and Class in Latin America During the National Period, sponsored by Cornell and Columbia Universities, New York City, December 16–18, 1965. Reprinted by permission of the author.

tones in the Wars of Emancipation were the revolutions of Hidalgo and Morelos in Mexico and the struggle in Venezuela in 1813 and 1814. In both, the real issues have escaped the apologetic-traditionalist historical school. In the traditionalists' view Boves, the royalist leader of the Venezuelan cowboys (*Llaneros*), is a personification of evil. On the other hand, some leftist writers have tried to assign to this warrior the role of popular redeemer. In a recent work, Germán Carrera Damas, a Marxist historian, calmly demonstrates the lack of documentary basis for either view. Sacking and pillage were normal means of financing war. In any case, examples of hatred between "Indians" and "whites," "pardos" and "criollos," abound in both Mexico and Venezuela and it is also clear that contemporaries for a moment thought a "racial war" absolutely imminent. Why did a struggle clearly fought along ethnic lines never take place at least in these two regions? My own impressions from reading published sources are that, in fact, the "white" leadership on both sides feared such tendencies and made what proved to be a joint effort to curb them. This would be the context in which to place Bolívar's ruthless executions of a Piar and a Padilla. It also seems to me, however, that a thorough study of the ethnic aspects of the struggle for emancipation remains to be done, as also an unbiased study of the ethnic attitudes of the principal protagonists. Surprisingly enough, it seems that not even Bolívar's somewhat contradictory views on race have been submitted to a systematic and objective analysis. Also, during the postemancipation era, ethnic tensions seem to have expressed themselves occasionally in Latin American politics, as during the Federal War of Venezuela, and in the revolution of northeastern Brazil between 1832 and 1848. But they are difficult to assess.

The tendencies toward a struggle along ethnic lines during the Wars of Emancipation and later should be clearly distinguished from the participation of dark-skinned elements in the wars. It is evident that during the Wars of Emancipation, on both sides, Indians, Negroes, and "Castas" usually provided the bulk of the fighting forces. But their role was only "passive," completely subordinated to the aims dictated by the "white" leadership. Their neglected history should be written in this way. For instance, it is surprising to find how seldom it is mentioned in the literature that about a third of San Martín's army at Maipú and the Chacabuco were Negroes. For the Negro slaves, recruitment provided the way to freedom — but the casualties they suffered were heavy. The rapid decrease in the percentage of slaves and corresponding increase in that of free Negroes, but also the absolute diminution of the African element in continental Spanish America in the early nineteenth century must be seen against this background, as recognized by José Luis Masini and Ildefonso Pereda Valdés.

The wars provided the opportunity for many individuals with dark skin to climb the social ladder by virtue of their military merits. This is verified easily in the biographies of men such as Santa Cruz or Agustín Gamarra. An even better example, on a more modest level, is the Chilean mulatto "Sargento Mayor" José Romero (1794–1858), described by Guillermo Feliú Cruz. A more systematic study of the function performed by the wars in promoting upward social mobility (and ethnic passing) would probably be different (since a great many individuals would have to be thoroughly reviewed), but probably rewarding. Of course, this phenomenon is not restricted to the period of Emancipation but became a continuing and positive side effect of Latin American militarism. Neither have serious studies as yet been undertaken on the rest of the nineteenth century.

The study of the abolition of the legal framework of "Caste Society" seems not to present great problems. A succinct account of this process in Argentina has been presented recently by Orlando Carracedo. The texts of the laws and constitutions are usually clear enough; also, the legislative debates preceding them in part have been made available in modern editions. Apart from the constitutions enacted in Latin America, the Cadiz constitution of 1812 is also worthy of attention, because so many Spanish American deputies participated. Furthermore, the ethnic composition of the overseas population became a hotly debated issue in Cadiz, on the problem of constructing the popular basis for the new representative system of the new Spanish constitutional monarchy. The excellent study of James F. King illumines this topic.

The era of emancipation introduces a new kind of source material on the social history of Latin America: the travelogues written by non-Iberian foreign visitors, whether merchants, scientists, diplomatic agents, or mercenary soldiers. Even the few earlier examples of this genre, Alexander V. Humboldt and others, are sufficiently close to the time of Emancipation as to serve as sources for the same kind of materials. Though the observations of the foreign travelers — especially the Anglo-Saxon ones — are often quoted, their works should, more than hitherto, be submitted to critical analysis. When the background, experiences, and attitudes of the authors are better known and their evidence, on ethnic conditions, for instance, is duly compared, they will probably prove a better source of knowledge.

D. The End of the Revolutionary Period

5. The Great Landed Estates Remained

R. A. HUMPHREYS

The fall of the empire is the second great revolution on which modern Hispanic America is founded. Like the conquest, it was written in blood. And like the conquest, it has been shrouded in myth. "The War for Independence," declared Alberdi, "endowed us with a ridiculous and disgraceful mania for the heroic." And while, on the one hand, heroes and demigods were made to dominate the stage, on the other, the revolutions of the first quarter of the nineteenth century were seen as great popular movements leading to the triumph of the idea of liberty as against the defenders of a dark colonial past.

Heroism, of course, there was, and not on one side only. But though much was said of the sovereignty of the people, the revolutions which transformed into independent states the Hispanic-American societies that had been evolving since the conquest were "popular" revolutions only in a very restricted sense. They did not represent the sudden release of the resentments of a native people, or even of a large cross-section of a colonial population, against a European oppressor. Nor were they essentially democratic. On the contrary, most of them began, quite simply, as the revolt of one Spanish minority against another Spanish minority, of creoles, in the language of the day, against *peninsulares*. Their aim was self-government for creoles, not necessarily for the mixed races, for Indians, and for negroes, who, together, made up four-fifths of the population of

From *Tradition and Revolt in Latin America* by R. A. Humphreys (London: The Athlone Press, 1965), pp. 9–16, *passim.* Reprinted by permission.

Spanish America. And with the political emancipation of creoles was coupled their economic emancipation, the destruction, that is, of the commercial monopoly of Spain and the opening of the ports of the continent to the trade of the world.

But revolutions are not made in a day. Nor is it easy to control them. Conflicts of interests quickly appeared, and divergencies also of ideas and aims — between capital cities and provincial cities, for example, between conservatives and radicals, and between the reforming ideals of the "age of enlightenment" and its revolutionary ideals. Creoles fought Spaniards. But Spanish Americans also fought each other. And while rebels and royalists alike appealed to, and exploited, the illiterate masses, the struggle once begun released incalculable forces, was waged with ruthless violence, and left desolation in its wake. A few areas — Paraguay was one — escaped comparatively lightly. Coastal cities, such as Buenos Aires and Valparaiso, grew and flourished on the new currents of foreign trade. But, though the extent of the damage varied from region to region, in general, the economic life of Spanish America was disrupted and the prosperity which had marked the closing years of the colonial period destroyed. Trade routes were abandoned, mines deserted, crops and livestock laid waste. The labour supply was dislocated, capital put to flight.

As the economic life of Spanish America was disrupted, so also political stability was undermined. The Crown had been the symbol of a political control which extended to almost every aspect of colonial life. Naturally it was not always obeyed. But it supplied a unifying, cohesive force, and, in theory at least, it was invariably respected. Its disappearance left a vacuum. This the creoles had expected to fill with a new republican authority, safeguarded in written instruments of government. Instead, as Lord Acton remarked, the habits of subordination departed with the Spaniard. The wars themselves encouraged the military not the civilian virtues; and, while generals who had commanded armies aspired to govern countries, the consequences of that lack of experience in self-government which, with whatever limitations, the English colonies in North America had enjoyed became fully apparent. "Until our countrymen," wrote Bolívar, in his famous Jamaica Letter in 1815, "acquire the political talents and virtues which distinguish our brothers of the north, entirely popular systems, far from working to our advantage, will, I greatly fear, come to be our ruin." His disillusion and despair as, fifteen years later, he neared his tragic end, he summed up in a still more famous phrase: "For us America is ungovernable. He who serves a revolution ploughs the sea."

The social results of the revolutions are more difficult to estimate. This also is a field of enquiry in which much work remains to be done. But the clash of race and class was clearly marked during the wars of independence. In Mexico the great Indian and mestizo rebellions led by Hidalgo and Morelos were revolts of the dispossessed against the possessing classes. The elements of racial war were plainly visible in Venezuela, and, in what Sarmiento described as the warfare of the countryside against the town, a conflict of cultures was equally evident in Argentina. Heirs to the traditions of the eighteenth-century enlightenment, many of the revolutionary leaders, notably Bolívar and San Martín, Santander in Colombia, O'Higgins in Chile, and Rivadavia in Buenos Aires, were concerned with social and humanitarian, as well as with political and economic, reform. And though their efforts were not always successful, it is obvious that some social consequences of great importance did flow from the revolutions. Negro slavery and the slave trade were in most countries restricted or abolished, in contrast to what happened in the old Portuguese colony of Brazil. The legal disabilities affecting the mulattos and other inferior castes were removed. New men, creoles and mestizos, rose by the revolutions to enter the ranks of the ruling class. And the all-pervading influence of the Church, hitherto an arm, or at least an ally, of the State was weakened.

The relation of the social classes to one another, already changing in the late eighteenth century, was thus further modified by the revolutions. But the hierarchical structure of society remained intact. Apart from the wild Indian tribes of the interior the whole population of Spanish America in 1825 was no greater than that of England, Wales and Scotland at the time of the first Reform Bill. The Indians were by far the largest element, and after them the mestizos. But the coming of independence meant little or nothing to the Mexican peon, the Peruvian Indian or the Chilean *inquilino,* and the social and economic power of a small territorial aristocracy was in no way diminished. "The distinctively Mexican economy," Professor Woodrow Borah observes, "was already organized on the basis of latifundia and debt peonage" at the end of the seventeenth century. It was still so organized at the end of the nineteenth century. There were differences, certainly. New blood had again entered the ranks of the landed gentry. The agricultural labourer was probably still worse off at the end of the century than he was at the beginning. And the great estates, now "little principalities," had become more numerous. In Chile O'Higgins had attempted to abolish entail. In Chile, however, it was not the entailed estates that disappeared, but O'Higgins. The *inquilinos* continued to be tied to the soil as serfs, and the great estates retained their pre-eminence until well after the middle of the century. In Venezuela, where the colonial aristocracy had been reduced both in numbers and importance, nevertheless its style of life remained, and the great estates passed into the hands of a new creole and mestizo oligarchy. As for Argentina, a neglected peripheral region of the empire till after the middle of the eighteenth century, there land had endowed its holder with social rather than economic power. It was to give both in the nineteenth century, and political power also; and it was in the nineteenth century that the great estates were built up. "We are all descendants of tradesmen or of ranchers," says a character in a well-known Argentine novel: " — this we know very well. But everyone tries to forget it, and the one who is furthest from his grandfather — who might have been a country storekeeper, a clerk, a shoemaker, or a shepherd — is the most aristocratic."

The conventional picture of Latin America in the half century after the establishment of political independence is that of a continent of disorder, in which anarchy was tempered only by despotism and despotism only by revolution. Already by 1830 the faith in the future which had animated so many of the great revolutionary leaders had been dimmed — like those visions of El Dorado which had captivated the imaginations of the British merchants. "I blush to say it," wrote Bolívar, "but independence is the sole good which we have gained at the cost of everything else." "The labour and the blood given for the independence of America," San Martín declared, twelve years later, "have been, if not wasted, at any rate unfortunately spent in most of the new states." And the opinion expressed by Hegel to his students in Berlin, that in South America "the republics depend only on military force; their whole history is a continued revolution," was to become a widespread belief in Europe.

It cannot be denied that there was much truth in this picture. But it was not the whole truth. It did not hold for Brazil, for example. Portuguese America, of course, differed markedly from Spanish America, and the differences were nowhere more strikingly illustrated than in the manner in which the two great colonial areas won their independence. What was violently achieved in Spanish America was peacefully achieved in Portuguese America. There was no sudden break with the colonial past, no prolonged and devastating civil war. The heir to the crown of Portugal himself became the Emperor of Brazil, endowed the country with its constitution, and secured its entry into the family of nations. And the throne thus peacefully established was to survive for more than sixty-five years. Nor did this picture of chronic instability hold for Chile. Chile, like Brazil, had its domestic disorders, most serious in Chile in the eighteen-twenties and in Brazil in the eighteen-thirties. But Chile, like Brazil, early succeeded in establishing stable political institutions; and these rested, in both countries, on the support of a landed aristocracy, which in Chile, at least, was remarkably successful in assimilating new elements.

But the empire of Brazil and the "aristocratic republic" of Chile were exceptional. In Mexico, in the thirty years before the great civil wars of the middle century began, the executive office changed hands forty-six times. Argentina fell under the long dictatorship of Rosas and still had to face war between Buenos Aires and the provinces before the country could enter on the full and natural development of its economic life in 1862. And not till the end of the nineteenth century did Uruguay shake off its turbulent past. There were, of course, enlightened despots and unenlightened despots, liberal revolutions and illiberal revolutions. But for many years, and over large parts of Spanish America, it was the law of force, not the force of law, that held most governments in power; and, since force could only be met by force, revolution became an essential element in the political system. Venezuela is said to have experienced fifty-two major revolutions, in all, in the first century of its independent life, and Bolivia more than sixty — by 1952, indeed, more than a hundred and sixty.

Yet few of these nineteenth-century revolutions led to any fundamental changes in the structure of society or the sources of social and economic power. In Mexico the great movement of the *Reforma* in the eighteen-fifties stripped the Church of much of its temporal power; in the name of nineteenth-century liberalism it transferred ecclesiastical estates, often unbroken, into the hands of lay landlords; and, in the name of nineteenth-century individualism, it tried, without much success, to substitute private for collective ownership of land in the Indian villages. But what other revolutionary movement resembled this? In general, the revolutionary tradition in politics was combined with a conservative tradition in society. What invites the attention of the historian in Latin America, indeed, is not sc much the instability of politics as the extraordinary stability of social institutions. The landed gentry, it is true, were less successful in resisting political, personal, or military pressures in Mexico than in Chile, or in Bolivia than in Peru. As politicians they failed again and again. But they preserved their way of life. One dictator succeeded another; in some countries a mestizo oligarchy gradually replaced a creole oligarchy; but the great estate remained at the basis of the social and economic system.

6. Further Reflections

CHARLES C. GRIFFIN

Although our preliminary study . . . revealed some important economic and social differences between viceregal and independent Hispanic America, it also left some doubts. Were the changes observed the direct consequence of the revolution, or were they merely the result of time and chance? Would a similar study on the last decades of the colony or on the years immediately following independence show changes of equal importance? The last possibility raises, another point that merits discussion: the question of the chronological limits of the independence movement. Perhaps the war years, considered as a definite period, do not permit us to prove that great transformations occurred; but, if we broaden our historical vision to include the last years of the reign of Charles IV and the period immediately after Ayacucho, the difference between the beginning and the end of the era will become much more evident. The wars of independence, together with the subsequent wars of republican consolidation, might then be considered as the military aspect of the evolution of Hispanic America from an Hispanic colonial civilization, modified of course by Indian influences, to an autonomous, creole Hispanic-American civilization, in which the original Iberian forms receded in many cases before new influences from Western Europe and even from the United States.

In a work on the social history of the United States, the volume called *The Completion of Independence* deals with the period from

From *Los temas sociales y económicos en la época de la independencia* by Charles C. Griffin (Caracas: Fundación John Boulton & Fundación Eugenio Mendoza, 1962), pp. 20–74, *passim*. Reprinted by permission.

1789 to 1830 and discusses efforts to create an autonomous nation and culture after the achievement of political independence. The study of Hispanic American independence might be broadened in the same way, for the new nations were not created all at once nor in the space of a few years. These nations, which had been developing within the increasingly restrictive confines of the imperial system, were subsequently born in the clash of war and baptized themselves upon declaring their independence. In reality, however, many patriots did not become Venezuelans, Chileans, Argentines, or Mexicans until nearly a generation had elapsed. Thus, just as the geographical boundaries of the new republics remained fluid, so sentiments of nationality remained incomplete.

Whether or not this is the best way of approaching the independence period, we already have a strong documentary and monographic base on which to rest our study of socio-economic changes, without the need for going beyond the years between 1810 and 1830. . . .

In this first lecture I will have time only to underline some of the results of the most recent studies, especially with respect to the social achievements of the political leaders of the period, a subject which has received insufficient recognition in the past. The men of second and third rank were not overly concerned with this problem, but the efforts of the giants — among them Bolívar, Santander, San Martín, O'Higgins, and Rivadavia in South America and Miguel Hidalgo and José María Morelos in Mexico — were extraordinary. These men of genius knew that a social program was needed if their struggles to achieve independence and liberty were to be successful. It was necessary to give justice to the Negro and the Indian; the poor had to be educated and to be made to feel a commitment to the new regimes that were interested in them and in their problems. This program of social action was also due to the fact that *independence was sought for a purpose* — not merely to satisfy the ambitions of the leaders, to show off new banners, or to create new bureaucracies. Independence carried with it the ideal of justice and of a government conscious of its duty to work for the general welfare. . . .

If what I have just stated is true, how can we explain the lack of interest or concern among historians for this subject until now? There are several ways of answering this question. In the first place, the lack of concern has not been total. It may be said, instead, that this subject was studied as an aspect of the biography of celebrated men or as a chapter of national history, and not as a facet of Emancipation. Moreover, I believe that historians were unlikely to attach much importance to studies of enterprises that were later almost completely undone by a series of obstacles, for it is true that a large part of the social program of the independence period was deferred, left unfinished, or destroyed. It is also possible that its importance was diminished by the skeptical or disillusioned attitude of the Liberator himself. Everyone knows that at the end of his career he said: "We have ploughed the sea." Why, then, should the elements of social evolution be sought in such anarchical conditions? I also believe that Marxism has had a positive effect in deflecting our vision of the independence period. Because the revolution for independence was not the uprising of an oppressed class (except in some isolated cases) and much less the struggle of a proletariat that did not exist at the time, writers of a Marxist tendency have tried to minimize the results of the movement. For a majority of the Marxists, the revolution for independence was a frustrated revolution in which the masses did not achieve a single one of their goals. As a result, the class conflict of the period has been exaggerated, as well as the lack of social consequences.

The insistence of the Marxists on this last point and above all on the continued preeminence of a governing class dominated by landowners has influenced even liberal historians and social scientists who are not Marxists. Many sociological studies of Hispanic-American countries emphasize the idea that no social evolution has occurred since the conquest and that a form of "feudalism" survives in Hispanic America, except in Mexico and a few other countries which have recently experienced social revolution. No one can deny the continuity of history nor that the exploitation of rural laborers persists. However, it is erroneous to believe that their position in our century or in the past century is the same as it was during the colonial period. The insistence that society stood still for four centuries distracts the attention of scholars from a series of important changes that took place during the nineteenth century, including several in the independence period. If some reformist endeavors were unsuccessful, their history is nevertheless a part of the history of the period. They also served as stimuli to other efforts later on. In any case, they should not be ignored. . . .

In my first study . . . I stressed the disastrous [economic] effects of the war. Today, without completely denying these effects, I believe that the ravages to agriculture were far less severe than to other branches of production. The activities of small landowners

and subsistence farmers were not greatly affected. The large haciendas suffered, above all when they lost their slave labor force, but
they were hurt less in areas where Indian or mestizo workers were
used, as in the Andean regions of Venezuela and New Granada. With
respect to mining and cattle raising, there is no reason to alter my
previous opinion regarding the severity of the losses sustained.

The changes due to free trade were many and numerous, but they
did not bring wealth and general well-being except where it was
possible to increase the production of raw materials for export. Elsewhere these changes modified society, but they enriched only certain
sectors while 'hey ruined others. Nevertheless, although the economic results of free trade were varied, it must be admitted that
without it it would have been much more difficult for the patriots to
win military victory.

Recent investigations also point up (1) the efforts on behalf of
agrarian reform by means of foreign colonization, distribution of
land to the Indians, and the sale of public lands, though these programs had little or no success; (2) the many innovations in fiscal and
monetary systems; and (3) the attempts to spur economic development by means of concessions to foreign capital. The economic ideas
of the period were strongly influenced, but not completely dominated, by liberalism and laissez faire. In many places a form of neo-
mercantilism, derived from the reign of Charles III, was retained.

At present I would also attach more importance than in previous
years to the new relationship between Hispanic America and the
international economy of the West that developed through the
agency of English bankers, merchants, industrialists, and sailors.
Most of the manufactured articles introduced into the Hispanic
American countries in that period were of English origin; the capital
invested in the mining industry was also English; and the loans that
were negotiated were contracted in London. Thus Hispanic America entered into a new phase of its economic evolution, one that
would last for a large part of the nineteenth century. . . .

What conclusions may we hazard [about the social content of the
revolution]? In the first place — as we saw in the previous lecture
with reference to economic changes — the situation was not the
same in all Hispanic America during this period. Three distinct
revolutions may be identified:

1. The Mexican revolution. It began as a social revolution but was
forced by misfortune and defeat to reach a compromise with the

conservative and land-owning creole class in the famous Plan of Iguala, in which only a nominal acceptance of its social objectives was achieved.

2. The revolution of northern South America (eventually that of Gran Colombia). The revolution began as a movement of the upper-class creoles in favor of autonomy and soon afterwards of independence. Because of the hostility of the mulattoes (*pardos*), Bolívar and his lieutenants had to give the revolution a social content to which they were already inclined by the influence of liberal ideology. This policy was successful in attracting the masses to the patriot cause, but in the last years of Gran Colombia there occurred a reaction that again subordinated the masses.

3. The revolution of Southern America. From the Rio de la Plata to Peru, there was no social content of importance in the revolution, which was carried out by the upper classes, who succeeded in winning the adherence of the masses without the need for great concessions. We see the beginning of class conflict only in those wars of irregular armed bands from 1820 on, which finally became part of the Argentine civil wars of the Rosas era.

In spite of these differences in the rhythm and progress of the revolution, it is interesting to see how the tendencies noted in various regions show a convergence. The differences are based mainly on the intensity and rapidity of the transformation. I have tried in this lecture to set forth the social changes in schematic form by examining the different regions of Hispanic America in order to see if it is possible to find a comparative formula, but none is completely satisfactory. I think that this is due in part to the fact that many important transformations were initiated during the independence period, but few were completed. In my opinion, nearly all the socio-economic changes of the nineteenth century can be detected in an embryonic state. The makers of independence wished not only to transform the political institutions of Hispanic America but also to improve society as a whole. They were naturally unable to be completely successful in achieving this generous aim. Indeed, it is surprising that in the midst of so much violence and poverty these men had the courage and intelligence to attempt so much. . . . May our generation, which confronts problems as difficult as those of the independence period, be more fortunate.

E. Brazil

7. The Uniqueness of Brazil

C. H. HARING

Among all the new-born nations of the American hemisphere in the nineteenth century, only Brazil was able successfully to preserve the institution of monarchy. From 1822, the year in which the Brazilians separated from the mother country, Portugal, until 1889, they were governed by emperors under a constitutional regime.

Brazilians were not alone in this desire to retain in the New World the institutions with which they had been familiar in the Old. Other Latin American communities in their struggle for independence harbored the idea of setting up a native or American monarchy. One actually made the experiment — Mexico — without success. Brazil alone accomplished it. In Chile, Argentina, and Peru many of the conservative, land-owning class thought along similar lines. Most of them wanted political independence — that is, escape from the political, economic, and social inferiority imposed upon them by their colonial status. But many believed that monarchy was what the popular masses really understood and respected. To many it seemed to be the only guarantee of political and social stability. It would commend itself more readily to the monarchical governments of Europe whose diplomatic recognition they devoutly hoped for. It would also preserve the aristocratic framework of society with which their personal interests, economic and social, were identified. . . .

Brazil repudiated Portuguese rule in 1822, when upper-class Brazilians decided that the time had come to fend for themselves as an independent nation. The masses, for the most part illiterate, were scarcely yet a segment of the body politic. A nationalistic sentiment,

Reprinted by permission of the publishers from C. H. Haring, *Empire in Brazil* (Cambridge, Mass.: Harvard University Press), Copyright, 1958, by the President and Fellows of Harvard College.

a feeling of separateness from Europe and Europeans, had been growing in Brazil for a long time. Brazilian historians carry it back at least to the middle of the seventeenth century, when the Dutch West India Company seized and held for a quarter century the coastal area in the northeast around Pernambuco; just as contemporaneously they established themselves in North America in the valley of the Hudson River. These Dutch intruders were ultimately expelled from Brazil by the efforts, almost unaided, of the colonists themselves. And this achievement gave to the Portuguese Americans an enhanced sense of their own self-sufficiency, and some disillusionment perhaps with their Portuguese cousins in Europe.

On several occasions in the following century and a half there were armed conflicts between American-born and European-born Portuguese; protests usually against the privileged position occupied by the latter in government and trade, or against the social inferiority in which Americans were held by Europeans generally. There is no doubt that the example of the thirteen English continental colonies in achieving independence from Great Britain had considerable influence on the minds of contemporary Brazilians, as had the new concepts of liberty and equality released by the French Revolution. Cultural relations were intimate between Portugal and France, and the catastrophic course of events in Paris was followed closely by intellectual circles in Brazil. In short, the early years of the nineteenth century were a time of conflicting ideologies, of social turmoil and change, under any regime old or new. The parallel with our own age is obvious enough. And the Portuguese Brazilians, with their own special grievances, responded to the spirit of the times.

These forces were at work in all the American colonies, Spanish and Portuguese, and in both Portuguese and Spanish America the course of events culminating in political independence was occasioned and fashioned by the situation in Europe, more specifically by the seizure in 1807–08 of both Portugal and Spain by the armies of Napoleon Bonaparte. In Spanish America the effect was a bitter military struggle of some fifteen years' duration before independence of the continental colonies was finally achieved. In Brazil the course of events was very different. The first impulses to independence were in fact received from the Portuguese royal family itself.

When a French army under General Junot approached Lisbon near the end of November 1807, the royal family and the court fled overseas to Brazil under the protection of a British fleet. Portugal for a

century had been to all intents and purposes an economic protectorate of England, and in the gigantic struggle then involving all of Europe, a choice had to be made between the military imperialism of
Napoleon and the economic imperialism of Great Britain. At the
Portuguese court there were sharply opposing currents, one English,
the other French. In this painful dilemma, the Portuguese crown and
its chief advisers, after last-minute hesitations, chose to remain loyal
to their traditional allies. The sovereign at this time was Maria I,
but she was insane, and the actual government was in the hands of
her son and heir, the Prince Regent Dom João. When Junot approached the city gates, the royal flight had the appearance of a
panic, but it evidently had been discussed and decided upon in
detail, for treasure, archives, and all the apparatus of administration
were on board the fleet when the hesitant Prince Regent finally embarked.

After a brief sojourn in the ancient city of Bahia, the exiles
sailed on to Rio de Janeiro in March 1808. Rio became the temporal
capital of the Portuguese Empire. As Oliveira Lima has remarked,
the event was unique: the emigration of a European court overseas,
the transfer across the Atlantic of the seat of one of the great empires of the Old World, an empire that still included, besides Brazil,
the islands of Cape Verde, Madeira, and the Azores, the vast unex-
plored territories of Angola and Mozambique in Africa, and establishments in India, China, and Oceania.

The change was a great boon to Brazil. The old mercantile monopolies of Portugal associated with colonialism were swept away.
On the advice of the governor of Bahia, the Conde da Ponte, and of
José da Silva Lisboa, devoted follower of Adam Smith and Brazil's
most distinguished economist of his time, Brazilian ports were immediately thrown open to the trade of all friendly nations — to the
special advantage of England, it need scarcely be added, especially
when a treaty of trade and navigation two years later gave British
merchants tariff concessions greater than those accorded to Portugal
itself. The step in any case was inevitable, for trade with the metropolis occupied by French armies was impossible, and foreign commerce was essential to sustain what was now the head of Empire.

A variety of other reforms in Brazilian economic and cultural life
were sanctioned, freeing them from old colonial restrictions: promotion of communications by land and water between the widely
separated population centers; some improvement of the administration of justice and taxation; establishment of the first bank, merci-

lessly exploited by the government, and of a naval academy and a college of medicine and surgery; opening of the royal library of 60,000 volumes to the public; establishment of a botanical garden, or garden of acclimatization, of especial interest to the Prince Regent, and visited by tourists today; even a printing press was acquired for the first time in Brazil, in the beginning for official use only, but the first step toward the emergence of a public press. Measures were at the same time taken for the improvement of agriculture. It was in this period that the production of coffee began to expand under royal protection, and in the Botanical Garden was introduced the cultivation of oriental tea. A Brazilian iron industry had its beginnings at this time, as well as the production of textiles, which was to be Brazil's most important manufacture in the nineteenth century. . . .

But there was another side to the picture. With the crown came a host of exiled aristocrats, courtiers, officials, generals, hangers-on, who had lost their properties in Portugal, some fifteen thousand, it is said. Many of them arrogant, avaricious, they monopolized the offices and sinecures in the government. Rio de Janeiro, a squalid, unhealthy tropical city of 130,000 inhabitants, without waterworks or sewers, where daily life had been simple and uneventful, had suddenly to lodge and maintain a throng of strangers accustomed to a much more sophisticated existence. Even the housing of these newcomers was a problem, and many Brazilians were constrained to vacate their residences in Rio to make room for them. Discomforts and grumblings on both sides were inevitable. Taxation too was necessarily heavier, for now it was left to Brazil alone to support a royal court and an army. In earlier days the occupation of Brazil had never been a military one. It had been practically impossible for the metropolis to maintain a numerous garrison in the widely scattered overseas provinces, and such forces as there were had been mostly Brazilian, a well-organized system of local militia. So many of the native Americans were gradually alienated. A latent hostility between Creole and Portuguese, between American and European, was intensified. And it appeared even among army officers.

It was also in part a racial question, for most of the Brazilians, even of the upper class, were of mixed ancestry. The mingling of races had been a characteristic of Brazilian society from the early days of the colony. In the beginning, when European women were few, Indian women became the mothers of the children of the Portu-

guese adventurers. And very soon Negroes were brought in as
slaves from Portuguese possessions across the Atlantic in west Africa.
Negro slaves became very numerous on the plantations in the sugar-
growing area of Pernambuco and Bahia, and far outnumbered the
whites. The white planter, besides his white family, often had a
numerous colored progeny as well, who were frequently treated as
the sons of their father and sometimes were educated. The Portuguese, in fact, have displayed little or no aversion to the so-called
colored races, biologically or socially. Racial prejudice of the sort
common among Anglo-Saxons has never existed in Portuguese
countries.

The consequence was that most Brazilians, to a slight or greater
degree, were of mingled European and Indian or African extrac-
tion, and the racial complexion varied from one region to another.
In Amazonia the prevailing element was Indian, in the pastoral area
of the northeast and the interior provinces of Mato Grosso and
Goiás it was *mameluco* (Indian and white), along the sugar-producing coast from Rio de Janeiro to Pernambuco and Paraíba and in
the mining region of Minas Gerais it was Negro and mulatto, and
south of Rio there was a mingling of all three races with an increasing predominance of the European. The Portuguese who followed
the court to Brazil were inclined to look down upon these Americans
as mere colonials, but also as Indian or African, and jealousy and
hostility between them were only aggravated.

The Prince Regent and the court had been driven from Portugal
by the onslaught of the armies of Napoleon. After the reconquest of
the Iberian peninsula by the forces of the Duke of Wellington and
the exile of Napoleon, the Portuguese royal government might have
been expected to return to Lisbon. But Dom João elected to remain
in Brazil, despite the urgings of Lord Strangford, the British minister,
that he restore normalcy in the old country and rejoin the galaxy of
restored sovereigns in Europe. Dom João liked Brazil. Indeed he
seems to have fallen under the influence of his American environment to a degree surprising in a sovereign born to absolute rule. In
correspondence with Thomas Jefferson, President of the United
States, he alluded to the "well-founded liberal principles, religious
as well as political, that we both possess," and to the "most perfect
union and friendship which I hope will continue without interruption
between the nations that occupy this new world." Rio de Janeiro
itself, before it was embellished with wide avenues, manicured
beaches and ultra-modern skyscraper apartments, although less

healthful than today, must with its incredible natural environment have possessed even greater fascination and charm.

The Brazilians, as might be anticipated, bitterly opposed Dom João's departure, for fear that they might lose all that they had gained by the presence of the crown. Indeed Dom João in December 1815, in order to normalize the situation in the eyes of the European sovereigns meeting at the Congress of Vienna, was persuaded to elevate the colony to formal and legal equality with the mother country. In the following year the mad queen died, and the Prince became King as João VI of the "United Kingdom of Portugal, Brazil and the Algarve." Meantime Portugal was administered by a Council of Regency presided over by the British minister, Sir Charles Stuart, while a British general, Marshal Beresford, was Commander in Chief of the Army. If the Brazilians feared that the King would return to Europe, the Portuguese in Europe were as profoundly discontented at seeming to remain an appendage of their former colony and under alien rule. Moreover the disappearance of the old colonial trade monopoly had grievously affected Portugal's economic prosperity. Commercial treaties following that with Great Britain in 1810 had induced an active correspondence of Brazil with Europe and the United States, and the balance of trade with Portugal, formerly very favorable to the metropolis, was sharply reversed. Here was a dangerous dichotomy which the crown was never able satisfactorily to resolve.

As circumstances in Napoleonic Europe had started a course of events that culminated in the emergence of Brazil from its former colonial status, so it was again political developments in Europe that gave occasion for the complete separation of Brazil from the mother country.

The year 1820 was a time of political upheaval in southern Europe. In Spain, Portugal, Italy, and Greece there were armed protests against the monarchical absolutisms that prevailed generally after the fall of Napoleon. In Portugal the liberal elements, fired by the example of revolution in next-door Spain, irritated by their continued bondage to an "English" regency, demanded a constitution and the return of their king. Uprisings first in Oporto and later in Lisbon, during the temporary absence of Beresford in Brazil, forced the Regency to summon a national parliament or Cortes, which took steps to elaborate a modern democratic constitution, by which Brazilians were to be accorded representation in the parliament.

The liberal movement, although not anti-Brazilian in the beginning, with the continued postponement of the King's return became the medium of the pent-up resentments of the Portuguese. It soon appeared that the Portuguese liberals, once they had their king back and their own liberties secure, were determined to reduce the American realm to its former condition of an exploited dependency. In Brazil the news of these events of 1820 produced a profound repercussion. Both groups, the Portuguese and the native American, displayed strong sympathies with the revolution in Lisbon. The Portuguese courtiers felt no strong attraction to a liberal constitution, but were intensely interested in returning with the King to their estates in Europe. The Brazilians hailed the constitution, but wanted to retain their king. Many preferred separate constitutions for the two kingdoms under the same crown, i.e., home rule for Brazil. And so there were demonstrations in all the principal cities, while in some of the provinces liberal juntas were chosen to replace the old captains general.

Dom João, well-meaning but temperamentally timorous and irresolute, knew not which way to turn. He was an old man, who by education and inheritance possessed little understanding of the constitutionalism fashionable at that time. But if he returned to Portugal, it was clear enough that he might lose Brazil. If he remained in Brazil, he would certainly lose Portugal. Meantime, although some representative Brazilians appeared in the Lisbon assembly and eloquently upheld their cause, all attempts at conciliation failed. The new constitution sharply repudiated the system of dual monarchy devised by Dom João VI.

In February 1821, the King, pressed by the Portuguese about him and by his son, the Crown Prince Dom Pedro, and threatened by mutiny in the garrison at Rio, issued a decree approving the Portuguese constitution (although it was unfinished and its exact terms were unknown), and a fortnight later announced his approaching departure. The British government threw its influence on the side of departure, and even prepared to send a squadron to Rio to convey him back to Europe.

Dom João also summoned Brazilian electors to a meeting in Rio to choose deputies to the Cortes in Lisbon. This assembly met on April 21, but it immediately proceeded, *ultra vires*, to announce a separate constitution for Brazil — the celebrated Spanish Constitution of 1812 — and to insist on the King's remaining in Brazil. These decisions the King, who so far had clutched at any pretense to avert the dreaded voyage back to Portugal, accepted next day. However on the following day the military stepped in, dispersed the assembly, and forced the unhappy monarch to reproclaim the Portuguese constitution. To complete the confusion, some believe that Dom João was himself privy to the whole stratagem. At any rate, on April 24 he boarded a warship and two days later sailed for Europe, taking with him most of the cash in the Bank of Brazil and all the jewels he could collect, and accompanied, it is said, by some three thousand of the Portuguese party. He left behind his son and heir, Dom Pedro, as regent in his place. In a famous letter addressed to Dom Pedro he anticipated the secession of Brazil, and advised him to take the crown for himself before some adventurer seized it.

Dom João VI was a genial, democratic, if rather weak and vacillating autocrat, but in general his government was enlightened and liberal. Although born to rule as an absolute sovereign, he was tolerant, clairvoyant, and fortunate in his choice of ministers. He "had the rare quality of being able to discover merit, and the rarer quality of not being jealous." He left Brazil with regret, and Brazilians remember him with affection and gratitude as the ruler who, by raising Brazil out of its colonial abasement, made national independence inevitable.

A peculiar role was played in these episodes by the Crown Prince Dom Pedro, then twenty-four years of age. He was the favorite son of his father, to whom he was generally devoted, but of very different personality. Ardent, impulsive, courageous, with considerable native intelligence but with little formal education, he liked to identify himself with the liberalism then current. But temperamentally he was a child of eighteenth-century absolutism. In the incidents of February and April 1821, he is suspected of complicity with the Portuguese party in forcing the King's departure, although it was contrary to the desires of the Brazilian liberals. He was ambitious to remain behind as regent, as actually transpired. In fact, there is considerable evidence that Dom João VI had an understanding with his son that continued to the day of the King's death in 1826: that the only way the House of Braganza could retain control of the two countries was by Brazilian secession under Dom Pedro's leadership, with the expectation that the latter, retaining his right of succession in Portugal, would ultimately reunite the two crowns.

Thereafter events moved rapidly, impelled by the actions of the Cortes in Lisbon, which increasingly betrayed the intentions of even the liberals in Portugal to subject Brazil to its former colonial bondage. Decrees were issued abolishing the organs of central government at Rio and making the provinces individually responsible to Lisbon, with the obvious intention of playing upon interprovincial jealousies and rivalries and preventing unity of action among the Brazilians. Another decree peremptorily ordered Dom Pedro to return at once to Portugal and prepare for a tour of Europe to complete his political education. At the same time Brazilians were by edict excluded from political and military offices. Dom Pedro in letters to his father noted the universal popular discontent, the profound agitation throughout the country, and the danger that extremists would conspire to establish a republic whether he was present or not. In Portugal the old King, completely intimidated by the liberals, spied upon, in fear of his life, his correspondence violated, gave way to their least demands.

The instructions from Lisbon Dom Pedro, after some hesitation, refused to honor. And on January 9, 1822, in response to memorials and petitions from the provinces of São Paulo and Minas Gerais and from the Municipality of Rio de Janeiro urging him to remain with them in Brazil, he gave his celebrated promise: "As it is for the good of all and the general felicity of the nation, say to the people that I will remain." This is the famous *Fico* of Brazilian annals. It was a formal, public rejection of Portuguese authority and avowal of alliance with the American patriots, "the turning of a page in Brazilian history."

Two days later the Portuguese garrison in Rio retorted by demanding the Regent's compliance with the orders from the Cortes and threatening to bombard the city. Citizens and militia rushed to arms. The Portuguese commander, intimidated by the crowd, capitulated next day and moved the regiments across the bay to Niteroi. And a month later, for a price, he sailed with the garrison back to Europe.

At the same time Dom Pedro called into a newly formed Council of Ministers perhaps the most distinguished Brazilian of his day, José Bonifácio de Andrada. José Bonifácio was a native of São Paulo. He had studied at the Portuguese University of Coimbra and with eminent scientists elsewhere in Europe and had become a scholar and mineralogist of note. He lived for many years in Portugal where he held important official positions. He was a professor at Coimbra, perpetual secretary of the Academy of Sciences in Lisbon, and a member of many other European learned societies. He returned to Brazil in 1819 and soon rose to be the political leader of his native province. Early in 1822 he came to Rio de Janeiro to urge Dom Pedro to defy the Portuguese parliament and remained to be his chief minister. And it was his experience, energy, and statesmanship that guided the last steps to independence.

As remarked above, events moved rapidly. In February 1822 Dom Pedro published a decree creating a consultative council or junta to consist of representatives of all the provinces. In May he accepted from the Municipality of Rio the title, "Perpetual and Constitutional Defender of Brazil." In June he issued a call for a constituent assembly for Brazil in order to "establish the bases on which should be erected its independence." In August, in a series of proclamations, he urged the people to resist coercion, forbade the landing of Portuguese troops without his permission, and addressed a circular to the diplomatic corps announcing that Brazil was almost ready to proclaim its independence under the Braganzas. The final step was taken on September 7. While on a journey through São Paulo to unify resistance in that province, as he had already done successfully in the province of Minas Gerais, Dom Pedro was overtaken near a small stream called Ipiranga by a messenger from the Council in Rio with the latest Portuguese dispatches. The Cortes had revoked as rebellious the orders for the assembly of representatives of the provinces, had annulled all the acts of the Regent, and declared his ministers guilty of treason. There also arrived letters from his wife, the Princess Leopoldina, and José Bonifácio insisting that the decisive moment had come.

Dom Pedro read the dispatches, and before his escort and with show of great indignation, crumpled them and ground them under his heel, drew his sword, and cried out, "The hour has come! Independence or death! We have separated from Portugal!" This was the famous "Cry of Ipiranga" of Brazilian history. There was no official act confirming this gesture. In fact, several earlier dates, in January, May, June, and August, were almost equally significant. But September 7 remains the Independence Day for all Brazilians.

Section II

Juan Manuel de Rosas: Bloody Tyrant, or Founder of Argentine Unity and Defender of the Nation's Independence?

The rise and fall of dictators has long been a basic theme of Latin American history. Though Columbus may not have been the first dictator, which some believe he was, there is no doubt that the institution still flourishes south of the Rio Grande. What causes dictators, how they maintain themselves in power, and what they accomplish are highly controversial questions, for no magnum opus has yet been written on the subject. The latest historian analyzing this puzzling but persistent phenomenon in Latin American life emphasizes "the rich variety of dictatorial types and the multitude of factors that conditioned their existence."[1]

It may be useful to examine one dictator from several angles of vision. Juan Manuel de Rosas, who ruled Argentina with an iron hand from 1835–1852, has been violently attacked and stoutly defended since he first established his power. Articulate exiles in Chile and Uruguay kept up a steady fire against him through newspapers, pamphlets, and books. To counteract these writers, such as Domingo Faustino Sarmiento and Juan Bautista Alberdi, Rosas employed the foreign journalist Pedro de Angelis, who mounted an efficient propaganda machine aimed at improving the dictator's image in Europe and elsewhere.[2] Inside Argentina various methods were perfected

---

1 Hugh M. Hamill, Jr., ed., *Dictatorship in Spanish America* (New York: Knopf, 1965), p. 5.

2 William S. Dudley, "Pedro de Angelis (1784–1859): Journalist, Propagandist, and Historian" (Master's Thesis, Columbia University, 1966).

to keep alive the pro-Rosas spirit. One foreign visitor reported that puppet shows, theater performances, and the opera were opened with a display of public enthusiasm. The principal performers would assemble on the stage and cry out in a loud voice: "Long live the Confederación Argentina," to which the chorus would reply: "Viva." Then the principal characters would shout again: "Death to the savage Unitarians" with an answering "Mueran" from the chorus, after which the performance began.[3]

Foreigners visiting Argentina during the Age of Rosas reacted in various ways. Charles Darwin was favorably impressed, at least at first, whereas the American Anthony King denounced him as an "evil genius."[4] French opinion was analyzed by the late William Spence Robertson, who established the study of Latin American history at the University of Illinois (Reading II.1). One of the prominent refugees from Rosas was Esteban Echeverría, a literary figure who published the first volume of poetry in Argentina, introduced romanticism to the country as a result of his experience in Paris, and wrote a famous polemic against Rosas, *The Slaughter House* (Reading II.2).

In the years after Rosas fell, while he lived (1852–1877) quietly as a country gentleman in England, Argentines continued to deplore his "tyranny," his personalization of power (Reading II.3). Only toward the end of the nineteenth century did historians such as Ernesto Quesada portray Rosas as a product of his times and not as a unique monster in their nation's history (Reading II.4).

The debate still goes on. The historian of Argentine political thought, José Luis Romero of the University of Buenos Aires, has pointed out that Rosas continued the authoritarian tradition of colonial times (Reading II.5), whereas the late Miron Burgin — whose early death removed an outstanding pioneer in Latin American economic history — stressed the steady support Rosas gave to the pastoral development of Argentina (Reading II.6).

Since World War I a new Rosas revisionism has arisen, directed by a group of bitter, ultranationalistic, antiforeign, antidemocratic writers who have attracted a wide reading public (Reading II.7). This pro-Rosas spirit still lives today, in the hearts of some Argen-

---

[3] Tom B. Jones, *South America Rediscovered* (Minneapolis: University of Minnesota Press, 1949), p. 26.

[4] Charles Darwin, *Journal of Researches into the Geology and Natural History of the Various Countries Visited by H. M. S. Beagle* (London, 1839), pp. 85–87; John Anthony King, *Twenty-Four Years in the Argentine Republic* (New York, 1846), pp. 422–431.

tines, as demonstrated by the decree promulgated in 1964 by a municipality in the Chaco, on the occasion of the official naming of an avenue in honor of "Brigadier General Juan Manuel de Rosas" (Reading II.8). This was the first municipal tribute rendered to Rosas since his defeat in 1852.

A. Contemporary Attitudes

1. Foreign Estimates of Rosas

WILLIAM SPENCE ROBERTSON

Among the enigmatical personages of the "Age of Dictators" in South America none played a more spectacular role than the Argentine dictator, Juan Manuel de Rosas, whose gigantic and ominous figure bestrode the Plata River for more than twenty years. So despotic was his power that Argentine writers have themselves styled this age of their history as "The Tyranny of Rosas." A political enemy named Rivera Indarte, who attacked the dictator from an asylum in Montevideo, alleged in his "tables of blood" that Rosas had assassinated 722 persons, shot 1,393, and beheaded 3,765. Indeed, until the close of the nineteenth century the name of Rosas was often anathema in his native land. A dispassionate survey of the dramatic career of this bizarre figure was indeed not made until 1898. In that year Ernesto Quesada, a lawyer, historian, and sociologist of Buenos Aires published a monograph entitled "The Epoch of Rosas" in which he developed the thesis that this dictator was typical of his age, and furthermore that he laid broad and deep the foundations upon which the Argentine nation was successfully erected.

Still, even today among the intelligentsia of Argentina there are doubters who are loath to yield this tardy tribute to the great dictator. To paraphrase an historical sociologist: if you ask an his-

From "Foreign Estimates of the Argentine Dictator, Juan Manuel de Rosas" by William Spence Robertson, *Hispanic American Historical Review*, X, 1930, pp. 125–137, *passim*. Reprinted by permission.

torian who was Juan Manuel de Rosas, he will say, a tyrant; if you ask a physician, he will respond, a neurotic; ask a descendant of one of Rosas's partisans and he will retort, a great man; a publicist will dub him a clever politician; philosophers will declare that he was a son of his age; while poets will denounce him as infamous. . . .

At least this is a case in which interesting sidelights may be obtained from the other shores of the Atlantic. In the *Revue des Deux Mondes* for 1835, M. Pavie contributed an article entitled "The Indians of the Pampas," in which he expressed the opinion that, because of the civil dissensions in which they had engaged, the generals who had won the independence of Argentina had made peace more dangerous than open warfare. Pavie proceeded to give his impressions of the dictator of the Argentine Confederation, whom he had observed during a recent carnival in Buenos Aires. "In fact," said the Frenchman,

no one can tame a colt, or break a savage horse, or hunt a cougar better than Rosas. He made a show of compelling his fine Chilean steed to gallop through the worst paved streets of the capital; then he would suddenly wheel about, retrace his steps, and pirouette over the slippery stones, dodging not only the buckets of water but also the eggs which on that day, according to custom, the women showered upon the passersby.

This clever sketch, as well as the allusions made by Pavie to the generals who had fought for Argentine independence, much provoked the government of Rosas. In a despatch to Paris, the Marquis de Peysac, the French consul at Buenos Aires, reported that both the dictator and Señor Arana, his minister of foreign relations, were full of resentment. In consequence, conferences were held between Arana and Peysac in which the latter felt called upon to inform the Argentinian that liberty of the press existed in France. But to allay the wrath of the Argentinians the marquis soon transmitted to his government an article refuting "the vile lies, and calumnious imputations concerning the political condition" of La Plata that had been published in the *Gaceta Mercantil* of Buenos Aires. This portrayal of the Argentine dictator by a partisan will perhaps serve as a foil for other characterizations.

The dexterity, agility, and hardihood of General Rosas in horsemanship and in exercises of strength are perhaps unequalled in the Republic, as well as his ability, experience, and knowledge with respect to all sorts of rural labors and customs. But I should add that to these estimable gifts he unites other eminent qualities; his talents, his vast knowledge, his political skill and judgment, and his valor in military campaigns have often saved the republic from ruin and desolation. Classic and luminous proofs of this truth are furnished by his public life from the memorable year 1820 until the present time. He is the only man among us who has known how to unite the administrative talents of a most consummate statesman with the intrepidity, agility, and bravery of a warrior, and with the traits of a most clever gaucho. Then we must add to this happy union of singular and necessary qualities, an unshakeable patriotism, a severe virtue, and a noble disinterestedness — a combination of qualities that makes him the most perfect exemplar of the politician, the hero, the warrior, and the great citizen.

Shortly after the Marquis of Peysac had reported an interview with Rosas concerning Pavie's skit, the Duc de Broglie, who had recently become minister of foreign affairs in his own cabinet, formulated his concept of the dictator in these words:

This general is not an ordinary man. The oddities of his manner or character do not prevent me from considering him as one of the most eminent chieftains brought forth by the revolutions in South America. It is to be hoped that the value which he seems to place upon the opinions of Europe will tend to restrain him from that misuse of power which men of the New World elevated to such a position are too often inclined to permit. I have gladly acceded to the wish that he expressed to you of having published in our journals a refutation of the article he has taken so much to heart which appeared in the *Revue des Deux Mondes*. You can read this counterblast in the *Moniteur* in a version that has been rendered less bitter and more veiled.

A more interesting estimate of Rosas was furnished in 1840 by an officer of the French fleet that had blockaded the coast of Argentina largely because of the dictator's policy of requiring military service from French subjects who were domiciled in that country. This officer avowed that Rosas still enjoyed the barbarous amusements that he had loved while he lived in the country with the gauchos.

In the secrecy of his home, where he had retired with companions of these farces, Rosas gave himself up to a thousand foolish notions which are repugnant to our ideas of elegance, but which charmed those men who had grown up on the pampas in the midst of horse races and of manners and customs altogether different from those of Europe. This man, who founded his power upon the affection of the people, did not feel that he was degrading himself when he engaged in diversions which they loved. But when he found himself in the presence of a distinguished foreigner, whose esteem he desired to gain, the rude gaucho disappeared: his language became refined, his sonorous voice pleased the ear, his eye caressed, and his attentive and intelligent glance captivated. Though he had never distinguished himself by any remarkable feat of arms, yet no one ever denied that he had courage. The deep regret that seized him upon the death of his wife, as well as the extreme solicitude which he displayed toward his daughter, seemed to indicate that tender feelings had not been altogether banished from his heart. He made this cherished daughter the depository of his most intimate thoughts and the heiress of his fortune. And because he had laid up great riches for her, he was accused of wishing to seat her upon a throne. . . .

After describing the terrible murders that had been committed by a secret society in Buenos Aires at the behest of Rosas, a French traveler who had resided some months in La Plata deemed it only fair to depict another side of the dictator's personality. This Frenchman did not maintain that by his truly great qualities Rosas had offset his disdain for life and liberty, because these were defects for which no compensation could be made. But we do recognize, he continued, that Rosas really has great qualities, and that he would have been able to render his country splendid service, if only Heaven had given him more light and a more humane heart.

His great qualities were all related to the nature of his domination. Rosas knew how to command: he possessed the secret of commanding obedience. By virtue of this quality he might have become the benefactor and saviour of his country. He indeed saw that the evil was in the anarchy which devoured the land, in the confusion of all governmental power, in the weakening of all the springs of authority, and in the insubordinate habits of soldiers and generals. Unfortunately he overemphasized the opposite tendency and gave to the power that had become irresistible in his hands an effect that was odious, destructive, and degrading. He substituted his personality for the existing institutions; he induced the entire population to adore his own portrait; he had incense burned before that portrait in the churches; he had himself drawn in a carriage by women, and by the most distinguished persons in the capital city; and he desired that discourses should be addressed to himself in public ceremonies. At least, if he did not direct this to be done, he encouraged these servile demonstrations which in their manifold forms have reduced the citizens of the capital to the moral condition of Asiatic people.

The French minister, Baron Deffaudis, who had been sent on an extraordinary mission to La Plata to settle the interminable dispute between his government and Rosas, furnishes a view from a different angle. On June 7, 1845, after an interview with the dictator, this envoy sent a dispatch to Paris conveying his impressions of that curious personage.

Despite the care which he takes to veil them, intelligence, artifice, and determination are deeply engraven upon his face. If one were not aware that he held the lives of his adversaries very cheap, one would perhaps never divine this at all; but when one knows this, one is not in the least astonished at his physiognomy. On the other side, age begins to leave its mark upon him. His postures are awkward and somewhat weak. His body is ten years older than his face. One does not notice in him the agility, skill, and vigor that placed him, as he once said, at the forefront of the gauchos. He has the air of a townsman endowed with a strong constitution, who has become corpulent and enervated by a sedentary life. In fact, he scarcely leaves his apartments, particularly when he is in the city, and only takes the air on the terrace of his house. Then, too, he has been attacked by a cruel malady, the gravel, which leaves him only certain intervals of repose. I further believe that those Europeans who represent him as rather disposed to spring into a saddle to resume the vagrant life of the pampas than to yield to the more just and moderate demands of foreign diplomacy are interpreting him by traits that are out of date.   . . .

Each successive day General Rosas is becoming more and more a man of the cabinet: in this role he is now more redoubtable than as a gaucho. In the cabinet, in fact, he is a man full of will and perseverance as well as of astuteness and suppleness. He is absolutely indifferent about the nature of the means by which to gain success and clever to find the means which are suitable to his ends. He believes that men are full of vices and weaknesses, and boasts of his ability to discern by the first glance of his eye the species of seduction or corruption to which any particular man is susceptible. An indefatigable worker, he spends his days in supervising the smallest details of ministerial affairs, in corresponding directly with the civil and military authorities of the provinces in matters touching his personal policy, and finally in dictating and even correcting with his own hand an infinite number of articles destined for journals not only in his own country but also in foreign lands. The object of these articles is above all to depict his administration in the most attractive colors, to repel the attacks which are made upon it from every quarter, and also to make the most bitter criticism of every act of those governments with which he finds himself in disagreement.

Another French diplomat, Count Walewski, who was later sent on an identical errand to La Plata, thus conveyed the impressions that General Rosas made upon him during an interview that lasted five or six hours.

General Rosas is ordinarily prolix and diffuse. His periods are long; and he departs with great facility from the main topic in order to engage in digressions that immeasurably lengthen the conversation. From time to time he tries the effects of eloquence or of gestures, and his intonations are cleverly calculated to impress the hearer.

The count affirmed that it was very difficult to pursue an argument with Rosas. "Warned in advance of this digressive tendency," said Walewski,

while listening religiously, I was forced constantly to lead him back to the question at issue, and it was only because of these persistent efforts on my part that we were able to consider the principal points in the negotiation. Otherwise twenty-four hours would not have been sufficient. Aside from this, the course of his argument was admirably arranged, and if his premises were well founded, there was nothing that could have been said against him.

These personages terminated their interview by an exchange of diplomatic courtesies. Rosas declared that he had always desired that his political conduct would meet with "the approval of France," and particularly with "the approbation of her king," for whose person he professed in lofty terms a high admiration. The dictator mellifluously avowed that he considered Louis Philippe as

the most enlightened of those sovereigns who today occupy the thrones of the world, and as the greatest statesman of the century.

An attache of the mission named Brossard, who was present at this interview, was more successful than his master in discerning the salient traits of Rosas. A few years later, on a broad canvas and with a variety of pigments, this diplomat painted what was perhaps the best portrait ever made of the crafty despot. Here it is:

General Rosas is a man of medium height, quite stout, and apparently endowed with great physical vigor. His features are regular; he has a light complexion and blonde hair, and does not at all resemble a Spaniard. One might well exclaim upon beholding him, "Here is a Norman gentleman." His physiognomy is a remarkable mixture of craft and force. He is generally tranquil, and even mild; but upon occasion, the contraction of his lips gives him a singular expression of deliberate severity. He expresses himself with much facility, and as one who is a perfect master of his thoughts and his words. His style in conversation varies: now he uses well-chosen and even elegant phrases; and again he indulges in trivial expressions. There is perhaps a little affectation in the way in which he expresses himself. His remarks are never categorical; they are diffuse and complicated by digressions and incidental phrases. This prolixity is evidently premeditated and intended to embarrass the interlocutor. In truth it is

quite difficult to follow General Rosas in the detours of his conversation. . . .

The dictator showed himself by turns to be a consummate statesman,
an affable individual, an indefatigable dialectician, a vehement and passionate orator; as the emergency arose, he displayed with rare perfection,
anger, frankness, and bonhomie. One realizes that, when encountered face
to face, he could intimidate, or deceive, or seduce.

Walewski's aide also contributed so discerning a political analysis
of Rosas that in quoting it one scarcely knows where to stop:

Endowed with a reflective and persistent will, Juan Manuel is essentially an absolute ruler. Although force — that is to say, the principle
of persons who have no principles — is the basis of his government, and
although he constantly consults in his policies the necessities of his personal position, yet he is much pleased to be considered as a man of well-
founded convictions. He professes a great horror for secret societies, *lojias*
as they are designated, even though the *Mazorca* which he founded was
nothing else than a secret society, which became publicly known because
of its excesses. He becomes indignant when one supposes that he has the
least affinity with revolutionists who are enemies of the social order; and
as a statesman he assumes in his maxims a great austerity that does not
exist in his private morals. "I know," he avowed in his interviews, "that a
good example should be highly esteemed by all people."

Up to a certain point he has justified his pretensions and his words by
reestablishing material order throughout the country and in the administration, by causing the civil laws to be obeyed, and by enveloping his
dictatorship with the constitutional forms that were observed before his
advent. He busies himself with all the details of administration and carefully supervises them; he labors assiduously from fifteen to sixteen hours
every day in the transaction of public business, and does not allow anything to pass without a minute inspection. Thus, as he has said, the entire
burden of governmental responsibility falls upon himself. . . .

Raised to supreme power by astuteness, General Rosas has seen his
domination violently attacked, and he has not known how to maintain
himself except by force. Vindictive and imperious by education and by
temperament, he was precipitated into despotism, and has cheapened in
the interior of the country that liberty of which he has spoken so much.
He resembles those men portrayed by Tacitus who placed liberty to the
fore in order thereby to overthrow the existing order, and, who, when they
became masters of the empire, turned upon their mistress. Because of this
tendency he has committed those sanguinary acts that have surrounded
him with an aureola of terror. Because of this tendency he has been
obliged to concede extravagant favors to abandoned men, who are bound
irrevocably to his chariot by their vices and crimes as well as by his favors
and whose prosperity is an insult to morale and to public misery. From

this tendency there has arisen the system of legal oppression by which he persecutes all his enemies, who, it must be said, compose the most polished and intellectual part of the nation.

A man from the country, Rosas has in fact been the leader of the reaction of the men of the campo against the predominant influence of the capital city. Imbued with the prejudice of Castilian pride, he detests *en masse* those foreigners whose labor and capital could enrich his country, and accords them only a niggardly hospitality. An agriculturist by birth, by education, and by taste, he does not appreciate industry. . . . Nourished in the monopolistic maxims of Spanish colonial law, he neither understands nor permits trade except when it is hemmed in by prohibitive tariffs and rigorous regulations.

On the other side, General Rosas is much occupied with the means by which a government may influence the morale of a people. Thus it is that he attaches great importance to matters concerned with public education; for he considers both education and religion as means of political influence. This same motive causes him to intervene actively in the periodical press. He subsidizes periodicals in France, in England, in Portugal, in Brazil, in the United States, and directs his journals of Buenos Aires, namely, the *Gaceta Mercantil,* the *Archivo Americano,* and the *British Packet.*

In the belief that persons of the so-called Latin race have an insight into each other's character that is often denied to Anglo-Saxons, I have purposely used estimates of Rosas that emanated from French contemporaries. They present the concepts of foreigners whose viewpoint though prejudiced was much more detached than that of Argentine observers. My study convinces me that the treasure trove of unexploited material in the French archives will cast a glow of interpretative light upon both the domestic and the foreign policies of the Hispanic-American nations. So far as Rosas is concerned, these inedited papers demonstrate that he was a consummate poseur. They convey hints that his iron constitution was corroding. These papers further reveal that the dictator maintained an insidious diplomatic as well as journalistic propaganda both at home and abroad. At many points they confirm the view of other contemporaries with regard to the personal methods, the genuine ability, the strength, the resourcefulness, the astuteness, and the unscrupulousness of the gaucho tyrant — traits which he possessed in a more marked degree than many other Hispanic-American tyrants. In truth he was compared by one contemporary with the gloomy Paraguayan dictator Francia, while another contemporary likened him unto the French nationalistic monarch Louis XI. The iteration and reiteration of the cruelty and ruthlessness of Rosas in these accounts indeed provoke the query whether in the rehabilitation of the tyrant the historic pendulum may not have been swung from the extreme of denunciation too far in the direction of justification, and whether as fresh and discriminating sources are utilized the historian of the future may not bring the pendulum back to a median position. In any event this brief study brings up the perennial problem of the good and the evil in dictatorial rule in Hispanic America.

2. The Slaughter House

ESTEBAN ECHEVERRÍA

The Convalescencia, or Alto Slaughter House, is located in the southern part of Buenos Aires, on a huge lot, rectangular in shape, at the intersection of two streets, one of which ends there while the other continues eastward. The lot slants to the south and is bisected by a ditch made by the rains, its shoulders pitted with ratholes, its bed collecting all the blood from the Slaughter House. At the junction of the right angle, facing the west, stands what is commonly called the *casilla*, a low building containing three small rooms with a porch in the front facing the street and hitching posts for tying the horses. In the rear are several pens of ñandubay picket fence with heavy doors for guarding the steers.

In winter these pens become veritable mires in which the animals remain bogged down, immobile, up to the shoulder blades. In the casilla the pen taxes and fines for violation of the rules are collected, and in it sits the judge of the Slaughter House, an important figure, the chieftain of the butchers, who exercises the highest power, delegated to him by the Restorer, in that small republic. It is not difficult to imagine the kind of man required for the discharge of such an office.

The casilla is so dilapidated and so tiny a building that no one would notice it were it not that its name is inseparably linked with that of the terrible judge and that its white front is pasted over with posters. "Long live the Federalists! Long live the Restorer and the Heroine Doña Encarnación Escurra! Death to the savage Uni-

From *El Matadero* (*The Slaughter House*) by Esteban Echeverría, trans. and ed. Angel Flores (New York: Las Americas Publishing Company, 1959), pp. 15–35, *passim*. Reprinted by permission.

tarians!" Telling posters, indeed, symbolizing the political and religious faith of the Slaughter House folk! But some readers may not
know that the above mentioned Heroine is the deceased wife of the
Restorer, the beloved patroness of the butchers, who even after her
death is venerated by them as if she were still alive, because of her
Christian virtues and her Federalist heroism during the revolution
against Balcarce. The story is that during an anniversary of that
memorable deed of the *mazorca*, the terrorist society of Rosas' hench-
men, the butchers feted the Heroine with a magnificent banquet in
the casilla. She attended, with her daughter and other Federalist
ladies, and there, in the presence of a great crowd, she offered the
butchers, in a solemn toast, her Federalist patronage, and for that
reason they enthusiastically proclaimed her patroness of the Slaughter House, stamping her name upon the walls of the casilla, where it
will remain until blotted out by the hand of time.

From a distance the view of the Slaughter House was now
grotesque, full of animation. Forty-nine steers were stretched out
upon their skins and about two hundred people walked about the
muddy, blood-drenched floor. Hovering around each steer stood a
group of people of different skin colors. Most prominent among them
was the butcher, a knife in his hand, his arms bare, his chest exposed,
long hair dishevelled, shirt and sash and face besmeared with blood.
At his back, following his every movement, romped a gang of children, Negro and mulatto women, offal collectors whose ugliness
matched that of the harpies, and huge mastiffs which sniffed, snarled,
and snapped at one another as they darted after booty. Forty or more
carts covered with awnings of blackened hides were lined up along
the court, and some horsemen with their capes thrown over their
shoulders and their lassos hanging from their saddles rode back and
forth through the crowds or lay on their horses' necks, casting indolent glances upon this or that lively group. In mid-air a flock of
bluewhite gulls, attracted by the smell of blood, fluttered about,
drowning with strident cries all the other noises and voices of the
Slaughter House, and casting clear-cut shadows over that confused
field of horrible butchery. All this could be observed at the very beginning of the slaughter.

But as the activities progressed, the picture kept changing. While
some groups dissolved as if some stray bullet had fallen nearby or an
enraged dog had charged them, new groups constantly formed: here
where a steer was being cut open, there where a butcher was already
hanging the quarters on the hook in the carts, or yonder where a steer

was being skinned or the fat taken off. From the mob eyeing and waiting for the offal there issued ever and anon a filthy hand ready to slice off meat or fat. Shouts and explosions of anger came from the butchers, from the incessantly milling crowds, and from the gamboling street urchins. . . .

The slaughtering had been completed by noon, and the small crowd which had remained to the end was leaving, some on foot, others on horseback, others pulling along the carts loaded with meat.

Suddenly the raucous voice of a butcher was heard announcing: "Here comes a Unitarian!" On hearing that word, the mob stood still as if thunderstruck.

"Can't you see his U-shaped side whiskers? Can't you see he carries no insignia on his coat and no mourning sash on his hat?"

"The Unitarian cur!"

"The son of a bitch!"

"He has the same kind of saddle as the gringo!"

"To the gibbet with him!"

"Give him the scissors!"

"Give him a good beating!"

"He has a pistol case attached to his saddle just to show off!"

"All these cocky Unitarians are as showy as the devil himself!"

"I bet you wouldn't dare touch him, Matasiete."

"He wouldn't, you say?"

"I bet you he would!"

Matasiete was a man of few words and quick action. When it came to violence, dexterity, skill in the handling of an ox, a knife, or a horse he did not talk much, but he acted. They had piqued him; spurring his horse, he trotted away, bridle loose, to meet the Unitarian.

The Unitarian was a young man, about twenty-five years old, elegant, debonair of carriage, who, as the above-mentioned exclamations were spouting from these impudent mouths, was trotting towards Barracas, quite fearless of any danger ahead of him. Noticing, however, the significant glances of that gang of Slaughter House curs, his right hand reached automatically for the pistolcase of his English saddle. Then a side push from Matasiete's horse threw him from his saddle, stretching him out. Supine and motionless he remained on the ground.

"Long live Matasiete!" shouted the mob, swarming upon the victim.

Confounded, the young man cast furious glances on those ferocious men and hoping to find in his pistol compensation and vindication, moved towards his horse, which stood quietly nearby. Matasiete rushed to stop him. He grabbed him by his tie, pulled him down again on the ground, and whipping out his dagger from his belt, put it against his throat.

Loud guffaws and stentorian vivas cheered him.

What nobility of soul! What bravery, that of the Federalists! Always ganging together and falling like vultures upon the helpless victim!

"Cut open his throat, Matasiete! Didn't he try to shoot you? Rip him open . . . !"

"What scoundrels these Unitarians! Thrash him good and hard!"

"He has a good neck for the 'violin' — you know, the gibbet!"

"Better use the Slippery-One on him!"

"Let's try it," said Matasiete, and, smiling, began to pass the sharp edge of his dagger around the throat of the fallen man as he pressed in his chest with his left knee and held him by the hair with his left hand.

"Don't behead him, don't!" shouted in the distance the Slaughter House Judge as he approached on horseback.

"Bring him into the casilla. Get the gibbet and the scissors ready. Death to the savage Unitarians! Long live the Restorer of the laws!"

"Long live Matasiete!"

The spectators repeated in unison "Long live Matasiete! Death to the Unitarians!" They tied his elbows together as blows rained upon his nose, and they shoved him around. Amid shouts and insults they finally dragged the unfortunate young man to the bench of tortures just as if they had been the executioners of the Lord themselves.

The main room of the casilla had in its center a big, hefty table, which was devoid of liquor glasses and playing cards only in times of executions and tortures administered by the Federalist executioners of the Slaughter House. In a corner stood a smaller table with writing materials and a notebook and some chairs, one of which, an armchair, was reserved for the Judge. A man who looked like a soldier was seated in one of them, playing on his guitar the "Resbalosa," an immensely popular song among the Federalists, when the mob rushing tumultuously into the corrider of the casilla brutally showed in the young Unitarian.

"The Slippery-One for him!" shouted one of the fellows.

"Commend your soul to the devil!"

"He's furious as a wild bull!"

"The whip will tame him."

"Give him a good pummeling!"

"First the cowhide and scissors."

"Otherwise to the bonfire with him!"

"The gibbet would be even better for him!"

"Shut up and sit down," shouted the Judge as he sank into his armchair. All of them obeyed, while the young man standing in front of the Judge exclaimed with a voice pregnant with indignation:

"Infamous executioners, what do you want to do with me?"

"Quiet!" ordered the Judge, smiling. "There's no reason for getting angry. You'll see."

The young man was beside himself. His entire body shook with rage: his mottled face, his voice, his tremulous lips, evinced the throbbing of his heart and the agitation of his nerves. His fiery eyes bulged in their sockets, his long black hair bristled. His bare neck and the front of his shirt showed his bulging arteries and his anxious breathing.

"Are you trembling?" asked the Judge.

"Trembling with anger because I cannot choke you."

"Have you that much strength and courage?"

"I have will and pluck enough for that, scoundrel."

"Get out the scissors I use to cut my horse's mane and clip his hair in the Federalist style."

Two men got hold of him. One took his arms and another his head and in a minute clipped off his side whiskers. The spectators laughed merrily.

"Get him a glass of water to cool him off," ordered the Judge.

"I'll have you drink gall, you wretch!"

A Negro appeared with a glass of water in his hand. The young man kicked his arm and the glass smashed to bits on the ceiling, the fragments sprinkling the astonished faces of the spectators.

"This fellow is incorrigible!"

"Don't worry, we'll tame him yet!"

"Quiet!" said the Judge. "Now you are shaven in the Federalist style — all you need is a mustache, don't forget to grow one!"

"Now, let's see: why don't you wear any insignia?"

"Because I don't care to."

"Don't you know that the Restorer orders it?"

"Insignia become you, slaves, but not free men!"

"Free men will have to wear them, by force."

"Indeed, by force and brutal violence. These are your arms, infamous wretches! Wolves, tigers, and panthers are also strong like you and like them you should walk on all fours."

"Are you not afraid of being torn to pieces by the tiger?"

"I prefer that to have you pluck out my entrails, as the ravens do, one by one."

"Why don't you wear a mourning sash on your hat in memory of the Heroine?"

"Because I wear it in my heart in memory of my country which you, infamous wretches, have murdered."

"Don't you know that the Restorer has ordered mourning in memory of the Heroine?"

"You, slaves, were the ones to order it so as to flatter your master and pay infamous homage to him."

"Insolent fellow! You are beside yourself. I'll have your tongue cut off if you utter one more word. Take the pants off this arrogant fool, and beat him on his naked ass. Tie him down on the table first!"

Hardly had the Judge uttered his commands when four bruisers bespattered with blood lifted the young man and stretched him out upon the table.

"Rather behead me than undress me, infamous rabble!"

They muzzled him with a handkerchief and began to pull off his clothes. The young man wriggled, kicked, and gnashed his teeth. His muscles assumed now the flexibility of rushes, now the hardness of iron, and he squirmed like a snake in his enemy's grasp. Drops of sweat, large as pearls, streamed down his cheeks, his pupils flamed, his mouth foamed, and the veins on his neck and forehead jutted out black from his pale skin as if congested with blood.

"Tie him up," ordered the Judge.

"He's roaring with anger," said one of the cutthroats.

In a short while they had tied his feet to the legs of the table and turned his body upside down. In trying to tie his hands, the men had to unfasten them from behind his back. Feeling free, the young man, with a brusque movement which seemed to drain him of all his strength and vitality, raised himself up, first upon his arms, then upon his knees, and collapsed immediately, murmuring: "Rather behead me than undress me, infamous rabble!"

His strength was exhausted, and having tied him down crosswise, they began undressing him. Then a torrent of blood spouted, bubbling from the young man's mouth and nose, and flowed freely down the table. The cutthroats remained immobile and the spectators, astonished.

"The savage Unitarian has burst with rage," said one of them.

"He had a river of blood in his veins," put in another.

"Poor devil, we wanted only to amuse ourselves with him, but he took things too seriously," exclaimed the Judge, scowling tiger-like.

"We must draw up a report. Untie him and let's go!"

They carried out the orders, locked the doors, and in a short while the rabble went out after the horse of the downcast, taciturn Judge.

The Federalists had brought to an end one of their innumerable feats of valor.

Those were the days when the butchers of the Slaughter House were apostles who propagated by dint of whip and poignard Rosas' Federation, and it is not difficult to imagine what sort of Federation issued from their heads and knives. They were wont to dub as savage Unitarians (in accordance with the jargon invented by the Restorer, patron of the brotherhood) any man who was neither a cutthroat nor a crook; any man who was kindhearted and decent; any patriot or noble friend of enlightenment and freedom; and from the foregoing episode it can be clearly seen that the headquarters of the Federation were located in the Slaughter House.

B. Nineteenth-Century Historical Controversy

3. The Tyranny of Rosas

José Manuel Estrada

What was the tyranny? Is it true that it was a transitory phenomenon, a passing tendency of a people under the heel of a monster who never took root, a senseless despot who lived by chance, who tyrannized without plan and passed on without leaving any sign of his chains? In that case, Rosas would have been a conqueror, but not

From *Lecciones sobre la República Argentina*, 2nd. edition, by José Manuel Estrada (Buenos Aires: Librería del Colegio, de Pedro Igón y Cía., 1898), II, pp. 428–455, *passim*.

precisely a tyrant. Is it true that the fierce soul of Rosas did not harbor the sinister light in whose glow despots unfold the plans that realize the somber object of their passion? If he lacked the temperament of the true tyrant, how can we explain the slackening of republican fiber and the submission of a society transformed even in the exterior manifestations of culture to his extravagant whim? Great peoples are humiliated only by great tyrants. I will allow your own judgment to settle the question, gentlemen, after I have made some observations with respect to the system of Rosas, his plans, and the methods he employed to realize them.

Juan Manuel Rosas is portrayed in his works.

You know that the social dissolution which festered in the people after the civil war carefully stirred by his hand made him a dictator, elevated by the weariness of those who sought repose in obedience. The muse of Tacitus has not sufficed to teach society that the bondage of tyranny is far more destructive than anarchy. The rustic Caesar arrived, having been summoned on a day of discouragement. The brave and ardent city could not support the weight of the revolution. The personal government that had been spreading toward the mouth of the Plata from the slopes of the Cordillera and the plains of La Rioja settled heavily on its shoulders. But Rosas, who deserted the urban society in which he had been cradled for the gaucho, pastoral society which was his element by habit and by choice, did not represent — strictly speaking — the triumph of the rural areas over the cities, of primitive forces over the forces of civilization. Rosas was not the creation of gaucho culture in its ordinary manifestations. He was the child of the rural revolution, which he joined, identifying himself . . . with it in culture and morality, but dominating it and preserving his own character, passion, and originality. He introduced reforms to the pastoral industry and, without discarding those aspects of it which he considered barbaric and primitive, subjected it to a discipline that was new, severe, and marked by truly brilliant features. Rosas, having himself whipped by his foreman for having violated his own prohibition against the carrying of knives, is Napoleon rewarding the sentry who challenged him, Pedro the Cruel having himself hanged in effigy in the alley of Seville. He is the tyrant inculcating by extravagant example idolatrous adherence to his law, dominating by his personal authority the action and thought of others, the activity and individualism of those who obey him. . . .

A tyrant of such lofty stature could not exercise his despotism for the benefit of a social group or of a party. His ideal, therefore, was to personalize his power, using for this purpose whatever resource the contemporary demoralization of the people put at his disposal. · · · ·

Rosas recruited the blind instruments to carry out his commands in the slaughterhouses, where rudeness of occupation, cruelty of habits, and intellectual and moral depression were greatest, and elevated these men to the highest social rank, bedecking them with the glorious insignia of our armies. Guitiño and his partners in crime, part of the social potpourri with which Rosas and his daughter surrounded themselves, were the revered personages of the era.

Rosas had his court of intriguing women and of men who were worth even less. Through them he won the devotion of the lower class and, dazzling them with the prestige which he treacherously offered, used them to launch a secret police and a vast network of informers without equal in the history of tyranny. His daughter danced with the Africans at the base of the social pyramid; doña María Josefa Ezcurra intrigued tirelessly, making use of domestic servants, who betrayed the secrets of the home and sold them for the wretched pride which the tyrant's court awakened in their hearts. The upper class was the favorite target of his rage merely because in the universal humiliation which he envisioned, he wished to subdue and completely degrade the class that had the greatest resources of vitality because of education or wealth. · · ·

This system, gentlemen, had a double result. First, it terrified the object of his anathema. Second, it won the sympathies of the rabble. Did he love the masses, by chance? Was there some mysterious democratic sentiment in the depths of his soul? Not in the least. Democracy cannot advance by bringing anarchy to society or by lowering the level of culture; it advances by raising the disinherited classes to that middle elevation which harmonizes popular forces and renders them capable of loving and exercising common sovereignty. Rosas checked one class with the other. · · ·

An Argentine historian has cited as a fact of extreme transcendence in the history of tyranny one that I must not forget: the official and popular honors which Rosas caused to be offered to his wife after her death and the regal veneration that surrounded his daughter, who he indicated was worthy of succeeding him. These in effect were means of impressing on the masses the idolatry of absolutism in the person and kinsmen of the tyrant. It was more than the viceregal liturgy. It was the Aztec cult of personal power and sovereignty.

I am speaking about almost contemporary events, and I do not need lengthy references.

You are undoubtedly familiar with the parish celebrations of un-
forgettable and disgraceful memory. Yoked like beasts to the triumphal carriage in which the portrait of the tyrant was displayed,
magistrates, soldiers, citizens, and . . . their wives and daughters
dragged it through the streets. The portrait was placed on the sanctuary, while cowardly ministers of the Almighty entoned chants
to the God of holy meekness by celebrating the sacrifices of the implacable monster whom they held up to the worship of the rabble. . . .

The uniform abdication of personality had its external ritual: the
scarlet badge, the mottos of extermination, the horrible cries that
rocked cradles and profaned tombs, that embittered festivities and
degraded the sentiments. The watchman that called the hour in the
dead of night terrorized the holy vigil of the mother beside her
child's cradle: "Death to the savage Unitarians," he would shout in
the midst of the silence or of the fearful rumble of the storm. Children shivered with fear. "Death to the savage Unitarians" was the
eternal watchword of slavery. . . .

What could Rosas fear from the Assembly, which solemnly abdi-
cated in 1835? He mocked it with his resignations and had to be
begged on bended knee to pick up once more the scepter which no
hand dared to touch. In 1840 the legislature awarded him the titles
of "Hero of the Desert" and "Heroic Defender of American Independence." Rosas forbade their official use in 1843. October was
given the name "month of Rosas." Rosas banned it shortly afterwards.
He and his followers were exempted from all taxes. . . . The dele-
gations from the Assembly, on the occasion of each resignation,
went before the tyrant to renew their "patriotic federal offers," as
they said, of their lives and honor. Rosas frequently refused to see
them. The servile scenes of the Roman Senate, despised by Caesar,
who disdained their crowns and humble hymns, were reproduced
daily. But the fawning slave is incorrigible.

The cowardice of the public powers, the terror, the denunciations, the social disorder, isolated men from one another, and each
kept his complaints to himself. The spirit of association disappeared
in Buenos Aires to such an extent that it is barely beginning to be
reborn. Freedom of the press was dead, but the task of barbarization
did not stop there.

The revenues of the public educational establishments were abolished in 1840 and, thanks to the generous disinterestedness of some
noble professors, the "Athens of the Plata" did not present the spectacle of closing its university. After 1844 primary and secondary

schools had to submit their textbooks for official examination and request prior permission, which was renewed annually. Imagine the decadence of the interior provinces! Unable to communicate with Buenos Aires until March 1842 because of the suppression of the mails, they rotted in the tedium of their isolation. The blockades, the impressments, the persecution of their inert caciques, the difficulties of communication, annihilated their industries and forced them to submit. . . .

Rivera Indarte used to ask what Rosas had accomplished during his long domination. What law had he issued, what transcendental principle had been applied under his government, and to what end had he tried to remold society? Gentlemen, tyrannies are not means; they are in themselves the end. I will tell you what in my opinion Rosas did. He neutralized the democratic sentiments which had developed in the party struggles and in the disturbances of civil war. Reversing social order, erasing individuality, making himself adored as idol, sovereign, and majesty, he extirpated the revolution of May with all of its greatness and fecundity. Rosas created a political idolatry — the personalization of power — which had never existed in Argentine society, unless it be sought in the irregular armed bands. The extent to which he rooted it can be shown by the fact that it survived his tyranny . . . despite the incomplete precautions taken by the legislator, who imitated precepts of societies different from ours without realizing the enormity of the evil and the original and urgent remedies that were required. Power is still personalized. . . . This is the achievement of Rosas. This is the unhappy achievement of a great tyrant whose traces will be blotted out only by the time that heals and the education that redeems.

4. The "Middle Ages" of Argentine History

ERNESTO QUESADA

The crisis of 1820 gave birth to a historical period that might be called, by way of analogy, the "Middle Ages" of Argentina.

Just as the barbarian invasions destroyed the Roman empire and

From *La época de Rosas* by Ernesto Quesada (Buenos Aires: Instituto de Investigaciones Históricas, 1923), pp. 60–144, *passim*.

left its various members scattered throughout Europe without co-hesion or direction, abandoned as it were to the whims of chance, so in the Argentine Republic the crisis of 1820 dissolved the unity that existed throughout the entire country, annulled the central govern-ment, and left the provinces to their own devices amid the most horrifying anarchy.

In the Old World this period was characterized by the formation of more or less artificial groups subject to the rule of successful war-riors. They in turn relied upon their lieutenants, who exercised abso-lute control over the territory assigned to them. This was the origin of dynasties and nobility. Real and effective power resided in the nobility, which was in immediate contact with the population; royalty had to be satisfied at first with the shadow of power, exer-cised under the tutelage of the nobles, who regarded their fiefs as private property. . . .

Among us, too, each successful caudillo considered the region or province he dominated as his fief; in effect, the country was divided into great counties, inhabited by vassals and subject to true medieval lords, whose system of justice was based on the gal-lows and the knife and who exercised even the most fantastic rights of feudal potentates. They did not have recourse to the special forms of feudalism and did not swear fealty to an overlord, preferring to cloak themselves with the external forms of republican government, but the result was the same as in Europe: the masses supported and followed their caudillos because they protected them and guaranteed the precarious tranquility which they enjoyed. . . .

In Europe this period lasted for several centuries. Little by little the seaports and then the more populous towns became conscious of their strength. At the same time the unlimited power of the feudal lords made them excessively proud. There began the long and bitter struggle between royalty and nobility from which the crown was to emerge victorious. The result of this triumph was the humiliation of the haughty nobles, the dismemberment of the overly powerful fiefs, and the extension of privileges to the municipalities and the im-portant bourgeois centers. Thus the central power and the middle class united to overthrow the lords or caudillos.

This evolution also took place among us, precisely during the long Rosas era. However, the struggle between the provincial caudillos and the central power, which was aided by the natural influence of the metropolis — both a port and a populous center — was compli-cated here by rural jealousies that expressed themselves in a narrow

localist spirit and in the antagonism between provincials and *por-
teños*.

The anarchy of 1820 represented the triumph of "feudalism" in its
first stage. The new "barons" remained irresolute until the quadri-
lateral treaty and the pact of 1831 again gave life to national cohesion by nominally reconstructing the Confederation. But all this
would have been in vain and the rule of the caudillos would have
been strengthened instead of weakened if Rosas, a caudillo like the
others but with greater personal prestige, more intelligence, and a
more powerful fief, had not appeared on the scene. This was the
beginning of the arduous struggle, which lasted for twenty-five years,
between the central power of Rosas and the pride of the provincial
caudillos. Rosas, with unerring shrewdness, first pacified, then dominated, and finally reduced the feudal fiefdoms, making them
accustomed to respect the moral entity called the Argentine Confederation and later imposing on them the preeminence of the national government. . . .

In the paradoxical antithesis of "civilization" and "barbarism"
made popular by Sarmiento, the latter role is assigned to Rosas and
the federalists, who symbolize rural Argentina, while the former is
given to the Unitarians, who were eminently urban. This antithesis
has been converted into a cliché but it is so unfounded that Alberdi
himself has observed that "the symbol of barbarism is in reality the
symbol of civilization, that is, the wealth produced in the countryside, while the crafts, industry, sciences, and enlightenment were
excluded from the cities for centuries; the rural districts represent
what is most significant about South America for Europe." Metropolitan factions had nurtured and directed the Argentine revolution
for their own advantage and had completely neglected rural interests. The rural sectors reacted, with Rosas at their head. In order
to triumph, they had to dominate the cities and change the orientation of the government, for the metropolis was the site of the public
treasury, which constituted the nerve of power, whose nature is essentially economic. Rosas' supreme powers, the terror, and the other
incidents of his rule were but the means by which the real power of
the masses was consolidated, guaranteed by the economic power of
the government.

One must keep in mind, moreover, the unprecedented exacerba-
tion of the provinces after twenty years of ceaseless struggle, characterized by continuous disorganization and the absence of regular
administration, stable government, material security for life and

property, and the hope of improvement. Something like the wind of disenchantment that devastated the Old World in the Middle Ages was blowing across the Argentine pampas. Every kind of evil, terror, and phantasm visited the settlements of our gauchos; life no longer had any charm for them. They could no longer escape to the crusade of liberation, for the wars of independence had been transferred to a distant and unfamiliar theatre, and they lacked the exaggerated religiosity that would have counselled resignation or the cloistered life. As a result, the rural masses were in a state of ferment, ready to listen to the alarum of revolt in order to hurl themselves on the cities and on the social classes whom they dimly considered their oppressors and, aided by the fatalistic courage of the melancholy apathy, to demolish everything. They risked nothing since they had already lost everything. . . .

It is necessary, then, to keep these antecedents in mind in order to understand the nature of the savage reactionary impulse of the rural masses from 1820 to 1840 and the atmosphere which their leader would have to breathe. Rosas undoubtedly had the qualities needed to discharge his historic role; the mere fact that he held so prominent a place for so many years in itself indicates that he had an intelligence and a character of uncommon stamp. It is impossible, therefore, to ignore his psychology, which explains how the tendency of an entire era was so quickly personified in him.

Because of his background, his qualities, his aims, and his character, Rosas was the embodiment of his times, but . . . he did not twist or mold events to his taste. He made himself the leader of his generation, but he did this by taking advantage of existing trends which many before him had tried to exploit without success because they lacked the requisite qualities. . . . His acts were completely conscious; he governed autocratically because he realized that the times demanded it, and he was fully aware of his historical responsibility, which always concerned him and which he never refused. . . .

The great argument against Rosas, which has served to label his dictatorship as a "tyranny" was the nature of his implacable terrorism. But it should not be forgotten that the standard of the period was vengeance, regardless of the source or of the consequences. This condition explains, though it does not justify, the foreign alliances of the Unitarians and Sarmiento's encouragement to Chile to take possession of the Straits of Magellan, the starting point of the ill-fated Chilean-Argentine question. . . . The end justified the means, and the doctrines of the French Revolution, with its oceans of blood, constituted the underlying philosophy of the wars for independence and the civil wars. Rosas was a result of those doctrines, which he applied without quarter. The creoles Salomón, Cuitiño, and Parra were also unconscious imitators of Marat, Robespierre, and other leaders of the French Revolution, as was the rabble who hated the Unitarians, the allies of the foreigners. In addition, terror and vengeance were imbedded in the marrow of the people as a result of the colonial tradition. Cruelty was employed in the wars against the Indians during the Spanish regime and afterwards. How can one forget these antecedents in order to allow oneself the luxury of considering Rosas a phenomenon, a monster, the very incarnation of neurosis? . . .

How can one explain Paraguay under Francia, Chile under Portales, Ecuador under García Moreno, Mexico under Santa Anna, Mosquera in New Granada, Castilla in Peru, and the whole series of tyrants and petty tyrants in all the republics of Spanish origin? All had dictators of varying degrees of talent, but they were no doubt less celebrated than Rosas because no country had so large a group of emigrés nor one so addicted to the printing press; it was these spokesmen who created the exceptional notoriety of Rosas. Among us, what else were Quiroga, Aldao, Ibarra, and so many other provincial governors? Even General Urquiza organized and pacified the province of Entre Ríos by means of terror; as a result, that den of thieves became a hive of laborious people. . . .

What is interesting is that, after studying the evolution of Rosas, one arrives at a conclusion that at first sight seems paradoxical. Thanks to his gaucho diplomacy, he obtained what the haughty Unitarians were never able to achieve: the predominance of national power, the solidarity of the nation, and the recognition of the central government. What was the aspiration of the Unitarians, which they considered their ideal and for which — so they said — so much Argentine blood was shed? The triumph of civilization over barbarism. And, through a singular irony, the Unitarians succumbed in their quest, and it was Rosas, the "tyrant," who realized the dream. The Unitarian party had provoked the bloody crisis of 1820 because it wished to impose unity with cudgels, but none of its statesmen had the astuteness that Rosas displayed to attain the desired result.

In addition, Rosas reorganized public administration with Draconian severity and implanted an irreproachable integrity in financial affairs. The accounts of the treasury were published periodically and unfailingly; public employees worked with persistence and were paid with regularity. In the civil sphere, material security was complete, for Rosas pitilessly repressed banditry. National industry and prosperity were encouraged through his efforts; if his successes in this area were not very brilliant, it was due to the continuous warfare of the period. "Do not think that Rosas has not succeeded in stimulating the progress of the republic," Sarmiento, one of his most implacable enemies, admitted in 1845. "Rosas is a great and powerful instrument of Providence, who is achieving everything that concerns the future of the nation. The ideal of the Unitarians has been realized; only the tyrant is superfluous. The day that a good government is established, it will find local resistance conquered and everything prepared for union."

To be sure, the end does not justify the means. But it is a fact that . . . Rosas cemented national unity in a manner consonant with the federal creed, for respect for provincial autonomy was ensured and the powers of the provinces were held to be compatible with those of the nation. This was the total victory of federal doctrine; the victory was obtained by barbaric means, but it was so fundamental that the day after Caseros, the country could calmly promulgate, accept, and execute a federal constitution that still remains a model of its kind and seems perhaps a bit advanced for the present era.

C. Recent Interpretations

5. Rosas Continued the Authoritarian Colonial Tradition

José Luis Romero

Juan Manuel de Rosas was a powerful *hacendado* in the province of Buenos Aires, whose political prestige grew unchecked after

Reprinted from *A History of Argentine Political Thought* by José Luis Romero, introduction and translation by Thomas F. McGann, with the permission of the publishers, Stanford University Press. © 1963 by the Board of Trustees of the Leland Stanford Junior University.

1820. As an *estanciero*, he was able to count on great resources to gain control of the countryside; as the chief of a military force organized at his own expense — the "Colorados del Monte," or "Red Rangers" — he was able to influence decisively the events in the capital during the crisis brought on by Lavalle's seizure of power and the later execution of Dorrego. Rosas saw clearly that this was his chance to impose his authority, and he declared himself in favor of federalism. Henceforth his importance in the capital was unequalled, his power grew to near omnipotence, and at the end of 1829 he was made governor of the province.

His first government lasted until the end of 1832. In that period [General José María] Paz, who might have been his worthy rival, fell prisoner, and the League of the Interior, which Paz had organized, collapsed. At about the same time, the League of the Littoral was organized. With the disappearance of Paz, other provinces joined the new League, and they, like the original signatories of the pact, delegated to Rosas the conduct of the foreign relations of the country. Thus Rosas, on leaving power, had contributed to the establishment of a loose national regime — the Confederation — which merited the cooperation of the *caudillos* and permitted Buenos Aires to exercise a certain hegemony that did not. weigh greatly on the economy of the other provinces.

From 1832 to 1834, the provincial government of Buenos Aires was in the hands of men on whom Rosas could rely, yet who were zealously watched by his followers. His authority was by now unchallengeable, and it increased — as did his wealth — thanks to the campaign he led against the Indians of the desert. The popular masses and the most reactionary anti-Rivadavian groups supported him, especially the estancieros, whose interests Rosas rigidly defended, since they were also his interests. This coalition of forces propelled him to power for a second time, despite his tactics of pretended reticence by which he succeeded in obtaining the grant of "Extraordinary Powers," which was contrary to all republican tradition.

Events favored him, but he had the cunning to create favorable conditions for his own plans. Although he sought only to exercise exceptional powers as governor of Buenos Aires, he counted on obtaining de facto authority over the entire country. To that end, he conceived the plan to leave control of the provinces in the hands of caudillos who were all-powerful in local affairs, and later to bring those leaders under his own influence. The only obstacle to this plan of action was the presence of two caudillos who exercised notorious control over vast regions: Estanislao López and Juan Facundo Quiroga. But Rosas knew how to dominate them, and with a lucid mind, marked sagacity, and, above all, long patience and invincible tenacity, he accomplished his plans.

His views on the problems of the political organization of the country were expressed in two notable documents in 1834, shortly before his second ascent to power. As a result of a conflict between the governors of Salta and Tucumán, Quiroga was given the responsibility of mediating between the two men, and from the governor of Buenos Aires he received instructions that doubtlessly had been inspired by Rosas:

Señor Quiroga should take advantage of every opportunity to make all the people whom he will meet during his trip understand that a congress ought to be convened as soon as possible, but that at present it is useless to demand a congress and a federal constitution, since each state has not arranged its internal affairs and does not give, within a stable, permanent order, practical and positive proofs of its ability to organize a federation with the other provinces. For in this system, the general government is not united, but rather is sustained by union, and the State represents the people who comprise the republic in their relations with other nations; neither does the State resolve the disputes between the people of one province and those of another, but rather limits their activities in compliance with the general pacts of the federation — to watch over the defenses of the entire republic, and to direct their negotiations and general interests in relation to those of other States, since in cases of discord between two provinces, the constitution usually has an agreed way of deciding them, when the contenders do not arbitrate the dispute.

So expressed, this statement shows a sound and justifiable grasp of the situation. But these ideas have real significance only if one takes into account the fact that at last some of the caudillos — even Quiroga himself — were beginning to recognize the need to establish a national government, although under a federal system. Rosas' plan, therefore, was both the result of his interpretation of existing conditions and the disclosure of a scheme. His plan had been sketched out in the instructions that the mediator officially carried with him. But Rosas assumed that Quiroga was not convinced of the advantages of the plan, and tried to reinforce his arguments at a meeting; afterward he summarized his ideas in a letter he wrote to Quiroga in December 1834, at the Hacienda de Figueroa, before the two leaders separated:

After all that experience and evidence have taught and counseled, is there anyone who believes that the remedy is to hasten the constitutional organization of the State? Permit me to make some observations in this regard, since, although we have always been in agreement on such important matters, I wish to entrust to you with bold anticipation, and for whatever service it may be to you, a small part of the many thoughts that occur to me, and about which I must speak.

No one is more persuaded than you and I of the necessity to organize a general government as being the only means of giving responsible existence to our republic.

But who can doubt that this ought to be the happy result of employing all the means suited to its accomplishment? Who may hope to reach an objective by marching in the opposite direction? Who, in order to form an organized, compact entity, does not first seek out and arrange, by thorough, permanent reforms, the elements that ought to compose it? Who organizes a disciplined army from groups of men without leaders, without officers, without obedience, without rank — an army in which not a moment passes without internal spying and fighting, and thus involves others in its disorders? How may a living, robust being be created out of members that are dead, torn, and diseased by corrupting gangrene, since the life and strength of this new, complex being can be no greater than what it receives from the elements of which it must be composed? Please observe how costly and painful experience has made us see in a practical way that the federal system is absolutely necessary for us because, among other powerful reasons, we totally lack the elements required for a unified government. Furthermore, because our country was dominated by a party that was deaf to this need, the means and resources available to sustain the State were destroyed and annulled. That party incited the people, perverted their beliefs, set private interests against each other, propagated immorality and intrigue, and split society into so many factions that they have not left even the remnants of its common bonds. They extended their fury to the point of breaking the most sacred of those bonds, the only one that could serve to re-establish the others — religion. With the country in this pitiful condition, it is necessary to create everything anew, first laboring on a small scale and piecemeal, and thereby prepare a general system that may embrace everything. You will observe that a federal republic is the most chimerical and disastrous that can be imagined in all cases when it is not composed of internally well-organized States. Since each part preserves its sovereignty and independence, the central government's authority over the interior of the republic is almost nonexistent; its principal, almost its only role, is purely representative—to be the voice of the people of the confederated states in their relations with foreign governments. Consequently, if within each individual state there are no elements of power capable of maintaining order, the creation of a general, representative government serves only to agitate the entire republic over each small disorder that may occur and to see to it that an outbreak in one state spreads to all the others. It is for this reason that the Republic of North America has not admitted to its new confederation the new people and provinces that have been formed since independence, but rather has admitted them when they have put themselves in a condition for self-rule; meanwhile, they have been left without representation as States, and have been considered as adjuncts of the Republic.

Considering the disturbed condition of our people, contaminated as they all are by Unitarians, lawmakers, seekers after political power, the secret agents of other nations, and the great secret Lodges that spread their nets over all of Europe, what hope can we have of tranquility and calm for making a federal compact, the first step a congress of federation must take? And in the impoverished state to which political agitation has driven our people, with what funds can they pay for a permanent congress and a general administration?

Steadfast in his ideas, Rosas set out to maintain the status quo of the country, and he put off every attempt to organize the State. But if that was his intent in its legal aspect, his practical plans were quite different. What he sought was that the de facto power of the caudillos be brought under his own de facto power, on which there were no legal restrictions and for which there were no predetermined forms. Quiroga's death, which occurred on his return from his mission to the North, eliminated Rosas' most important rival, one whose goal seems to have been the prompt constitutional organization of the country. A few years later, in 1838, Estanislao López also died, in Santa Fe; henceforth, there was no one in the interior who could rival the governor of Buenos Aires, who exercised his authority over the whole country and progressively brought the caudillos under his control with threats, promises, or gifts. As Domingo F. Sarmiento wrote in 1845, in *Facundo:*

At last we have our centralized republic — and all of it bent under the arbitrary rule of Rosas. The old issues debated by the political parties of Buenos Aires have been stripped of all significance; the meaning of words has been changed; the laws of the cattle ranch have been introduced into the government of the republic, which was once the most war-like and the most enthusiastic for liberty, and sacrificed most to achieve it. The death of López delivered Santa Fe to Rosas; the death of the Reinafé brothers gave him Córdoba; Facundo's death gave him the eight provinces on the slopes of the Andes. To take possession of all these, a few personal gifts, some friendly letters, and some hand-outs from the treasury sufficed.

On this basis a national State with unusual characteristics took form, founded on a system of alliances and on the authority of an all-powerful chief — principally the latter, because, since Rosas' State lacked legal form, it was merely an extension of his personal power.

An analysis of the characteristics of this situation, and of the idea of power it involved, is highly suggestive. Intelligent — more than that, supremely astute and profoundly knowledgeable in the psychology of the creoles — Rosas had succeeded in creating among the people the deep-rooted conviction of his natural right to exercise authority. Only he appeared to be capable of restoring the traditional way of life and of putting an end to civil strife; this belief, which was held by his most devoted adherents, was corroborated by the plebiscite that he had demanded be taken before he accepted the grant of total authority. In effect, this belief was generally held, and his prestige quickly turned it into idolatry, and not without magical overtones pointing to the mysterious origin of his power:

> He, with his talent and his science
> keeps the country secure,
> and that is why he gets his help
> from Divine Providence.

So the people sang, and Rosas himself tried to make them believe it, allowing his image to appear in the churches, where it received popular homage. The vague awareness of the force behind his authority facilitated the shift to autocracy, and no person or thing altered his will or succeeded in decisively influencing his resolution. "During the time I presided over the government of Buenos Aires, charged with the foreign relations of the Argentine Confederation and holding total authority, as granted to me by law" — he wrote in 1870 — "I governed according to my conscience. I am solely responsible for all my acts, good or bad, and for my errors as well as for my successes." Rosas became so powerful that years later, his nephew, Lucio V. Mansilla, could say: "There was no discussion during the time of Rosas; no criticism; no opinion." His was a personal power, independent of that granted to him by law, and he was so sure that his authority sprang from himself alone that he once hinted at the possibility of transmitting his power to his daughter, Manuelita.

Despite the broad popular basis of his support, Rosas had many influential enemies. From the outset, he was opposed by the followers of Rivadavia, against whom he had fought as a federalist; later, he had enemies among all the groups that had any sense of honor, which was an obstacle to the submission that he demanded. Rosas was implacable with all his opponents: many fled to foreign lands, and many suffered violent persecution. As Paz said: "The historian who undertakes the job of narrating these events will be hard put not to give the appearance of exaggerating what happened, and posterity will have to work as hard to persuade itself that the events we have witnessed were possible." Thanks to the use of violence, thanks to the skill with which he managed the instincts and inclinations of the creole masses, Rosas obtained apparently unanimous support. He who was not unconditionally with Rosas was his enemy — "a savage, filthy Unitarian." The fact is that Rosas succeeded in planting in the minds of the people the conviction that all their enemies — among whom were doctrinaire Federalists and many old Unitarians who had later become convinced of the advantages of federation — made up a single group, characterized by unswerving centralist beliefs and by alien, anti-creole attitudes. And these qualities were precisely the most hateful ones to the masses.

Rosas' ideology stemmed directly from a colonial inheritance that is noticeable as early as the May Revolution. As Sarmiento wrote: "Where, then, did this man learn about the innovations that he introduced into his government, in contempt of common sense, tradition, and the conscience and immemorial practices of civilized peoples? God forgive me if I am wrong, but this idea has long possessed me: he learned them from the cattle ranch, where he has spent his whole life, and from the Inquisition, in whose tradition he has been educated." The author of *Facundo* was correct: not only was Rosas the culmination of the secessionist movement that had appeared after 1810 and that was, in a strict sense, more than mere federalism; also he was the distillation of the antiliberal movement that was part of the authoritarian tradition of the colony and that retained its vigor among the rural masses.

These trends may be clearly seen if one analyzes the symbols he employed with such marked success. Defense of the Catholic faith had been the order of the day of Quiroga, whose motto was "Religion or Death," and it was seemingly one of the basic objectives of the Rosas dictatorship. The ultramontane party, represented by men like Francisco Tagle and Father Gregorio Castañeda, had struggled hard to enthrone Rosas; their faithful followers were known as the "Apostolic Party," and when the people wanted to describe their enemies, they said that they were

> mocking religion; the result:
> heretics who had blasphemed

what is most holy, what most sacred
of our divine cult.

Ultramontane reaction was but one aspect of the antiliberalism that followed the revolution of 1830 in France. Anything that recalled the ideas of the men of the Enlightenment, of whom the followers of Rivadavia were the direct heirs, was violently condemned by the partisans of Rosas, as is conclusively shown by General Mansilla's comment to his son, Lucio, on the day he found him reading Rousseau: "My friend, when one is the nephew of Rosas, he does not read the *Social Contract* if he intends to remain in the country, or he gets out of the country if he wishes to read the book with profit." This antiliberalism, seen clearly in the political and economic views that Rosas put into effect during his long period of rule, was intermingled with creole reaction. If he was called the "Restorer of the Laws," it was not so much because the people regarded him particularly as the defender of legal norms, but because they felt he was the guardian of the traditions of the common folk and the zealous defender of a way of life that seemed to be condemned to extinction. This explains his political xenophobia, which was, nonetheless, compatible with his alliances with the governments of countries that traded with the estancieros and with the producers of hides and salted meats. It explains the devoted support given him by the masses, who were proud of their "Americanism," and who were by tradition and by inertia opposed to progress, and infatuated with the superiority of their virtues as a pastoral people — courage and manual dexterity.

Along these lines Rosas built the indisputable popular basis for his policies, and this support allowed the all-powerful governor of Buenos Aires and proprietor of its port to impose his authority on the Confederation, which was the elementary form in which he conceived the national State. No doubt he unified the country, as Sarmiento said, but he exhausted the Confederation's possibilities during his long rule, and gradually he awakened the desire to attain unity through a solidly founded constitutional system. It cannot be denied that he fulfilled a mission, despite the overtones of barbarism that darkened his labors as governor, although it is certain that he would have been able to achieve this result by other means if such violent prejudices and rancor had not been at work within him.

6. Rosas Assured the Continued Prosperity of the Pastoral Industries

MIRON BURGIN

In shaping the economic policies of his administration Rosas seldom ventured beyond the relatively narrow confines of the immediate interests of the province and the class he represented. To him as to the majority of *porteño* federalist leaders the concept of national economy was impracticable and even dangerous. National economy presupposed a degree of political and economic integration of the provinces that was not readily attainable and, from the point of view of Buenos Aires, undesirable. Buenos Aires could well afford to pursue an independent course in the field of economic endeavor. So long as the province was capable of producing export commodities in sufficient quantities and at reasonable prices, it remained relatively immune to the difficulties and maladjustments which afflicted the Interior and the Litoral. It was in foreign markets that Buenos Aires could dispose of the produce of its pastoral industries, and it was also there that the province could most advantageously satisfy its demand for manufactures and foodstuffs. Ever since the opening of Buenos Aires to foreign trade the province had been drawn into the orbit of European and North American economy. And at the same time the bond between Buenos Aires and the Interior, never too strong, had grown progressively weaker. It was toward the east and across the Atlantic that the province of Buenos Aires looked for its livelihood, and having once found its place in the world market it was determined to keep it at all costs.

From the earliest days of independence foreign trade had been relied upon to solve the economic problems of the country. Mariano Moreno had formulated the economic aspirations of Buenos Aires in terms of direct commerce with overseas countries. In the ten years following the Revolution of 1810 the principle of "free trade" was extended, until in the early twenties it became the cornerstone of the

Rodríguez-Rivadavia regime. Just as foreign trade brought Buenos Aires into closer contact with the outside world, so also could it become instrumental in attracting into the country capital, technical equipment, and skilled labor. Rivadavia and the unitary party were quite conscious of the economic backwardness of the young republic. They knew that the country's resources were insufficient to overcome the initial obstacle which the colonial regime had placed before it. But they were confident that with the help of foreign capital and enterprise the country's economic structure could be rapidly modernized. That in this revitalized national economy Buenos Aires should play the leading role seemed axiomatic, for Buenos Aires was not only the sole link between the Interior and the outside world, but also the most important commercial and financial center in the country.

It was precisely this emphasis upon national rather than provincial economic development which caused the porteño cattle breeders and landowners to distrust the unitary economic program and policies. In the federalist view the unitaries did not show sufficient concern for the welfare of the pastoral industry. Yet this industry was the mainstay of the provincial economy. Without it Buenos Aires could not hope to maintain its position of leadership in the national economy, all the more so since the country's foreign commerce was almost wholly dependent upon the produce of the pampa. Preoccupation with the problem of economic and political integration of the country prevented the unitaries from devoting more attention to provincial industries. The porteño federalists were not going to repeat the mistake of their adversaries. They proclaimed the principle of economic and political autonomy of the provinces; they disclaimed any intention of interfering in the internal affairs of the other provinces, but at the same time insisted upon complete freedom in shaping the economic destiny of Buenos Aires.

That destiny lay in the continued prosperity of the pastoral industries, and no one was more clearly aware of this than Rosas. The central problem facing cattle breeding in the early thirties was the growing scarcity of free land. Ever since the opening of Buenos Aires to foreign trade pressure upon grazing land had been steadily increasing, so that after twenty years grazing was rapidly approaching the limits of profitable expansion. Rivadavia attempted to solve the land problem . . . through the system of emphyteusis [extension of long-term leases of public lands to colonists], but the supply of such lands was limited, and the emphyteusis system did not always work to the advantage of the pastoral industry. At the same time cattle breeders were pushing southward into Indian territory in search of cheap land. But occupation and settlement of territories beyond the frontier was difficult and costly. Sustained and orderly expansion in these regions could not be hoped for unless the government was willing and able to insure safety against Indian attacks.

Rosas and other leaders of the federalist party recognized the importance of territorial expansion and land settlement. In 1830 the deputy government composed of Anchorena, Balcarce, and García spoke of settlement of the new frontier as "the solid foundation of provincial wealth and prosperity," and it assured the legislature that plans were being considered to meet the problem. Lack of funds prevented action at that time. In 1831 the provincial government reported that it had not been able to distribute the newly acquired territories in Bahía Blanca, Cruz de Guerra, and Federación, and it estimated the cost of settling these lands at about one million pesos. But colonization entered a new phase with the promulgation of the law of June 9, 1832. The government set aside nearly 360 square leagues in the vicinity of the forts Federación, Argentina, Bahía Blanca, and Mayo. This land was to be distributed among veterans of wars against the unitaries, and also among cattle breeders who were especially hard hit by the recent drought. The law further terminated all emphyteusis contracts in these areas and provided for indemnification of tenants on terms defined in the decree of September 19, 1829.

In 1833 Rosas organized the famous campaign against the Indians. He enlisted the coöperation of Córdoba and of the provinces of Cuyo, and induced Juan Facundo Quiroga to assume command of the expedition. The plan called for a simultaneous attack on the Indians in three columns: one under Félix Aldao in the Andean region; another under Ruiz Huidoboro in the Pampa Central; and the third column, led by Rosas, was to operate in southern Buenos Aires. The campaign was only partially successful. The armies of Cuyo and Córdoba were forced to withdraw from the field without accomplishing the main objective of the campaign. Lack of financial support from the provincial governments is to be blamed for this failure. But the porteño column under Rosas remained in the field. Within one year Rosas brought under military control vast territories until then inhabited by independent Indian tribes. The newly conquered area extended 200 leagues to the west as far as the Andes, and beyond the rivers Negro, Neuquén, and Lima, as far as Cape Horn, to the south. The campaign put an end to the military power of numerous Indian tribes who had for many years preyed upon porteño commerce and industry.

Once control over conquered Indian territory was more or less secured, the porteño government proceeded to transfer large tracts into private hands. In September of 1834, shortly after the campaign was concluded, the provincial legislature authorized distribution of 50 square leagues among the commanding officers of the expeditionary force. By law of May 10, 1836 the Junta de Representantes approved the sale of 1,500 square leagues of the public domain, whether unoccupied or held in emphyteusis. Land held in emphyteusis could not be sold to non-tenants, and leaseholders could not be forced to buy the land they held in emphyteusis, but rentals were to be doubled at the expiration of the emphyteusis period, i.e., in January 1838. The law established three price categories. In the region north of the Salado river the price was set at 5,000 pesos per square league; 4,000 pesos per square league was to be charged in the area between Río Salado and a line running from Sierra del Volcán y Tandil through Laguna Blanca, through Fuerte Mayo to Fuerte Federación; and, finally, land south of this line was to be offered at 3,000 pesos per square league.

The economic significance of the law of May 10, 1836 cannot be exaggerated. At one stroke the law released for economic exploitation vast tracts of grazing land. By fixing prices at a relatively low level the legislature hoped to stimulate expansion of grazing areas which until then were considered hardly suitable for cattle breeding. And at the same time the law foreshadowed eventual abolition of emphyteusis. The law of May 10, 1836 did not, it is true, cancel existing emphyteusis contracts, but it seriously weakened the fundamental principle of the emphyteusis system by offering public land for sale. Moreover, it allowed tenants to buy outright the land they held in emphyteusis. And, as if to make certain that tenants would avail themselves of the right to buy the land they leased, the legislature doubled the rent rates beginning with the new emphyteusis period. In July of 1837 the government took further steps to restrict the emphyteusis system. It decreed that lands returned to the state because of unpaid rentals would be withdrawn from emphyteusis and offered for sale. By another decree the government prohibited subdivision of land held in emphyteusis. Tenants were permitted to buy the land they leased, but they had to exercise this privilege within two months from the date of promulgation of the decree. On January

16, 1838 the rights of certain categories of tenants were declared forfeited and the land was offered for sale to the highest bidder.

At the time when emphyteusis contracts came up for renewal
(January 1838) the government made further inroads into the system.
By decree of May 28, 1838 renewals of emphyteusis contracts for a
period of 10 years were announced, but rentals were raised 100 per
cent payable half in currency and half in treasury bills. However, a
large area comprising the most populated and economically the most
valuable part of the province was not subject to the law of emphyteusis. All land in this area that was held in emphyteusis reverted to
the state and was subject to public sale in accordance with provisions
of the law of May 10, 1836. The government justified its decision to
limit emphyteusis to outlying areas of the province on the following
grounds. First, the provincial treasury was financially embarrassed
and was anxious to increase revenues; secondly, the government was
convinced that private ownership was more conducive to the welfare
of society and state; thirdly, there was increased demand for land as
a result of expansion of grazing; and, finally, the price set by the law
of May 10, 1836 was so reasonable that no hardship was involved in
the requirement that tenants buy the land they held in emphyteusis.

It is not possible to determine whether new emphyteusis contracts
were made after 1838. Information on this score is very scant. The
circumstance that no reference to emphyteusis is to be found in
Rosas' messages to the provincial legislature or in the more important compilations of provincial laws leads one to believe that the
practice of leasing land fell into disuse shortly after 1838. This should
not be surprising, for as currency depreciated to less than 4 per cent
of par the price of 3,000 or 4,000 pesos per square league was no
longer a serious obstacle to land ownership. Emphyteusis died a
natural although perhaps a lingering death.

The swing toward private ownership of land was motivated by
financial reasons as much as by considerations of economic order.
Both the provincial legislature and the government hoped to restore
the province's financial equilibrium with the proceeds from the sale
of public land. But these calculations proved to be erroneous. In the
seven months following the promulgation of the law of May 10, 1836
only 400 square leagues were sold for a total sum of about 1,500,000
pesos. After this first rush the demand for land slackened, and the
government sought other means of stimulating land distribution. It
could not reduce prices, which were fixed by law, but it did permit
payment in treasury bills and even in cattle, up to 50 per cent of the

value of land bought. Yet, even these concessions failed to produce satisfactory results. In a message to the legislature Rosas admitted that large areas remained unoccupied in spite of the fact that land values had risen sharply. The government's inability to distribute the public domain more quickly could be ascribed to technical as well as economic factors. Transfer of land titles was necessarily a slow and complicated process. Consummation of transfers frequently required the intervention of courts. The government tried to simplify the process of land acquisition by instituting systematic surveys of public lands. But such surveys consumed time, especially in the outlying districts. Even more important was the economic factor. Exploitation of land in the province was confined primarily to cattle breeding and to a lesser extent sheep breeding. But grazing depended ultimately upon foreign markets. Unless, therefore, foreign demand for hides and jerked beef or wool increased very considerably the pastoral industry was bound to reach the limit of profitable expansion very soon. Accessibility to foreign markets played of necessity an important part in the fortunes of the industry. Therefore, when in 1838 and 1839 the French fleet closed the Buenos Aires port, the demand for land declined to a minimum.

Within two years of the passage of the law of May 10, 1836 it became clear that the government would not be able to sell all the land at its disposal. The province continued to be the largest single landowner, without however deriving any financial or economic benefit from the vast public domain. If these areas were to produce any income at all they had to be incorporated into the economy. And since the land could not be sold the government decided to give it away. The mutiny of Dolores and Monsalvo on October 29, 1839 provided the occasion for a wholesale transfer of public lands to private ownership. Anxious to check the revolt as speedily as possible the Junta de Representantes promised land grants to loyal troops. The grants were defined in the law of November 9, 1839, and were put into effect in the middle of 1840 when Rosas ordered the Contaduría General to issue land certificates.

The decree of July 9, 1840 marked the culminating point of Rosas' land policy. From the viewpoint of the *estanciero* class that policy was highly successful. In a relatively short period Rosas had fully realized the most important postulates of the federalist economic program. He virtually abolished the system of emphyteusis; he extended the southern frontiers of the province; and he assured the pastoral industry of a plentiful supply of land at reasonable prices. On this score alone Rosas deserved well of the cattle breeder and meat and hide producers. No other social group derived greater benefits from the Rosas regime, nor was any other group more intimately interested in maintaining the regime intact.

Rosas' solicitude for the welfare of the pastoral industry contrasted sharply with his somewhat lukewarm attitude toward other sectors of the provincial economy. It would seem as if concern for this one industry exhausted the resources of the government, or else that Rosas and the federalist party were incapable of formulating an economic program and policy which envisaged a more balanced expansion of the provincial economy. The privileges accorded the pastoral industry had cost the treasury a good deal in revenues. Reduction or abolition of cattle taxes or of duties upon salt imports, for example, meant that other taxes, however burdensome, had to be retained and even increased. Excessive regard for the interests of the *estancieros* and the *saladeristas* forced the government to exercise extreme caution when it came to extending a helping hand to the farmer and the industrialist. Nor did Rosas and his collaborators succeed in reconciling the divergent tendencies in the provincial economy. Quite naturally, the federalist leaders tended to identify the interests of grazing industry with those of the province. Their economic program was based on the theory that what was good for the estanciero class was good for the society as a whole, and therefore also for each of its component parts. This was perhaps inevitable, but it was equally inevitable that political leaders of the Rosas regime should have become accustomed to view the economic issues of the day in a false perspective. It was unavoidable, also, that their policies should have been tinged with a strong admixture of opportunism.

The estancieros had realized most of their economic postulates even before Rosas began his second term in office. Henceforth his main objective was to guard against any radical changes in the established order, to maintain and to strengthen, if possible, the economic and political status quo. Both the government and the legislature were reluctant to strike out new paths of economic thought, and whenever the administration was forced under pressure to venture beyond the relatively narrow confines of the established economic pattern it did so half-heartedly and without conviction.

D. Revisionists and Revisionism

7. Discussions on Rosas Reflect the Swirling Currents of Argentine Life

CLIFTON B. KROEBER

[The "classical" or "liberal" school of Argentine history] which dominated the field until very recent years, was based on a kind of nineteenth-century liberalism of and for the landed upper class. These writers were dedicated to the Idea of Progress, to materialism and positivism, and thus to an almost infinitely optimistic view of the future of their nation. In writing political history, they exalted the program of their own party and class — justice under law, public education, civilian government, religious freedom, and a ready welcome for foreign businessmen and immigrants who would expand Argentina's economy. Most Argentine historical writing since the time of Mitre and López echoes these same ideals.

However, since 1880 there have been two important attempts to revise the prevailing liberal synthesis of Argentine history that has just been reviewed. These two movements, one lasting from about 1880 to 1914, the other from the early 1920's until the present, are commonly identified by the name "revisionism," in the view that they represent a single historical school with similar motives, methods, and objectives. But, in spite of some superficial resemblances, it now appears that Argentine "revisionism" includes two separate movements. Each has a standing of its own as to basic assumptions, motives and objectives, use of historical methods, and content of the writings. Each one appears to be part of a different literary context. Thus, in discussing the revision of Argentine history relating to the dictator Rosas we will first survey each movement, to show what it is and how it differs from the liberal historiography; then we will com-

From "Rosas and the Revision of Argentine History 1880–1955" by Clifton B. Kroeber, *Inter-American Review of Bibliography*, X, 1960, pp. 3–25, *passim*. Reprinted by permission.

pare the two revisionist schools, so as to establish meaningful similarities and differences.

The first important challenge to the prevailing liberal school of history came after 1880, as limited and moderate appeal for balanced judgment of the Rosas era. This new view appeared little by little, over more than thirty years, in the writing of men who had very different motives and political interests. There was no sense of group effort among these revisionists, even though it can be seen, after the fact, that their writings have much in common.

Their objectives were two in number: first, to give a more rational explanation of the Argentine civil wars, or "Age of the Caudillos," up to 1852 or even to 1880; and, second, to raise serious doubts as to Sarmiento's famous proposition that the population of the country-side represented "barbarism" in those days, while only the city — in fact, only the city of Buenos Aires — stood for "civilization."

These views were not entirely new in 1880, since a few writers, such as the acute José Hernández in his *Martín Fierro* and other works, had already questioned the liberal analysis of Argentine life. Probably more important, as a literary forerunner of the new historical revisionism, was Juan Bautista Alberdi, who was fundamentally a man without party. In the 1870's, his writings on the recent Argentine past were voluminous, and at that time he delivered one of the most blistering critiques of Sarmiento's work, *Facundo*, that has appeared. But it fell to another, Adolfo Saldías, to make the first thorough-going statement of historical revisionism concerning Rosas. In a long work of narrative first published between 1881 and 1887, Saldías argued that Rosas was not nearly as bad as pictured, that he should be understood as a manifestation of his disordered times, and that much could be said not only for his anticipation of national government but also for his strong defense of the national interest against foreign attacks (by Britain and France, 1838–1850). This argument was considered too daring by Bartolomé Mitre, who had now become the patriarch of Argentine intellectual life; but the work does express a legitimate point of view that soon recurred in more careful works of scholarship.

The next writer, who became even more influential than Saldías, was Ernesto Quesada, whose first essays on Rosas appeared in 1894, to be followed by a major work four years later. His argument ran along the same line as that of Saldías, but was more analytic and, to many readers, a more compelling literary statement. Like Saldías, Quesada argued that the Rosas era should be considered worthy of

its place in national history, in view of the constructive and permanent elements it had contributed to Argentine life. Rosas himself
should, therefore, also be included among the leading figures of the
Argentine past. Quesada proposed, for instance, that government
under Rosas, far from being a mere chaos of caudillos, was in fact a
confederation explicitly regulated by interprovincial treaties and
other laws. Thus Quesada felt that government in Rosas' time was a
basic precedent and source for the Argentine federal government of
his own day. . . .

The other group of revisionists took up again the apology for the
Rosas regime, and, for whatever reasons, they chose to emphasize the
least promising part of the work, namely, the rehabilitation of Rosas
himself. The beginnings of this trend are not clear, but it appears in
view shortly after World War I; and since that time the new Rosas
revisionism has attracted many writers and a wide reading public. As
a trend in historical and polemic literature, it has changed with the
times, gradually acquiring the bitter, ultra-nationalistic and antidemocratic dogma its writers employ today. This tendency soon became a self-conscious movement, as the older revisionism of 1900
never had. It founded its own organizations and came to share a common vocabulary and viewpoint. Rosas revisionism is not, then, an
academic school, but rather a group of writers highly conscious of
political developments and of such other considerations as national
pride and the nation's position in a world of great powers.

In fact, the Rosas revisionists see themselves as confronting a national emergency. In their writings, the emergency is variously identified as a decline of individualism, a national servitude to foreign
powers, a standstill in national progress due to governmental ineptitude, or a condition of oligarchical control of the national life by rich
people. Most of these writers also labor under the feeling that Argentina since 1852 has constantly been blocked from her place of greatness because of the machinations of traitors and enemies whom they
can easily identify for their readers. In short, this trend of writing
began in a vigorous new feeling of nationalism which since the early
1920's has gradually moved to the extreme of chauvinism.

The beginnings of Rosas revisionism were, in the few years just
before and after World War I, in the fact that the high optimism of
many younger men was shattered by the war and its aftermath. Domestic events must have played their part in this change of feeling
too; since in the decade following the war many Argentines became
discouraged with the Radical Party, which went into office in 1916

with much middle class and labor support, but which disappointed many of the people before 1930.

The optimism of young Argentines just before 1910 is remembered by one of their number, Roberto F. Giusti, who recalls that ". . . we proposed a vague internationalism. We believed, as the nineteenth century had believed, in indefinite Progress; and we had confidence — in spite of appearances to the contrary — in peace among nations and in universal peace." Even then, before the shock of disillusion and dismay occasioned by the war and the Versailles Treaty, there was a turn toward a new nationalist feeling — a thrust of nationalist assertion and self-pride, as Giusti felt it and as is seen in Ricardo Rojas' call for a sweeping reform of the teaching of national history in the schools.

How general this new feeling was by 1920 — the pre-war nationalism, now coupled with post-war disillusionment — it is hard to say. What does seem clear is that many writers went on into the 1920's and 1930's without that firm faith in nineteenth-century liberalism that had been so prevalent before the war. Thus the Rosas revisionism in history was but one phase of a chauvinistic trend in writing which touched the novel, poetry, and essays as well as histories. No one term can define the varying moods of the writers of all these works, and, indeed, it may be said that ebullience is seen in some and a certain sense of malaise in others.

A feeling of pessimism concerning the state of affairs is seen in such different individuals as Manuel Gálvez, Leopoldo Lugones, and, later, Carlos Ibarguren. They looked at the world about them and felt terrible doubts of Argentina's ability to continue with the social, economic and political organization she then possessed. Lugones, who had taken Buenos Aires by storm as a young poet from the provinces, now showed deep moods of depression. Much of the writing of his later years is to advocate military rule and social discipline in modern society. Gálvez, meanwhile, had long been oppressed by his feeling that Argentine society and government were in process of dissolution; now he watched the progress of Benito Mussolini in Italy and Primo de Rivera in Spain for whatever he might think useful for Argentina. Like Lugones, he saw a national emergency in a lack of social discipline and in the government's indecision both in foreign and in domestic policies. But Gálvez, and the others who were soon to become the leaders of Rosas revisionism, did not make their major statements until after 1930. Thus Carlos Ibarguren delivered a series of lectures in favor of Rosas, as early as 1922, from his chair of history at Buenos Aires; but his influential biography of Rosas appeared only in 1930.

In that year, the coup by General José F. Uriburu upset Hipólito Yrigoyen's Radical Party government, brought the upper class back into power, and delivered the military officer group out of its recent exile from national politics. These events offered only a brief hope to some of the Rosas revisionists, however. Soon, with the effects of world economic depression widely felt in the country, they, in common with many other Argentines, evidenced a deeper sense of emergency. The Rosas revisionists sharpened their demands for a remedy to what they saw as a national crisis. In so doing, they slipped further into the habit of accusing their historical and their contemporary enemies of bad faith and treachery. These tendencies, still mild in Ibarguren's book of 1930, became much more marked in the works that appeared after the early thirties.

Now the prediction made almost a century before by an enemy of Rosas, General Tomás de Iriarte, was to be borne out: Rosas would be presented as a hero to twentieth-century Argentines. In 1930, Julio Irazusta was beginning the research which soon made him the leading student among Rosas revisionists. In 1934, Manuel Gálvez contributed obliquely to this new history with a forceful book on what he saw as the social and political emergency, *Este Pueblo Necesita,* which reads as if the model for much of Perón's later propaganda. In 1940, Gálvez followed with his vastly popular historical novel, *Vida de Don Juan Manuel de Rosas,* from which a generation of young readers had acquired basic views of their nation's history. In 1941, Irazusta's major opus, a heavily annotated edition of Rosas' political documents, began to appear. Meantime, the other major figure of this school, Vicente D. Sierra, had issued his small book on Rosas as political leader.

Already in 1938, this group of writers had established a historical institute of its own, with a scholarly review devoted to Rosas and his regime. The line of attack on the liberal school of history was clearly drawn, and the revisionists had already attracted bitter criticism from writers within and without the liberal tradition.

As for their general feeling of discontent and impatience with the state of Argentine affairs, the Rosas revisionists were not alone. We have referred to Lugones as writing along lines parallel to those followed by Gálvez and Irazusta; but such a writer as Eduardo Mallea, who had nothing in common politically or aesthetically with these others, mirrored something like the same sense of despair in his writings of that period. So also did the bitter critic Raúl Scalabrini Ortiz, and so also the leader of the Partido Demócrata Progresista, Senator Lisandro de la Torre, of Santa Fe Province. These writers were inveighing against the same sort of ills they saw in Argentine society, and against a government which allowed "British domination" of the economy to continue unchecked. That those feelings were genuine, not simply self-interested propaganda, there is little doubt. The most dispassionate observer of the trends of historical revisionism stated, not long afterward, that the new Rosas revisionism had arisen in large part because of the twentieth-century changes in theories concerning the state: "Thus the renewal of the Rosas spirit responds to deep causes. It would be foolish to see in this merely a resurrection of family feeling or a simple passing fancy; it is a sign of the times in which we live."

During the early 1930's, then, one clear difference between the liberal school of history and the new revisionism lay in their opposed ideas of the governmental function and of relationships between people and the state. During the late 1930's and early 1940's, the Rosas revisionists were part of a large sector of feeling in the country which would soon play its part in paving the way for the military rulers, Ramírez, Farrell, and Perón, from 1943 to 1955.

A few — but by no means all — of the Rosas revisionists actively supported the Perón regime, and, for his part, Perón did not adopt this school of writers as his spokesman in the field of history. Nor did Perón place any significant number of these historians in high positions in universities, archives, or museums.

Why Perón's coming did not meet with more enthusiasm from the revisionists is not at once explainable. His program included a plan of economic development and a full measure of economic nationalism; a strong executive control of government; and a marked emphasis on Argentine nativism. All of these were points the revisionists had stressed. There were also some historical viewpoints in common. Both Perón and the revisionists habitually blamed the political leaders since 1852 for having "given away" the Argentine economy to foreigners. Both proclaimed that the record of the past proved the need for a strong government that would solve Argentina's problems. Still, no accommodation was made, perhaps because the revisionists' differences with Perón in matters of history were too important for them to overlook. He did not raise Rosas to primacy among national heroes, for instance, but further exalted José de San Martín, to whom he dedicated many things including the whole year of 1950. Also, Perón leveled a constant barrage of propaganda against the large landowners, whom he identified as the "oligarchy" whose influence in the nation must be utterly destroyed. Nor did he present a pessimistic view of the present and future of Argentina, but instead stressed the improvements in ordinary life which his regime was supposedly achieving. So also in reference to foreign affairs, his propaganda used the history of economic colonialism in Argentina only as a counterpoint for the new freedom from foreign influence that he maintained he had already achieved. Perón's history was, all in all, too optimistic and too conventional for the revisionists' taste.

Meanwhile, the Rosas school remained as pessimistic as before in all that related to Argentina's past, present, and future. Although their writing continued in an increasing stream through the years of Perón to 1955, no new points of view, no new synthesis appeared. These writers seemed unlikely to make new statements until their work be informed by broader interests and archival research. Thus the revisionist feeling that had been gathering ever since the early 1920's seemed to have stabilized, and may be compared and contrasted with that earlier revisionism that had evolved between the 1880's and about 1914.

As for motives, there is a noticeable difference between the earlier and later writers. The revisionists of 1900 sought a conciliation of feelings, as well as recognition for the provinces' contributions to Argentine democracy. Living and writing so soon after 1850, they tended to believe that the distinctions between *unitario* and *federal* represented permanent, not passing, political tendencies, and that the objectives of both these parties needed to be understood and respected in the best interests of all Argentines. By contrast, the revisionists in our time are mainly interested in a regeneration of the Argentine spirit that would result in an extremely nationalistic feeling and in certain sweeping changes in social, economic, and political life. The one group was satisfied with its Argentina; the other is not. Members of both groups tended to belong to minority parties in politics; but the earlier revisionists seem to have felt that they were of the political process, whereas the present-day writers appear to belong to fringe groups, and their writings seem to echo the resentment of those who have not played meaningful roles in politics.

All this suggests a major contrast between the two groups as to the subject matter of their writings, aside, of course, from their common interest in Rosas. The earlier writers were concerned with the Argentine provinces as sources of national tradition and as scenes of political initiative. They knew that by 1900 Buenos Aires had long since won the political struggle for control of the country, but they wanted it remembered that the other provinces had also helped to create the democratic tradition in Argentina. Today's writers, however, draw their topical interests from their views of current problems; and they see little importance in the old nineteenth-century issue of the capital city versus the provinces. We can suppose that this variation of interest merely reflects the two different worlds in which these writers exist. The earlier revisionists could remember, personally or through family tradition, a time when provincial authorities did possess substantial powers. Personally, they still felt the impact of the struggle for national power which had died out only after 1880. But the Rosas revisionists are, like most of us, creatures of a central government and of its very great power. They have no feeling for the historical issue of provincial autonomy, and they see no place for such a thing in Argentina today. They have not touched this issue in any serious way in their writings.

As to methods, there is more difference than similarity. The older writing is apologetic, both in its selection of data and in its discussion of those data; but the recent writers are more inclined to go to logical conclusions in argument, and thus to extreme viewpoints. Such differences are clearly seen in the use of source materials. The older writers selected data from a broad pattern of sources and histories, most of them friendly but some unfriendly to their own views. The newer school is much more inclined to base arguments on the propaganda legislation, and political correspondence that Rosas himself issued during his regime. Likewise, they will admit fewer doubts and almost no neutral or hostile writers. Finally, both groups of revisionists are weak insofar as resort to archives or any unpublished sources is concerned; and both are somewhat weak in analysis if only because they both are writing, to some degree, within a closed system of thought. Even here there is a difference, since the thought of the earlier school is apologetic, while the later writers are evangelical in the sense of seeking to establish a secular faith.

As to fundamental assumptions, there are similarities but many more differences, as one might expect in two groups of writers separated by the great socio-economic and political changes of a half century. The present writers, for instance, are strongly Romantic in their view of Argentina's past. To most of them, if not all, the past was better than the present. Vicente Sierra phrased one small part of this feeling as follows:

> One cannot deny that the great cancer of Argentina is urbanism, devourer of persons and breeding ground of all the directives that are destructive of the liberty of man. It is in the cities where the politicians, creations of civilization and foreign to Western culture, pervert the population in mass. Spengler says that the countryman is the "only organic man remaining"! . . .

This view, that Argentina was better when she had few cities and many gauchos, extends to the extreme hinted at by some writers, that personal liberty was present in Argentina in 1840 but absent in 1940. The older writers knew better than this. They were under no illusion that life in 1900 was worse than it had been in 1850. Indeed, the early revisionism was a positive statement almost in entirety. Its only negative emphasis came in showing that Rosas' enemies were at least as violent as he was.

The revisionists today are rarely positive in view, and more than usually pessimistic. They employ a number of major arguments that were absent from or unimportant in the earlier literature of revisionism. Class and group resentment, for example, is writ large across these recent histories. The "oligarchs," meaning men of large business in the cities, sometimes also the Jews and Freemasons, and almost always the "liberals" and foreigners — these are the scapegoats of the newer revisionism. They are lumped together with the *unitarios* of the 1820's as traitors to the nation.

The Rosas revisionists of today picture Argentine life as in danger of disaster; and their effort is to find the roots of this danger, to tell the bad story of national decline since Rosas' time. In so doing, these writers use loaded terms, just as the liberal school once employed other epithets to damn the acts and intentions of Rosas. The favorite revisionist words in our time are such as *traición, entrega, vendipatria, antinacional, extranjerizante;* and *claudicaciones, desvíos,* and *supercheria.* Even as early as 1930, in Ibarguren's biography of Rosas, one finds that the Unitarist party of Buenos Aires, when trying to unify the country during the 1820's, consisted of "an aristocratic oligarchy directed by a criminal [Masonic] lodge of anarchists, who were threatening the social order."

This bitterness against one's enemies, present and past, is always present whether in specific statements or by implications. There is, for instance, an implicit assumption that Argentina's troubles result in large part from a conscious plot among her enemies, foreign and domestic. The plotters are usually identified as British imperialists and Argentine commercial magnates, with all those who assist them. The helpers are variously identified as university people, Jews, leftists, Socialists, Communists, but always as "liberals" since the name "liberal" is anathema to this school, which has been at some pains to show that liberalism is always a mistake in Argentina. The one important group escaping condemnation is the large landowners, presumably because Rosas himself was a leader of the *estanciero* party in Buenos Aires Province. Of equal importance here is the fact that the modern revisionists do not see the landowners as a menace to the stability of Argentine life today.

The extreme views and the bitterness just discussed remind us of that feeling of nationalism which has been increasing in Argentina since the early years of this century. While the revisionists of 1900 were also nationalists, theirs was the same liberal sort of national feeling that pervaded the upper class during the latter nineteenth century. That feeling, so characteristic of the Generation of 1880, did not include any marked sense of inferiority or resentment toward foreign nations. Today's nationalism, by contrast, is seen at its extreme in the works of the Rosas revisionists, with the simplified dogmas and overly simple historical explanations employed at that extreme.

The most notable historical oversimplification in this school of writing is the insistence that Argentina before 1852 was a static society in which social equality and political democracy reigned as never before or since. Such a view is not that of the generality of Argentine writers today, since it overlooks the complexities of life as lived either today or one hundred years ago.

In this respect there is a similarity between revisionists both in 1900 and in 1940 or 1950; that all of them tend to exalt the leader in politics and in society. The older writers, intending to rehabilitate Rosas, seemed also to approve of personalism in politics, at least for Argentina as it was before 1852. But the present-day revisionists go much further. They are remaking Rosas a very great man by weaving about him a charismatic myth. Thus it is often stated that these writers are trying to resurrect a tradition of personalism in Argentine history and politics, at a time when professional historians are doing so much to dispel that feeling.

The older revisionists imparted the view that human affairs involve choices, sometimes very difficult choices, among alternatives. Thus Peña showed that men of much the same background and politics acted differently during the civil wars. Álvarez assumed that men and parties of different principles might follow the same policies, if their economic interests remained the same. Those older writers were also aware that life in Argentina had changed over the half century intervening between the events they described and their own day. They made few blanket denunciations or endorsements of the historical figures they discussed. In all these respects, the older revisionism contrasts with the Rosas school of today, which gives little idea that life might involve complex choices, that men are not necessarily all bad or all good, and that conditions have changed during the past one hundred years.

In summary, it may be said that the older revisionism was a moment of balance in historical writing, occurring between two swings of the pendulum of nationalism. By the 1880's, the pendulum had swung far upward, in the overly exuberant and uncritical spirit of that age of material prosperity. That was the generation which gloried in the new national unity and the power that came with it. Then some Argentine writers took a somewhat sober look at their history since independence; this was the moment of revision that lasted until about the time of the First World War. Finally, the increasing complexity of twentieth-century life has, especially since the 1930's, impelled a numerous company of writers to explain their national history in terms of failure in the past and pessimism for the future. This, up to the fall of Perón in 1955, was the spirit of the newer revisionism in Argentine history.

8. Rosas Still Lives in the Hearts of Some Argentines!

Whereas: The naming of streets has always had as its purpose the commemoration of the attitudes, deeds, or conduct of personalities who have distinguished themselves in ways the remembrance of which should not be neglected; and

Considering: That it is therefore proper to honor the name of one of the forgers of our nationality and that this resolve is all the more fitting because the province to which this city belongs has been one of the last to be integrated as a Federal State within the vast Argentine Fatherland;

From Clifton B. Kroeber, *Rosas y la revisión de la historia Argentina*, trans. by J. L. Muñoz Azpiri (Buenos Aires: Fondo Editor Argentino, 1965), pp. 87–90. Reprinted by permission.

That the heroes of our National Organization effected the triumph of the Argentine Confederation already perfected and founded by Brigadier General Juan Manuel de Rosas by means of the Organic Pact of 1831;

That the said Confederation was sustained by its founder for more than two decades while he struggled against internal conspiracies and foreign coalitions under conditions that would have discouraged any other ruler or military leader;

That as governor of the province of Buenos Aires, Juan Manuel de Rosas created, by means of novel systems for the production, distribution, and commercialization of goods, useful sources of employment for the rural and proletarian workers, thereby materially improving the general welfare to which the constitution of 1853 refers;

That the rancher, businessman, and exporter Juan Manuel de Rosas founded . . . the so-called "mother industry of the country" — cattle-raising — the products of which he exported in ships flying the Argentine flag and belonging to the first Argentine National Merchant Marine, whose tonnage was surpassed only in 1943;

That he dignified the worker by assuming with national pride the name of "gaucho," which was used at that time to refer disdainfully to humble Argentines;

That he caused this name to be respected by the powers of the earth through the exercise of intelligence and arms;

That he initiated the first ordinance of national economic independence in the famous Customs Law of 1831, which provided financial controls and protection for our industries and crafts;

That he professed to be permanently honored "with the friendship of the poor" and to hold himself aloof from the privileges of the so-called oligarchy of Buenos Aires;

That he recovered thousands of leagues from the wilderness and founded the centers of civilization called Bahía Blanca, Junín, and 25 de Mayo;

That during twelve years of international conflict he defended Argentine sovereignty with immortal dignity, preserving it "as whole and unblemished as when it left the hands of the Almighty," and he fulfilled and for the first time brought about the true fulfillment of the oath of July 9, 1816;

That he declared the ninth of July a national holiday;

That he enjoyed the admiration of the world's leading statesmen and publicists, who considered him the champion of the rights of South American sovereignty;

That he brought dignity to the name of Argentina because of his irreproachable conduct in his personal and private life and his scrupulous management of public funds;

That he strengthened the privileges of the Church and revoked measures of persecution against Catholicism which had been dictated by previous doctrinaire governments, thereby fortifying Argentina's civil unity, one of the sources of which is the strength and solidarity of the Christian faith;

That he made the Argentine Army a specialized and technical body, providing it with industries and laboratories and establishing the bases of military manufacturing in the model barracks and workshops of Santos Lugares;

That he converted our fledgling diplomatic service into a corps of professionals and specialists in international politics and in the art of negotiation, among them Arana, Guido, Manuel Moreno, and Mariano Balcarce;

That he was the first to honor the Father of the Country by decreeing that a plaza in Buenos Aires bear the name of the Liberator during his lifetime;

That the name of Juan Manuel de Rosas survives in the bosom of this region, the latest to be recovered from the wilderness of the Argentine Chaco, as the symbol and epitome of the purest national essence;

That his heroic name, pronounced by the humble and patriotic hearts of Argentina's generous soil, will always prevent humiliations or slights to our Fatherland;

That he deserved the highest posthumous honors that any Argentine citizen has hitherto received upon setting forth on his voyage to the tomb, accompanied by the sword of San Martín and the flag of Arenales;

That the present resolution fulfills one of the desires of the Father of the Country, General José de San Martín, who in a letter to General Rosas dated on May 6, 1850, in Boulogne sur Mer expressed the hope "that upon ending his public life he would be overwhelmed by the just gratitude of every Argentine."

For all these reasons:

The Municipal Council of Roque Saenz Peña directs that:

Article 1. The name Brigadier General Juan Manuel de Rosas be given to the present Avenue of Labor along its entire length.

Article 2. The Subsecretariat of Public Works take action to put up the appropriate street signs.

Section III

Economic Entrepreneurs
in the Mid-Nineteenth Century

Recent emphasis on the problems of economic underdevelopment in Latin America in the twentieth century has obscured the spirit of enterprise which was to be found in a number of countries in the nineteenth century. Following the wars for independence, from about 1830 on, many attempts were made to bring capital and techniques to Latin America. Usually these attempts to modernize the economies have been considered the work of foreigners, but Frank Safford of Northwestern University points out in a closely reasoned essay that in Colombia "native entrepreneurs matched foreign innovators step-for-step" (Reading III.1). Howard F. Cline of the Library of Congress shows that the same spirit of enterprise was active in Mexico and gives as a convincing illustration the story of the textile factory called the "Aurora Yucateca" in the distant province of Yucatan (Reading III.2).

Chile manifested a steady development economically, even before the War of the Pacific (1879–1883) enabled it to make a dramatic leap forward. And J. Fred Rippy, professor emeritus of the University of Chicago, Fredrick B. Pike of the University of Notre Dame, and Jack Pfeiffer show that both Chileans and foreigners were involved in the attempts to establish industries, exploit mines, and otherwise strengthen the country's economy (Reading III.3). Sometimes foreigners did exercise a special influence, as Professor Rippy makes clear in his account of the remarkable exploits of that "Yankee Pizarro," Henry Meiggs, in building railroads in the mountains of Peru (Reading III.4).

A. Colombia

1. There Was No Lack of Individual Enterprise

FRANK SAFFORD

Most English language writings on Latin American economy in the nineteenth century have tended to stress the role of foreign and particularly British and American innovators. British bankers and mining companies and American engineers and *empresarios* figure strongly in the literature. The native upper class generally is pictured as the passive recipient of Anglo-American technical and organizational advances.

There can be no doubt that foreign investors and innovators did play an important role in many of the Latin American countries, and particularly in Argentina, Brazil, Peru, and Mexico. British capital and technology rejuvenated the mining industries of Mexico, Peru, and Bolivia. A British company took control of and organized the guano fertilizer industry in Peru. British banks, railways, and utilities dominated Argentina, Brazil, and Mexico. In Peru and Chile, the figure of the American railroad empresario Henry Meiggs clearly stands out.

Nevertheless, investigation of one case, that of Colombia, indicates that native entrepreneurs matched foreign innovators step-for-step. Secondly, it appears that native entrepreneurial leadership came almost entirely from the established landed upper class. There is no clear evidence that a struggling minority group — whether foreign-born or native — took business leadership because of deprivation of status within Colombian society or for any other emotional reasons.

In comparing the activities of foreign and native entrepreneurs in

From "Foreign and National Enterprise in Nineteenth-Century Colombia" by Frank Safford, *Business History Review*, XXXIX, 1965, pp. 503–526, *passim.* Reprinted by permission.

Colombia, this article will discuss their respective roles in new enterprises, evaluate their relative strengths and weaknesses, and examine the nature of their relations. The article also suggests explanations of the differing economic roles of some of the various regional groups within the Colombian society.

In the nineteenth century, Colombia stood in the middle rank of Latin American countries. Her population, through most of the nineteenth century, was the third largest in Latin America — rising from slightly over 1,600,000 in the 1830's to more than 2,200,000 at mid-century, to more than 4,100,000 in 1895. Only in the 1890's did the population of Argentina begin to surpass that of Colombia. Aside from being large in absolute size, Colombia's population was also relatively dense by New World standards. At the end of the 1870's, with 3.5 inhabitants per square kilometer, her population density was less only than those of Chile (6.6), Mexico (4.9), and Central America (4.0). Most other Latin American countries had population densities of less than two persons per square kilometer. On the other hand, Colombia was not distinguished by impressive urban centers. The capital at Bogotá had by far the largest urban population, growing from 20,000 to 100,000 during the nineteenth century. But at no time was Bogotá more than half the size of Mexico City, Havana, Rio, or Buenos Aires. Even in the most densely populated regions the Colombian population was markedly rural.

Despite her relatively large and dense population, Colombia was commercially poor. In value of foreign trade between 1821 and 1880 she usually ranked no higher than seventh or eighth among Latin American countries. At the end of the 1870's, Colombia's exports were officially valued at no more than $11,000,000, while Brazil was exporting almost $90,000,000 worth, Peru and Argentina had exports of more than $45,000,000, and Mexico and Chile of $25,000,000 to $30,000,000. In total value of foreign trade, Colombia stood in a middle group, roughly on a par with Venezuela and Central America, clearly ahead of Bolivia and Ecuador.

Weakness in foreign trade meant that Colombia lacked capital, both public and private, as the export economy in most of Latin America provided the greatest increments of capital and credit in the nineteenth century. Colombia's national revenues, tied like those of other Latin American countries to customs collections, stood at about the same rank as her foreign trade. Colombia's combined national and state government revenues amounted to about $10,000,000 at the end of the 1870's, as contrasted with more than $50,000,000 in

Brazil, more than $65,000,000 in Peru, and more than $16,000,000 each in Chile, Argentina, and Mexico.

The private sector was almost equally poor. By the standards of Rio, or Mexico, or Lima, the Colombian upper class was an indigent lot indeed. Upper-class incomes in Bogotá in the first half of the nineteenth century frequently amounted to no more than $5,000 per annum, and the number of individuals in Bogotá with a capital of more than $100,000 could be counted on the fingers of one hand. Incomes of the middle and lower classes were correspondingly small. The small middle class, composed of lower army officers, small tradesmen, and artisans, earned between $150 and $700 per year. The great mass of agricultural labor, as well as domestic servants and unskilled urban labor, earned between $70 and $75 per year. The low income of the peon class would provide only the weakest incentive for mass production of consumer goods. And the puny capital resources of the upper class would make the undertaking of large enterprises of any kind difficult indeed. This was particularly true given the lack of banking institutions through which their limited capital might be expanded.

Colombia's poverty can be explained largely as a consequence of the country's geographical situation. Colombia lies entirely within the tropics, from the equator to 13 degrees north latitude; the country below 3,000 feet tends to be hot and uncomfortable. In the nineteenth century, the "hot country" presented a constant danger of death by fever and dysentery. The great bulk of Colombia's population for this reason chose to live in the cooler climate created by the three branches of the Andes running on a southwest-to-northeast axis from the Ecuadorean border to the Caribbean. The temperate climate which prevailed in these mountains made possible the development of relatively dense (though predominantly rural) population clusters in the regions of Bogotá, Tunja, and El Socorro in the easternmost range and in Antioquia and the Cauca Valley in the western part of the country.

On the other hand, the three mountain chains badly divided the country. Each of the three principal chains breaks into many subbranches, each of which rises sharply above deep-running mountain gorges or rivers. Most of the country's main-traveled roads pitched off down the sides of steep mountain ranges, taking gradients which only mules could negotiate. Tropical rain storms, occurring at various times in the year but in seasons covering half the year, frequently washed out whatever trails had been cut through mountainous regions. In many places, mules sank to their girths in mudholes. In others, clay made footing slippery as soap, particularly after rains. Over mountain roads, freight costs through most of the nineteenth century averaged from 30 to 50 cents per ton mile in the dry season, 70 cents or more after heavy rains.

The condition of the mountain roads also affected transportation over relatively level territory. As the most important roads could be used only by mules, Colombians tended to send goods by muleback even in the occasional places where the terrain made the use of carts possible. Only slowly did wheeled vehicles come into use in the few places where this was practicable. As a result, land transportation costs remained high even in level places, generally above 25 cents per ton mile in the middle of the nineteenth century.

Such transportation conditions naturally inhibited the development of a national market. Nevertheless, until the middle of the nineteenth century, durable and semi-durable manufactures, as well as some regionally specialized foods, were traded over great distances. The highlands of the eastern belt (Bogotá, Tunja) sent wheat flour, potatoes, cotton and woolen cloth, and some iron to the western provinces (Antioquia, the Cauca Valley) more than 300 miles away, as well as to consumers in the nearby sugar-producing hot country. Cacao grown in the Cauca Valley as well as in the province of Santander, was taken an equal distance for sale in Bogotá. Cattle, bred in the eastern Llanos, were fattened in the Magdalena Valley, and slaughtered in the highlands. Most staples — such as maize, plantains, manioc [yuca], and sugar products — were traded over shorter distances only because they could be cultivated in practically every part of the country. But for manufactured goods and some foods, the interior provinces of Colombia offered a market containing 1,500,000 to 2,000,000 people.

The existence of a national market, at least for some manufactures, was made possible by the fact that until the end of the 1840's, the various provinces of New Granada were as isolated from the outside world as from each other. The interior provinces' one route for foreign trade was the Magdalena River. Until 1849, the 600 miles from the Caribbean coast to the interior port of Honda were served primarily by keelboats poled by boatmen against a current which in many places was both strong and treacherous. Using the poled boats, it cost about twice as much to bring goods to Honda up the river from the Caribbean as down the trail from Bogotá. This fact effectively eliminated Cartagena and other towns of the Caribbean coast from the national market. But it also made it possible for entrepreneurs to conceive of competing with European manufactures in the interior provinces, poor and rugged as these were.

On the assumption that the traditional interior market would remain more or less intact, the government of New Granada up to the 1840's attempted to encourage national manufacturing. Between 1821 and 1845, tariffs were moderately protective. Enterprises considered particularly meritorious were conceded loans from the government's exiguous treasury. Entrepreneurs attempting to develop internal communications and manufacturing were granted limited monopoly privileges, of ten to twenty-five years in duration. Those granted the privileges were given sole right to produce a commodity by a modern factory process; traditional cottage manufactures were not barred, nor were imported goods.

The more or less nationalist bent of the earlier period gave way during the 1840's to free trade policies which prevailed for most of the rest of the century. The free trade current was encouraged by the mediocre showing of local manufacturers, the growing efficiency of overseas competitors, the expanding European market for tropical products, and the influence of English policy. But an important factor was the breakdown of the interior's geographical protection with the definitive establishment of steamboats on the Magdalena River and in ocean transportation in the middle of the nineteenth century. These improvements in marine transportation made it cheaper to bring goods to the western provinces from Liverpool than from Bogotá. Thus, New Granada's national market became fragmented, and each segment of the interior carried on its principal economic dealing with Europe.

Colombian businessmen naturally responded to these changing conditions. Before 1845, their energies were directed to a notable extent toward domestic agriculture and manufacturing; after 1845 they tended to focus more on the production and export of tropical products and on the importation of foreign manufactures. The interior provinces, previously dependent upon the export of gold to earn foreign exchange, now could rely in addition on tobacco, cinchona bark, and many other minor commodities to make their payments to Europe. Though most of the leading Colombian agricultural export commodities between 1845 and 1870 had only fleeting success in European markets, the export economy throughout this period remained a mania among the Colombian upper class. After persistent experimentation with various commodities, Colombian exporters finally found a winner in coffee in the years after 1865. The focus of entrepreneurial activity, therefore, changed radically during the nineteenth century, moving from an emphasis on internal development in the early decades to virtually single-minded devotion to the export economy in the second half of the century.

Foreign Enterprise — From the first moments of Colombian independence, the government made efforts to promote the immigration of Europeans. Upper-class politicians, against the opposition of the church, legislated a species of religious toleration; naturalization was permitted after only two years' residence; land was granted to immigrants on easy terms. Despite these measures, Europeans migrated to Colombia in relatively small numbers during the nineteenth century. At mid-century, there were fewer than 850 Europeans and North Americans in Colombia. Nevertheless, these few immigrants had an influence disproportionate to their numbers because most of them were more-or-less skilled. Many of them were merchants, as is indicated by the concentration of Europeans and North Americans at the principal commercial centers. Almost half of them resided in Panama, and the rest were grouped in the capital at Bogotá, in the river port and mines near Honda, and in the ports of the Caribbean. Most other Europeans and North Americans lived by technical skills either as artisans or as technicians in larger enterprises. Thus, while the number of foreigners in Colombia was not large, they were almost all well-endowed either with capital or skills, and therefore played an important part in local enterprise.

Foreign enterprisers were particularly prominent in Colombia at the beginning of the republican period. During the 1820's English adventurers in particular flocked in great numbers, each apparently expecting to find his own El Dorado. In the Wars of Independence some 4,000 soldiers from the British Isles had come to fight for the patriots; a number of their officers stayed in Colombia to undertake various enterprises. Even more important in economic activities, however, were the many merchants who came from England, Jamaica, and the United States, and established themselves in most of Colombia's ports, some of them arriving well before the Spanish armies had been driven from the field. After Colombian independence was assured, significant British and other foreign investments were made in mining, manufacturing, and communications. . . .

With the exception of ventures in agriculture and the export-import trade, most of the early British enterprises failed. In some cases they were afflicted by political problems. Colombia's nineteenth century was characterized by almost continuously acrid political disputes between the Liberal and Conservative parties. These erupted in major civil disturbances or in civil war: in 1828–1831, 1839–1842, 1851, 1854, 1860–1863, 1876, 1885, 1895, and 1899–1903. Many other minor conflicts, confined to one or two provinces, occurred, particularly between 1864 and 1880, when politics (and therefore civil war) were to some extent decentralized.

The early wars, particularly during the 1820's and 1830's, appear to have caused some direct losses to foreign businessmen, through forced contributions or seizure of property. But after 1841, foreigners generally were free from arbitrary exactions. This was in part because of the latent threat of gunboat diplomacy on the part of the British and United States governments, but even more because of Colombia's desire to attract foreign capital. . . .

Foreign businessmen did occasionally suffer from discrimination. For a brief period in the early 1820's, foreign merchants were forbidden to enter the import trade; as a result they were forced to use Colombian merchants as frontmen. There are a number of instances of Colombians with political influence using their connections to force their way into participation in foreign enterprises. In 1836, when Charles Biddle of Philadelphia proposed to construct a railroad or canal across the Isthmus of Panama, the leading merchant-capitalists in Bogotá formed a competing company in order to oblige Biddle to buy them off. On various other occasions foreigners could obtain rights of construction only by buying them from initial concessionaries, who happened to be Colombian politicians. But there are also numerous instances of government contracts or monopoly privileges being awarded to foreigners in preference to higher Colombian bids.

It appears that discrimination against foreign empresarios lessened as the early spirit of economic nationalism subsided and Manchesterian liberalism came to the fore. In steamboat navigation on the Magdalena River, for example, the Colombian government in the early period proved sporadically jealous of the rights of nationals. Juan Bernardo Elbers, after having invested more than $250,000 in his steamboat enterprise between 1823 and 1827, was suddenly stripped of his monopoly privilege in 1829. Though the privilege was restored to Elbers in 1831, it was again abrogated in 1837, in part because he had not provided the service stipulated, but also because a competing Colombian enterprise was being organized. Later, between 1846 and 1852, Colombian law forbade the navigation of foreign-owned vessels on national waters. During the 1850's, however, a complete reversal of policy occurred, and between 1855 and 1864 a large proportion of the river steamboats were foreign-owned and operated. Generally speaking, both government policy and public opinion were highly receptive to foreign enterprise, particularly between 1850 and 1880.

Perhaps as important as political discrimination in deterring foreign enterprise was the difficulty of adjusting to a Spanish, Roman Catholic cultural environment. Some American businessmen found it hard to abide the rigid Roman Catholicism which characterized Bogotá and many other towns in the Colombian interior. Hostility was occasionally quite marked among the priesthood and the masses over which they held sway.

But foreign businessmen were generally well received by Bogotá's upper class. Because of their cultural equipment, many foreigners who arrived in Colombia with little capital quickly became important in economic activities and consequently members of the upper class. Clerk or artisan to capitalist within a decade was a familiar story for those European fortune-seekers who came to Colombia in the nineteenth century. Those who had the wit to adjust sufficiently to the Colombian style were among the most respected people in the country, and precisely because of their economic acumen.

The most troublesome cultural problem for foreign businessmen was presented by traditional Spanish catch-as-catch-can economic relations. Anglo-American businessmen who were accustomed to prompt payment of obligations found Colombian casualness on this point somewhat wearing.

Some foreign entrepreneurs also had difficulty in handling native labor. One of the British managers of the salt mines of Zipaquirá was murdered, allegedly because he had refused to permit workers to steal salt. John Steuart, who attempted to establish a hat factory in Bogotá in 1837, complained that Colombian workers were dilatory, did not follow instructions, lied and stole, and could not be won over by fair treatment.

Many other foreign observers, however, testified that Colombian labor, properly trained, promptly paid, and patiently treated, could be loyal, hard-working, and quite productive. The supposed indolence of the lower class often was attributed to a tradition of mistreatment at the hands of employers or to wages which were too low to offer an incentive for work. Charles Biddle stated that he had never known a "more hard-working and industrious people . . . whilst they have a prospect of reward to stimulate them . . . but like the inhabitants of all other countries they are not fond of working for amusement." North American workmen, he noted, would not perform half the labor of a Granadan worker for double the pay. J. D. Powles, an English merchant of long experience in New Granada, declared that Colombian workers would do anything that could reasonably be expected of them, as long as they were paid regularly, "a point of great interest to them." . . .

Most of the early foreign enterprises failed not so much for cultural or political reasons as for purely economic ones. Foreign investors and managers, in the spirit of inflated optimism which characterized most British investments in newly independent Latin America as a whole, had greatly overestimated Colombia's immediate economic potential during the 1820's. It was widely assumed by Anglo-Americans that Colombia was a rich country which had been kept poor by misguided Spanish colonial policy. With independence it was believed that the natural springs of production would be released. During the 1820's and 1830's, however, many foreign empresarios found that the country's economic horizons were quite restricted. . . .

Others failed simply because the market and the volume of trade in Colombia were so small. Juan Bernardo Elbers' steamboat enterprise was hampered by political difficulties, and had to bear the cost of innovation on a tropical river with tricky navigation. But he also found his enterprise unprofitable because the Magdalena at the time did not carry enough traffic to support more than one steamboat. Similarly, foreign businessmen who attempted to manufacture consumer goods found that the local market simply was not big enough. John Steuart's hat factory and a women's comb factory established by two Americans both failed because the upper and middle classes which might consume these items were very few in number. The discovery between 1825 and 1839 that Colombia's immediate economic potential was relatively limited appears to have been an important factor in restricting the migration of Europeans to the country.

National Enterprise — Just as the flow of European businessmen slowed to a trickle, so did that of European capital. At the same time, in periods of political disturbance the larger Colombian capitalists transferred their capital from Bogotá to foreign parts or to regions of the country which were not affected by civil wars. As a result, the area with the greatest population, around Bogotá, fell into a deep depression during the 1830's. In this region, prices fell to half their levels of the 1820's, and interest rates in Bogotá rose to between 2 and 5 per cent per month.

It was in this period of acute depression, just as the interest of foreign capitalists was flagging, that the Colombian upper class took up the burden of entrepreneurial leadership. After 1830, foreigners, particularly Englishmen, Germans, and Americans, continued to supply technical skills. But the Colombian elite provided most of the capital and business organization. It is worth emphasizing that these entrepreneurial Colombians were distinctly upper class — of traditionally respected landed and commercial families. There is no evidence whatsoever of a pariah, or deprived minority, group within Colombian society assuming entrepreneurial leadership. Whether they came from Bogotá or from Medellín, Popayán, or other provincial towns, Colombia's business leaders until at least 1890 were almost entirely members of families whose upper-class position had been established before the end of the colonial period and was recognized throughout New Granada.

Early examples of elite entrepreneurial leadership can be found in efforts to establish modern factory manufacturing in the Bogotá area between 1830 and 1845. The participants in the local manufacturing movement of this period were predominantly large landowners in the Bogotá region and descendants of colonial administrators. Ignacio Gutiérrez Vergara, investor in an ironworks and promoter of Bogotá's first industrial fair, was the grandson of one of the biggest *hacendados* in the Bogotá region and the son of a lawyer in the *audiencia* of Santafé, both of whom later became patriot leaders; ancestors on both sides had held high administrative posts in the seventeenth and eighteenth centuries. Rafael and José María Alvarez, who invested in the ironworks and in a china factory, were the descendants of Manuel Bernardo Alvarez, chief accountant of the vice-royalty (1803–1810), President-dictator of Cundinamarca in 1814, and subsequently superintendent of the mint; and of the Lozano family, greatest landowners on the Sabana de Bogotá at the end of the colonial period. Colonel Joaquín Acosta, son of the *corregidor* of Guaduas and inheritor of 80,000 pesos' worth of land in the Guaduas area, invested a portion of his capital in the china factory and in a paper mill. . . .

In retrospect, some of these ventures appear suicidal — particularly given the poor state of Colombian communications and the rapid improvements being made in transportation systems and in manufacturing technique in England. At the time, however, Bogotá's upper-class enterprisers undoubtedly found encouragement in the protection afforded by high transportation costs up the Magdalena River. The motive of economic patriotism also entered in, many Colombian leaders believing that the country should remain behind in no type of economic activity. There was also a strong element of *noblesse oblige* — the establishment of factories would provide useful employment to the many beggars and vagrants in the capital, and thus serve to "moralize" the society. The elite expected, however, to make a profit while doing their moralizing. In the latter part of the 1830's, all of Bogotá's industrialists joined in asking the Colombian Congress to pass a law establishing forced apprenticeship in factories, child labor being cheaper than adult. . . .

It is not entirely clear what reasoning went into the selection of the various types of manufacture tried by the Bogotá elite. In many cases raw materials were readily available: coal and iron ore for the ironworks, high quality clay and feldspar for china, abundant wool for the woolen mill, and rags and forests for paper. Cotton yarn, on the other hand, was not obtainable by local mill-owners in the quality or at the low cost possible for English competitors. The glass factory lacked an adequate supply of potash, sodium, and lead oxide, and most of these materials had to be imported.

Market conditions were not especially favorable for the manufacturers. Iron had a potential market in all types of agriculture, but it had to be developed, as the high cost of imported iron in the colonial period had conditioned Colombians to the use of wooden substitutes. Glassware, similarly, had not yet come into general use; and the upper classes which might use it represented only a tiny proportion of the population. China and woolen textiles, though more generally consumed, had to compete with the prestige of goods manufactured in Europe. The crude cotton textiles manufactured in Bogotá had a broad potential market among the large peasant class. But cottons faced devastating competition from lower-priced British cloth. In addition, cottage weavers in the province of El Socorro already supplied most of the domestic market with crude cottons. As cotton was grown in El Socorro, while it had to be carried some 200 miles to Bogotá, the cottage weavers could hold their own with the small mill in the capital.

The factories established in Bogotá between 1821 and 1860 were modest by comparison with European and North American establishments. Capital in the larger plants amounted to no more than $50,000. This investment, measured in dollars, was smaller than that found in contemporary mills in the United States. In addition, this amount of capital would buy much less equipment in Bogotá because of the high cost of transporting machinery by mule (or by teams of Indian bearers in the case of pieces over 250 pounds) up the steep mountain road from Honda to Bogotá. One of the largest plants, a water-powered cotton mill, had only fifteen looms. The early Colombian factories were thus comparable to, though slightly smaller than, the textile mills established in Brazil in the middle of the nineteenth century. . . .

Though the Bogotá elite assumed clear leadership in early manufacturing enterprises, none of them was completely free from foreign participation. The first industrial venture of the Colombians was to buy out and reorganize an ironworks established by a French physician, Bernard Daste, after its first years of failure in the 1820's. The ironworks was finally made profitable during the 1830's through the efforts of an English merchant, Robert Bunch. The bulk of the capital, and the organization of distribution, however, were supplied by the Bogotá upper class. The china factory established in the 1830's also featured English technical aid in cooperation with Colombian capital. First experiments in firing were made with foreign help, but the enterprise was carried to success through the perseverance of a single Bogotá aristocrat, Nicolás Leiva. The Bogotá firm of Sánchez, Ponce initially used foreign technical assistance, particularly in purchasing machinery, in founding their woolen mill in 1856. Some other enterprises involving foreign technicians and local capital did not work out well. A glass factory in Bogotá failed in part for lack of a sufficient market, but also because French glassworkers imported for the purpose proved completely ungovernable.

While it is true that in most areas Colombians relied heavily on foreigners for technical advice, they also showed considerable interest in undertaking their own mechanical innovations. Beginning in 1841, annual industrial fairs were held in Bogotá, in which prizes were given for new inventions and productions. It cannot be claimed that any of the inventions submitted were of world-shaking importance, but the interest and the activity were there.

Though practically all Colombian economic innovation involved borrowing and adapting European techniques, not all new developments required the intervention of foreign personnel. Banking, for example, was largely home-grown. One of the first important experiments with banking was the establishment in Bogotá between 1839 and 1841 of a "house of exchange and discount." This rather primitive commercial bank was founded by Judas Tadeo Landínez, a businessman-politician from the backward interior provincial town of Tunja. It is not clear how Landínez happened to conceive of this project. He appears not to have visited Europe or the United States before founding his establishment; his previous experience in banking, therefore, could not have extended beyond simple moneylending. In any case, his operations, while quite complicated, were not characterized by a high degree of organization. Landínez simply issued commercial bills under his name; these circulated at par with silver coin, as he had succeeded in establishing his credit through prompt payment, at the time a novelty in Bogotá. Aided by a loan of $450,000 from Antioquia, Landínez' operations took on considerable scale. During the year of 1841, Landínez carried on transactions involving a great proportion of the real property surrounding Bogotá in a radius of a hundred miles — buying haciendas, houses, shares in factories or other companies at inflated prices and interest rates, and then selling them again. Landínez' speculation soon whirled out of control, and he went into bankruptcy with $2,000,000 in obligations and only $500,000 in assets. In the process he brought most of the Bogotá elite to temporary ruin; property not lost directly in Landínez' crash was wasted in dozens of prolonged and complicated lawsuits. Perhaps Bogotá's bitter experience with Landínez' brief but heady speculations was one factor in delaying the establishment of other commercial banks.

After the Landínez episode, Bogotá's next experiment with credit institutions was the creation of a savings bank. The first, and most successful, savings bank in Colombia was established in the Caribbean port of Cartagena in 1844. In the following year, however, a savings bank was founded in the capital, from which the movement spread to Santa Marta, Medellín, Neiva, and lesser provincial towns. The Bogotá savings bank was founded as an institution to be administered by the upper class on behalf of the lower. The bank was to encourage the saving habit among the poor, who otherwise would dribble away their few reals in the consumption of aguardiente. In theory the bank's funds were to go to worthy, but small, enterprises — no loan could exceed 1,000 pesos.

The Bogotá elite gave the bank strong administrative support.

The first junta of administrators was composed of sixteen of the most prestigious politicians, hacendados, and merchant-capitalists in the capital; the director was the Minister of Finance, Lino de Pombo, and his assistants included the Archbishop of Bogotá. The aristocratic administrators devoted their Sundays, by turns, to receiving deposits. The upper class at first also gave the bank financial support, with merchants and other elite types making some relatively large deposits. By the end of the 1850's, however, few large merchants were contributing, and the bulk of the fund was provided by the middle artisan class. In 1859, its fourteenth year, the savings bank had capital amounting to only a little more than $200,000.

Throughout the period from 1821 to 1870, Colombian merchants and politicians sporadically discussed the desirability of forming national banks of issue, mortgage banks, and other commercial banks. These innovations were believed to be of pressing importance because much of the interior chronically suffered from a shortage of circulating media, as well as of credit. All of the projects before 1870 failed, however, because civil wars stripped the national government and many private citizens of the capital or foreign credit needed to establish an initial fund. . . .

The first commercial banks in Bogotá which survived the nineteenth century were established in the 1870's, under the leadership of native Bogotanos, and without notable foreign assistance. In the first of these banks, the Banco de Bogotá, founded in 1870, only 9 of the 93 original shares appear to have been held by men of foreign birth. The first Colombian insurance company, the Compañía Colombiana de Seguros, was founded in 1874 by Pedro Navas Azuero, a native Bogotano, with the support of most of the notable local merchant-capitalists.

While the manufacturing and banking enterprises attempted in Bogotá between 1821 and 1870 were either failures or only modest successes, in the gold-rich region of Antioquia a number of mining enterprises were proving quite lucrative. As in the case of manufacturing in Bogotá, developments in mining in Antioquia were the joint work of native capitalist-entrepreneurs and foreign technicians. In the period between 1800 and 1820 the yield of many mines in Antioquia had fallen and local miners lacked the technique required to exploit relatively low-grade ore. In the 1820's, Francisco Montoya and four other leading citizens of the Antioquia town of Rionegro, formed a mining company for the purpose of introducing the best European techniques into the mines of Santa Rosa. They procured the services of an English engineer, Tyrell Moore, who brought new ore mills which permitted use of lower-grade ores. The increased productivity permitted by Moore's innovations was responsible for the great prosperity which characterized Antioquia in the 1830's, when most other regions of the country were deep in depression.

Wealth accrued from the mines of Antioquia between 1830 and 1860 played a dominant role in the founding of many new enterprises in other areas of the country, most notably the development of steam navigation on the Magdalena and of tobacco exporting. Leadership in both of the latter developments was provided, more than by any other single man, by Francisco Montoya, one of the five developers of the mines of Santa Rosa. Member of a distinguished Rionegro family, Montoya had fought in the patriot armies in 1815–1816, attaining the rank of colonel. During the period of Spanish repression between 1816 and 1819, he lived in Jamaica, where he carried on commercial activities. In 1824, already a rich man, he negotiated a loan of £4,750,000 in London for the Colombian government, for which service he and an Antioqueño associate, Manuel Antonio Arrubla, received a commission of more than $200,000. After forming the mining company in Antioquia, he assumed leadership of many enterprises in Bogotá, where he resided from the middle 1820's to his death in 1862. In 1836 he led the group of Colombian capitalists who obtained a franchise to construct a transit line across the Isthmus of Panama by road, rail, or water. Montoya also headed a firm (composed mostly of fellow Antioqueños) which practically monopolized keelboat transportation on the Magdalena, at the same time building roads and engaging in land freighting between the Magdalena River and Bogotá. Between 1837 and 1839 he formed a company to place a steamboat on the Magdalena; the company provided service between 1839 and 1841, when its lone steamboat was seized and destroyed during civil war. After this setback, Montoya and other Antioqueños who worked with him again turned to keelboat service on the river. In 1847, when a group of forwarding merchants in Santa Marta founded the first successful river steamer company, they found it necessary to buy Montoya's keelboats, giving him a large share of the steam company stock.

An important factor in the success of steam navigation was the development of tobacco exports from the region of Ambalema, on the banks of the Upper Magdalena. Tobacco had been cultivated in this region since at least the middle of the eighteenth century.

But the amount of production had been controlled by a government monopoly, both in the colonial period and under the republic. Beginning in the 1830's, the government of New Granada adopted the policy of encouraging the export of this tobacco. Particularly after 1845, production for export increased markedly. The export of tobacco provided increased downstream freight for steamboats, and brought 'new exchange which permitted the expansion of imports, and thus upstream traffic.

The development of tobacco production for export was the work of both British and Colombian entrepreneurs. William Wills played an important role in the early stages. In the early 1830's, as representative of the English house of Powles, Illingworth, he began systematic testing of Granadan tobacco in European markets. In this period Wills accumulated important information on European requirements for curing and packing, which guided the industry for the next four decades.

The second important step in developing the tobacco industry was executed by Francisco Montoya and his family, five members of which composed the firm of Montoya, Sáenz. In 1845, the government of New Granada contracted out production of tobacco for the monopoly to Montoya, Sáenz, in the belief that a private businessman with credit resources superior to those of the government could expand production more efficiently and effectively. As producer of tobacco for the government monopoly between 1845 and 1849, Montoya, Sáenz established a system of centralized curing, inspection, and packing, and insisted on the most careful selection and quality control. Contemporaries generally credited Montoya and family with developing the reputation of Ambalema tobacco as being second only to Cuban leaf for cigar wrappers.

Most Colombian export commodities were developed by Colombians without noteworthy foreign assistance. Bogotanos took the lead in the cultivation of indigo in the 1860's. Colombians from the eastern provinces were also entirely responsible for the production and export of straw hats, principally to the Caribbean islands and to the southern United States. Bogotanos also made efforts, with varying success, to develop exports of cowhides and of such forest products as vegetable ivory, medicinals (sarsaparilla, ipecacuanha, ratan root), and assorted dyewoods. . . .

Comparison — In many respects, the performance of foreign businessmen in Colombia differed very little from that of native Colombians. The main difference between them lay in the fact that the foreigners generally had superior technical knowledge. In almost any activity requiring new types of machinery, foreign technicians played a vital role. Foreigners played a critical part in improving the mechanics of mining and manufacturing. Until the 1860's, river steamboats were almost exclusively built and captained by foreigners. But in all of these activities Colombians provided entrepreneurial initiative, business organization, and capital.

In other respects, foreign and national businessmen were very much alike. As manufacturers, they both tended to overestimate the domestic market. Foreigners, in fact, erred more than natives in this respect, for the Colombians generally attempted to produce staple goods, while foreign enterprisers tended to gravitate to luxury products having a very limited consumer base.

As exporters, English and Colombian merchants also operated similarly. English and Colombian tobacco exporters both failed to maintain quality control in Ambalema. After the collapse of Montoya, Sáenz in 1857, Ambalema was dominated by the British house of Frühling and Goschen. It was precisely during the period when the English house was the biggest exporter that Ambalema tobacco became discredited in the Bremen market. As exporters of cinchona bark and other commodities, English merchants proved themselves not a whit more adept than their Colombian counterparts.

It does not appear that foreign businessmen in Colombia showed any markedly greater genius for successful economic calculation than did native merchants. A great many foreign ventures in Colombia were marked by a tendency to over-extension. This was true of the British-owned Colombian Mining Association. It was true of Juan Bernardo Elbers' early efforts in steamboating. It was true of the American manufacturers of combs and beaver hats. It was true of the activities of the Bank of London, Mexico, and South America.

It is possible, of course, to view the foreigners' recklessness as evidence of entrepreneurial dash, contrasting it with Colombian caution and lack of interest in innovation. On the other hand, it can also be said that the Colombians appraised economic conditions more realistically and were thus less likely to be drawn into quixotic adventures. Colombian merchants were cautious because experience had revealed to them the limitations of the local market. Experience also had taught them the danger of committing capital to new enterprises in an environment of political strife. They could anticipate that during civil wars materials or markets might be cut off, or that workers or products might be seized for use by contending factions. Finally, many Colombian businessmen were cautious simply because they lacked capital and it was more difficult for them to borrow than it was for European entrepreneurs with connections in London.

In nineteenth-century Colombia it appears that the most important requisite for entrepreneurial leadership was the ability to procure capital. Englishmen and Antioqueños were frequently found at the head of large new enterprises because capital was available to them in larger quantities and at cheaper cost than to Colombians from the poorer interior provinces. In the poorer areas, the upper class had little capital beyond the land. And, lacking banks, this capital was hard to mobilize. In this situation, the liquid capital controlled by merchants from gold-rich Antioquia would be a powerful economic lever. The Antioqueños, alone among Colombian businessmen, could stand up to British merchants with credit in London. As they already had considerable capital, upper-class Antioqueños were able to obtain credit from British banks more easily than any other group. The largest private British loans before 1870 were made to the Antioqueño tobacco exporter, Montoya, Sáenz, by the firms of S. Rucker & Sons and Frühling & Goschen.

Distinctive cultural characteristics probably played some role in English and Antioqueño leadership. Bogotanos and other Colombians respected both groups as especially enterprising. The English were thought to be distinguished for their persistence in the face of adversity, the Antioqueños for their general industriousness. Nevertheless, other investment groups displayed many of the same characteristics. The inhabitants of the province of Santander shared with the Antioqueños a restless energy which carried them to distant parts of the country in search of new economic opportunities. The merchants of Santa Marta were the equal of the Antioqueños in shrewdness and business skill and in the ability to cooperate imaginatively in major community enterprises. Colombians from these poorer regions were constantly engaging in new endeavors, whether in manufacturing, exporting, or transportation. But their activities generally were carried out on a smaller scale and, therefore, have attracted less notice than those of the Antioqueños or of foreign investors.

Within the limits imposed by their capital resources, by the domestic market, and by the political environment, merchant-capitalists in many regions of Colombia gave a good account of themselves. The fact that their country failed to develop in any significant way during the nineteenth century can be ascribed primarily to geographical and political factors. In some areas, cultural factors, such as a weak associative spirit, played a role in inhibiting development. But among the upper class in many par's of Colombia, there was no lack of individual enterprise.

B. Mexico

2. The Spirit of Enterprise in Yucatan

Howard F. Cline

Its founder, Pedro Sainz de Baranda y Borreiro, asserted that the "Aurora Yucateca" was the first completely mechanized textile factory in Mexico to use steam power. His descendants, Yucatecan contemporaries, foreign travelers, and later writers have echoed the claim. The "Aurora" was designed to use modern equipment for ginning, spinning, and weaving into yard-goods the cotton grown locally. Its labor force was drawn from Maya Indians and mestizos. On March 8, 1833, the Yucatecan congress extended to Baranda a five-year monopoly on the use of steam-driven textile machinery. Shortly thereafter the factory was producing cloth on an experimental basis.

Entirely unsubsidized, the "Aurora" was a private enterprise, a completely Yucatecan undertaking. The mill did not reach full or even profitable production until about 1839, but thenceforth it flourished until the death of Baranda in 1845. Not long after his demise the city of Valladolid and its surrounding district, site of the "Aurora" and its source of raw materials, were devastated by rebel Maya in a savage uprising known in Yucatecan annals as the War of the Castes. The fact that the "Aurora" had operated in the area had little to do with the revolt, which broke out in 1847, but the

From "The 'Aurora Yucateca' and the Spirit of Enterprise in Yucatan, 1821–1847" by Howard F. Cline, *Hispanic American Historical Review*, XXVII, 1947, pp. 30–60, *passim*. Reprinted by permission.

double blow, death of its founder and outbreak of the long struggle, crushed any hope that the factory would operate uninterruptedly in other hands.

The spirit which moved Baranda to establish the "Aurora Yucateca" was not wholly confined to Yucatan. There, however, impulses to change and novelty were surging strong in many fields. All over the Republic of Mexico men of like stamp had similar ideas. From mixed motives of patriotism, hope of gain, desire for prestige, perhaps merely satisfaction derived from overcoming the numerous obstacles in their way, other Mexican capitalists of the era turned to textile ventures at about the same time Baranda did. Political disorders, and the fact that funds with which to launch industrial ventures could be had only at ruinous rates of interest (12 to 24 per cent) hampered their activities; but by 1843, in addition to the "Aurora Yucateca," there were already some fifty-seven cotton-spinning mills scattered widely over the republic. Their 125,362 spindles and 2,609 looms hummed and clattered from Sonora to Veracruz. The similarity of names testifies to like aims; thus the "Aurora Industrial" of Puebla presumably expressed the hope of that area, just as the "Aurora Yucateca" did for the peninsula.

Whether or not the Yucatecan bid for industrial precedence in Mexico is valid seems relatively unimportant. Counter-claims undoubtedly could be presented for other places, and perhaps ultimately the matter can be settled by investigators of the commercialization and industrialization of Latin America, a theme of recently growing interest. For present purposes the "Aurora Yucateca" is significant as a symbol and as a case history which illuminates facts of some importance. Its relatively early establishment indicates that a fairly general shift in ideas and activities had taken place on Yucatan, and that by the first third of the nineteenth century there was a climate of opinion saturated with the spirit of enterprise. This was in direct contrast to the spirit of the times reported in late colonial days: investigators in 1766 lamented that Yucatecans were completely apathetic to ideas of commerce or change, that they were much less addicted to "trade and war than to love, inaction, and repose." There is a two-fold purpose in relating details of the "Aurora" — to provide specific material on an early factory, and to utilize it as a point of departure for sketching rapidly some of the other notable shifts that were transpiring under the pressures which a newly arisen spirit of enterprise was creating in Yucatan following its independence. These latter are important;

they conditioned and affected historical development there, most dramatically by heightening tensions between the numerically preponderant Maya population and the handful of white creoles who were attempting to bring Yucatan abreast of the modern world.

Not only some insights into the economic origins of the Yucatecan Caste War may be gleaned from examination of changes in the peninsula, but there seem to be even broader implications. The generation that directed the first footsteps of the newly emancipated province and republic was an enthusiastic and generally able one. Its real achievements are sometimes obscured in the murk of political polemic and of the history based upon it. Partisan and factional bickerings did generate political anarchy, but all life of the epoch was not confined to political arenas and forums. There also existed social and economic leaders with ability and vision, only loosely attached to a political group. Baranda seems such a figure, but like others of the era, when nearly any man of talent was likely to be pressed into political service, he succumbed to the demands made on him, though his chief interest lay in his other enterprises. But standing somewhat apart from small coteries, each obsessed by notions of gaining and holding political power, were other groups, pioneers in social, intellectual, and economic lines. Collectively they were apparently moved by sincere and usually fervent zeal to free their provinces and country from a colonialism which others had combated on the battle fields. By substituting national achievement and aims for a discredited mercantilism, such figures labored to put solid foundations under the political liberty so recently won.

With supreme confidence that economic gains accompanied and inspired desirable advance in other fields, Mexicans who matured from 1821 to perhaps 1850 attacked an enormous task with fervor and high hope. Their general object was to convert an outmoded and now disdained economy and civilization based on Spanish imperial policies into a commercial, possibly industrial, economy and a modern society premised on national sovereignty and self-determination. In many aspects the United States, Great Britain, sometimes France, whose important political thought and economic philosophies were accepted, served as suitable models. The enthusiasm and aspirations of their peoples glow through their writings with an exultation and optimism most nearly comparable to that engendered in Russian authors who praise the Soviet five-year plans.

In the Yucatan of the period, politicians, educators, inventors, artists, plantation owners, traders, and others were extending new social and economic frontiers far beyond colonial bounds. In one important respect, however, they overlooked a major problem, or at least deferred its consideration until too late. With but few exceptions their new hopes and activities excluded the native population, a vast mass of Maya whose forbears had erected the sophisticated civilization, the ruins of which dot southern Mexico, but who under the colonial regime had served as a mute and docile labor force, retaining scarcely any memory of their illustrious past. . . .

That planners and men of action from 1821 to 1847 failed to grapple with a major element and to integrate the exploited Indians into their dream of progress does not wholly obscure some positive achievements of the era. These remain as important pioneering steps, products of a protean spirit of enterprise which at once was probably chiefly responsible for the Caste War, but simultaneously for creation of solid foundations on which later intellectual, social, and economic edifices could be built. Debatable indeed is the question of whether the one result counterbalanced the other. Here emphasis is placed on the more positive side, particularized to discussion of Baranda's "Aurora Yucateca" as a typical result of the reigning urge to progress, and to brief indications of some other manifestation of the same spirit in contemporary economic changes which led ultimately to the Caste War.

Though in most ways a child of his age and locale, Pedro Sainz de Baranda was unlike some of his fellow citizens in that his hopes and aims did not wholly outstrip his ability to realize them. By background, experience, and temperament he was fitted to undertake, with some assurance of success, a relatively complex project like founding a cotton mill in the hinterland of a backward peninsula. Though he was competent himself, whatever the personal traits he may have lacked to become an accomplished businessman may well have been supplied to the enterprise by his close associates, John L. MacGregor, a Yucatan Scot, and John Burke, an American from New York. The combination proved a winning one until first MacGregor, then Baranda died, and the Caste War erupted.

The Baranda family was a distinguished one in Old Spain, and its Yucatecan branches did not dim its record. In addition to his career as an entrepreneur, Pedro Sainz de Baranda had been a Spanish and Mexican naval figure; and he held high civil posts, including governorship, in Yucatan. His sons both became state governors; one, Joaquín, was an intellectual, a lawyer, and an able administrator, while another, Pedro, was chiefly instrumental in creating the separate state of Campeche and also acquired glory as a professional soldier. . . .

Viewed at this time and distance, some of the many virtues attributed to Baranda by eulogists have their luster somewhat dimmed, but he remains an attractive and typical figure of an important transitional period in Yucatan. Urbane, sophisticated, and able, sincerely patriotic and loyal to his province, he compares well with other of his compatriots — Justo Sierra, Andrés Quintana Roo, Lorenzo Zavala, Manuel Barbachano — who rendered valuable services to Mexico and Yucatan, their homeland. As a group they were widely traveled, alert to adopt new ideas and developments of interest and value to their struggling province and nation.

Unfortunately only scanty information is available on John L. MacGregor, Baranda's silent partner in the "Aurora." Each subscribed half the initial investment of forty thousand dollars which it required, having agreed that Baranda would receive for his active administration an annual salary of one thousand pesos. Since in 1844 Baranda listed his co-partners as heirs of MacGregor, presumably the father had died. The latter's descendants included sons who have left minor traces in the records of the day, and who became linked to the Baranda family through marriage. Apparently both the Barandas and the MacGregors were included in the group of cosmopolitan citizens whose polylingual households and attention to refinement, culture, and business gave Campeche an air of briskness which travelers thought equal to the best in Europe and perhaps unmatched in Mexico.

John Burke left no literary remains, and data on him are few. He succeeded four Americans who had accompanied the "Aurora's" equipment from New York, to install it and to instruct native workmen; two died in Yucatan from malaria, and the other pair seemingly soon left. Burke entered Baranda's employ in 1835 and acted as mill superintendent until at least 1844. When Stephens talked to him in Valladolid in 1842, Burke had already nearly forgotten English, but was otherwise typically American in dress, appearance, and outlook. His career after 1844 is hazy in detail, but was evidently profitable, since he is said to have died in New York, leaving an estate of four million dollars.

With their capital Baranda and MacGregor purchased machinery to set up a small but quite up-to-date textile factory which performed all operations necessary to convert raw cotton brought from nearby fields to finished cloth. Their yard-goods compared favorably in quality, less so in price, with products from New England and Great Britain. Aside from the important fact that the "Aurora" existed at all so early in an apparently backward area of isolated Yucatan, Baranda's management policies consciously or unconsciously formed a model pattern. They indicated that exploitation need not necessarily accompany economic development. His workers, fifty-three mestizos and native Maya, were paid on a piece-work basis and earned twice the prevailing wage for agricultural workers and artisans, figured usually at one *real* (0.125 pesos) and three cents worth of maize a day. In addition Baranda contracted with sixty-four Indian families to provide wood for his boilers, paying them the standard wage of a *medio* (half a real, 0.063 pesos) a load. Like others, he found it difficult to change the Indian way of doing things and therefore conformed to it; he preferred unsplit logs, but for generations the Maya had split them, and so perforce he got split logs. A compatriot, Simon Peón, likewise discovered persistent native refusal to modernize when Indians on his hacienda would not use a patented American churn.

Aside from the 117 local families supported by the "Aurora," there was an unspecified number of Maya around Valladolid who grew cotton for it. These were independent agriculturists. They cultivated cotton in their unplowed patches known as *milpas,* which at the same time provided them with maize, beans, and a number of subsidiary products. For the unginned cotton Baranda paid them from eight to twelve reales (1.00 to 1.50 pesos) for a load of thirty-two pounds. At current wage rates the Indians made perhaps 100 per cent profit at that price and had maize and other products from their milpas as bonus, by-products of cotton culture. By March, 1844, the "Aurora" had used nearly three hundred tons of cotton (580,000 pounds) and had thus contributed a respectable sum to the Maya cotton growers. Whether these idyllic conditions, contrasting sharply with cotton production by slave labor on American plantations, would have continued had Yucatan developed a full-fledged industry is very questionable, but it seems to Baranda's credit that even when competition from smuggled goods undercut his prices and drove his product from the peninsula he did not try to meet it by exploitation of the native growers.

The plant of the "Aurora" was a neat, efficient-looking establishment. It consisted of a series of buildings surrounded by a ten-foot fence on a lot which faced the plaza in Candelaria, a *barrio* or suburb of Valladolid. Its area was 150 by 200 feet, within which the buildings were grouped around an open patio. Four warehouses formed the side nearest the plaza, divided by a gate which led to the patio. At the extreme end of the patio were maintenance units, a smithy and a carpenter's shop. These and all the other buildings were solid structures, of whitewashed rubble and mortar, roofed with tile. . . .

Salable products included thread and yard-goods. The former was reckoned by weight, the latter by yardage and number of pieces. Daily capacity of the "Aurora" was from four to five hundred yards of medium-fine cotton cloth, plus a hundred pounds of thread. By March, 1844, the factory had produced 13,256 pieces of cloth, amounting to about 395,000 yards, and about 1,700 pounds of No. 16 thread.

The factory did not immediately begin profitable production. By 1835, at an estimated cost of eight thousand dollars over capital investment, it had produced only eighteen yards of cloth. The difficulties were due mainly to technical troubles which seemingly were cleared up after Burke got on the job. In the three years from 1840 through 1842, the factory output amounted to about 200,000 yards of cloth, and 7,000 pounds of thread. Since cloth from the "Aurora" sold for 18½ centavos per vara (33½ inches), gross income from that alone would amount to 37,000 pesos. Raw materials probably cost about 27,000 pesos, leaving the difference to labor, Baranda's salary, other overhead, and profits, if any. Production was much less a problem than was distribution, for in the latter Baranda ran afoul of political snarls.

Because of competition from British Honduras, Baranda had to seek markets outside Yucatan. British cloth, produced in Manchester, could be smuggled into Yucatan via Belize and sold for 12½ centavos a yard, as opposed to Baranda's 18½ per vara, a differential of about 40 per cent in favor of British goods. When Baranda looked abroad for sales, he was trapped, after 1843, by a political impasse between Yucatan and Mexico.

Yucatan twice had cut itself loose from Mexican control following 1839. Once it had returned voluntarily without coercion, and once, in 1843, it soundly thrashed Mexican troops, but then joined the union on Mexican promises that Yucatecan goods might enter Mexican Gulf ports without duty. Mexico was to publish such a list of "natural products" of Yucatan which a treaty arranged in December, 1843, prescribed. When Mexican authorities published the list, nearly all Yucatecan money crops and products had been dropped or omitted from it; among them were sugar, henequen, salt, and textiles. As the situation existed in 1844, and thereafter for some time, these goods shipped from Yucatan were considered by Mexican port officials as merely trans-shipments from foreign ports, and therefore subject to regular tariff levies.

Earlier Baranda had run into the same type of difficulty. At Vera-cruz and Tampico his yard-goods had been categorized as "foreign" despite their Yucatecan trademark, because port officials refused to believe that Yucatecans could produce such cloth; it appeared to them English, marked locally to avoid duty. Even after this matter had been cleared at those places, officials at Tabasco charged full tariff on samples Baranda sent there. But omission from the free list in early 1844 was a rude blow. Contemporaries hinted that Mexican factories feared Baranda's competition and had brought pressure to bear to ruin him. In any event, before the difficulty was finally cleared in 1848 Baranda was dead, and the "Aurora" was serving embattled creoles as a fortress to withstand Maya assaults. Its ruins remained standing for many years.

The "Aurora" brings to the fore some of the problems that entrepreneurs of the time had to face, and which Baranda solved as well as one man could. His relations to native and mestizo workmen seem irreproachable, but in carrying out a humane and enlightened policy he lost a large local market. The financial difficulties that destroyed many another textile enterprise — Lucas Alamán's as a notable example — were overcome through the help of MacGregor. Technical problems were often solved by empiricism, such as more solid construction of the main building after its two collapses, or by the importation of foreign experts like Burke. Yet one man alone could not regulate the political environment; that required group action, as did numerous other subsidiary elements.

Transportation, for instance, was a conditioning factor. Until roads had been completed from the port of Sisal to Mérida, and thence to Valladolid, the heavy machinery, carried to Baranda's "Aurora" in special carts purchased in New York, could not have been moved inland, nor the finished product out, except at prohibitive cost. Yet if the mill were placed elsewhere, added cost for transporting raw cotton to it would have been equally restrictive.

It seems clear that the "Aurora" was not an isolated phenomenon of individual enterprise, when viewed in this context. Preceding it and accompanying it were other developments which made possible its appearance in 1833, but whose unchecked acceleration led to the Caste War in 1847. Probably that ugly wave of revolt would have obliterated the "Aurora" even had Baranda not died in 1845.

C. Chile

3. Economic Development Before the War of the Pacific
FREDRICK B. PIKE

Mineral Wealth and Social Transition — The Portales era commenced on a resounding note of economic good luck. The Chañarcillo silver mine began operation in 1832 — a mine that yielded 450,000,000 of the 891,000,000 pesos worth of silver produced in nineteenth-century Chile. The mining boom had commenced, and the age of fabulous silver strikes continued until 1870, the date of the discovery of the northern Caracoles vein. By the time of the Caracoles find, Chilean nitrate production had begun, and the country was already saddled with a dependence on extractive industries that rendered unlikely a balanced economic growth. In 1864, approximately 70 per cent of Chile's exports consisted of mine products, while by 1881 the figure had risen to 78.5 per cent.

Behind these statistics lie many stories of personal vision, daring, energy, and often ruthlessness, that rival the success tales of men like Vanderbilt, Carnegie, and Rockefeller. In 1845, Juan Mackay, a man of redoubtable spirit, began Chilean coal exploitation. Seven years later Matías Cousiño appeared upon the scene, married the widow of Miguel Gallo, who had himself been a mining millionaire, and shortly began the work that would make him the principal figure in the Chilean coal industry. All of Cousiño's patience, confidence, influence, and wealth were necessary to bring about successful production in the Lota and Coronel fields south of Concepción. But the capitalist-adventurer overcame the long odds

From *Chile and the United States, 1880–1962: The Emergence of Chile's Social Crisis and the Challenge to United States Diplomacy* by Fredrick B. Pike (Notre Dame, Ind.: University of Notre Dame Press, 1963), pp. 4–8. Reprinted by permission.

against him, and by the later years of his life was investing some of his coal millions in northern nitrate operations. He had become perhaps Santiago's most colorful millionaire, living in one of the more lavish of the many mansions constructed in the capital city during the mining bonanza.

By the 1870's, increasing numbers of Chileans were gaining fortunes in northern nitrate operations. One of them was José Santos Ossa, a daring explorer of the desert and the discoverer of the Antofagasta nitrate deposits. Santos Ossa was also active in establishing the *Compañía de Antofagasta* which became the main nitrate operation in South America. It was almost exclusively a Chilean venture, with the principal founders being, in addition to Santos Ossa, Agustín Edwards Ross, Alfredo Ossa, and Juan Francisco Puelma.

As early as the 1850's, a new aristocracy, its wealth based on commerce, industry, banking, and above all on mining, was coming to occupy positions of social and political importance formerly reserved to landowners who could trace their lineage back to early colonial times. Agustín Edwards Ossandón, Gregorio Ossa, Tomás Gallo, and naturally Matías Cousiño, were the first outstanding representatives of this new class. In 1857, the traditional landlord aristocracy suffered a rude blow with the abolition of *mayorazgos* (roughly equivalent to combined primogeniture and entail), which facilitated redistribution of landed estates. A depression from 1858 to 1860, moreover, caused a disastrous decline in agrarian land values, impoverished many members of the old order, and permitted the new rich to acquire land and, thereby, social prestige and acceptance.

By mid-nineteenth century Chile was revealing a remarkable tolerance for allowing entry of new blood into the ranks of the social elite. Even more striking, by the latter part of the century the aristocracy was studded with the names of foreigners whose grandfathers had arrived in the country only around the time of the independence movement. From the United Kingdom had come settlers with the names of Ross, Edwards, Lyon, Walker, MacClure, Garland, MacIver, Jackson, Brown, Price, Phillips, Waddington, Blest, Simpson, Eastman, Budge, Page, and others; from France came the Cousiño, Subercaseaux, and Rogers families, while from Slavic and German areas had come the Piwonkas and the Königs. A survey of Chilean biographical encyclopedias, of membership lists for such aristocratic organizations as the *Club de la Unión,* or of the roll of the stock-market founders, and a scanning of prominent names in diplomacy, politics, and the fine arts will reveal the prominence that these names have enjoyed from the mid-to-late nineteenth century to the present time. A conspicuous factor in this development was the "well-known preference" of Chilean ruling classes for marrying their children to financially successful immigrants and their descendants.

The rapid transformation in Chilean society was noted by the leading Valparaíso daily, *El Mercurio*, in May of 1882. Of the fifty-nine personal fortunes in Chile of over one million pesos (of forty-eight pence), twenty-four were of colonial origin, and the remainder belonged to coal, nitrate, copper, and silver interests, or to merchants, all of whom had begun their march toward fortune only in the nineteenth century.

Other Aspects of Economic Development — In the 1850's, the first of the true banks appeared in Chile. The year 1855 saw the establishment of the Bank of Valparaíso, which accepted deposits and engaged in discount activities. The famous agricultural mortgage credit agency (*caja de crédito hipotecario*) was founded in the same year, for the purpose of providing long-term loans. The man who devised the basic patterns of this agency — long a landmark in Latin-American agricultural finance — was a young economist, Wenceslao Vial y Guzmán, who later played a leading role in founding the National Bank of Chile. On the eve of the War of the Pacific, banking deposits had risen to close to sixty million pesos. A law of 1860, extremely favorable in its provisions to bankers, had facilitated the dramatic rise of the Chilean banking system.

Between 1845 and 1860, the volume of Chilean commerce tripled. A great boon to commerce was the completion in 1863 of the Valparaíso to Santiago railroad — a feat for which the Yankee speculator and railroad builder Henry Meiggs was principally responsible. By 1874 the total of Chile's foreign trade, exports and imports, had soared to 157 million pesos. Great Britain took close to two thirds of the annual exports, and supplied the country with approximately one third of its imports. Following Great Britain in importance of commercial relations were France, Germany, and Peru. The United States, an insignificant factor in the commercial picture, was in eighth place.

The mid-nineteenth century witnessed also the inception of scientific livestock raising, under the direction of such men as Ricardo E. Price, Tomás Eastman, Tomás Gallo, Agustín Edwards, José

Tomás Urmeneta, Guillermo Brown, Manuel Bunster, and Tomás Bland. General agricultural production matched the gains of animal husbandry. During the 1844–1880 period, the value of agricultural exports was nearly one half that of the extractive industries. Wine production was also becoming increasingly important, with the vineyards of Manuel Antonio Tocornal, José Tomás Urmeneta, and Magdalena Vicuña Subercaseaux gaining wide renown. By 1865, moreover, there were twenty-six breweries in Chile.

Utilization of new land and encouragement of immigration, especially the attempt to lure Germans to the southern area around Lake Llanquihue, added also to the nation's economic development. Instrumental in making a reality of President Manuel Montt's (1851–1861) dream of German settlements was Vicente Pérez Rosales, an adventurer and writer of ingratiating style who had been at one time or another a farmer in Boldamávida, a producer of *aguardiente* in Colchagua, a merchant, a painter of theatrical posters and decorations, an herb doctor, a contrabandist on the Argentine pampas, a miner in Copiapó, and a gold-seeker in California. Pérez Rosales accepted the post of colonization agent in the early days of the Montt administration and thereafter worked indefatigably to attract German immigrants, as well as to prepare a suitable settlement for them at Valdivia. He procured land for the first group of colonists to arrive in the South, among whom was Carlos Anwandter, destined to found a distinguished family in Chile. In 1852 while seeking new settlement sites, Pérez Rosales helped found Puerto Montt and Puerto Varas, and his paintings of this area are considered almost as valuable as his charmingly written *Recuerdos del pasado,* in which he described the early German colonization efforts.

Still, Chile did not attract large-scale immigration. In the periods immediately preceding and following 1880, complaints were often voiced that more people left Chile in search of better opportunity than came to the land.

4. The Dawn of Manufacturing in Chile

J. Fred Rippy and Jack Pfeiffer

In Chile, as in other countries, the handicraft production by the individual, or by the individual family, of kitchen utensils, pottery, footwear, simple tools, or woven goods was the forerunner of manufacturing industry. The development was slow everywhere, and the market was limited at first to families in the immediate vicinity, then to the nearest village, and finally, when methods had improved enough to produce a larger surplus, it expanded to other villages. In Chile, the process was longer and slower than in the United States and England.

One of the first observers of the backward condition of Chilean manufactures was a Yankee printer named Samuel Johnson, who had gone to Chile in time to witness the struggle against the Spaniards for independence. Johnson, in his diary dealing with the period from about 1811 to 1818, notes that the Chileans were dependent on foreign commerce for almost all their manufactured goods except blankets.

Another on-the-spot observer, who told essentially the same story, was Lady Maria Callcott, an English widow and friend of Thomas Cochrane, who resided in Chile in 1822 and had the following comments to make about the state of Chilean manufactures:

The people of the country are still in the habit of spinning, weaving, dyeing, and making every article for themselves in their own houses, except hats and shoes. . . . The stuffs of the country are seldom to be purchased in a shop because few are made but for domestic consumption.

Lady Callcott was a shrewd observer, who seems to have possessed a true woman's curiosity about the ways of others, a curiosity which gives one an insight into the whole of the Chilean manufacturing system (manufacturing in the sense that we now consider it of being the production of surplus goods, of articles destined for more

From "Notes on the Dawn of Manufacturing in Chile" by J. Fred Rippy and Jack Pfeiffer, *Hispanic American Historical Review*, XXVIII, 1948, pp. 292–296. Reprinted by permission.

than simple home use). She speaks of the manufacture of earthen jars in Valparaíso, where she found that the potters had no regular establishment, no division of labor, and that they did not even use the potter's wheel — a great surprise even for a woman not particularly familiar with industrial life. She also gives one of the first reports on the earliest of all manufacturing establishments in Chile, a factory for making gunpowder which the Spanish royal government had erected at La Chimba, near Santiago, and which had been destroyed by leaders of the movement for Chilean independence. This mill had made use of water to run its equipment, thus foreshadowing what was soon to become one of the chief methods of producing motive power in many of the Chilean industries.

Waterpower was being used at the time of her ladyship's visit to move the machinery of many of the numerous Chilean flour mills. In fact, John Miers, an Englishman who, with his family, was well acquainted with Lady Callcott while she was in Chile, and who later wrote of his own experiences, spoke of the utilization of such power in the flour mill which he built.

In addition to manufacturing flour, Miers was a pioneer in the manufacture of milling equipment in Chile, for he had made all of the equipment needed for a flour mill, with the exception of the millstones, which had to be imported from France. Lady Callcott, in speaking of Miers, adds that he was utilizing a circular saw to make barrel staves, and that this put him "about a hundred years ahead of his time" in Chile. Both of these early English visitors took note of the soap-making, tanning, wine, brewing, and candle-making industries in existence at the time.

Miers, being engaged in manufacturing himself, naturally observed other such establishments. He described a lime works at Polpayco, a small village on the road between Valparaíso and Santiago, which had crude smelting furnaces built in the side of a hill. The type of furnace used and the method of charging it were strikingly similar to the "log furnaces" and the methods employed in connection with such furnaces in the lead mines of Missouri, which were coming into prominence at this time. Miers also observed that the sugar industry, which quite early became one of the best developed Chilean manufacturing enterprises, had been tried out at an *ingenio* north of Santiago, but had been abandoned.

An interesting aspect of the early manufacturing situation was the position taken by the Chilean government. Both Lady Callcott (possibly because she was so friendly with the Miers family) and

Miers were disgusted with the national government. Miers had good reason to be, for his purpose in leaving England had been:

> To erect a very extensive train of machinery in that country for refining, rolling, and manufacturing copper into sheathing. . . . I dispatched for Chile, in different vessels, about one hundred tons' weight of machinery, . . . [and] embarked with my wife in a merchant brig, . . . with about 70 tons of machinery, implements, and baggage; taking with me several very skillful workmen, engineers, millwrights, and refiners.

But Miers never accomplished his purpose — in fact he lost, according to his own figures, $40,000 on this enterprise.

The major part of Miers's troubles were encountered in trying to get legal possession of a site for his copper factory; but even if he had succeeded in this, his hopes regarding the success of the plant were not very bright. According to his version, the Chilean government would offer inducements to foreign manufacturers to establish themselves in Chile, and then would tax them out of existence. In substantiation of this, Miers offered the case of an Englishman who was operating one of the few successful breweries of Chile, but who was so heavily taxed that the establishment was unprofitable. Another early manufacturing enterprise that fell by the wayside was a plant, also erected by a foreigner, which was designed to manufacture copper vessels for export to Peru. Taxes forced the plant into bankruptcy. Regarding government policy Lady Callcott made the following observation:

> The duties on all these [importations] are so high, as in many cases to amount to a prohibition, with the view of protecting home-manufactures, forgetting that, excepting hats and small beer, there is not a single manufactory established in Chile; for we can hardly call such the soap-boiling and candle-dipping of the country. And because a man in Santiago has made a pair of stockings in a day, no more foreign stockings are to be introduced; so the ladies must learn to knit or go barefoot.

Despite the handicaps, foreigners continued to try their luck at manufacturing in Chile. According to Miers, however, the only successful foreign manufacturer was a German who was operating a plant to make hemp bags. This plant was located in Santiago, and Miers asserted that it was using machinery to manufacture its product. But Miers's views seem to be a bit severe, especially since he was able to stand the loss of $40,000 without being crushed. His flour mill must have been somewhat profitable even after the government taxes were paid.

The influence of foreigners — in all of the principal industries, such as flour milling, smelting, soap and candle making, and bag making — persisted through the years as manufacturing developed in Chile. From the outset of Chile's industrial life, industries that were of any importance were nearly always controlled, not by natives, but by foreigners. And as new industries were introduced, or as the old ones grew, they were usually owned, controlled, or operated by foreigners.

The extent of the industries that were developed in Chile by 1850 is not clearly evident. One way to get some idea of what they were is to examine the lists of Chilean exports during that period to see if the products listed give any indication as to what industries had developed far enough to produce a surplus that went into foreign trade. A list published by the United States Government for 1837 contained the following goods imported from Chile: 695 gallons of various wines, 102 pounds of cordage (the Chilean hemp industry had its beginnings back in 1822), 315 dollars' worth of leather manufactures, and one gross of glass bottles. (The chief imports of the United States from Chile during these years were the semi-manufactured — "processed" — mineral products of Chile — copper, gold, and silver.) One must not try to derive too much from such data, however, for the list also shows that the United States received from Chile 1,400 square feet of window glass, $2,192 worth of dyed or printed cotton goods, and some silk goods! All of these were probably re-exports, or goods transshipped via Chile, and for that reason they appear on the United States government list as "imports" from Chile. The situation remained about the same up until 1850 — the only available sources being the United States lists as given in *Commerce and Navigation*. In the lists for 1846, 1847, and 1848, hats, caps, and bonnets were added to the previous articles. (The manufacturing of hats was among the first Chilean enterprises mentioned by Lady Callcott.)

The following observations are ventured in regard to the state of Chile's industry by the middle of the nineteenth century: (1) There were, despite comments by travelers to the contrary, several true manufacturing industries with a firm foothold in Chile — flour mills which used water for power, wineries, tanneries, and soap and candle factories. (2) There were, in addition, manufactories connected with the mineral industries, many, if not most, of them dominated by foreigners. (3) The government of Chile displayed an increasing interest in the promotion and protection of home industry. (4) There were indications of the types of establishments that would become a permanent part of the Chilean manufacturing system, such as those making pottery, hemp products, copper utensils, and sugar.

D. Peru

5. Henry Meiggs, Yankee Pizarro

J. FRED RIPPY

Henry Meiggs was perhaps the most remarkable railroad builder who ever appeared on the Latin-American scene. Landing in Chile early in 1855, a stranger and "like a thief in the night," he obtained his first railway contract three years later, and by the end of 1867 had managed the construction of nearly 200 miles, a good part of it across the Chilean coastal range. In 1868 he went to Peru, where the railway era was at its dawn, with less than 60 miles in operation. At his death in Lima on September 30, 1877, Peru had approximately 1,200 miles of track, more than 700 miles of which had been built under Meiggs's direction. . . .

As early as 1862 the Peruvian minister in Chile had urged that Meiggs should be induced to come to Peru and build its railroads. Five years later Meiggs sent his first proposals to the Peruvian government; but his first railway contract in Peru was not awarded until April 30, 1868, three months after his arrival in Lima. A few weeks afterward he set his engineers and labor crews to work on the Arequipa line.

Already his fame was so great that no further evidence of his capacity was required. Three additional contracts were almost thrust upon him before the Arequipa road was finished. By the end of 1871 the total of his contracts mounted to seven, which required the construction of some 990 miles of railway. The aggregate contract price, in cash and in bonds taken by Meiggs at considerably below par, was more than 130,000,000 Peruvian *soles;* and at that time a Peruvian sol was almost the equivalent of a United States gold dollar.

Not only did nearly all the Meiggs railways in Peru run up steep canyons into the giant Andes or along lofty plateaus higher than the highest passes of the North American Sierras and Rockies; floods or scarcity of water accentuated these baffling topographical barriers. The seven railroads, their length, and the dates of the contracts signed with Meiggs are as follows:

1. Mollendo to Arequipa, 107 miles, April 30, 1868.
2. Callao to Oroya, 136 miles, December 18, 1869.
3. Arequipa to Puno, 218 miles, December 18, 1869.
4. Pacasmayo to Magdalena, 91 miles, December 13 and 24, 1870.
5. Ilo to Moquegua, 63 miles, January 12, 1871.
6. Chimbote to Huaraz, 166 miles, October 31, 1871.
7. Juliaca to Cuzco, 210 miles, December 2, 1871.

On February 3, 1877, Meiggs was awarded his eighth and last railway contract. It provided for the construction of a railroad from Oroya to the Cerro de Pasco silver and copper mines, a distance of some 85 miles.

Meiggs did not live to complete these railways. Only the Arequipa, the Puno, and the Ilo-Moquegua lines were finished at his death. He had managed, however, to build the major part of the others, except the Juliaca to Cuzco and the Oroya to Cerro de Pasco roads. No doubt he would have built them all if the national finances had not failed. He made a tremendous attack on the formidable Andes; and often he dreamed of laying rails down their rugged eastern slopes to the mighty Amazon.

The most difficult of the Meiggs railroads to build were the lines from Mollendo to Arequipa and from Callao to Oroya. The longest was the line from Arequipa to Puno, with hardly a mile of its 218 lower than 7,500 feet above the sea and with two passes at an altitude of more than 14,500 feet — higher than Pikes Peak or Mount Evans. But the terrain, in this case, was comparatively smooth and the climate fairly healthful.

Most of the Mollendo-Arequipa line had to be pushed through desert and mountains. The cost of providing a water supply for the railway after it was finished was nearly two million soles, to say nothing of the expense of transporting it during the period of construction. The mountains and canyons required, of course, many fills, excavations, curves, bridges, and culverts. On one stretch tons of drifting sand were confronted and mastered. Disease and accidents took a heavy toll of the laborers — 2,000, it is said — and bloody fights sometimes occurred between the Chilean and Peruvian workers.

The Oroya Railway arouses the admiration of all who see it. After a journey over the road in the 1930's Christopher Morley declared that Meiggs "was one of the world's great poets," for he "built a rhyme loftier than Lycidas." A Peruvian journalist, many years before, had called the enterprise a great hymn with notes running all the tones from "the dull blow of the pickaxe . . . to the shrillest whistle of the locomotive." Some have called it the "railway to the moon." It is, to say the least, a marvelous railroad. The first thirty miles or so run over a gradually rising coastal plain; but the railway then enters the narrow, deep gorge of the River Rímac, as formidable as any on earth. There are 61 bridges, 65 tunnels, and 26 switchbacks; the passenger hardly knows whether he is coming or going. The towering, artistic Verrugas bridge, destroyed years later by an avalanche, was the pride of Peru. The Galera Tunnel runs under Mount Meiggs at an elevation of 15,645 feet. The construction of the road is said to have cost ten thousand lives. Fatal accidents were numerous; mortal fever swept repeatedly through the ranks of the workmen. Only 87 miles were in operation at Meiggs's death.

The gauge of all the Meiggs roads except the Chimbote line was standard: four feet, eight and one half inches. Yet he sent the locomotives higher than they had ever gone before.

Meiggs was the last man to claim exclusive credit for what he did. He was not a trained engineer; he was merely a great executive and a dynamic personality. He imported his experts from all the skillful nations of the world, but mostly from the United States. Some of the managers and technicians were his kinsmen, his brother John G. Meiggs and his nephew Henry Meiggs Keith among them. Prominent among his construction engineers were John L. Thorndike and William H. Cilley. He also employed a few Peruvian technicians who had learned how to build railways. Among his physicians were George A. Ward, Juan Martínez Rosas (a Peruvian), Henry Kinney, Isaac T. Coates, and Edwin R. Heath, who was later to make himself famous by his explorations in the Amazonian jungle. The hard labor was done mostly by Peruvians, Chileans, Bolivians, and Chinese coolies — all employed on a scale seldom witnessed in Latin America. As many as twenty or twenty-five thousand were working for Meiggs at the height of his construction enterprises in 1872.

Meiggs paid his laborers well and was seldom indifferent about their welfare. They were exposed, of course, to the hazards of precipices, landslides, rolling boulders, falling stones, and work trains, as well as to those of climate and disease; but their food was better than they had been accustomed to, and while the medical service was often clearly inadequate it was superior to any they had known before. Of the Chilean *rotos* whom he employed both in their home country and in Peru, Meiggs once said: "I have treated them like men and not like dogs, as is the custom, for they are good if one knows how to direct them." Sometimes his peons were roughly handled by labor bosses or Peruvian soldiers; but that was almost unavoidable in view of the Latin-American attitude toward the lower classes at the time. Criticized in some quarters because of the high death rate among the men working on the Oroya, Meiggs once remarked that people were accustomed to die in Peru as elsewhere. The remark did not signify, however, that he was not grieved. He was careful regarding the food of even the Chinese.

Meiggs had to import nearly everything he used in building his railroads. Peru furnished only the powder for blasting, the rights-of-way, rock for ballast, and a part of the food, medicines, and clothing for the workers. Purchasing agents were located both in England and the United States; but all of the rolling stock and most of the tools, machinery, and materials for construction came from the United States. The bulk of the ties and lumber was shipped in from Washington, Oregon, and California.

Meiggs knew how to win Latin-American sympathies. He was a great dramatist and a great orator. His banquets, celebrations, and charities were long remembered both in Chile and Peru. A Chilean declared that he was a true philanthropist. He distributed thousands of pesos and soles among the poor and the victims of earthquakes. He spent tens of thousands on ceremonies and entertainments, chiefly in connection with his railways.

Work was begun on the Valparaíso-Santiago Railway with a gorgeous fiesta; interrupted to dedicate a monument created by Meiggs himself to the memory of a Chilean Revolutionary hero; concluded with magnificent ceremonies that extended from one end of the line to the other. Trains received the blessings of the higher clergy; Chileans drank toasts to Don Enrique Meiggs the Great Builder; Meiggs compared the Chilean officials of the day with the intrepid founders of the nation, paid glowing tribute to his railway experts, and praised the Chilean *roto* to the skies. For five years thereafter he was a social lion in Chile.

One of the banquets Meiggs gave in Lima during the celebration that marked the beginning of work on the Oroya Railway was attended by 800 of the double cream of society. On that occasion he promised eternal fame to the top-flight officials who were soon to collaborate in unlocking the treasure vaults of the nation and expanding its role in history:

This happy event proclaims . . . a great social revolution whose triumph and whose benefits are entrusted to the locomotive, that irresistible battering ram of modern civilization. At its pressure will fall those granite masses which physical nature until today has opposed to the . . . aggrandizement of the Peruvian nation. Its whistle will awaken the native race from . . . [its] lethargy. . . .

Peru, ever noble and generous, will . . . inscribe in the book of its glorious history, at the head of its lofty benefactors, the names of all the illustrious citizens to whose indefatigable exertions and patriotism is due the establishment of this iron road.

The Peruvians called Meiggs the "Messiah of the Railway." After the elaborate ceremonies ended he published an apology in the newspapers to those whom "unintentionally" he had failed to invite to the feast. . . .

Two weeks of celebration marked the opening of the Arequipa Railway to public traffic late in 1870. Four steamers were required to transport Meiggs's guests to Mollendo and five trains were employed to haul them up to Arequipa. The president and all the members of the cabinet and Congress were in the party. The locomotives received a sprinkling of holy water from the bishop. Many speeches were made at both ends of the line.

At Mollendo, Meiggs spoke with deep emotion of the cost of his technological triumph. "I do not refer to money," he said. "I speak of the blood and the lives poured out by hundreds of Chileans, Peruvians, Bolivians, Frenchmen, Irishmen, and even Anglo-Americans who have died on this work. Let us drink here in silence to the memory of those who died. . . ." The Bolivian minister called Meiggs a "colossus of fortune and credit," a "contractor without fear," a wizard who had come to Latin America to erase the word "impossible" from all the dictionaries, a miracle-man who had joined Valparaíso and Santiago and brought Arequipa down to the sea, and who would on the morrow place Puno, Cuzco, Oroya, perhaps even distant Potosí and "dear" Sucre "close to the breakers of the Pacific." After the banquet was over the guests began to dance. They spent the night in Mollendo, their temporary abode the railway buildings; they were provided by Meiggs with food, drinks, good mattresses, pillows, sheets, and — for the ladies — even mosquito nets.

In Arequipa, which recently had been gravely damaged by an earthquake, the railway was described as a "present from heaven to compensate for the sufferings of the past." Almighty God, President José Balta, and Henry Meiggs were praised and thanked. Handing Balta the hammer and the last spike, Meiggs declared:

Be certain, most excellent sir, that as you place the last rail . . . the civilized nations will look upon you as the collaborator of Newton, Fulton, and Humboldt in science, and that the history of the fatherland will open to you its pages alongside those which Bolívar and San Martín occupy, because the steam and the iron with which you are endowing your country affirm also the liberty and independence of nations.

Always less fluent than most Latins, Balta was almost speechless with elation. He gazed about for a moment in silence, then spoke a few words and drove home the golden spike that completed the first of Meiggs's Peruvian railroads. After more feasting, oratory, poetry, and dancing the party returned to Lima, where they left with Meiggs many souvenirs of their profound appreciation.

Such pageantry was never surpassed even in the glittering days of the colonial viceroys. Much of the Latin temperament seems to have entered Meiggs's soul. He was welcomed into the best social circles of Peru.

The closing scene of the Meiggs drama was most impressive. He died poor. The debts he left behind probably exceeded the value of his mortgaged property. He could build no more railways and there was no more money for charity. But twenty or thirty thousand people, the majority of them Peruvian peons, came to witness the last rites. The ceremony took place in La Merced, a Catholic church in Lima, and the body was buried in a private cemetery on the Meiggs estate. As the corpse was being transferred from the church to the flower-covered hearse drawn by four white horses a great crowd of humble people surged forward. They demanded the privilege of bearing the metal casket to the open grave, two or three miles away, and took the heavy burden on their tired shoulders. "Harry" Meiggs must have enjoyed his funeral.

Meiggs's spectacular career is not free from the stain of dishonesty and corruption. Having overspeculated in California real estate, he sold forged warrants and issued unauthorized stock in an effort to save himself and his friends. When his crime was about to be discovered he fled to Chile to avoid prosecution — perhaps even execution — by irate citizens determined to take "justice" into their hands. Although his record in Chile is untainted and it is said that he later made amends for his financial sins in California, he has been accused of resorting to large-scale bribery in Peru. He is also charged with major responsibility for bankrupting the nation.

The millions spent on his railways and others of the period did bring Peru at least to the very brink of bankruptcy; and the unsuccessful war with Chile that followed in 1879–1883 sent the country over the precipice. In 1890 the Peruvian Corporation, an English enterprise organized to bail out European bondholders and salvage the wreck of Peruvian finances, took over most of the railways of the nation. And the Peruvian railways are still dominated by this English corporation. In the midst of their calamities it was natural for the Peruvians to search for a scapegoat, and some of them found one in Henry Meiggs.

Meiggs probably bribed several politicians. Bribery seems to have been the custom in those days, not only in Peru but in a number of other countries. It is likely that Meiggs had to buy some of the Peruvians in order to obtain permission to build the railways. And the drive for bribes, along with the Meiggs pageantry, no doubt contributed to the railway boom. But other factors were involved. The earning capacity of railroads and their power to stimulate economic development were vastly overestimated — perhaps honestly so by many — and enthusiasm for the new means of transportation was already tremendous among the members of the ruling class before Meiggs reached Lima. It is doubtful whether he originated a single railway project upon which he actually began construction. Certainly most of the lines he finished or started had been discussed for years before he arrived in Peru.

The conclusion seems clear. Peruvian leaders must share much of the blame for the nation's calamities. At times Henry Meiggs was a scoundrel; but he had his good traits and he built some remarkable railways. Few have ever accused him of shoddy workmanship or the use of any but the best of materials. His iron roads may not last as long as the Inca palaces; but they are sure to endure for many years.

Section IV

Negro Slavery in Brazil

Slavery hangs like a heavy cloud over the history of nineteenth-century Brazil. Many of the important movements and events — immigration, the growth of republicanism, the onset of modernization, the War of the Triple Alliance, the fall of the monarchy — were directly or indirectly related to the fate of "the peculiar institution." The many travelers from Europe and the United States who visited this huge country almost always discoursed upon Negro slavery, in much the same way that visitors to our antebellum South did. No Latin American country has a richer travel literature for this period than Brazil, and a few samples are given in this section which will surely whet the reader's appetite for more.

Henry Koster, the English merchant who traveled about in the period 1808–1818, principally in the northeast, believed that Brazilian slaves were less abused than those in the British West Indies and gave his reasons (Reading IV.1). But he also attested to the brutality of the slave trade, and noted the large number of suicides among Brazilian slaves.

Robert Walsh, an English clergyman who lived in Brazil from 1828–1829, described the "horrid traffic" and the frightful conditions of life on the slave ships (Reading IV.2).

The importation of slaves into Brazil became illegal in 1830, but the traffic did not stop despite the steady pressure and threats of Great Britain. William D. Christie, the British Minister, estimated that one million slaves had been unlawfully landed in Brazil between 1830 and 1852.[1] British consuls throughout the country kept

[1] William D. Christie, *Notes on Brazilian Questions* (London, 1865), p. 81.

155

London informed of conditions, and typical of such reporting were the despatches by the veteran consul Robert Hesketh in 1831 on the slaves and their life in the northern provinces (Reading IV.3).

The American Protestant missionaries Kidder and Fletcher wrote probably the most popular book on Brazil ever published in the United States, and attempted to give a balanced picture of Negro slavery, particularly as it existed in Rio de Janeiro in the years immediately following the cutting off of international traffic in 1850. Slavery was doomed in Brazil, they felt, and they were convinced Brazilian Negroes had greater opportunities for advancement than those in the United States (Reading IV.4).

Herbert H. Smith, the American naturalist who saw all the major regions during 1874–1878, was one of the many scientists who have been attracted to Brazil by the tremendous variety of flora and fauna there. He also observed slavery, and emphasized the harm it did to the masters by influencing them toward "indolence and pride and sensuality and selfishness" (Reading IV.5).

Travelers see only a part of the reality they attempt to describe; it remains for the historian to sift all essential sources in order to present a more comprehensive view of the past. Stanley J. Stein of Princeton University does this in detailing "The Patterns of Living" as a part of his monograph on a coffee plantation (Reading IV.6).

Slavery was abolished in 1888 by imperial decree. This act freed three quarters of a million slaves, brought ruin to many landowners, and was one of the principal causes of the fall of the monarchy in 1889. The late Percy Alvin Martin of Stanford University, a pioneer in Brazilian history in the United States, addressed himself a quarter of a century ago to the question of why the popular Emperor Pedro II was forced to abdicate.[2] Now a younger Brazilianist, Richard Graham, considers the same subject, and brings — as historians often do — new evidence and a fresh viewpoint to help us understand the old problem.[3] Another valuable review article on the fall of the monarchy, more general in scope, has been published by George C. A. Boehrer of the University of Kansas.[4]

[2] Percy Alvin Martin, "Causes of the Collapse of the Brazilian Empire," *Hispanic American Historical Review*, IV (1921), pp. 4–48.

[3] Richard Graham, "Causes for the Abolition of Negro Slavery in Brazil: An Interpretative Essay," *ibid.*, XLVI (1966), pp. 123–137.

[4] "The Brazilian Republican Revolutions. Old and New Views," *Luso-Brazilian Review*, Winter (1967). For an older interpretation, see Vicente Licinio Cardoso, "A margem do Segundo Reinado," *Revista do Instituto Histórico Geográfico Brasileiro*, LXXXXVIII (1925), pp. 1039–1087. A recent interpretation

During the last decades the University of São Paulo produced a vigorous school of sociologists and historians whose researches have laid the basis for a new approach to the study of Negro slavery. The conclusions of one of these scholars, Emília Viotti da Costa, indicate the trend (Reading IV.7).

Consideration of the fate of Negro slaves in Brazil has frequently led to a comparison with slavery in the United States and elsewhere in the Americas. Gilberto Freyre and other writers have maintained that slavery in Brazil was relatively mild. This view is now challenged by a younger scholar, Robert Conrad of the University of Illinois in Chicago, as the result of his recent researches in Brazilian archives and libraries (Reading IV.8). This debate will doubtless grow in intensity, and may well lead to a re-evaluation of the history of slavery in the Western Hemisphere.

A. How Foreigners Viewed Negro Slavery

1. Slaves in Brazil Have More Tolerable Lives Than Those in Other Countries

HENRY KOSTER

The general equity of the laws regarding free persons of colour in the Portuguese South American possessions, has been, to a certain degree, extended to that portion of the population which is in a state of slavery: and the lives of the slaves of Brazil have been rendered less hard and less intolerable than those of the degraded beings who drag on their cheerless existence under the dominion of other

From *Travels in Brazil in the years from 1809–1815* by Henry Koster (Philadelphia: M. Carey and Son, 1817), II, pp. 189–217, *passim*.

by Luís Martins considers the revolution as a revolt against, and a slaying of, a father by his sons. See his *O patriarca e o bacharel* (São Paulo: Martins, 1953). See also Charles Willis Simmons, *Marshal Deodoro and the Fall of Dom Pedro II* (Durham: Duke University Press, 1966).

A recent view of how slaves were treated has been given by Fernando Henrique Cardozo, "A sociedade escravócrata. Realidade e mito," in his *Capitalismo e escravidão* (São Paulo, 1966).

nations. The Brazilian slave is taught the religion of his master: and hopes are held out of manumission from his own exertions: but still he is a slave, and must be guided by another man's will; and this feeling alone takes away much of the pleasure which would be felt from the faithful discharge of his duty, if it was voluntarily performed. . . .

Slaves, however, in Brazil, have many advantages over their brethren in the British colonies. The numerous holidays of which the Catholic religion enjoins the observance, give to the slave many days of rest or time to work for his own profit: thirty-five of these, and the Sundays besides, allow him to employ much of his time as he pleases. Few masters are inclined to restrain the right of their slaves to dispose of these days as they think fit: or, at any rate, few dare, whatever their inclinations may be, to brave public opinion in depriving them of the intervals from work which the law has set apart as their own, that their lives may be rendered less irksome. The time which is thus afforded, enables the slave, who is so inclined, to accumulate a sum of money: however this is by law his master's property, from the incapability under which a slave labours of possessing any thing which he can by right call his own. But I believe there is no instance on record in which a master attempted to deprive his slave of these hard-earned gains. The slave can oblige his master to manumit him, on tendering to him the sum for which he was first purchased, or the price for which he might be sold, if that price is higher than what the slave was worth at the time he was first bought. This regulation, like every one that is framed in favour of slaves, is liable to be evaded, and the master sometimes does refuse to manumit a valuable slave: and no appeal is made by the sufferer, owing to the state of law in that country, which renders it almost impossible for the slave to gain a hearing; and likewise this acquiescence in the injustice of the master proceeds from the dread, that if he was not to succeed, he would be punished, and that his life might be rendered more miserable than it was before. Consequently a great deal depends upon the inclinations of the master, who will, however, be very careful in refusing to manumit, owing to the well-known opinion of every priest in favour of this regulation, to the feelings of the individuals of his own class in society, and to those of the lower orders of people: and likewise he will be afraid of losing his slave. He may escape with his money: and the master will then run much risk of never seeing him again, particularly if the individual is a creole slave. In general, therefore, no doubts are urged, when application is made for manumission by a slave to his master; who is indeed oftentimes prepared for it by the habits· of industry and regularity of his slave, and by common report among the other slaves and free persons upon the estate, that the individual in question is scraping together a sum of money for this purpose. The master might indeed deprive the slave of the fruits of his labour: but this is never thought of; because the slave preserves his money in a secret place, or has entrusted it to some person upon whom he can depend, and would suffer any punishment rather than disclose the spot in which his wealth lies concealed. A still more forcible reason than any other, for the forbearance of the master, is to be found in the dread of acting against public opinion: in the shame which would follow the commission of such an act; and perhaps the natural goodness which exists in almost every human being, would make him shun such gross injustice, would make him avoid such a deed of baseness.

A slave is often permitted by his owner to seek a master more to his liking; for this purpose a note is given, declaring that the bearer has leave to enter into the service of any one, upon the price which the master demands being paid by the purchaser. With this the slave applies to any individual of property whom he may wish to serve; owing to having heard a good report of his character towards his slaves, or from any other cause. This is a frequent practice; and at least admits the possibility of escape from a severe state of bondage to one that is less irksome.

A considerable number of slaves are manumitted at the death of their masters: and indeed some persons of large property fail not to set at liberty a few of them during their own life-time. A deed of manumission, however simply it may be drawn out, cannot be set aside. A register of these papers is preserved at the office of every notary-public, by which any distress that might be occasioned by the loss of the originals is provided against; for the copy, of course, holds good in law. A slave who has brought into the world, and has reared ten children, ought to be free, for so the law ordains. But this regulation is generally evaded: and besides, the number of children is too great for many women to be benefited by it. The price of a new-born child is 5l. (20,000 mil-reis), and the master is obliged to manumit the infant at the baptismal font, on the sum being presented. In this manner, a considerable number of persons are set at liberty; for the smallness of the price enables many freemen who have had connections with female slaves to manumit their offspring; and instances occur of the sponsors performing this most laudable act. Not unfrequently female slaves apply to persons of consideration to become sponsors to their children, in the hopes that the pride of these will be too great to allow of their god-children remaining in slavery. Thus by their own exertions, by the favour of their masters, and by other means, the individuals who gain their freedom annually, are very numerous. . . .

All slaves in Brazil follow the religion of their masters; and notwithstanding the impure state in which the Christian church exists in that country, still such are the beneficent effects of the Christian religion, that these, its adopted children, are improved by it to an infinite degree; and the slave who attends to the strict observance of religious ceremonies, invariably proves to be a good servant. The Africans, who are imported from Angola, are baptized in lots before they leave their own shores: and on their arrival in Brazil they are to learn the doctrines of the church, and the duties of the religion into which they have entered. These bear the mark of the royal crown upon their breasts, which denotes that they have undergone the ceremony of baptism, and likewise that the king's duty has been paid upon them. The slaves which are imported from other parts of the coast of Africa, arrive in Brazil unbaptized, and before the ceremony of making them Christians can be performed upon them, they must be taught certain prayers, for the acquirement of which one year is allowed to the master, before he is obliged to present the slave at the parish church. The law is not always strictly adhered to as to the time, but it is never evaded altogether. The religion of the master teaches him that it would be extremely sinful to allow his slave to remain a heathen: and indeed the Portuguese and Brazilians have too much religious feeling to let them neglect any of the ordinances of their church. The slave himself likewise wishes to be made a Christian; for his fellow-bondmen will, otherwise, in every squabble or trifling disagreement with him, close their string of opprobrious epithets with the name of *pagam* (pagan). The unbaptized negro feels that he is considered as an inferior being: and although he may not be aware of the value which the whites place upon baptism, still he knows that the stigma for which he is upbraided, will be removed by it; and therefore he is desirous of being made equal to his companions. The Africans who have been long imported, imbibe a Catholic feeling; and appear to forget that they were once in the same situation themselves. The slaves are not asked whether they will be baptized or not. Their entrance into the Catholic church is treated as a thing of course: and indeed they are not considered as members of society, but rather as brute animals, until they can lawfully go to mass, confess their sins, and receive the Sacrament.

The slaves have their religious brotherhoods as well as the free persons: and the ambition of the slave very generally aims at being admitted into one of these, and at being made one of the officers and directors of the concerns of the brotherhood. Even some of the money which the industrious slave is collecting for the purpose of purchasing his freedom, will oftentimes be brought out of its concealment for the decoration of a saint, that the donor may become of importance in the society to which he belongs. The negroes have one invocation of the Virgin (or I might almost say one virgin), which is peculiarly their own. Our Lady of the Rosary is even sometimes painted with a black face and hands. It is in this manner that the slaves are led to place their attention upon an object in which they soon take an interest, but from which no injury can proceed towards themselves, nor can any through its means be by them inflicted upon their masters. Their ideas are removed from any thought of the customs of their own country; and are guided into a channel of a totally different nature, and completely unconnected with what is practised there. . . .

The Portuguese language is spoken by all the slaves: and their own dialects are allowed to lie dormant until they are by many of them quite forgotten. No compulsion is resorted to, to make them embrace the habits of their masters: but their ideas are insensibly led to imitate and adopt them. The masters at the same time imbibe some of the customs of their slaves: and thus the superior and his dependant are brought nearer to each other. I doubt not that the system of baptizing the newly imported negroes, proceeded rather from the bigotry of the Portuguese in former times than from any political plan: but it has had the most beneficial effects. The slaves are rendered more tractable. Besides being better men and women, they become more obedient servants. They are brought under the controul of the priesthood: and even if this was the only additional hold which was gained by their entrance into the church, it is a great engine of power which is thus brought into action. . . . .

The slaves of Brazil are regularly married according to the forms of the Catholic church. The banns are published in the same manner as those of free persons: and I have seen many happy couples (as happy at least as slaves can be) with large families of children rising around them. The masters encourage marriages among their slaves; for it is from these lawful connections that they can expect to increase the number of their creoles. A slave cannot marry without the consent of his master; for the vicar will not publish the banns of marriage without this sanction. It is likewise permitted that slaves should marry free persons. If the woman is in bondage, the children remain in the same state: but if the man is a slave, and she is free, their offspring is also free. A slave cannot be married until the requisite prayers have been learnt, the nature of confession be understood, and the Sacrament can be received. Upon the estates the master or manager is soon made acquainted with the predilections of the slaves for each other: and these being discovered, marriage is forthwith determined upon, and the irregular proceedings are made lawful. In towns there is more licentiousness among the negroes, as there is among all other classes of men. . . .

The great proportion of men upon many of the estates, produces, of necessity, most mischievous consequences. A supply is requisite to keep up the number of labourers. The women are more liable to misconduct, and the men imbibe unsettled habits. But if an adequate number of females are placed upon the estate, and the slaves are trained and taught in the manner which is practised upon well-regulated plantations, the negroes will be as correct in their behaviour, as any other body of men: and perhaps their conduct may be less faulty than that of other descriptions of persons, who have less to occupy their time, though their education may be infinitely superior. That many men and many women will be licentious, has been and is still the lot of human nature, and not the peculiar fault of the much injured race of which I speak.

I shall now state the manner in which the Africans are transported from their own country to Brazil, and the disposal of them on their arrival in South America; the characters of the several African nations with which the ships are loaded; the condition of those who are employed in Recife — upon the sugar-plantations — in the Mata or cotton estates — and in the Sertam or cattle districts.

As the voyage from the coast of Africa to the opposite shores of South America is usually short, for the winds are subject to little variation, and the weather is usually fine, the vessels which are employed in this traffic are generally speaking small, and are not of the best construction. The situation of captain or master of a slave ship is considered of secondary rank in the Portuguese merchant-service: and the persons who are usually so occupied, are vastly infe-

rior to the generality of the individuals who command the large and
regular trading vessels between Europe and Brazil. The slave ships
were formerly crowded to a most shocking degree; nor was there
any means of preventing this. But a law has been passed for the
purpose of restricting the number of persons for each vessel. However, I more than suspect, that no attention is paid to this regulation
— that means are made use of to evade the law. On the arrival at
Recife of a cargo of slaves, the rules of the port direct that they shall
be disembarked, and taken to St. Amaro, which is an airy spot, and
sufficiently distant from the town to prevent the admittance of any
infectious disorder, if any such should exist among the newly imported negroes; and yet the place is at a convenient distance for
the purchasers, St. Amaro being situated immediately opposite to
Recife, upon the inland bank of the expanse of waters which is
formed by the tide, on the land side of the town. However, like many
others, this excellent arrangement is not attended to: and even if the
slaves are removed for a few days to St. Amaro, they are soon conveyed back to the town. Here they are placed in the streets before
the doors of the owners, regardless of decency, of humanity, and of
due attention to the general health of the town. The small pox, the
yaws, and other complaints have thus frequent opportunities of
spreading. It is probable, that if the climate was not so very excellent
as it is, this practice would be discontinued; but if it was not put a
stop to, and the country was subject to pestilential complaints, the
town would not be habitable.

In the day-time, some of the streets of Recife are in part lined
with miserable beings, who are lying or sitting promiscuously upon
the foot-path, sometimes to the number of two or three hundred.
The males wear a small piece of blue cloth round their waists, which
is drawn between the legs and fastened behind. The females are
allowed a larger piece of cloth, which is worn as a petticoat: and
sometimes a second portion is given to them, for the purpose of covering the upper parts of the body. The stench which is created by
these assemblages is almost intolerable to one who is unaccustomed to
their vicinity; and the sight of them, good God! is horrid beyond any
thing. These people, do not, however, seem to feel their situation,
any farther than that it is uncomfortable. Their food consists of salt
meat, the flour of the mandioc, beans, and plantains occasionally.
The victuals for each day are cooked in the middle of the street in
an enormous caldron. At night, they are driven into one or more
warehouses: and a driver stands to count them as they pass. They

are locked in: and the door is again opened at day-break on the following morning. The wish of these wretched creatures to escape from this state of inaction and discomfort is manifested upon the appearance of a purchaser. They start up willingly, to be placed in the row for the purpose of being viewed and handled like cattle: and on being chosen they give signs of much pleasure. I have had many opportunities of seeing slaves bought; for my particular friends at Recife lived opposite to slave-dealers. I never saw any demonstrations of grief at parting from each other: but I attributed this to the dread of punishment, if there had been any flow of feeling, and to a resigned or rather despairing sensation, which checks any shew of grief, and which has prepared them for the worst, by making them indifferent to whatever may occur: besides, it is not often that a family is brought over together: the separation of relatives and friends has taken place in Africa. It is among the younger part of the assemblage of persons who are exposed for sale, that pleasure is particularly visible at the change of situation, in being removed from the streets of the town; the negroes of more advanced age do whatever the driver desires, usually with an unchanged countenance. I am afraid that very little care is taken to prevent the separation of relations who may chance to come over in the same ship: and any consideration on this point lies entirely with the owner of the cargo. A species of relationship exists between the individuals who have been imported in the same ship. They call each other *malungos:* and this term is much regarded among them. The purchaser gives to each of his newly bought slaves a large piece of baize and a straw hat; and as soon as possible marches them off to his estate. I have often in travelling met with many parties going up to their new homes, and have observed that they were usually cheerful — any thing is better than to sit at the door of the slave merchant in Recife. The new master, too, does every thing in his power to keep them in good humour at first, whatever his conduct may afterwards be towards them. . . .

The slaves who are employed in Recife, may be divided into two classes; household slaves, and those which pay a weekly stipend to their owners, proceeding from the earnings of some employment which does not oblige them to be under the immediate eye of the master. The first class have little chance of gaining their freedom by their own exertions; and are subject to the caprice and whims of their superiors. But some few are manumitted by the kindness of those whom they have served: and the clothing and food which is afforded to them is generally better than that which the other class obtains. This second class consists of joiners, shoemakers, canoemen, porters, &c. and these men may acquire a sufficient sum of money to purchase their own freedom, if they have the requisite prudence and steadiness to allow their earnings to accumulate. But too often, the inducements to expend them foolishly are sufficiently powerful, to make these people swerve from their purpose. They generally earn more each day than the master exacts, and have besides the Sundays and holidays as their own: and if the slave feeds and clothes himself, to these are added the Sundays of every week. I think that allowing largely for him to supply every thing requisite for his support and decent appearance, and yet something for what may to a person in such a rank in life be accounted luxury, a slave so circumstanced may in ten years purchase his freedom. If his value is great, it is because his trade is lucrative; so that these things keep pace with each other. The women have likewise some employments by which they may be enabled to gain their liberty. They make sweetmeats and cakes, and are sent out as cooks, nurses, house-keepers, &c.

Creole negroes and mulattos are generally accounted quicker in learning any trade than the Africans. This superior aptitude to profit by instruction is doubtless produced by their acquaintance from infancy with the manners, customs, and language of their masters. From the little experience, however, which I have had, and from the general remarks which I have gathered from others, who might be judged better acquainted than myself with slaves, I think that an African who has become cheerful, and seems to have forgotten his former state, is a more valuable slave than a creole negro or mulatto. He will be generally more fit to be trusted. Far from the latter submitting quietly to the situation in which they have been born, they bear the yoke of slavery with impatience. The daily sight of so many individuals of their own casts, who are in a state of freedom, makes them wish to be raised to an equality with them: and they feel at every moment their unfortunate doom. The consideration with which the free person of mixed casts are treated, tends to increase the discontent of their brothers who are in slavery. The Africans do not feel this; for they are considered by their creole brethren in colour, as being so completely inferior, that the line which, by public opinion, has been drawn between them, makes the imported slave feel towards the creoles as if they had not been originally of the same stock.

Miserable objects are at times to be seen in Recife, asking alms in various quarters of the town, aged and diseased. Some of these persons have been slaves: and when, from infirmity they have been rendered useless, their masters have manumitted them: and thus being turned away to starve in their old age, or in a crippled state, their only resource is to beg in the public streets. These instances of gross injustice and depravity in masters, are not many: but that they should occur, is sufficient to cause the aid of law to be called in, that the *existence* of them should be prevented.

2. "A Horrid Traffic": Life on a Slave Ship

ROBERT WALSH

After about an hour standing towards us she [a suspected slaver] tacked, as if not liking our appearance, and alarmed at our approach, and stood away directly before the wind. We crowded all sail in chase. The breeze freshened, and at four bells we had neared so much that we had a distinct view of her hull, and we were now certain she was a slaver, and also perhaps a pirate, and that she had at least five or six hundred slaves on board. This opinion was formed on that sagacity that a long experience on the coast of Africa, and a familiar acquaintance with such vessels had imparted. We were, therefore, all on the alert, exulting in the prospect of liberating so many fellow-creatures, and bartering and bargaining for our share of the ransom-money, for it seemed almost certain that she could not escape us. She resembled, however, a fox doubling in all directions, and every moment seeming to change her course to avoid us.

The captain now ordered a gun to be fired to leeward, and the English union flag to be hoisted; we had the wind right aft, and were running right down upon her, distant about four miles. She took no notice of our gun and flag, and another was fired with as little effect. Orders were then given that one of the long guns at the bows should be shotted and sent after her. We all crowded to the forecastle to witness the effect. The ball went ricochetting along the waves, and fell short of her stern; in a little time afterwards she hoisted a flag, which we perceived was Brazilian. Two shot more were sent after her with as little effect, and the wind again dying

From *Notices of Brazil in 1828 and 1829* by Robert Walsh (London: Richardson, Lord & Holdbrook, 1831), pp. 476–494.

away, our coming up with her before dark seemed very doubtful. To increase the way of the ship, the long guns of the bows were brought midships, but without effect; we were evidently dropping astern. We kept a sharp look-out with intense interest, leaning over the netting, and silently handing the glass to one another, as if a word spoken would impede our way. At length the shades of evening closed on us, and we applied night-glasses. For some time we kept her in view on the horizon, but about eight o'clock she totally disappeared.

All night we were pointing our glasses in the direction in which she lay, and caught occasional glimpses of her, and when morning dawned, we saw her like a speck on the horizon, standing due north. We followed in the same track, the breeze soon increased our way to eight knots, and we had the pleasure to find we were every moment gaining on her. We again sent long shot after her, but she only crowded the more sail to escape; and we observed her slinging her yards, that is, hanging them with additional cords, that they might be supported if the proper lifts were shot away.

We could now discern her whole equipment; her gun streak was distinctly seen along the water, with eight ports of a side; and it was the general opinion that she was a French pirate and slaver, notorious for her depredations. At twelve o'clock, we were entirely within gunshot, and one of our long bow-guns was again fired at her. It struck the water alongside, and then, for the first time, she showed a disposition to stop. While we were preparing a second, she hove-to, and in a short time we were alongside her, after a most interesting chase of thirty hours, during which we ran 300 miles.

The first object that struck us, was an enormous gun, turning on a swivel, on deck, the constant appendage of a pirate; and the next, were large kettles for cooking, on the bows, the usual apparatus of a slaver. Our boat was now hoisted out, and I went on board with the officers. When we mounted her decks, we found her full of slaves. She was called the *Veloz*, commanded by Captain José Barbosa, bound to Bahia. She was a very broad-decked ship, with a mainmast, schooner-rigged, and behind her foremast was that large formidable gun, which turned on a broad circle of iron, on deck, and which enabled her to act as a pirate, if her slaving speculation had failed. She had taken in, on the coast of Africa, 336 males, and 226 females, making in all 562, and had been out seventeen days, during which she had thrown overboard fifty-five. The slaves were all enclosed under grated hatchways, between decks. The space was so low, that they sat between each other's legs, and stowed so close together, that there was no possibility of their lying down, or at all changing their position, by night or day. As they belonged to, and were shipped on account of different individuals, they were all branded, like sheep, with the owners' marks of different forms,

These were impressed under their breasts, or on their arms, and, as the mate informed me, with perfect indifference, "queimados pelo ferro quento — burnt with the red-hot iron." Over the hatchway stood a ferocious looking fellow, with a scourge of many twisted thongs in his hand, who was the slave-driver of the ship, and whenever he heard the slightest noise below, he shook it over them, and seemed eager to exercise it. I was quite pleased to take this hateful badge out of his hand, and I have kept it ever since, as a horrid memorial of reality, should I ever be disposed to forget the scene I witnessed.

As soon as the poor creatures saw us looking down at them, their dark and melancholy visages brightened up. They perceived something of sympathy and kindness in our looks, which they had not been accustomed to, and feeling instinctively that we were friends, they immediately began to shout and clap their hands. One or two had picked up a few Portuguese words, and cried out "Viva! viva!" The women were particularly excited. They all held up their arms, and when we bent down and shook hands with them, they could not contain their delight; they endeavoured to scramble upon their knees, stretching up to kiss our hands, and we understood that they knew we were come to liberate them. Some, however, hung down their heads in apparently hopeless dejection; some were greatly emaciated, and some, particularly children, seemed dying.

But the circumstance which struck us most forcibly, was, how it was possible for such a number of human beings to exist, packed up and wedged together as tight as they could cram, in low cells, three feet high, the greater part of which, except that immediately under the grated hatchways, was shut out from light or air, and this when the thermometer, exposed to the open sky, was standing in the shade, on our deck, at 89°. The space between decks was divided into two compartments, 3 feet 3 inches high; the size of one was 16 feet by 18, and of the other 40 by 21; into the first were crammed the women and girls; into the second, the men and boys: 226 fellow-creatures were thus thrust into one space 288 feet square;

and 336 into another space 800 feet square, giving to the whole an average of 23 inches, and to each of the women not more than 13 inches, though many of them were pregnant. We also found manacles and fetters of different kinds, but it appears that they had all been taken off before we boarded.

The heat of these horrid places was so great, and the odour so offensive, that it was quite impossible to enter them, even had there been room. They were measured as above when the slaves had left them. The officers insisted that the poor suffering creatures should be admitted on deck to get air and water. This was opposed by the mate of the slaver, who, from a feeling that they deserved it, declared they would murder them all. The officers, however, persisted, and the poor beings were all turned up together. It is impossible to conceive the effect of this eruption — 507 fellow-creatures of all ages and sexes, some children, some adults, some old men and women, all in a state of total nudity, scrambling out together to taste the luxury of a little fresh air and water. They came swarming up, like bees from the aperture of a hive, till the whole deck was crowded to suffocation, from stem to stern; so that it was impossible to imagine where they could all have come from, or how they could have been stowed away. On looking into the places where they had been crammed, there were found some children next the sides of the ship, in the places most remote from light and air; they were lying nearly in a torpid state, after the rest had turned out. The little creatures seemed indifferent as to life or death, and when they were carried on deck, many of them could not stand.

After enjoying for a short time the unusual luxury of air, some water was brought; it was then that the extent of their sufferings was exposed in a fearful manner. They all rushed like maniacs towards it. No entreaties, or threats, or blows, could restrain them; they shrieked, and struggled, and fought with one another, for a drop of this precious liquid, as if they grew rabid at the sight of it. There is nothing which slaves, in the mid-passage, suffer from so much as want of water. It is sometimes usual to take out casks filled with sea water, as ballast, and when the slaves are received on board, to start the casks, and refill them with fresh. On one occasion, a ship from Bahia neglected to change the contents of the casks, and on the mid-passage found, to their horror, that they were filled with nothing but salt water. All the slaves on board perished! We could judge of the extent of their sufferings from the afflicting sight we now saw. When the poor creatures were ordered down again, several of them came, and pressed their heads against our knees, with looks of the greatest anguish, at the prospect of returning to the horrid place of suffering below.

It was not surprising that they should have endured much sickness and loss of life, in their short passage. They had sailed from the coast of Africa on the 7th of May, and had been out but seventeen days, and they had thrown overboard no less than fifty-five, who had died of dysentery and other complaints, in that space of time, though they had left the coast in good health. Indeed, many of the survivors were seen lying about the decks in the last stage of emaciation, and in a state of filth and misery not to be looked at. Evenhanded justice had visited the effects of this unholy traffic, on the crew who were engaged in it. Eight or nine had died, and at that moment six were in hammocks on board, in different stages of fever. This mortality did not arise from want of medicine. There was a large stock ostentatiously displayed in the cabin, with a manuscript book, containing directions as to the quantities; but the only medical man on board to prescribe it was a black, who was as ignorant as his patients.

While expressing my horror at what I saw, and exclaiming against the state of this vessel for conveying human beings, I was informed by my friends, who had passed so long a time on the coast of Africa, and visited so many ships, that this was one of the best they had seen. The height, sometimes, between decks, was only eighteen inches; so that the unfortunate beings could not turn round, or even on their sides, the elevation being less than the breadth of their shoulders; and here they are usually chained to the decks, by the neck and legs. In such a place, the sense of misery and suffocation is so great, that the negroes, like the English in the black-hole at Calcutta, are driven to frenzy. They had, on one occasion, taken a slave vessel in the river Bonny: the slaves were stowed in the narrow space between decks, and chained together. They heard a horrid din and tumult among them, and could not imagine from what cause it proceeded. They opened the hatches, and turned them up on deck. They were manacled together, in twos and threes. Their horror may be well conceived, when they found a number of them in different stages of suffocation; many of them were foaming at the mouth, and in the last agonies — many were dead. A living man was sometimes dragged up, and his companion was a dead body; sometimes, of the three attached to the same chain, one was dying, and another dead. The tumult they had heard, was the frenzy of those suffocating wretches in the last stage of fury and desperation, struggling to extricate themselves. When they were all dragged up, nineteen were irrecoverably dead. Many destroyed one another, in the hopes of procuring room to breathe; men strangled those next them, and women drove nails into each other's brains. Many unfortunate creatures, on other occasions, took the first opportunity of leaping overboard, and getting rid, in this way, of an intolerable life.

They often found the poor negroes impressed with the strongest terror at their deliverers. The slave dealers persuaded them that the English were cannibals, who only took them to eat them. When undeceived, their joy and gratitude were proportionately great. Sometimes, a mortal malady had struck them before they were captured, from which they never could recover. They used to lie down in the water of the lee scuppers, and notwithstanding every care, pined away to skin and bone, wasted with fever and dysentery; and, when at length they were consigned to the deep, they were mere skeletons. Unlike other impressions, habit had not rendered these things familiar, or hardened the hearts of my companions. On the contrary, the scenes they had witnessed made them only more susceptible of pity on the present occasion; and the sympathy and kindness they now showed these poor slaves, did credit to the goodness of their hearts.

When I returned on board the frigate, I found the captain of the slaver pacing the deck in great agitation; sometimes clasping his hands, and occasionally requesting a drink of water; and when asked whether he would have any other refreshment, he replied, turning his head and twisting his mouth, with an expression of intense annoyance, "nada, nada — nothing, nothing." Meantime, his papers were rigidly examined, to ascertain if they bore out his story. He said that he was a Brazilian, from Bahia, and that his traffic was strictly confined to the south of the line, where, by treaty, it was yet lawful; that he made Bengo bay, on the coast of Angola, nine degrees south of the line, traded along that coast, and took in all his slaves at Cabinda, and was returning directly home; that his ship had only received on board the number allowed by law, which directs that five slaves may be taken in for every two tons; and that his complement was under that allowance. All this, his chart and log corresponded with. As the tale, however, could be easily fabricated, and papers were written to correspond, a strict scrutiny was made into other circumstances. Some of the poor slaves said they came from Badagry, a place in six degrees north latitude. Two of the crew, whose persons were recognized by some of our people, confessed they were left at Whida, by another ship, where they had been seen; and above all, the slave captain had endeavoured to escape by every means in his power, as conscious of his guilt; and it was not till after a persevering chase of 300 miles that he was at length taken, and that too, sailing in a northerly direction, when his course to Bahia would have been south-west. He said, in reply, that the slaves might have been originally from Badagry, and sent, as is usual, to Cabinda, where he bought them; that the two men entered at Cabinda, to which they had been brought in a Spanish ship from Whida; and finally, that he did not bring-to when required, because he imagined the *North Star* to be one of the large pirates which infest these seas, whom he endeavoured to escape from by every means in his power; and in fact in his log, our ship was designated "hum briganda." All this was plausible, and might be true.

The instructions sent to king's ships as to the manner of executing the treaty of Brazil, are very ambiguous. They state in one place that "no slave ship is to be stopped to the south of the line, on any pretext whatever." Yet in another, a certain latitude is allowed, if there is reason to suspect that the slaves on board "were taken in to the north." By the first, the ship could not be detained at all, and it was doubtful if there was just reason for the second. Even if there were the strongest grounds for capturing and sending her to Sierra Leone for adjudication, where the nearest mixed commission sat, a circumstance of very serious difficulty occurred. It would take three weeks, perhaps a month or more, to beat up to windward to this place, and the slaves had not water for more than half that time and we could not supply her. A number had already died, and we saw the state of frenzy to which the survivors were almost driven from the want of this element. On a former occasion, a prize of the *North Star,* sent to Sierra Leone, had lost more than 100, out of a very small complement, while beating up the coast, notwithstanding every care; and it seemed highly probable that in this case but few could survive. Under these doubtful circumstances, then, it appeared more legal and even more humane to suffer them to proceed on their course to Bahia, where it is probable, after all, the remnant left alive would be finally sent, after an investigation by the commissioners, as having been taken in, within the limits of legal traffic. It was with infinite regret, therefore, we were obliged to restore his papers to the captain, and permit him to proceed after nine hours' detention and close investigation. It was dark when we separated, and the last parting sounds we heard from the unhallowed ship, were the cries and shrieks of the slaves, suffering under some bodily infliction.

It should appear, then, that notwithstanding the benevolent and persevering exertions of England, this horrid traffic in human flesh is nearly as extensively carried on as ever, and under circumstances, perhaps, of a more revolting character. The very shifts at evasion, the necessity for concealment, and the desperate hazard, cause inconvenience and sufferings to the poor creatures in a very aggravated degree. The restriction of slaving to the south of the line was in fact nugatory, and evaded on all occasions. The number of slaves recaptured and liberated by our cruisers, appears a large amount; and certainly, as far as it goes, has rendered most important services to humanity. Captain Arabin was on the station three years; and from August, 1826, to May, 1829, visited vessels, having on board 3,894 slaves; of these, nine bearing the Brazilian flag, three the Spanish, one the Portuguese, and one the French and Dutch, in all fourteen, containing 2,465 slaves, were detained, and sent to Sierra Leone for adjudication. The whole number captured by all our cruisers, and afterwards emancipated, for nine years, from June, 1819 to July, 1828, was 13,281, being about 1,400, on an average, each year. During that period, it is supposed that nearly 100,000 human beings were annually transported as slaves from different parts of the coast, of which, more than 43,000 were in one year legally imported into one city alone. It is deeply to be regretted, therefore, that the proportion of the good to the evil is so small. On the 23d of March, 1830, however, the permission to Brazil will expire; the whole of this ransacked and harassed coast will then be protected, and every slaver on any part of it, will be seized and treated as a pirate.

Two difficulties, however, will yet remain, which ought to be removed for the final and effectual prevention of this traffic. By treaties with Spain, Portugal, the Netherlands, and Brazil, mutual right of search is allowed to the cruisers of each nation, and mixed commissions for adjudication reside at Sierra Leone, Havannah, Rio de Janeiro, and Surinam; but no right of mutual search exists with France or North America, and slaves are continually transported with impunity under their flags. Surely, if nations are sincere in this great cause of God and man, they will no longer suffer the little etiquettes of national vanity to oppose it.

It also happens that the right of capture is cunningly evaded by the slavers, as vessels are only liable to seizure when they have actually slaves on board. Ships frequently enter the mouths of rivers, or other parts of the coast, having every apparatus on board for the reception of slaves, which are collected in the vicinity, and ready to embark on the first opportunity. This is known to our ships, who often watch them for a considerable time, while the slaver remains quietly and securely at anchor. When from any cause the attention of the cruiser is called away, the slaves are all embarked in one night; and when the cruiser resumes his station, the slaver has disappeared with her full cargo. The cruiser has little chance of overtaking the slaver, even though she should be in the immediate neighbourhood. The superior class of vessels employed by the Spaniards, is so well calculated for escape in this way, that our ships of war have no chance of overtaking them at sea. To defeat this, an additional article in the treaty with the Netherlands provides, that all vessels are to be considered as slavers, and treated as such, when they have an apparatus evidently intended for the reception of slaves, even though none be found on board.

If therefore, when the whole coast of Africa is protected from this commerce, and no vessel of any nation is permitted to traffic on any part of it, the right of mutual search is acknowledged, and acted on by all civilized nations, and every ship found with the damning proofs on board be confiscated, and the crews treated as pirates, then, and not till then, can we hope to see this horrid traffic finally abolished.

3. A British Consular Report on Slavery in Northern Brazil (1831)

ROBERT HESKETH

I will attempt to describe the condition of slave population, and that of the free people of colour in the northern provinces of Brazil. This description must be confined to a general outline, as many of the statistical returns, essential for a minute description, are not obtained by the Government in that quarter, and the few that exist

From *Correspondence with Foreign Powers, Relating to the Slave Trade, 1831, Presented to Both Houses of Parliament, by Command of His Majesty* (London, 1832), pp. 29–32.

are not accessible. With such obstacles, I am reluctantly obliged to estimate the extent of population from enquiries I made in the country; it cannot, therefore, be exactly correct, but is more likely to be below than above the amount of the existing slave population.

			Slaves.				
In the	Province of	Maranham	180,000	of which	½	are creoles	and mulatos.
"	"	Piaùtry	60,000	"	⅔	ditto	ditto.
"	"	Searà	30,000	"	¾	ditto	ditto.
"	"	Parà	70,000	"	½	ditto	ditto.
			340,000				

This slave population may be divided into two distinct classes, those who are employed in agriculture (by far the most numerous), and those occupied in towns. The slaves on estates are composed either altogether of African negroes, of creoles, or of both, which is more generally the case. In large well-established estates, slaves are well fed, and mildly treated. They have comfortable habitations, and the time allowed them, from the numerous Saint days in the Roman Catholick Calendar, enables them to cultivate plots of ground. The children are attended to, as well as the sick. The increase of slaves in such an estate, by births alone, is about 25 in every 100 in every 5 years. But in small estates, and particularly those where a planter is making his last struggles to continue his agricultural pursuits, the misery of the slaves, from hardships and privations of every kind, as will be seen, are extreme. Till within the last 3 and 4 years, planters were becoming wealthy by growing cotton; but since then, the diminished value of that produce, added to their improvident habits, has in a great measure impoverished them; and, therefore, the condition of the slaves is gradually becoming worse.

But it is not to this accidental fluctuation in markets alone that the misery of slaves is to be attributed. The real cause is easily to be traced to the existing law of inheritance, and to the oppressive taxation on agriculture in that country. The slaves of an estate are, like all other property, equally divided amongst the surviving children of the original proprietor; these, by law, have a right to their respective shares; the parents have only each 1/6th of the whole property at their disposal by will. For the sake of elucidation, I state the following as an instance of every day occurrence. A proprietor resides on a well-established estate, consisting of 600 slaves, and obtains, by the resources derived from such a community, not only every necessary for his family and slaves, but even luxuries, although far removed from any town; turning the labour of his slaves to a profitable cultivation of the land, as well as to the production of good and sufficient food for them. But at the decease of such a proprietor, his surviving family of 6 sons and daughters (perhaps half of them married) and his widow, have all a right to have their respective shares of the whole estate ascertained; and supposing, which is often the case, that they disagree as to the minute particulars of such a division, and insist upon its immediate execution, and that, after some expensive law suits, the widow, by keeping the deceased husband's portion and her own, remains with 200 slaves, and the remaining 400 are divided between the other 6 members of the family: then the resources of the estate are at once paralized, not only with respect to the extent of crops, but also the comforts and consequent efficient labour of the slaves. But when, at the decease of the widow, the full shares of the whole estate are completed to each of the 6 remaining members of the family, and when these establish themselves on different parts of the original extensive estate, with their respective quotas of slaves, some idea will be formed of the cruel change 5/6ths of the original slaves must experience, when thus forced to leave the old established estate, and labour for their second and young master, now, perhaps, rearing a family, and depending for its support on the activity and economy of his agricultural pursuits, a slave being thus exposed to increased labour and privation, as he advances in years. But if this law thus subjects so many slaves to misery, it also places many in a situation to attain with facility their emancipation. This constant division and subdivision of estates, added to the rude system of agriculture at present pursued in that country, tends to impoverish the class of planters; the succeeding heirs to estates being sooner or later reduced to a state of poverty, according to the size of such estates. A person with few slaves must live in a state of poverty, while pursuing agriculture as a means of support; whereas, by coming into a town, the income derived from such slaves, hired as labourers or tradesmen, affords a much more comfortable livelihood: this is the method ultimately pursued by the descendants of once opulent planters; and it will be seen with what facility slaves, under such circumstances, if industrious, can pay their weekly hire, and save enough to purchase ultimately their freedom from the impoverished master.

The class of slaves employed in towns as artificers and labourers are to a much greater degree free agents than those on estates, for they are generally left to select their employers, having only to bring a stated sum weekly to their masters. This class of slaves, taken as a body, are industrious, and chiefly direct their efforts to accumulating a sufficient sum for the purchase of their freedom. The law of the country is particularly favourable to them in this regard, for slaves of both sexes can have their value legally ascertained, and, on depositing the amount, can force the owner to emancipate them. The greatest portion of slaves, which have become in this manner free, are creole negroes, and mulatos, African negroes, for the most part, preferring to emancipate their offspring instead of themselves. These emancipated slaves prove a much better conducted race of people, than could be expected from the institutions of the country, and the examples of the white population; they prove the most contented and industrious class; their increase alone from births is much greater than amongst slaves; they form a large portion of the population in all towns and villages, and are spread over the interior districts. The troops are chiefly recruited from the descendants of this class, and some are found in every profession, even in the church. An emancipated slave can hold any species of property, and of late their political rights as citizens have been made equal to those of the white population. Many of these emancipated slaves own land, but most of them become to some extent householders and owners of slaves. The gradual increase of this class is certain, as also that from it will be derived the chief population of the country. The law thus facilitating emancipation, proves a beneficial stimulus to the good conduct and industry of creole slaves; and its result of blending the coloured with the white population, has mainly contributed to the security of the latter from insurrection amongst slaves, a calamity which has sometimes partially occurred, but which fortunately found a speedy check.

While stating the facility with which slaves merge into the free population of that quarter of Brazil, it may be right to specify, that in all cases, when by the Slave-trade Treaties slaves ought to have been emancipated, the local Authorities have hitherto neglected every step which could ensure their freedom; and that while empty forms were complied with, the negroes alluded to continue in a condition worse than slaves.

The condition of slaves in the northern provinces of Brazil would be ameliorated, if the present system of agriculture were improved, but this cannot be expected to take place, so long as the present

heavy export duties on produce, independent of a 10 per cent tax
on its market value, so far diminishes profit, as to prevent the employment of capital in agriculture.

Estates about Maranham have been lately sold with from 200 to
300 slaves with the most productive lands, at credits, for an amount
which would be a 6 years' purchase, calculating that the price of
cotton was maintained at about 6½d. per pound at the sea port,
which was a customary price for the planters a few years since.
But not half that amount can reach the planter's pocket at present,
nor will 4,000 Reis per annum of 32 pounds, under the present
duties, remunerate the planter. The above-mentioned purchases,
apparently so favourable, must prove unfortunate; and, in fact,
under the present system of export duties and local taxes, all planters are impoverished. The point of rendering the trade of Brazil
more vigorous, by fostering the agricultural interests of that country, would seem to justify an alteration in the existing Commercial
Treaties. At the commencement of the trade, the duties on British
imports were lightened, and this favourable concession has been
gradually extended to every flag, while the deficiency in the revenue
is extorted from the agricultural labour of the country; and its commercial field is now nearly exhausted, to the detriment of all these
states, which have so far reaped the temporary advantages of a
trade founded on a principle opposed to its extension and per-
manency.

Under the present system of trade the agricultural class will become impoverished, the slave population gradually working out,
through misery, their emancipation, and ultimately the population
of the country will consist of a coloured race without either a
wealthy or much enlightened class.

State of the Slave-trade in the Northern
Provinces of Brazil

The slave-trade on the northern coast of Brazil was commenced
with Portuguese capital; and the agents at Maranham, acquiring
property, also embarked in that trade. *Bona fide* Brazilian capital
has not yet been employed in the slave-trade in that quarter of
Brazil. The importation of slaves has been on the decline ever since
the year 1820. The total number landed at Maranham that year was

2,844, and the following, only 1,761 slaves were landed in that port. During the 4 years, from 1821 to 1824, both inclusive, there were 6,242 slaves landed at Maranham. After Brazil was separated from Portugal, slave-vessels to that coast were chiefly navigated under the Brazilian flag, but the numbers imported still continued to decrease: for, in the 4 years from 1824 to 1828, both inclusive, there were 2,098 slaves imported by Brazilian, and 106 by Portuguese vessels, into Maranham, being a decrease of 4,038 slaves during the last-mentioned 4 years. Notwithstanding this decrease, and the approaching termination of the trade, there was but little demand for slaves in the period from 1823 onwards. In 1824 Mozambic negroes were sold chiefly to the poorer class of planters, in lots of 100 to 200 of both sexes, and of all ages, under very long credits, at 100,000, and even 90,000 each. There were 2 or 3 cargoes of this description of negroes sold; and it is a melancholy fact, that, at the close of 1828, there were very few of them living; being of weak constitutions, and unused to labour, they sunk under hardships, and a diet to which they were not accustomed.

The slave-dealers, finding it impossible to carry on the trade with negroes from Southern Africa, commenced, about the end of the year 1825, to obtain, at all risks, negroes from the prohibited African ports to the northward of the Line. These negroes being accustomed to labour in Africa, and to a diet similar to that given by planters at Maranham as most economical, being chiefly rice, were looked upon by the planters as equal to creole negroes, and they were accordingly tempted to purchase them at exorbitant prices, particularly under the expectation that every cargo was the last. Many of this description of slaves were imported into Rio de Janeiro, Bahia, and Pernambuco, under every species of subterfuge, which could screen them in the evasion of the Slave Treaty, and undoubtedly with the connivance of the local Authorities; some of these slaves were ultimately landed at Maranham, from the southern Brazil ports.

On the arrival of vessels at Maranham from the Cape de Verd Islands, with prohibited negroes, the local Authorities, notwithstanding every subterfuge, being pressed to enforce the Treaties, a check was given to the open continuance of the trade; but small vessels were subsequently employed to smuggle slaves into unfrequented rivers and bays on the northern Brazil coast, which slaves were brought chiefly from the Cape Verd Islands, and also from the neighbouring African shores. This was the manner in which the slave-trade was pursued on the northern coast of Brazil, at the time the Treaty prohibited it altogether. But, by frequent reports from Maranham, it appears that these slave-dealers still persevere in transporting the above-mentioned description of negroes, a traffick which these smugglers pursue at all risks, more as the means of profit, than from any positive necessity on the part of the Brazilian planter; and, should the extensive range of the northern Brazil coast be left, as heretofore, open to the undisturbed operations of these lawless adventurers, means will soon be found to introduce these negroes, once surreptitiously landed, into the vast interior districts of Deiras and Minas Geraes, and an extensive field will be allowed for smugglers under every flag.

In the northern provinces of Brazil, the system of agriculture is, to clear each year a fresh plot of forest; estates are consequently at great distances from each other, and, when on a small scale, are exposed to great privations; the laws operate against the existence of large estates, and favour emancipation; therefore, if in this state of things planters are to be annually purchasing, at high prices, the most civilized negroes from Africa, they are, in a most prejudicial manner to themselves, trying to counteract a drain in the slave population, which is the natural result of the existing laws in that country.

If there were a great necessity for slaves, the most opulent would purchase from the poor planter; but, instead of that, planters prefer going into a slave market of fresh-imported negroes, so long as such exists, under the impression that creole slaves are troublesome to manage, and that though healthier and more expert than Africans, yet that the latter are more saleable. On the other hand, so long as the slave-trade was allowed, planters purchased under advantageous credits; but now, when the importation is to be carried on by smugglers, planters cannot expect this advantage, and will more than ever feel the severity of the terms at which they purchase such labour. It may be asserted that the evil will correct itself; but before it does, the remaining wealth of an already distressed class, and one on which the commercial stamina of the country depends, will have passed into the possession of lawless adventurers.

It is, therefore, to be deduced, that for some years past the importation of slaves into the quarter of Brazil, above alluded to, has been prejudicial to the planters, and that such importation has been only induced by the avaricious employment of Portuguese capital.

4. Slavery Is Doomed in Brazil

D. P. KIDDER AND J. C. FLETCHER

The subject of slavery in Brazil is one of great interest and hopefulness. The Brazilian Constitution recognises, neither directly nor indirectly, color as a basis of civil rights; hence, once free, the black man or the mulatto, if he possesses energy and talent, can rise to a social position from which his race in North America is debarred. Until 1850, when the slave-trade was effectually put down, it was considered cheaper, on the country-plantations, to use up a slave in five or seven years and purchase another, than to take care of him. This I had, in the interior, from intelligent native Brazilians, and my own observation has confirmed it. But, since the inhuman traffic with Africa has ceased, the price of slaves has been enhanced, and the selfish motives for taking greater care of them have been increased. Those in the city are treated better than those on the plantations: they seem more cheerful, more full of fun, and have greater opportunities for freeing themselves. But still there must be great cruelty in some cases, for suicides among slaves — which are almost unknown in our Southern States — are of very frequent occurrence in the cities of Brazil. Can this, however, be attributed to cruelty? The negro of the United States is the descendant of those who have, in various ways, acquired a knowledge of the hopes and fears, the rewards and punishments, which the Scriptures hold out to the good and threaten to the evil: to avoid the crime of suicide is as strongly inculcated as to avoid that of murder. The North American negro has, by this very circumstance, a higher moral intelligence than his brother fresh from the wild freedom and heathenism of Africa; hence the latter, goaded by cruelty, or his high spirit refusing to bow to the white man, takes that fearful leap which lands him in the invisible world.

In Brazil every thing is in favor of freedom; and such are the facilities for the slave to emancipate himself, and, when emancipated, if he possess the proper qualifications, to ascend to higher eminences than those of a mere free black, that *fuit* will be written

From *Brazil and the Brazilians* by D. P. Kidder and J. C. Fletcher (Philadelphia: Childs & Peterson, 1857), pp. 132–139.

against slavery in this Empire before another half-century rolls
around. Some of the most intelligent men that I met with in Brazil
— men educated at Paris and Coimbra — were of African descent,
whose ancestors were slaves. Thus, if a man have freedom, money,
and merit, no matter how black may be his skin, no place in society is refused him. It is surprising also to observe the ambition
and the advancement of some of these men with negro blood in
their veins. The National Library furnishes not only quiet rooms,
large tables, and plenty of books to the seekers after knowledge,
but pens and paper are supplied to such as desire these aids to
their studies. Some of the closest students thus occupied are mulattoes. The largest and most successful printing-establishment in Rio
— that of Sr. F. Paulo Brito — is owned and directed by a mulatto.
In the colleges, the medical, law, and theological schools, there is
no distinction of color. It must, however, be admitted that there is a
certain — though by no means strong — prejudice existing all over
the land in favor of men of pure white descent.

By the Brazilian laws, a slave can go before a magistrate, have
his price fixed, and can purchase himself; and I was informed that
a man of mental endowments, even if he had been a slave, would
be debarred from no official station, however high, unless it might
be that of Imperial Senator.

The appearance of Brazilian slaves is very different from that of
their class in our own country. Of course, the house-servants in
the large cities are decently clad, as a general rule; but even these
are almost always barefooted. This is a sort of badge of slavery.
On the tables of fares for ferry-boats, you find one price for persons
wearing shoes (*calçadas*), and a lower one for those *descalças*, or
without shoes. In the houses of many of the wealthy Fluminenses
you make your way through a crowd of little wooly heads, mostly
guiltless of clothing, who are allowed the run of the house and
the amusement of seeing visitors. In families that have some tinc-
ture of European manners, these unsightly little bipeds are kept in
the background. A friend of mine used frequently to dine in the
house of a good old general of high rank, around whose table
gambolled two little jetty blacks, who hung about their "*pai*" (as
they called him) until they received their portions from his hands,
and that, too, before he commenced his own dinner. Whenever the
lady of the house drove out, these pets were put into the carriage,
and were as much offended at being neglected as any spoiled only
son. They were the children of the lady's nurse, to whom she

had given freedom. Indeed, a faithful nurse is generally rewarded by manumission.

The appearance of the black male population who live in the open air is any thing but appetizing. Their apology for dress is of the coarsest and dirtiest description. Hundreds of them loiter about the streets with large round wicker-baskets ready to carry any parcel that you desire conveyed. So cheaply and readily is this help obtained, that a white servant seldom thinks of carrying home a package, however small, and would feel quite insulted if you refused him a *preto de ganho* to relieve him of a roll of calico or a watermelon. These blacks are sent out by their masters, and are required to bring home a certain sum daily. They are allowed a portion of their gains to buy their food, and at night sleep on a mat or board in the lower purlieus of the house. You frequently see horrible cases of elephantiasis and other diseases, which are doubtless engendered or increased by the little care bestowed upon them.

The coffee-carriers are the finest race of blacks in Brazil. They are almost all of the Mina tribe, from the coast of Benin, and are athletic and intelligent. They work half clad, and their sinewy forms and jetty skins show to advantage as they hasten at a quick trot, seemingly unmindful of their heavy loads. This work pays well, but soon breaks them down. They have a system among themselves of buying the freedom of any one of their number who is the most respected. After having paid their master the sum required by him daily, they club together their surplus to liberate the chosen favorite. There is now a Mina black in Rio remarkable for his height, who is called "The Prince," being, in fact, of the *blood-royal* of his native country. He was a prisoner of war, and sold to Brazil. It is said that his *subjects* in Rio once freed him by their toil: he returned, engaged in war, and was a second time made prisoner and brought back. Whether he will again regain his throne I know not; but the loss of it does not seem to weigh heavily on his mind. He is an excellent carrier; and, when a friend of mine embarked, the "Prince" and his troop were engaged to transport the baggage to the ship. He carried the largest case on his head the distance of two miles and a half. This same case was pronounced unmanageable in Philadelphia by the united efforts of four American negroes, and it had to be relieved of half its contents before they would venture to lift it up-stairs.

From time to time the traveller will meet with negroes from those portions of Africa of which we know very little except by the reports of explorers like the intrepid Livingstone and Barth. I have often thought that the slaves of the United States are descended not from the noblest African stock, or that more than a century of bondage has had upon them a most degenerating effect. We find in Brazil very inferior spiritless Africans, and others of an almost untamable disposition. The Mina negro seldom makes a good house-servant, for he is not contented except in breathing the fresh air. The men become coffee-carriers, and the women *quitandeiras,* or street pedlars.

These Minas abound at Bahia, and in 1838 plunged that city into a bloody revolt — the last which that flourishing municipality has experienced. It was rendered the more dreadful on account of the secret combinations of these Minas, who are Mohammedans, and use a language not understood by other Africans or by the Portuguese.

When the delegation from the English Society of Friends visited Rio de Janeiro in 1852, they were waited upon by a deputation of eight or ten Mina negroes. They had earned money by hard labor and had purchased their freedom, and were now desirous of returning to their native land. They had funds for paying their passage back again to Africa, but wished to know if the coast were really free from the slavers. Sixty of their companions had left Rio de Janeiro for Badagry (coast of Benin) the year before, and had landed in safety. The good Quakers could scarcely credit this last information, thinking it almost impossible that any who had once been in servitude "should have been able and bold enough to make so perilous an experiment"; but the statement of the Minas was confirmed by a Rio ship-broker, who put into the hands of the Friends a copy of the charter under which the sixty Minas sailed, and which showed that they had paid four thousand dollars passage-money. A few days after this interview, Messrs. Candler & Burgess received from these fine-looking specimens of humanity "a paper beautifully written in Arabic by one of their chiefs, who is a Mohammedan."

In Rio the blacks belong to many tribes, some being hostile to each other, having different usages and languages. The Mina negroes still remain Mohammedans, but the others are nominal Roman Catholics.

Many of them, however, continue their heathen practices. In

1839, Dr. Kidder witnessed in Engenho Velho a funeral, which was of the same kind as those curious burial-customs which the African traveller beholds on the Gaboon River. You can scarcely look into a basket in which the *quitandeiras* carry fruit without seeing a *fetisch*. The most common is a piece of charcoal, with which, the abashed darkey will inform you, the "evil eye" is driven away. There is a singular secret society among the negroes, in which the highest rank is assigned to the man who has taken the most lives. They are not so numerous as formerly, but from time to time harm the unoffending. These blacks style themselves *capoeiros,* and during a festa they will rush out at night and rip up any other black they chance to meet. They rarely attack the whites, knowing, perhaps, that it would cost them too dearly.

The Brazilians are not the only proprietors of slaves in the Empire. There are many Englishmen who have long held Africans in bondage — some for a series of years, and others have purchased slaves since 1843, when what is called Lord Brougham Act was passed. By this act it is made unlawful for Englishmen to buy or sell a slave in any land, and by holding property in man they are made liable, were they in England, to prosecution in criminal courts. The English mining-company, whose stockholders are in Great Britain, but whose field of operations is S. João del Rey in Brazil, own about eight hundred slaves, and hire one thousand more.

Frenchmen and Germans also purchase slaves, although they have not given up allegiance to their respective countries.

If it be asked, "Who will be the laborers in Brazil when slavery is no more?" the reply (given more at length in the account of a visit to the colony of Senator Vergueiro) is that the supply will come from Germany, Portugal, and Azores and Madeira, and other countries.

It is a striking fact that emigrants did not begin to arrive from Europe by thousands until 1852. In 1850 and '51 the African slave-trade was annihilated, and in the succeeding year commenced the present comparatively vigorous colonization. Each year the number of colonists is increasing, and the statesmen of the Empire are now devoting much attention to discover the best means for thus promoting the advancement of the country.

Almost every step in Brazilian progress has been prepared by a previous gradual advance: she did not leap at once into self-government. She was raised from a colonial state by the residence of the Court from Lisbon, and enjoyed for years the position of a constituent portion of the Kingdom of Portugal. The present peaceful state of the Empire under D. Pedro II was preceded by the decade in which the capabilities of the people for self-government were developed under the Regency. The effectual breaking up of the African slave-trade is but the precursor of a more important step.

Slavery is doomed in Brazil. As has already been exhibited, when freedom is once obtained, it may be said in general that no social hinderances, as in the United States, can keep down a man of merit. Such hinderances do exist in our country. From the warm regions of Texas to the coldest corner of New England the free black man, no matter how gifted, experiences obstacles to his elevation which are insurmountable. Across that imaginary line which separates the Union from the possessions of Great Britain, the condition of the African, socially considered, is not much superior. The Anglo-Saxon race, on this point, differs essentially from the Latin nations. The former may be moved to generous pity for the negro, but will not yield socially. The latter, both in Europe and the two Americas, have always placed merit before color. . . .

Thus far reason and Christianity have proved impotent in rooting out this prejudice, or in doing away with these social hinderances, which, more than slavery, will ever render the black man "a hewer of wood and a drawer of water" to the Anglo-American, and which, unjust as they are, I fear can never be eradicated. These insurmountable obstacles, it seems to me, like plain providences, point to Liberia as the nearest land where the North-American-born negro may enjoy the full freedom and the social equality enjoyed by the African descendants in the most enlightened Government of South America.

5. Slavery Is a Curse for Both Negroes and Whites

HERBERT H. SMITH

I came to Brazil, with an honest desire to study this question of slavery in a spirit of fairness, without running to emotional extremes. Now, after four years, I am convinced that all other

From *Brazil: The Amazons and the Coast* by Herbert H. Smith (New York: Charles Scribner's Sons, 1879), pp. 466–470.

evils with which the country is cursed, taken together, will not compare with this one; I could almost say that all other evils have arisen from it, or been strengthened by it. And yet, I cannot unduly blame men who have inherited the curse, and had no part in the making of it. I can honor masters who treat their slaves kindly, albeit they are owners of stolen property.

In mere animal matters, of food and clothing, no doubt many of the negroes are better off than they were in Africa; no doubt, also, they have learned some lessons of peace and civility; even a groping outline of Christianity. But it would be hard to prove that the plantation slave, dependent, like a child, on his master, and utterly unused to thinking for himself, is better, mentally, than the savage who has his faculties sharpened by continual battling with the savage nature around him. Slavery is weakening to the brain; the slave is worse material for civilization than the savage is, and worse still with every generation of slavery.

That is not the main evil, however. The harm that slavery has done to the black race is as nothing to the evils it has heaped upon the white one, the masters. If every slave and free negro could be carried away to Africa, if every drop of cursed mixed blood could be divided, the evils would be there yet, and go down to the children's children with a blight upon humanity.

Indolence and pride and sensuality and selfishness, these are the outgrowths of slavery that have enslaved the slavemakers and their children. Do you imagine that they are all rich men's sons, these daintily clad, delicate young men on the Ouvidor? The most of them are poor, but they will lead their vegetable lives, God knows how, parasites on their friends, or on the government, or on the tailor and grocer, because they will not soil their hands with tools. "Laborers!" cries Brazil. "We must have labor!" and where will she get honest workmen, if honest work is a degradation? Slavery has made it so. For generations the upper classes had no work to do, and they came to look upon it as the part of an inferior race. So they have kept their hands folded, and the muscle has gone from their bones, and indolence has become a part of their nature. Still, they will be sham lords, if they cannot be real ones; so their money — what they have of it — goes for broadcloth coats and silk hats, and sensuality; a grade below that, they are yet shabby-genteel figures, with an eye to friendly invitations to dinner; and below that, they sink out of sight altogether, from mere inanition.

The rich men's sons are not parasites; sharp enough, many of them are, to keep the money they have, and double it. But from their cradle, the curse of slavery is on them. The black nurse is an inferior, and the child knows it, and tyrannizes over her as only a child can. The mother is an inferior, by her social station, and she does not often venture to thwart the child. The father, with whom authority rests, shirks it back on the irresponsible ones, who may not venture to lay sacrilegious hands on the heir of power. The amount of it is, that a child's training here consists in letting it have its own way as much as possible; and the small naughtinesses and prides develop into consuming vanity and haughtiness. It is characteristic of the Brazilians, this vanity; it may come out in snobbism, or over-confidence, or merely a fiery sensitiveness; but there it is plainly; in the best of them. Slavery is to blame for it; black slavery, and woman slavery that gives the mother no authority.

Of the sensuality that comes from slavery, the mixed races that overrun Brazil are a sufficient witness, as they are in our Southern States. But in Brazil, the proportion of these mixed races is vastly greater; I am safe in saying that not a third of the population is pure-blooded; social distinctions of color are never very finely drawn, though they are by no means abolished, as some writers would have us believe.

People who talk of "amalgamation," as a blessing to be hoped for, should study its effects here, where it is almost an accomplished fact. The mixed races are invariably bad; they seem to combine all the worst characteristics of the two parent stocks, with none of the good ones; and the evil is most apparent where the "amalgamation" is most complete. A light mulatto, or an almost black one, may be a very decent kind of a fellow; but the brown half-and-half is nearly always lazy and stupid and vain. So with the whites and Indians, or the Indians and blacks; the *mamelucos* are treacherous, and passionate, and indolent; the *mestiços* are worse yet; but a dash of mixed blood may not spoil the man that has it.

The treatment of slaves in Brazil depends, of course, on the master; largely, too, on the district. In the provinces north of the São Francisco, I am bound to say that they are treated with great kindness; on the Amazons, they would be, from necessity, if not from choice, for every ill-used slave would run off to the woods, as many have done, out of mere laziness; freedom, considered abstractly, is not likely to have much influence on the negro mind. But around Rio and Bahia, where the vast majority of the slaves are now owned, there are masters who treat their servants with a severity that is nothing short of barbarism. We shall see something of this, when we come to study the coffee-plantations.

Yet Brazil should have a certain credit above other slave-holding countries, present and past; for she alone has voluntarily set herself to getting rid of her shame. Other nations have done it by revolutions, or because they were forced to by a stronger power, or because the system died out of itself. But Brazil, among all, has had nerve to cut away the sore flesh with her own hand; to cut it away while it was yet strong, while it seemed her best vitality. Would to God that she could cut away the scar as well! But the scar will be there, long after emancipation has done its work.

By the present law, slavery will cease to exist in 1892; essentially, I think, the northern provinces will free their slaves before that time. At Pernambuco, especially, the emancipation-spirit is very strong; it has come out in the form of an abolition society, which embraces nearly every prominent man in the place; many slaves have been freed by subscription, at the meetings of this society; there, and elsewhere, the masters frequently celebrate days of public rejoicing, by releasing some old servant. Sometimes a rich man frees his entire household, by testament.

The slaves have been drained into the southern provinces for years. It is common to find three or four hundred of them on the Rio coffee-plantations; rarely, there will be as many score on the sugar-estates of Pernambuco or Pará. Now mark the result. At Rio there is a constant cry for workmen; the slaves are not sufficient, yet free laborers cannot compete with the forced ones; the planters work their negroes as they would never work their mules, yet complain that they reap no profits. In the northern provinces, there is free labor, enough and to spare; poor men have a chance in the world; rich ones are content with the fair returns that their money brings them; society is far more evenly balanced, and the level of private character is far higher than in the south. Of course, there are humane masters at Rio also; the city, in this instance, is better than the country around. Many of the negro porters are slaves; great, brawny fellows, who run in gangs through the streets, each one with a hundred and thirty pounds of coffee on his head. Sometimes we see five or six of them, trotting together, with a piano; the weight evenly distributed on the woolly craniums; the men erect, moving in time to the leader's rattle, and to a plaintive chant. The porters pay their masters a certain sum per day; what they earn over this, is their own. The best of them sometimes buy their freedom from their savings.

B. Analysis by a Historian

6. Patterns of Living on the Vassouras Plantation

STANLEY J. STEIN

Slave life on the average Vassouras plantation of approximately eighty to one hundred slaves was regulated by the needs of coffee agriculture, the maintenance of *sede* [the plantation buildings] and *senzallas* [slave quarters], and the processing of coffee and subsistence foodstuffs. Since the supply of slaves was never adequate for the needs of the plantation either in its period of growth, prosperity, or decline, the slaves' work day was a long one begun before dawn and often ending many hours after the abrupt sunset of the Parahyba plateau.

Cooks arose before sunup to light fires beneath iron cauldrons; soon the smell of coffee, molasses, and boiled corn meal floated from the outdoor shed. The sun had not yet appeared when the overseer or one of his Negro drivers strode to a corner of the *terreiro* [coffee drying terraces] and reached for the tongue of a wide-mouthed bell. The tolling of the cast-iron bell, or sometimes a blast from a cowhorn or the beat of a drum, reverberated across the terreiro and entered the tiny cubicles of slave couples and the separated, crowded *tarimbas*, or dormitories, of unmarried slaves. Awakening from their five- to eight-hour slumber, they dragged themselves from beds of planks softened with woven fiber mats; field hands reached for hoes and billhooks lying under the eaves. At the large faucet near the senzallas, they splashed water over their heads and faces, moistening and rubbing arms, legs, and

ankles. Tardy slaves might appear at the door of senzallas mutter-
ing the slave-composed *jongo* [slave work song] which mocked the
overseer ringing the bell:

> That devil of a *bembo* taunted me
> No time to button my shirt, that devil of a bembo.

Now, as the terreiro slowly filled with slaves, some standing in
line and others squatting, awaiting the morning *reza* or prayer,
the senhor appeared on the veranda of the main house. "One
slave recited the reza which the others repeated," recalled an ex-
slave. Hats were removed and there was heard a "Praised-be-Our-
Master-Jesus-Christ" to which some slaves repeated a blurred "Our-
Master-Jesus-Christ," others an abbreviated "Kist." From the master
on the veranda came the reply: "May-He-always-be-praised." The
overseer called the roll; if a slave did not respond after two calls,
the overseer hustled into the senzallas to get him or her. When orders for the day had been given, directing the various gangs to
work on certain coffee-covered hills, slaves and drivers shuffled to
the nearby slave kitchen for coffee and corn bread.

The first signs of dawn brightened the sky as slaves separated
to their work. A few went into the main house; most merely placed
the long hoe handles on their shoulders and, old and young, men
and women, moved off to the almost year-round job of weeding
with drivers following to check stragglers. Mothers bore nursing
youngsters in small woven baskets (*jacás*) on their backs or carried
them astraddle one hip. Those from four to seven trudged with
their mothers, those from nine to fifteen close by. If coffee hills to
be worked were far from the main buildings, food for the two meals
furnished in the field went along — either in a two-team ox-cart
which slaves called a *maxambomba*, or in iron kettles swinging on
long sticks, or in wicker baskets or two-eared wooden pans (*gamel-
las*) on long boards carried on male slaves' shoulders. A few slaves
carried their own supplementary articles of food in small cloth bags.

Scattered throughout the field were shelters of four posts and a
grass roof. Here, at the foot of the hills where coffee trees marched
up steep slopes, the field slaves split into smaller gangs. Old men
and women formed a gang working close to the rancho; women
formed another; the men or young bucks (*rapaziada nova*), a third.
Leaving the *moleques* [Negro or mulatto male children] and little
girls to play near the cook and assistants in the rancho, they began
the day's work. As the sun grew stronger, men removed their shirts;

hoes rose and fell slowly as slaves inched up the steep slopes. Under the gang labor system of *corte e beirada* used in weeding, the best hands were spread out on the flanks, *cortador* and *contra-cortador* on one, *beirador* and *contra-beirador* on the other. These four lead-row men were faster working pace-setters, serving as examples for slower workers sandwiched between them. When a coffee row (*carreira*) ended abruptly due to a fold in the slope, the slave now without a row shouted to his overseer "Throw another row for the middle" or "We need another row"; a *feitor* [plantation overseer] passed on the information to the flanking lead-row man who moved into the next row giving the slave who had first shouted a new row to hoe. Thus lead-row men always boxed-in the weeding gang.

Slave gangs often worked within singing distance of each other and to give rhythm to their hoe strokes and pass comment on the circumscribed world in which they lived and worked — their own foibles, and those of their master, overseers, and slave drivers — the master-singer (*mestre cantor*) of one gang would break into the first "verse" of a song in riddle form, a jongo. His gang would chorus the second line of the verse, then weed rhythmically while the master-singer of the nearby gang tried to decipher (*desafiar*) the riddle presented. An ex-slave, still known for his skill at making jongos, informed that "Mestre tapped the ground with his hoe, others listened while he sang. Then they replied." He added that if the singing was not good the day's work went badly. Jongos sung in African tongues were called *quimzumba;* those in Portuguese, more common as older Africans diminished in the labor force, *visaría.* Stopping here and there to "give a lick" (*lambada*) of the lash to slow slaves, two slave drivers usually supervised the gangs by criss-crossing the vertical coffee rows on the slope and shouting "Come on, come on"; but if surveillance slackened, gang laborers seized the chance to slow down while men and women slaves lighted pipes or leaned on their hoes momentarily to wipe sweat away. To rationalize their desire to resist the slave drivers' whips and shouts, a story developed that an older, slower slave should never be passed in his coffee row. For the aged slave could throw his belt ahead into the younger man's row and the youngster would be bitten by a snake when he reached the belt. The overseer or the master himself, in white clothes and riding boots, might ride through the groves for a quick look. Alert slaves, feigning to peer at the hot sun, "spiced their words" to comment in a loud voice

"Look at that red-hot sun" or intermixed African words common to slave vocabulary with Portuguese as in "*Ngoma* is on the way" to warn their fellow slaves (*parceiros*), who quickly set to work industriously. When the driver noted the approaching planter, he commanded the gang "Give praise," to which slaves stood erect, eager for the brief respite, removed their hats or touched hands to forehead, and responded "Vas Christo." Closing the ritual greeting, the senhor too removed his hat, spoke his "May He always be praised" and rode on. Immediately the industrious pace slackened.

To shouts of "lunch, lunch" or more horn blasts coming from the rancho around 10 A.M., slave parceiros and drivers descended. At the shaded rancho they filed past the cook and his assistants, extending bowls or *cuías* of gourds split in two. On more prosperous *fazendas* [plantations], slaves might have tin plates. Into these food was piled; drivers and a respected or favored slave would eat to one side while the rest sat or sprawled on the ground. Mothers used the rest to nurse their babies. A half hour later the *turma* [work group] was ordered back to the sun-baked hillsides. At 1 P.M. came a short break for coffee to which slaves often added the second half of the corn meal cake served at lunch. On cold or wet days, small cups of *cachaça* [sugar brandy] distilled from the plantation's sugar cane replaced coffee. Some ex-slaves reported that fazendeiros often ordered drivers to deliver the cachaça to the slaves in a cup while they worked, to eliminate a break. *Fanta* or supper came at 4 P.M. and work was resumed until nightfall when to drivers' shouts of "Let's quit" (*vamos largar o serviço*) the slave gangs tramped back to the sede. Zaluar, the romantic Portuguese who visited Vassouras, wrote of the return from the fields: "The solemn evening hour. From afar, the fazenda's bell tolls Ave-Maria. (From hilltops fall the gray shadows of night while a few stars begin to flicker in the sky). . . . From the hill descend the taciturn driver and in front, the slaves, as they return home." Once more the slaves lined up for roll call on the terreiro where the field hands encountered their slave companions who worked at the plantation center (sede).

Despite the fact that the economy of the fazenda varied directly with the success of its coffee production, a high percentage of plantation slave labor, which some estimated at fully two-thirds, others at one-half of the labor force, was not engaged directly in field work. "On the plantation," Couty judged, "everything or almost everything is the product of the Black man: it is he who has built the houses; he has made the bricks, sawed the boards, channeled the water, etc.; the roads and most of the machines in the *engenho* [mill] are, along with the lands cultivated, the products of his industry. He also has raised cattle, pigs, and other animals needed on the fazenda." Many were employed in relatively unproductive tasks around the sede as waiters and waitresses, stableboys and cooks, and body servants for the free men, women, and children.

Throughout the day in front of the house could be seen the activity of the terreiro. From his shaded veranda or from a window the fazendeiro watched his slaves clean the terreiro of sprouting weeds, or at harvest time revolve the drying coffee beans with wooden hoes. Until the hot sun of midday drove them to the shade, bare-bottomed black and mulatto youngsters played under the eye of an elderly "aunt" and often with them a small white child in the care of his male body servant (*pagem*) or female "dry nurse." In a corner slaves might butcher a pig for the day's consumption while some moleques threw stones at the black turkey buzzards which hovered nearby. Outside the senzalla a decrepit slave usually performed some minor task or merely warmed himself in the sun. From the engenho came the thumping sound of the pilões [pestles — parts of the coffee processing machinery] and the splash of water cascading from the large water-wheel. In the shade of the engenho an old slave wove strips of bamboo into mats and screens. Washerwomen, beating and spreading clothes to bleach in the sun, worked rhythmically "to the tune of mournful songs."

Behind the main house, the páteo enclosed on all sides offered a shelter from outsiders' eyes, a place to be at ease. Here and in the rooms around it the lives of the free and slave women blended together. Washerwomen chatted as they dipped their arms into the granite tank in the center of the páteo or stretched wet clothes to bleach on the ground, and through the door of the kitchen slaves occupied with the unending process of food preparation could be seen at long wooden work tables. From a small porch opening on the páteo, or from the dining-room window, the mistress of the house, *sinhá* (or more informally, *nhanhá*), in a dressing gown, leaned on the railing and watched, maintaining a flow of gossip with her slaves or reprimanding some. Yet, despite the close contact between free and slave, locks on the doors of pantries and cupboards and the barred windows of both gave mute testimony to the faith of the mistress in her slaves. Life for the female house slave often seemed easier in comparison with that of a field hand; indeed, many of the *mucamas* or household female slaves were chosen from the field gangs. Yet they felt they had less liberty than the field hands since they were constantly supervised. A former pagem put the case succinctly: "Of course life in the household was always better. But many a sinhá beat her mucamas with a quince switch."

The dining room, with its close relation to kitchen, páteo, and sleeping rooms, was probably the general place of family congregation on those fazendas which did not have special sewing and sitting rooms. Bedrooms were small and sparsely furnished and, in the case of the windowless alcovas, entirely dark. In the house the younger women and maiden aunts sewed and embroidered, gossiped, and made delicacies for feast days, while the mistress of the household took a direct hand in the management of affairs. Usually an active sinhá carried the keys to pantries, which were opened twice daily to dole out food for the household's main meals, and to linen, china, and silver closets. Under her direction, slaves made beds, arranged disorder, swept, and moved dust from one point to another with feather dusters, while nursemaids took charge of the younger children and wet nurses satisfied squalling infants.

At meal times, which occupied a large part of the day, diners sat on both sides of the long extension table, the fazendeiro at its head. When guests were present talk was largely between them and their host, while the children and dependent relatives ate in silence, speaking only when addressed. The senhor tapped his plate with a spoon to remind the waiter to change plates. A demitasse of coffee closed the meal which was followed by the inevitable toothpick taken from a silver holder. After the noon meal, while the free retired to their nap, the household slaves ate their meal, gossiped, and yawned through the washing of dishes and silverware, and, when finished, resumed the *bate-papo* [small talk] unless the mistress or master kept them busy with small biddings.

At evening roll call (*formatura*) slaves were checked and sent to evening tasks to begin what one Vassouras planter termed the "brutal system of night tasks" (*serão*), sometimes lasting to 10 or 11 P.M. During winter months the principal evening task — the sorting of dried coffee beans on the floor of the engenho or on special tables — was continued in the light of castor-oil lamps or woven *taquara* [bamboo] torches. Preparation of food for humans and animals was the next most important job: manioc was skinned by hand, scraped on a huge grating wheel, dried, and then toasted for manioc flour. Corn cobs were thrown to pigs, while slaves beat other ears on tables (*debrulhadores*) with rods to remove kernels to be ground into corn meal. Women pounded rice in mortar and pestle to hull it. Coffee for the following day's consumption was toasted in wide pans, then ground. Slaves were sent out to gather firewood, and moleques walked to nearby abandoned groves to drive in the few foraging cows, oxen, mules, and goats. A light supper ended the serão.

In the dwelling house slaves cleared the supper table and lit castor-oil lamps or candles. The planter's family retired soon to their rooms, followed by the mucama "whose job was to carry water to wash the feet of the person retiring." She departed immediately to return after a short wait, received a "God-bless-you" and blew out the light.

And now field hands straggled from the engenho to slave senzallas where they were locked for the night. Household help too was locked in tiny rooms located in the rear of the house near the kitchen. For the slaves it was the end of a long day — unless a sudden storm blew up during the night while coffee was drying on the terreiros; then they were routed out once more by the jangling bell to pile and cover hurriedly the brown beans. Except for the patrollers (*rondantes*), moving in groups on the roads and through the coffee groves to pick up slaves out without passes (*guías* or *escriptos*) to visit nearby plantations or taverns, activity ceased.

With the arrival of Saturday evening and Sunday — awaited with much the spirit of the American South's "Come day, go day, God send Sunday" — came the only interruption of the work routine of plantation life. On Saturday the evening stint was usually omitted to give the labor force an opportunity to live without close supervision. Near a fire on the drying terrace, to the beating of two or three drums, slaves — men, women, and children — led by one of their master-singers, danced and sang until the early morning hours.

Even Sunday too was partially devoted to work. In morning chores, lasting until 9 or 10, field hands attended to the auxiliary tasks of the plantation: hauling firewood from clearings, preparing pasture by burning the grass cover, clearing brush from boundary ditches, repairing dams and roads, and killing ever-present *saúva* ants with fire and bellows. Sunday was the day for distribution of tobacco cut from a huge roll of twisted leaf smeared with honey, and of clean clothing for the following week's work. Chores completed, the master "gave permission" — permitted slaves to dispose of the remainder of the day until the line-up at nightfall. It was also common for planters to "give permission" on days other than Sunday to stagger the weekly day off and prevent slaves from meeting with friends from nearby plantations.

Many now scattered to small *roças* [small cultivated plot] near the plantation center, where they raised coffee, corn, and beans. Planters gave them these plots for various reasons: they gave the slave cultivators a sense of property which, known or unknown to Brazilian masters, continued an African tradition and softened the harsh life of slavery; they provided subsistence foodstuffs which planters failed to raise in their emphasis on one-crop agriculture; and, by offering cash for the produce, planters put into slaves' hands small change for supplementary articles not provided by the plantation. Often planters insisted that slaves sell only to them the coffee they raised. Slaves obtained cash too when the custom became widespread among planters to pay for Sunday or saints'-day labor.

Where male and female slaves cohabited, men often were accompanied to the roças by their children, while women washed, mended, and cooked, bringing the noon meal to their mates in the field. The single men brought firewood for the cook to prepare their meal, returning at eating hours. Other slaves used the free time to weave sleeping mats or cut and sew clothing for sale. With cash or corn or beans, slaves went on Sundays to trade at nearby saloons (*tabernas*) or small country stores. On a visit to a fazenda of the province of Rio, the Swiss Pradez entered a fazenda-owned *venda* [country store] run by an aging slave "aunt" of the fazendeiro's confidence where he found the typical stock: tobacco and cachaça (particularly attractive to slaves), notions including mirrors, straw hats, and clothing cut from cotton cloth (*Petrope*) of a quality slightly better than the coarse cloth furnished by the plantation. Outside the confines of the fazenda, he found a white taberna proprietor who served Negroes with cachaça at a *vintem* per glass. In friendly fashion the white man, to Pradez's surprise, discussed with a slave the weather, the crops, and his master, as though the slave were a "client to be maintained."

C. Recent Interpretations

7. Why Slavery Was Abolished

EMÍLIA VIOTTI DA COSTA

In 1822 Brazil achieved political independence, but her traditional economic structure continued essentially unchanged. Some
of the leaders of Independence made conscious if somewhat timid
attempts to create domestic industries, but these were very quickly
frustrated. The industries died at birth, unable to withstand the
invasion of European manufactured goods, especially English ones,
which had been favored by commercial treaties. Brazil's colonial
destiny was reaffirmed: she seemed fated to supply Europe with
primary products and to receive manufactured goods. . . .

The country became organized as an independent nation. Parliament discussed the theoretical formulas of the representative system. Opinion was divided over the form for popular participation
in the government, over federalism, and over the limits of royal
power. The doctrinal controversies which agitated the European
public had their repercussions among us. In Parliament the liberal
credo was recited. The Constitution of 1824 included the formulas
consecrated in the Declaration of the Rights of Man. Individual
guarantees were assured. Laws were declared to be the expression
of the will of the people. Theoretically, privileges were abolished
and all were made equal before the law, but by protecting property, a contradiction was maintained which would generate numerous conflicts: revolutions were made in the name of freedom,
but the nation kept more than a million people enslaved in the
name of the right of property.

This profound contradiction did not worry the majority of politi-

From "O escravo na grande lavoura" by Emília Viotti da Costa in *História Geral
da Civilização Brasileira: Tomo II, O Brasil Monarquico*, Sérgio Buarque de
Holanda, ed. (São Paulo: Difusão Européia do Livro, 1967), pp. 135–188,
passim. Reprinted by permission.

cians. There were not many in that period who denounced the evils
of the slave system and urged its extinction. . . .

[The half century following Independence saw some economic
and social changes, which help to explain the growing strength of
the abolition movement after 1870.]

Because of changes in the system of production, a group of plantation owners emerged — in the Northeast as well as in the South —
who were not tied to the slave system. They were receptive to the
abolitionist movement and, in certain cases, their interests were
directly linked to the extinction of slavery. The adherence of this
group to the ideas of free labor made the final victory of abolition
possible in Parliament and explains in great part the relatively practical character of the movement. In general, however, traditional
large-scale agriculture — that is, the more backward parts of agriculture — was hostile to abolitionism, sometimes even to the point
of armed resistance. To the very end, some sectors were opposed
to abolition, which implied not only modification of the labor system but also abandonment of the seignorial world view and the
relinquishing of a series of values related to it. For many, abolition
would represent the loss of social status.

Abolitionist ideas found greater support in urban areas, among
the social groups least tied to slavery.

There was no clear dividing line between the bourgeoisie and the
rural aristocracy in Brazil during this period. Many of the lawyers,
doctors, engineers, teachers, and government functionaries came
directly from the seignorial class. When they were not linked to it
by family ties, their economic and financial interests operated
within its orbit. Thus at times they too were compromised by the
seignorial world view. They were not, however, directly dependent
on slave labor and therefore could face abolitionist propaganda with
some equanimity.

In general, abolition was favored by the representatives of the
urban classes, which were gaining importance because of economic
changes taking place in Brazil, such as the development of the railroads, the appearance of the first industrial enterprises, insurance
companies, credit organizations, and the increase in retail commerce. Equally favorable to the liberation of the slaves were the
artisans: free workers, Brazilian or foreign, who found new opportunities for work. Their collaboration was decisive in the revolutionary action unleashed in the 1880's. The followers of Antônio
Bento who acted in São Paulo, inciting slaves to flee from the plan-

tations, worrying the landowners, threatening the overseers, beating the men sent out to catch runaway slaves, were recruited primarily from the following groups: lawyers, journalists, printers, coachmen, railroad workers, doctors, and businessmen.

The abolitionist movement was essentially urban, even when it reached the slave quarters inciting the slave masses to insurrection in order to speed the necessary reforms. The rural population remained, in general, indifferent to the fate of the slaves. [Joaquim] Nabuco, in 1884, bitterly criticized the attitude of those classes which did not know their own interests: "It is not with us, who raise the cry of abolition, that these impassive victims of the monopoly of land by the few join, but with the others who raise the cry of slavery — slavery which oppresses them without their realizing it because it has crushed them from the cradle."

The behavior of the immigrants was more conscious. Many of them were caught indoctrinating slaves, inciting them to insurrection, holding forth on the injustices of captivity. With the exception of some Portuguese merchants and a small number of North Americans [Confederate exiles] in São Paulo, the greater part of the foreigners living in Brazil favored abolition.

The Negroes and freedmen had an important role in the abolitionist movement. Despite the indifference of many former slaves toward the fate of those still in bondage, a great number were attracted to the movement. Rebellion in the slave quarters during the last years of slavery was a decisive factor in the final disintegration of the system.

Abolitionist propaganda and the prospect of liberation made captivity more difficult to endure. The existence of free labor alongside slavery only served to emphasize the injustice of the institution. Travellers in the provinces of São Paulo and Rio de Janeiro in 1883 had the impression that a social revolution was imminent. There were signs of unrest everywhere; escapes, revolts, and crimes committed by slaves increased the tension. Negroes were refusing to obey orders and were frequently finding aid and sympathy among the free population.

As the economic bases of the slave system weakened, abolitionist arguments gained influence. No one dared any longer to make a doctrinaire defense of slavery. All said that they favored emancipation; however, the slave owners' spokesmen insisted upon emphasizing that the situation in which the slave lived was superior to that of the European laborer. They made a point of stressing that in

Brazil slavery was milder than in other countries, that here the masters were benevolent, and that the relations between masters and slaves were paternal in tone. They even argued that the slaves had been happy up to the moment in which subversive ideas spread by the abolitionists had created discontent. They accused the abolitionists of painting too dark a picture of slavery. Theoretically, they were in favor of gradual emancipation provided that property rights were safeguarded, that is, provided that the owners were indemnified. But whenever any measure aiming at emancipation was suggested, it was vehemently opposed. They invoked the right of property, they accused the abolitionists of being "communists" and agitators who had nothing to lose, and of jeopardizing public security and national prosperity. They said that the abolitionist movement had no support from public opinion, that it was an artificial movement promoted by an anarchistic group which preached illegal and subversive doctrines threatening the highest national interests which had been created and maintained under the protection of national laws. They always considered premature any emancipatory measure which had not been prepared for by prior studies, statistics, and far-reaching reforms, such as colonization and the construction of railroads and canals.

In 1871 the project designed to free the children born of slave mothers was labelled a crime, robbery, theft, and communist-inspired. One deputy affirmed, in a style much to the taste of the rhetoric of the period, that the proposal "unfurled its sails on an ocean also navigated by the pirate ship *International.*" The government was accused of seriously compromising the future of the nation by even permitting the question to be debated in Parliament. There was talk of the social agitation and the misery which would result if slavery were abolished.

The abolitionists were no less vehement. They said that slavery created an obstacle to the economic development of the country, impeded immigration, inhibited the mechanization of agriculture, and created a false wealth well described by the proverb "rich father, noble son, poor grandson." They repeated the arguments which had been heard so many times since Independence: slavery corrupted society and the family, encouraged laziness and wastefulness, degraded the masters, debased the slaves, corrupted the language, religion, and *mores*, and violated natural law. To the traditional arguments provided by the thought of the Enlightenment and by the doctrines of romanticism and classical economics, arguments derived from positivism were now added. Slavery, said the positivists, was an anachronistic and transitory state which was destined to be eliminated.

Ideology, however, bowed to economic interests. The positivist group was divided. There were some, such as Miguel Lemos, who favored abolition without indemnification while others like Pereira Barreto and Ribeiro de Mendonça urged gradual emancipation. All of them invoked the fathers of positivism to justify their positions.

Until the 1860's, antislavery ideas had little influence on public opinion. Projects introduced in Parliament seeking to improve the conditions of life of the slaves aroused strong opposition. Literature, which for quite some time had presented a conventional picture of the Negro, slowly became more aware of the problems created by slavery. Among the poets, Castro Alves best exemplifies this tendency. In prose, Macedo in *Vítimas e Algôzes* is the best example of militant literature during the period. Beginning with the Paraguayan War [1864–1870], the number of works in this genre increased; stories, novellas, plays, novels, feuilletons, and pamphlets were written with the purpose of fighting slavery. The number of abolitionist newspapers grew. The press prepared public opinion to accept abolitionist ideas. . . .

The abolitionist movement intensified after 1880. From this period onward a clear opposition developed in the Chamber between the majority of deputies from the Northeastern provinces, who favored discussion of the slavery question in Parliament and extension of emancipatory measures, and the representatives of the coffee-growing provinces, the majority of whom favored the maintenance of the status quo.

The abolitionists organized an intense campaign, promoting speeches, bazaars, fund raising parties, and public meetings. More violent and effective were the activities of certain groups which promoted the escape of slaves. Labor on the plantations was becoming disorganized. In order to retain their slaves, plantation owners found themselves forced to grant them freedom with clauses requiring that they serve as hired workers for various periods of time.

In the provinces least tied to the slave system, emancipation advanced rapidly. In 1884 slavery was abolished in Amazonas and Ceará. Parliament discussed the question once again. Opinion was divided. Among the abolitionists there were those who believed gradual emancipation by prudent means to be the most advisable course while others wanted total and definitive abolition and called for slave revolts as the most effective way of achieving it. For some, such as Nabuco, the cause had to be won in Parliament; for others, such as Patrocinio and Lopes Trovão, it had to be fought in the streets and slave quarters. The activities of the agitators prepared and strengthened the action of the moderate members of Parliament.

In the areas which had the greatest concentration of slaves, such as the sugar-growing region of Campos and the coffee-growing parts of Rio de Janeiro and São Paulo, tension between slave owners and abolitionists grew. In some areas the plantation owners, with weapons in their hands, sought to defend their threatened property and attacked the abolitionists. They established secret clubs and organized a militia. The judges and functionaries who favored the slaves were threatened, the abolitionists persecuted and at times expelled from rural areas. Parliament was flooded with petitions against the abolitionist movement. . . .

Slavery, however, was doomed. From this point onward the disintegration of the slave system proceeded rapidly. An important factor in this process was the mass escape of slaves from the *fazendas* — often observed with indifference by the troops called to recapture them. Clashes increased between the people and the authorities who were trying to guarantee order and suppress the escapes. The plantation owners, unable to prevent the slaves from running away, preferred to free them on the condition that they continue working for their former masters. In this way the plantation owners hoped to be able to count on a labor supply for some years to come. Even so, many were still unable to retain their workers. The slaves, encouraged and led by abolitionists, continued to leave their work and go to other fazendas where they were hired as salaried laborers. The plantation owners, even the most reluctant, saw themselves forced to accept this situation, which was imposed upon them by the tumult which had spread through the rural areas. In São Paulo, the Republican Party, which was largely made up of coffee plantation owners from the western part of the province and which had equivocated for some time on the slavery question, ended up in 1887 by approving a report deciding that the republicans would free their slaves by July 14, 1889. The process of abolition accelerated. Agitation grew. In Parliament in 1887, Nabuco appealed to the army urging it to rebel against the job of catching runaway slaves which was being given to it. Shortly thereafter, the military decided to request Princess Isabel that they be relieved of this dishonorable task.

Slavery was losing its last bases of support. Things had reached such a point that in São Paulo the provincial assembly requested Parliament to carry out abolition. Disorder and turmoil had created a situation in the economic and social life of the province which was dangerous and unbearable.

Upon reopening in 1888, the Chamber of Deputies was faced with a de facto situation: João Alfredo, who had organized a new cabinet at the request of the Princess Regent, announced the introduction of the government's proposal that the immediate and unconditional abolition of slavery be enacted into law.

Only nine deputies voted against the proposal, eight of whom represented the province of Rio de Janeiro. This was the last protest by the agricultural interests of that province, which was the one most affected by abolition.

The law of May 13th [1888, abolishing slavery] was the death blow to an economy already in crisis and meant the loss of status for the majority of coffee plantation owners from the older areas as well as for a large number of Northeastern sugar growers. The areas which had kept their archaic structure and traditional production methods were the ones most affected by the extinction of slavery.

With abolition came a shift in political power. The decadence of the traditional oligarchy which had held power during the Empire and identified itself with the monarchy was accelerated. The social bases of the monarchical system in Brazil were shaken and in the following year the Republic was proclaimed. Economic power became concentrated in the more dynamic areas. In western São Paulo coffee grown in the *terras roxas* produced harvests never before seen. The methods of processing coffee had been improved, railroads had revolutionized the transportation system, and free labor had been tried out. A new social group had been formed — a new oligarchy which would control political power during the First Republic [1889–1930].

After abolition, the dreary prophecies of national catastrophe were not fulfilled. Despite the temporary disorganization of labor and the rapid decline of certain areas, the pace of economic development in Brazil accelerated. With the removal of obstacles to the entry of immigrants, they flowed in large numbers to the newer areas. They thus served the needs of an expanding agriculture and made possible the organization of plantations along more modern and rational lines. However, the conditions of life of the rural workers did not change substantially. The coffee plantations were organized as large exporting units whose income continued to depend in large part on price fluctuations in the international market. Many of the prejudices developed during the period of slavery remained unchanged.

Nevertheless, new possibilities for upward social mobility were opened. The beginning of the urbanization process and the attempts to develop industry, the construction of the railroads, the organizations of credit institutions, and the increase in commerce, all opened up new horizons. At the same time, the expansion of coffee and the moving of the economic frontier westward favored social mobility.

The immigrants took advantage of these new opportunities. The former slaves, marked by the heritage of slavery, were with very few exceptions unable to compete with foreigners in the labor market. The majority continued at their hoes, in a style of life like that they had lived before abolition. Some, attracted by the mirage of the city, gathered in the urban centers where they came to live by their wits, taking on the lowest tasks. Others left the plantations and went into subsistence agriculture. Freedom for them meant the possibility of choosing with whom, when, and how they were going to work and especially the right to do nothing at all. The pattern of life to which they had been accustomed made it difficult for them to adapt to free labor conditions. The Negro was to become a marginal man and develop forms of behavior typical of such marginality.

Since abolition had been more the result of a desire to free Brazil from the problems of slavery than of any wish to emancipate the slaves, the dominant social groups did not concern themselves with the Negro and his integration into a class society. The ex-slave was left to his own fate. His difficulties in adjusting to new conditions were taken as proof of the incapacity of the Negro and of his racial inferiority. It was even said that he was happier as a slave than as a free man since he was incapable of leading his own life.

Contemporaries differed in interpreting abolition. Some, identified with the abolitionist movement, considered it the result of the action of a handful of idealists. Others, more identified with the rural classes, saw abolition as the will of the Emperor and the

Princess Isabel. Some said that the 1888 law had been wise and opportune; others said that it had driven the rural classes into misery. These subjective evaluations interfered with the analysis of the process. Historians studied abolition as an exclusively political phenomenon, marked by judicial stages. They based their studies on the testimony of contemporaries and relied primarily on parliamentary evidence. For some time the ties between the disintegration of the slave system and the economic and social changes at work in Brazil during the second half of the century passed unperceived. Similarly, the relationship between the development of industrial capitalism and the end of slavery as a labor system was given inadequate attention.

Later, starting from viewpoints less compromised by the seignorial view of the world, revision began of the myths which seignorial society elaborated to justify the slave system. Only then was it possible to analyze slavery and the abolitionist movement in a new light.

Abolition represented a stage in the process of the liquidation of Brazil's colonial economy, which involved an extensive revision of the life styles and values of our society. It did not, however, mean a definitive break with the past. The development of coffee cultivation kept the country subject to a new type of colonial domination, tied to international industrial and capitalist trends. The rationalization of production methods, the transition from a seignorial to an entrepreneurial society, the improvement in the standard of living of rural workers, the real emancipation of the country are all part of a process still under way.

8. The Brazilian Slave

ROBERT CONRAD

A mildness and humaneness of character have sometimes been attributed to Brazilian slavery, which are not supported by a close study of nineteenth century documents. It is inaccurate to say that the persons, "men of stone or of iron," in the words of Mendes, who

This material forms a part of the doctoral dissertation of Robert Conrad ("The Struggle for the Abolition of the Brazilian Slave Trade, 1808–1853," Columbia University, 1967). Used by permission of the author.

survived all of the arduous stages . . . from their place of enslave-
ment in Africa to their place of employment in Brazil, were finally
compensated for these harsh experiences by their introduction into
the most humane of slave systems, where they were protected and
loved by wise, patriarchal masters and introduced into an all-
embracing faith. After his long, hard voyage the slave arrived in a
strange and hostile land possessing an economic and legal system,
customs and prejudices not designed for the gratification of his
needs and pleasures, or even favorable to his personal survival. He
was taken to Brazil to work and to produce commodities for export
to Europe, and he was an expendable element in the process. He
was an instrument of production first and a human being and prospective convert to Christianity only incidentally, though the slave
trade and slavery itself were often justified by the conversion from
idolatry to Christianity purported to be a salutary by-product of
slavery. If the slave was treated with human kindness, this was an
incident of chance – an individual human experience – but in the
broader economic and social scheme of things he was a tool, to be
maintained at lowest possible cost and to be replenished cheaply.
He was a beast of burden, an object of investment and commerce,
an item on a balance sheet. The slave represented wealth, transfer-
able property, mortgage collateral, to be traded, auctioned, bar-
gained for, listed as merchandise for sale or rental in the daily
press, shut up like cattle at night, shipped as perishable merchandise at the lowest possible cost, beaten into submissiveness or into
action like a mule or an ox.

Yet it was possible, as Gilberto Freyre has stressed, for the individual slave to cease being a slave, and to rise to a higher level in
the stratified Brazilian society, but it was not for this purpose that
the African was seized and transported thousands of miles to a
foreign country. Eventual liberation was in fact extremely impossible, particularly for the African-born slave who was less likely to
gain his master's sympathy than were those native to Brazil. Individuals did manage to purchase their freedom. Others were liberated
upon the death of their masters. Others were given the opportunity to purchase the freedom of close relatives, as was the case
of one Adrianna who in 1826 was authorized by a letter from her
mistress to become a public beggar for the purpose of purchasing
the freedom of her son Belino, valued at 100,000 [sic]. Many slaves
were freed voluntarily, though often with the provision that they
serve their master until the latter's death. Yet rarely if ever, except

during the last years of Brazilian slavery, in 1887 and 1888, when the slave system was in a state of collapse, were individual manumissions so common that freedmen made up a large portion of the Brazilian population, and even then such manumissions were usually granted with the provision that the newly freed person serve his master for a stated number of years. Even the abolitionist movement failed in its first years to stimulate this form of philanthropy enough to create impressive statistics. Of a total slave population of 1,532,926 registered under the provisions of a law of 1871, only 87,221 were reported to have been freed gratuitously by 1885. Though at first glance this may seem a large number, it was an annual average of about 6,700, or, at best, about one in every 180 slaves in an era when the idea of abolition was beginning to be popular, and was having a truly impressive effect in such provinces as Ceará, Amazonas and Rio Grande do Sul.

Furthermore, during much of the century, voluntary manumissions could be revoked for "ingratitude" if, among other reasons, a freedman was disrespectful to his former master, wounded or laid hands on him, acted in such a manner as to prejudice his business, or failed to comply with commitments made in exchange for his freedom. The Brazilian Legal Code stated that the former master could revoke the liberty of a freedman whom he had released if he committed "some personal ingratitude in his presence, or in his absence, either verbal or in deed." The "ingratitude" of the freedman to his former master was designated a "crime" and his re-enslavement the "punishment" for that crime.

Furthermore, a very large number of persons held as slaves in Brazil were legally free, perhaps at times during the nineteenth century almost as many as half of the persons so held. This was true of hundreds of thousands of Africans brought into the country after 1831 who, by a law of November 7 of that year, were declared free men. It was true of their descendants. It was true of hundreds of Africans removed from slave ships and declared free by British Brazilian Mixed Commissions who subsequently were absorbed into the slave masses, despite Article 179 of the Criminal Code which provided for prison sentences of from three to nine years for reducing a free person to slavery. It was undoubtedly true of hundreds and perhaps thousands of free Negroes, Indians and persons of color whose liberties were not easily protected in rural areas where the power of the landlord was almost total. . . .

The Brazilian slave system was based theoretically on Roman

law and on specific regulations and statutes which had grown out of the Brazilian experience, some of which, when put into practice, eased the conditions under which slaves lived and labored. But most of the customs and legal practices followed in Brazil were fashioned to ensure the owner's control of his human property.

The Brazilian master, in fact, possessed an almost total control over the life and person of the slave, and was in few ways responsible to authority. The slave was legally "a man who has lost the right of property over his person, this right having been transferred into the possession of another person or society, which . . . can dispose of him as with any other asset or property." Theoretically, the master had the right to obtain from his slave the maximum profit possible in exchange for the obligation to feed, clothe and cure him, while remaining ever conscious of the human character of his charge. Like other forms of property, slaves were inheritable. As in the case of domestic animals or other possessions able to reproduce or to give forth fruit, the offspring of the slave women belonged to their masters. By law, persons who stole slaves were subject to the penalties established to punish theft. Furthermore, the Constitution of the Empire, promulgated in 1824, fully guaranteed the right to possess property, without distinctions as to kind, permitting its confiscation only in the event of public need, and then only with full and previous indemnification.

In theory, the slave acquired nothing for himself and everything for his master, though a form of property known as a *peculio* or *peculium*, to use the Latin term, was sometimes allowed to him in a vague practical recognition of the Roman precedent. On some plantations slaves were allowed to cultivate land on Sundays and holidays, both to subsist and to produce a surplus for sale at a local market. Some slaveowners in cities and towns permitted their slaves to hire themselves out to others, paying their masters a certain daily stipend and keeping the remainder for themselves, in this way acquiring a peculio, with which they sometimes were able to purchase their freedom. Yet there was nothing in Brazilian law which guaranteed to the slave the possession of his peculio or the right to make free use of this form of property, and nothing which forced a master to accept a cash payment from his slave in exchange for his freedom. . . .

As a class, Brazilian slaves were always subjected to harsh conditions, but, prior to the abolition of the African slave trade in the mid-nineteenth century, the concern of slaveholders for the health, comfort, and lives of their property was minimized by the ease and cheapness with which they could acquire replacements. No less an authority than a Special Commission of the Brazilian Chamber of Deputies reported on May 12, 1871:

When the importation of African laborers was legal, abundant, and at a low price, the well-being of those cheap machines, whose existence was equivalent to that of a domestic animal, was neglected; all labor was assigned to those workers, and for the whites was reserved dull laziness. With the slaves beginning to grow scarce, and increasing ten-fold in price, they represented considerable capital; from which cause originated much improved care for the conservation of elevated values and of instruments of labor irreplaceable in the same form. . . .

A majority of male slaves lacked the encouragement and comfort which a wife might have contributed in these hard circumstances, and many presumably were denied even normal sexual experiences. Marriages were not much encouraged among slaves, says Perdigão Malheiro, and, at any rate, adult males outnumbered females by perhaps two to one during at least the first half of the nineteenth century. In the captaincy of Minas Gerais in 1786 there were reported to be 116,291 male slaves and only 57,844 females, while the free population was more naturally and harmoniously divided at a little over 94,000 persons of each sex. In the province of Rio de Janeiro in 1840, male slaves outnumbered females by 137,873 to 86,139, while the free population of 183,720 was almost equally divided by sex. This imbalance among the slaves, which was of course generally limited to the adults, was a result simply of the preponderance of males in the cargoes of slave ships, due in turn to the greater usefulness of males in the hard work of plantation production. . . .

The high proportion of males to females, the infrequency of marriages, the impermanence of families, frequent abortions, the lack of care for slave children, and the hard physical conditions of slave life combined to prevent the maintenance of the slave population through natural reproduction. . . .

. . . In 1798 the slave population is reported to have been about 1,582,000. Between 1800 and 1850 probably about 1,600,000 slaves were carried into the country. If, therefore, the population had been maintained through natural reproduction (which admittedly was impossible due to the lack of females), the slaves of Brazil should have numbered very close to three million persons in 1871, the year when a law of the Empire freed all children of slave women born thereafter. Yet only 1,541,819 slaves were registered under the provisions of that same law. In comparison, the slave population of the United States was increasing by half a million slaves per decade in the era before the Civil War.

The key to the slave system, the one thing that made it function, was the whip and the threat it symbolized. The slave knew only obedience, in the words of one Brazilian observer of the servile system. He was passive and mute before his master, "because he fears the physical punishment which is inflicted upon him whenever . . . he tends to leave the straight orbit which is traced out for him." The owner of a plantation in Bahia explained to the Archduke Maximilian that punishment and the threat of punishment enabled a few isolated white men to maintain their "moral ascendancy" in the midst of hundreds of rebellious slaves. . . .

Brazilian slaves reacted to this environment in a number of ways. Most were meek, obeying, working and trying to survive. Others committed suicide. Some killed their masters or their overseers. Others rebelled, and a very large number fled. About 1818, Thomás Antonio da Villanova Portugal described the relationship between the masters and the slaves as "a state of domestic war" which weakened the nation. Half of the energies which should have been applied to the service of the sovereign, complained this Minister in the government of João VI, were diverted to the security of the masters living among their slaves. So common was physical violence on the plantations that in 1829 the Emperor Pedro I, after hearing the opinions of his Council of State, decreed that all sentences pronounced against slaves who took the lives of their masters were to be carried out immediately, "independent of ascending to My Imperial Presence," which summary punishment he justified by "the quite repeated homicides practised by slaves on their own masters, perhaps due to a lack of prompt punishment." In 1833, a project was presented to the Chamber of Deputies to authorize the death penalty for slaves killing their masters, an unpopular solution among men for whom such offenders, however dangerous, constituted assets. To counter this objection, Honório Hermeto Carneiro Leão of Minas Gerais recommended an amendment to reimburse masters from the public treasury for slaves condemned to death, but the project failed to gain support. Finally, however, on June 10, 1835, perhaps as a result of the extraordinarily violent slave revolt of the preceding January in Bahia, the Regency of the Empire decreed the death penalty for all slaves of either sex "who kill by any means whatever, offer poison to, gravely wound or commit any serious physical offense against their master, his wife, descendants or elders . . . , the administrator, overseer, and their wives." . . .

There was much genuine fear among the slaveholding class that their chattels were conspiring to revolt on a grand scale, seize power, and exterminate or drive them from the country, as had once happened, many persons remembered, on the distant island of Haiti. Fear of revolt was particularly great in Bahia and Pernambuco, where slaves were ethnically and linguistically more homogeneous than in the south. Particularly dangerous, from the point of view of the slaveholders, were the Africans of the Mina Coast, the Yorubas, Ewes, Hausas and Fulah or Fulani, all influenced to a greater or lesser degree by Islam, and commonly brought to Bahia in the early nineteenth century. Possessing organized societies and elected chiefs wherever they came together in sufficient numbers, these slaves were reputed "remarkable for their habits of order, their serious and dignified deportment, their economy, their prevision, and their sullen courage."

Many slave revolts, in fact, erupted, some planned and some spontaneous, and many unsuccessful conspiracies came to light, particularly in the north, where Moslem slaves or Africans influenced by that religion were responsible for most of the frequent incidents of insurrection which occurred in Bahia in the first half of the nineteenth century, ending in the conflict of January 24, 1835, in which slaves clashed with their masters in the city streets. . . .

Far more common than revolts, which were dangerous, hard to organize, and unlikely to succeed, was the simple alternative of fleeing the master's tyrannical presence. Thousands of offers to reward the capture and return of runaway slaves appearing daily in hundreds of Brazilian newspapers over a period of six decades are convincing proof that flight was the slave's most common solution to his predicament.

The problem of runaway slaves placed a permanent claim on the energies and assets of the slaveholding class. The loss of the slave's labor for weeks, months, or even permanently was merely the first and most obvious injury arising from his departure. Advertisements and rewards for his capture and return, the salaries of policemen, slavehunters and judges paid from public revenues, fees for punishment and cure, or lodging at the local jail, outlays for arms, the loss of livestock and other assets in raids by bands of fugitives, and the immeasurable toll of insecurity and human lives were an immense drain on the assets, patience and comfort of the slaveholding class as long as they maintained the slave system. Few wealthy owners were without runaways listed on their slave rolls, and even the slaves of the State and of the Imperial Family, presumably better placed than most, sought recourse in flight from their slave status. Of forty-seven slaves, including children, listed on the rolls of the Imperial Plantation of Santa Cruz and at the Imperial Iron Foundry of São João de Ipanema in 1844, twelve, or slightly more than twenty-five per cent, had opted to depart without formal permission. . . .

Slaves abandoned their masters for a precarious and difficult life in the jungles and mountains on the outskirts of large cities, and near plantations and other settled places where alone they could acquire certain necessities through purchase, barter, theft or armed raids. In the 1820's the major cities of Brazil were virtually surrounded by such clusters of refugees, established in small or larger settlements called *quilombos,* preying on plantations and travelers. Efforts to destroy them were often without success, though long campaigns were sometimes waged against them. . . .

An objective comparison of the condition of Brazilian slaves with that of their counterparts in the plantation colonies of other European nations would probably show that in some ways their situation was better and in other ways it was worse, but it would not turn up a numerous class of enlightened and kindly masters surrounded by docile and happy slaves. It would show that a comparatively mild and permissive ideology of race in Brazil was balanced by rigid and cruel class concepts injurious to all men of low rank, to Indians, to slaves, and to poor free men, white or black. It would reveal in Brazil, as in the other colonies or countries where plantation slavery existed, a system of unremunerated forced labor based on coercion and punishment producing good things for the tables of Europe and North America and creating in its victims the need to take retaliatory or compensatory measures for relief, revenge, and self-preservation.

In the early nineteenth century this system, which dominated the life of the nation, came under serious attack for the first time in its long existence, principally from abroad, but was found to possess sufficient vigor to survive criticism and opposition for almost the entire century, while less formidable slave systems fell apart and dissolved. Like the mangrove trees of Brazilian coastal swamps, slavery had thrived in the climate and thrown out roots. Its eradication would require persistent effort and substantial changes in the economic and social environment which made it flourish.

Section V

The Chilean Revolution of 1891:
The Beginning of National Frustration

For a civil war that cost 10,000 lives and well over $100 million, the successful revolution by the "Congressional" Party against President José Manuel Balmaceda of Chile has not been given much space in the history books. This colorful, dynamic leader had been elected president at a time when the Chilean victory over Bolivia and Peru in the War of the Pacific (1879–1883) had induced exuberant confidence in the country, as Fredrick B. Pike of the University of Notre Dame explains (Reading V.1). But few of the politically powerful Chileans were willing to follow Balmaceda in his plans to stimulate economic expansion by temporary deficit spending. The conservative moneyed class was scandalized, mounted a successful attack, and forced him to leave office in August, 1891. In September he sought asylum in the Argentine Legation and there committed suicide.

Seventy-five years later historians still dispute the figure of Balmaceda and the "origins, character, and consequences of the revolution" as Harold Blakemore, secretary of the Institute of Latin American Studies of the University of London, makes clear (Reading V.3). Dr. Blakemore is in part replying to the largely economic interpretation of the Chilean Marxist Hernán Ramírez Necochea (Reading V.2), but he also provides a sober and balanced view of this complicated event.

Though controversy exists on the Revolution itself, no one denies that Balmaceda's defeat ushered in the dismal period of Chilean history known as the pseudoparliamentary regime. During this period the landed aristocracy and the rising middle classes joined forces: "upper and middle classes, old and new or potential aristocrats, rural and urban sectors united in regarding the lower classes, wherever found, as fair prey."[1] This was also the time of a dramatic population shift to the cities, Santiago alone increasing 52 per cent from 1885 to 1907. The depressed rural workers who rushed to the cities found urban conditions as miserable as life on the great estates, with the added disadvantage that they no longer had patrons to afford them some protection. Thus were built up the explosive social forces that were brought to the surface by Arturo Alessandri in 1920, whose election began the long period of economic and social uncertainty in which Chile still finds herself almost half a century later. If Balmaceda had won, Professor Pike suggests, Chile might have escaped "many of the horrors of the social problem that today threatens stability and progress." But he adds that Chile could have put into effect Balmaceda's program only by ignoring the nation's tradition of political freedom. The real question, he believes, is why those who overthrew him were so indifferent to the nation's welfare.[2]

Another significant result of the 1891 revolution lies in inter-American relations. The congressionalists resented Washington's apparent preference for the "dictator" during the civil war, and they considered United States Minister Patrick Egan both incompetent and unfair to them. A reservoir of bitterness thus formed, which helps to explain the nasty incident that occurred on October 16, 1891, when American sailors on shore leave from the *Baltimore* engaged in a free-for-all with Chileans in the tenderloin district of Valparaiso. The *"Baltimore* Incident" gets short shrift in the work that was for many years a standard authority on United States relations with Latin America. President Benjamin Harrison represented a new Manifest Destiny spirit and his paramount purpose was strengthening political and commercial relations with Latin America, but Professor Bemis states that he was "diverted by an absurd war crisis with the distant republic of Chile arising from a murderous mob attack on United States sailors on shore leave in Valpa-

---

[1] Fredrick B. Pike, "Aspects of Class Relations in Chile, 1850–1960," *Hispanic American Historical Review,* XLIII (1963), p. 21.

[2] Pike, *Chile and the United States, 1880–1962: The Emergence of Chile's Social Crisis and the Challenge to United States Diplomacy* (Notre Dame: University of Notre Dame Press, 1963), p. 46.

raiso."[3] The Chilean judge who investigated the case had an entirely different explanation, and the standard history of Chile gives a more temperate and more accurate account of this unlovely episode in Chilean-United States relations.[4] President Harrison blustered out an ultimatum on January 25, 1892, although the affair had been practically settled by diplomats earlier; Chile agreed to pay an indemnity to the families of the two sailors who died. But the Chileans did not accept this humiliation easily:

> To this day, the majority of Chileans can whip themselves into an anti-Yankee frenzy by recalling the martyred *Teniente* Carlos Peña. The legend of Carlos Peña — and despite the wide credence it enjoys, it is pure legend — has it that final settlement of the "Baltimore" affair necessitated the sending of a Chilean warship either to Valparaíso or San Francisco, California, depending on the version, to strike its colors in atonement. Lieutenant Peña volunteered to perform the onerous task of actually lowering his country's flag. As the standard touched the deck, he turned to the band and directed it to play the Chilean national anthem. Then, clutching the flag to his breast, he shot himself through the heart.[5]

President Harrison may have taken his high-handed action to brighten his image as a stalwart defender of United States citizens everywhere as preparation for the 1892 elections, as many in Chile believed. Others judged that the United States was announcing to Latin America and the world that the Colossus was now supreme in hemisphere affairs, as Secretary of State Richard Olney stated during the 1895 Venezuela boundary controversy.[6]

One more aspect of this apparently minor Chilean Revolution of 1891 has been obscured because United States writers tend to emphasize United States relations with individual Latin American countries rather than the more complicated story of relations among these nations themselves. Robert N. Burr has begun to repair this neglect,[7] which may be partly explained by the fact that Latin American nations do not normally allow access to their diplomatic archives. As Bryce Wood remarked at the conclusion of his detailed examination of armed conflicts in Latin America from 1932 to 1942:

---

[3] Samuel Flagg Bemis, *The Latin American Policy of the United States* (New York: Harcourt, Brace, 1943), p. 126. Apparently Professor Bemis did not use any Chilean sources for this episode.

[4] Luis Galdames, *History of Chile*, Tr. by I. J. Cox (Chapel Hill: University of North Carolina Press, 1941), pp. 402–403.

[5] Pike, *Chile and the United States*, p. 81.

[6] *Ibid.*, p. 82.

[7] Robert N. Burr, *By Reason or Force: Chile and the Balancing of Power in South America, 1830–1855* (Berkeley: University of California Press, 1965).

" 'History is too important to be left to historians' appears to be the motto of diplomats and officials of foreign offices who jealously guard the fundamental records."[8]

Intense diplomatic activity went on throughout 1891 and 1892. Bolivia and Peru, still smarting from their dramatic defeat by Chile in the recent War of the Pacific, helped to defeat President Balmaceda. Chile received accurate reports from Washington and European capitals, and Argentina naturally followed the *Baltimore* incident with keen interest, since her relations with Chile have often been tense. In December, 1892, the "rumor began to circulate in high Chilean government circles that Argentina had offered the United States an offensive-defensive alliance" in case war came between Chile and the United States. As lately as 1963 Professor Pike, discussing this rumor, wrote: "Never reliably confirmed, and indeed quite effectively denied, these rumors nonetheless were, and still are widely believed in Chile."[9]

At just about the time Professor Pike's book was published, however, a Chilean diplomatic historian, José Miguel Barros had uncovered — not in Argentina or Chilean archives, but in the National Archives in Washington, D.C. — proof that the rumored Argentine offer to the United States was actually made, through a confidential despatch to the Secretary of State by the United States Minister in Buenos Aires on January 25, 1892.[10] The Minister's subsequent cable of January 30 included the core of the message:

Confidential. Argentine Minister for Foreign Affairs frankly assures me full moral support for United States against Chile. Is ready to declare publicly if I ask this. Indicates how Argentine Republic cattle and supplies to us at Antofagasta in six days. Says Prussian Major passed by here twenty-four last month in order to mount guns in the harbors Valparaiso, Iquique, Talcahuano. Owing to trouble last week in Argentine-Chilean boundary commission Argentine fleet moving; cruiser "Twenty-fifth May" went south on Wednesday. Relations between countries very critical; have

---

[8] Bryce Wood, *The United States and Latin American Wars, 1932–1942* (New York: Columbia University Press, 1966), p. 394.

[9] Pike, *Chile and the United States*, p. 84.

[10] José Miguel Barros, "Don Estanislao Zeballos y el incidente del 'Baltimore,' " *Mapocho*, I (Santiago de Chile: Biblioteca Nacional, 1963), No. 2, pp. 218–224. Barros had previously published a monograph on the incident, *Apuntes para la historia diplomática de Chile. El caso del Baltimore* (Santiago: Universidad de Chile, 1950).

In the *Mapocho* article he translates the confidential despatch of the Minister, John R. G. Pitkin, of January 25, 1892, as well as his cable of January 30. Both documents are in the National Archives, Washington, D.C. (Microcopy 69, Roll 24).

advised admiral of the [United States] fleet Montevideo also concerning
the full artillery, cavalry, infantry armament of Chile confidentially
described to me by the Minister of Foreign Affairs. Will you authorize
acknowledgment favorable to perfect close relations.[11]

The Argentine proposal to join forces with the United States
against Chile if war came is easily understood because of the
strained Argentine-Chilean relations over the years. But Argentina
had also just begun her vigorous anti-United States campaign at
the first Pan American Congress in 1889.[12] More revelations and a
fuller understanding of this episode and many others of intra-
American relations will surely result when diplomatic archives in
Latin America are open to historians.

The Chilean Revolution of 1891, when seen in all its ramifica-
tions, strikingly illustrates the complexities of a single historical
incident and the difficulties historians encounter in gaining access to
the facts. A study of the defeat of President Balmaceda by the
Congressionalists shows the limitations of the purely economic interpretation of the civil war and also helps to illuminate Chile's
subsequent domestic development, Chilean-United States relations, and Argentine-Chilean rivalry.

11 My text comes from a microfilm copy of the original in the National Archives,
Washington, D.C. (Microcopy 69, Roll 24).
12 Thomas F. McGann, "Argentina at the First Pan-American Conference,"
Inter-American Economic Affairs, I (1947), No. 2, pp. 21–53.

A. Background of the Revolution

1. An Era of Exuberant
Confidence

FREDRICK B. PIKE

Chileans Respond to Signs of National Greatness — The Treaty
of Ancón, signed on October 20, 1883, was a milestone in Chilean

From *Chile and the United States, 1880–1962: The Emergence of Chile's Social
Crisis and the Challenge to United States Diplomacy* by Fredrick B. Pike (Notre
Dame, Ind.: University of Notre Dame Press, 1963), pp. 31–46, *passim.* Re-
printed by permission.

history, and the culminating point in a series of military victories that was nothing short of fantastic. At the outset of the War of the Pacific in 1879, the Chilean army of 2,400 had been pitted against 13,200 Peruvian and 3,232 Bolivian troops. (The Bolivian forces included over one thousand officers.) And yet, within four years, Chile had humiliated her combined adversaries, had vastly expanded her national boundaries, had established her sovereignty over nearly 25,000 new subjects, and, most important, had acquired control over rich nitrate deposits, destined to constitute the principal source of national income for the next three to four decades. While all of this was transpiring, ordinary governmental services had not been interrupted. Between 1880 and 1883, for example, the number of public schools increased by eighty-three, and the ratio of schools to students changed from 1:217 to 1:170.

Traditional procedures of civilian government had proved their merits by maintaining domestic development and tranquility while simultaneously providing competent direction to the military effort. By the end of the war, then, the political institutions that had been evolving since 1830 were more firmly established than ever before. Because of this, newly appearing military heroes had little opportunity of capitalizing on war-won glory to gain political dominance. Instead, the army was content to find its full measure of satisfaction in its professional accomplishments, while leaving politics to the civilians. The sense of military professionalism was enhanced by the arrival in 1886 of a German training mission led by Emil Körner. The tremendous economic boom touched off by the successful war also helped to stifle any overflow of military activity into the political sphere. Expanding economic opportunities existed on so vast a scale that ambitious middle-class elements did not have to turn to military careers as a means of gaining security and perhaps an entry into politics. The military remained, therefore, strictly military, and Chile escaped one of the worst impediments to political maturity that has beset the majority of other Latin-American republics. . . .

The economic development that accompanied and followed the War of the Pacific was so remarkable that Marxist writers feel justified in alleging that Chile's great military adventure was instigated by self-seeking capitalists in order to bring their country out of the business stagnation that had begun in 1878. However absurd this allegation, the truth is that the war did provide Chile with the economic means for coming of age. Manuel Guillermo

Carmona, Chief of the Commercial Statistics Office, sensed this fact when in 1881 he observed that economic advances had been no less spectacular than those of the Chilean army in Peru. Three years later the Central Office of Statistics noted that the total value of general commerce — exports and imports — had soared to over 129 million pesos, compared to roughly 83 million in 1875. With only 5.4 per cent of the Latin-American population in 1887, Chile conducted 13 per cent of the entire area's commerce and enjoyed the highest per-capita income of any republic south of the Rio Grande. More surprising still, the per-capita value of exports was higher than that of the United States. Bank deposits also reflected the economic upsurge. Approximately 60 million pesos on the eve of the war, they had risen to double this amount by 1890. A bright economic future seemed assured, and the claims of the Society for Industrial Development (*Sociedad de Fomento Fabril*) that Chile could soon be largely self-sufficient even in the production of finished products seemed perfectly reasonable to many of the nation's capitalists.

The federal government shared with private capitalists in the spiralling national prosperity. Treasury income rose from 65 to 75 million pesos of eighteen pence between 1880 and 1890. For this last year, nearly 15 million pesos of the national budget were allotted to public works. And in the decade following the outbreak of the War of the Pacific, the value of nitrate exports jumped from 25 to 80 million pesos. Increasingly, the government came to depend on nitrate export taxes for its revenue. In 1880, export taxes produced only 4.7 per cent of government revenue, while in 1890 they accounted for over 46 per cent of the national treasury's income. . . .

With a background of military victory, an outer show of political stability and representative civilian government, and head-turning economic progress, Chileans came to regard themselves as something of a master race in Latin America. An editorial in *El Ferrocarril* averred in 1880 that Chile's military victories were winning for it the attention and admiration of the world, and would soon attract armies of immigrants and guarantee the realization of a glorious destiny. Military success also called forth heightened pride in political institutions, as various newspapers suggested that the heroic feats would have been impossible without the stability of legal and constitutional administration which Chile, alone among Latin-American nations, had known how to achieve.

Minister of Interior (and soon-to-be-president) Domingo Santa María noted with justifiable pride in mid-1880 that it had not been necessary to alter constitutional order to achieve military triumph: "The integrity of the legal regime, preserved amidst such exceptional circumstances, is a source of glory for the republic, and an eloquent testimony to the patriotism of the Chilean people." A little later, a patriotic writer noted with approval that Argentina was beginning to advance toward stability by emulating Chile's political institutions. "By developing along these lines," he declared, "Argentina has now attained the right to aspire to friendship with Chile on the basis of equality."

Other observers tended to attribute success to the superior virtues of the Chilean nature. A newspaper editorial stated: "Our triumphs are owing to the fact that . . . we are a people accustomed to overcoming grave difficulties by our habits of great industry and labor." In a different paper, an article concluded: "It is reserved to Chile, land of peaceful habits, incessant labor, humanitarian sentiments and tranquil disposition . . . to give to our sister republics an example of what patriotism and dedication to work can accomplish." Then, there was the editorial that affirmed: "Chile, through the effort and labor expended since the attainment of independence, has achieved a reputation of virtue and industry not equalled by another country of this continent." The all-pervasive spirit of self-satisfaction ushered in during the early 1880's was probably best expressed in the Valparaíso daily, *El Mercurio*: "Chile's greatness is now immense and all other nations acknowledge it. . . . How could its glory be greater? Is there any other American nation that has accomplished so much?"

Combined with pride in past attainments was an unbounded confidence in the future, and a conviction that Chile was well on the way to becoming one of the world's great powers. This attitude was in the 1880's as much a part of the national outlook as was ever Manifest Destiny in the United States. Unfortunately, added to the natural exuberance and optimism of a young republic whose accomplishments provided a legitimate source of pride and emotional nationalism was a view of race that would, as the years passed, establish itself as one of the more significant features of upper- and middle-class attitudes. In more than one of the contemporary editorials may be found at least the implication that Bolivia and Peru were mere Indian pygmies trying to stand in the way of white Chile's destiny. Suggestions were further advanced that racially heterogeneous nations in the American Hemisphere could never aspire to the heights which Chile was destined to attain. Journalists also ascribed the allegedly scandalous conduct of Peruvian leader Nicolás Piérola to his Indian blood, and described a Peruvian general as a typical Indian: false, dissimulating, ostentatious, and fatuous.

Some Signs of Economic Imbalance — The spirit of the 1880's was hardly conducive to reform, and the warnings of a few concerned observers went largely unheeded. A blistering editorial denouncing the slum conditions in which urban lower classes lived, and demanding that something be done about cleaning streets so that city dwellers would not have to breathe polluted air, produced no response. Equally ignored was a plea that adulteration of food and liquor be halted.

Still, for those willing to probe beneath the surface, there were disturbing indications that not all was well, not even economically. The Society for Industrial Development warned that nitrate prosperity was ephemeral, and that only industrialization could guarantee the nation's future economic strength. In 1884, Manuel Aristides Zañartu, later to serve as Minister of Treasury under President Balmaceda, published the first volume of *Luis Ríos*, in which he preached the need for economic nationalism, urged especially that tariffs be enacted to encourage new industries, and cautioned the nation against merely living off its nitrate wealth. From still other sources came essentially the same message, advising economic diversification, particularly industrialization, and pleading that Chile encourage technical education rather than cling to the educational goals of the Renaissance. In a country that still suffered from an illiteracy rate of 65 per cent, and in which an increasing urban proletariat would inevitably become disillusioned and restive unless provided with expanding economic opportunities, there were ample grounds for this advice, regardless of how little impact it created.

A few writers also grew wary of increasing British influence in the nitrate industry, and admonished their countrymen not to let their economic future fall into the hands of foreign monopolies. Even by the early 1880's, British financiers were actively initiating the process which by the middle of the next decade would place them in control of some 43 per cent of Chile's nitrate capital. . . .

Chile's most eminent economist and long-time champion of

laissez faire, Miguel Cruchaga Montt, grew alarmed about the situation. In the pages of the *Revista Económica,* which he had founded in 1886, he began to argue for national control over nitrates. His crusade was short-lived, for he died the year after founding his distinguished economics journal. But the cause was soon taken up by Francisco Valdés Vergara, one of Chile's best economic writers in the late nineteenth and early twentieth centuries. In 1889 Valdés published *La crisis salitrera y las medidas que se proponen para remediarlo.* The book denounced foreign monopolistic control over nitrates, and called for government action to end it.

The attention of other economic worriers was fixed upon the currency problem. Some of them found ominous the fact that even in a decade unrivaled in national history for its prosperity, the foreign debt increased from 93 to nearly 125 million pesos. Furthermore, in the course of the War of the Pacific, the government had directly issued 28 million pesos in paper money, and this mildly inflationist step helped produce a decline in the peso's international exchange rate. The money problem became more severe after 1885, when the world prices for such Chilean exports as copper, wheat, guano, and nitrates declined appreciably. The Santa María administration (1881–1886) began to plan for retiring paper money, and for converting to metallic currency. The matter was still under discussion, however, when the Balmaceda regime was installed in 1886. . . .

Internal Dissension and Civil War — Background Considerations. Inaugurated as president at the age of forty-six, the tall, slender, and handsome Balmaceda was descended from the colonial aristocracy. As a young politician he had associated in the *Club de la Reforma* with such advocates of change as Lastarria and Matta, and the Gallo and Arteaga Alemparte brothers. He had been influenced by the political ideas of such French thinkers as Rousseau and Montesquieu. For his economic concepts, however, Balmaceda turned away from the classically liberal French school as popularized in Chile by Juan Gustavo Courcelle-Seneuil, and took to heart the state interventionist theories of Georg Friedrich List. The new president desired greatness for his nation with a fervor matched by few of the renowned nationalistic patriots of the 1880's. But he was remarkable for his times in assuming that a splendid future for Chile was not inevitable. In order to realize the full national potential, he was convinced that Chileans must critically analyze their situation, reject many traditional procedures, carefully plan for the future, and be prepared to make greater sacrifices for the nation's welfare.

While unquestionably a man of unusual vision and patriotic zeal, Balmaceda seemed excessively theatrical to many of Chile's aristocrats — men who have always been suspicious of spectacular, colorful, out-of-the-ordinary, and even unusually talented personalities. Balmaceda was also an extreme egotist, who, as his ideas encountered opposition, came to look upon himself more and more as the only man who truly understood what was best for his country. If he could not sell his ideas by persuasion, then he would enforce them. Power became more and more an obsession with the president, and to maintain it he appeared willing to utilize almost any expedient. It is possible that many of the most noteworthy measures he supported in the last period of his rule were not the products of a rational projection of principle so much as they were desperate attempts to gain support from some new quarter as the leaders of the traditional political and pressure groups tended more and more to desert him.

Politically Motivated Opposition to Balmaceda. Increasingly restive during the past several administrations, the Conservatives under the Balmaceda regime determined to make an all-out effort to end what for them had become an intolerable situation. They rallied behind a plan advanced by Manuel José Irarrázaval for establishing a political structure based on autonomous municipalities. Irarrázaval, a great idealist and something of a utopianist, apparently sincerely believed that autonomous communities constituted the best means by which every member of society might most fully develop his full, God-given, human potential. Many other Conservatives probably regarded the plan simply as a convenient method of curbing the power of a central government that had become unfriendly, and of utilizing whatever influence the Church still maintained on the local level to establish a political system aimed essentially at protecting the interests of the Conservatives. Regardless of their sources of motivation, Conservatives were enraged by Balmaceda's evident desire to augment, rather than to diminish, presidential authority. And remembering Balmaceda as a one-time champion of anticlerical legislation, Conservatives distrusted the conciliatory attitude toward the Church that he adopted upon becoming president.

Through its Central Committee (*Junta Central*), the Radical Party in 1889 announced its opposition to the strong-president ambitions of Balmaceda: ". . . our system of government is, and ought constitutionally to be, parliamentary, or the government of the cabinet." As with the Conservatives in their support of the autonomous community, so also with the Radicals in their espousal of parliamentarism, motivation was highly varied. Some Radicals thought only of political expediency. In recent years, their party had made notable headway in local and provincial politics. If presidential intervention should end, the party could certainly elect a considerable bloc of national legislators. But so long as an absolutist president out of sympathy with their cause maintained power, the political future for the Radicals seemed bleak. Other Radicals, and Manuel Antonio Matta was certainly one of them, were devoted to parliamentary government because of principles and ideals, convinced that it was the most perfect of all political forms.

The Liberal Alliance [which had supported Balmaceda in the 1886 election] was itself split by personality issues, with several factions supporting the political aspirations of different men. Nearly all of the factions were outraged by what they considered presidential interference when Balmaceda began to groom his close collaborator and cabinet member Enrique Salvador Sanfuentes to succeed to the chief executive office. Nor were they mollified when Sanfuentes withdrew his candidacy upon accepting a new cabinet post, that of Minister of Interior, in 1890. The time had come, felt most politicians, to end once and for all presidential violation of the free electoral process.

A new political organization that appeared upon the scene in 1887, the Democrat Party (*Partido Demócrata*) distrusted all previously existing parties, and doubted that Balmaceda actually had the national good at heart. Led by the lawyer Malaquías Concha, who was concerned over the decline in purchasing power of urban labor income during the 1880's, the Democrats demanded solution to what they described as deplorable social problems. They criticized the Conservatives as representing landlord interests, the Nationals as being only concerned with bankers and the higher bureaucrats, the Liberals as defenders exclusively of landowners and mine operators, and the Radicals as the champions solely of southern *latifundistas*, northern mine owners, and the professional sectors. Their charge that Balmaceda did not really worry over the worsening plight of the laborers gained substance when during the massive 1890 strike in Iquique the president sent national troops to disperse the aroused workers. The resultant violence led to some three thousand casualties.

To mounting political opposition, Balmaceda responded by ruling in an ever more arbitrary and authoritarian manner. He was condemned by every major newspaper — excepting the government-published *La Nación* — ranging from the Conservative *El Estandarte Católico* to the anticlerical *El Ferrocarril*, when in early 1890 he began to purge government agencies of his critics. "Is this political persecution madness, or is it crime?" asked *La Epoca*. "The president [is] trampling on constitutional provisions . . . ," charged *La Patria* in Valparaíso. And in the same city, *El Heraldo* concluded that the president no longer deserved the benefit of the doubt which the paper had previously extended him. Opposition intensified during the remainder of the year. *El Ferrocarril* charged that the presidential message of June 1 did not contain adequate guarantees for free elections. When a few days later the president announced he would retain his cabinet despite lack of parliamentary confidence in it, *El Independiente*, *La Tribuna*, *La Libertad Electoral*, and *La Epoca* all joined with *El Ferrocarril* in charging tyranny. Even before this, the Santiago press had delighted in running quotations made by Balmaceda when he had served from 1881 to 1882 as Minister of Foreign Relations to the effect that ministers must obey the wishes of congress.

Writing to his Foreign Office in late 1890, Baron von Gutschmid, the Imperial Germany envoy in Chile, observed that Balmaceda's opponents included the most honored members of all political parties and even the hero of the War of the Pacific, General Manuel Baquedano. The Baron noted also the cool reception Balmaceda had received in Valparaíso, Talcahuano, and Concepción during a recently concluded tour of the South, and reported signs of active hostility upon the president's return to Santiago. The Chilean populace, stated von Gutschmid, was making apparent how ". . . little disposed it was to support the authoritarian internal policies that obtain at present."

On January 1, 1891, Balmaceda delivered a "Manifesto to the Nation," declaring that as the national congress would not cooperate with him and refused to approve his budget, he would proceed to enact the provisions of his proposed budget, even in the absence of constitutionally required legislative approval. The president noted that elections for national deputies were only sixty days away, at which time the electorate would have the chance to endorse or repudiate his policies. But the opposition, perhaps not anticipating honest elections, would not wait. On January 7, against government orders, the fleet in Valparaíso weighed anchor and headed north, under the command of Jorge Montt. Accompanying the rebelling naval forces were Waldo Silva, vice-president of the Senate, and Ramón Barros Luco, president of the Chamber of Deputies. The now openly insurgent "congressionalists" declared their opposition to the president and called for the restoration of constitutional government. Balmaceda responded by promptly raising army salaries 50 per cent to assure loyalty. The civil war had begun.

Economically Motivated Opposition to Balmaceda. In his January 1 "Manifesto," Balmaceda had justified his position on the grounds that chronic ministerial crises resulting from legislative interference in the province of the executive made stable political administration an absolute impossibility. In this appraisal, the harassed president overlooked the real crux of the matter. To a large extent his quarrel with the opposition rested upon economic rather than political considerations. Once he was removed, his successors agreed among themselves on basic economic and social policies. This being the case, despite all manner of cabinet turnovers, they did at least succeed in providing their country with political stability.

In essence, the Balmaceda approach to Chilean material development rested on a belief in the necessity of an expanding economy under government stimulus and supervision. The president apparently was undismayed by temporary deficit spending and forced currency expansion, feeling confident that the inflationist tendencies of these measures could be more than absorbed by the economic expansion resulting from a deliberate pump-priming process. These fiscal beliefs also led Balmaceda toward a policy of government control over banking activities. In addition, he insisted adamantly that nitrate income be used to finance special national development projects, and that the costs of ordinary government administration and services be paid for by a series of additional internal taxes.

The major obstacle to implementation of these policies was that the moneyed classes accepted laissez faire as the inevitable law of economic progress — a law that could not be artificially stimulated or hurried by government manipulation. They were scandalized by the president's notions. Had not economic individualism and national budgets that were generally balanced resulted already in remarkable prosperity? What need was there to experiment with new expedients? Why not use nitrate export taxes to finance ordinary government administration and services, avoid all measures of planned expansion, and allow the upper classes to go tax-free? In the final analysis, what country riding the crest of an apparent boom, with a small population, with no bitter social cleavage yet apparent, with vast, newly-opened frontier lands, with the prospect of further discovery and exploitation of natural resources, would seriously consider embarking, as Balmaceda urged, upon a policy of centralized social and economic planning? The times seemed to suggest quite the opposite approach. Anarchy, wildly liberal ideas, and economic disruption had, at the inception of the Portales period, demanded that social and political leaders curb their individualism and cooperate in a tightly centralistic and often arbitrary administrative structure. Now, the wealth of the 1880's, combined with political stability so firm that it had withstood even the challenge of war, seemed to permit at last a loosening of the reins of government, and a certain license for individuals and regions to conduct affairs as they saw fit, and if they chose, simply to luxuriate in indolence.

If Balmaceda had succeeded in imposing his economic policies, there is little question that Chile would in the twentieth century have been in vastly better condition. The nation might even have escaped many of the horrors of the social problems that today threaten stability and progress. But Chile could have implemented the Balmaceda program only by crushing genuinely precious qualities in the national tradition: regard for political freedom and liberty of expression, fundamental revulsion for dictatorship, and distrust of self-proclaimed saviours. Balmaceda fell because the 10 per cent or less of the population that constituted an effective body politic would not accept dictatorial imposition of basically distasteful policies. The vast majority of Chileans who were politically inarticulate served merely as uninterested spectators of the political drama.

The central question of modern Chilean history is not why anything so inevitable as the fall of Balmaceda occurred. Rather, it is why those who overthrew him, many of them high-minded and self-sacrificing, were able to do no more than to lead their country into a period of apathetic drifting. Because of the palpable failure of those who overthrew and followed him in power, Balmaceda's vague and often chameleon program, which evolved in *ad hoc* manner toward extremes of central planning, was assumed by a later generation of Chileans to have borne the stamp of genius.

B. Interpretations of Historians Today

2. Balmaceda's Economic Ideas Differed Fundamentally from Those of the Bankers, Businessmen, and Landowners

HERNÁN RAMÍREZ NECOCHEA

The Motives of the Anti-Balmaceda Opposition and the Promoters of the Civil War — In order to better understand the events that provoked the civil war, it would undoubtedly be useful to determine the motives that induced the anti-Balmaceda opposition to assume the attitude which they sustained with so much enthusiasm and fervor. It is also of singular importance to identify the promoters of this violent disturbance. In other words, it would be helpful to know whether the purpose expressed publicly on numerous occasions corresponded in truth to a solid political conscience, or whether purely circumstantial factors induced the opposition to uphold ideological postulates which were pleasing to public opinion but which concealed other intentions. One would like to know, moreover, whether it was the entire nation that rose against the President, or merely certain sectors that had special reasons for doing so.

In dealing with these questions of supreme importance for determining the true character of the civil war, a perspicacious student of our political history, Alberto Edwards, affirms that because Balmaceda wanted to consolidate the principle of authority, he had "to clash with the traditional ruling class of Chile." He therefore concludes that in the struggle between Congress and Balmaceda,

From *La guerra civil de 1891: Antecedentes económicos* by Hernán Ramírez Necochea (Santiago: Editora Austral, 1951), pp. 206–220, *passim.* Reprinted by permission. A second, revised edition has appeared under a different title: *Balmaceda y la contrarrevolucion de 1891* (Santiago: Editorial Universitaria, 1958).

not only were purely doctrinal questions at stake, but also the desire of certain groups to impede the establishment of an authority which would be superior to theirs and which would have an orientation different from their own. . . .

Ricardo Salas Edwards, author of one of the most thorough works on the civil war, writes: "The business sectors and the productive classes of the country viewed with satisfaction the fall of a defective political regime that did not reflect the true interests of the nation, even though this was accomplished by extra-legal means." This author immediately adds that the supporters of Congress included "a very large bloc of parties and influential intellectuals, who were allied with the principal businessmen and land-owners." . . .

Finally, an English journalist, Maurice Hervey, in an interesting book published in England in 1892 with the title *Dark Days in Chile: An Account of the Revolution of 1891*, indicates that the traditionalist and affluent classes of Chile, in particular the land-owners and the bankers, were opposed to Balmaceda. He adds: "By the large foreign element resident in Chile, Balmaceda was regarded with very general aversion, and more especially by the British. He was known to entertain many views by no means consistent with the uninterrupted advancement of foreign interests."

These opinions of relatively impartial authors or of definite supporters of Congress and the antecedents presented in previous chapters permit us to reach the following conclusions:

1. Balmaceda's political acts gave to Congress only the ostensible motive — that is, the pretext — for creating the conflict with the Executive.

2. The ambitions of the individuals and groups which dominated the political parties and Congress were the cause of the conflict.

3. The following elements acted in opposition to Balmaceda: the great land owning families and the native and foreign bankers, industrialists, businessmen, and miners. With them were allied the majority of the clergy, as well as some intellectuals and politicians whose socio-economic interests coincided with those of the landed aristocracy, the native plutocrats, and the foreign capitalists.

The participation of these elements in the promotion and direction of the civil war can be seen even more clearly in the financing of the rebel forces. In effect, until the end of May 1891, the Junta of Government in Iquique financed its expenditures with the help of Chilean and foreign capitalists. "The expenditures made in Europe, during the first months of the revolution, for the cause of Congress were taken care of by us (Matte and Ross) with funds of the Bank of A. Edwards & Co. Despite the size of the remittances sent from Iquique beginning in May 1891, they not only failed to cover these outlays but they did not take care of necessities." It should be recalled that the bankers Edwards, Matte, and Ross were among the promoters of the civil war; later they were its beneficiaries. Nevertheless, they did not give a single cent to the cause they defended so disinterestedly. In the report cited above, we find the following paragraph, which confirms this fact: "We then resolved to open an account on the Delegation of Congress for the expenditures we would make in its name; it was to reimburse us as soon as its financial situation permitted, or once a legal regime had been established in Chile." Contributions similar to these were made by the rebel leaders, and all of them recovered their loans with the corresponding interest. Like good businessmen, they confined themselves to making a profitable "investment." An exception was a small group of persons who donated the sum of $272,496.60; among these the greatest contributor was Alfredo Délano, Treasurer-General of the Army and Navy, who was closely connected with the nitrate industrialists and bankers and who donated the sum of $100,000.

In a report made to his government by the United States minister in Santiago [Patrick Egan], the following statements can be found: "I may mention as a feature of much interest the fact that the revolution has the undivided sympathy, and in many cases the active support, of the English residents in Chile. . . . It is known that many English houses have subscribed liberally to the revolutionary fund. Among others, it is openly stated by the leaders of the revolution, Mr. John Thomas North contributed the sum of £100,000."

From this note it can be deduced that the foreign capitalists cooperated financially in the unfolding of the rebellion against the government. This is not strange if one keeps in mind that when North was in Chile in 1889, "one gentleman urged the Nitrate King to finance a revolution in a neighbouring State." Since North had no interests in any Latin-American country besides Chile, it is very probable that he was asked to finance a movement in Chile. The aforementioned English journalist, Maurice Hervey, shared this suspicion.

In synthesis, it can be affirmed categorically that the Congressional majority did not act in accordance with the dictates of ideology nor even with the purpose of perfecting our republican institutions. Their acts were determined by considerations of a purely economic and social order, as their opposition to Balmaceda's economic policy shows. Nevertheless, the Congressional bloc knew how "to spread among its followers the idea, well calculated to produce momentary fanaticism, that it was struggling to achieve public liberties once and for all, making Chile one of the leading democracies of the world. The opposition, then, had found a postulate capable of causing an intense seething of civic passion."

Opposition to Balmaceda's Economic Policy — . . . [Balmaceda's] economic ideas differed fundamentally from those of the bankers, businessmen, and landowners, who were supporters of free trade. Balmaceda, on the other hand, was a protectionist; therefore, he identified himself with those who sought the economic transformation of the nation so that Chile's economic structure might rest on manufacturing and on industrialized agriculture and mining. He represented, accordingly, a serious attempt to make Chile an industrial society in which capitalistic forms would prevail. This naturally presupposed the destruction of the agrarian society in which the dross of a seignorial economy existed together with a nascent financial and commercial capitalism and in which the first manifestations of imperialist penetration were being felt.

In our first chapter we indicated that the landowning oligarchy was hurt by the public works program put into effect by the government and by its agrarian policy and its encouragement of manufacturing and immigration since they modified the bases on which the oligarchy's economic, social, political, and even cultural power rested. In addition, Balmaceda's financial policies were likely to interrupt the expansion which the banking oligarchy was realizing at the expense of the state and of the productive capacity of the Chilean economy.

All of this necessarily had to produce deep distress among those whose vital interests were being affected by the policies of the government, a distress . . . that would influence both the leaders of the parties and the attitudes that the different groups would assume before the government of the republic. Such a reaction, moreover, was easy to encourage since the landowners, bankers, and businessmen held the positions of leadership in all the parties of the period when they were not their only components. . . .

In addition, foreign capital, dominated primarily by English entrepreneurs, was threatened by the anti-imperialist overtones of President Balmaceda's nitrate policy. . . . Unable to act directly in Chilean politics, the nitrate magnates sought and found the support of the most prominent public figures for the defense of their interests. . . .

To sum up, the political parties were dominated by the economic and social classes against which Balmaceda's policies were oriented. It is in this association of powerful interests that one may find the basis of the opposition organized in 1889 to contain or alter the action of the government for its own benefit.

It is noteworthy that this opposition was formed in 1889, that is, the culminating year of the economic action of the Balmaceda government. It should be kept in mind that the public works program was in full development in 1889; in addition, in the same year the President announced that the metallic conversion so keenly desired by the bankers would be indefinitely postponed, and he also set forth his plan to nationalize the railroads that crossed our territory. This was also the year of his encounter with Colonel North and of the formulation of his nationalistic nitrate policy. That is, there is a strange coincidence of time between the formation of the oppositionist movement and the initiation of what might be considered the second — and most decisive — stage of Balmaceda's economic policy. . . .

The True Character of the Civil War — In the light of all the antecedents set forth, there is not the slightest doubt that the civil war of 1891 cannot be considered a conflict provoked by purely political considerations. Phenomena of this type, no matter how important they may be, cannot determine movements of the magnitude of the conflagration of 1891. Moreover, political struggles . . . are merely the expression of deeper conditions; they are generally the result of social antagonisms aroused by the existence of opposing economic interests. As a result, if one wishes to find the explanation of a historical phenomenon, it is not enough to seek its political or ideological antecedents; it is necessary to penetrate the economic and social phenomena that determine these antecedents.

This has been the standard followed during the investigation set forth in this book. And as a result of it, it can be affirmed categorically — because there is sufficient proof — that the civil war of 1891 was nothing but a violent reaction to the economic policy carried out by President Balmaceda with enthusiasm, tenacity, and clear-sightedness and without vacillation. Those who saw their social and economic interests threatened and did not desire the changes that Chilean society required, took up arms against a statesman who was truly ahead of his time and who had "no concern except for justice, no love except for good, and no passion except for his country."

This evaluation of the most violent disturbance in Chilean history is also confirmed by the events that followed the civil war. In 1894 Francisco Valdés Vergara, in a study on the economic condition of Chile, wrote the following:

"The liquidation of the revolution brought the following results:

1. Expenses of more than $100,000,000.

2. The emission of $20,000,000.

3. The loss of 10,000 men who would have been useful in economic activities.

4. Serious dislocation of the fiscal and commercial credit of Chile.

5. Predominance in the financial leadership of the republic of a small group of persons who represented great fortunes and whose interests became identified with those of the country."

And Valdés Vergara, a severe judge of the revolutionaries whom he had enthusiastically aided, added: "It is painful to confess, but it is certain that with the best intentions of serving the country, of stimulating its growth, of purifying its politics, the men who made the revolution and those of us who served it, have caused evils greater than the promised benefits. . . ."

Meanwhile, an economic policy diametrically opposed to Balmaceda's was put into effect. In 1892 a metallic conversion was attempted which redounded only to the benefit of the banks, and three years later there was carried out a conversion that failed completely, though after some years it brought fat profits to the banking institutions. In addition, the denationalization of the nitrate industry proceeded apace through the sale of state holdings. Thus around 1898 there was the formation of "a small circle or guild of nitrate entrepreneurs constituted by the foreign monopoly that now dominates the industry; this monopoly manages production according to its own interests and not those of the state, takes from us control over foreign exchange and thereby disturbs the economy of the country, deprives the Treasury of millions of *pesos* in export taxes, hinders the development of the industry and threatens its very life by arti-

ficially raising prices, and endangers our national integrity, which
has been converted by its riches into a source of foreign power."

In other areas it can be observed that after 1891 the state abandoned plans for national economic development. In 1892, for example, the minister in charge of development declared before the
Senate that "the government believes the moment has come to suspend colonization. The country has derived considerable benefit
from what has been done up to now. In a region which was unin-
habitable ten years ago, European centers have been founded which
contained no less than 5,000 inhabitants, who are a lesson and a
model for Chilean settlers."

If one were to make a complete study of the orientation as well
as of the achievements of Chilean economic policy after 1891, one
would have evidence that it was in truth diametrically opposed to
that of President Balmaceda. These facts prove, from another aspect,
the thesis upheld by this book: the civil war of 1891 was nothing but
the product of the reaction provoked by the economic policy put
into practice by the Chilean state during the administration of President José Manuel Balmaceda.

3. A Purely Economic Interpretation Is Dangerous

HAROLD BLAKEMORE

Discussion of the Chilean revolution of 1891 has been in progress
for almost three-quarters of a century, yet, despite this considerable
period of investigation and interpretation, the origins, character and
consequences of the revolution and the figure of José Manuel Balmaceda, protagonist of the revolutionary drama, are still subjects of
much dispute among historians. . . .

Historians differ primarily on the question of responsibility for
the revolution, but whereas the great majority see the struggle between Balmaceda and his Congress as a battle of political principles
in which the contestants were activated by genuine conviction,
others, who see the springs of political action primarily in social and
economic circumstances, consider the basic issues in the conflict to

From "The Chilean Revolution of 1891 and Its Historiography" by Harold
Blakemore, *Hispanic American Historical Review*, XLV, 1965, pp. 393–421,
passim. Reprinted by permission.

have been about the economic organization and development of the republic. It is, therefore, possible and, indeed, convenient to speak of a dichotomy in the historiography of the revolution between "constitutional" historians on the one hand and "economic" historians on the other. These terms are not always mutually exclusive, but while the "constitutional" historian may not altogether ignore social and economic factors in the genesis of the revolution he does consider them relatively unimportant, whereas the "economic" historian. may grant some validity to constitutional factors while still regarding them largely as a veneer.

For many reasons, the sources on the constitutional side bulk larger than on the social and economic. In the first place, social and economic issues in the Chile of 1891 had not yet provided scope for the organization of political parties along those lines, and it was not until the twentieth century, particularly with the growth of an industrial working class, that Chile's political form really began to reflect changes in her social structure. Secondly, many interpretations of the revolution are part of the biography of the Chilean aristocracy, that unique social body which largely controlled the national life; it was natural, therefore, as the antagonists of 1891 were members of a homogeneous class proud of its political self-consciousness, that ideological differences should be stressed by historians, many of whom examined the same evidence afresh and came to individual conclusions. Again, contemporary propaganda at the outset of the revolution was primarily constitutional in tone: Balmaceda appealed to the written constitution, the Congressionalists to unwritten practice, and both sought support and sympathy by claiming to be the true representative of the nation's wishes. Indeed, to argue in such terms was a prime duty of the Congressional agents abroad during 1891, and one basis of the widespread international interest in the conflict was precisely the belief that the civil war was a genuine struggle of constitutional ideas. This belief was fostered by the similarity of approach of both sides in justifying their conduct which may be illustrated by two contemporary pamphlets, indicating the position adopted by Congress and Balmaceda, the Legislative and Executive powers respectively, to defend their alleged prerogatives.

The Congressional view was summarized by Pedro Montt in the pamphlet he wrote in the United States. He based his argument on the assumption that as Congressional approval was necessary for the passage of essential laws, "no minister can carry on the government or exercise its functions without the . . . confidence of the legislative body." This essential element of a parliamentary system, Montt continued, had been accepted even by Balmaceda, but the latter had broken with the practice in order to engineer the election of his chosen successor. Moreover, Congress had the power to remove the president if he were "unfit to discharge the duties of his office by reason of infirmity, absence or other grave cause." In Balmaceda's case, the "grave cause" was his openly unconstitutional act in declaring as laws the Appropriations and Forces Bills for 1891 which Congress had declined to pass in 1890. Montt asserted, in fact, that owing to the growth of unwritten precedent, a parliamentary system had developed in Chile which Balmaceda, for ulterior reasons, refused to acknowledge; he was, therefore, the real revolutionary and Congress the defender of the constitutional *status quo*.

Typical of the Balmacedist counter-argument on constitutional lines was the pamphlet of Eulogio Allendes which was published in English during the civil war. He interpreted the events of 1890 and 1891 in terms of Chile's written constitution, seeking thus to justify Balmaceda's final and admittedly unconstitutional act. "The Constitution," he said, "in none of its provisions empowers the House of Representatives to suspend the collection of taxes." Balmaceda, then, faced with a recalcitrant Congress refusing to perform its constitutional duty, was forced to arrogate to himself powers not strictly his to maintain government. Furthermore, Congress itself had acted unconstitutionally long before Balmaceda in that, having been called in Extraordinary Session in 1890 for the exclusive purpose of passing specified and essential laws, it had exceeded this mandate and passed votes of censure against Balmaceda's ministers. But the real crux of the question, said Allendes, was the presidential succession and control of the electoral machinery, and the revolution had really arisen from the desire for power of the Congressional opposition.

Historiographically, both of these *ex parte* pamphlets are significant for their emphasis on constitutional and political matters, and neither dilates upon economic and social factors in the genesis of the revolution. Much other contemporary material bears the same stamp. The Congressional records for 1890, the year of crisis before the revolution, testify to the seriousness of the constitutional differences between president and Congress, and little space is devoted to economic issues. Finally, though perhaps most significant of all, in both his Manifesto to the Nation of January 1, 1891, and in his Political Testament of September 18, 1891, written shortly before his suicide, Balmaceda himself expressly stated that the issues involved in the war were political and constitutional, and in neither of these magisterial documents did he so much as mention social and economic factors.

Not surprisingly, therefore, much of the history of the revolution is written in terms of constitutional ideas and political maneuvers, and when Balmaceda, in one of his final letters, entrusted to Julio Bañados Espinosa the task of justifying his conduct to posterity, he unwittingly ensured that much of the revolution's historiography would follow primarily constitutional lines.

The work of Bañados is the first important study of Balmaceda, not least because the author was in a unique position to write it. Despite its partisanship it is detailed and erudite and, as a discussion of the constitutional issues of the revolution, it has not been superseded. Bañados claims that the apparent causes of the revolution — Balmaceda's alleged denial of free elections, parliamentary rights, and individual liberties — were mere pretexts for Congressional action; the real causes were "political ambition in some and interest in others," for the history of the Balmaceda administration was "a struggle between men and circles to obtain predominance in the Government and to decide the candidature for the Presidency of the Republic in the election of 1891." He refutes Congressional arguments based on the written constitution of Chile, the opinions of eminent jurists, and the example of other states with similar systems. Bañados, however, also makes a number of allegations about the influence of foreign capital in Chile, asking rhetorically what influence the nitrate concessionaires had in the revolution. He also hints darkly at the link between the opposition to Balmaceda and the principal nitrate capitalist, John Thomas North. But he does not answer the tantalizing questions he poses, pleading the lack of such exact documentary evidence as would allow him to give other compromising details. It is noteworthy, however, that these questions and innuendo occupy a very small space in his book and, indeed, he devotes a mere twenty of his fifteen hundred pages to foreign interests in Chile, the emphasis throughout being on the personal ambitions of Chilean politicians. . . .

But the most avowedly constitutional interpretation appeared long after the political passions of the 1890's had died away: the study of Ricardo Salas Edwards is notable for its impartiality, seeking to justify Congress and to vindicate Balmaceda, each according to their lights, and seeing the revolution as inevitable. Thus, neither side was directly culpable, for "the heterogeneous opposition . . . was not fighting for a caudillo, neither was Balmaceda struggling to retain . . . power . . . both . . . claimed that they were the true and only defenders of traditional constitutional practice." The revolution was a clash between opposing interpretations of the written constitution and of practices of government which had grown up in the nineteenth century. Salas Edwards also refutes the view that the revolution was suborned by financial interests and he denies that it was also a simple struggle for power by a class which believed in its hereditary right to rule, but he does not investigate either assertion very thoroughly. . . .

Little positive advance in the constitutional interpretation was made until Yrarrázaval's careful study of Balmaceda took a significant stage further the argument on precedent and the constitution so warmly debated by previous writers. His basic contention was that

the primary aim of the opposition parties, temporarily united against Balmaceda — with some acting from lofty and disinterested motives and others . . . moved by opportunism — was to put an end to the traditional interference of authority in elections.

With this thesis as his guide, Yrarrázaval, in subsequent articles, categorically refuted the view that both foreign nitrate capitalists and native bankers had been so antagonized by Balmaceda's economic policies that they took up arms against him.

Any discussion of the Chilean revolution of 1891 must include the voluminous and controversial history of Francisco A. Encina. For him, the origins of the revolution stretch far back into Chile's past, but the immediate cause of crisis lay also in the character of Balmaceda. Encina argued that, throughout the nineteenth century, the autocratic structure of government was gradually weakened and the process was marked by an idealization of electoral liberty, by a doctrinaire attitude to politics and by conflicts on religious issues. Reform of the constitution of 1833 and an end to interference in elections became invested by the Congressional opposition with the ideal character of a universal panacea but, unfortunately, this movement of opinion and ideas reached its apogee under Balmaceda, a man who never realized the character or strength of the forces against him, who, fixing his eyes on the goal of Chile's material

greatness, moved in a utopia unrestricted by realities, and whose
character, complex and grandiose in the extreme, brought to a head
the conflict between the political tendencies of the aristocracy and
the established system of government. Balmaceda's errors crys-
tallized the problem: on the one hand stood the Congressional majority, now seeking to bend him to its will and implant electoral
liberty and parliamentary government, on the other the President
and his supporters, convinced that the opposition was activated
solely by sordid ambitions and selfish desires, fighting to preserve
and perpetuate a system of government long since doomed. For
Encina also, the revolution was not inspired by economic forces;
in its origins it was "political and sentimental and not one of interests." Any belief in the influence of North's gold and the antagonism of bankers and landowners to Balmaceda as motivating forces
in the revolution is completely misleading and utterly wrong. . . .

Apart from the avowedly partisan work of Bañados, and allowing
for differences of emphasis on personal and political factors, all the
above interpretations of the revolution share the characteristic of
either ignoring or refuting the belief that economic interests, both
national and foreign, played a part in the genesis of the crisis. The
"economic" aspect of its historiography derives from the conscious
dissatisfaction of some historians with these views in the light of
what they hold to be unequivocal material to suggest that economic
and social factors were not only prominent in 1891 but may even
have been paramount. This reaction to the "traditional" view has
more than intrinsic interest in that its emergence is closely bound
up with twentieth-century developments in both Chile and the outside world. First, Chile's changing social and economic character
under Alessandri and the Popular Front threw new emphasis on the
revolution of 1891, for the striking contrast between the nineteenth-
and twentieth-century history of Chile has caused some historians
to regard the revolution as the real turning-point if not, indeed, the
great tragedy of the republic. The tendency to speculate on the
possible consequences of a Balmacedist victory has proved irresistible, and today Balmaceda is often regarded as a great national hero
who was brought down by a nefarious combination of selfish
and unpatriotic Chilean economic interests and acquisitive foreign
capitalists, particularly British, both of whom felt threatened by
Balmaceda. In a wider context, few historians today would deny
the significance of economic and social factors in historical development while not necessarily espousing the Marxist historicist

thesis. But the latter has had a profound effect where it is easy, often at a superficial level, to fit a country's history into such an ideological framework, and Chile can be made to conform to this kind of treatment. Again, to a Marxist, it can appear that individuals are so unaware of the true motivation of their actions that the influences which move them are largely different from the reasons they would consciously formulate. This convenient, because unprovable, doctrine, if applied to the revolution of 1891, leads to the view that simply because the social and economic interests at stake are less apparent than the clash of personalities and the conflict of political ideas, this is insufficient ground for believing they are less important.

In fact, however, some facets of the Chilean revolution of 1891 seem to establish *a priori* reasons for investigating social and economic issues, though here a few examples must suffice. In March, 1891, Patrick Egan, the American Minister to Chile, reported home that John Thomas North had alone contributed £100,000 to the revolutionary cause. Earlier the British Minister had written:

It is at present the policy of the Government to ascribe the revolutionary movement to the desire of the Opposition to secure the riches of the province of Tarapacá (the nitrate region), and the Government newspapers are full of abuse of Colonel North and of rich individual Chileans who are alleged to have corrupted Chile by having developed the resources of Tarapacá.

The special correspondent of *The Times* of London, Maurice Hervey, made scarcely veiled references to North when he wrote from Chile:

Without quoting names, some of which are as well known upon the London Stock Exchange as the cardinal points of the compass, . . . the instigators, the wire-pullers, the financial supporters of the so-called revolution were, and are, the English or Anglo-Chilean owners of the vast nitrate deposits of Tarapacá.

And he repeated these allegations in his subsequent account of his adventures in Chile in 1891. Balmaceda's government itself put out propaganda on similar lines, arguing that the Chilean aristocracy, bankers, and foreign capitalists had plunged the country into bloody civil war. . . .

These random examples of contemporary statements implying the operation of economic factors in the genesis of the revolution can be multiplied, and they have been much used by later historians who are not satisfied with the "constitutional" interpretation. But the "economic" historiography of the revolution was really launched by Joaquín Villarino in his study of the Balmaceda administration. He asserted that the revolution, besides being a clash of ideas, was also a conflict of an economic and social kind with a sinister part being played by "the English nitrate entrepreneurs . . . with their lawyers and their deputies bought with high salaries." Balmaceda had offended the landowners, affronted the clergy, disturbed the bankers, and worried the nitrate capitalists, particularly North, who had been thwarted in his desire to make a kind of "South American India" of Tarapacá. Similar assertions, especially about the corrupting influence of foreign gold, were made by a more prominent Balmacedist, José Miguel Valdés Carrera, a former Finance Minister, who, in a pamphlet written in exile, alleged that North and others had spent large sums of money in Chile to bribe public men to defend foreign interests at the expense of those of the state.

These Balmacedist *apologias* were the starting-point of an "economic" interpretation of the revolution, though, in fact, this aspect of the historiography did not have the continuity of the "constitutional" view. Perhaps naturally, considerable attention has been paid by later writers to the alleged role of foreign nitrate capitalists in 1891 and, in this connection, it is interesting to note that the Chilean Radical Party declared in 1936 "that the enslaving of Chile to the foreign conquerors has only been made possible because of the treachery of a reactionary oligarchy, sold out to the gold of London and New York . . . ," a declaration remarkably similar in spirit, if not exactly in circumstance, to the Balmacedist propaganda during 1891. But substantive evidence is lacking and, consequently, some writers assert much but prove little. Thus, H. B. Williams claims that Chilean politicians could not accept Balmaceda's policies for the nitrate industry because they derived such benefits from foreign nitrate companies, but he offers no substantiation. E. Frei Montalva points out that Balmacedist propaganda was on economic as much as constitutional lines, but does not dispute the validity of it.

By far the most convincing theses on economic lines are those of the late Osgood Hardy and the Chilean historian, Hernán Ramírez Necochea. Hardy held that there was enough evidence to show that "British nitrate interests played a significant part in inspiring the *Congresionalistas* to rebel against the *Balmacedistas*." After an excellent survey of the growth of the British nitrate industry and North's key role in it, he went on to argue that Balmaceda had a policy for nitrates inimical to North's interests, and concluded that the latter and others helped to finance the revolution which replaced Balmaceda by those more favorable to the nitrate capitalists.

Unlike Hardy, who used mostly secondary sources, Ramírez brought in new material to support his case. The main argument of his first study of the subject was admirably expressed in the foreword by Guillermo Feliú Cruz, who stated that

a coalition of bankers and landowners, mine-owners and industrialists, opposed to the financial and economic policy of Balmaceda which was rooted in nationalism, opposition to laissez-faire and in favour of the definite intervention of the state in the economic organization of the Republic, proposed — at the same time as defending the rights of the Constitution — to consign these ideas of Balmaceda to oblivion. . . .

The author was, however, less concerned with Chilean nationals than with what he calls "English imperialism" in Chile, incarnated in John Thomas North, and here he traced in detail the network of personal and professional relationships built up between foreign capitalists and leading Chilean political and forensic figures. Ramírez then analyzed Balmaceda's policies and concluded, with the support of a wide range of contemporary and later comments, that "the political parties were dominated by all the social and economic elements to which Balmaceda's Government and policy were opposed." The civil war of 1891 was no more than a violent reaction by these elements to Balmaceda's economic policy. This is the most sustained and convincing attempt to explain the revolution essentially in social and economic terms.

The development of a modern "economic" interpretation of the revolution has been valuable, for it has focussed attention on factors hitherto largely neglected, and it has broken away from the somewhat sterile controversy between the Congressionalist and Balmacedist viewpoints in terms of the constitution. The purely "constitutional" argument was never entirely convincing, for the appeal of the antagonists and their apologists to principles, real or imagined, may well have obscured the fact that behind such an appeal were often less ideal motives and more personal interests than the desire for constitutional change. It is often easy for those who do not enjoy political power to confuse a well-founded theory of its limitation with mere objections to its exercise by their opponents. Thus the Congressionalist claim that Balmaceda thwarted cabinet responsibility was false, as that practice had never been established. In 1892 the British Minister pointed out that, before Balmaceda, the regimen had never been called parliamentary, a term implying cabinet responsibility to the legislature; it was the Congress which first raised this issue, not so much to secure desirable reforms as to obtain control of the government. "The Chilean Revolution," he went on, "may be described as an interested movement of political parties for obtaining power. The question of principle found but little space in the struggle. . . ." This was, of course, the Balmacedist view, but it ignored an equally vital point in arguing that Congress forced Balmaceda to act unconstitutionally by failing to pass the essential laws for 1891. For, if the Constitution of 1833 ever intended to give Congress any control over the executive, it did so in the supervisory mandate over appropriations. In fact, the simple explanation may be that the Chilean founding fathers did not, perhaps could not, envisage the possibility of serious conflict between the branches of government, as each represented the aristocracy.

To return, however, to the contribution of such writers as Hardy and Ramírez to the historiography of the revolution, it is important to recognize that, whatever their value, they are a reaction to views long held, and it is characteristic of such reactions that often no clear distinction is drawn between probabilities and possibilities. Simply because an interpretation is new is no criterion of its superior validity to the old. The remainder of this article, therefore, will attempt to put the economic interpretation of the revolution into perspective before finally considering whether some synthesis of the two aspects of its historiography is not now possible.

In the first place, the reliability of two key contemporary observers in 1891 on the role of British nitrate interests may be questioned, as both of them, Patrick Egan and Maurice Hervey, have been quoted approvingly by a number of historians. Egan's remarks must be set against his background and his purpose in Chile. His earlier relations with the British can hardly be called cordial, for he was a former Treasurer of the Irish Land League and a defendant of Charles Stuart Parnell at his trial in 1880. This connection had brought him into the news again shortly before his appointment to Santiago when, in 1888–1889, *The Times* accused Parnell of complicity in the notorious Phoenix Park murders of 1882. Secretary of State James G. Blaine appointed Egan to Chile partly to flatter Irish voters, but also because Egan probably seemed eminently suitable to forward Blaine's ideas for a more dynamic commercial policy in an area where British interests predominated. During 1891 Egan's sympathy for Balmaceda was used by the latter to put pressure on Great Britain, though the American minister was almost alone among the diplomatic corps in leaning towards the president. The occasion arose when Balmaceda decreed the Congressional-held northern ports closed to shipping in April, 1891, but both the British and German ministers refused to accept this "paper" blockade which Balmaceda could not enforce. Egan, however, undertook to induce his government to recognize it. . . . . How far Egan's attitude was prompted solely by considerations of national interest is conjectural, but it seems reasonable to question, in the light of it, his past history, and the purposes for which he had been appointed, whether he may really be considered an impartial witness, especially when his statements about North's alleged complicity in the revolution derived from Balmacedist sources.

Stronger doubts are permissible about Hervey. He was appointed special correspondent of *The Times* with orders "to report faithfully, and without unfair bias in favour or against any particular interest or view." He reached Chile in March and stayed there four months, during which, according to Kennedy:

He appeared to avoid his countrymen and also all those who were not partisans of the President . . . he identified himself too closely with the cause of the President . . . and accepted as Gospel truths statements which certainly are arguable.

Now, Hervey's first dramatic report was written in Santiago on March 19. We have his own testimony that he left Buenos Aires on March 5, reached Mendoza three days later and crossed the Andes on March 10–11, so that, whatever his precise timetable thereafter, he cannot have been in Santiago much more than a week before he was emphatically convinced of the truth about the revolution. His later and more sensational reports drew a strong protest from the leading British commercial houses in Chile. Only one, Antony Gibbs & Sons, had nitrate interests, and this was the very firm which had attacked North's Nitrate Railway Company in representations to the Foreign Office in 1890. The head of another, Williamson, Balfour & Co., also wrote to *The Times* in March, pointing out Hervey's lack of knowledge of Chile and suggesting that he seemed to be "under the influence of the President and his associates." This writer, Stephen Williamson, had no regard for North, for in a letter to his manager at Valparaiso in 1889 he described North as a "regular charlatan," said that the nitrate interests had so abused their privileges in Chile that some check should be placed on them, and recommended expropriation of the Nitrate Railway. To the present writer, there is some significance in the fact that British interests in Chile who had no brief for the *parvenu* North should, nevertheless, come to the latter's defence against Hervey, who, incidentally, told his paper that Williamson had been "bought by the Nitrate interest." Hervey was recalled in April, 1891, because his reports were so at variance with all other sources of information. He was subsequently given leave to stay in Chile to make a trip with the Balmacedist torpedo-boats, but was finally recalled on May 28 and requested to bring back proofs of his allegations against British capitalists. Though, in his book, Hervey cited *verbatim* most of the telegrams he received from *The Times* in 1891, of the last he noted that he was requested to "start at once for London with certain documentary evidence," but did not mention nitrates or British capitalists in this context at all. Dismissed by *The Times* in August, shortly after his return, Hervey then wrote the book which has exercised considerable influence on the "economic" historians of the revolution.

This *caveat* against two oft-quoted contemporary witnesses on economic issues in the revolution applies also in part to later writers who have used them, notably Hardy and Ramírez. Villarino and other contemporary Balmacedists who argued on economic lines are not in the same category, their work being largely a continuation of the wartime diatribes of the government, polemical in tone, apologist in intent, and singularly lacking in proof. It is, however, some measure of their contribution that Hardy and Ramírez deserve serious consideration, though both can be challenged on grounds of detail and interpretation.

Hardy begs the question at the outset in speaking of "the causative effect of the Atacama Desert's nitrates" in the genesis of the revolution. But he seems to the present writer to go further in unwarranted assumption in dealing with Balmaceda's alleged economic nationalism and North's antagonism to it as factors in the revolution. His evidence is, first, the cancellation of the Nitrate Railway concession in January, 1886, which was the subject of a protracted lawsuit; secondly, Balmaceda's speeches during 1889, and, thirdly, the meetings that year between the president and North which Hardy construes as having been distinctly unhappy for the latter. Considering this "evidence," it should be noted that Hardy's treatment of the Nitrate Railway issue is inaccurate in detail. He says:

In 1885, immediately after his election, Chile's chief executive had stated that Tarapacá should have competing railroads, and the following year, on

January 29, 1886, the Chilean Minister of Justice announced the cancellation of the concessions upon which North's Tarapacá railroad rested.

Actually, Balmaceda was not elected president until six months later,
and he was not even in the ministry under Santa María when the
concession was annulled. Moreover, North did not become involved
with the Railway Company until 1887 and Chairman of its Board
until 1889. And, while Hardy is right in claiming the issue to be
a bone of contention between Balmaceda and North, he over-person-
alizes it, as opposition to the Railway's monopoly owed as much to
other British nitrate interests as it did to the government. More
important, Hardy's interpretation of Balmaceda's speeches on the
nitrate industry suggests that he did not consider them as a whole.
Thus, of the most famous speech at Iquique on March 9, 1889, he
says that Balmaceda "outlined in clear terms his attitude towards
the nitrate problem," which he summarizes under three headings:
nationalization of the industry, prohibition of any monopoly which
might limit production to raise prices, and expropriation of the
Tarapacá railroads. But Balmaceda explicitly rejected nationalization, saying that "an industrial monopoly of nitrate is not an undertaking for the State, whose fundamental mission is to guarantee the
rights of property and liberty . . . ," though he added that the state
should conserve forever enough nitrate grounds to frustrate "an industrial dictatorship." As to the railway, Balmaceda hoped that
all the lines in Tarapacá would become national property, with the
qualification that "the railway question ought to be equitably arranged without injuring lawful private interests or harming the
convenience and rights of the State." And, in fact, the government's method of solving the Nitrate Railway question was to award
a concession for a competing line to the Agua Santa Company in
which the controlling interest was held by the British firm of Camp-
bell, Outram and Co. This obeyed political as well as economic
objectives in that several Chilean politicians, interested in the Agua
Santa Company, gave their support to Balmaceda, probably in return for the concession, when he was in acute political difficulties in
1890. One of them, Lauro Barros, became Minister of Finance in
Balmaceda's "personal" ministry of October, composed when Balmaceda's differences with Congress had reached a nadir from which
they never

recovered. Furthermore, by this action, the government ignored the advice
of the Deputy Luis Martiano Rodríguez, an adviser of the Nitrate Rail-

way Company, who, in Congress, had urged that the competing line should be built by the state itself rather than by a private firm.

If Hardy's interpretation of this issue is somewhat misleading, a similar criticism may be made of his treatment of other matters. For example, he says that

Balmaceda did not change one whit from the views expressed in his Iquique speech. When North tried to "reach" the President through a third party and privately proposed the sale of government-owned nitrate fields he was informed: "The state must conserve forever sufficient nitrate fields to maintain through its influence, production and sale. . . ."

Here he follows Salas Edwards, but omits to point out that this statement was part of the Iquique speech, made on a public platform nine days before North set foot in Chile to begin his celebrated tour of 1889.

A close consideration, however, of Balmaceda's speeches and actions on nitrates suggests an alternative picture to that of the economic nationalist threatening foreign interests. It is true that in 1887 he had said that the Government would study what practicable measures could be taken "to nationalize Chilean interests which are, at present, chiefly of benefit to foreigners." Again, in November, 1888, he asked:

Why does the credit and the capital which are brought into play . . . in our great cities, hold back and leave the foreigner to establish banks at Iquique, and abandon to strangers the exploiting of the nitrate works of Tarapacá . . . the foreigner explores these riches, and takes the profit of native wealth . . . to give to other lands and unknown people the treasures of our soil, our own property and the riches we require.

Such speeches, including the one at Iquique, excited some attention, if not apprehension, in foreign business circles. Yet Balmaceda's government did little or nothing to carry out his implied threats, and, while there is certainly a paucity of evidence to show that he had a consistent policy on nitrates, there is some to suggest that such policy as he did have was limited in its objectives and obeyed transitory motives. . . .

There is one other reason why Hardy's interpretation is not convincing, apart from this suggested alternative. This turns on his view that the meetings between Balmaceda and North in 1889 left the latter "with the knowledge that the foundations of his kingdom were not entirely secure," for this is largely subjective since firsthand sources are strictly limited. William Howard Russell, who was present in 1889, reported that

> the President declared that he was desirous of giving every facility to the introduction of foreign capital . . . the gist of the interview was that he had not the smallest intention of making war on vested interests. . . . Colonel North was much gratified by the assurances . . . the interview was . . . most satisfactory to him.

Hardy, however, doubts the validity of this, preferring to accept the view of Hernández Cornejo, who was not present, and arguing that North "must have been chagrined at President Balmaceda's refusal to accept the Colonel's personal gift of some horses." But Hernández does not cite his source, and on the meeting his precise words are: "it is said that Balmaceda received the Nitrate King coldly." This is not a trivial point as it is on such minor details that Hardy's case is constructed, and it is, therefore, justifiable to criticize minutely both the sources he uses and the way he uses them, without detracting in any way from the important service he has performed by raising the economic issue in the revolution of 1891.

The work of Ramírez Necochea is much more detailed and, at first sight, convincing. His study of the development of the nitrate industry is well-documented and sound, apart from its Marxist overtones; his survey of Balmaceda's policies is full of interesting facts, and his material on the relations between Chilean public men and foreign capitalists shows in detail what relationships existed. But his thesis seems to the present writer rather to strain the evidence to fit the case, and to ignore or minimize the value of material which might prove embarrassing to it. A few examples will illustrate these points, though it is not proposed to deal with his treatment of Balmaceda's alleged nitrate policy, which largely follows Hardy in giving Balmaceda credit for a cohesive policy he did not possess.

A major argument advanced by Ramírez for the view that economic interests were dominant in the revolution turns on the links between Chilean public figures and foreign nitrate capitalists, and he has shown incontestably that many of the former, some of whom played a significant role in 1891, were employed by the latter as legal advisers in Chile. "Some," he says, "were seduced by foreign gold to put their prestige and influence at the service of the leading nitrate entrepreneurs." He asserts that foreign capital was menaced by Balmaceda and argues that after the latter's defeat, the nitrate industry was denationalized so that by 1898 the industry was completely dominated by foreigners. The patent inference is that the relationship between Chileans and foreigners was a major factor in the genesis of the revolution, and that the nitrate capitalists reaped their reward for services rendered after the revolution. It is a plausible and neat interpretation, cogently argued, but, while the present writer accepts completely the fact of the relationship described, he questions the conclusion that such ties were necessarily nefarious, and he believes that it is pure speculation to consider them as major factors in the genesis of the revolution.

Ramírez examines the Nitrate Railways Corruption Case of 1896–1898 which was reported in the Chilean press and which he holds to be significant proof of his thesis. Briefly, in 1896–1897, shareholders in the Nitrate Railways Company forced the Directors to submit to a detailed examination of the Company's activities in Chile since 1882. Among other things, the enquiry revealed that the Company had paid lawyers and public men in Chile some £93,000 from 1887 to 1895 in defence of its interests. Robert Harvey, North's close associate in nitrates from the early days, was startlingly frank about his attitude to the question:

The course of justice is not based on that high standard of purity that it is in this country. I do not say that money is absolutely required to bribe the Judges, but I think that very many impecunious members of the Senate derived some benefit from some of this money in order to give their votes, and to keep the Government from absolutely declining to listen to any of our protests and appeals.

No doubt both Harvey and North, who dominated the Company's Board until his death in 1896, believed this was so, but the reports of the enquiry created a furore in Chile and "great public indignation." The Chilean Legation in London issued a statement refuting the evidence heard at the enquiry, and pointed out that no Chileans had been named but simply referred to by initials. But to anyone acquainted with the Company, the Mr. Z. most often mentioned was easily identified as Julio Zegers, the Company's counsel in Chile for ten years and a prominent lawyer-politician. Zegers himself petitioned the *Comisión Conservadora* of the Chilean Congress for a full investigation, but one was never held, and he lived out his life in the shadow of public scandal.

At first glance this case might seem to show conclusively that Chilean public men were corrupted by foreign gold to act in ways inimical to their country's interest, but it is not quite so simple.

First, the amount spent by the Company in Chile was spread over eight years, during which the Company was involved in the costly and protracted lawsuit to preserve its monopoly in Tarapacá. Secondly, a considerable proportion of the money was spent after 1891, when Balmaceda's successors showed they were determined to liquidate the monopoly, contrary to the Company's expectations, a fact which Ramírez singularly ignores. Thirdly, the Company's more honest advisers recommended the Directors to recognize the inevitable long before the revolution. One of them, Mr. E. Manby, told the enquiry that Enrique MacIver, one of their lawyers, "averred that Congress and people would never tolerate a Bill prolonging or confirming our monopolies" as early as 1889. There were two basic reasons why so much was spent in the Company's supposed interest: North's dominant personality, liberality, and wrongheaded optimism, and Zegers' insistence that all might be saved even when the monopoly was clearly doomed. The Company's manager in Chile, Mr. Rowland, advised in December, 1890, that Zegers was not trustworthy, but, despite this, the latter continually applied for and received, on North's recommendation, large sums of money as late as 1893 onwards. A reading of this evidence, therefore, far from supporting the view that Chilean lawyers were "seduced by foreign gold," rather raises the suspicion that British capitalists were being heavily "blackmailed" by Chilean lawyers, and it certainly leaves open to doubt the notion that relationships between British nitrate interests and Chilean forensic figures were important factors in the genesis of the revolution. . . .

Two other examples show how misleading this approach can be. As has been noted, Ramírez argues that Balmaceda's policies were opposed by a Congress representing social and economic interests threatened by him. It should be noted that Balmaceda retained little support from members of Congress in 1891 and in 1890 89 of 126 congressmen signed the document deposing him. While material for a detailed investigation of the economic interests of his supporters is lacking to the present writer, a cursory glance at the membership of the rump Congress of 1891 shows that it includes landowners like Ricardo Cruzat, Alejandro Maturana, Alfredo and Ruperto Ovalle, also the owners of rich silver mines, Santiago Pérez Eastman and Ignacio Silva Ureta. All these might be called millionaires, and so might Víctor Echaurrén, Manuel García de la Huerta, Juan Mackenna, and others. The question is how far the economic and social interests of these Balmacedists differed from those of the Congressionalists against whom the government thundered during 1891. Much more detailed investigation is necessary on this isuue before it can be concluded that the interests of the aristocracy were threatened by Balmaceda or that the revolution divided Chilean politicians along social and economic lines. The present writer believes that economic factors were much less significant than Ramírez suggests and that personal and political allegiances within the governing class were the principal determinants of conduct.

Finally, although it is logically necessary for Ramírez to assert that the results of the revolution were favorable to the interests which allegedly suborned and supported it, not least the nitrate capitalists, in neither of his books on the revolution does he deal in detail with the period after 1891. Had he done so he would have found convincing evidence that under President Jorge Montt, 1891–1896, the Chilean government pursued nitrate policies which, following Ramírez, one can only describe as Balmacedist. . . .

More space would permit the citation of other aspects of the thesis put foward by Ramírez which show similar traits of *suggestio falsi*, for example his treatment of Balmaceda and banking interests. But perhaps the above is sufficient to cast some doubts on a total acceptance of his economic interpretation. It seems to the present writer that the only reasonable verdict possible at present on such questions as the collusion of British nitrate interests and antagonism between Balmaceda and his Congress on economic grounds as motivating forces in the revolution is "not proven." However important new lines of approach may be, historical interpretation demands rigorous attention to detail and a willingness to modify *a priori* assumptions where the evidence conflicts with them.

Finally, is a synthesis of the "constitutional" and "economic" interpretations of the revolution now possible? The answer must be a qualified "no," for a number of prerequisites are still lacking. We need a series of studies on such issues as the social structure of Chile in the nineteenth century, most imperatively a detailed investigation on biographical lines of the aristocracy and its economic interests such as land, banking, and mining; the role of professional men — lawyers, journalists, and commercial figures — and their political outlook and affiliations; the precise part played by foreign capital in Chilean development, and Chile's place in a wider world economy, and, not least, a whole range of regional studies which might well throw light on much more than regional issues. The *raison d être* of such studies would obviously not be limited to adding to our knowledge of the revolution of 1891, but they would manifestly contribute to our interpretation of it, and that event has some ground for being considered as the critical one in the modern history of the republic, in which many tendencies and developments of the nineteenth century reached their climax and from which flowed consequences still felt in the national life. For these reasons, it is hoped that it will continue to engage the attention of historians in the future as much as it has done in the past.

Section VI

Porfirio Díaz, Dictator of Mexico

No nineteenth-century caudillo has been so much written about as Porfirio Díaz, who first became provisional president of Mexico in 1876 by revolting with the cry "No re-election" and then by 1884 had the country so thoroughly dominated that he was able to get himself "elected" term after term until the Mexican Revolution overthrew him in 1911. The *Porfiriato*, as this long period is called, produced peace and some economic progress, but these were achieved only at a great price.

The intellectuals did not go into exile as they had when Juan Manuel Rosas held sway over Argentina, and in fact General Díaz received strong support from the positivists. As one Mexican historian explains:

His figure came to symbolize the order and peace for which the men trained in positivism had clamored. Materialism and dehumanization were converted into models of life for the generation which developed during his regime: industry, money, railroads, and always more money. Progress definitely seemed to triumph. The social evolution seemed to be moving forward with gigantic steps, but . . ·. freedom was forgotten, the very thing for which it was said that order had been established.[1]

The fault was by no means his alone, but in his long years of power the people as a whole did not advance and remained illiterate. While the celebrants of the centenary of Mexican independence and of the dictator's eightieth birthday drank twenty carloads of champagne and consumed many delicacies, the masses verged on

[1] Leopoldo Zea, *The Latin-American Mind*, Tr. by James H. Abbott and Lowell Dunham (Norman: University of Oklahoma Press, 1963), p. 284.

starvation, for they had suffered a steady reduction in their in-
credibly low living standards during the long Porfiriato. Yet in
many ways Díaz was a great man; one of his severest United States
critics concludes:

> He accomplished what none of his countrymen had been able to do be-
> fore him — to maintain a generation of peace. . . . But the overshadow-
> ing fact — to remember — is that the Mexico he left in 1911 had all its
> problems, the problems of four centuries, still to solve.[2]

During the Porfiriato, Americans began to go to Mexico in ever-
increasing numbers — to invest money, to build railroads, to buy
ranches, to write books, to report for newspapers, or just to pay a
tourist visit. The publicist James Creelman traveled "nearly four
thousand miles from New York to see the master and hero of modern
Mexico" and published in 1908 in *Pearson's Magazine* a panegyric
(Reading VI.1), which included the dictator's unexpected remark
that he would welcome an opposition because he was retiring in a
couple of years from the presidency. But when another American,
John Kenneth Turner, issued his harsh attack on the aged dictator
two years later, Díaz was still in the saddle (Reading VI.2).

Knowledge of modern Mexican history has greatly increased in
recent years under the impetus supplied by Daniel Cosío Villegas
and his colleagues at the Colegio de México. Representative selections from recent collections of documents are an editorial on the
desirability of foreign investment in Mexico (Reading VI.3); a
résumé of the report of the first agrarian congress (1904) sponsored
by the Bishop of Tulancingo, which illustrates the concern of some
churchmen over the plight of the rural masses (Reading VI.4); the
objectives of the Liberal Party led by Ricardo Flores Magón, as
they were set forth in a program published in 1906 in the United
States (Reading VI.5); and an appeal to Mexican laborers not to go
to the United States (Reading VI.6).

The Porfiriato is also inextricably linked to the Revolution, for
it was the background for this violent period, as Charles Cumberland of Michigan State University shows (Reading VI.7). And any
fair appraisal of Díaz's influence on Mexico must include the ten
years of chaos that followed his fall.[3] For one appraisal, we turn
to Cosío Villegas, who has been responsible for opening up in a decisive and competent fashion the history of modern Mexico (Reading

---

[2] Ernest Gruening, *Mexico and Its Heritage* (New York: Century, 1928), p. 65.
[3] *Ibid.*, p. 64.

VI.8). Thanks to his investigations and to his stimulus, we now begin to see the true Porfirio Díaz; a dictator, yes, but also a patriot who defended well some of the national interests of Mexico.[4]

[4] For a judicious statement on past and present interpretations of Díaz, see Martín Quirarte, *Historia Mexicana*, XV (1965–1966), Nos. 2–3, pp. 416–422.

A. Contemporary Interpretations

1. President Diaz: Hero of the Americas

JAMES CREELMAN

From the heights of Chapultepec Castle President Diaz looked down upon the venerable capital of his country, spread out on a vast plain, with a ring of mountains flung up grandly about it, and I, who had come nearly four thousand miles from New York to see the master and hero of modern Mexico — the inscrutable leader in whose veins is blended the blood of the primitive Mixtecs with that of the invading Spaniards — watched the slender, erect form, the strong, soldierly head and commanding, but sensitive, countenance with an interest beyond words to express.

A high, wide forehead that slopes up to crisp white hair and over- hangs deep-set, dark brown eyes that search your soul, soften into inexpressible kindliness and then dart quick side looks — terrible eyes, threatening eyes, loving, confiding, humorous eyes — a straight, powerful, broad and somewhat fleshy nose, whose curved nostrils lift and dilate with every emotion; huge, virile jaws that sweep from large, flat, fine ears, set close to the head, to the tremendous, square, fighting chin; a wide, firm mouth shaded by a white mustache; a full, short, muscular neck; wide shoulders, deep chest; a curiously tense and rigid carriage that gives great distinction to a personality

From "President Diaz: Hero of the Americas" by James Creelman, *Pearson's Magazine*, XIX, March 1908, pp. 231–277. A facsimile reproduction of the in- terview, together with a Spanish translation, appears in *Entrevista Díaz-Creel- man* (Cuadernos del Instituto de Historia, Serie Documental, No. 2; Mexico: Universidad Nacional Autónoma de México, 1963).

suggestive of singular power and dignity — that is Porfirio Diaz in his seventy-eighth year, as I saw him a few weeks ago on the spot where, forty years before, he stood — with his besieging army surrounding the City of Mexico, and the young Emperor Maximilian being shot to death in Querétaro, beyond those blue mountains to the north — waiting grimly for the thrilling end of the last interference of European monarchy with the republics of America.

It is the intense, magnetic something in the wide-open, fearless, dark eyes and the sense of nervous challenge in the sensitive, spread nostrils, that seem to connect the man with the immensity of the landscape, as some elemental force.

There is not a more romantic or heroic figure in all the world, nor one more intensely watched by both the friends and foes of democracy, than the soldier-statesman, whose adventurous youth pales the pages of Dumas, and whose iron rule has converted the warring, ignorant, superstitious and impoverished masses of Mexico, oppressed by centuries of Spanish cruelty and greed, into a strong, steady, peaceful, debt-paying and progressive nation.

For twenty-seven years he has governed the Mexican Republic with such power that national elections have become mere formalities. He might easily have set a crown upon his head.

Yet to-day, in the supremacy of his career, this astonishing man — foremost figure of the American hemisphere and unreadable mystery to students of human government — announces that he will insist on retiring from the Presidency at the end of his present term, so that he may see his successor peacefully established and that, with his assistance, the people of the Mexican Republic may show the world that they have entered serenely and preparedly upon the last complete phase of their liberties, that the nation is emerging from ignorance and revolutionary passion, and that it can choose and change presidents without weakness or war.

It is something to come from the money-mad gambling congeries of Wall Street and in the same week to stand on the rock of Chapultepec, in surroundings of almost unreal grandeur and loveliness, beside one who is said to have transformed a republic into an autocracy by the absolute compulsion of courage and character, and to hear him speak of democracy as the hope of mankind.

This, too, at a time when the American soul shudders at the mere thought of a third term for any President.

The President surveyed the majestic, sunlit scene below the ancient castle and turned away with a smile, brushing a curtain of scarlet trumpet-flowers and vine-like pink geraniums as he moved along the terrace toward the inner garden, where a fountain set among palms and flowers sparkled with water from the spring at which Montezuma used to drink, under the mighty cypresses that still rear their branches about the rock on which we stood.

"It is a mistake to suppose that the future of democracy in Mexico has been endangered by the long continuance in office of one President," he said quietly. "I can say sincerely that office has not corrupted my political ideals and that I believe democracy to be the one true, just principle of government, although in practice it is possible only to highly developed peoples."

For a moment the straight figure paused and the brown eyes looked over the great valley to where snow-covered Popocatapetl lifted its volcanic peak nearly eighteen thousand feet among the clouds beside the snowy craters of Ixtaccihuatl — a land of dead volcanoes, human and otherwise.

"I can lay down the Presidency of Mexico without a pang of regret, but I cannot cease to serve this country while I live," he added.

The sun shone full in the President's face but his eyes did not shrink from the ordeal. The green landscape, the smoking city, the blue tumult of mountains, the thin, exhilarating, scented air, seemed to stir him, and the color came to his cheeks as he clasped his hands behind him and threw his head backward. His nostrils opened wide.

"You know that in the United States we are troubled about the question of electing a President for three terms?"

He smiled and then looked grave, nodding his head gently and pursing his lips. It is hard to describe the look of concentrated interest that suddenly came into his strong, intelligent countenance.

"Yes, yes, I know," he replied. "It is a natural sentiment of democratic peoples that their officials should be often changed. I agree with that sentiment."

It seemed hard to realize that I was listening to a soldier who had ruled a republic continuously for more than a quarter of a century with a personal authority unknown to most kings. Yet he spoke with a simple and convincing manner, as one whose place was great and secure beyond the need of hypocrisy.

"It is quite true that when a man has occupied a powerful office for a very long time he is likely to begin to look upon it as his personal property, and it is well that a free people should guard themselves against the tendencies of individual ambition.

"Yet the abstract theories of democracy and the practical, effective application of them are often necessarily different — that is when you are seeking for the substance rather than the mere form.

"I can see no good reason why President Roosevelt should not be elected again if a majority of the American people desire to have him continue in office. I believe that he has thought more of his country than of himself. He has done and is doing a great work for the United States, a work that will cause him, whether he serves again or not, to be remembered in history as one of the great Presidents. I look upon the trusts as a great and real power in the United States, and President Roosevelt has had the patriotism and courage to defy them. Mankind understands the meaning of his attitude and its bearing upon the future. He stands before the world as a statesman whose victories have been moral victories. . . .

"Here in Mexico we have had different conditions. I received this Government from the hands of a victorious army at a time when the people were divided and unprepared for the exercise of the extreme principles of democratic government. To have thrown upon the masses the whole responsibility of government at once would have produced conditions that might have discredited the cause of free government.

"Yet, although I got power at first from the army, an election was held as soon as possible and then my authority came from the people. I have tried to leave the Presidency several times, but it has been pressed upon me and I remained in office for the sake of the nation which trusted me. The fact that the price of Mexican securities dropped eleven points when I was ill at Cuernavaca indicates the kind of evidence that persuaded me to overcome my personal inclination to retire to private life.

"We preserved the republican and democratic form of government. We defended the theory and kept it intact. Yet we adopted a patriarchal policy in the actual administration of the nation's affairs, guiding and restraining popular tendencies, with full faith that an enforced peace would allow education, industry and commerce to develop elements of stability and unity in a naturally intelligent, gentle and affectionate people.

"I have waited patiently for the day when the people of the Mexican Republic would be prepared to choose and change their government at every election without danger of armed revolutions and without injury to the national credit or interference with national progress. I believe that day has come. . . .

"In the old days we had no middle class in Mexico because the minds of the people and their energies were wholly absorbed in politics and war. Spanish tyranny and misgovernment had disorganized society. The productive activities of the nation were abandoned in successive struggles. There was general confusion. Neither life nor property was safe. A middle class could not appear under such conditions."

"General Diaz," I interrupted, "you have had an unprecedented experience in the history of republics. For thirty years the destinies of this nation have been in your hands, to mold them as you will; but men die, while nations must continue to live. Do you believe that Mexico can continue to exist in peace as a republic? Are you satisfied that its future is assured under free institutions?"

It was worth while to have come from New York to Chapultepec Castle to see the hero's face at that moment. Strength, patriotism, warriorship, prophethood seemed suddenly to shine in his brown eyes.

"The future of Mexico is assured," he said in a clear voice. "The principles of democracy have not been planted very deep in our people, I fear. But the nation has grown and it loves liberty. Our difficulty has been that the people do not concern themselves enough about public matters for a democracy. The individual Mexican as a rule thinks much about his own rights and is always ready to assert them. But he does not think so much about the rights of others. He thinks of his privileges, but not of his duties. Capacity for self-restraint is the basis of democratic government, and self-restraint is possible only to those who recognize the rights of their neighbors.

"The Indians, who are more than half of our population, care little for politics. They are accustomed to look to those in authority for leadership instead of thinking for themselves. That is a tendency they inherited from the Spaniards, who taught them to refrain from meddling in public affairs and rely on the Government for guidance.

"Yet I firmly believe that the principles of democracy have grown and will grow in Mexico."

"But you have no opposition party in the Republic, Mr. President. How can free institutions flourish when there is no opposition to keep the majority, or governing party, in check?"

"It is true there is no opposition party. I have so many friends in the republic that my enemies seem unwilling to identify themselves with so small a minority. I appreciate the kindness of my friends and the confidence of my country; but such absolute confidence imposes responsibilities and duties that tire me more and more.

"No matter what my friends and supporters say, I retire when my present term of office ends, and I shall not serve again. I shall be eighty years old then.

"My country has relied on me and it has been kind to me. My friends have praised my merits and overlooked my faults. But they may not be willing to deal so generously with my successor and he may need my advice and support; therefore I desire to be alive when he assumes office so that I may help him."

He folded his arms over his deep chest and spoke with great emphasis.

"I welcome an opposition party in the Mexican Republic," he said. "If it appears, I will regard it as a blessing, not as an evil. And if it can develop power, not to exploit but to govern, I will stand by it, support it, advise it and forget myself in the successful inauguration of complete democratic government in the country.

"It is enough for me that I have seen Mexico rise among the peaceful and useful nations. I have no desire to continue in the Presidency. This nation is ready for her ultimate life of freedom. At the age of seventy-seven years I am satisfied with robust health. That is one thing which neither law nor force can create. I would not exchange it for all the millions of your American oil king."

His ruddy skin, sparkling eyes and light, elastic step went well with his words. For one who has endured the privations of war and imprisonment, and who to-day rises at six o'clock in the morning, working until late at night at the full of his powers, the physical condition of President Diaz, who is even now a notable hunter and who usually ascends the palace stairway two steps at a time, is almost unbelievable.

"The railway has played a great part in the peace of Mexico," he continued. "When I became President at first there were only two small lines, one connecting the capital with Vera Cruz, the other connecting it with Querétaro. Now we have more than nineteen thousand miles of railways. Then we had a slow and costly mail service, carried on by stage coaches, and the mail coach between the capital and Puebla would be stopped by highwaymen two or three times in a trip, the last robbers to attack it generally finding nothing left to steal. Now we have a cheap, safe and fairly rapid mail service throughout the country with more than twenty-two hundred post-offices. Telegraphing was a difficult thing in those

times. To-day we have more than forty-five thousand miles of telegraph wires in operation.

"We began by making robbery punishable by death and compelling the execution of offenders within a few hours after they
were caught and condemned. We ordered that wherever telegraph
wires were cut and the chief officer of the district did not catch the
criminal, he should himself suffer; and in case the cutting occurred
on a plantation the proprietor who failed to prevent it should be
hanged to the nearest telegraph pole. These were military orders,
remember.

"We were harsh. Sometimes we were harsh to the point of
cruelty. But it was all necessary then to the life and progress of the
nation. If there was cruelty, results have justified it."

The nostrils dilated and quivered. The mouth was a straight line.

"It was better that a little blood should be shed that much blood
should be saved. The blood that was shed was bad blood; the blood
that was saved was good blood.

"Peace was necessary, even an enforced peace, that the nation
might have time to think and work. Education and industry have
carried on the task begun by the army." . . .

"And which do you regard as the greatest force for peace, the
army or the schoolhouse?" I asked.

The soldier's face flushed slightly and the splendid white head
was held a little higher.

"You speak of the present time?"

"Yes."

"The schoolhouse. There can be no doubt of that. I want to see
education throughout the Republic carried on by the national Government. I hope to see it before I die. It is important that all citizens
of a republic should receive the same training, so that their ideals
and methods may be harmonized and the national unity intensified.
When men read alike and think alike they are more likely to act
alike."

"And you believe that the vast Indian population of Mexico is
capable of high development?"

"I do. The Indians are gentle and they are grateful, all except the
Yacquis and some of the Mayas. They have the traditions of an
ancient civilization of their own. They are to be found among the
lawyers, engineers, physicians, army officers and other professional
men."

Over the city drifted the smoke of many factories.

"It is better than cannon smoke," I said.

"Yes," he replied, "and yet there are times when cannon smoke is not such a bad thing. The toiling poor of my country have risen up to support me, but I cannot forget what my comrades in arms and their children have been to me in my severest ordeals."

There were actually tears in the veteran's eyes.

"That," I said, pointing to a hideously modern bull-ring near the castle, "is the only surviving Spanish institution to be seen in this landscape."

"You have not noticed the pawnshops," he exclaimed. "Spain brought to us her pawn-shops, as well as her bull-rings." . . .

There are nineteen thousand miles of railways operated in Mexico, nearly all with American managers, engineers and conductors, and one has only to ride on the Mexican Central system or to enjoy the trains de luxe of the National Line to realize the high transportation standards of the country.

So determined is President Diaz to prevent his country from falling into the hands of the trusts that the Government is taking over and merging in one corporation, with the majority stock in the Nation's hands, the Mexican Central, National and Inter-oceanic lines — so that, with this mighty trunk system of transportation beyond the reach of private control, industry, agriculture, commerce and passenger traffic will be safe from oppression.

This merger of ten thousand miles of railways into a single company, with $113,000,000 of the stock, a clear majority, in the Government's hands, is the answer of President Diaz and his brilliant Secretary of Finances to the prediction that Mexico may some day find herself helplessly in the grip of a railway trust.

Curiously enough, the leading American railway officials representing the lines which are to be merged and controlled by the Government spoke to me with great enthusiasm of the plan as a distinct forward step, desirable alike for shippers and passengers and for private investors in the roads.

Two-thirds of the railways of Mexico are owned by Americans, who have invested about $300,000,000 in them profitably.

As it is, freight and passenger rates are fixed by the Government, and not a time table can be made or changed without official approval.

It may surprise a few Americans to know that the first-class passenger rate in Mexico is only two and two-fifths cents a mile, while the second-class rate, which covers at least one-half of the whole passenger traffic of the country, is only one cent and one-fifth a mile — these figures being in terms of gold, to afford a comparison with American rates.

I have been privately assured by the principal American officers and investors of the larger lines that railway enterprises in Mexico are encouraged, dealt with on their merits and are wholly free from blackmail, direct or indirect. . . .

More than $1,200,000,000 of foreign capital has been invested in Mexico since President Diaz put system and stability into the nation. Capital for railways, mines, factories and plantations has been pouring in at the rate of $200,000,000 a year. In six months the Government sold more than a million acres of land.

In spite of what has already been done, there is still room for the investment of billions of dollars in the mines and industries of the Republic.

Americans and other foreigners interested in mines, real estate, factories, railways and other enterprises have privately assured me, not once, but many times, that, under Diaz, conditions for investment in Mexico are fairer and quite as reliable as in the most highly developed European countries. The President declares that these conditions will continue after his death or retirement.

Since Diaz assumed power, the revenues of the Government have increased from about $15,000,000 to more than $115,000,000, and yet taxes have been steadily reduced.

When the price of silver was cut in two, President Diaz was advised that his country could never pay its national debt, which was doubled by the change in values. He was urged to repudiate a part of the debt. The President denounced the advice as foolishness as well as dishonesty, and it is a fact that some of the greatest officers of the government went for years without their salaries that Mexico might be able to meet her financial obligations dollar for dollar.

The cities shine with electric lights and are noisy with electric trolley cars; English is taught in the public schools of the great Federal District; the public treasury is full and overflowing and the national debt decreasing; there are nearly seventy thousand foreigners living contentedly and prosperously in the Republic — more Americans than Spaniards; Mexico has three times as large a population to the square mile as Canada; public affairs have developed strong men like José Yves Limantour, the great Secretary of Finances, one of the most distinguished of living financiers; Vice-president Corral, who is also Secretary of the Interior; Ignacio

Mariscal, the Minister of Foreign Affairs, and Enrique Creel, the brilliant Ambassador at Washington.

And it is a land of beauty beyond compare. Its mountains and valleys, its great plateaus, its indescribably rich and varied foliage, its ever blooming and abundant flowers, its fruits, its skies, its marvelous climate, its old villages, cathedrals, churches, convents — there is nothing quite like Mexico in the world for variety and loveliness. But it is the gentle, trustful, grateful Indian, with his unbelievable hat and many-colored blanket, the eldest child of America, that wins the heart out of you. After traveling all over the world, the American who visits Mexico for the first time wonders how it happened that he never understood what a fascinating country of romance he left at his own door.

It is the hour of growth, strength and peace which convinces Porfirio Diaz that he has almost finished his task on the American continent.

Yet you see no man in a priest's attire in this Catholic country. You see no religious processions. The Church is silent save within her own walls. This is a land where I have seen the most profound religious emotion, the most solemn religious spectacles — from the blanketed peons kneeling for hours in cathedrals, the men carrying their household goods, the women suckling their babies, to that indescribable host of Indians on their knees at the shrine of the Virgin of Guadalupe.

I asked President Diaz about it while we paced the terrace of Chapultepec Castle.

He bowed his white head for a moment and then lifted it high, his dark eyes looking straight into mine.

"We allow no priest to vote, we allow no priest to hold public office, we allow no priest to wear a distinctive dress in public, we allow no religious processions in the streets," he said. "When we made those laws we were not fighting against religion, but against idolatry. We intend that the humblest Mexican shall be so far freed from the past that he can stand upright and unafraid in the presence of any human being. I have no hostility to religion; on the contrary, in spite of all past experience, I firmly believe that there can be no true national progress in any country or any time without real religion."

Such is Porfirio Díaz, the foremost man of the American hemisphere. What he has done, almost alone and in such a few years, for a people disorganized and degraded by war, lawlessness and comic-opera politics, is the great inspiration of Pan-Americanism, the hope of the Latin-American republics.

Whether you see him at Chapultepec Castle, or in his office in the National Palace, or in the exquisite drawing-room of his modest home in the city, with his young, beautiful wife and his children and grandchildren by his first wife about him, or surrounded by troops, his breast covered with decorations conferred by great nations, he is always the same — simple, direct and full of the dignity of conscious power.

In spite of the iron government he has given to Mexico, in spite of a continuance in office that has caused men to say that he has converted a republic into an autocracy, it is impossible to look into his face when he speaks of the principle of popular sovereignty without believing that even now he would take up arms and shed his blood in defense of it.

Only a few weeks ago Secretary of State Root summed up President Diaz when he said:

It has seemed to me that of all the men now living, General Porfirio Diaz, of Mexico, was best worth seeing. Whether one considers the adventurous, daring, chivalric incidents of his early career; whether one considers the vast work of government which his wisdom and courage and commanding character accomplished; whether one considers his singularly attractive personality, no one lives to-day that I would rather see than President Diaz. If I were a poet I would write poetic eulogies. If I were a musician I would compose triumphal marches. If I were a Mexican I should feel that the steadfast loyalty of a lifetime could not be too much in return for the blessings that he had brought to my country. As I am neither poet, musician nor Mexican, but only an American who loves justice and liberty and hopes to see their reign among mankind progress and strengthen and become perpetual, I look to Porfirio Diaz, the President of Mexico, as one of the great men to be held up for the hero-worship of mankind.

2. The Diaz System

JOHN KENNETH TURNER

The slavery and peonage of Mexico, the poverty and illiteracy, the general prostration of the people, are due, in my humble judg-

From *Barbarous Mexico* by John Kenneth Turner (Chicago: Charles H. Kerr & Company, 1910), pp. 120–137, *passim*.

ment, to the financial and political organization that at present rules
that country — in a word, to what I shall call the "system" of General Porfirio Diaz.

That these conditions can be traced in a measure to the history
of Mexico during past generations, is true. I do not wish to be unfair to General Diaz in the least degree. The Spanish Dons made
slaves and peons of the Mexican people. Yet never did they grind
the people as they are ground today. In Spanish times the peon at
least had his own little patch of ground, his own humble shelter;
today he has nothing. Moreover, the Declaration of Independence,
proclaimed just one hundred years ago, in 1810, proclaimed also
the abolition of chattel slavery. Slavery was abolished, though not
entirely. Succeeding Mexican governments of class and of church
and of the individual held the people in bondage little less severe.
But finally came a democratic movement which broke the back of
the church, which overthrew the rule of caste, which adopted a
form of government as modern as our own, which freed the slave
in fact as well as in name, which gave the lands of the people back
to the people, which wiped the slate clean of the blood of the
past. . . .

It was under Porfirio Diaz that slavery and peonage were re-
established in Mexico, and on a more merciless basis than they had
existed even under the Spanish Dons. Therefore, I can see no injustice in charging at least a preponderance of the blame for these
conditions upon the system of Diaz.

I say the "system of Diaz" rather than Diaz personally because,
though he is the keystone of the arch, though he is the government
of Mexico more completely than is any other individual the government of any large country on the planet, yet no one man can stand
alone in his iniquity. Diaz is the central prop of the slavery, but
there are other props without which the system could not continue
upright for a single day. For example, there is the collection of
commercial interests which profit by the Diaz system of slavery and
autocracy, and which puts no insignificant part of its tremendous
powers to holding the central prop upright in exchange for the special privileges that it receives. Not the least among these commercial interests are American, which, I blush to say, are quite as
aggressive defenders of the Diaz citadel as any. Indeed . . . these
American interests undoubtedly form the determining force of the
continuation of Mexican slavery. Thus does Mexican slavery come
home to us in the full sense of the term. . . .

In order that the reader may understand the Diaz system and
its responsibility in the degradation of the Mexican people, it will
be well to go back and trace briefly the beginnings of that system.
Mexico is spoken of throughout the world as a Republic. That is
because it was once a Republic and still pretends to be one. Mexico
has a constitution which has never been repealed, a constitution
said to be modeled after our own, and one which is, indeed, like
ours in the main. Like ours, it provides for a national congress, state
legislatures and municipal aldermen to make the laws, federal, state
and local judges to interpret them, and a president, governors and
local executives to administer them. Like ours, it provides for man-
hood suffrage, freedom of the press and of speech, equality before
the law, and the other guarantees of life, liberty and the pursuit of
happiness which we ourselves enjoy, in a degree, as a matter of
course.

Such was Mexico forty years ago. Forty years ago Mexico was at
peace with the world. She had just overthrown, after a heroic war,
the foreign prince, Maximilian, who had been seated as emperor by
the armies of Napoleon Third of France. Her president, Benito
Juarez, is today recognized in Mexico and out of Mexico as one of
the most able as well as unselfish patriots of Mexican history. Never
since Cortez fired his ships there on the gulf coast had Mexico enjoyed such prospects of political freedom, industrial prosperity and
general advancement.

But in spite of these facts, and the additional fact that he was
deeply indebted to Juarez, all his military promotions having been
received at the hands of the latter, General Porfirio Diaz stirred up
a series of rebellions for the purpose of securing for himself the
supreme power of the land. Diaz not only led one armed rebellion
against a peaceable, constitutional and popularly approved government, but he led three of them. For nine years he plotted as a common rebel. The support that he received came chiefly from bandits,
criminals and professional soldiers who were disgruntled at the anti-
militarist policy which Juarez had inaugurated and which, if he
could have carried it out a little farther, would have been effective
in preventing military revolutions in the future — and from the
Catholic church. . . .

In defiance of the will of the majority of the people of Mexico,
General Diaz, thirty-four years ago, came to the head of government. In defiance of the will of the majority of the people he has
remained there ever since — except for four years, from 1880 to
1884, when he turned the palace over to an intimate friend, Manuel

Gonzalez, on the distinct understanding that at the end of the four years Gonzalez would turn it back to him again.

Since no man can rule an unwilling people without taking away the liberties of that people, it can be very easily understood what sort of regime General Diaz found it necessary to establish in order to make his power secure. By the use of the army and the police powers generally, he controlled elections, the press and public speech and made of popular government a farce. By distributing the public offices among his generals and granting them free rein to plunder at will, he assured himself of the continued use of the army. By making political combinations with men high in the esteem of the Catholic church and permitting it to be whispered about that the church was to regain some of its former powers, he gained the silent support of the priests and the Pope. By promising full payment of all foreign debts and launching at once upon a policy of distributing favors among citizens of other countries, he made his peace with the world at large. . . .

Take, for example, Diaz's method of rewarding his military chiefs, the men who helped him overthrow the government of Lerdo. As quickly as possible after assuming the power, he installed his generals as governors of the various states and organized them and other influential figures in the nation into a national plunderbund. Thus he assured himself of the continued loyalty of the generals, on the one hand, and put them where he could most effectively use them for keeping down the people, on the other. One variety of rich plum which he handed out in those early days to his governors came in the form of charters giving his governors the right, as individuals, to organize companies and build railroads, each charter carrying with it a huge sum as a railroad subsidy.

The national government paid for the road and then the governor and his most influential friends owned it. Usually the railroads were ridiculous affairs, were of narrow-gauge and of the very cheapest materials, but the subsidy was very large, sufficient to build the road and probably equip it besides. During his first term of four years in office Diaz passed sixty-one railroad subsidy acts containing appropriations aggregating $40,000,000, and all but two or three of these acts were in favor of governors of states. In a number of cases not a mile of railroad was actually built, but the subsidies are supposed to have been paid, anyhow. In nearly every case the subsidy was the same, $12,880 per mile in Mexican silver, and in those days Mexican silver was nearly on a par with gold.

This huge sum was taken out of the national treasury and was supposedly paid to the governors, although Mexican politicians of the old times have assured me that it was divided, a part going out as actual subsidies and a part going directly into the hands of Diaz to be used in building up his machine in other quarters.

Certainly something more than mere loyalty, however invaluable it was, was required of the governors in exchange for such rich financial plums. It is a well authenticated fact that governors were required to pay a fixed sum annually for the privilege of exploiting to the limit the graft possibilities of their offices. For a long time Manuel Romero Rubio, father-in-law of Diaz, was the collector of these perquisites, the offices bringing in anywhere from $10,000 to $50,000 per year.

The largest single perquisite whereby Diaz enriched himself, the members of his immediate family, his friends, his governors, his financial ring and his foreign favorites, was found for a long time in the confiscation of the lands of the common people — a confiscation, in fact, which is going on to this day. Note that this land robbery was the first direct step in the path of the Mexican people back to their bondage as slaves and peons.

. . . The lands of the Yaquis of Sonora were taken from them and given to political favorites of the ruler. The lands of the Mayas of Yucatan, now enslaved by the *henequen* planters, were taken from them in almost the same manner. The final act in this confiscation was accomplished in the year 1904, when the national government set aside the last of their lands into a territory called Quintana Roo. This territory contains 43,000 square kilometers or 27,000 square miles. It is larger than the present state of Yucatan by 8,000 square kilometers, and moreover is the most promising land of the entire peninsula. Separated from the island of Cuba by a narrow strait, its soil and climate are strikingly similar to those of Cuba and experts have declared that there is no reason why Quintana Roo should not one day become as great a tobacco-growing country as Cuba. Further than that, its hillsides are thickly covered with the most valuable cabinet and dyewoods in the world. It is this magnificent country which, as the last chapter in the life of the Mayas as a nation, the Diaz government took and handed over to eight Mexican politicians.

In like manner have the Mayos of Sonora, the Papagos, the Tomosachics — in fact, practically all the native peoples of Mexico — been reduced to peonage, if not to slavery. Small holders of every tribe and nation have gradually been expropriated until today their number as property holders is almost down to zero. Their lands are in the hands of members of the governmental machine, or persons to whom the members of the machine have sold for profit — or in the hands of foreigners.

This is why the typical Mexican farm is the million-acre farm, why it has been so easy for such Americans as William Randolph Hearst, Harrison Gray Otis, E. H. Harriman, the Rockefellers, the Guggenheims and numerous others each to have obtained possession of millions of Mexican acres. This is why Secretary of Fomento Molina holds more than 15,000,000 acres of the soil of Mexico, why ex-Governor Terrazas, of Chihuahua, owns 15,000,000 acres of the soil of that state, why Finance Minister Limantour, Mrs. Porfirio Diaz, Vice-President Corral, Governor Pimentel, of Chiapas, Governor Landa y Escandon of the Federal District, Governor Pablo Escandon of Morelos, Governor Ahumada of Jalisco, Governor Cosio of Queretaro, Governor Mercado of Michoacan, Governor Canedo of Sinaloa, Governor Cahuantzi of Tlaxcala, and many other members of the Diaz machine are not only millionaires, but they are millionaires in Mexican real estate.

Chief among the methods used in getting the lands away from the people in general was through a land registration law which Diaz fathered. This law permitted any person to go out and claim any lands to which the possessor could not prove a recorded title. Since up to the time the law was enacted it was not the custom to record titles, this meant all the lands of Mexico. When a man possessed a home which his father had possessed before him, and which his grandfather had possessed, which his great-grandfather had possessed, and which had been in the family as far back as history knew; then he considered that he owned that home, all of his neighbors considered that he owned it, and all governments up to that of Diaz recognized his right to that home.

Supposing that a strict registration law became necessary in the course of evolution, had this law been enacted for the purpose of protecting the land owners instead of plundering them the government would, naturally, have sent agents through the country to apprise the people of the new law and to help them register their property and keep their homes. But this was not done and the conclusion is inevitable that the law was passed for the purpose of plundering.

At all events, the result of the law was a plundering. No sooner had it been passed than the aforesaid members of the governmental machine, headed by the father-in-law of Diaz, and Diaz himself, formed land companies and sent out agents, not to help the people keep their lands, but to select the most desirable lands in the country, register them, and evict the owners. This they did on a most tremendous scale. Thus hundreds of thousands of small farmers lost their property. Thus small farmers are still losing their property. . . .

Another favorite means of confiscating the homes of small owners is found in the juggling of state taxes. State taxes in Mexico are fearfully and wonderfully made. Especially in the less populous districts owners are taxed inversely as they stand in favor with the personality who represents the government in their particular district. No court, board or other responsible body sits to review unjust assessments. The *jefe político* may charge one farmer five times as much per acre as he charges the farmer across the fence, and yet Farmer No. 1 has no redress unless he is rich and powerful. He must pay, and if he cannot, the farm is a little later listed among the properties of the jefe politico, or one of the members of his family, or among the properties of the governor of the state or one of the members of his family. But if he is rich and powerful he is often not taxed at all. American promoters in Mexico escape taxation so nearly·invariably that the impression has got abroad in this country that land pays no taxes in Mexico. Even Frederick Palmer made a statement to this effect in his recent writings about that country.

Of course such bandit methods as were employed and are still employed were certain to meet with resistance, and so we find numerous instances of regiments of soldiers being called out to enforce collection of taxes or the eviction of time-honored landholders. . . .

. . . Hardly a month passes today without there being one or more reports in Mexican papers of disturbances, the result of confiscation of homes, either through the denunciation method or the excuse of nonpayment of taxes. . . .

Graft is an established institution in the public offices of Mexico. It is a right vested in the office itself, is recognized as such, and is respectable. There are two main functions attached to each public office, one a privilege, the other a duty. The privilege is that of using the special powers of the office for the amassing of a personal fortune; the duty is that of preventing the people from entering into any activities that may endanger the stability of the existing regime.

Theoretically, the fulfillment of the duty is judged as balancing the harvest of the privilege, but with all offices and all places this is not so, and so we find offices of particularly rosy possibilities selling for a fixed price. Examples are those of the jefes politicos in districts where the slave trade is peculiarly remunerative, as at Pachuca, Oaxaca, Veracruz, Orizaba, Cordoba and Rio Blanco; of the districts in which the drafting of soldiers for the army is especially let to the jefes politicos; of the towns in which the gambling privileges are let as a monopoly to the mayors thereof; of the states in which there exist opportunities extraordinary for governors to graft off the army supply contracts.

Monopolies called "concessions," which are nothing more nor less than trusts created by governmental decree, are dealt in openly by the Mexican government. Some of these concessions are sold for cash, but the rule is to give them away gratis or for a nominal price, the real price being collected in political support. The public domain is sold in huge tracts for a nominal price or for nothing at all, the money price, when paid at all, averaging about fifty Mexican *centavos* an acre. But never does the government sell to any individual or company not of its own special choice; that is, the public domain is by no means open to all comers on equal terms. Public concessions worth millions of dollars — to use the water of a river for irrigation purposes, or for power, to engage in this or that monopoly, have been given away, but not indiscriminately. These things are the coin with which political support is bought and as such are grafts, pure and simple.

Public action of any sort is never taken for the sake of improving the condition of the common people. It is taken with a view to making the government more secure in its position. Mexico is a land of special privileges extraordinary, though frequently special privileges are provided for in the name of the common people. An instance is that of the "Agricultural Bank," which was created in 1908. To read the press reports concerning the purpose of this bank one would imagine that the government had launched into a gigantic and benevolent scheme to re-establish its expropriated people in agriculture. The purpose, it was said, was to loan money to needy farmers. But nothing could be farther from the truth, for the purpose is to help out the rich farmer, and only the richest in the land. The bank has now been loaning money for two years, but so far not a single case has been recorded in which aid was given to help a farm that comprised less than thousands of acres. Millions have

been loaned on private irrigation projects, but never in lumps of
less than several tens of thousands. In the United States the farmer
class is an humble class indeed; in Mexico the typical farmer is the
king of millionaires, a little potentate. In Mexico, because of the
special privileges given by the government, medievalism still prevails outside the cities. The barons are richer and more powerful
than were the landed aristocrats before the French Revolution,
and the canaille poorer, more miserable.

And the special financial privileges centering in the cities are no
less remarkable than the special privileges given to the exploiters of
the *hacienda* slave. There is a financial ring consisting of members
of the Diaz machine and their close associates, who pluck all the
financial plums of the "republic," who get the contracts, the franchises and the concessions, and whom the large aggregations of
foreign capital which secure a footing in the country find it necessary
to take as coupon-clipping partners. The "Banco Nacional," an institution having some fifty-four branches and which has been compared flatteringly to the Bank of England, is the special financial
vehicle of the government camarilla. It monopolizes the major portion of the banking business of the country and is a convenient
cloak for the larger grafts, such as the railway merger, the true significance of which I shall present in a future chapter.

Diaz encourages foreign capital, for foreign capital means the
support of foreign governments. American capital has a smoother
time with Diaz than it has even with its own government, which is
very fine from the point of view of American capital, but not so
good from the point of view of the Mexican people. Diaz has even
entered into direct partnership with certain aggregations of foreign
capital, granting these aggregations special privileges in some lines
which he has refused to his own millionaires. These foreign partner-
ships which Diaz has formed has made his government international
insofar as the props which support his system are concerned. The
certainty of foreign intervention in his favor has been one of the
powerful forces which have prevented the Mexican people from
using arms to remove a ruler who imposed himself upon them by
the use of arms.

When I come to deal with the American partners of Diaz I mention those of no other nationality in the same breath, but it will be
well to bear in mind that England, especially, is nearly as heavily
as interested in Mexico as is the United States. While this country
has $900,000,000 (these are the figures given by Consul General
Shanklin about the first of the year 1910) invested in Mexico, Eng-

land (according to the South American Journal) has $750,000,000. However, these figures by no means represent the ratio between the degree of political influence exerted by the two countries. There the United States bests all the other countries combined. . . .

In this chapter I have attempted to give the reader an idea of the means which General Diaz employed to attract support to his government. To sum up, by means of a careful placing of public offices, public contracts and special privileges of multitudinous sorts, Diaz absorbed all of the more powerful men and interests within his sphere and made them a part of his machine. Gradually the country passed into the hands of his officeholders, their friends, and foreigners. And for this the people paid, not only with their lands, but with their flesh and blood. They paid in peonage and slavery. For this they forfeited liberty, democracy and the blessings of progress.

B. Contemporary Documents

3. Mexico Needs Foreign Capital (1897)

"El Economista Mexicano"

It has become a frequent practice among some newspapers of the Mexican press to decry the use of foreign capital in the nation's development as being dangerous to our territorial integrity or damaging in the economic sphere because it is said that all our riches are going to end in foreign hands. Accordingly, there is bitter criticism of the expansion of North American and European capital that has recently made itself felt in the country.

L'Écho du Mexique has taken on the job of refuting these hoary fears, putting matters in their true light. We are going to paraphrase some of the arguments set forth by our intelligent French colleague and add some words of our own on this issue, which is of genuine interest now that a laudable upsurge of development is being felt everywhere.

From *Historia documental de México,* ed. Ernesto de la Torre Villar, Moisés González Navarro, Stanley Ross (Mexico: Universidad Nacional Autónoma de México, Instituto de Investigaciones Históricas, 1964), II, pp. 391–393. Reprinted by permission.

Foreign capital employed here in any kind of enterprise — agricultural, industrial, or mining — is not harmful to the country, nor can any criticism of its expansion be justified. It is true that the returns from this capital go abroad and do not circulate among us, but this is the only lamentable feature — not a necessarily censurable one — that the use of such capital in Mexico offers. But the funds employed in business dealings, tools, buildings, machinery, etc. serve to increase the country's wealth, just as the wages and salaries paid by these enterprises spread among the proletarian class. The benefit to the country is obvious, especially if the enterprise or business in question had not been previously undertaken by Mexican entrepreneurs or if there had been no hope that it would be undertaken. If the choice is one of not having businesses in certain areas of production or of having them based on foreign capital, the latter is preferable, especially since, regardless of the object of the business, it always yields a portion that belongs to the country in which it is established and leaves benefits in its wake, even when the products and profits are divided among foreign stockholders.

There is another aspect to this question. Foreign capital, accustomed to the industrial movement of the United States or Europe, can take over and direct enterprises which we would consider impossible because of our customary timidity. Thus our natural resources are developed, and unknown sources of wealth are revealed which would never appear otherwise. Are all the enterprises in which foreign capital participates profitable? Are they all sources of stupendous earnings? Obviously not. Many go bankrupt and fail, but even so they leave some benefit because they give us a sound lesson which in turn becomes part of our public wealth. A failure of this type means little to a foreign corporation, we suppose, because investments, even some that are audacious and foolish, are constantly being made abroad; but these investments are considered vehicles for the operation of capital, bringing some benefit and later serving as an example. How often a company that fails serves to show the true path to its successor, which reaps a bountiful harvest!

Therefore, the opinion that rejects the foreign capital which comes to develop our natural resources is ill-founded. Even if one concedes that the expansion of such investments could harm us in some way, we do not understand why the censure is directed at the investors and not at those who being able to avoid them do not do so.

We do not have the attitude of the famous dog in the manger

which did not want to eat but would allow no one else to eat; on the contrary, we want the banquet of our wealth to be prepared, the field being open as it is to all activities and to all honorable and wholesome labor. Criticism of the use of foreign capital should in fact be directed against our men of wealth who completely ignore the innumerable means that the country offers for making money; instead, they devote themselves only to enterprises that are familiar and safe and demand little effort. But the vigor that our natural elements are acquiring will soon leave the safe businesses of our capitalists behind. In the future when they look for returns of some importance for their funds, they will no longer be able to obtain them in the same easy manner as at present, and they will find the best doors closed and the best places filled.

Criticism, then, ought to take as its point of departure our national indolence, which abandons our great resources in their period of development, and not foreign capital, which, though it may leave its profits in foreign hands, increases our wealth and shows us the firm and sure path of the future.

4. A Catholic Conference Discusses
Agrarian Problems (1904)

TRINIDAD SÁNCHEZ SANTOS

The lawyer Trinidad Sánchez Herrera tells us in his report that the peon is a drunkard because of his need to offset his hunger, because of custom, exploitation, ignorance, the hypocrisy of the authorities, and a tendency toward idleness. The rural wage-earner abandons the fields for two-fifths of the year, and during this entire period brutishly surrenders himself to drunkenness.

The second section has made dreadful revelations regarding the family among the wage-earners with whom it deals. In reality, the family does not exist, and since domestic society is and must be the source and basis of civil society, it is very clear that this enormous mass of persons does not constitute a society . . . but a horde with less cohesion than a gypsy tribe. . . .

From *Historia documental de México*, ed. Ernesto 'de la Torre Villar, Moisés González Navarro, Stanley Ross (Mexico: Universidad Nacional Autónoma de México, Instituto de Investigaciones Históricas, 1964), II, pp. 400–403. Reprinted by permission.

The commission tells us that this proletarian rural class, shunning lawful marriage, normally gives itself up to concubinage characterized by a constant changing of partners; and Sr. González, in the judicious work adopted by the commission, details with unusual exactitude the disastrous consequences of this troglodytic savagery. The man abandons the woman as soon as he feels the weight of his offspring, and to seduce another woman he moves from his place of residence. . . .

The third section describes the truly chaotic ignorance of the masses and presents us with a plan for regional school organization which you did well in accepting because it is excellent from a technical point of view; to be fruitful, however, it demands the vigorous completion of [the workers'] uneven development. I have already said it before the distinguished Society of Geography and Statistics: the regional school, a form of normal school identical to that proposed by the section, will be empty so long as the father earns twenty-five cents a day, so long as these twenty-five cents are pocketed by the renter of the [local] store, so long as the renter is exploited by the store owner, by the wholesaler, and by the tax collector. The school will be empty so long as the father . . . cannot support his children and forces them to support themselves from the time they take their first steps. . . . I do not know how anyone can go to school before, during, or after fourteen hours of work and sun, and I do not know how anyone can go to school without eating. I do not understand how we can think about grammar without first thinking about the tortilla.

Throughout the world the home developed before the school. And if the second section tells us — and our own eyes confirm its report — that the family does not exist among the workers, the first thing we ought to do is to create it so that the home may grow out of it, and from the home the school, which is actually a collective representative of the home.

This is so true that the fourth section, which was given the task of studying means to end the poverty of the rural workers, in a practical report, stopped short before the hurdle of child labor, which is necessary for the subsistence of children. . . .

Finally, the fifth section, as if gathering all the black drapery of this gloomy scene, depicts a positive hell in its study of the physical, moral, and intellectual condition of the rural working class. . . .

In order to combat alcoholism, the first section proposed and the congress approved, among other conclusions, education and

antialcoholic propaganda; establishment of recreation centers on
the haciendas where leisure hours may be spent; written contracts
between master and peon imposing fines for those who get drunk;
and petition to the state legislature [of Hidalgo] for the adoption
of Tlaxcala's legislation of this matter.

To combat concubinage and the shocking rate of child mortality,
which, according to the learned Dr. Galindo, reaches seventy-five
per cent, several very effective conclusions have been approved, including those that the Bishop [of Tulcaningo, José Mora del Río]
supported with ample economic concessions to facilitate marriage
and those which shall be requested of the governor of the state with
respect to civil ceremonies. In addition, extensive vaccination and
action by the Board of Health in so serious a matter.

To combat ignorance, regional schools; to combat poverty, employment records, bonuses, savings banks, and other proposals you
have heard.

But without denying the effectiveness and wisdom of all that has
been approved, I believe that the group which truly put its finger
in the sore — though timidly because the sore is so sensitive — was
the fourth section, which asked that wages be increased.

This, gentlemen, is the basis of all the changes that the congress
seeks to encourage. The section asks for a wage of only thirty-seven
cents. This is insufficient, it is unjust, it is contrary to the interests
of the worker and the owner. So long as the wage-earner does not
eat meat, so long as he cannot support his children while they
finish their schooling, so long as he has no needs other than the
dirty rag that half clothes him, so long as he is a legal slave in
bondage for a loan of two hundred *pesos*, he will not be a civilized
man, and we shall have no agriculture. Some landowners assert that
it is impossible to pay a higher wage. This is not true. . . .

But in any case, even if this project is abandoned, history will say
that it was a Bishop who, inspired by apostolic and patriotic ardor,
appealed to you in time to hold back the storm; he appealed to you
in time to encourage a great work of justice and salvation, and he
put you face to face with your duties toward God, your children,
and your country.

5. Program of the Liberal Party (1906)

Every political party that struggles to acquire effective influence in the direction of the public affairs of its country is obliged to declare to the people, in a clear and precise form, the ideals for which it fights and the program that it proposes to put into practice if it is favored by victory. This duty might even be considered an advantage to honorable parties, for their objectives, being just and beneficent, will undoubtedly win the sympathy of many citizens, who will adhere to the party inspired by such objectives in order to attain them.

The Liberal Party, dispersed by the persecution of the Dictatorship, weak, and nearly moribund for a long time, has succeeded in healing its wounds and is now in the process of organizing itself. The Liberal Party is struggling against the despotism that today rules our country and, sure as it is of finally triumphing over the Dictatorship, believes that it is time solemnly to declare to the Mexican people in detail the desires it proposes to realize once it obtains the influence it seeks in the orientation of our national destinies. . . .

Since all the amendments that have been made to the constitution of 1857 by the Government of Porfirio Díaz are considered illegal, it may seem unnecessary to call for the reduction of the presidential term to four years and a ban on re-election. However, these points are so important and were proposed with such unanimity and forcefulness that it has been deemed fitting to include them explicitly in the Program. The advantages of the alternation of power and of not surrendering it to one man for an excessively long time do not have to be proven. . . .

Compulsory military service is one of the most odious of tyrannies, incompatible with the rights of the citizen of a free country. This tyranny will be suppressed. In the future, when the National Government will not need, as the president Dictatorship does, so many bayonets to sustain it, all those who are forced to bear arms today will be free, and only those who wish to will remain in the army. . . .

From *Breve historia de la revolución Mexicana*, by Jesús Silva Herzog (Mexico: Fondo de Cultura Económica, 1960), I, pp. 76–108, *passim*. Reprinted by permission.

The education of children ought to receive very special attention from a Government which truly desires the advancement of the country. The basis of the greatness of a people lies in the primary school, and the best institutions are of little value and run the risk of being destroyed if alongside them there do not exist thousands of well-equipped schools where the citizens who will safeguard those institutions may be formed. . . . The need to create as many new schools as are required by the country's school-age population will be immediately acknowledged by everyone who is not an enemy of progress. . . .

It is pointless to declare in the Program that the Mexican should be given preference over the foreigner, other conditions being equal, for this is already part of our constitution. As a means of effectively avoiding foreign domination and guaranteeing our territorial integrity, no measure seems more fitting than to consider all foreigners who acquire real estate as Mexican citizens. . . .

The Catholic clergy, exceeding the bounds of its religious mission, has always attempted to make itself a political power and has brought great evils upon the country, either as co-ruler of the state with conservative governments or as a rebel against liberal governments. This attitude of the clergy, inspired by its savage hatred of democratic institutions, produces a similar attitude in honorable governments which will not permit religious encroachments on civil power nor patiently tolerate the continuous rebelliousness of clericalism. If the Mexican clergy would emulate the conduct of its counterparts in other countries, such as England and the United States . . . no government would disturb it or take the trouble to keep it under surveillance. . . . The aggressive attitude of the clergy toward the liberal state compels the state to make itself respected energetically. If the Mexican clergy, like that of other countries, always remained within the religious sphere, political changes would not affect it. But since it is at the head of a militant party — the conservative party — it must resign itself to suffer the consequences of its conduct. . . .

A Government that is interested in the effective welfare of the entire people cannot remain indifferent toward the very important question of labor. Thanks to the Dictatorship of Porfirio Díaz, which puts its power at the service of all the exploiters of the people, the Mexican worker has been reduced to the most wretched conditions; wherever he lends his services, he is obliged to work long and hard for a daily wage of a few cents. The sovereign capitalist imposes, without appeal, the conditions of labor, which are always disastrous for the worker, who has to accept them for two reasons: because poverty forces him to work at any price or because the bayonets of the Dictatorship take care of subduing him if he rebels against the abuses of the rich. Therefore, the Mexican worker accepts jobs of twelve or more hours a day for salaries of less than seventy-five cents, and finds himself obliged to endure discounts from his miserable wage for medical services, religion, civil or religious holidays, and other things, in addition to the fines that are imposed on any pretext.

The rural worker is in an even more deplorable situation than the industrial worker, for he is a veritable serf of the modern feudal lords. In general, these workers are supposedly given a daily wage of twenty-five cents or less, but they do not even receive this meager sum in cash. Since the masters have taken pains to burden the peons with more or less nebulous debts, the former collect the latters' wages as interest and provide them with some corn and beans only to keep them from dying of hunger. . . .

A work day of eight hours and a minimum daily wage of one *peso* is the least that can be sought so that the worker will at least be rescued from poverty, so that fatigue will not drain him of all his energy, and so that he may have the time and desire to seek education and diversion after his work. . . . What is being sought now is to uproot the abuses of which the worker is a victim and to put him in a position to struggle against capital. . . . If the worker were left in his present situation, he would barely manage to improve, for the black poverty in which he lives would continue to oblige him to accept all the conditions of the exploiter. On the other hand, if he is guaranteed fewer hours of work and a higher salary . . . his yoke will be lightened, and he will be able to fight for greater gains, to unite and organize and strengthen himself in order to wrest new and better concessions from capital. . . .

The improvement of working conditions on the one hand and, on the other, the equitable distribution of land, with facilities for cultivating and developing it without restrictions, would produce inestimable advance for the nation. Not only would the classes directly benefitted be saved from destitution and acquire certain comforts, but there would be great development of our agriculture and industry and of all the sources of public wealth, which are today stagnant because of our widespread poverty. In effect, when the people are too poor, when their resources are enough only to eat badly, they consume only articles of prime necessity, and on a small scale at that. How can industries be established, how can textiles, furniture, and similar objects be produced in a country in which the majority of the people cannot obtain any of the comforts of life? . . . But if these starvelings get enough to eat, if they are in a position to satisfy their normal needs, in a word, if their labor is well or at least adequately remunerated, they will consume an infinity of articles of which they are today deprived, and large-scale production of these articles will become necessary. When the millions of pariahs that today vegetate in hunger and nakedness eat less badly, use clothing and shoes, and no longer have mats as their sole furniture, the now insignificant demand for thousands of objects will increase in colossal proportions, and industry, agriculture, and commerce will all be impelled to develop on a scale which will never be reached so long as the present conditions of general poverty continue. . . .

Mexicans: Make a choice between what despotism offers you and what the Program of the Liberal Party offers! If you prefer shackles, poverty, humiliation before the foreigner, the gray life of the debased pariah, support the Dictatorship that gives you all this. If you prefer liberty, economic betterment, the dignity of Mexican citizenship, the proud life of the man who is his own master, come to the Liberal Party, which fraternizes with all worthy and virile men. Unite your efforts with those of all who fight for justice, in order to hasten that glorious day on which the tyranny shall fall forever and the long-awaited democracy shall rise with all the splendors of a star that shall never cease to shine in the serene horizon of the fatherland.

6. Mexican Workers, Do Not Go to the United States! (1910)

"El Imparcial"

Thousands of workers are being hired in the mining district of Parral, Chihuahua, and it is calculated that at least 2,000 more can be easily employed in construction work on the great haciendas

From *Historia documental de México*, ed. Ernesto de la Torre Villar, Moisés González Navarro, Stanley Ross (Mexico: Universidad Nacional Autónoma de México, Instituto de Investigaciones Históricas, 1964), II, pp. 427–429. Reprinted by permission.

connected with the railroads that will link various mines. The wages being paid are the highest in the Republic, and the cost of living this year will be very low in comparison with previous years because of the prospect of a good crop of corn and beans.

These lines, which we excerpted from a letter written to us, offer a contrast to the bitter complaints that we receive every day from Mexicans who, dreaming of the promised land, cross our northern border to enter the United States. It is untrue that, as some suppose, there is an extraordinary demand for laborers in the United States; it is untrue that Mexican workers are paid wages that are really higher than those paid here; it is untrue, in a word, that they are paid and treated better there than in their own country.

Emigration is generally due to one of two causes: the excessive poverty of the soil or an oversupply of workers. And in Mexico the soil is not so poor that it cannot satisfy the needs of fourteen million inhabitants, nor are laborers so numerous (we refer to those who work, not to those who remain inactive) that they cannot all find employment. But, without exaggeration, over 50 per cent of the Mexicans spend the year in idleness; the benign climate requires only that they half cover their nakedness; the fertile soil asks only that, when the rainy season draws near, they sow a handful of corn which will give them enough to eat for twelve months.

And while this is going on in rural areas, industry is short of manpower. There are firms which find themselves obliged to hire foreign workers, and so we see our workers leaving the field to foreigners and emigrating when they could find sufficient elements of life here. The mirage of the United States with all its marvelous delights, which usually turn into the cruelest deceptions, is what induces our compatriots to leave their homes and families in search of magnificent salaries which they never receive. The only things they find are bad treatment, irritating injustices, and continuous humiliation. They must constantly be told: Mexican workers, don't go to the United States! While there is a job for you here, stay in your own country!

C. Later Views

7. The Díaz Regime as Background for the Revolution

CHARLES C. CUMBERLAND

When in September, 1910, Mexico played host to the embassies of the world at the magnificent spectacle celebrating a century of Mexican independence, the special delegates vied with one another in extolling the virtues and strength of the Díaz regime. General Porfirio Díaz was completing his seventh term as constitutional president of Mexico, having been the dictator of his country for thirty-four years, and was then about to embark upon his eighth term. His nation was honored and respected; as a head of state Díaz had been phenomenally successful in stabilizing Mexico and bringing her material prosperity. The power and prestige of the aged dictator, who appeared to be hale and vigorous in spite of his eighty years, had never been greater; his government was believed to be impervious to attack, his power unassailable, his country assured of a peaceful future. And yet, within the space of eight months the Díaz government crumbled, the dictator and most of his chief advisors fled into exile, and a revolution of tremendous force began.

That the Díaz government was a dictatorship no one denied. Even its strongest supporters freely admitted that the Constitution of 1857 had been perverted, that the branches of government were nonexistent inasmuch as Díaz was the final arbiter in all questions, and that "democracy" was merely a term used indiscriminately. As Francisco Bulnes expressed it, the question was not whether Díaz was a dictator, since the Mexicans in the past had possessed neither liberty nor democracy, but whether he was a good or a bad dictator. His task, on assuming control in 1876, had been to weld the Mexican people into a peaceful unit, to stabilize the government

From *Mexican Revolution: Genesis under Madero* by Charles C. Cumberland (Austin: University of Texas Press, 1952), pp. 3–28, *passim*. Reprinted by permission.

and pacify the country, and to bring material gain and prosperity to
the nation. Each part of the task impinged on the other; failure in
one would have meant almost inevitable failure in the other
two. . . .

Within a relatively short time after coming to power, Díaz managed to obtain the active or tacit support of the great majority of
the Mexican people of all classes by attempting to meet the special
interests of each class. Through this practice, supplemented by a
policy of harsh repression against revolutionaries and bandits, he
brought peace to Mexico, the first peace the nation had known since
the colonial period, and laid the foundation for an amazing material development. Railway lines, which in 1876 had been negligible, totaled more than fifteen thousand miles in 1910. During the
same period, exports and imports increased nearly tenfold, with a
favorable balance of trade in most years. Smelting of precious and
semiprecious metals increased fourfold, petroleum production became a major industry, textile mills were built by the hundreds,
sugar mills sprang up in the southern states, and numerous smaller
but important industries began. The prosperity of the epoch was
reflected in the favorable relationship between national debt and
national income, and in the foreign-credit standing. Mexican bonds
on foreign markets sold at a premium, the national debt declined
until in the early 1900's it was the smallest in the country's history,
revenues increased more than tenfold, and reserves accumulated
annually. The domestic and foreign financial standing of the Mexican government, under the direction of the dictatorship, was very
sound. . . .

It was the economic advances and their by-products . . . that
served as a stimulus for most of the support of, and much of the
opposition to, the dictatorship. In view of the general financial condition of Mexico and her people when Díaz came to power — the
government was heavily in debt and the people had little cash reserve for new investment — it was absolutely necessary to encourage
a flow of foreign capital to Mexico if there was to be material development. From the beginning of his administration, Díaz deliberately
fostered foreign investment on terms highly advantageous to the
investor. The policy brought money to Mexico, but the zealous regard for the interests of the foreigner created another class in Mexican society and added to the already prejudicial social and economic stratification. The foreigner, particularly the American, was
now considered the most important element in society, with much

of the economic legislation framed to favor his group. The concessions made to foreigners, especially in the changes in the mining code, worked to the grave disadvantage of the nation, inasmuch as the government's proportion of income from the mines was lessened and speculation in mining properties was encouraged. The preference granted to foreigners was constantly humiliating to the nationals and was one of the most irritating facets of the dictatorship. On the other hand, often the robber was robbed, for the majority of foreigners who invested in Mexico were victimized by ignorance and sharp dealing, even though many of those who came to the country did amass fortunes.

The emphasis on industrialization had other evil effects as well, for with the development of monopolies the already clearly defined difference between rich and poor became even more marked. Mexico's economy was largely controlled by a small group of businessmen and financiers who completely dominated money and credit, controlled the most lucrative concessions, and soon became the "arbiters of the prosperity of the Mexicans." For example, of the sixty-six financial, transportation, insurance, and industrial corporations listed in the 1908 report of the Banco Central Mexicano, thirty-six had common directors from a group of thirteen men; and nineteen of the corporations had more than one of the thirteen. One of the thirteen men was on the boards of nine banks, one railroad, one insurance company, and four industrial concerns. This tight control by a small group led to many of the economic and social abuses of which the Díaz government was accused, and brought into being what a Díaz opponent called "mercantilism." "It was this 'mercantilism,'" he said, "which overwhelmed the nation, increased despotism, despoiled the people, implanted degrading speculation, and sustained infamous and depraved governors." As the monopolists became more opulent, they were blinded by their own prosperity and became less able than ever to see the needs of the less fortunate. Their own prosperity, too, bolstered by the statistics of production, foreign trade, and finances, convinced them that Mexico as a nation was prosperous and that their own interests were synonymous with national interests.

In the last decade of the nineteenth century, a few men representing the new moneyed class banded together under Díaz' father-in-law, Manuel Romero Rubio, into a group which soon came to be called the Científicos. Hardly a political party at its inception, the organization was nonetheless allied closely with a political party formed in 1892 and came to exercise all the functions of a party. The group soon determined that the most effective means of guaranteeing a continuation of the economic system that had developed would be to control the government in so far as possible during Díaz' life and absolutely after his death. Until the formation of the Científicos, Díaz had maintained his early policy of meeting the demands of the mestizos; but as the Científicos grew in power, they successfully drew him away from the mestizos and convinced him of the necessity for supporting the creoles. Looked upon by many in the nineties and in the early years of the new century as the hope for a regenerated Mexico, the Científicos came to be feared and hated, even by men who had previously been their ardent supporters. . . .

There were many evidences, tenuous to be sure, of economic instability after 1904, even in [Minister of Hacienda José Ives] Limantour's own special province — banking. Adoption of the gold standard in 1905, followed by the 1907 money panic in the United States and an export price decline, brought shrinking national revenues, which necessitated foreign borrowing, and at the same time placed a heavy strain on domestic financial institutions. The banks, although outwardly prosperous, demonstrated symptoms of instability which endangered the entire Mexican financial structure. Limantour himself recognized the symptoms and called a national conference of bankers early in 1908 for the purpose of studying the situation and proposing new laws to rectify the existing weaknesses. The banks had obviously been indulging in speculation, lending enormous sums on poor security; institutions authorized to issue bank notes were particularly at fault, engaging in practices which sometimes brought large returns but which were generally unsound. As a consequence of the conference and Limantour's recommendations, a new banking law to correct some of the dangerous policies and to encourage the establishment of investment and mortgage banks was passed in the summer of 1908.

The new regulations, however, did not correct all the evils. Less than a year later the Banco Central Mexicano, the central reserve institution, was in a condition that approached the critical. The weakness of the bank was largely the responsibility of the government itself, which at various times had "suggested" to the bank that loans be made to administration friends. When the public learned that the central bank had absorbed enough worthless paper to impair its capital, confidence in all credit and financial institutions was seriously undermined. . . .

As might be expected in such a financial situation, inflation was rampant during most of the latter part of the Díaz regime. The cost of most items, particularly the staples on which the mass of the population depended, increased enormously; there was not a corresponding increase in the wages of agricultural and industrial workers. The wage earners were therefore forced into a constantly deteriorating position. What was happening to corn, a basic part of the diet of 85 per cent of the population, indicates the trend. Between 1893 and 1906 the value of corn per unit increased on the average by 50 per cent, and after 1906 the increase was more rapid. Occasionally the government would sell corn at "much lower prices than those established by the speculators," to use Díaz' words, but these sales were temporary expedients only and were usually confined to the capital itself. Somewhat the same trend was noted in other staples. Even more destructive of the well-being of the masses was the violent fluctuation in the price of staples from day to day and from place to place; a change of 400 per cent in a matter of days was not unusual. The government, in spite of the obvious need for price stabilization, did nothing permanently constructive. . . .

While basic commodity prices were on the increase, there was no ascertainable rise in salaries. In the early nineteenth century Baron Alexander von Humboldt had estimated the average daily wage to be approximately twenty-five centavos; in 1891 the prevailing wage was between twenty-five and fifty centavos, with the average nearer the lower figure; in 1908 the daily wage was almost exactly what it had been one hundred years earlier. In sum total, the static wage and the increasing cost of commodities meant a drastic decline in real wages. . . .

In the face of his rapidly deteriorating economic position, the laborer was helpless. Not only were there no labor laws to aid the worker but as Díaz became more closely allied with the creoles and their interests he became less sympathetic to the predicament of the mestizos and Indians, who composed the working class. A cheap labor supply being one of the principal assets which Mexico could offer to foreign investors and Mexican industrialists, and the general standard of work among the laborers being rather poor, the government never considered that protection of the laborer was either necessary or desirable. In vain did some intellectuals demand an improvement of conditions; in vain did Wistano Luis Orozco, scholar and humanitarian, insist that the lower classes were the brothers of the remainder of society and had a right to demand improvement, "morally and physically." The alliance between government and special privilege was too strong. Labor organizations were practically unknown before 1900; and even if the workers had been organized, they would have found it almost impossible to act in their own behalf. In most states and territories the laws forbade strikes; in the Federal District heavy fines and imprisonment could be imposed on any person attempting to use physical or moral force for the purpose of increasing salaries or wages. Even in areas where no specific law applied to striking, various means were used, often with the aid of public officials, to defeat the aims of the workers.

But these industrially idyllic conditions, in which the laborer worked for a pittance without question, could not continue indefinitely. The syndicalist and anarchist concepts, though late in penetrating into Mexico, became known after the turn of the century through the work and writing of Spaniards and Mexicans, the most important of whom was the Mexican Ricardo Flores Magón. Accordingly, the workers, "better taught than before to look out for their own interests, resented . . . oppression and resolutely aspired to improve their condition." Beginning in 1906, the laborers insisted that wages be raised and hours shortened; as a result of the industrialists' adamant refusal to meet these demands, a period of unrest developed. Although the strikes were defeated in most cases through government intercession, most industrial centers saw strife of varying intensity, and the workers were at last beginning to realize their potential strength, even though industrial labor constituted only a small proportion of the country's total labor force. . . .

The poor condition in which the industrial worker found himself had its counterpart, perhaps exaggerated to a degree, in the situation of the vast number of Indians whose primary source of livelihood was the land. The rural inhabitants, largely Indian, had been at the mercy of the Spaniard and the creole during the colonial epoch and continued in that state after independence. But many Indian villages had been allowed to retain the community holdings which were in their possession prior to the Conquest, and many more had been granted land by the Spanish crown. These areas, called *ejidos* though actually divided into five distinct classifications, served as a guarantee of partial independence for members of the community, but in the immediate postindependence period considerable difference of opinion arose among liberals over the question of the Indian and his relation to the land. Some, arguing that the Indian did not have a European concept of ownership, insisted that the village ejidos be left undisturbed; others, convinced that communal holding was evidence of backwardness and was not conducive to progress, favored a distribution of village land among the inhabitants of the village, with the individuals holding the parcels in fee simple. It was this last contention which prevailed when the triumphant liberals, after defeating Santa Anna and his conservative supporters in the Revolution of Ayutla, drafted the Constitution of 1857. The Ley Lerdo, which had been passed the previous year and which prohibited civil or religious corporations from owning real property not directly necessary for the functioning of the corporations, was written into the constitution. The village lands were therefore open to distribution among the members of the communities.

In the meantime the haciendas, enormous holdings of land often poorly and incompletely cultivated, were becoming increasingly important as an institution — economic, social, and political — in the rural areas. Many haciendas dated from the colonial period, but with the application of the Ley Lerdo and the Reform Laws effectuated a few years later, and with the confiscation, during both the War of Reform and the French Intervention, of much of the property belonging to the losing factions, the hacienda system was extended and a new hacienda class developed. . . .

It was on this foundation that the Díaz land system developed, and it was in the agrarian field that the Díaz government recorded one of its greatest failures. In a nation which depended heavily on agriculture, the Díaz government made no attempt to improve agricultural production through education or experimentation. Although much of the country was arid or semiarid and needed irrigation planning on a national scale, the government did practically nothing. It did not attempt to relieve the critical food shortage by encouraging increased production of cereals or other items consumed by the masses; although statistics indicate an annual increase in agricultural production, the increase was largely in items for export and gave little aid to the mass of the population. These were errors of omission; much more serious were the errors of commission in land legislation.

Díaz was not completely responsible for the development which robbed the villages of their land and forced the major portion of the Indian population into economic slavery; previous legal and constitutional provisions had set the pattern. The first interpretations of the constitutional provision had stipulated that the *suertes,* or

terrenos de común repartimiento — agricultural lands attached to
the villages at the time of the Conquest — were not subject to parceling, and as long as that interpretation prevailed many villages in
the heart of the agricultural districts would retain their independence. By successive decrees in 1889 and 1890, however, Díaz
brought all village lands within the categories to be parceled, and
from that time forward the laws were more stringently applied.
The new owner, unaccustomed to thinking in terms of private
ownership and not given proper protection by the government, was
easily victimized by unscrupulous officials and by individuals who
legally or illegally gained control of the land. In the final analysis,
the Indian villager too often found that as a result of the distribution he no longer had access to any land of his own and was forced
to seek employment at the nearest hacienda.

Not all the Indian villages, however, lost their land through the
instrumentality of the distribution law; many were victimized outright by a variety of other means. In some cases grasping government officials, charged with the responsibility of parceling the land
and dispensing justice to the villagers, merely sold all village
property to a company or an individual; such sales were irregular
and illegal, of course, but the despoliation was effectuated nevertheless. In many cases the village was destroyed when an outsider
gained control of the water supply and forced the village to sell.
But the most disastrous practice, in so far as the loss of village lands
was concerned, resulted from a series of surveying laws passed in
1863, 1883, and 1894. Under these laws, each more advantageous
than the last to the surveying companies and demanding fewer
responsibilities from them, national lands were surveyed by individuals and companies and the surveyors allowed to gain control of
enormous amounts of land. Under the 1894 law any parcel to which
a legal title could not be produced could be declared *terrenos
baldíos*, or untilled national lands, and any individual could file a
claim to purchase the property at a set cash price. . . . Through
the operation of the laws, and through official or quasi-official
chicanery, enormous quantities of land came under the control of a
small group of men or companies. One estimate indicates that over
two and one-quarter million acres of good land, representing the
means of livelihood of tens of thousands of Indians, passed from
the Indian communities to the *hacendados;* this was in addition to
the untold millions of acres of bona fide national lands which were
alienated.

A combination of the above forces and practices meant disaster to the Indian village, and tremendous growth to the haciendas. The free agricultural village — one in which the majority of the residents had access to sufficient lands to make a living — was disappearing, and concentration of land ownership was intensifying. Between 1881 and 1889, 14 per cent of the arable land was concentrated in twenty-nine companies or individuals; by 1894, more than 20 per cent was controlled by fewer than fifty holders; and by 1910, less than 1 per cent of the families owned or controlled about 85 per cent of the land. . . .

Had the land acquired by the haciendas been profitably used, and had the villagers now forced to work for the haciendas been properly treated, the situation would not have been so disastrous. But the haciendas were not economically successful: they left too much arable land uncultivated, and they were not so productive, proportionally, as the smaller holdings. The rapid development of the hacienda system under Díaz constituted a burden on, and a retrogression of, the agricultural economy, rather than, as its proponents insisted, an improvement. . . .

Díaz' attitude toward rural and industrial labor is indicative of his loss of political perception. In contrast to his remarkable acumen in recognizing the paramount interest of each important group and in catering to those interests before 1900, after the turn of the century he was no longer able to see the forces or to adjust his policies accordingly. Labor was rapidly becoming a factor to consider in national politics, and yet Díaz and his advisors could think of nothing more constructive than suppression. When confronted with somewhat the same condition in 1876 with respect to bandits, Díaz had adroitly obtained the support of a sufficient number to counterbalance those who were recalcitrant. To labor he made no concession at all, and after 1900 labor constituted a greater potential force than had the bandits in 1876. . . .

Díaz was also unconcerned with the nationalism which had been developing rapidly in the latter part of the nineteenth century. The constant condescension displayed by the President and his government to everything Mexican, and the near adulation for everything foreign, were irritating to the younger generation. The foreigner was treated with the deference of an invited guest, the mining laws governing concessions and subsoil rights were reframed to conform with foreign concepts and practices, enormous areas of land were sold or practically given to foreigners, and foreigners were regularly favored in Mexican courts. Since citizens of the United States were the most numerous among the foreigners, one bitter critic summed it up by saying that the regime "destroyed national honor in the face of Yankee demands." Díaz was not alone in his preference for foreigners; most of the social elite were prejudiced in favor of foreign goods, foreign literature, and foreign ideas. Industrial concerns, whether under the control of Mexicans or aliens, regularly paid higher wages to foreign employees than to natives; the policy was probably justified by the foreigners' greater technical skill, but it did not endear the government or the industrialists to the laborers. All those who were proud to be Mexicans resented the rank favoritism which seemed to be common.

Even the upper classes were mixed in their support of the government after 1900. Díaz, consistently refusing to allow widespread political participation to the social and economic plutocracy, destroyed the public spirit of the class and weakened it as a bulwark of the regime. To be sure, the moneyed groups gave unstinting praise to Díaz' government, but they were without organization and without leadership other than that formed by the government. In his anxiety to protect himself against the political ambitions of this group, Díaz had enervated a potentially powerful support.

Without quite realizing what had happened, Díaz gradually lost the active support of most elements in Mexican society. Many mestizos were alienated by his gradual orientation toward creoles and foreigners, as well as by the treatment accorded labor and small proprietors. The proprietors, allied with the labor leaders, became a solid core of opposition before the end of the regime. The Indians, while not openly hostile except in rare instances, generally were becoming more and more restive as a result of agrarian developments which either threatened their independent existence or left them destitute. Members of the upper class not directly connected with the regime were either not allowed to render public service or were driven into partial opposition by the government's bland assumption that all able men served the government and that all who questioned the policies were either knaves or fools. Added to the insult was the economic injury which seemed to be impending; the rather precarious economic situation after 1905 forced many men who previously had been staunch Díaz supporters to question the safety of the Mexican economy under Díaz' continued administration. The group whose economic interests were in danger did not always actively oppose the administration; but when the revolution came, the plutocracy gave Díaz little help.

Díaz still had strong support, particularly among those who profited directly, or hoped to profit, from his government. More important to the future of the nation, and more widespread, than the support to Díaz himself was the belief in his philosophy of government. Many of those who turned against the Díaz administration, or who no longer supported it, did so because they detected weaknesses in his government rather than because they opposed the principles upon which he acted. These men, including many of the great hacendados and financiers, were quite willing to see Díaz removed from office, even though they looked with horror upon fundamental changes in the governmental or social structure. They were the men who made possible a successful revolution against Díaz, but at the same time their attitude would make it difficult for a reform government to function. As a class they foresaw a revolution, but they did not foresee the nature of the struggle; they believed it would take place after Díaz' death and would be nothing more than a quarrel over political power among the upper class. They did not recognize the symptoms of a social revolution developing in Morelos, for example, where "ragged plebeians, with their thin veneer of rudimentary civilization, were acting like savage gluttons of human carrion" during the 1908 gubernatorial election. They were unconcerned with the needs of the masses, and being unconcerned they were ignorant of the potential of those masses.

8. The Porfiriato: Legend and Reality

Daniel Cosío Villegas

The Porfiriato must have been, as the legend has it, an era of consolidation. The tranquility of the period suggests that divisions or differences were neither so violent nor so irreconcilable as to lead to war. It was, moreover, an era in which means of communication improved significantly, thereby increasing opportunities for Mexicans to become acquainted and have contact with one another. Finally, one suspects that consolidation was also furthered by the undeniably authoritarian character of the regime, for extraordinary power makes itself felt on everything and everyone, impressing a uniform cast on the entire society.

From "El porfiriato, era de consolidación" by Daniel Cosío Villegas, *Historia Mexicana*, XIII, 1963, pp. 76–87, *passim*. Reprinted by permission.

Such must have been the Porfiriato. To be certain, however, one would have to ask whether the process of consolidation was general or selective. According to the legend, the regime was notably successful in promoting the consolidation of two areas at least: Mexican nationality and institutions. . . .

The consolidation of the Mexican nation has been the result of a very long process. Perhaps it dates from the incipient imperialism of the Aztecs, which . . . imposed some unity on the political and cultural diversity of the numerous Indian groups of the period. The conquest and domination of the Spaniards, despite the elements of profound disparity which they introduced, gave to the native civilizations elements of community, language, religion, and government which they had hitherto lacked. The consequences did not take long to appear, for the first clear manifestations of a spiritual nationalism were evident in the eighteenth century. But it was above, all during that calumniated first half of the nineteenth century that the process of national formation was accelerated, precisely because of the misfortunes that befell the newly born nation. . . . The war with the United States and the very loss of territory helped, like few other events, to consolidate our nationality, first through the sensation of danger and the feeling of hatred for the aggressor — sentiments which constitute a negative force but a tremendously effective one when a weak people is involved. Secondly, no matter how unjust and painful the loss of half of our national territory was, it is undeniable that it drastically reduced the material and spiritual task of forging the nation, as well as the time that would be needed to accomplish this task. Finally, this unhappy war also taught us that when our internal struggles passed certain limits of rancor and persistence, the danger of aggression and the irreparable loss of the nation would become real and substantial.

It does not seem that the country made use of this sad but beneficial lesson, for in a very short time, during the wars of the Reform and Intervention, the two contenders, blinded by immediate partisan interests, appealed for foreign aid. But this occurred for the last time because it became apparent that with the aid came the foreign soldier, that is, the flesh-and-blood enemy of Mexican nationhood. These two wars fought so bitterly that, by way of a reaction, they created a conciliatory climate that bore fruit throughout the entire period of the Restored Republic. . . .

[By 1876], then, Mexico, as a result of so many painful and seemingly sterile struggles, was beginning to gather the positive fruits of its misfortunes; it had gone a long way toward placing general interests before partial interests.

Does all this mean that the Porfiriato did not contribute in any way to the task of consolidating the Mexican nation? By no means. It merely means that the process was lengthy, that it was initiated a long time before 1876, and that the principal direct contributions had been made previously. The contribution of the Porfiriato, while it was very important, seems to me to have had an indirect character. With the railroads, telegraph, and telephone, with the general improvement of communications and transportation, particularly of the press, the circulation of Mexicans, as well as of their wealth, ideas, and sentiments, also improved.

It is less easy to define and very difficult to assess another factor in the consolidation of the nation which appeared in a singularly active manner during the Porfirian age. Mexico had always lived under the thumb of regional caciques; accordingly, federalism had a reality that was political, social, and economic, as well as geographic and ethnic. Only Juárez emerged in 1867 as a great national figure; but the impossibility of preserving the unity of the liberal party and Juárez' need to lead his own faction in order to defend himself and prevail over the factions of Lerdo and Díaz made him lose to a large extent the general and superior character of a national figure. Díaz, on the other hand, less scrupulous in his political practices and born of a revolutionary coup and not of lawful elections, had far more liberty of action. Finding the field already sowed and blessed with better luck, he at length succeeded in putting an end to the regional caudillos and in transforming himself into the sole caudillo, that is, into the national caudillo. To this must be added the popular aura that Díaz always had, the memory of his glorious campaigns against the foreign invader, his very age, his granite-like physical appearance, and his conscious effort to acquire and exhibit the air of a man who was superior to petty and fleeting passion; his was the air of the guardian of the permanent interests of the country, the air of a monarch who receives homage not only from his own subjects but also from the outside world, the civilized world.

But Porfirio Díaz did not become merely a decorative national symbol, like the flag or anthems which evoke and exalt patriotic sentiments upon reaching the eyes or ears, not even in the more intellectual sense of serving as a symbol of national unity, like the English monarch. He was also authority, and in many respects the sole authority; he was power, and in many respects the sole power. Family disputes were laid before him, as well as disputes involving towns, authorities, or interests. All the organs of public power depended on him: legislatures, courts, judges, governors, political and military chiefs. Not only was he seen everywhere, like God, but he also made himself felt everywhere. . . .

There can be no doubt that, as the legend claims, juridical, economic, and social institutions were consolidated to some extent. One merely has to consider the peacefulness, prosperity, and longevity of the regime to admit this; when there is peace, wealth, and time, there are opportunities and resources for the undertaking of projects that in turbulent periods are left for "better times." Unfortunately, history requires more than generalities; it requires analysis and a body of facts.

With respect to juridical institutions, the work had already begun. The first great bodies of law antedated the Porfiriato: the constitution itself, the organic law of public instruction (1867), the law governing juries in criminal cases (1869), the organic law on the recourse of *amparo* (1869), the penal code (1871), the civil code (1871), the code of civil procedure (1872), the code pertaining to aliens (1876), etc. But these were few in number and limited in influence, in part because most of them could be applied only in the Federal District and in part because the conditions of the country were not sufficiently normal for their beneficial influence to be felt. During the Porfiriato, these same codes were revised, made more consistent, and complemented with new ones . . . while important legislation, such as the law on credit institutions, was also enacted. To this body of true juridical creation, there ought to be added the regulatory and administrative achievement. These gains placed the country on the path to a normal, regular existence, which in many respects became ideally impersonal. In addition, the law in general appeared to attain a respectability, a stature, that made it impervious to human negation or threats.

All this is very well, but how can one forget that political institutions are a part of juridical institutions? Can it be sustained that political institutions were consolidated during the Porfiriato? They simply disappeared, and something that does not exist is not susceptible of consolidation or dispersion.

In this matter there is no defense or qualification. No Porfirista — not even the most passionate, nor the most timid, nor the most shameful, nor the most cynical — has ever dared to affirm that

Mexico progressed politically during the Díaz regime. This is the explanation of [Rafael de] Zayas Enríquez: the people of Mexico voluntarily ceded their political rights to Porfirio Díaz so that he might return them little by little as the Mexicans learned how to be free. This is the opinion of [Francisco] Bulnes: "it passes the limits of stupidity to assail General Díaz for not having done the impossible — to be a democratic president in a nation of slaves." . . .

According to Emilio Rabasa, one of the few Mexican political writers of true talent, "the dictatorship of Díaz was characterized, *above all*, by respect for *legal forms*, which he always preserved in order to keep alive in the people the sentiment that their laws were respected even though they were not enforced, and that they remained on the books so that they might recover their ascendancy in the not-too-distant future." This is the point that truly deserves investigation, for on it depends the answer to the question of whether political institutions were consolidated during the Porfiriato.

Is it possible to respect a law that is not enforced? Can a law which is not enforced remain in force? Can a law which is not enforced someday recover its ascendancy? To me, it is as clear as daylight that a law which is not enforced provokes mockery, compassion, but never respect; a law which is not enforced is a dead law, and what is dead can never remain in force; a law which is not enforced has no power and in consequence can never recover what it never had. Finally, to describe as the "not-too-distant future" an era which, like that of Díaz, lasted for thirty-five years is to forget that in so long a time a whole generation was born and raised in the delightful atmosphere of the law that is not enforced but is respected. I would say exactly the opposite of Rabasa: that nothing degrades and demoralizes a people so much as the constant, repeated, daily spectacle of the non-enforcement of the law. . . .

It is this attitude toward the law, especially the political laws, that indicates the gulf between Porfirio Díaz and the great liberals of the Reform. The latter had a blind faith in the law as a pick-axe to strike down old and noxious institutions and in the law as a cherished mould for shaping new ones. For this reason they respected the law, and to preserve or change it, they were capable of risking their lives or their futures. . . .

Porfirio Díaz, who fought for the liberal cause from his boyhood, who once accused Juárez of conservatism, did not have that respect and veneration for the law which was the very essence of Mexican liberalism. For Díaz, the law was a dead letter and consequently

lacked spirit. For him, the *fact* was the instrument of change, and
the fact, of course, was power and might. Because he despised the
law, he did not change it or trouble himself about it; he simply for-
got it and sought power in the invincible fact of being stronger than
everyone else. . . .

The conclusion of all this seems obvious to me, as well as logical.
Some juridical institutions were consolidated during the Porfiriato,
and some were not. Those that were consolidated were the secondary
ones, while the major ones — the political institutions — simply disappeared.

Section VII

The Great Debate: Cultural Nationalism, Anti-Americanism, and the Idea of Historical Destiny in Spanish America

For students and teachers of Latin American history in the United States, one of the most difficult topics to discuss is the tension between Latin America and the United States in cultural matters. Chauvinism and ignorance sometimes play leading roles when "Yankee" and "Latin" values are compared, for the gulf of misunderstanding that separates the United States from Latin America has never been fully or even adequately bridged. In part, this situation was created by the hand of history, for European economic, political, and religious struggles had established some prejudices and predispositions in the minds of most emigrants who crossed the Atlantic to both continents of the New World.

Once the Latin American nations had liberated themselves from European political domination, they were faced with the enormous problem of developing their own way of life. Throughout the nineteenth century many Latin Americans observed the material progress of the United States with great interest; some hoped their own countries would emulate the Yankees while others questioned or attacked mere economic improvement as dangerous to their way of life. By the end of the century, positivists who had enjoyed considerable influence in Brazil, Mexico, and elsewhere found less fertile ground for propagating their views on the beauty of material progress.

Beginning with the turn of the century, a new and powerful senti-

ment began to be widely expressed in Latin America: the fear that
the United States would increasingly intervene to transform the
Caribbean into a North American lake dominated by dollars and
Marines. Just at this time the Uruguayan José Enrique Rodó published *Ariel,* which became both a source and a symbol of misunderstanding. Within ten years this beautifully written book went
through eight editions, and became a kind of bible for those Latin
Americans intimidated by North American power, because Rodó
affirmed their own potential. The recent war against Spain through
which the United States had acquired more territory and more
power was itself an example of the triumph of brute force, according
to the Argentine Manuel D. Pizarro, who prophesied a dark future:
"todo es materia y fuerza."[1]

Although *Ariel* was not primarily an attack upon United States
materialism, and in fact is an example of moderation, other Latin
Americans showed no such restraint in interpreting Rodó's message.
The Mexican Carlos Pereyra, the Argentine Manuel Ugarte, and the
Venezuelan Rufino Blanco Fombona all gave Rodó's message an
anti-American twist. *Ariel* has come to be looked upon as a symbol
for all who would exalt the "spiritual" qualities of Latin Americans
and depreciate the "money-grubbing Yankees."

Yet Rodó's true message was not this: Rodó used *Ariel* as a symbol not of Latin American reality but of the qualities to which Latin
America and the United States as well should aspire. Rodó's Prós-
pero stressed that the youths to whom he addressed himself must
be patient and not expect results even in their lifetime; he portrayed
Latin America as languishing in a relatively primitive condition. If
Rodó had believed that Latin America had already achieved spiritual
eminence he would not have felt the need to admonish its youth. He
was not trying to assert Latin America's superiority to the United
States in a defiant posture; his purpose was to exhort, not to extol.[2]
Nor did Rodó identify the United States with Caliban, but felt that
it, too, could and should aspire to a greater idealism even as he
exhorted the youth of Latin America to do.

The vision Rodó presents in *Ariel* (Reading VII.3) must be considered together with the efforts that had been made since Bolívar's

[1] *El conflicto hispanoamericano. Las repúblicas de Sud-América. Cartas de Manuel D. Pizarro* (Córdoba, Argentina: Imprenta La Minerva, 1898), p. 35.
[2] Richard Stillinger, "Ariel: Source and Symbol of Misunderstanding." Mr. Stillinger's paper, prepared as a term paper at Columbia University, has been very helpful in the preparation of this section.

day to create a new and distinct civilization in Latin America. The Peruvian sociologist César Graña of the University of California, Davis, provides a broad base for a study of the historical destiny idea in Spanish America particularly, and of the way thinkers in many parts of this great area have looked upon their countries as a part of the American Dream (Reading VII.1). Graña's interpretation will not satisfy some Latin Americans. The view held by Waldo Frank, one of the best known North American intellectuals in Latin America from the publication of his widely discussed book *America Hispana* (1931) until his death in January, 1967, is much closer to the image many Latin Americans have of their own culture (Reading VII.2).

Graña and Frank do not discuss Rodó in any detail, for their purpose is to give a broad treatment of the theme, but Rodó has attracted more attention than any other *pensador*, and his *Ariel* still speaks to some Latin Americans, according to Kalman Silvert of New York University (Reading VII.4). And the two Americas still do not understand each other. Indeed, Richard M. Morse of Yale University believes that professors in the United States who study Latin America are particularly in need of enlightenment (Reading VII.5). Even though Rodó and *Ariel* may be passé, Latin Americans continue their search for their own expression, their distinctive contribution to the culture of the world. The government of Chile sponsored a Congreso de la Comunidad Cultural Latinoamericana in 1966, and Mexico supported the second meeting of this group in 1967.[3]

Cultural nationalism in Latin America is part of the variety of nationalism so powerful in the world at large. As a case study of how nationalism has grown in Mexico and how closely connected it has been to anti-Americanism, Frederick C. Turner of the University of Connecticut describes the development of xenophobia there (Reading VII.6).

---

[3] For the list of Latin American intellectuals who participated in the Congreso and the program, see the booklet published by the Comisión Nacional de Cultura y Junta de Adelanto de Arica, *Congreso de la Comunidad Cultural Latinoamericano* (Arica, 1966). The Chilean Foreign Minister Gabriel Valdés delivered the closing address.

A. General

1. Cultural Nationalism: The Dreams of Spanish-American Intellectuals

César Graña

Early Stages of Cultural Nationalism in Spanish America — In the case of Spanish America, the particular atmosphere surrounding the claims of a cultural and historical destiny is evident in the very words which Spanish Americans choose to discuss that destiny. "Americanism," we learn from *Webster's Dictionary*, refers to American customs, characteristics, singularities of language, and to a devotion or preference for American traditions and ideals. It is a concept clearly within the reach of folklorists, ethnologists, linguists, anthropologists, historians, sociologists, literary observers, and very much what in the Spanish American sense is meant by *Americanismo*. But the air changes the moment one tries to grasp the intentions of another term, for which there is no true English equivalent — *Americanidad*, which means literally "Americanity." Americanidad is not related to the concrete historical, political, or sociological stamp of Spanish America. It is not even a signpost to some *je ne sais quoi* — the effect or ring of Spanish America as a social spectacle, aesthetic image, or cultural personality. It is no one actuality but a felt Presence. It is an ultimate reality which events echo and toward which they move. A force pressing so to speak from behind time into the future, as well as toward the as yet unfilled mold into which Spanish America will in the end be poured to become a finished historical and spiritual fact.

Given the intellectual style implicit in such concepts as Americanidad, we should not be surprised to find in a recent book by Emilio Uranga on the Mexican national character that the author at once

From "Cultural Nationalism: The Idea of Historical Destiny in Spanish America" by César Graña, *Social Research*, XXIX, Winter 1962, pp. 395–418 XXX, Spring 1963, pp. 37–52, *passim*. Reprinted by permission.

moves into the language of metaphysics to speak of the "substance" and "accidents" of "Mexicanity" and the importance of making use of the "ontological method" as the means of revealing the issue of "Mexicanity" as the "constitutive" fact of Mexican society. The book is typically entitled *An Analysis of Mexican "Being."* Uranga, like other Spanish American thinkers, has been greatly influenced by European existentialists, like Martin Heidegger, from whom he has adopted an untiring responsiveness to certain words like Being and Non-Being when used within a system of peculiarly arranged intuitions, implications, and suggestions. But actually Spanish American thinking about the future has been overhung with an air of high implication from the very beginnings of Spanish American national history. Indeed, the earliest example of such thinking is part of the life of Simón Bolívar, and it links the vision of America to the legend of the *Libertador* in a characteristic scene of incandescence and revelation.

When Bolívar, as a wealthy twenty-two-year-old colonial making the grand tour of Europe, visited Rome in the company of his tutor Simón Rodríguez in 1805, he found himself one summer evening looking down on the city from the side of Aventine Hill. In the spirit of historical retrospection and musing almost *de rigueur* in that setting, he and his teacher sat on the base of a fallen column talking of the ancient world and the new. Suddenly, according to Rodríguez, Bolívar stood up and "breathing heavily, his eyes glistening, his face reddened, almost in a fever," he swore "by God and by my honor" never to rest "arm or soul" until Spanish America had been freed. Now, although Bolívar was a learned and eloquent designer of constitutional and political plans, he was not blind to the realities of Spanish American society. It lacked, he thought, the heritage of civic morality and political experience possessed by the United States. And although he said that he wished "more than anyone else to see formed in America [again in the Spanish sense] the greatest nation in the world," he did not think, at least as late as 1815, that all the countries of Spanish America would ever be gathered under one sovereign state. Still he could never abandon the prophetic voice he had assumed on the Aventine hillside. In 1824, having become President of Greater Colombia (the name given to the union of Venezuela, Colombia, and Ecuador which Bolívar had created between the years 1819 and 1822) and Dictator of Peru, he called for a congress at Panama to launch the federal union of the new nations. He spoke of the Panamanian isthmus as the new Corinth, and wondered whether history would not choose it for the capital of the world, placed as it was at the center of the globe, facing Asia on one side and Europe and Africa on the other. Later, in a letter to Rodríguez, he assumed the tone of the oracle and, in some sense, the mythologist of Spanish American civilization: "Come to Mount Chimborazo. Tread with daring foot the stairway of the titans, the crowned of the Earth, the invincible watch tower of the new universe. From its height you will gaze upon the miracle of terrestrial creation, and you will say: there are two eternities before me, the one that is past and the one [that] is to come, and this throne of Nature, equal to its Author, will be as lasting, indestructible, and eternal as the Father of the Universe. . . . In that declining world [Europe] you have seen but the relics and the remnants of an Old Mother. There she lies, bent by the weight of her years and her ailments. And here stands this Maid, immaculate and beautiful, garlanded by the very hand of the Creator."

Perhaps because of the early revolutionary experience of Northern South America, and perhaps also because of the millennarian atmosphere surrounding Bolívar, and in part created by him, the first auguries of Spanish American civilization come from Ecuador and Venezuela. José Olmedo, an Ecuadorian poet (1780–1847), combined theatrical adulation of Bolívar with a vision of Spanish America as the haven of liberty — both apparently based on French artistic and intellectual models. His description of Bolívar as a young Achilles riding the storm, victory flashing from his sword, thunder and lightning in his voice and eyes, reads like a literary transposition to the cult of the *Libertador* of the pictorial glorification of young Bonaparte by artists like David, Gross or Géricault. His conception of political liberty as a creation of Greek and Roman antiquity was certainly a borrowing from the French Revolution. It was Olmedo's thought, however, that if liberty had been born on the banks of the Eurotas and the Tiber, it would now build its altar by the Rimac and the Magdalena. Another, and far weightier, literary figure of this period who also addressed himself to the future was the Venezuelan Andrés Bello (1781–1865). Bello occupied political and diplomatic posts early in the struggle for independence, but his place is above all that of a prototype of the Spanish American self-made universalist, the *pensador*. He founded and was the first president of the University of Chile. He was also a legal and classical scholar, a grammarian, and an educator. And he wrote about America's nature, America's gifts, and its place in the world. These thoughts, with their praises and promise, are contained in two famous poems,

"Ode to the Agriculture of the Torrid Zone" and "Call to Poetry."
The "Ode" is a nature song to the tropics, a celebration of its fruits,
and a didactic pastorale ending with this hope and admonition:

> Honor the fields, honor the simple life
> Of the farmer and his frugal plainness
> Thus there will always be in you
> A dwelling for liberty
> A bridle to ambition, a temple for the law

Coming from a New World poet, and written at a time of revolution,
one might, without discomfort, call these words Jeffersonian. Actually, however, the poem's style and its content — the idealization of
the countryside as the home of piety and virtue, and the rejection of
the vulgarity, vanity, demagoguery, and greed of city life — come
from Virgil's *Georgics*. By itself this use of a classical idyll to construct a New World version of the natural world as conducive to the
goodness of man is not yet a true American prophecy. But at the
poem's end we find the following:

> Oh young nations
> Whose heads crowned with early laurels
> Are raised above the astonished West

These lines take us into the "Call to Poetry," which is written in that
tone of sumptuous portent already seen in Bolívar's Chimborazo
letter, and, like it, has as its theme the unveiling of Spanish America
as an historical creature. The premises of the "Call to Poetry," both
as to literature and as to ideology, are the premises of European
Romanticism. Reason and an excessive civility will turn experience
and imagination to dust. Poetry — which stereotypically rises out of
grottoes, forests, and mountain tops — is the utterance of Life in its
wholeness and flow. Bello thought that "cultivated" Europe had
become too spent and too sterile to contain the unspoiled thrust of
the poetic impulse. Poetry should, therefore, flee to the "great stage"
of America where nature itself was epic and human grandeur still
possible. But if the poem is historical, it is not political. It speaks of
the youthful deeds of the recently freed nations, and of the episodes
of Aztec and Inca antiquity. But it says nothing about liberty and
democracy, which were near inescapable items in the public rhetoric
of the period. Above all, America was "of the Sun the young bride,
and of the ancient ocean's youngest daughter." This full-blown,
untried energy in a land where birds sang "no learned song" made

of it a poetic fact of nature intended for the unfolding of magnificence.

Magnificence and splendor are, indeed, the words for Bello's image of Spanish America, rather than social and political greatness. This image of an awe-ridden land, an arena for vast and transcendent action or contemplation and marvelling, is obviously charged with force and exaltation. But it is essentially poetic and nonsecular, to be manifested in memorable episodes or the glory of beauty, rather than in the construction of a virtuous daily life. Edmund Burke indicted all of modernity when he said that the age of chivalry had ended and the age of calculation begun. Bello, at least in "Call to Poetry," used the word "philosophy" to symbolize the forsaken orderliness of a purely rationalistic universe to which he opposed the ultimate supremacy of life-feeling. In this he may have provided the beginnings of what was to become the Spanish American version of the romantic soul's great public drama — the war between creativity and philistinism. As we know, this war was waged, not only between individuals and classes, but between soulful and soulless nations. The role of the nobly embattled protagonist, victim of its own deference to beauty was now to belong, of course, to Spanish America. The villain was the familiar one found in the European account of the contest; the raw materialism and large but commonplace energy of the United States.

Perhaps the first writer to speak of the nature of Spanish American civilization by comparing it with that of the United States was the Chilean Francisco Bilbao (1823–1865). Bilbao was an excitable, grandiose, and naive *penseur* on social and historical subjects, as well as a political pamphleteer and agitator. (Like countless other Spanish American intellectuals, he was deported from his country in 1851 after a frustrated revolt.) He was also a poet, a critic, and a religionist of beauty in the nineteenth century fashion. This last, however, was coupled with a democratic passion and trust in the masses rare among aestheticians of this period, at least in Europe. Bilbao looked upon the Spanish past with repugnance and resentment; it was an inheritance of darkness, superstition, feudalism, and indolence which could only be stamped out by a great social and psychological revolution. He wanted for the Spanish American countries political reform and strength together with the stability that would come with political unification; in this respect he was an almost envious admirer of the United States. He had nothing of the polemical bitterness of the writers of the later Theodore Roosevelt era, and he dispassionately compared the orderliness and economic growth of North America with the chaos, poverty, and endemic despotism of the South American countries. He regarded North Americans as the paragon of political virtue. He thought the Puritans "sublime" and the United States the "new Greece." Yet his tone changed the moment the continental power of the United States began to assert itself with the annexation of Texas. His political admiration was still there, but he now sought to stake a claim for Spanish America which was uniquely her own. He writes:

There lives in our regions something of an ancient and divine hospitality, and in our breast there is room for love of mankind. We have not lost the tradition of the spirituality of man's destiny. We love and believe in everything that unites. We prefer the individual to the social, beauty to riches, justice to power, art to commerce, poetry to industry, philosophy to the textbook, the pure spirit to calculation, duty to self-interest. We are of those who believe in art, in the enthusiasm for the beautiful regardless of the consequences. We do not see in this earth, the ultimate end of man. . . . It is this that the citizens of South America dare to place on the scales next to the pride, the riches, and the power of North America.

We recognize easily in Bilbao an example of the enthusiast of Love and Beauty. The enmity between the individual and the mass, sensitivity and gain, creativity and productivity, intellectual flight and rote learning, spirituality and calculation, are all items from the romantic code book. Still Bilbao is significant because he gives Bello's aesthetic praise of Spanish America a social dimension. All of the subjects of Bilbao's homage have, as we know, been employed to discredit the cultural consequences of democracy which was thought inimical to them. But Bilbao was at once a stereotypical romanticist and a sentimental populist. And he could be these by making cultural nationalism meet the needs of his literary fervors. Thus he made the Spanish American *people* the carrier of every sensitive, noble, and soul-freeing value. European romantics had looked in the Orient, in medieval reveries and in countries of the mind — like Baudelaire's *Cocagne* where even the cuisine was lyrical — for a social reality that embodied their aesthetic ideals. What Bilbao, and other Spanish American writers, did was to transport to the Western Hemisphere the stock literary battle between the idealist and the materialist, the creative spirit and the bourgeois, the intuitive and the prosaically rationalistic. By implication in the case of Bilbao, and ardent conviction in the case of others, the United States always found itself on the wrong side of this ledger; Spanish

America became an engagingly bohemian, yet lofty, civilization, a poet civilization, and a collective noble dreamer.

Bilbao's intellectual vision flows into the language of political struggle in the writings of the great Cuban patriot José Martí (1853–1895). As with so many other Spanish American figures of the nineteenth century Martí's career is pieced together from an extraordinary miscellany of exertions. He was a doctor of law, a magazine editor in Mexico, a professor of political science in Guatemala, and a consular agent for a number of South American nations in the United States. He was also an orator of celebrated emotional powers and a precursor of the so-called "modernista" movement in poetry. Historically, however, he earned his place as the unwearying "apostle" of Cuban freedom for which he ultimately died in one of the early battles of the Cuban war of independence. Martí's prose has been described as "forest-like" and "Wagnerian" in scale. As a political thinker he was steeped in the nineteenth century notion of the man of genius as a mixture of enormous personal powers and a somnambulistic obedience to the forces of history; and who was, therefore, able to foresee in detail what others could anticipate only in outline. Speaking with a kind of solemn humility, rather than a simple vainglory, he said of himself that he was a people, not a man, speaking. And, one should add, he looked not only on Cuba but on all of Spanish America as a collective personage charged with the noblest of historical fates. In a speech to a New York literary society in 1889, he said:

> Our America, resourceful and indefatigable, triumphs over all obstacles, and her standard rises ever higher, from sun to sun, by the power of the soul of the land, harmonious and artistic, created out of the music and the beauty of our nature. . . . This is so because of the millennial power with which this natural order and greatness have overcome the disorder and meanness of our beginnings. This is so because of the expansive and humanitarian liberty, above place, race, or sect, which came to our republics in their seminal hour . . . a liberty which, perhaps, finds no dwelling place so generous as this. Would that my lips were branded by the fire of what *is* to be! For our lands are being readied boundlessly for honorable effort, loyal solicitude, and true friendship.

We are faced here, of course, with a rhapsodic ambiguity, a mingling of wish, sentiment, speculation, description, and exhortation, which is beyond unravelling. Still one could see this statement as a version of the American dream, in the sense that such an expression has in the United States: the expectation of an embracing humaneness granting liberty to all regardless of social ancestry and condition. There is in it, however, the peculiar Spanish American aesthetic posture, the insistence on Spanish America, not only as an historical but as an artistic miracle. And there is more. In his surrender to the grandness of nature, Martí takes us back to Bello. In his assumption that there is lodged in the Spanish American world a loving libertarian humaneness, he recalls Bilbao. But there is also an attempt to relate these historical and psychological virtues to an "earth-force" explanation; to make of them an emanation of the "soul of the land" anticipating highly literary forms of geographical determinism found later.

Spanish American Self-Conceptions — But before dealing with this geographical nativism (and we shall see that it occurs among poets, social essayists, and cultural interpreters) one should consider the appearance of two other persistent themes on the list of Spanish American self-conceptions. One is the response to the expansion of North American power in the Western Hemisphere, already broached by Bilbao. The other is the idealization of Spanish America, not as a nature queen or the home of social benevolence, but as a particularly triumphant species of cultural pageant with Indian, ancient, and Christian motifs. We encounter both themes in the Nicaraguan Rubén Darío (1867–1916), who is regarded by many critics as the single greatest revolutionary in the history of Spanish American poetic styles. Darío is the Oscar Wilde of Spanish American literature (with something of Edgar Allan Poe and Scott Fitzgerald), at least at the point where personality and biography meet in ironic conflict. A man of the most mercurial egotism and sensitivity, dwelling in the most expensive aesthetic fantasies, whose life, brilliantly and self-destructively squandered, ends in sordid disaster. Although Darío was of Indian ancestry, there is nothing nativistic in his personal or literary tastes. He was a disciple of the French symbolists, lived mostly away from his own country (Paris, not Managua, was his chosen home), and was as conscientiously cosmopolitan and unprovincial as only a provincial can be. His poetry suggests a curious revival in an obscure ex-colony of the aristocratic spirit of Watteau's painting. It contains the same aesthetic glorification of the luxurious garden party, the same atmosphere of mannered eroticism among marble and satin surroundings. In actuality, however, Darío would not have survived without his friends in the publishing business, such as the editors of the Buenos Aires daily *La*

Nación who, by making him a "foreign correspondent," virtually subsidized his long stays in Europe. During his early life Darío dragged himself through years of itinerant work. Later, after becoming famous, he was sporadically kept in high style by diplomatic sinecures. He finished his life as an impenitent alcoholic, an exhibit on the lecture circuit, and the personal charity of the Nicaraguan dictator.

This discordance between Darío's life and his poetry should be mentioned as a parable of a larger reality. For both his pro-Spanish Americanism and his anti-North Americanism were the product of a strained intellectual posture that chooses to ignore the uglier truths. The sight of the provincial retracing his steps to Europe is, of course, not an unfamiliar one in North American literature, as witness Henry James, Henry Adams, and T. S. Eliot. What these men wanted, however, was wisdom, poise, propriety, or certain reverent ways of the imagination that they did not find at home. Darío's search was more frivolous. He was essentially an intellectual voluptuary who saw Europe as a treasure trove of cultural possessions. His poetic world, a realm of swans, peacocks, colonnades, silk rustlings, the purple and swords of chivalry, and glossy versions of antique mythology, could have been constructed only in full flight from the political and social realities of nineteenth century Spanish America — just as only the most willful and parochial snobbery could account for his contrast between the graciousness and impressive glamor of Spanish America and the sweaty pragmatism of the United States. This fabled antagonism is the subject of Darío's "To Roosevelt" which is addressed, of course, to Theodore, and is one of the best known pieces of verse in Spanish America. The poem, in which Darío calls Roosevelt a mixture of Alexander and Nebuchadnezzar and the United States the cultist of Hercules and Mammon, ends with these lines:

> But our America,
> The one who had poets since the old Netzahualcoyotl,
> The one who, on an ancient day learned Pan's alphabet,
> Who consulted the planets that Atlantis knew,
> Atlantis whose name since Plato's day has echoed
> Through the centuries.
> This America, since the first of its days,
> Has lived of light, of fire, of perfume, of love.
> The America of the great Montezuma, of the Inca,
> Fragrant America of Christopher Columbus.

This America . . . Man of Saxon eyes and barbarous soul.
This America lives.
And it dreams, and it loves and is vibrant.
She is the daughter of the Sun.
Beware. Spanish America lives!
The Spanish lion has a thousand cubs.   . . .
You have everything but one, God.

As should be clear, this cry is motivated by what Darío conceived as the nature of the cultural question, rather than by any political or economic indignation caused by American interference. One of its features is a crudely romanticized element of racial pride; Saxon eyes and a barbarous soul are one and the same thing. This, of course, borrows from stock South European affectations about the barbaric North. "Spanish," on the other hand, is offered as a self-evident epithet signifying spiritual high caste. But, as in Bilbao and Martí, we find also the theme of Spanish American emotional munificence, what Darío calls broadly "love." In the other writers, however, this has the implication of a fund of humane and brotherly passions. In Darío it is nothing but an effusion of enthusiasm for its own lyrical sake, just as "vibrancy" is offered as an unspecified gift for sensitive and imaginative responsiveness.   . . .

Darío's "Ode to Roosevelt" is easily the classical statement of the literary view of Spanish America as a continent-poet and the United States as a successful bore. The Hispanic countries become as a whole creatures and votaries of *l'art pour l'art*. North America, heavy with wealth and power, is also cursed with dullness and greed. Andrés Bello spoke of *divina poesía*, a more or less inescapable gesture of the romantic artist. Bilbao spoke of Spanish America as the home of "divine humanity," which can be understood within the modern rhetoric of social piety from Kant to Victor Hugo. Darío renders Spanish America wholly "poetic" and, therefore, wholly "divine," concluding his ode with an unanswerable piece of glorification: God is on the side of the Latins.

Sharing Darío's place as the major figure of the early twentieth century Spanish American poets was the Peruvian José Santos Chocano (1875–1934). In the tradition of the great literary egocentrics, Chocano saw himself as an international eroticist, and was fired from a diplomatic post in Madrid for lurid indiscretions. He served as a literary hack for Central American dictators and, reputedly, as an agent for Pancho Villa in the United States. He killed a literary rival and was himself gunned while riding a tramway in Chile.

Writing in the preface to Chocano's first book of verse, Rubén Darío called him "the muse representative of our culture, of our modern Spanish American soul." This was also Chocano's view. He regarded his willfulness and bombast as a spark from an historical force and his imagination as a rumbling vortex of Moorish fancy, Spanish blood, and Incan pulse.

Chocano's great aim was to mix in his style gorgeous lyricism and epic intonation, which he thought appropriate to the rivers, jungles, prairies, palaces, exotic populations, and flashing historical romance of Spanish America. In his prose writing — chiefly as a raconteur of travel experiences and literary camaraderies — this results in an annoying and embarrassing failure. He seemed unable to separate thinking from artifice and posturing; in his *Memorias,* for example, he cannot rise above a clutter of hasty and indiscriminate phrase-making which drowns all really sensitive observations of fact. As a poet, however, he could make his verse swell and break; although, except for the best of it, it always leaves the reader with an uncomfortable sense of ephemeral excitement. Yet Chocano is a representative writer. His poetry reveals, not only pride in the face of the North American specter, but, when looked at closely, a deep frustration which must be quieted by avenging dreams. Darío has been called, quite correctly, an essentially escapist artist. Chocano, on the other hand, was sensitive to the question of power and the avenues of power in the Western Hemisphere. His political ideas were fabricated of blithe aphorisms, which are improvised and often dictated by personal predicament or convenience. But he wanted for Spanish America the things of the modern world: highways, schools, productivity, railroads, exports, a solid currency, and an unassailable national sovereignty. Curiously, his continental nationalism was based on a profoundly negative view of the Spanish American people. He regarded them, as did others, as a "sick" people, verbose, will-less, racially predisposed to excitability, ineffectuality, and credulity. This made him look favorably upon bloody revolutions as a means of cleansing out torpor and upon dictatorship as a way of getting things done. It also explains why he put so much reliance upon the primitive force of Spanish American nature as a defense against the thrust of the United States. Speaking of the planning of the Panama Canal in a poem entitled "The Epic of the Pacific," he writes:

> Let us distrust the blue-eyed man
> When he attempts to steal from us

> The warmth of the home-fire
> When he attempts to dazzle us
> With his buffalo blankets.   . . .
> But let us not weep over a future conquest.
> Our jungles will not acknowledge a master race.
> Our Andes disdain the whiteness of the White.
> Our rivers will laugh at the greed of the Saxon.

The poem also promises miasma, fever, swampland, reptiles, and the sun's fire to the blond race. The Americans might pay for the Canal, but they could not cut the Spanish American earth with their own hands. This would have to be done, Chocano says, by the dark Eastern and Latin races, by black-skinned West Indians, or by the descendants of:

> The builders of the Pyramids,
> Of Alexandria's lighthouse
> Of the Temple at Jerusalem
> Those whose blood was spilled
> On the Colosseum's sand.   . . .

It may seem strange to spend so much time discussing the erratic beliefs of a poet about race and climate as part of the study of a social and cultural concept. But a mixture of racial, geographical, poetical, mythical, and historical ideas has not been exceptional in Spanish America, even among academic intellectuals. One of the most widely read men exemplifying this blend of thought is José Vasconcelos (1882–1959), a veteran figure of the Mexican Revolution and one of the cultural personages of Mexico in this century. Vasconcelos was the founder of the ministry of education in 1922 as well as minister of education, director of the National Library, and rector of the University of Sonora and the National University. In addition, he wrote approximately twenty books on philosophy, literary criticism, and history including two interpretations of Spanish American culture, *Indologia* and *La Raza Cósmica,* that were regarded as signal by the intellectuals of the 1920s and the 1930s. Throughout his writings Vasconcelos assumes an unhesitating prophetic tone which is broad enough to embrace the historical origins of Spanish American civilization, the discovery of America itself, and even the presumed geological beginnings of the continent. As an example, even though Christopher Columbus might not at first have known that he had in fact "discovered" America, the event should nevertheless be regarded as a "treasure of fruitful suggestions." Vasconcelos means by this that, regardless of his early misconceptions, Columbus *did* discover America in the higher and ultimate sense: In "christening with the name of Indies, those lands which are today ours, a breath of the same illumination which led him to discover new routes in the sea, Columbus raised himself to the conception of a new era of civilization, an era in which collective life was to crystallize in universal and definitive form."

Like Darío, Chocano, and others to be discussed later, Vasconcelos spoke with a special proprietary solemnity about the tradition of Atlantis as a portent of Spanish American destiny. He, as the others, wanted to believe that Atlantis was America, and that this was to be taken as a measure of the continent's historical lineage and the antiquity of its intended greatness. In the poets we may suspect a metaphor; in Vasconcelos' *La Raza Cósmica* the Atlantis and its meanings are literal: "If we are then ancient, both in our geology and in our traditions, how can we accept the fiction, invented by our European ancestors, of the newness of a continent which existed at a time when the land whence conquerors and discoverers came had yet to appear upon the surface of the earth?" Vasconcelos chooses to forget that, since many people in Spanish America are of European ancestry, they could hardly claim for themselves the past ages of Atlantis. Furthermore, the relative antiquity or novelty of the continent could only be of importance to its present inhabitants if the mere fact of such antiquity constituted a promise for the future. Yet this is, of course, precisely what he thinks. The matter, he added, was of the greatest importance "to those who search [for] a plan in history."

Spanish American Racial Theories — Vasconcelos' view of the main cultural role of Spanish American nature is as broad as his view of historical forces. The difference in physical environment, he said, was alone sufficient to explain the "corresponding differences" separating the people of the Northern and Southern portions of the Western Hemisphere. Equally resounding are the ethnic theories contained in the famous *La Raza Cósmica*. In fact, one can say that Vasconcelos' thinking about the sources of Spanish American civilization is made up of generalizations so radical as to render all others superfluous. Before becoming too critical of Vasconcelos' racial beliefs, however, it should be repeated that some form of racial thinking has been present in Latin America as a whole (and not only the Spanish countries), even among sociologists and anthropologists. (In the United States, on the other hand, the latter group would certainly be most likely to reject this kind of thinking.) This is true of men of the stature of Gilberto Freyre (born 1900), professor of anthropology and sociology at the University of Brazil, and possibly the most renowned cultural anthropologist in Latin America. In the preface to his famous *Casa Grande e Sensala,* translated into English as *Masters and Slaves,* Freyre announces that his studies under Franz Boas at Columbia University had emancipated him from racial theories of social behavior. Yet in the same preface he speaks of "the Semitic tendencies of the Portuguese adventurers inclining them towards trade and barter." This statement is itself contradicted later when Freyre says that the patriarchal feudalism of the frontier plantations represented the truly typical Portuguese style of colonial settlement.

Vasconcelos' own racial ideas are particularly luxuriant. Racial mixture in Spanish America, he says, resembles "the profound scherzo of a deep and infinite symphony" made up of the "abyss in the Indian soul; the Negro's eagerness for sensual happiness; the Mongol, whose oblique eyes make him see everything in unexpected perspectives; the Judaic strains in the Spanish blood [a quality left undefined]; the melancholy of the Arab; and the [rationality of the] White, whose thought is as limpid as his skin." It should give anyone a start to think that these things (a pastiche of the most conventional racial legends) could have been said by a man of Vasconcelos' titles — he was once proclaimed "Master to the Youth of Spanish America." But one thing may be claimed for them; they represent a turn of ethnic thinking, not infrequent in Spanish America, that may be called the theory of positive racialism. Contrary to everything that anthropologists have been able to discover, this view holds that race can explain specific psychological and "spiritual" characteristics of given groups. But it also regards miscegenation as a good thing because it enriches the cultural variety of a civilization. The situation is different from that of the United States in certain interesting respects. For example, the ideological basis of the demands made by Negro communities in the United States is clearly that the Negroes are as a "race" the equal of the whites because they are also equal to the social, economic, political, and technological tasks that the United States expects of its citizens. (This argument is aside from constitutional issues and moral arguments such as human justice.) And public officials, sometimes quite honestly, sometimes for the record; intellectuals; and social scientists by and large agree that this is so. Even in the South itself politicians hesitate these days to state publicly that Negroes are as a race inferior. In short, social science assumes, and political talk by and large agrees, that once historic and artificial handicaps are removed, it will be shown that Negroes are capable of the same degree of discipline, efficiency, seriousness, and dependability as whites in all civic, economic, managerial, and technical aspects of life.

North Americans, then, argue for the social equality of races on the grounds that all of them are capable of the kinds of performances required in a rational society, using the term rational society in the sense that sociologists give to it: a society in which men have clearly tangible social aims, and in which these aims are gained by a systematic, explicitly understandable sequence of performances. Obviously, however, such a society could make very little use of the "abyss" of the Indian soul, the "obliqueness" of the Oriental mind, or the "leaping sensuousness" of the Negro. This means that in order to accept something so contrary to the American outlook as the coexistence between ideas of racial difference and an advocacy of racial mixing, and to understand why Vasconcelos regards Spanish America as racially more advanced, one must see that his view rests on a fundamentally aesthetic rather than a rationalistic vision of social life; a view that is concerned with the transcending gestures of a culture to the disregard of its more daily and secular aspects. . . . ·

By comparing Vasconcelos with his contemporary, the Peruvian Francisco García Calderón (1883–1953), one sees that a lack of distinction between social analysis and utopian forecasts can emanate out of different social premises and preferences. Author of a classic commentary on Spanish American social history, entitled *La Creación de un Continente*, Calderón in his political, sociological, and racial ideas was a severe Westernizer who regarded Indians and Negroes as retarding influences. He saw civilization as the creation of the masses of European immigrants — those "ancient and energetic races" — that would erase Spanish America's passing inferiority and turn it into a Europe of their own. He spent most of his life in France and a number of his works are written in French. In fact, he was a spokesman for the Europeanized urban upper classes of his generation, and he noted hopefully, but incorrectly, that Indians and Negroes were being pushed out of the cities as civilization advanced. Because of this *La Creación* is at the same time optimistic and apologetic; the work of a cosmopolitan from the ex-colonies eager to dissociate himself from the colorful indignity of the banana republic, and to file his own and his society's credentials for the consecrated values of Western culture.

Since he wanted to see in the New World a replica of the historic achievements of Europe, such things as the obvious violence and disorder of Spanish America had to be interpreted by him as the early turbulence of a vital young society not yet sure of its way. He added a routine, romantic element to this interpretation by suggesting that such turbulence was the price to be paid for Spanish American artistic sensitivity, a virtue whose existence he took for granted. And since he was, after all, writing of the future of new men and their countries, he vacillated between subservience to Europe and pride in national assimilation. At the close of his book he ultimately resolved all these ambivalences by veering into a fortissimo of prophetic expectations which sweeps without pause through nineteenth century evolutionism, a touch of Nietzscheanism, Virgil's Fourth Eclogue, Plato's Atlantis, and the "Visionary of the Caravels" (i.e., Columbus). He ends as follows: "Perhaps she [America] has been destined from the beginning of time to give birth upon her wide plateaus to the Child of the Sun — as in the imperial legends of the Incas — to the master of proud mountains and venerable rivers. To Superman solitary and irresistible." . . .

. . . Though the basis may be "spiritual," geographic, Iberian, Latin, or racially "Cosmic," the conviction dominating a great deal of Spanish American historical and cultural theory is that it refers, and *must* refer, to a world of values which is all-embracing in its contents, purpose, and the course of its development. One more example of this, coming from a source as high as any other, is provided by the works of Ricardo Rojas (1882–1957), dramatist, historian, literary critic, one of Argentina's senior men of letters, and for many years president of the University of Buenos Aires. Like his contemporary José Vasconcelos, and in something like the same broad and dramatic way, Rojas believes in the significance of race and race mixtures, and in what he calls the "metaphysical forces" of racial inheritance. . . .

The terminology of Rojas' discussion is rather formidable. He conceives a national culture as the outcome of the twin identities of individual and collective personality, the second being the "metaphysical" extension of the first; a true culture is the expression of this collective soul manifesting itself through time. He speaks without hesitation of the angelic *numen* of a culture, of the powers of the *genius loci* of a culture inhabiting the earth and creating the unity of a race and the continuity of its traditions and its social types. In the case of Spanish America such gods, having reigned at the time of the Incas, fled frightened by the crimes of the Conquerors and the exorcisms of the Church; spoke again through the founders of independence; but again fled before "the materialistic appetites of the immigrant and the materialism of the men of science." Nevertheless, says Rojas, there are clear indications in our day that the gods of America "are once more hovering over us, suggesting new aesthetic and moral forms, as though they wanted to leave their metaphysical exile to re-enter the necessary torment of history."

The purpose of the historical and social analysis of ideas is to understand their sources and function. One must, therefore, restrain perplexity and discomfort at the seriousness of Rojas' mythological language, and notice instead that it introduces a new element in the social interpretation of spiritual questions. Spanish American nature, which in Andrés Bello was a beneficent stage for new cultural glories, and in José Santos Chocano a terrifying guardian of sovereignty, is in Rojas (as it was in José Martí) the cradle of mystically powerful energies creating the moral and aesthetic aspects of social life. But since these forces find themselves in conflict with the materialistic temptations of the modern age, the Spanish American spectacle of a soul-filled civilization endangered by shabby and greedy influences is once again before us. In writers like Rubén Darío the portrayal of this struggle had been found in the fable of the philistine ogre of the North and the radiant presence to the South. But Darío was a provincial from an isolated and unchanging country who, having chosen Spanish America to stand for his rather chic version of high culture, also chose himself to speak for both.

In Rojas, on the other hand, there is a more immediate concern — and one with more direct political implications — to be explained by the fact that Rojas was writing in Argentina, a nation which had led all other Spanish American countries in the modernization of social life and absorbed the greatest number of immigrants. According to Rojas the "genie-souls" of the Spanish American countries which by themselves would produce nothing but dignity and beauty were faced with certain inimical influences. These, however, were not outside but inside the fabric of Spanish American life. Rojas' opposition to what he calls materialistic science is in the tradition of modern literary hatred for technology as the inducer and the servant of the gross and superficial aspirations in men and the destroyer of a living and reverent relationship to nature. But Rojas also attacks *social* materialism. Here his racial and geographical mysticism seems only the language with which to defend aristocratic, ancestral, and leisurely values — the values of a landed elite or the traditionally oriented urban upper classes — and to oppose the social newcomers with their presumed acquisitiveness, self-serving spirit, and their callousness or ignorance toward past loyalties, memories, and venerable manners. In Rojas, then, the battle of materialism versus non-materialism has become an internal social question. A question, in fact, of social classes, of natives and foreigners, of country versus city.

The nature of this conflict is very apparent in another Argentinian, Eduardo Mallea (born 1903) who, in addition to his work as critic and literary editor for some of the important publications in Argentina, is also one of the Spanish American essayists and novelists in highest regard at the present time. Elegiacally in his autobiography *Historia de una Pasión Argentina,* Mallea contemplates the dissolution of the "spiritual physiognomy" of Argentina under the drive for wealth and gratification which, like Rojas, he blames chiefly on the immigrant masses. He understands, he says, the poverty, social disorder, and political conditions these immigrants escaped; nonetheless, he condemns the readiness with which they reached for the superficial, the "visible," rather than the "deeper" Argentina. Mallea is as critical of the new elites as he is of the new masses. He acknowledges the excitement and brilliance of urban life in Buenos Aires, but sees something feigned, unsound, even treacherous in its cultural vitality. An Indian in the fields is truly "cultured" because for him culture is a state of being and not a usable or an exhibited possession. The cosmopolitan man, for all his intellectual skillfulness, can never escape the temptations of a nervous, yet bloodless faddism, or, worse, the self-betrayals of opportunism. Mallea is particularly despairing of the new leading men of Argentinian life, the lawyers, doctors, teachers, art patrons, academicians, the "cultured public" — all of them "successful or merely pretentious, but no longer able to live like men, suffer like men, hate like men, have men's devotions, passions. . . ."

Time and a different sensitivity separate Rojas and Mallea. As frequently happens with the Spanish American penseur, Rojas' writing takes the form of a conspicuous montage of historical generalizations and cultural prescriptions. His view of Spanish American history is that of the drama of the native soul divided into four acts: the Indian, assimilated into colonial civilization; the Spanish, assimilated into family and language; the *creole* elements, which go into political existence and art; and, finally, the re-forging of all of these into a way of life at once universal and national. It is a large lesson in cultural programming, resting on vague, aphoristic (and questionable) concepts, delivered in a momentous public tone. Mallea's *Pasión* is a more private record of experience. It is, in fact, a modern literary document speaking for forms of literary unhappiness nearly universal in our time; a story of self-discovery in the midst of a world which conspires to hide itself from its own sham. What Mallea laments are the cultural consequences of democratization; the acquisitiveness which frequently accompanies social mobility; the corrosion of personal relations under what the German sociologist Georg Simmel calls the "unmerciful matter-of-factness" of the urban market place; and the appearance as a general type of the person capable of that ardent, profuse, but depthless socialization expected of men in a world where many people are brought together under loosely defined standards. . . .

Rojas wanted to breed cultural fullness out of carefully selected materials. Mallea looked for a human type capable of what he called "a severe exaltation of life." That is to say, a dignified form of human energy free of the shallow and wasteful impulses of contemporary life. But what he and Rojas expected of social personality, and the way in which they went about discovering it, are virtually the same. The key to Rojas' concept of cultural integrity is the theory that the social mind is born out of the collectivization of individual personalities. This was possible, however, because in a true culture individual personalities were so immersed in common values that they produced social characters as a "metaphysical extension" of themselves. This is, of course, a tautology. For if individual personalities can be that homogeneous we could just as well say that the individual psyche is the metaphysical extension of the collectivity. Mallea's "interior march," in the moral and psychological meaning, toward the deeper Argentinian led him to the geographical interior; to the La Plata hinterland; and to the Argentinian "natural man," the farmer and the gaucho. These, he declared, should become "the national monad," a spiritual matrix which would relate itself to all specific manifestations of cultural life "as the seed to the stem and the foliage." The determination is obvious on the part of both writers to employ any method, learned or obscure, historical, rhetorical or intuitive, in order to arrive at a sense of cultural unity and decisiveness. Mallea's prescription for the discovery of this principle, in particular, may be called a Platonic version of cultural anthropology. "What we need at all times is a reminiscence, that is an a priori knowledge of our destiny; in the origin of our destiny is the origin of our temper, of our mode of behavior, our nature. Our becoming is potentially combined in our natural origins."

This strain to bring off an act of absolute self-discovery, and thus to create an unbreakable life-frame within which culture will stream uncontroverted into the future, is universal in Spanish America, whether the language used is that of "race," "soil," "soul," or "conscience." Victor Raúl Haya de la Torre (born 1895), the Peruvian writer and political figure, though himself not an Indian, can say that "the Indian subconscious . . . lives in us all." The Colombian historian and literary critic Germán Arciniegas (born 1900), in a work he regards as "sociological," looks upon the volcanoes of Spanish America as "the bonfires of (its) earth-spirit." One can measure the tyranny of the drive toward self-revelation by the hypnotic burden placed upon the language accompanying it. Alberto Zum-Felde (born 1889), an Uruguayan literary critic and historian who has also been director of the National Library, restates Mallea in a transparent tautology which takes the form of a string of onto-logical-sounding nouns and adjectives. The problem of Spanish American culture, he says, is "identical with the definition of our original Self" as an "a priori historical imperative" residing in the "radical subliminal zone." Like Rojas, he is convinced that such reality "pre-exists and pre-acts" through the powers of the "Sublime Unconscious" to give societies their specific characteristics. And, like Alfonso Reyes, he knows that the spirit of Spanish America is "moving its necessary destiny with the infallibility of a sign." According to a recent book of the Mexican philosopher Emilio Uranga, historical and philosophical investigation are actually the same, and the present historical task of Mexico consists in sifting out from within itself the "morphology and dynamics" of its "being"; "onto-logical hunches," says Uranga, are one of the ways of performing this task. Speaking of José Rodó, the celebrated Uruguayan essayist, Emilio Oribe (born 1883), who is also an Uruguayan and a professor of philosophy at the University of Montevideo, writes the following which shall be its own commentary:

What is not to be doubted is that, in the essential sense, the work of Rodó becomes merged with the spiritual destiny of an idea-producing America as she may be envisioned as an ultimate transcendental finality. In the most secret recesses of Rodó's thinking we may find the nurturing nebulae of that which will be the rationally formulable future of these lands: the reign of intelligence linked with beauty, the creativeness of the individual resting in the profound freedom of Being. The inevitable verdict of our destiny rests upon the knee of the divine, upon reason, science and freedom. . . .

It is always in some ways unfair to rake passages out of whole works in order to illustrate a common theme or expose a special point. And it is true that the quotations given here do not sound quite so extravagant when read within the atmosphere of these writings, which is that of a soliloquy embracing history, anthropology, philosophical speculation, and personal commentary used as a means of raising some pressing rhetorical questions. Still, the reason that they appear so unfrugal is, of course, that their premises naturally induce self-incantation and climax by suggestiveness. It is also clear that this literature can prosper by attending only to the conventionally elevated facts of history and civilization: philosophical and artistic ideals, the pageantry of great events, and souls of peoples and nations. Its outlook is, therefore, aristocratic, at least in the intellectual sense, even though some of the men who practiced it may have been politically to the left. And it is also essentially aesthetic, looking for a society which could be *contemplated* in the sense of artistically appreciated. One is here reminded of the statement of the Mexican philosopher Antonio Caso that things exist in this world in order to be *seen*. (Italics added.)

In the case of the poets they may have conceived it as their obligation to be grand and to be noble. Bello, being a profoundly academic man, made America a reflection of his own desires, a new garden for the promenades of the cultivated mind. Darío was clearly too manneristic a writer to have any footing in social actuality, just as his whole life is a long episode of flight from his social and national beginnings. Yet, even in writers like Martí, who were immersed in the political struggle, their temptation is to look at the materials of Spanish American civilization in an aesthetic perspective. Martí's famous essay, *Nuestra América*, which attacks false erudition, empty cosmopolitanism, and artificial institutions and laws, is dominated by poetic imagery in its portrayal of the native society: "Can Hamilton's theories stop the charge of *llanero's* colt? Can a phrase from Sieyes make the frozen blood of the Indian run again?" Or, ". . . the password of our generation is 'create.' Let our wine be banana wine; and if it turns sour, it is *our* wine." Vasconcelos' racial theories are really a discourse on the natural endowment of the Spanish American populations for aesthetic sensitivity. García Calderón, for all his concern with the "advances of civilization" in the commonplace sense of this term, ends in a pure note of Nietzschean aesthetic heroics: the future Spanish American as the master of Andean peaks and jungle rivers, "over-whelming and lonely." Rojas treats every element in Spanish American history as a specific component of the artistic imagination of the society; what he wants to construct is a temple in which each one of those elements will be a part of the supporting arch. Even Mallea's "national monad," while ostensibly a moral antidote to the spread of modern pharisaical ambition, is also an aesthetic figure, a quiet monument of human completeness in its simplicity, harmoniousness, and self-effacing dignity. Having dealt, like Plato, in reminiscences, Mallea seemingly concluded, like Plato, that good conduct is graceful and graceful conduct good. Indeed, the search for a cultural archetype is itself an aesthetic expectation which shows the structural and the ideological aspects of these theories to be inseparable; looking at society and culture as a finished architecture implicitly promises the existence within that society and culture of a unifying and lasting spiritual principle. This, however, raises the question of how so elevated a quest could have survived the daily surroundings of Spanish American life: the perennial stumbling in the solution of social problems, economic stagnation, unpredictable politics, and international impotence. The answer is, obviously enough, that such speculations are one of the few answers available to such realities. The prophetic aestheticism of "ontological" views of culture, therefore, has an underside of profound anxiety, an anxiety which, uncontrollably, breathes next to all the words of brave expectancy. Mallea, in search of Argentina, tells us that "of this anguish was born this reflection." Luis Alberto Sánchez (born 1900), the Peruvian literary critic and historian, says of his book, ¿Existe la América Latina? that it was written as a way of "putting the finger in the wound." Alberto Zum-Felde speaks at one moment of the infallibility and imperative nature of Spanish America's destiny, and concedes at the next moment the "anguish of the problem, our culture.". . . This is the same mournful and haughty condition of Spanish America which José Martí had also recognized: "There is no fatherland in which a man can take greater pride than in our sorrowful republics."

Conclusion — In the single most accurate criticism of the philosophical schools of Latin America, the Brazilian Euryalo Cannabrava described them as the product of a "superstitious attitude towards the inner life" and an "attempt to reduce philosophy to an exercise in verbalistic ingenuity or to the vindication by argument of purely instinctual beliefs." And he might have added that, as theories of culture, they also constitute extraordinarily, if unconsciously, ingenious forms of intellectual procrastination. They demand the unearthing of essences, but seldom tell us exactly what they are. And they define the object of their expectations, the character of Spanish American civilization, in such a way as forever to postpone its coming; although, of course, the hope always presumes the necessity of its fulfillment. There are two kinds of reasons for this: some ideological in a broad sense, some sociological in a narrow occupational sense. When one glances at the careers of Spanish American men of letters one cannot avoid the impression of an improvised miscellany of tasks and intellectual interests. Men who are poets are also political essayists, historians, philosophers, academics of various kinds, heads of governmental offices, diplomats, and librarians. These facts have been used to suggest in these men a devotion to universality, and the respectful support of intellectual work by the institutions of their society. What they really suggest, however, is the dependence of the intellectual upon political accommodation and literary piecework in a society devoid of a large and dependable reading public or a sufficiently broad and well-paid system of higher education. In addition, this means that intellectual work is done in an atmosphere of haste which invites dilettantism and a conviction that all questions may be embraced by a sufficiently elevated rhetoric. This is the other side of what García Calderón calls, praisefully, the Spanish American "cult of general ideas."

The challenge of insecurity, however, is not only personal and economic, but cultural. For no society which meets in some measure the expectations of its intellectuals need be asked to deliver its cultural promises on such an utopian scale as the Spanish Americans demand. And it is, perhaps, as an answer to the actual denials of their environment that one can account for what may be called the spiritually *nouveau riche* character of Spanish American cultural

speculation. By this I mean the stubborn notion that one cannot discuss social meaning, or be subtle, or develop and communicate insight except through a language of obvious intellectual expenditure,
of "first class" mental travail; a language full of words like "sublime,"
"a priori," "inner," "destiny," "Being," "imperative," and, of course,
the ever recurrent "ontology." The Spanish-speaking countries of
this hemisphere have always regarded themselves as part of the
American Dream. But their notorious difficulties in fulfilling their
part of this mission has turned this promise into a painful paradox,
naggingly deepened by the successes of the United States and by
the profound inroads into their world of American economic and
political power. Because of this history Spanish American intellectuals have had no workaday feeling of cultural development, of the
flowering of many particular aspects of social life, or of that "sense
of secure and sustained growth" which H. G. Wells attributed to
the United States. "We are those who believe in art, in the enthusiasm for the beautiful regardless of the consequences," wrote Francisco Bilbao. But Vasconcelos, turning away for a moment from
ethnic self-congratulation, had this comment to make: "Let us admit that it was our misfortune not to have developed the cohesion of
that extraordinary breed to the North, which we cover with insult
because it has beaten us at every game in the secular struggle."

The power and plenty of the United States has excused American
intellectuals, certainly since the Civil War, from the necessity of
being nationalists (with the significant exception of the defeated
South). But, if anything is true of the Spanish American intellectuals,
it is the opposite. The voice of their cultural dreams whether mellif-
luous, querulous, or melodramatically utopian, is the voice of a
repressed, yet never spent, nationalistic passion. Cultural ontology
in Spanish America is the metaphysics of cultural frustration.

2. The Hispano-American's World

Waldo Frank

Divergences — Malaise clouds the good-will with which our country turns to the peoples south. We have the intuition that we should

From "The Hispano-American's World" by Waldo Frank, *The Nation*, May
24, 1941, pp. 615–618. Reprinted by permission.

be close, not for mere reasons of defense and commerce, but because we *are* close; and yet that we lack the key for understanding. America Hispana is a world enormously farther from us in culture than Europe; at the same time it is a world deeply and dynamically closer to us than Europe. This is a paradox — a truth, that is, hidden under divergent symptoms. And the best way to get at it is to know the differences: which means, first of all, to cut beneath the rhetoric and sentimentalism, vague or vicious, that are supposed to "unite," but merely dupe, us.

Ethnic. Our dominant stock, of course, is European; our minor elements were Europeanized before they came here (like the Jews), or are held in strict subjection (like the Negroes), or are long since nullified (like the Indians). The ethnic scheme south is infinitely more complex, not only because of the many strains which have been kept culturally alive, but because these strains have created new ones with new psychological traits. In Mexico, Central America, except Costa Rica, and the Andean countries, the mestizos and Indians are dominant. Along the Pacific coast down to Chile, mixtures of Negro with Indian (*zambo*) and of Negro with mestizo (*cholo*) have significantly shared in history and culture. And in Brazil a new Afro-Creole race that is neither Negro nor Portuguese shapes the life and, although it has not yet wrested political power from the "Aryan" minority centered in six southern states, *must rule the destiny* — if it is to be more than colonial — of the vast nation. None of the important countries is predominantly Western European except Chile and Argentina; and even here there are significant suffused non-European forces. The Chilean temperament, for instance, reveals traits of the Auracana Indians — as distinct from the Indians of Argentina as the Andes from the pampa; the Negro strain in Buenos Aires, entirely assimilated because never suppressed, continues to nourish and form the people in that profoundest of folk-dances and folk-complines, the tango. (I am not referring to the corrupt concoctions of our radio and night clubs.)

Cultural. Our country's culture stems from the late stages of the English Protestant Reformation and its bastard children — empirical rationalism and the Industrial Revolution. It has, therefore, in the main, the traits of the eighteenth and nineteenth centuries, and is indigenous to our dominant race. The culture of America Hispana, insofar as it is European, derives from the Catholic Renaissance of sixteenth- and seventeenth-century Hispana (the term includes Portugal); in energy and values it is a direct transplantation of

Queen Isabel's crusade against the Moors. It is therefore much older
and enormously different. But its European parts were at once complicated by the deep Indian cultures closer to Asia than to Europe —
Aztec, Toltec, Maya, Chibcha, Quechua, Aymara — which the Conquistadores encountered from Mexico to north Chile and Argentina.
Even this is too simple. The effect of Protestantism, which soon
made alliance with empirical rationalism, was to suppress ethnic
intuitions and personal emotions that did not conform with the
march of the pioneer. The Hispanic Renaissance, although it conquered, at the same time preserved and transfigured.

Strictly speaking, there are no true survivals of Indian cultures,
even in the remotest Andes; there are *transformed* beginnings of a
culture with Indian and Catholic roots. Neither Spain nor pre-
Conquest America exists in America Hispana. This holds with the
Negro elements. The blacks, for instance, who fought in the wars of
independence against Spain were already American; the "African"
note in arts as distinct as the intellectual prose of Cuba, the folk-
music of Brazil, the courtly verse of Peru, is not to be found in
Africa. A unique virtue of Hispanic imperialism, setting it high above
that of Britain, was that its ruthless "charity of the sword" kept alive,
in new forms, the intuitions and spiritual tongues of the conquered
and exploited peoples.

Geographical. There were other complications. Our Thirteen
Colonies were a comparatively flat and friendly expanse of temperate forest and low mountain. The men who settled there, and on
the way had to fight Indians of low resistance, took two and a half
centuries to reach the Pacific. The Spaniards — they were ahead of
the Portuguese in sailing from the Andes down the Amazon — in fifty
years flung their passionate search from Chile to California. And they
were opposed not only by stubborn native cultures that submitted
and never surrendered but by some of the vastest mountains, jungles,
and deserts in the world. Still another barrier opposed them: the
stern purpose of the mother country to prevent colonial intercom-
munication. Each colony was dependent on the metropolis and
otherwise self-sufficient. And within each frontier were these huge
accumulations of conflict — ethnic, cultural, economic, enhanced by
natural divisions.

Psychological. As the new generations were born, *all these conflicts came to be stratified within every individual.* This is a point
difficult, yet absolutely essential, for us to grasp. A citizen of Mexico,
Brazil, Peru, may be of "pure" Hispanic descent or "pure" Indian; he

may be entirely of West European stock (Italo-Hispanic-German). He has nevertheless within him the whole complexity of his country and his continent. Past differences of race, religion, culture, have become actively present traits in a new human nature.

Political. By 1776, within our comparatively simple, expanding world, the people were divided into three great sections: the North with its free-labor farms and free-artisan towns; the slave-planter South; and the frontier. It took less than three generations to fuse them in the final act of civil war. Cultural homogeneity had already long been more than potential. Our entire people, able to read the same papers and listen to the same speeches, going to churches whose variety canceled them into impotence against the prevailing economic trend, was ready for political democracy. And with the directly inherited political genius and empirical philosophy of Britain, they got it. The revolutions from Mexico to La Plata were bewilderingly different, and far less simple. True democracy is a goal inherent in the aims of a literate, economically integrated, culturally harmonious people. We were not ready for it in 1776, nor have we achieved it now — nor ever will achieve it until we outlive *both* our economic system and our shallow vision of life. But the main elements were there, and had been prepared by two centuries of simple growth. The trend was in us. Britain was preventing a homogeneous people from going ahead. Our revolution freed us so the trend *toward integration* could proceed. The revolutions south freed the people *into chaos.* Spain, with her iron laws that forbade trade except from each colony to her, with her controlled church that fought the contact of the native clergy with the people, with her clumsy military rule, was holding the peoples from what had to be their first stage of growth: acceptance of the turmoil and conflicts within them. Worlds are born from chaos. And this was literally a new world in the making. America Hispana had to be free of Spain and Portugal in order to enter into the creativity of chaos.

And now another tragic paradox. The Hispanic colonies, boiling over with unsolved problems of religious, economic, and social life, had to take on some political form. None of their own was ready. They accepted the political design imposed on them by their soldiers, who, unlike ours, were political romanticists and idealists schooled largely by *our* statesmen. Our republic from the start was an organic form in which we proceeded to grow up. Their republic, at best, was a defensive armor against reaction — a theoretic form in which the people could at least begin to work out their chaos.

The Century of the Mestizo — This is the key to the first century of the southern republics. We might call it the "century of chaos," if the thousand proofs were clear to us that this is a chaos pregnant of a great world. I prefer "the century of the mestizo," because the mestizo, born of the marriage of Spain and Amerindia, is the incarnate symbol of this creative chaos. Not everyone has liked this term; and when I first used it in my book "America Hispana" many a critic from Mexico to Argentina objected. Of course, there are whole nations, among the most important, with little mestizo trace; and there are other mixtures. But in the dynamic character of the marriage of the European with the Indian girl — a union part lust, part tenderness, part devil, and part Christ — I see the perfect symbol for the inward complexity of all Hispano-Americans, and of their first century of independence.

The reader must not suppose that this chaotic gestation period — a very brief one, in view of the immensely complex elements involved — had no cultural fruits, no moments of political peace. There were significant arts in the republics; fascinating projections of the high genius of colonial and pre-colonial days. And lands as remote as Mexico and Argentina produced successful statesmen. But the expression was of primitive parts of the whole, as the folk music and dance, or of simplifications of the chaos, as the work of a Juárez in Mexico, of a Sarmiento in Argentina. Neither in its political nor in its cultural life was America Hispana ready before our generation to come to grips with its whole self as an organic, potentially integral culture.

The world of the Hispano-American writers is still largely this "century of the mestizo." Nevertheless, their *essential* conditions for work are better than ours. For these reasons among others: (1) The Catholic culture creates an atmosphere of respect for literature and art that was already waning in Britain at the time of Swift. (2) It impregnates the people with that tragic sense of life, inherent in all great art (including comedy), which our sleazy eighteenth- and nineteenth-century optimism rubbed out; and with a receptivity to general ideas conspicuous for its absence in our historians, our critics, our anti-philosophical philosophers. (3) Most important of all, it prepares the mind to conceive life as organic and whole. (4) This Catholic attitude survives the Catholic faith (not many of the best writers of America Hispana have been church members; most, even in the nineteenth century, were radicals or socialists) and harmonizes with the intuitive values of the Indian and mestizo peasant, with the pantheism and aesthetic genius of the pre-Conquest cultures. From all this is derived a fact of paramount importance: the Hispano-American student can *speak* with the illiterate peasant. In the knowledge of the unity and of the tragedy of life, in the knowledge of the immediate conduits between the self, the soil, and the cosmos, peon and intellectual are close together. This knowledge, the source of all aesthetic work, prepares the Hispano-American writer for the overwhelming problems of his people, and tends to humanize and deepen his adaptation of economic and political creeds from Europe.

On the other hand, as both Sánchez and Mallea made clear in their essays, the *environmental* condition of the Hispano-American writer is far worse than ours. The peasant, although instinctively and spiritually close, cannot read him; the lack of communication which, until the airplane, made the shortest line between Mexico and Panama run through New York, often restricts his public to a few friends within his own frontiers. Only Brazil and Argentina have thus far produced writers, not the best, who can live by their literary work. Every good Hispano-American writer is a journalist, a professor, a lawyer, a government clerk — unless fame gives him a consular or diplomatic position.

But, on the other side of the picture, every educated man in America Hispana tries to be a writer. The poetic ferment has been stupendous. I am no statistician, but I'll wager that more little sheaves of verse·are published in a year in America Hispana than in England and the United States in a lustrum. Most of it, of course, appears in humble, privately printed volumes; but if little is important, surprisingly little is emotionally or technically dead. And from this ferment has issued the greatest poetry of the Western Hemisphere.

José Hernández in 1872 created "Martín Fierro," the rebellious epic of the gaucho against "respectable" Buenos Aires over which the schoolmaster genius, D. F. Sarmiento, author of "Facundo," was presiding. "Martín Fierro" is the best modern folk poem in the world; to find its equal one must go back to the dawns of English, Spanish, and German narrative verse. A generation later, Rubén Darío appeared in Nicaragua, possibly the one poet of indubitable first world rank that the Americas have produced.

Novels and tales are also often privately printed, and of late years have become a flood almost equaling the verse. So that it might be said that America Hispana has had more writers than readers. It has no novel equal in depth and furious power to "Moby Dick"; no colossus of virtuosity like the later Henry James. But it has far more profoundly expressed the frontier. Our best in that field, I suppose, is "Huckleberry Finn." Compare it with "Don Segundo Sombra," by the Argentine Güiraldes. Here too is the tale of a boy, wandering, not down a symbolic river, but on horseback through the pampa. His companions, instead of being adults of equally infantile soul and mind, are gauchos of whom the leader is a noble, unsentimental man whose great dignity, without transcending the rough terms of frontier life, reveals the depth of the potential American culture.

The Organic Century — History, needing dates, may say that the "century of the mestizo" began to die about 1910. The Mexican Revolution under political leaders like Madero, Carranza, Obregón, and, greatest of all, Lázaro Cárdenas, under cultural leaders like Vasconcelos, Manuel Gamio, Reyes, Rivera, Orozco, Siqueiros, Chávez, Revueltas, marks the beginning of an organic movement that has its counterpart in other nations — for instance, in Argentina, under President Hipólito Irigoyen. The reader will have noted the difference in the generations of poets described by Reyes and Mallea. For a Darío the abyss was too huge between the chaotic actuality and the ideal forced on his world by the romantic soldiers — of whom Bolívar was only the greatest among many. Hence literary power took a perpendicular and prophetic trajectory. With the generation of Pablo Neruda, the creative energy tends to suffuse and illumine the daily life of the people.

In the literary art most dependent on an immediate audience, the drama, America Hispana barely begins — in Buenos Aires, as was to be expected. In criticism the lack of communication between artist and readers has worked a havoc of false perspectives almost as bad as, with us, the atmosphere of ballyhoo and the refusal to face life in its depths, which are at once unitary, tragic, and divine. Nevertheless, men of creative critical power appeared in the "century of the mestizo"; and always they were men of action. In Argentina there were Alberdi, Sarmiento, the socialist Esteban Echeverría. Peru at the close of the nineteenth century produced the socialist poet Manuel González Prada. In Cuba, José Martí and Enrique José Varona; in Puerto Rico, Eugenio María de Hostos, inspired a whole generation of keen historical and cultural critics. Mexico gave, among others, José Vasconcelos, who, as Secretary of Education under Obregón, was midwife to a painters' renascence, founded the still thriving rural schools, and wrote books whose passionate amalgam of Christian, Hindu, and socialist ideas made him a leader of youth in all America Hispana, until his political ambitions betrayed him. From Colombia came the essayist Baldamiro Sanín Cano, spreading, not only with his works but with his warm personal contacts as a diplomatic envoy, his noble continental vision. Finally Peru produced a man whom Mallea might have named, even if he did not live to carry out his promise. José Carlos Mariátegui (1895–1930) wrote in "Siete Ensayos de Interpretación de la Realidad Peruana" a treasure store and a model of revolutionary American criticism. His awareness of the primacy of religious, aesthetic, and psychological factors in the organic problem of social reconstruction teaches a lesson that our socialists and liberals have yet to learn.

The Common Ground — . . . Despite barriers and divisions, a deep common spirit unites the writers of America Hispana and makes of their works a common ground. Identity of problems and of aims has preestablished harmony between them. Even in mood, they are brothers. They share the dilemma of the rifts between ancient religious and modern political-economic needs; they share confusion within ethnic contrasts and an unwieldy opulent world that is overborne and menaced, more than ever, by foreign lusts; they share the sense of destiny — to create a true new world — and bewilderment before the enormous forces, internal and external, they must master to create it.

This harmony of the Hispano-American writers reveals a basic harmony with ours. (I have meant, throughout, of course, by *writers* the creative men, the artists, the knowers, the seers; not the clowns, the "informers," the dealers in slick shoddy who crowd every modern literary market.) No wonder the writers of the South read Jefferson, Whitman, Emerson, Thoreau, as soon as ours. And we too, like them, have our voiceless masses struggling for a true new world, although the jungle that overwhelms us is the jungle of the machine, the jungle voice of radio-movie-journal. And our masses are even more remote from our writers than the illiterate Indians of the Andes are from the makers of their potential Word. So the circle closes: harmony between our writers and theirs; harmony between our publics, who can know themselves and each other chiefly through the writers. Here is the body of a true alliance.

The Hispano-American writer has his enemies chiefly at home (this must not be forgotten; foreign imperialisms can never succeed without domestic allies). They are the same categories there as here:

the foes, aggressive or implicit, of creative experience and creative thinking; the exploiters, the money-men, the political lackeys, the professional and professorial parasites, the prostitute-artists. In America Hispana you will find them, as here, in the usual places of power — from government bureau to rich journal, from church to school. There as here they are the rule, with occasional illustrious exceptions.

Most of our efforts for "better inter-American relations," including plans for defense against Europe's fascist forces, have been negotiations between members of these suspect categories: between men and institutions who stand *between* and implicitly *against* the interests of the peoples. Hispano-American business men and politicians are just as little concerned for the happiness and health of their people as are our own business men and politicians. But men of these categories in the southern republics will go along with their North American brothers as long as the going is good. If Hitler loses, and the United States emerges as the dominant power in an Anglo-Saxon axis, they will come to us anyway; and we could have saved our money. If Hitler wins, or a fascist Europe, our money is wasted. Facts — facts of trade and price, in so far as they mean pesos in the pocket — are what count with these minorities; even as dollars, and the power of which the dollar is the symbol, are what count with the oligarchy that sits firm in the American saddle. And let us not fool ourselves: in so far as men of these categories in *both Americas* are concerned with ideology at all, their hearts belong to reaction, even though they fight Hitler: they distrust democracy, even though they quote Jefferson and Bolívar.

Our true allies in America Hispana are the people, and their true spokesmen are the writers. Our efforts to make alliance with them, to undertake nutritive exchange with them, have been criminally weak. In this urgent need America Hispana has been more advanced than we. Its writers have learned from our teachers, have been nourished by our poets. They have shown aptitude and capacity to digest our strengths, far beyond ours even to guess at their values. Perhaps this is only natural, since their life is rooted in deeper cultures; since, for all their divisions, they have been far less disintegrated by the machine — or rather by our shallow philosophies that let the machine be master — and have preserved far better the contact with self, with soil, and with the people that is life and the beginning of wisdom. But it is time we did something about it.

B. Ariel: Source and Symbol
of Misunderstanding

3. Ariel Embodies the Mastery of Reason and of
Sentiment Over the Baser Impulses of Unreason

José Enrique Rodó

On that evening the venerable old master whom we used to call
Prospero, after the wise sage of Shakespeare's "Tempest," was bid-
ding good-bye to his young scholars, met about him for the last
time after a long year of task work.

They had come to the lofty hall of study, where a taste at once
refined and austere sought to do honour to the noble presence of
books, Prospero's faithful companions. But the leading note of the
hall — like a divinity, serene in its nimbus — was a finely wrought
bronze, representing Ariel in "The Tempest."

It was the manner of the Master to sit close by this bronze statue,
and that was why he was called by the name of the magician who
in the play is loved and served by the spirit of fancy that the sculp-
tor had sought to embody.

But perhaps, as well in the manner of his teaching, or in his character, there were a reason for the nickname, in profounder sense.
Ariel, genius of the Air, represents, in the symbolism of Shakespeare
the noble part — the spirit with wings. . . . For Ariel embodies the
mastery of reason and of sentiment over the baser impulses of un-
reason. He is the generous zeal, the lofty and disinterested motive in
action, the spirituality of civilization, and the vivacity and grace of
the intelligence; — the ideal end to which human selection aspires;
that superman in whom has disappeared, under the persistent chisel
of life, the last stubborn trace of the *Caliban,* symbol of sensuality
and stupidity. . . .

From *Ariel* by José Enrique Rodó, translated by F. J. Simpson (Boston
Houghton Mifflin Company, 1922), pp. 3–148, *passim.* Reprinted by permission
of the publisher.

Prospero passed his hand, thoughtfully, over the head of the little statue; then, gathering a group of young men about him, with a firm voice — the voice of the Master, which, to pass its ideas and grave them deeply in the minds of the disciples, can employ either the clear penetration of a ray of light or the sharp blow of a chisel on the marble, the stroke of the painter's brush on canvas or the touch of the wave upon the sands to be read in fossils by future genera- tions of men — the Master, as his scholars waited with affectionate attention, began to speak:

Near this statue where you have seen me preside each day over our talks as friends — talks which I hope have succeeded in dispel- ling from the work of teaching any touch of austerity — I have once more to speak to you, that our parting hour may be like the seal stamped upon our agreement both in feeling and in ideas. So I in- voke Ariel as my divinity, and I could wish to-day for my lecture the most gentle and persuasive force that ever it has had, for I think that to speak to youth of noble motives, of lofty ideas, whatever they are, is as a kind of sacred oratory. I also think that the spirit of youth is as a generous soil, where the seed of an opportune word may in a short time return the fruits of an immortal harvest. I earnestly wish to cooperate with you in a page of that programme which, in preparing yourselves for the free air of action, you have doubtless formed in your inner thought for the end of your efforts, the object to which each personality shall devote his life. For that intimate, personal programme — which rarely is formulated or written out, but more usually stays within the breast until it is revealed in outer action — fails never in the spirit of those peoples or those persons who are something above the rabble. If, with relation to individual liberty, Goethe could say so profoundly that only he is worthy of liberty and life who can conquer it for himself each day; with much more reason might I say that the honour of every human generation requires that it shall conquer for itself, by the persevering activity of its own thinking, by the effort of its own will, its faith in the deter- mined, the persistent manifestation of the ideal, and the place of the ideal in the evolution of all ideas. And in conquering your own you should begin by recognizing as the first object of faith your own selves. The youth which you love is a power whose application you must work yourselves, and a treasury for the use of which yourselves are responsible. Prize that treasure and that power; see that the lofty consciousness of its possession stays radiant and effective in yourselves. I say to you with Renan: "Youth is the discovery of that

immense horizon which is life." And the discovery which reveals unknown lands must be made complete with the virile force which
shall rule them. No spectacle can be imagined more fit to captivate
at once the interest of the thinker and the enthusiasm of the artist,
than that which a human generation presents when it goes to meet a
future all vibrant with the impatience of action, of lofty front, with
a smiling and high disdain for deceit, the soul purified by sweet and
distant mirages which wake in it mysterious impulses, like the
visions of Cipango and Eldorado in the heroical chronicles of the
Conquistadores. . . .

The divergence of individual vocations will impress divers directions upon your activities and cause to predominate in each one of
you a disposition of mind predetermined by a definite aptitude. Some
will be men of science, others of art, others still, of action. But over
all the inclinations which may bind you severally to different tasks
and ways of life, you should guard in your inner soul the consciousness of the fundamental unity of our nature, which demands that
every human being be, above and before all, the unspoiled pattern
of a man in whom no noble faculty of the mind be obliterated, and
no lofty interest for all men have lost its communicative virtue. Before all modifications of profession and training stands the fulfilment
of the destiny common to all rational beings. "There is one universal
profession: — to be a man," says Guyau. And Renan, remembering
à propos of unbalanced and imperfect civilizations, that the end of
the human creature cannot be only either to know or to feel or to imagine, but to be entirely and really human, defines the ideal of perfection to which he should bend his energies, as the possibility of
offering in the individual type an abbreviated picture of the whole
race.

Try, then, to develop so far as possible not any single aspect, but
the plenitude of your being. Shrug not your shoulders before any
noble and fecund manifestation of human nature, under the pretext
that your own individuality ties you of preference to a different one.
Be attentive spectators where you may not be actors. When that
false and vulgarized idea of education, which thinks it subordinate
wholly to utilitarian ends, takes upon itself to mutilate by such
materialism the natural fulness of our minds, and by a premature
specialization to proscribe the teaching of anything that is disinterested or ideal, it fails to avoid the danger of training for the
future minds that have become narrow, incapable of seeing more
than the one aspect of a thing which immediately touches them,

separated as by a frozen desert from other minds that in the same society have chosen other aspects of our life. The necessity of devoting ourselves each one to some determined activity, some special form of learning, surely need not exclude the inclination to realize, for the intimate harmony of our spirit, that destiny which is common to all rational beings. That special activity must be but the basic note of that harmony. The famous line in which the slave of the old play affirmed that nothing human was strange to him, being human himself, forms part of that cry of the heart which is eternal in the human consciousness because its meaning is inexhaustible. Our capacity to understand must only be limited by the impossibility of understanding souls that are narrow. To be unable to see more than one phase of nature, more than one human interest or idea, is like living in the shadow of a dream pierced by a single ray of sunlight. That intolerance, that exclusiveness, which when born of tyrannous absorption in some high enthusiasm or flowing from some disinterested ideal may merit justification or even sympathy, becomes converted to the most abominable of inferiorities when in the circle of vulgar life it betrays the narrowness of a mind incapacitated to reflect on more than the partial appearances of things.

Unfortunately, in the very times when civilization reaches its highest level of culture is the danger of this limitation of minds most serious and its results most to be feared. For the law of evolution requires, as it appears in societies as well as individuals, an ever-increasing tendency to heterogeneity, which as the general culture of society increases limits individual activities more and more and restricts the field of action of each one to an ever narrower specialty. And though it be a necessary condition of progress, this development of the notion of specialization brings with it visible evils which not only lower the horizon of the eye of thought, thus distorting its image of the universe, but come to injure also the spirit of human solidarity by the particularization of individual habits and affections. . . .

To that conception of human life which is formed on the free and harmonious development of our nature, and therefore includes among its essential objects the satisfaction of our feeling for the beautiful, is opposed — as a rule for human conduct — the conception called utilitarian, under which our whole activities are governed by their relation to the immediate ends of self-interest. The blame of a narrow utilitarianism as the only monitor of the spirit of our century, meted out to it in the name of the ideal with all the rigours of Anathema, is based in part in the failure to recognize that its Titanic efforts for the subordination of the forces of Nature to the human will and for the extension of material well-being are a necessary labour to prepare, as by the laborious enrichment of an exhausted soil, for the flowering of future idealisms. The transitory predominance of that function of utility which has absorbed the agitated and feverish life of the last hundred years with its most potent energies explains, however, although it does not justify, many of the painful yearnings, many discontents and grievances of the intelligence, which show themselves either by a melancholy and exalted idealization of the past, or by a cruel despair of the future. For this there is one fruitful and well-adventured thought in the proposition of a certain group of thinkers of these last generations, among whom I need only cite again the noble figure of Guyau, who have tried to seal the definitive reconciliation of the conquests of the century with the renovation of many old human devotions, and have put into this blessed work as many treasures of love as of genius.

Often you will have heard attributed to two main causes that torrent of the spirit of utility which gives its note to the moral physiognomy of the present century, with its neglect of the aesthetic and disinterested view of life. The revelations of natural science, whose interpreters, favourable or the reverse, agree in destroying all ideality for its base, are one; the other is the universal diffusion and triumph of democratic ideas. I propose to speak to you exclusively of this latter cause; because I trust that your first initiation in the revelations of Science has been so directed as to preserve you from the danger of a vulgar interpretation. Upon democracy weighs the accusation of guiding humanity, by making it mediocre, to a Holy Empire of Utilitarianism. This accusation is reflected with vibrant intensity in the pages — for me always full of a suggestive charm — of the most amiable among the masters of the Modern Spirit: the seductive pages of Renan, to whose authority you have often heard me refer and of whom I may often speak again. Read Renan, those of you who have not done so already, and you will have to love him as I do. No one as he, among the moderns, appears to me such a master "of that art of teaching with Grace" which Anatole France considers divine. No one so well as he has succeeded in com-

bining irony with pity; even in the rigour of the analysis he can put
the unction of the priest. And even when he teaches us to doubt, his
exquisite gentleness sheds a balsam over the doubt itself. His
thoughts ring in our minds with echoes ineffable, so vague as to remind one of sacred music. His infinite comprehension makes critics
class him among those dilettantes of a light scepticism who wear the
gown of the philosopher like the domino of a mask; but, once you
penetrate his spirit, you will see that the vulgar tolerance of the mere
sceptic differs from his as the hospitality of a worldly *salon* from the
real spirit of charity.

This master holds, then, that high preoccupation with the ideal
interests of our race is irreconcilable with the spirit of democracy.
He believes that the conception of life in a society where that spirit
dominates will gradually come to seek only material welfare, as the
good most attainable for the greatest number. According to him,
democracy is the enthronement of Caliban. Ariel can but be van-
quished by its triumph. Many others who most care for aesthetic
culture and select spirit are of a like mind. Thus Bourget thinks that
universal triumph of democratic institutions will make civilization
lose in profundity what it gains in extension. He sees its necessary
end in the empire of individual mediocrity. "Who says democracy
voices the evolution of individual tendencies and the devolution of
culture." These judgments have a lively interest for us Americans
who love the cause and consequence of that Revolution which in our
America is entwined with the glory of its origin, and believe instinctively in the possibility of a noble and rare individual life
which need never sacrifice its dignity to the caprices of the rabble.
To confront the problem one must first recognize that if democracy
does not uplift its spirit by a strong ideal interest which it shares with
its preoccupation by material interests, it does lead, and fatally, to
the favouring of mediocrity, and lacks, more than any other social
system, barriers within which it may safely seek the higher culture.
Abandoned to itself, without the constant rectification of some active
moral sanction which shall purify and guide its motives to the dig-
nifying of life — democracy will, gradually, extinguish the idea of
any superiority which may not be turned into a more efficient training for the war of interests. It is then the most ignoble form of the
brutalities of power. Spiritual preference, exaltation of life by unselfish motive, good taste and art and manners, and the admiration of
all that is worthy and of good repute, will then alike vanish unpro-

tected when social equality has destroyed all grades of excellence without replacing them with others that shall also rule by moral influence and the light of reason.

Any equality of conditions in the order of society, like homogeneity in nature, is but an unstable equilibrium. From that moment when democracy shall have worked its perfect work of negation by the levelling of unjust superiorities, the equality so won should be but a starting-point. Its affirmation remains; and the affirmation of democracy and its glory consist in arousing in itself by fit incentives the revelation and the mastery of the true superiorities of men.

With relation to the conditions of the life of America, that duty of attaining the true conception of our social state is doubly needful. Our democracies grow rapidly by the continual addition of a vast cosmopolitan multitude, by a stream of immigration which is merged with a nucleus already too weak to make active effort at assimilation and so contain the human flood by those dikes which an ancient solidity of social structure can alone provide, a secured political order, and the elements of a culture that has become deeply rooted. This rapid growth exposes our future to the dangers of a democratic degeneration which smothers under the blind force of the mass all idea of quality, deprives the social consciousness of all just notion of order, and, yielding its class organization to the rough hands of chance, causes the triumph of only the most ignoble, unjustifiable supremacies. . . .

The utilitarian conception as the idea of human destiny, and equality at the mediocre as the norm of social proportion, make up the formula which in Europe they call the spirit of Americanism. It is impossible to think on either of these as inspirations for human conduct or society, while contrasting them with those which are opposed to them, without at once conjuring up by association a vision of that formidable and fruitful democracy there in the North, with its manifestations of prosperity and power, as a dazzling example in favour of the efficacy of democratic institutions and the correct aim of its ideas. If one could say of utilitarianism that it is the word of the English spirit, the United States may be considered the incarnation of that word. Its Evangel is spread on every side to teach the material miracles of its triumph. And Spanish America is not wholly to be entitled, in its relation to the United States, as a nation of Gentiles. The mighty confederation is realizing over us a sort of moral conquest. Admiration for its greatness, its strength,

is a sentiment that is growing rapidly in the minds of our governing
classes, and even more, perhaps, among the multitude, easily impressed with victory or success. And from admiring it is easy to pass
to imitating. Admiration and belief are already for the psychologist
but the passive mood of imitation. "The imitative tendency of our
moral nature," says Bagehot, "has its seat in that part of the soul
where lives belief." Common sense and experience would suffice of
themselves to show this natural relation. We imitate him in whose
superiority and prestige we believe. So it happens that the vision of
a voluntarily delatinized America, without compulsion or conquest,
and regenerate in the manner of its Northern archetype, floats already through the dreams of many who are sincerely interested in
our future, satisfies them with suggestive parallels they find at every
step, and appears in constant movements for reform or innovation.
We have our *mania for the North*. It is necessary to oppose to it
those bounds which both sentiment and reason indicate.

Not that I would make of those limits an absolute negation. I well
understand that enlightenment, inspiration, great lessons lie in the
example of the strong; nor do I fail to realize that intelligent attention to the claims of the material and the study of the useful, directed abroad, is of especially useful result in the case of people in
the formative stage, whose nationality is still in the mould. . . .

Still, the dispassionate study of that civilization which some would
offer to us as a model, affords a reason no less potent than those
which are based only on the indignity and unworthiness of mere
imitation to temper the enthusiasm of those who propose it as our
model. . . . And now I come to the very theme of my discourse,
and the relation to it of this spirit of imitation. Any severe judgment
formed upon our neighbours of the North should begin, like the
courteous fencer, by lowering a rapier in salute to them. Easy is this
for me. Failure to recognize their faults does not seem to me so in-
sensate as to deny their qualities. Born — to employ Baudelaire's
paradox — with the innate experience of liberty, they have kept
themselves faithful to the law of their birth; and have developed,
with the precision and certainty of a mathematical progression, the
fundamental principles of their organization. This gives to their
history a unity which, even if it has excluded the acquirement of
different aptitudes or merits, has at least the intellectual beauty of
being logical. The traces of its progress will never be expunged from
the annals of human right, because they have been the first to evoke

our modern ideal of liberty and to convert it from the uncertainty of experiment and the visions of Utopia into imperishable bronze and living reality. For they have shown by their example the possibility of extending the immovable authority of a republic over an immense national commonwealth, and, with their federal organization, have revealed — as de Tocqueville felicitously put it — the manner in which the brilliancy and power of great states may be combined with the felicity and peace of little ones. . . .

Theirs are many of the most daring deeds for which the perspective of time shall distinguish this century; theirs is the glory of having revealed completely the greatness and dignity of labour, thereby accentuating the firmest note of moral beauty in all our civilization; that blest force which antiquity abandoned to the abjection of slavery, and which to-day we identify with the highest expression of human dignity, based on the consciousness and the exertion of its own merit. Strong, tenacious of purpose, holding inaction as opprobrious, they have placed in the hands of the mechanic of their shops and the farmer of their fields the mystic key of Hercules, and have given to human genius a new and unwonted beauty, girding it with the leathern apron of the handworker. Each one of these presses on to conquer life as his Puritan ancestors did the wilderness. Persistent followers of that creed of individual energy which makes of every man the artificer of his destiny, they have modelled their commonwealth on a kind of imaginary population of Crusoes, who, as soon as they have roughly attended to their training in the art of taking care of themselves, will turn to the making of themselves into a stable State. And, never sacrificing to this their conception of the sovereign Individual, they yet have known how at the same time to make of their association the most admirable instrument of their grandeur and empire; they have got from the sum of their energies, as devoted to research, industry, philanthropy, results that are the more marvellous in that they were secured with the most absolute integrity of their personal liberty.

They have a sleepless and insatiable instinct of curiosity, an impatient eagerness for the light; and, carrying a fondness for public education almost to the point of monomania, have made the common school the surest prop of their prosperity, believing that the mind of the child should be the most cherished of their precious things. Their culture, while far from being spiritual or refined, has an admirable efficiency so far as it is directed to practical ends and their immediate realization. And, while they have not added to the acquisitions of science a single general law, one new principle, they have done wonders in its application to new inventions and made giant strides in its service to utilities; in the steam boiler, the electric dynamo, are now billions of invisible slaves who centuple for their Aladdin the power of the magic lamp. The growth of their greatness and power will astonish future generations. By their marvellous gift for improvisation they have found a spur to time, so that in a few years they conjure, as it were from a desert, the fruitage hitherto the work of centuries.

And that Puritan liberty which gave them light in the past unites with that light a piety which still endures. Beside the factory and the school it has erected churches whence ascend the prayers of millions of free consciences. They have been able to save from the shipwreck of all the idealities that which is the highest of all, and kept alive the tradition of a religious sentiment which, if it does not uplift on wings of the highest idealism, spirituality, at least maintains over the utilitarian stampede some rein of the moral sense. Also, they have known how to maintain a certain primitive robustness even amidst the refinements of a highly civilized life; they hold to the pagan cult of health, sanity, and strength; they preserve in strong muscles the instrument of a strong will; obliged by their insatiable ambition to employ all human energies, they fit the torso of the athlete over the heart of the free man. And from all this springs a dominant note of optimism, confidence, faith, which makes them face the future with a proud and stubborn assurance; the note of "Excelsior" and the "Psalm of Life," which their poets have opposed as a balsam to melancholy or bitterness of spirit.

Thus it is that their Titanic greatness impresses even those made most distrustful by their exaggerations of character and the recent violences of their history; and I, who do not love them, as you see, admire them still. I admire them, first, for their formidable power of *desire;* I bow before that *"school of will and work"* — which Philarete Chasles tells us they have inherited from their forbears.

In the beginning was Action. With these famous words of Faust the future historian of the great Republic may begin; the Genesis, not yet concluded, of their national existence. Their genius may be defined as the universe of the *Dynamists:* force in movement. Above all, it has the capacity, the enthusiasm, the fortunate vocation, for doing things; volition is the chisel which has shapen this people from hard rock. Their characteristic points are manifestations of the willpower, originality, and audacity. Their history is above all a very paroxysm of virile activity. Their typical figure should be entitled, not Superman, but He who wants. And if anything saves them collectively from vulgarity, it is that extraordinary *verve* of energy which they always show and which lends a certain epic character to even the struggles of self-interest and the material life. . . .

North American life, indeed, describes that vicious circle which Pascal remarked in the ceaseless seeking for well-being when it has no object outside of oneself. Its prosperity is as immense as its incapability of satisfying even a mediocre view of human destiny. Titanic in its enormous concentration of human will-power, in its unprecedented triumph in all spheres of material aggrandizement, its civilization yet produces as a whole a singular impression of insufficiency, of emptiness. And if man's spirit demands, with all the reason that thirty centuries of growth under classic and under Christian influence have conferred upon it, *what* are in this new world the dirigent principles, — the ideal substratum, the ulterior end of all this concernment with the positive interests that so informs that mighty multitude, — he will only be met, as a definite formula, by that same exclusive interest in material triumphs. Orphaned of the profound tradition that attended his birth, the North American has not yet replaced the inspiring ideality of his past with any high unselfish conception of the future. He lives for the immediate reality of the present, and for this subordinates all his activities in the egoism of material well-being, albeit both individual and collective. Of all his aggregation of the elements of wealth and power, one might say, what Bourget said of the intelligence of his character the Marquis Norbert, "a mountain of wood to which they have not yet known how to set fire." The vital spark is lacking to throw up that flame of the ideal, restless, life-giving, from that mountain of dead wood. Not even the selfishness of patriotism, for want of higher impulses, nor the pride of race, both of which transfigured and exalted in ancient days even the prosaic hardness of the life of Rome, can light a glimmer of ideality or beauty in a people where a cosmopolite confusion and the atomism of a badly understood democracy impede the formation of a veritable national conscience. . . .

Sensibility, intelligence, manners — each is marked in that enormous people by a radical unaptness for selection; and this, with the mechanical ordering of their material activities, makes a chaos of all that pertains to the realm of the ideal. It were easy to follow this unaptness from its most obvious manifestations to the more intimate and essential ones. Prodigal of riches — for meanness is not his fault — the North American has learned only to acquire by them the satisfaction of his vanity and material luxury, but not the chosen note of good taste. In such a surrounding true art can only exist as the rebellion of an individual. Emerson, Poe, are as estrays of a fauna expelled from their true habitat by some geological catastrophe. In "Outre Mer" Bourget speaks of the solemn tone in which the North American utters the word Art, when he, a self-made man, has achieved riches which he now desires to crown with all the human refinements; but he never has felt the divine frenzy of poem or picture; he would buy but to add to his collection a new toy, to satisfy at once his vanity and his acquisitive instinct. That in it which is disinterested, chosen, rare, he ignores, despite the munificence with which he scatters his individual fortune to found schools of art, form popular taste, build splendid museums, patronize huge expositions, and deck his cities with monuments and his streets with bronze and marble. And if one had to characterize his taste, in a word, it would be that which in itself involves the negation of great art; strained brutality of effect, insensibility to soft tones or an exquisite style, the cult of bigness, and that sensationalism which excludes all noble serenity as incompatible with the hurry of his hectic life.

The ideal of beauty does not appeal to the descendants of the austere Puritan, nor even a passionate worship of the truth; they care little for any thinking that has no immediate practical object — it seems to them idle and fruitless; even to science they bring no selfless interest for discovery, nor do they seem capable of loving its truths only because they are true; investigation is merely the necessary antecedent of practical application. Their praiseworthy efforts to extend the benefits of popular education are inspired with the noble motive of communicating the rudiments of knowledge to the masses; but it does not appear that they also concern themselves over-much with that higher education which shall rise above the general mediocrity. And so the outcome is that of all their struggle with ignorance the only gain has been a sort of universal semiculture and a profound indifference to the higher. . . . As fast as the general ignorance decreases, so, in the air of that giant democracy, decreases the higher learning and vanishes genius itself. This is why the story of their intellectual activity is of a retrogression in brilliance and originality. For while at the era of their Independence and Constitution many famous names illustrate their history in thought as well as in action, a half-century later de Tocqueville could say of them, the Gods are disappearing. And, when he wrote his master work, there still radiated from Boston, the Puritan home, the city of learning and tradition, a glorious pleiad which holds in the intellectual story of our century a universal fame. Who since has picked up the heritage of Emerson, Channing, Poe? The levelling by the middle classes tends ever, pressing with its desolating task, to plane down what little remains of *intelligentsia:* the flowers are mown by the machine when the weeds remain.

Long since their books have ceased to soar on wings beyond the common vision. To-day the most actual example of what Americans like best in literature must be sought in the gray pages of magazines or periodicals which seldom remind one that that mode of publication was employed in the immortal "Federalist." . . .

As fast as the utilitarian genius of that nation takes on a more defined character, franker, narrower yet, with the intoxication of material prosperity, so increases the impatience of its sons to spread it abroad by propaganda, and think it predestined for all humanity. To-day they openly aspire to the primacy of the world's civilization, the direction of its ideas, and think themselves the forerunners of all culture that is to prevail. The colloquial phrase, ironically quoted by Laboulaye, "America can beat the world," is taken seriously by almost any virile Westerner. At the bottom of their open rivalry with Europe lies a contempt for it that is almost naïve, and the profound conviction that within a brief period they are destined to eclipse its glory and do away with its spiritual superiority; thus once more fulfilling, in the progress of civilization, the hard law of the ancient mysteries, whereby the initiated shall put to death the initiator. It were useless to seek to convince them that, although their services to inventions and material advance have been doubtless great, even rising to the measure of a universal human obligation, they do not of themselves suffice to alter the axis of the earth. It were useless to seek to convince them that the fires lit upon European altars, the work done by peoples living these three thousand years gone by about the shores of the Mediterranean, though rising to glorious genius when bound with the olive and the palm of Athens, a work still being carried on and in whose traditions and teachings we South Americans live, makes a sum which cannot be equalled by any equation of Washington plus Edison. Would they even revise the Book of Genesis, to put themselves upon the front page? . . .

All history shows a definite relation of growth between the progress of utilitarian activity and the ideal. And just as the former can be turned into a shelter and protection for the latter, so the ideas of the mind often give rise to utilitarian results, above all when these latter are not sought directly. For instance, Bagehot remarks that the immense positive benefits of navigation might never have been attained for humanity if in earliest times there had not been dreamers, apparently idle — and certainly misunderstood by their contemporaries — who were interested solely in the contemplation of the movements of the stars.

This law of harmony bids us also respect the arm that labours arduously in what seems a barren and prosaic soil. The work of North American positivism will also at the end serve the cause of Ariel. That which this people of Cyclops have achieved for the direct purpose of material advantage, with all their sense for what is useful and their admirable faculty of mechanical invention, will be converted by other peoples, or later, even by themselves, to a wealth of material for the higher selection. Thus that most precious and fundamental invention of the alphabet, which gives the wings of immortality to the spoken word, originated in Phœnician shops, the discovery of merchants who only desired to keep their accounts. Using it for purposes merely mercenary, they never dreamed that the genius of a superior race would transfigure and transform it to a means of perpetuating the light and the learning of their own being. The relation between material good and good that is intellectual or moral is thus only a new aspect of that modern doctrine which we call the transformation of energy: material well-being may be transformed into spiritual superiority.

But North American life does not as yet offer us any new example of this indiscutable relation, nor even dimly suggest it as the triumph of the generation to come. . . .

Already there exist, in our Latin America, cities whose material grandeur and apparent civilization place them in the first rank; but one may fear lest a touch of thought upon their exterior, so sumptuous, may make the shining vessel ring hollow within; lest our cities too — though they had their Moreno, their Rivadavia, their Sarmiento, cities which gave initiative to an immortal revolution that, like a stone cast on water, spread the glory of their heroes and the words of their tribunes in ever-widening circles over a vast continent — may end like Tyre or Sidon, or as Carthage ended.

It is your generation that must prevent this; the youth which is of to-day, blood and muscle and nerve of the future. I speak to you, seeing in you those who are destined to guide the others in coming battles for a spiritual cause. The perseverance of your strength must be in you as your certainty of victory. . . .

Can you not picture to yourselves the America we others dream of? Hospitable to things of the spirit, and not only to the immigrant throngs; thoughtful, without sacrificing its energy of action; serene and strong and withal full of generous enthusiasm; resplendent with the charm of morning calm like the smile of a waking infant, yet with the light of awakening thought. Think on her at least; the honor of your future history depends on your keeping constantly before your eyes the vision of that America, radiant above the realities of the present like the rose window above the dark nave of a cathedral. . . . In dark hours of discouragement may it [the statue of Ariel] rekindle in your conscience the warmth of the ideal, return to your hearts the glow of a perishing hope. And Ariel, first enthroned behind the bastion of your inner life, may sally thence to the attack and conquering of other souls. I see the bright spirit smiling back upon you in future times, even though your own still works in shadow. I have faith in your will and in your strength, even more in those to whom you shall transfer your life, transmit your work. I dream in rapture of that day when realities shall convince the world that the Cordillera which soars above the continent of the Americas has been carved to be the pedestal of this statue, the altar of the cult of Ariel.

4. Rodó Still Touches Chords of Sympathy and Desire in Latin America

Kalman H. Silvert

For its time *Ariel* was obviously very advanced. To use it as a model half a century later is of doubtful validity. A grateful *pas-*

From *The Conflict Society: Reaction and Revolution in Latin America* (rev. ed.) by Kalman Silvert (New York: American Universities Field Staff, Inc., 1966), pp. 139–142. Reprinted by permission.

tiche of Comte, Carlyle, Nietzsche, humanism, Gallican Catholicism, and the Latin American cult of youth, Rodó's comments have their appealing side. But he is typical of the *Philosophe*, of the *pensador*, the man who could be inflamed, who could mold the ideas of others and propagate them, but who could not pass into the truly creative stage of putting systematized questions to his materials and thus proposing their possible answers within a system of method and not of yearning. Time has long since passed by much of his political commentary, but "Rodonism" and *arielismo* remain important parts of the mystique of Latin youth, whether they have read this work or not. The point is that Rodó still touches chords of sympathy and desire in Latin America.

There is something sad in the construction of a stereotype which doesn't quite come off. The essence of a stereotype is that it is partly true; therefore, it is also partly false. His belief that the Germans would help solve the cultural deficiencies of the Americans demonstrates the wellsprings of his kind of idealism, as well as the pitfalls of stereotypical views.

An illustrious thinker who compared the slaves of ancient societies to particles undigested by the social organism might perhaps find a similar comparison to characterize the situation of that strong colony of German ancestry who, established in the states of the Mid- and the Far West, conserve intact in their nature, their sociability, and in their customs the imprint of the Germanic spirit which, in many of its most profound and vigorous characteristic conditions, must be considered a true antithesis of the American genius.

Rodó's half-truth is the Germany of Goethe, Hegel, Beethoven, and Schiller. How unfortunate it is that the half-falsity should have so well obscured for Rodó that Germany which gave rise to Hitler and Goebbels. But still his largely unrevised rendering of the United States remains the stock in trade of the Latin American idealistic and intellectual nationalist.

I do not deny the right of Latin American intellectuals to attack the United States or any other country as they will. But two things must be insisted on if their opinions are to be respected: accuracy of commentary and observation, and covert motives at the same level of generosity as their avowed ideals. My purpose is not to belabor Rodó for his generalizations or to point out the factual failings of other Latin Americans as they construct their views of the United States. Nor is it my purpose to accomplish the same attack through the back door, condemning Latin America's thinkers by making selective and invidious comparisons with their counter-parts in the United States.

The tragedy of the Latin American intellectual is his necessary constriction by the context within which he lives. He desperately wants to be what he cannot be – a universalist – in societies just learning to be national. He complains about the United States from the posture of the Greek Stoic, and not from that of the contempo-rary man trying to get at least some of his view of the present from forecast. The clamoring demands throughout Latin America for the useful and potentially liberating claptrap of modern civilization have made Rodó's Hellenic yearnings obsolete. The tragedy is that their contextual obsolescence is not even yet recognized by the Latin intellectuals who can support their yearnings for the contemplative and spiritual life *as they define it* only at the cost of a Greek-like social organization, slaves and all. And yet they are dedicating their lives – and some do so with great abnegation – precisely to com-batting social inequities as they see them.

I am reminded here of a biting *New Yorker* cartoon showing an analyst jumping up and shouting at his patient, "Dammit, you *are* inferior!" My desire at this point is to jump up and say to the arielistas, "But dammit, señores, you *are* underdeveloped!" Amer-icans overseas have been carefully taught that the term "underde-veloped area" refers only to economic matters, and not at all to cultural and intellectual attainments. But of course the term has something at least inferential to say about intellectual and artistic matters. An economically poor country cannot support symphony orchestras, cannot provide competent university training to quali-fied persons, and cannot pay for the research necessary to the kind of contemplation this century demands.

Even more hampering to the Latin American intellectual is that to be economically underdeveloped is also almost invariably to be non-national in culture. As a result the thinkers of underdeveloped areas find it difficult to compete on the international market of ideas and art, for their expressions often lack the limited kind of universality understandable within the universe of the citizen of the nation-state. The Latin American pensador, with his pull toward the great outer world, is an effective instrument for the absorption of European trends and their translation into the terms of his homeland. But when it comes time for him to return what he has borrowed with the interest of his country's special cultural point of view, he finds that nobody is listening because what he has to say is either not significant or not fresh in a different cultural context. It is not that "fault" lies with one side or the other; it is basically that there is a break in the complete circuit of communications. This is caused in part by the representative of the economically industrialized area, who — with his different outlook — finds it hard to understand what the man from the underdeveloped area is saying.

The major exceptions to my statements come out of Mexico and Brazil, where the nationalism which has seized on large parts of the population has been fed its distinctive flavor by a new ethnic amalgam expressed within intriguing (for the rest of the national world) physical surroundings. The other major area of exception is in the general field of literature, but again, the few Latin American novels, for example, which have had the widest circulation are of the genre of the novel of protest, an area of obvious universalistic appeal both in function and, usually, in description of the clash of cultures and of desires.

It hardly needs to be added that nation-state status will not automatically produce hordes of creative Ariels. The factors of the accident of the individual and then his training and his stimuli are still to be taken into account. There is little doubt that Uruguay has national attitudes in ample measure, but playing against it is its smallness, its overreadiness to ingest European ideas, and its physical isolation from the mainstreams.

The frustration of the anti-imperialistic intellectual in Uruguay is a sorry thing to behold, and his brusqueness must be understood in terms of this frustration.

It is very often said that anti-imperialist movements must not be confused with democratic ones, as witness so many cases in Africa, Asia, and Latin America. In the short run, I suppose the argument is correct; in the longer run, the usual way of looking at the matter has been to say that democracy cannot flourish except in conditions of national independence. But is it possible that misdirected anti-imperialism may not also make the development of broadening democratic institutions more remote? It is convenient and easy to direct frustrations to the outside, but one inevitable result is to create a climate of fear and impotence with respect to local problems truly subject to solution from within. If anti-imperialism serves to paralyze the will and thus reduces the area of possible action, it is at the very least antisocial. My feeling is that what I have seen of the Uruguayan anti-imperialists puts them into the category of the self-destructive ones, at least for the time being. They would be shocked to hear it said, but if their rationale is still *arielismo* and their effect is to limit choice, then they are, of course, reactionary in the truest sense of the word.

But Uruguay remains fortunate in the depth of its traditions and in the complexity of its society. And if we isolate and describe a certain kind of intellectual, it does not by any means follow that we have described the entire society. But even if it is true that a solid majority of Uruguayans objects to American society, objection is not enough. Anti-imperialism which is not mere *antiyanquismo*, Third Positionism which also is not mere antiyanquismo, attitudes with an affirmative content, selected and expressed with respect for data — these are what Latin American politics sorely need. The politicized Latin American intellectual has his task clearly presented to him. If he is to justify the goodly measure of leadership and respect he now has, he must begin to speak in terms of *specific* wants, *specific* programs, and *specific* capabilities. To do so he must learn techniques of research to find out what is possible to satisfy what he thinks is desirable. He must leave his ivory tower and dirty his intellectual hands, finding solutions within himself and within his society.

In answer to this argument about the necessity for techniques and data in order to solve pressing public problems, an Argentine intellectual told me, "No, no, social knowledge reveals itself." Speaking of Greeks, I wonder what Aristotle would have replied to such a comment.

5. The Two Americas Are Far Apart

RICHARD M. MORSE

. . . The defects of Latin-American studies in the United States are largely attributable to a fundamental alienation between the two Americas. By alienation I do not gently mean unfortunate misunderstandings which might be remedied by a bit more knowledge and good will. What concerns me is the fact that for many of our Latin-Americanists the intensive study of their subject merely kindles their subconscious hostility to it. The heart of the matter is that here are

From "The Strange Career of 'Latin-American Studies'" by Richard M. Morse, *Annals of the American Academy of Political and Social Science*, Vol. 356, 1964, pp. 106–112, *passim*. Reprinted by permission.

two cultures whose historic spiritual trajectories are not merely different — this would not produce backlash when the attempt is made to "understand" — but diametrically opposed.

At this point it will be said that I am victimized by the stereotype of the Uruguayan *penseur*, J. E. Rodó. In 1900 Rodó wrote an essay in the most limpid Parnassian style imaginable to suggest that Latin America (symbolized by Ariel) may aspire to the path of culture, moral heroism, and saintliness, while North America (Caliban) wallows in vulgarity, utilitarianism, and egalitarian mediocrity. This image has become one of the dearest bits of bric-a-brac in the Latin-American psychic storeroom, and our own behavior for two-thirds of a century has not allowed much dust to settle upon it.

At the moment, though, I am not on Rodó's side. For one thing, the specialists in colonial psychology would now tell us that we are the paranoid magician (Prospero) with his wand of technology (Ariel), while poor Latin America is Caliban, not for being objectively brutish, but for being unintelligible and inarticulate from Prospero's point of vantage — for being indeed a colonial. But the historic schism which inhibits our study of Latin America needs to be mapped more directly than is possible by literary analogy. Before attempting this, let me clarify some assumptions.

1. I assume that, whatever the difficulties of Far Eastern, Indian, or African studies in our country, those who design them can count on the relative innocence of their audience, on the student's willingness to suspend judgment and to clamber, however gracelessly, into a new cultural universe. Latin America is deceptively recognizable — to novitiate and "expert" alike — as a poor and slightly disreputable Western cousin. Across our common borders, we freely exchange millions of tourists for millions of wetbacks and bus boys. Latin America professes what is for many Americans a familiar and slightly *déclassé* brand of Christianity; its languages — as Marianne Moore said of "plain American" — are ones "which dogs and cats can read."

2. I am concerned with liberal or speculative studies, not with technical or activist programs. The benefits that applied knowledge derives from a formal education are either less important or more subtle than the pundits axiomatically assume. Our central question is: Why are the Hispano-Catholic mind-set and social system so baffling for American scholarship? and not the question: How can agricultural extension services in Iowa be adapted for highland Peru? The activist who rolls these two sorts of questions into one ball of wax acquires more grace for his social dealing in Latin Amer-

ica, but he may overinterpret and overreact to prosaic human problems.

3. I must arrange the academic disciplines in concentric circles of relevance to my purpose. In practice, a Latin-American "area studies program" embraces whatever regionally oriented courses a university has on the books at the moment of fund-raising. They can range from development economics to basic English for foreigners, from pre-Columbian archaeology to tropical agriculture. Given my concern with the cultural premises of personality and society, however, I must place history and history of ideas, literature and the arts, and — in some of their phases — the social sciences in the innermost circle. At varying removes from the center come — not necessarily in the order given: archaeology and prehistory, ethnology of isolated tribes, statistical and quantitative studies, the natural sciences, and the applied or "tool" courses. If our assumption is true that the premises of Latin-American culture have been inaccessible to American scholarship, we may expect that academic quality improves as we move from the center to the rim of this circle.

That the wheel of Latin-American studies has a clay hub can by and large be confirmed. It is a commonplace, for example, that the American academic milieu supports scarcely any intellectually mature activity in Latin-American literary history or literary criticism. Pedagogical and technological innovations in methods of language-teaching have far outpaced any renovation in the understanding and teaching of literature. The amount of serious attention given to Latin-American art and music is miniscule.

Activity in the social sciences has been sporadic and generally unproductive of academic landmarks. It is, perhaps, not far off target to say that sociology has been the most laggard and its sister, anthropology, the most productive of the social science disciplines. Even if one sets aside contributions in archaeology, prehistory, and tribal ethnology, the balance of the anthropological contribution is substantial. Within the context of American scholarship, it offers perhaps the only firm and broadly based point of departure for exploring personality, culture, and the logic of institutions within the Latin-American ethos. That so much has been achieved by this discipline is remarkable, given its anti-theoretical tendencies, and given miscellaneous recent pressures which drive anthropologists into consultantships and applied programs. A possible explanation is that anthropologists "backed into" standard Latin-American creole culture via the non-Hispanic or partly Hispanic tribal or Indian-village communities. This may have helped them preserve a certain innocence of vision. Moreover, it is interesting that the occasional theoretical or interpretive thrusts of our anthropological research in Latin America are often toward generalized formulae — "folk-urban continuum," "the culture of poverty" — and not toward identification of special characteristics of the Latin-American social milieu.

The work of American historians on Latin America is too voluminous to be characterized briefly — although if a single word were required, it might be "humorless." Moving onto still thinner ice, I venture that as of now the most important American contribution to Latin-American historiography has been in the realm of "services": bibliographic compilation, devising of research aids, and build-up of library collections. Our historians' lack of intellectual or spiritual involvement with Latin America is evident from any cursory comparison of the best work done by North and Latin-American historians during, say, the last thirty years. . . .

The American historian's lack of concern with — and, presumably, lack of respect for — cultural and intellectual trends in Latin America is symptomatic of his sober pursuit of "objective themes and purposes." He recommends a research project not because it is inherently interesting, but because "it needs to be done" to fill out the academic jigsaw puzzle.

By the foregoing, I do not intend to trundle out the old stereotype of an American culture that is long on practicability and method, and short on philosophic substance and vision. Rather, I am asking whether there are special historical and cultural factors which inhibit mobilization of the best resources of North American scholarship when the object of study is Latin America.

A preliminary point to be made is that through the years our contact with Latin America has been largely a utilitarian, backdoor relation. American trade with the Hispanic world trended sharply upward after the American Revolution, and the first college course in Spanish in this country was offered at the University of Pennsylvania in 1766. Yet in 1817 the *North American Review* still questioned whether the Spaniards had "taken a step in the right road of learning since the days of the Cid." Many loan-words which have penetrated American English from south of the border — *desperado, bronco, hombre, sombrero, vamoose* or *mosey, buckaroo, hoosegow,* and *calaboose* — seem somehow sweaty and uncouth, as though they emanated from a contraband or culturally marginal world.

I am not bemoaning the lack of "cultural relations" with Latin

America, for I am never sure what is implied when people insist that these be established, or improved. It is just that Latin America — unlike most parts of the world — has never given us the sense that somewhere, protected from its money marts, its civil violence, its unwashed masses, it possesses privileged sanctums where national aspirations are purified and perpetuated. The North American knows of no Florence in Latin America, no Weimar, no Taj Mahal, no exquisite gardens with arching footbridges and clumps of dwarf pine. (He is therefore forced to "invent" his own Taxco.) For us the Latin-American is the peon or *pistolero,* and not — as he might be for occasional Frenchmen — the poet or jurist.

Because of signposts in their own culture, therefore, gifted young Americans on the threshold of intellectual careers fail to discern in Latin America any worthy targets of endeavor. It holds out for them no shaped ideals, no noble mysteries. Much later, in the course of other pursuits, they may glimpse the riches of the Latin-American tradition, but by then it is too late. Who is the trimmer who would submit to being "retreaded" — that abusive new term of ours — by a grant from a busybody commissar? Thus Latin America is left for our academic Prufrocks.

Beyond all this, however, the story has deep spiritual entanglements. It is of enduring consequence that our country was founded in revolt against Catholicism, against the layered and corporative society, against casuistical justice, against tolerance of sin in the human community, against individual eccentricity and affective release — against the whole late-medieval world which Huizinga recreated for our century and which is still largely a reality for Hispanic peoples. Seventeenth-century Ibero-America stood for everything which Anglo-America had set itself fiercely against. History is not so capricious that this situation has radically changed. Our present *doctrinal* diversity and toleration obscure for us the fact that we are integrally a Protestant nation, insensitive and vaguely hostile to the *sociological* and *psychological* foundations of a Catholic society. We assume that Calvin and Locke are a point of departure for "American studies" — while would-be Orientalists, I gather, must sweat over Buddha, Confucius, and Lao-tse. Yet how seriously have any of us dared require a steeping in St. Thomas, Dante, and Suárez for those who would understand Latin America?

In 1699 Cotton Mather made an entry in his diary which, were it not for its honesty and clarity, might have been written by a modern expert, planner, or program assistant. It deserves being quoted as a reminder of the recalcitrancies of history:

About this Time, understanding that the way for our Communication with the *Spanish Indies*, opens more and more, I sett myself to learn the *Spanish Language*. The Lord wonderfully prospered mee in this Undertaking; a few liesure [*sic*] Minutes in the Evening of every day, in about a Fortnight, or three weeks Time, so accomplished mee, I could write very good Spanish. Accordingly, I composed a little Body of the *Protestant* Religion, in certain Articles, back'd with irresistible Sentences of Scripture. This I turn'd into the Spanish Tongue; and am now printing it, with a Design to send it all the wayes that I can, into the several parts of *Spanish America*; as not knowing, *how great a matter a little Fire may kindle*, or whether the Time for our Lord Jesus Christ to have glorious churches in *America*, bee not at hand.

We must, of course, recognize that Latin-American, or more broadly Hispanic studies have had their moments of promise in America. The outstanding one was the era of Irving, Prescott, and Bryant, the years when the Smith Professorship of French and Spanish, established in 1816 at Harvard, was held successively by Ticknor, Longfellow, and J. R. Lowell. Whatever spark of cultural generosity or potion of Moorish enchantment gave us this moment, it was important, not for cornerstones of scholarship, but for the spectacle, never again repeated, of a constellation of our nation's leading writers bringing things Hispanic to central prominence on our literary and academic scene.

A subsequent generation — Lea, Moses, Bourne, and others — was more professional, had better "understanding." But the flair, style, and romance were gone. The subject could not be powerfully related to the core of American life. The center of the stage was lost. Since then our Latin-Americanists have "cultivated, sung, groaned, and loved" — to borrow Ortega's phrase for the Spanish masses: they have done all that was under the circumstances to be done. Despite sometimes useful or even handsome accomplishments, Latin-American studies have, since the 1920's, been a faintly ridiculous tail to a politico-commercial kite. In the groves of Academe the scholar lies down in darkness with the former diplomat, the casual pundit, the entrepreneur.

Now, however, the situation becomes menacing. For now our past mistakes are to be rectified — as if historic cultural commitments were a corrigible misdemeanor. Millions of dollars are dangled each year before harassed and thirsty university administrators. Like the golden apple which Eris cast among the gods, they cause tumult and rancor rather than rewarding "the fairest." They also create programs, centers, and institutes that hasten the amputation of Latin-American studies from the main trunk of American scholarship. And they subsidize cadres of gimlet-eyed graduate students who plunge into archives or field interviews without having lingered over Kant or Troeltsch or Huizinga or Wölfflin, or whatever sources of perspective and wisdom might have proven congenial.

One pay-off for these new benefactions is that scholarship on Latin America will now "catch up" with that in other fields. Take the case of poor political science. Hitherto, it is said, our political studies of Latin America have been largely journalistic interpretation, constitutional analyses, and excursions into diplomatic history. Now there is dutiful mobilization to produce "scientific" studies of party systems, interest groups, and voting behavior. The mechanical transference of research designs from California or Canada to Chile or Colombia makes the next ten or twenty years of political inquiry predictable, and therefore drab. We of course assert that within Latin America itself the serious study of political science is almost nowhere cultivated. Yet, ironically, the Latin-Americans have produced first-class studies in political theory, philosophy of law, and the history of political institutions. These are precisely the realms from which we should be taking our cues. An inquiry into voting behavior should presuppose understanding of the relation of conscience to natural law in the Hispano-Catholic tradition. An analysis of the decision-making process should presuppose knowledge of the moral function of casuistry in a Catholic society.

The examples could be multiplied. But it remains to peel off one more layer of the onion. We have mentioned the sociology of international contact. We have mentioned philosophic and spiritual commitments. This can only lead us to a question in the domain of collective psychology. For we must conclude that the North American who looks South wrestles with an insidious doubt. Even in the face of the cruelty, poverty, and tumult of Latin America, he cannot escape the lurking suspicion that *it is just barely conceivable that his own ancestors may have taken a wrong turn in the sixteenth and seventeenth centuries*. We never had the opportunity to be Japanese or Hindu. But once upon a time we *were* within the mother Church. Whatever we gained by leaving it, we were forced to cauterize some of those early instincts, to abandon some of that immemorial social wisdom, in which the Latin-American world abounds. Latin America confronts us with much that we swept under the rug, with much that might still have been ours. Can it be, can it possibly be, that our several strategies for keeping Latin America at an intellectual and psychic remove were devised so as to obscure this simple fact?

C. A Case Study: Xenophobia in Mexico

6. The Roots of Nationalism

Frederick C. Turner

The Extension of Xenophobia — Xenophobia as a passion which forcefully and predominantly shapes thought and action is a phenomenon of comparatively short duration without repeated provocation. A North American traveling in Mexico today as a tourist, student or businessman may — depending more upon his own character than upon his national origin — find in the friendliness of Mexicans of all social classes little to remind him of the anti-Americanism which flared in Mexico from 1910 to 1917. When individual Mexicans resent United States influence, resentment tends to focus on phenomena such as Madison Avenue advertising or unpleasant experiences with individual North Americans rather than on the United States itself. Since the Good Neighbor policy of Franklin Roosevelt and the revered presidency of John Kennedy, Mexicans have had ample cause to stop fearing American policy as far as Mexico is concerned. Although xenophobia has abated and resentment is now less visible, however, the xenophobia which gripped Mexico during the Revolution has significantly shaped the growth of the Mexican national community. It implanted a distinct feeling of national separation on the Mexicans who felt it, and it still implants a feeling of separation to the Mexicans who year by year become aware of the events of the period.

Xenophobia became intermittently weaker after 1917. Despite the genuine affection which Mexicans came to feel for Ambassador Dwight Morrow, an underlying antagonism shaped largely by the

From Frederick C. Turner, "The Roots of Mexican Nationalism" (Ph.D. dissertation, Fletcher School of Law and Diplomacy, 1965), pp. 424–479, *passim.* Used by permission of the author. The University of North Carolina Press is publishing a revised version of this dissertation under the title *The Dynamics of Mexican Nationalism* (1968).

earlier American interventions labeled even this outstanding representative of the new American policy of active cooperation as a *yanqui* responsible for halting the social progress of the Mexican Revolution. Lázaro Cárdenas' nationalizations of foreign oil properties in 1938 rejuvenated xenophobic attitudes. It became a commonplace to denounce pre-1910 events in terms which show them to be foreign and non-national, as when José Luis Martínez denounces the Díaz regime by accusing it of imposing a "Prussian discipline," a "French urbanity" and a "dictatorial government in the Hispanic-american style."

A strong undercurrent of anti-yankee feeling remains in Mexico today. Mexicans who experienced the xenophobia of the Revolutionary years are being replaced by younger generations, and many of the most violently anti-American tracts of the 1910 to 1917 period received only limited printings and today gather dust on library shelves, read by scholars but largely ignored by the general Mexican public. Revolutionary participants have conveyed attitudes to their children and grandchildren, however, and the ideas of the early anti-American books still appear in a great variety of popular genres. Mexicans still resent examples of North American "presumptuousness," of the smug boasting and display of material wealth, the tourist's insistence on speaking English in Mexico without even an attempt to learn Spanish, or the distasteful attitudes of racial or religious superiority found in some Americans. Heightened by leftist propaganda which depicts the "economic imperialism" of Yankee capitalism, anti-gringo sentiment finds support in the American invasions and xenophobia of the past. Mexicans who remember the North American invasions of their country hold out against breaking relations with Fidel Castro's Cuba even under concerted pressure from the Organization of American States. Although anti-American rantings in such magazines as the Communist organ *Política* represent only a small fraction of the Mexican people, the equally consistent and more clever anti-yankeeism in each issue of *Siempre!* accurately reflects the sentiments of a large part of the Mexican national community.

An anti-yankeeism taken in part from the interventions in Mexico has also shaped the spirit of "Latin Americanism" which theoretically competes with Mexican nationalism. In providing an excellent focus for xenophobia, the United States has encouraged Latin American states to maintain a feeling of comradeship rather than xenophobia toward the other states of Latin America. Common fear of the

United States has in fact been one of the principal causes for that degree of Latin American solidarity and camaraderie which now exists — more important perhaps than the dubious if often reiterated ties of common language, geography and history. Latin Americans continue to face what appears to be economic and cultural if no longer political danger from the northern colossus, and discord within the area would seriously fragment its influence on United States policies. The spirit of Latin Americanism has in no sense seriously challenged nationalism for the effective loyalty of the Mexican people, however. Xenophobia, in conjunction with the social bases of Mexican nationalism, has made nationalism a far more potent and pervasive force.

Literature and Nationalism — Literature both registers growing awareness of nationalism among the inhabitants of a given territory and cumulatively increases that awareness as successive generations develop common attitudes from "their own" literature. Mexican literature, in its various genres, is a primary source by which we may measure the extent and nature of nationalism in consecutive periods of Mexican history, considering the extent to which the cumulative growth of nationalistic expression has in turn stimulated national consciousness both during and after the period of composition. The relationship between literature and nationalism encompasses what literature fails to say as well as what it says, so that the lack of emphasis upon indigenous art forms and the extent of extra-Mexican thematic and stylistic material during the nineteenth century evidences an absence of full cultural autonomy in Mexico before 1910. Mexican literature, music and art in both the nineteenth and twentieth centuries have contained an abundance of introspective and romantic material which bears virtually no relevance to nationalism. The beginning of conscious formulation of a national literature coincided in the nineteenth century, however, with literary works which either directly or indirectly furthered the individual attitudes which made an enlarged national community possible. During and since the events of 1910 to 1917, moreover, in novels, histories, plays, poetry, films, murals and popular ballads, Mexicans have both memorialized the events themselves and pleaded the cause of national solidarity and social justice for which they have made the events stand. . . .

School Textbooks. School textbooks have become an introduction to national history for a majority of young Mexican citizens today.

The growth of nationalism in Mexico as elsewhere has given added importance to scholars and teachers, many of whom no longer simply seek knowledge or instruct youth but also in their writing and teaching give their national community the propagandistic justification which facilitates communication and social interaction within it. Textbooks are particularly important in Mexico, because Mexicans get their first detailed impressions of civics and history from them and because many students lack the opportunity to pursue studies beyond the textbook level. Poverty and the pressures of a rapidly expanding population force many Mexicans to drop out of school before reaching the sixth grade, while with the increasing technological complexity of Mexico's emerging society most of the students who go on to study medicine, agriculture, science or even literature have little time to pursue historical studies beyond the level of a *secundaria* text. The ideological as well as the material requirements of Mexican society thus add key importance to the content of its textbooks.

On the cover of many of the government textbooks, which are distributed free to children in primary school, appears the figure of a beautiful woman with flowing black hair and slightly Indian characteristics who carries an unfurled Mexican flag. As an insert on the title page of each book tells the children, the woman "represents the Mexican nation advancing with the impetus of her history with the triple impulse — cultural, agricultural, industrial — which the people give her." *Primaria* textbooks and workbooks amplify this idea of the Mexican nation. The geography texts, for example, give schoolchildren a very good idea of the physical proportions of the motherland, as they place heavy stress on Mexican geography and significantly treat the geography of Mexico as a whole rather than pointing up differences between Mexican states. Typically, the fourth grade geography book has 59 colored pictures which show the physical characteristics of Mexico with only two pictures which indicate any state divisions. Supplementing the geography texts, the third year workbook contains eight pictures of Mexico which the children can color, while the fourth year workbook contains 31.

For second grade students, a reading book provides an initial concept of the national community through descriptions and colorful illustrations of Cuauhtémoc, Hidalgo and the *Niños Héroes* who died fighting the United States in the War of 1847. With a striking, full page sketch of Aztecs circling lake Texcoco to see a huge eagle on a cactus with a snake in his mouth and claws, the reader explains the legend of the founding of Mexico City which forms the basis for the central symbolism of the Mexican flag. A separate section even gives second graders a sense of Mexican racial unity. With pictures of red, brown and white hands joined together and of five boys of distinctively different colors and racial characteristics holding their arms around each other in comradeship, the section entitled "Comrades" says encouragingly that "all the boys who are part of the second year group are friends and play together at recess."

Second grade workbooks support the approach of the reader. Here children can color pictures of the national coat of arms, the founding of Mexico City, Cuauhtémoc and Cortés, Sor Juana Inés de la Cruz, Hidalgo, Morelos, Vicente Guerrero, the Niños Héroes, the full career of Benito Juárez, Justo Sierra, Francisco Madero and Belisario Domínguez. Domínguez, the anti-Huerta martyr, is included according to the workbook text "as an example of the valiant men who fight, sacrificing themselves, without other arms than their thoughts and their words." Suggesting that "in the community, we must all give aid," the workbook shows a Mexican policeman, soldier, doctor, teacher and forestryman aiding their country. With places for the children to write in the colors of the flag and the verses of the national anthem, the workbook concludes that "Mexico is a home. It is the home of all Mexicans."

The third year course continues the nationalist indoctrination at a slightly advanced level. In the third grade reading book a section with a colored picture of a fluttering Mexican flag makes the flag speak in the first person, saying "young Mexicans, look well at my three colors: green, white and red. . . . I represent the Motherland, this Mexican land in which you saw light for the first time." The book details Mexico's "civic calendar" and separately enumerates the patriotic significance of such events as Juárez' birthday on March 21, Soldier's Day on April 27, Labor Day on May 1, the May 5 celebration of the 1862 victory over the French invaders at Puebla, and Hidalgo's ringing of the Independence bell on September 15. The reader explains with colorful pictures how the Mexican Navy protects the Motherland and contains the familiar references to Cuauhtémoc's valor when the Spaniards tortured him. It makes a particular point of exemplifying the patriotic heroism of Mexican youth. Besides recounting the story of the Niños Héroes of Chapultepec, it shows *el Pípila*, the boy who burned down the doors of the Alhóndiga for Hidalgo in 1810. Here too is the story of Narciso Mendoza, the boy cannoneer, who at twelve years of age in February

1812 fired a cannon on his own initiative at the Spanish to aid José María Morelos in the siege of Cuautla.

The history textbook of the fourth grade again praises national heroes and illustrates each step of national history with large color pictures. It places the blame for the War of 1846 to 1848 squarely on the United States. Summing up the accomplishments of the 1910 Revolution, it defines progress in such fields as land distribution, irrigation, health, public education, social security and industry to be the work of the Revolution of 1910. The Revolutionary interpretation here follows that of the third grade civics text which has already shown Madero as the "Martyr of Democracy," Carranza as leader of the triumph of "the people," Zapata as champion of the *campesinos,* and the 1917 Constitution as the supreme law and "the basis of Mexican democracy."

Secondary school textbooks, like textbooks of the *Porfiriato,* add a strong note of xenophobia to evocations of nationalism. José R. del Castillo's *Curso elemental de historia patria,* a government endorsed textbook issued just before the turn of the century when the Díaz government was already opening Mexico wide to foreign investment, arouses nationalism first through ordinary, non-xenophobic descriptions. One of 20 small chapter biographies claims that for Mexico the name of Juárez "is a symbol, it represents patriotism and integrity, it means love of liberty and of the people, it signifies heroism and suffering, it embraces these three words: *Independence, Republic* and *Liberty.*" The Castillo text also glorifies Mexico's past opposition to foreigners, however. Mexican troops are described as giving heroic combat to General Taylor's troops at Palo Alto in the rout of May 8, 1846, while Mexican citizens and soldiers are repeatedly praised for their "extraordinary valor" and "heroic opposition" to the advancing armies of Taylor and Scott. The cadets who defended their military college in Chapultepec Castle, already part of the national mystique as the Niños Héroes of Chapultepec, are honored as having "sealed with their blood the oath which they had made to defend their flag and their motherland."

Contemporary *secundaria* textbooks display still more violent xenophobia although foreign investment has nevertheless increased again. Angel Miranda Basurto's long standard textbook, for example, emphasizes how the United States tried to steal the Mexican provinces of Texas, New Mexico and California even before Mexico gained her independence. It claims that in the War for Texan Independence the United States sent not only military supplies but also "deserters" from the American Army to aid the separatists. Finding that President Polk ordered General Taylor to let Mexicans attack first only to give the false impression that Mexico was the aggressor in the War of 1846 to 1848, it describes many alleged abuses of North American soldiers and their looting of jewels from Mexican churches after the taking of Mexico City. A large map graphically demonstrates the extensiveness of the huge provinces which the United States took from Mexico. The textbook also stirs resentments against later interventions. Proudly noting that Maximilian's intervention cost France "900 million francs and the lives of 65,000 imperialists," Miranda Basurto reminds his young Mexican readers that the French intervention was important for Mexico "because during the development of the struggle the people were becoming unified and awakening their *national consciousness*." He finds that "North American capitalism" used Ambassador Henry Lane Wilson to provoke the fall of Madero and claims that American capitalists instigated each North American intervention in Mexico between 1910 and 1917. Praising the heroic resistance of the Mexican people and the naval cadets to the landing of United States Marines in 1914, he repeatedly praises Carranza for his implacable resistance and unification of the Mexican people "in the face of yankee imperialism." Textbook history written from this national standpoint — in whatever country it may be found — quite naturally gives secondary school students a sense of pride in the separateness of their national community.

Popular Literature. Numerous types of popular literature reinforce these attitudes of school textbooks. A number of children's books, for example, closely resemble the textbooks. *La bandera de México*, a children's book with a huge, forward-rushing Mexican flag on the cover which overspreads both Mexicans brandishing rifles and a serene view of Mount Popocatepetl in the background, traces the history and significance of the national flag. A set of special coloring books illustrate the physical and human geography of the diverse Mexican regions to give young students a comprehensive idea of their nation. Supplementing Revolutionary comic books like the *Leyendas de Pancho Villa,* the *Biografías Selectas* comic books emphasize that Mexican youth can be heroes of the nation with special issues devoted to el Pípila, the boy cannoneer, and the Niños Héroes. Other comic books in the series glorify the whole gallery of national heroes from Guadalupe Victoria and doña Josefa Ortiz de Domínguez to Benito Juárez and Venustiano Carranza.

One of the most interesting mediums through which Mexicans ac-

quire pride in the events of their common history is a series of colorful foldout pamphlets and pictures which cover such subjects as the
winning of national independence, the War of 1847, the national
anthem, and the careers of national heroes. With eight or more pictures in brilliant colors on a long sheet and lengthy descriptions of
each picture on the reverse side, small pocket-size pamphlets sketch
historical events in a highly nationalistic manner. One pamphlet
describes the events of the Maderista revolution and variously shows
Madero with his wife formally accepting the presidency from León
de la Barra, discussing conditions in Morelos with Zapata, under
arrest before h:s murder, and riding above the masses against the
background of the Mexican flag. Juárez appears in his boyhood as a
shepherd in Oaxaca, as a student, and as a triumphal national leader
in his simple black coach of the war against the French. In one of
the most violent picture pamphlets fierce Mexican soldiers are shown
slashing, strangling and shooting North American soldiers in the War
of 1847. The Niños Héroes here defend a battered Chapultepec
Castle, and Cadet Juan Escutia wraps himself in the Mexican flag
and appears in the famous death leap which he took from the walls
of the Castle in order to save the flag from the American invaders.
Pamphlets of the Independence period similarly recount the various
heroic exploits of Hidalgo, Morelos, el Pípila and doña Josefa Ortiz
de Domínguez. Supplementing the small pamphlets are large, full
color pictures of national heroes with accounts of their exploits on
the back. Sold in Mexico all year long, these pamphlets and pictures
are particularly popular at the time of national holidays such as the
sixteenth of September, at which time myriads are sold along with
the red, white and green bunting, flags and pendants which decorate
houses, stores, trucks and bicycles throughout the Republic.

Nationalist handbooks and advertising campaigns add to the national content of the Mexican milieu. An effective inculcator of
nationalism, which has sold over 130,000 copies in its three editions
and is now officially approved for use in schools by the Mexican
Ministry of Education, is Francisco Vargas Ruiz' nationalist's handbook, *Yo soy mexicano; Lo que todo ciudadano debe saber.* In
addition to an up-to-date copy of the Mexican Constitution and the
various "plans" of Revolutionary leaders, it contains biographies of
twenty-one national heroes and describes the lives of all the heroes
buried in the *Rotonda de Hombres Ilustres.* Sold inexpensively and
at reduced bulk rates, it also provides Mexicans with a series of
national statistics, a copy of the national anthem, and a long calendar

of all the important days in Mexican history. In addition to literature like the handbook, even the advertising techniques of modern sales campaigns promote Mexican nationalism. As a promotional device to stimulate sales, a leading Mexican bank recently issued a scrapbook in which depositors paste brightly colored stamps which show Mexican troops in action, the architectural and industrial achievements of modern Mexico, and pictures of Mexico's heroes, monuments and murals. Upon filling the book with the stamps which they receive for regular deposits, Mexicans receive a 256 page history, *La nación mexicana*. In this type of sales campaign, advertising devices designed to promote sales have the same nationality-arousing effect as the patriotic histories, textbooks and popular paraphernalia which stir Mexican nationalism.

Section VIII

Imperialism, Intervention, and Communism in the Caribbean

The Caribbean area up to about 1900 was the cockpit of the Americas, where competing nations sought for power and plunder. At the end of the Spanish American War the United States assumed new responsibilities toward Cuba and Puerto Rico. The construction of the Panama Canal brought a powerful strategic consideration into United States policy. William Graham Sumner, the Yale University sociologist, was not far wrong when he delivered a Phi Beta Kappa address in 1899 on "The Conquest of the United States by Spain," in which he set forth the startling proposition that although Spain had lost the war, she had given over to the United States her imperial ambitions and burdens.

The twentieth-century history of the Caribbean remains to be written, but it is obvious that the United States' actions and its conception of its role there will be a dominant theme. The United States has supervised elections, sent in the Marines, installed customs offices, conducted health campaigns, moved in whole teams of experts to provide a variety of programs, trained constabulary forces, organized invasions such as the Bay of Pigs fiasco, and in many other ways tried to maintain stability or defend what a particular government in Washington conceived to be in the national interest.

The conception of United States national interest has varied. President Calvin Coolidge announced in April, 1925, that "the person and property of a citizen are part of the general domain of the nation, even when abroad. . . . There is a distinct and binding

370

obligation on the part of self-respecting governments to afford protection to the persons and property of their citizens, wherever they may be."[1] This was no idle threat or new doctrine, since in 1910 the United States minister to Cuba had been instructed to inform the Cuban government that if it was unable or failed to protect the lives or property of American citizens, "the Government of the U.S., pursuant to its usual custom in such cases, would land its own forces for this purpose."[2]

The subject of the United States in the Caribbean is so large and complicated that only a few of the major aspects may be touched upon here. To understand United States action, the exuberant and complacent mood of many Americans from 1900 onward must be seen as an essential part of the story. Even so outspoken an anti-imperialist as Professor Sumner believed that the creation of empires was the inevitable "penalty of greatness" that obliged "the ascendant nation to extend law and order for the benefit of everybody."[3] A bias against colored peoples was also involved, and many in the Caribbean are colored. The remarks by George W. Crichfield in his popular work of 1908, appropriately entitled *American Supremacy*, convey effectively the feeling of superiority toward Latin Americans and the determination to do something for them whether they liked it or not (Reading VIII.1).

Such actions roused opposition in the United States, especially in academic circles, and in many parts of the world were condemned as "dollar diplomacy." Professor Harry Elmer Barnes directed a series of studies on American financial imperialism,[4] and Professor Lawrence F. Hill denounced what he called the protectorate system in these words:

In its mature form, the system demanded governmental setups in Cuba, Santo Domingo, Haiti, Panama, Nicaragua and elsewhere amenable to

[1] As quoted by Herbert Feis, *The Diplomacy of the Dollar: First Era, 1919–1932* (Stamford, Conn.: Archon Books, 1965), p. 29.

[2] Milton Offut, *The Protection of Citizens Abroad by the Armed Forces of the United States* (Baltimore: The Johns Hopkins Press, 1928), p. 160.

[3] James P. Shenton, "Imperialism and Racism," in *Essays in American Historiography: Papers Presented in Honor of Allan Nevins*, Donald Sheehan and Harold C. Syrett, eds. (New York: Columbia University Press, 1960), p. 230.

[4] Leland Hamilton Jenks, *Our Cuban Colony: A Study in Sugar* (New York: Vanguard Press, 1928); Melvin M. Knight, *The Americans in Santo Domingo* (New York: Vanguard Press, 1928); Margaret Alexander Marsh, *The Bankers in Bolivia: A Study in American Foreign Investment* (New York: Vanguard Press, 1928).

orders from Washington. If the natives of these countries were unable or indisposed to carry out dictation from Washington, they were displaced by "expert" administrators from the United States — which had an excess of them. These "expert" administrators from the fields of government, military science, finance, education, and many others, were all politicians willing to execute mandates from the Potomac, and occasionally to execute Latin American natives as well. In its worst manifestations, the system led to brutal military intervention, complete obliteration of native customs and institutions, and selfish financial control by New York bankers. In all cases, the European investors were paid off or choked off and the Yankees assured a monopoly. This was the system allegedly established to fend off Old World dangers; this was the system allegedly invoked in defense of the Monroe Doctrine. And sad to relate, this was the system that brought to the United States the ill will of two thirds of the Western Hemisphere.[5]

Dana G. Munro, who served in several diplomatic posts in the Caribbean before beginning his academic career at Princeton University, has recently combatted the view that United States policy was sordid or sinister (Reading VIII.2). Whatever our motives may have been it is clear, maintains the political scientist Theodore Paul Wright, Jr., that the United States practice of trying to promote political stability by supporting "free elections" has failed (Reading VIII.3).

Cuba and the Dominican Republic represent the most serious challenges to United States policy in the Caribbean. Many nations have sought to dominate Cuba, but after 1900 United States influence became increasingly powerful. How Fidel Castro managed to triumph in 1959 and escape from the orbit of Uncle Sam remains one of the great stories of the twentieth century, some of it still shrouded in mystery. Hugh Thomas, the British writer who produced one of the best books on the Spanish Civil War, has drawn up a carefully argued explanation of the coming of Castro (Reading VIII.4).

Generalíssimo Rafael Trujillo represents the nadir of all Caribbean dictators. Nevertheless, President Franklin D. Roosevelt supported him; the resulting "stability" was won, however, according to Raymond H. Pulley of the University of Virginia, only at a very high price (Reading VIII.5). How high that price was may be seen from the comments of a British scholar, Gordon Connell-Smith

---

[5] Lawrence F. Hill, "Our Present Peril," in *Hispanic American Essays: A Memorial to James Alexander Robertson*, A. Curtis Wilgus, ed. (Chapel Hill: University of North Carolina Press, 1942), pp. 375–376.

of the University of Hull, on the crisis in inter-American relations provoked by the unilateral intervention there of the United States in April, 1965 (Reading VIII.6).

A. General

1. The United States Is Honor Bound to Maintain Law and Order in South America

GEORGE W. CRICHFIELD

Our people believe in justice, and in the liberty which carries the torch of civilization over the earth. They have always earnestly desired to see stable republics established in South America. They do not believe in monarchies. They believe in "a government of the people, by the people, and for the people." Our people enthusiastically upheld President Monroe when he declared that European monarchies should not extend their territory on American soil, and each succeeding administration, without exception, has striven to aid in the establishment, maintenance, and development of decent republican governments in these countries.

When our State Department has seen revolutions, anarchy, and crime rampant in South America, foreigners being looted, robbed, and murdered (Americans suffering worse than any other class), infamy, perfidy, intrigue, and scoundrelism covering Spanish America as with a pall — it has not shut its eyes to the facts. On the contrary, no father ever watched over his wayward offspring with more care, sorrow, and anxiety than has the beneficent government of the United States observed these countries, studying by what means it could bring order out of chaos, decency out of crime.

For three quarters of a century this has been our policy, followed with patience and a spirit of philanthropy to which history affords

From *American Supremacy: The Rise and Progress of the Latin American Republics and Their Relations to the United States under the Monroe Doctrine* by George W. Crichfield (New York: Brentano's, 1908), I, pp. 7–544; II, pp. 635–644, *passim*.

no parallel. As one bandit government after another has appeared on the horizon of South America, our government has counselled it to exercise moderation, to walk in the paths of civilization, to respect the lives and property of foreigners; and we have stood between these so-called "governments" and the civilized powers of Europe.

In spite of all that our country has done for them, the incontestable fact remains that Venezuela, Colombia, Ecuador, Bolivia, Santo Domingo, Hayti, and practically all of Central America are in a worse condition to-day, politically, socially, commercially, and deeper in barbarism, than they were three quarters of a century ago. Dilettante philosophers, reactionists who are against every policy which has made the United States the peerless giant which it is, will go on shouting in behalf of our "poor oppressed Sister Republics." On such people the facts stated in the following pages will have no effect. But Americans — the hardy, brainy, practical race which has founded the Great Republic, before the tremendous power of whose solemn and deliberate judgment governments must stand or fall — that innumerable army of men who have made and who constitute "God's country" — men who hate brigand governments (all the more if they assume the name of Republics), who love justice and truth, and hate wickedness whatever may be its form — should know these Spanish-Indian-Negro countries as they actually are. If they could see Americans and American enterprises wiped off the face of the earth by the aggregations calling themselves Republics, it would not be long before the machinery of the government of the United States would be diverted towards bringing about a most thorough renovation in their conditions.

To many people it may seem impossible that in this day and age, and on the Western hemisphere, there could exist such conditions of semi-barbarism in Colombia, Venezuela, Santo Domingo, and Central America as are here disclosed. To know a country thoroughly one must have lived in it and done business in it. Distinguished writers have written admirable descriptive works of South America — of landscapes, of cities and rivers and lakes, of mountains and llanos, with a coloring of individual incident and interesting anecdote; they are admirable productions of scholarly men. One may describe a landscape from the window of a Pullman car, but one cannot in such a manner apprehend the social and political problems of the peoples through whose country the railroad passes. However brilliant a traveller may be, however acute his power of observation, it is not possible that he can probe into the depths and analyze the character and capabilities of a people, except by long and varied intercourse with them. . . .

It will be found that practically all Latin Americans exhibit the following peculiarities to a degree greater than that possessed by any other people with which I am familiar: (1) a lack of thoroughness, exactness, definiteness of aim; (2) inability to apply themselves persistently and continually to the mastery of a subject; (3) carelessness and lack of foresight; (4) contempt for the drudgery of ordinary work and a disposition to shirk it; (5) a desire to make a great display, to pretend to be what in fact they are not; (6) satisfaction with the outward appearance of knowledge, with no real desire to get at the heart of any proposition; (7) lack of initiative, invention, creative energy; (8) possession of a multitude of impracticable theories and ideas which are a nuisance, but of which it is impossible to rid them; (9) complete absence of a sense of responsibility; (10) ignorance of the most elementary methods of doing things; (11) a disposition to talk, rather than to act; (12) a disposition to do work in the showiest manner possible, but to produce what is really shoddy and worthless; (13) a disposition to make money by intrigue rather than in legitimate business; (14) a very scant respect for the property or personal rights of others, particularly foreigners; (15) absolute indolence and lack of genuine ambition, and opposition to progress.

All of these will be recognized as characteristics of large sections of our own country; and indeed they cannot be set down as the exclusive peculiarities of any people, or as all of them applying to any one section of any people. Yet in their entirety they come nearer applying to the Latin Americans than to any European race. . . .

National Ingratitude — The United States has befriended the Latin-American countries in ten thousand ways; it has defended them against civilized powers for eighty years; it has submitted to outrages committed on its flag and on the persons and property of its citizens, outwardly without protest; it has declared in the presence of the world, untruthfully, but nevertheless declared it, that these countries are civilized republics, and their courts worthy the same consideration as are the courts of England or our own; it has called them "Sister Republics," and stood with its army and navy ready to defend them, at the grave risk, on more than one occasion, of having a war on its hands with the whole civilized world. In view of all this, it might reasonably be inferred that Americans are popular in

South America; but it is not so. Americans are robbed more than are either Germans or Englishmen; more outrages are committed against Americans than against any other class of foreigners.

If ingratitude is the index of a criminal, then these fighting, quarrelling, intriguing, murdering communities should be classed as criminals. . . .

Latin American Types — The military Jefe is the most noted Latin-American type which impresses itself upon a visitor. The Jefe may be colonel, general, comandante, or any of the other numerous military grades. As a rule, he is a man without conscience, of unbridled ambition, cruel and relentless, and a dangerous citizen generally.

Closely allied with the military Jefe is the civil politician. This man can write pronunciamentos, and hair-raising essays on liberty and patriotism. He also fixes up the decretas for the military Jefe to sign. A considerable portion of the graft is allotted to this type of politician. He is merely a schemer for the Jefe with his army of macheteros.

The doctors of Latin America are as numerous as the generals. They are a much more amiable class of men. While their pretensions to learning are exaggerated and amusing, nevertheless, they are a respectable element of society. Ignoring their idiosyncrasies and pretensions of refinement and culture, we may sincerely like and admire these men, most of whom are very decent fellows and a large number of whom are first-class gentlemen of a high type.

Throughout Mexico, Argentina, and Chili there are enormous plantations or tracts of land called *haciendas,* the owner of which is known as a *hacendado.* This man is easily, in my opinion, the highest type of Latin-American gentleman. He has not the literary ability or the refinement and culture of the doctors, but he is an all-round man of affairs, a good business man, and really forms the backbone of the nation. It is the hacendado who gives to Mexico, Chili, and Argentina their stability and higher governmental excellence. The hacendado is usually the supporter of the government, unless it be in fact very vicious, because it is to his interest to maintain the established order of things. He does not want his property overrun by revolutionary hordes, and he knows that it is better to submit to the exactions of a corrupt government than to run the risk of losing all by siding with anarchy. These great plantations are not cultivated thoroughly, and enormous tracts of land lie fallow or in their primeval condition. No opportunity is afforded to the small man to become a landed proprietor, and this constitutes the real element of weakness in the hacienda system. The inconceivable strength of the United States is due to the fact that we have millions of home owners. A comparatively poor man with us can own his own house and farm. Not so in the countries mentioned. A landed proprietor there is necessarily a man of wealth. The coffee plantations of Venezuela and Colombia afford a somewhat similar system to that of the great landed estates in the other countries mentioned, but owing to the frequent uprisings and the despoliation by predatory bands, these plantations are usually run down and neglected.

There are many special types in Central and South America which are very interesting to a foreign observer. They may be briefly mentioned. The *arierro*, or mule-driver, is a picturesque fellow. He directs the burros in their never-ending work of transporting the products of Latin America. These burro trains by the hundreds can be found in all parts of Latin America, each animal carrying loads of two hundred or two hundred and fifty pounds, over mountains and valleys, wading rivers, climbing where it would seem to be impossible for an animal to step, going on journeys for days or even for weeks. The arierro is utterly oblivious to the suffering of his beasts. He is ordinarily not a bad fellow, but is entirely indifferent to pain, and ignorant with regard to every subject except the matter in hand. The *gaucho*, or cow-boy, of the great interior plains of Argentina, Brazil, and Southern Venezuela is a most daring rider, an excellent shot, and makes one of the hardiest soldiers in the world. He loves ornaments in dress, is disposed to drink a great deal of bad liquor and indulge in gambling, and is generally a citizen with whom one must be careful in dealing. . . . The beggar is another distinctive type in Latin America which impresses itself upon the visitor with a vividness and distinctiveness which can never be obliterated. One day a week, usually Saturday, is set apart particularly for the beggars, in which they make their rounds of all the houses and streets, soliciting alms. The utter hopelessness of this type is pitiable and pathetic. They live in indescribable squalor and misery, diseased, deformed, helpless, and hopeless. There are hundreds of thousands of all ages and both sexes belonging to this type in Latin America. The enormous percentage of dire helplessness is one of the saddest features which an observer encounters in every Latin-American country. . . .

Protection of Civilized Men in America — The United States is in honor bound to maintain law and order in South America, and we may just as well take complete control of several of the countries, and establish decent governments while we are about it. Peru, Chili, and Argentina are already fairly responsible governments. We ought not to interfere with them so long as they conduct themselves in a reasonably satisfactory manner. Mexico is an excellent government, and worthy of our best friendship. A stricter surveillance should be exercised over Costa Rica, Brazil, Uruguay, and Paraguay. These governments are not as advanced or as worthy of recognition as those named, but they are not wholly bad. There are evidences of genuine efforts at improvement, and some regard for the amenities of civilization and international rights, and a rather more decent spirit towards foreigners. Whether they will ever amount to anything or not, time alone will tell. They should be kept under the strictest friendly supervision by the United States. No marked internal or external policy should be permitted without our consent. They should be held under a quasi-protectorate, yet with such a minimum of interference with their affairs as would secure perfect security for life and property, and a reasonable measure of material and intellectual progress. . . .

The Dictatorships Should Be Placed Under a Civilized Government — Now, what shall be said of Venezuela, Colombia, Ecuador, Bolivia, Santo Domingo, and Haiti, and the rest of Central America?

They have sinned away their day of grace. They are semibarbarous centres of rapine in an age which boasts of enlightenment. They are a reproach to the civilization of the twentieth century.

It is a waste of time to argue in connection with these States about sovereign rights. The United States should take immediate possession and jurisdiction of each and every one of them, without waiting for a pretext. It should govern them in precisely the same way as it governs other territory of the United States. The century of intrigue and bloodshed and bad faith in these countries should be brought to a close, and a new era ushered in more in harmony with the sentiments of the age. With the United States in control of South America, I venture to predict that within ten years we could take a Pullman car at Maracaibo and go straight through to Buenos Ayres without change, and in ten years longer it might be that we could step into another car and go to New York. Under the present régime such conditions would not be brought about in ten thousand years.

There are doubtless many persons who would concede that this ought to be done and yet hesitate to commit the United States to such a policy on account of the apparent magnitude of the task. Our people have not yet got over the idea that the taking of Porto Rico and the Philippines under our wing was a mighty feat, and the ravings of the "antis" have rather accentuated that belief. As a matter of fact, the Philippines and Porto Rico are only specks in the ocean in comparison with the immensity of England's colonial possessions.

If the United States were to take possession of the whole of the Western Hemisphere, from the Rio Grande to Cape Horn, the total area of its territory would be only about equal to that of the British Empire, and its population not more than one third as great.

What Englishmen can do Americans can do. The United States, with vastly greater territory and population, is as truly a breeding-place of creative energy, of originating and productive enterprise, as England or any other country. . . .

No very great argument should be required to show the incomparable benefit to the United States as a nation in controlling these great territories. It is a curious thing that the English, who are in all ordinary business matters extremely slow and conservative in comparison with Americans, should in this one matter so completely outstrip us in foresight and in a true apprehension of the right policy to pursue. If we are to become a great manufacturing nation, we must have outlets for our goods, and those outlets must be in countries where there is money to pay for them and the disposition to buy them. To develop the continent of South America properly will require twice as many tons of steel rails as it has required to develop the United States, for it is twice as large. It will require as much mining machinery, for the natural mineral resources of South America are unquestionably as great and as valuable as those of North America. The people who are now scantily clothed would, under proper conditions, be large consumers of our manufactured products. The manufactured production of the United States is now running parallel with the domestic consumption, and in a short time will overleap it. We must have markets, vast markets; for our productive capacity is great. If our workingmen are to be kept employed, if the prosperity of the United States is to continue, we must look ahead, and provide ourselves for outlets of our products. It has been truly said that when we export a million dollars' worth of goods, at least $800,000 of money has been paid to our own people for the labor of their production. I am aware that every

effort of far-seeing statesmen to establish our future commercial
prosperity on a sound basis calls forth protest from a certain
class of mugwumps, who join the words "commercialism," "militarism," and "imperialism" as though they constitute a trinity of
horrors. . . .

Importance of Civilized Control — It seems unnecessary to emphasize the beneficent effects upon the people of those South American countries which would result from placing them under the
American flag. One immediate and very important consequence
would be that a man could go to sleep at night without fear of
being assassinated. No one, unless he has slept for some years
with one eye open and an automatic revolver within reach, can
appreciate the delight of unmolested sleep.

Another blessing scarcely less appreciable would be the privilege
of working and reaping the results of one's efforts. To-day, in South
America, military Jefes will not work, nor will they let any one else
work. The enormity of this wrong can be only partially appreciated
by those people in the United States who have personally observed
the tyranny of the labor boss as displayed in its unvarnished ugliness in certain localities.

As fully explained in another chapter, the great majority of the
people of South America are good people — incapable of self-government, but fully capable of marvellous development under decent
conditions. To those who wish to live in peace and accumulate a
little property against old age or death, the American flag would
be a beacon of hope. Rascals, intriguers, and the semi-bandit governing class are the only people whose liberties would in any wise be
curtailed by the control of the United States.

Do I need to multiply examples in order to prove my contention?
Is there any American so blind that he cannot to some extent perceive the blessings that have accrued to each successive territory
which has come under the beneficent control of the United States?
Look at that magnificent State, Texas, and that incomparable garden of the world, rich and beautiful California, and the rest of the
splendid commonwealths which have been created out of the territory wrested from Mexico.

Suppose that territory had remained in the exclusive control of
Mexico and Mexicans, and that the enterprise and capital of Americans had never entered it. Does any sane man believe it would ever
have attained a fraction of its present prosperity? Even the progress
of Mexico itself is due mainly not to internal activity, but to the stim-

ulus of external enterprise exercised within its borders. Nor can any fault-finder truthfully assert that the rule of the United States in Porto Rico and the Philippines is any less promising. The mediæval systems of a century are not to be swept away in a moment, and the complete regeneration of a people is a question of time; but already much has been accomplished in both those colonies. Never before were they so well governed, never were they so clean, never was education so well looked after, public improvements so actively pushed, happiness and security of the people so thoroughly safeguarded, or such contentment and evidences of future prosperity as at the present time.

Size, distance, or inaccessibility of these countries constitutes no valid objection against this program. The world is apparently destined to be divided up among five or six great powers. The time has passed when we can permit the famines and pestilences and revolutions which grow out of barbaric or semi-barbaric conditions to destroy millions. With the world under the control of half a dozen civilized powers, wars would be unknown, and the chief function of the military would be its police duties. On this hemisphere the power which controls should be the United States. . . .

What shall be the final destiny of these countries no man can tell. What part the United States is to take in the mighty onward march of affairs is likewise shrouded in the future. But any reasonable man must see clearly that the present condition of anarchy cannot continue indefinitely in Spanish America. It is not they alone who suffer, but the whole world; and not they alone, but the whole world, would be benefited by the United States taking possession of them.

2. United States Policy Was Not Inspired by Sinister or Sordid Motives

DANA G. MUNRO

To many observers the policy which culminated in the military occupation of Haiti and the Dominican Republic and interference to a lesser degree in the internal affairs of other nearby countries seemed little different from the imperialism of European powers

From Dana G. Munro, *Intervention and Dollar Diplomacy in the Caribbean, 1900–1921* (Princeton, N.J.: Princeton University Press, 1964), pp. 530–546. Reprinted by permission of Princeton University Press.

in Africa and the Far East. The American intervention in the Caribbean aroused a hostility throughout Latin America that still affects our relations with the other countries of the hemisphere. What happened might have been forgotten after the repudiation of the intervention policy by Presidents Hoover and Franklin Roosevelt, had it not been for the belief that the policy was inspired by sinister and sordid motives, which might well reassert themselves at some future time. This belief has contributed materially to the myth of North American imperialism, political and economic, which is assiduously kept alive today by hostile propaganda.

The persistence of this belief in Latin America is not surprising, because the same ideas about the motives behind the intervention policy have often found expression in the United States. Many liberal North Americans were shocked when they realized that American marines were killing Haitians and Dominicans who resisted the occupation of their countries by foreign forces, and thought that the policy which led to such a situation must be wrong. Writing at a time when historians were prone to assume that all governments were unprincipled and that governmental actions must be explained by economic considerations, "anti-imperialist" authors assumed that the United States could only have been acting for the benefit of American financial interests, and they found enough in the story of dollar diplomacy to convince them that their assumption was correct. One still hears it said that the marines were sent to the Caribbean "to collect debts," an idea that seems somewhat incongruous when one reflects that it was Woodrow Wilson who ordered the more important interventions. For several years after 1920 most of the books written about Caribbean affairs, some of them the work of honest and competent historians, reflected this point of view.

It would be impossible to deny that many of the American government's actions were ill-judged and unfortunate in their results. As we look back on the story, however, it seems clear that the motives that inspired its policy were basically political rather than economic. What the United States was trying to do, throughout the period with which this study has dealt, was to put an end to conditions that threatened the independence of some of the Caribbean states and were consequently a potential danger to the security of the United States. Revolutions must be discouraged; the bad financial practices that weakened the governments and involved them in trouble with foreigners must be reformed; and general economic and social conditions, which were a basic cause of instability, must be improved. The Platt Amendment was an effort to achieve these purposes in Cuba, and the Roosevelt Corollary to the Monroe Doctrine meant that the United States would seek to achieve them in other Caribbean states.

The same purposes inspired the policy of successive administrations from Theodore Roosevelt to Woodrow Wilson. The methods used in attempting to achieve them varied from one administration to another, but more because of accumulating experience and increasing involvement than because of any difference in the ultimate goals. Each successive Secretary of State took up Caribbean problems where his predecessor had left them, in most cases making no abrupt change in the way in which they were being handled. . . .

Throughout the period between 1901 and 1921, the first objective of American policy in the Caribbean was to discourage revolutions. Revolutions, and the interstate wars that often rose out of them, were the chief cause of controversies with European powers because they endangered foreign lives and property and disrupted the government's finances so that it could not meet foreign claims. Frequent civil wars were also an obstacle to any sort of material or social progress. A government that had to devote all of its resources simply to maintaining itself in power could do little road building and little for public education, and an atmosphere of insecurity discouraged private enterprise in agriculture or industry.

The improvement of economic conditions was a second objective. There could be little basic improvement in the political situation while the masses of the people were poverty stricken and illiterate. A part of the Dominican bond issue of 1908 was used for public works, though little was accomplished, and the proposed loan for Nicaragua was to have provided funds to build a railroad. In Haiti and the Dominican Republic the occupation authorities had ambitious programs of roadbuilding, port improvement, and sanitation. All economic development, however, had to be carried on with the limited funds available from the countries' own revenues or from loans, because it would hardly have been possible before 1921 to ask the United States Congress to make grants of aid to another country.

In discussing their policy, officials in the State Department sometimes held out the hope of increased trade and new fields for American investment as a third objective. It is doubtful, however, whether these considerations really had any great influence in the formulation of policy. There is little evidence that the American government made any important effort to promote trade, and with the exception of Cuba the countries which the United States tried particularly to help were too small and too poor in natural resources to offer attractive opportunities for foreign enterprises.

These objectives, whatever we may think of the way in which the American government tried to attain them, were neither sinister nor sordid. Many critics of the United States' policy, however, maintained that there was a fourth purpose: to forward the selfish interests of American businessmen and bankers. To what extent this charge is justified is one of the questions that must be considered in any study of dollar diplomacy and intervention.

Certainly many American citizens who lived in Caribbean countries did benefit from the establishment of more orderly conditions and from the increased influence and prestige of the United States, which made their lives and property more secure. The American government, like other governments, thought that it had a duty to intercede for its nationals when they were the victims of violence or injustice in a foreign country, and it showed somewhat more interest in protecting them after 1900 than it had in the past. Warships were sent to Caribbean ports not only to influence the local political situation but to prevent injury to Americans and other foreigners. The State Department also tried to bring about the settlement of American claims, and in Nicaragua, Haiti, and Santo Domingo it urged the establishment of mixed commissions for this purpose. The benefits derived from these, however, were dubious, for all claims, and especially those of Americans and other foreigners, were usually arbitrarily scaled down and many claimants were compelled to accept awards which they considered unfair. A study of the work of the claims commissions hardly supports the idea that the purpose of the Caribbean interventions was to collect debts. . . .

Except in Cuba, little new American capital went into the countries where the United States intervened. The occupation in Santo Domingo and the treaty officials in Haiti tried to encourage investment in new agricultural or industrial enterprises, in Santo Domingo by setting up the land courts, which improved the chaotic state of land titles, and in Haiti by abrogating the constitutional provision against foreign land ownership. The results were not particularly impressive, though the sugar companies in Santo Domingo, some of which were American, found it easier to obtain new acreage and considerably increased their production. A few new foreign agricultural enterprises were started in Haiti, most of them after 1921, but only one or two of them were ever profitable. Little foreign capital went into Nicaragua.

Dollar diplomacy might have brought profits to American bankers if it had been more successful, but its purpose, under Taft as well as under Wilson, was purely political. Both administrations were interested in loans as a means of stabilizing Caribbean governments and bringing about the establishment of American customs collectorships, and as a way to provide funds for economic development. They also wished to eliminate European financial influence in the area. Disputes over unpaid debts were always likely to provide an excuse for European intervention, and it was thought that the exploitation of the Caribbean countries by European interests was one cause of their backwardness.

In most cases, it was the State Department that took the initiative in bringing forward projects for loans. The bankers, however, were usually glad to participate in them and sometimes competed for the privilege, because they assumed that they would be sound business ventures. At times, a desire to cooperate with the State Department and the fascination exerted by projects for the development of strange and distant countries led the bankers into ventures which at least cost them far more in time and trouble than the profits could justify, but they would have been subject to merited criticism if they had gone into transactions where there was not a prospect of a reasonable profit. . . .

If we dismiss as unfounded the charge that the purpose of dollar diplomacy was to enrich a few North American businessmen, we must still inquire whether the broader Caribbean policy of which it was a part was wise and profitable. The policy did eliminate, for the time being, the danger of European intervention. Perhaps neither Germany nor any other power seriously entertained the idea of territorial expansion in the Caribbean, but there is little doubt that European interference would have taken forms unacceptable to the United States and possibly dangerous to the independence of the countries involved if the American government had not acted as it did in Santo Domingo in 1905 and in Haiti after 1910. Before 1914 the vital importance of defending the approaches to the Panama Canal made any unfriendly activity in the Caribbean a much more serious matter than it seemed to be after the First World War, when the naval power of the United States was so much greater.

It is more difficult to assess the benefits and disadvantages to the Caribbean countries themselves. The policy of the United States certainly reduced, though it did not end, the bloodshed and turmoil that had kept the Caribbean states so backward before 1900. It stopped international wars between the five Central American states and made internal revolutions less frequent and destructive. Except for the *caco* uprising in Haiti, that country and the Dominican Republic had a long period of peace. Unless one has seen something of the terror and the misery caused by a civil war in a small Caribbean country, it is difficult to appreciate what peace meant to all classes of the people. It was certainly the first requisite for any sort of economic progress.

We have seen that the amount of economic progress actually achieved down to 1921 in the countries where the United States intervened was not very great. There were, nevertheless, some material benefits. The customs receiverships, which continued in Nicaragua, Haiti, and Santo Domingo for several years after 1921, helped commerce by eliminating favoritism and corruption in the customhouses and strengthened the financial position of the governments. These three countries were among the very few in Latin America that continued to pay interest on their foreign bonds during the depression. Some other administrative reforms introduced by American officials and advisers were of lasting value. Much-needed roads were built in Haiti and the Dominican Republic, and there was a notable improvement in sanitary conditions in the larger cities of both countries. More might have been achieved if the public works programs had not had to be financed entirely from the scanty resources of the local governments. For various reasons, the substantial foreign loans which the customs receiverships were to have made possible did not materialize, and the United States government could give little help.

The replacement of the old inefficient and corrupt armies by better-trained police forces, in Haiti and the Dominican Republic, helped to maintain peace but had unfortunate consequences after the American occupations ended. The efficiency and discipline of these organizations gave their officers a potential political power which only the ablest of the old style *caudillos* had had. In Santo Domingo, General Trujillo, the chief of the new force, took control of the government in 1930 and ruled the country despotically until 1961. In Haiti, too, the *Garde* has at times been the master of the government rather than its servant. It is perhaps less unpleasant to live under the tyranny of a comparatively efficient military force than under the equally tyrannical but irresponsible and inefficient rule of the old type of local *comandantes,* but the evolution of the constabularies was a disappointment to those who hoped that they would help to promote republican government.

It can hardly be said, in fact, that the American government's policy did very much to promote republican government in other ways, except insofar as the maintenance of peace and some economic progress created an atmosphere more conducive to the gradual development of democratic institutions. The support of constituted governments and the discouragement of revolutions meant in practice that one party might stay in power indefinitely. A government that felt secure in its position was less likely to mistreat its opponents or to curtail civil rights, and it could devote more energy and resources to constructive work; but it would be no more inclined to permit its opponents to win elections. . . .

The failure to insist on fair elections in Cuba and in Nicaragua unquestionably gave the opposition parties reason to feel that they were unfairly treated. The opposition parties in several other Caribbean states could likewise complain that the discouragement of revolutions and the policy of refusing recognition to governments coming into office by the force was unreasonable when they had no other means of changing an unsatisfactory regime. Officials at Washington, however, might well have hesitated before committing themselves to any general policy of compelling the holding of fair elections. No supervision could be effective without assuming control of or supplanting the military forces and the civil authorities and the courts in all functions connected with the electoral process. The governments in power would have had to be coerced into accepting this sort of intervention, and this would be unfair because it would hurt the prestige and probably cause the defeat of the government party, even in cases where it might otherwise have majority support. It would be difficult to find qualified people to conduct the supervision, and there was a practical problem: the State Department had very little money which it could use for such purposes. It is not surprising that there was not a more strenuous effort to change the way in which the Caribbean governments had always conducted their elections, even though there was an inconsistency in preventing revolutions against governments that perpetuated their control in obviously undemocratic ways. It could be argued that the maintenance of peace was first requisite for the sort of progress that would ultimately make real elections possible, and that it would be futile to try to force democratic practices on people who were not ready for them.

One unfortunate consequence of the American government's efforts to improve political conditions in the Caribbean was that the local leaders got into the habit of looking to Washington for the settlement of political problems. A belief that the faction favored by the United States would usually come out on top, and even that an established government which the United States disliked might not be able to stay in office, gave an excessive importance to every indication or fancied indication of the attitude of American officials. Rumors about American policy were fabricated and circulated for political effect, and even ordinary courtesies extended by the State Department or the American legations were given an exaggerated significance. Under such conditions, many of the local leaders tended to feel less responsibility for the settlement of their own problems.

The willingness of many political leaders to accept American help made it more difficult for the State Department and its representatives to appreciate the resentment their actions were causing. If the American government's policy after 1909, as we look back on it, seems increasingly callous in its disregard of local sentiment, we must remember that those who directed it thought that they had the support of important groups in the countries with which they were dealing. In the State Department's correspondence, one frequently encounters the idea that the truly patriotic leaders, and most of the solid and intelligent people, wanted peace and reform, and that the opposition came from "corrupt politicians" and "professional revolutionists." Had it not been for the belief that the United States must help the decent element against evil men who wished for their own selfish reasons to perpetuate anarchy and misgovernment, it would have been more difficult for Taft to send the Marines into Nicaragua in 1912 and for Wilson to order the military occupation of Haiti and Santo Domingo.

Important groups in the community often did welcome American interposition. In countries where there had been long periods of disorder, property owners and businessmen were glad to have peace restored, and many humbler citizens were glad to be free from the oppression and hardship that always accompanied civil strife. When the United States prevented a revolution, only those who had hoped to get possession of the government were really distressed. There were many patriotic people who approved of the reforms which the State Department urged and who wished for American help in road-building and education and economic development. The spirit of economic nationalism, which had already made its appearance in Mexico after 1910, was much less evident in the smaller Caribbean republics, where many people hoped that the development of their natural resources by foreign capital would help them to emerge from the backward conditions that made their lives unattractive.

As the American policy developed, however, it met with increasing opposition. There had always been much distrust and traditional dislike of the United States and some suspicion of American motives. This suspicion grew stronger as the American government intervened more and more in purely internal affairs and began to seek actual control of important governmental functions. The use of force or the threat of force to settle political problems or to compel reforms was offensive to people who were jealous of their independence. The occupation of the country by American military forces, in Haiti and the Dominican Republic, was of course still more offensive.

The hostility and distrust that it aroused, not only in the Caribbean but throughout Latin America, was the worst result of the intervention policy. The full extent of this feeling was not apparent until after the First World War, when Haitian and Dominican opponents of the American occupations began to carry on a propaganda campaign in South America and in the United States. A realization of the reaction in Latin America and of the unpopularity of intervention at home led to a gradual change of policy at Washington after 1921, but suspicion of North American "imperialism" continued to be a major obstacle to inter-American cooperation throughout the 1920's. Even today the recollection of what happened in the first decades of the century provides useful material for anti-American propaganda.

The American government was necessarily interested in what happened in the Caribbean, especially after the decision to build the Panama Canal, and it had sound reasons for wishing to do away with the internal disorder and financial mismanagement that endangered the independence of some of the Central American and West Indian republics and the security of the United States. In trying to correct these conditions the statesmen who directed the policy of the United States in the Roosevelt, Taft, and Wilson administrations were dealing with exasperatingly difficult situations, where their best efforts were often defeated by the unpredictable and irresponsible conduct of local *caudillos* and their followers. We may well hesitate to criticize them too severely, but since it is clear that their policies had bad results, and since we are still faced with similar problems, it would be regrettable if we did not learn something from the story.

One fact that stands out is the inadvisability of sending incompetent diplomatic representatives to countries where the United States had great interests and heavy responsibilities. No policy could succeed when its implementation was in the hands of ministers who were too ignorant or too senile to command respect. The State Department repeatedly had to make decisions on the basis of information and recommendations received from persons who knew little about what was really happening, and it had to entrust these same persons with the conduct of its negotiations. Several of its representatives were, of course, not so incompetent, but few of them, especially after 1913, were fitted for their positions by training or experience. Many mistakes and unfortunate incidents could have been avoided if there had been able ministers at each post.

The bad results of the American government's policy, however, cannot be attributed wholly to diplomatic ineptitude. What made the policy offensive, in the Caribbean and in South America, was the use of coercion to compel the acceptance of American control in internal affairs and to obtain reforms that the United States considered desirable. Imposition of this sort would have been intolerable, however efficiently and tactfully it was carried out. . . . With a policy of persuasion and cooperation the moral influence of the United States might have accomplished more than attempted compulsion did.

Had it not been for the effort to impose controls unacceptable to any people who prized their independence, there would have been less resentment of the vast influence which the United States necessarily exercised, and less resentment even when the American government used force to back up its efforts to end armed strife and to protect foreigners. Natives, as well as foreigners, were usually glad to see a warship appear at a port where fighting was imminent, and a show of force to stop a war caused little lasting bad feeling if it led to a fair settlement with no continuing offensive American interference in the government's affairs.

With tactful persuasion, much could have been done to promote better administration and economic progress. Caribbean governments often voluntarily accepted the help and advice of foreign experts, though they naturally resisted efforts to give experts authority over their own officials. Aid in roadbuilding and education and sanitation would have been welcome if it was not accompanied by efforts to impose foreign control. In Haiti and Santo Domingo there would probably have been less progress in these fields than there was under the military occupations, but the gains that were made might have been more lasting. If the American government could have provided funds for economic development, as it does today, a great deal could have been accomplished.

A policy that relied on cooperation rather than compulsion would have required patience and self-restraint. Its success would have depended on the quality of the American diplomatic representation in the Caribbean, but the diplomats would not have had to be supermen. A minister or even a young chargé d'affaires could exercise a great influence in a Caribbean country simply because he was the representative of the United States, and this influence was still greater if he was liked and respected. It was dangerous to have an incompetent man in such a position, but a moderately able man could accomplish a great deal, both for his own government and for the people of the country where he was serving.

Such a policy would also have required a willingness to accept and to live with situations in some Caribbean countries that were far from satisfactory from the American point of view. American influence could not bring about free and fair elections in countries where the people had not learned to demand them and to run them; and so long as elections were not satisfactory governments would inevitably be ousted by force or threats of force from time to time. Other evils, like corruption and oppression of political opponents, would have continued to exist. The United States could have exercised a very great influence for better and more democratic government and for the peaceful settlement of political conflicts, but in countries which were and must remain independent political progress had to be made primarily through the efforts of the people themselves. Stable democratic government cannot be imposed by exhortation or outside pressure.

3. "Free Elections" Are Not the Answer

THEODORE PAUL WRIGHT, JR.

The United States has not deliberately embarked upon a policy of promoting democracy in other countries. It has supported free elections as an answer to certain concrete policy problems which accom-

From *American Support of Free Elections Abroad* by Theodore Paul Wright, Jr. (Washington, D.C.: Public Affairs Press, 1964), pp. 137–157, *passim*. Reprinted by permission.

panied its rise to world power. The chief of these has been how to prevent or halt revolutions. In practically every case related in this study, political stability was the direct or indirect goal of American electoral intervention. Even where the immediate problem has been the liquidation of American military occupation or the decision whether to recognize a new regime, the desire to foster stable government has been at its root. In situations of the former type, the United States has wished to leave the occupied state in a condition most conducive to peaceful acquiescence by the populace of their new government with a view to preventing a repetition of the disturbances which had caused American concern in the first place. In situations of the latter type in which the question was whether to recognize a new regime, the issue has arisen because nonrecognition was adopted previously as a technique for discouraging revolutions. The only exceptions to the anti-revolutionary goal of the United States policy have been the few cases such as Panama in 1903, Nicaragua in 1909, Guatemala in 1954, Hungary in 1956, Cuba in 1961 and South Vietnam in 1963 in which the immediate aim has been rather to validate uprisings which have been deemed favorable to our security.

Why this obsessive concern with the political stability of our neighbors? Primarily, it is because conditions of unrest and civil war may provoke or legally excuse intrusion by foreign powers hostile to us. Ever since the Monroe Doctrine, the United States has publicly proclaimed such interference in the Western hemisphere to be a threat to its security. Since 1898 we have been strong enough to combat it. With the Truman Doctrine we have extended our sphere of influence to large parts of the Eastern hemisphere.

Why promote political stability by supporting free elections? Why not simply strengthen the military dictatorships which have ruled many of the states in question? It could be argued against the latter course that even the best entrenched dictators must die or fall from power eventually and the disorders usually attendant upon the transfer of rule where force has been used to maintain a regime are liable to be explosively violent. What American policy makers have argued has been that the best way to stop revolutions led by the members of the parties out of power is to ensure that the elections already provided for in their constitutions should be free of fraud and violence. Americans tend to believe that the real cause of their neighbors' frequent revolutions is the indignation of the losers in elections over being coerced or cheated out of victory. That is what the representatives of "out" parties who troop to Washington to protest against the tyranny of the "ins" tell American officials. That is what rebels tell American mediators. There has been nothing in the recent historical experience or ideology of the United States to contradict this assumption. Secretary Root was a lone dissenter when he challenged the cherished American doctrine that government derives its just powers from the consent of the governed. The United States is itself the product of a successful revolution, so it can not consistently aid in suppressing uprisings against tyranny elsewhere. We have reasoned that the only way both to prevent revolutions and to determine whether they are justified if they do break out, is to guarantee free elections. . . .

The policy of supporting free elections evidently has not been very effective in achieving the goals of American policy makers for which it has been adopted. I have concluded above that the original and ultimate aim of the policy in most cases has been to preserve the security of the United States by promoting stability and discouraging revolution in certain strategically important areas. Americans have pursued this particular policy for that goal because they have mistakenly assumed, that fraudulent and coerced elections are the cause of revolutions in countries which already have democratic constitutions.

The policy has succeeded in creating stability only where our military and naval power has been exerted as in Cuba (1906–08), Panama (1903–31), Nicaragua (1912–25, and 1927–33), and the Philippines (1898–1946) or where the policy has had the unintended, ironical and self-contradictory result of paving the way for a strong dictatorship as in Nicaragua, Cuba, the Dominican Republic and Haiti after 1933 and South Korea and South Vietnam more recently.

Clearly there is something irrational about a policy which succeeds in its ultimate purpose, stability, only by failing in its ostensible immediate purpose — free elections. The reason for this lies in the nature of the politics of Latin America and other underdeveloped areas which make successful support of democracy as an end in itself impossible no matter how comprehensive the means employed. In order to understand this, it is necessary to take a brief look at these characteristics and the impact of American electoral intervention on them:

Imitation of the U.S. Constitution — All of the Latin American republics and some Asian ones have borrowed the presidential system from the United States in the course of the nineteenth and twentieth centuries. The superficial identity of institutions has meant that the burden of proof has lain on anyone who has proposed radically different forms of government even if the proposed forms would be more consistent with the actual conditions and practices there. Hence also the American prescription of legal reform for the faulty operation of the foreign copies when they haven't seemed to work. Because colonial revolutionists imitated our Constitution voluntarily they themselves have been at first ready to ask for and defend American intervention in an effort to make the borrowed institutions function properly. Only later when these idealists began to count the costs of "bringing in King Stork" have they resigned themselves to other solutions such as "guided democracy."

Fluidity of Factional Coalitions — Although the two major parties in most Latin American countries early in the century, Conservative and Liberal, were composed of different elements of the population and were divided by bitter partisan antagonism, Americans have been shocked to find no "real" issues debated in Latin American elections. Perhaps they had not observed their own election campaigns realistically! Since there seemed to be no deep convictions about principles behind party differences, Americans have finally concluded that the so-called parties must be only factions or cliques fighting for revenge and the spoils of office.

With nothing but personal ambitions represented in party rivalry, there should logically be as many factions as leaders, but the existence of the indivisible American-type executive necessitates the coalescence of the inimical factions into two ill-defined alliances at election time. Once "in," an alliance promptly splits up again into its component parts over the division of the spoils because there are never enough jobs to go around in an underdeveloped country. The pressure for government jobs is due to the lack of equally prestigious and remunerative alternative occupations in business and industry. In such a situation, the stakes at issue in an election are high: persecution, discrimination, confiscation, imprisonment or exile all too often await the losers. Because of this, the "ins" can not afford to let the "outs" win an election and the "outs" cannot accept defeat without an appeal to arms.

The consequence of these characteristics is a constant shifting of political alignments which has frustrated all American attempts to discover by free elections a stable majority which could enjoy the allegiance, or at least the acquiescence, of enough of the population to prevent successful revolutions until the next balloting. The "out" parties, especially in Cuba, Panama and Nicaragua, have claimed to represent an overwhelming majority of the people in their countries. The fact that there are always more dissatisfied jobseekers than satisfied jobholders has lent their claims some authenticity. The evidence they have offered that they enjoyed the confidence of a suppressed majority has been convincing enough at the time to bother American consciences and bring about supervised registrations and elections to determine the "real" size of the major parties.

The Problem of Reelection — In discussing the Central American treaties of 1907 and 1923 we have seen that Latin American preoccupation with the reelection of executives has gone far beyond our concern with it. The problem of the peaceful and periodic transfer of power in a presidential government has been aggravated by the nepotism and discrimination characteristic of their Latin culture and pre-modern economies. One observer of Latin American practices concluded from this that "the principle of rotation in office . . . has become one of the fundamental political traditions . . . and . . . [its failure] one of the underlying [causes] . . . of most revolutions in Central America. . . . A series of Executives may be dictators in form, but the very fact that they are changed periodically results in the introduction of new elements into the Government." From these facts has arisen the strict constitutional and treaty prohibitions against reelection which we have cited. It might be noted that it was the attempt of President Chamoun of Lebanon to change the constitution so that he might be eligible for reelection which precipitated the Lebanese civil war of 1958 in which the United States had to intervene.

From the late 1920s on, Latin American presidents turned from reelection to extension of their terms of office by constitutional amendment. Thus they could stave off the whole problem of elections until a more propitious time. Our State Department protested against this practice in the Dominican Republic (1927), Haiti (1927, 1930), Cuba (1927), and Nicaragua (1930), but with little effect except in the last case. "Continuismo" has more recently appeared in Asia and Africa.

The Use of Force in Politics — The result of nepotism, mutual distrust and animosity, the drive for spoils and the absence of the essential conditions for democracy in the population has been the use of force and fraud in elections by all parties, though the advantage, of course, has lain with the party which has controlled the electoral machinery. There has been utter lack of confidence that if a party's enemies should win office by election, the latter would thereafter respect the rules of the game and give the "outs" a fair chance of winning the next time. This has produced a vicious circle of government-controlled elections and revolt by the losers. Members of each party have come to believe that any means are justified to save their country, and themselves, from their opponent's rule. In a situation like this, where violence is ever near the surface, the army is naturally very powerful and independent of civilian control.

The Bandwagon Effect — The ordinary voter or small office holder in a political system in which "winner takes all and for keeps" has found the penalties of being on the losing side so high and the rewards of joining the prospective "ins" so important that he can not afford to take a position in accordance with any philosophic principles which he might imagine he finds in one party more than the other. He has had to estimate as late as possible in the campaign which side would win and then jump on the bandwagon. The consequence of this phenomenon is that very slight rumors or strained inferences from the words and actions of military and foreign power holders have been enough to precipitate an avalanche of votes for the favored side.

Uncontested Elections — Revolution thus has appeared to be the cheaper alternative to the leaders of the prospective losing side in an election since they can not expect a fair chance to win. At the very least they may abstain from voting, as a protest, to prevent the winners from claiming their allegiance on the ground of a legitimate victory. Such an uncontested election has usually been the signal for a rebellion.

The appearance of the United States on a political scene with the gap just described between formal rules of government and actual practice has produced a policy dilemma. The "ins" have used American guarantees of independence and stability to forestall revolts against their imposed elections. The "outs" have then appealed to the United States against such a tacit support of tyranny. They have asked that we either guarantee free elections or allow revolutions against fraudulent elections. If American intervention has not been forthcoming, the "outs" would start a revolution to force the hand of the North Americans. The losing side in a civil war, be it "in" or "out," has appealed for American aid because they felt, "rather the Americans than our opponents."

Because the American reaction to the above appeals has been unpredictable from time to time and from place to place, other consequences have followed. The United States has been eased into the position of naming candidates and presidents and vetoing others despite its repeated and earnest protestations of impartiality between candidates and parties. Each party has wanted a candidate who would meet with American approval, so the "center of political activity" of these countries has shifted to Washington. The position of Minister to the United States has become of almost equal importance to that of President in these circumstances.

The irritating uncertainty and loss of sovereignty implied by these results has led foreign politicians increasingly to lobby in the United States Congress and to propagandize through the Americans and their own press with a view to forcing us to give up our electoral interventions. Critics abroad have pointed to the inconsistency between American words and deeds, to the contradiction between present American opposition to revolution and our own revolutionary origin. They have pointed to examples of dishonesty in Uncle Sam's own backyard. With each change of party control in Washington, they have hoped for a reversal of policy. On occasion they may even have helped the "out" party in the United States with campaign material as in the 1920 election.

As foreign populations have experienced American intervention and occupation, inevitably friction has arisen and produced popular resentment. American racial prejudice has antagonized some and affronts to sensitive national honor and patriotism have alienated others. Therefore, Americans who have found no "real" political issues in the politics of some underdeveloped countries have been blind to the obvious paramount issue wherever American military, political and diplomatic intervention are felt: the extent and duration of that interference itself. Political leaders may be obsequious toward the United States in public but they have their own ways of standing up to us. If they believe that their opponents have the final endorsement of Washington, they can turn to stirring up the latent xenophobia of the populace as a last resort.

When open opposition to the United States has been impossible, those leaders who have solicited American help in elections have often tried to conceal their requests or to blame their domestic foes for the necessity of this affront to national honor and sovereignty. There has been a lot of maneuvering to get us to accept the onus of demanding publicly what they have themselves asked for in private. This has run counter to the State Department's determination to avoid criticism by acting only when foreign executives request our intervention. The fact that American interference itself has become the main political issue also accounts for the seeming ingratitude of its beneficiaries. Once a party is in power, it attacks all forms of American participation in their electoral processes even if the "ins" owe their success to foreign supervision of the previous election. If they did not play the ingrate in this way, they would be smeared as American puppets.

The policy dilemma, the bandwagon effect, and the exploitation of American intervention as a political issue all point to one conclusion: that impartial support of free elections is impossible. Since the impartiality of the supervising power is presumably a condition of any support of a really "free" ballot, we are driven to the further conclusion that the support of free elections as an end in itself is self-defeating in countries where genuine democracy has not already existed.

No matter how disinterested the American policy makers in Washington and their representatives in the field, every American word and action is bound to be misinterpreted as favorable to one side or the other in an election or civil war, given the political milieu unfolded above. Impartiality is inconceivable to people who have never known it from their own governments. In short, a technically "free and fair" election can never play the role assigned it by democratic theory — a real test of party strength — as long as American participation influences the minds and ballots of the voters.

B. The Coming of Castro

4. The Castro Revolution Was the Culmination of a Long Series of Thwarted Revolutions

HUGH THOMAS

The present Cuban explanation of events is that Cuba, previously a semi-colonialist society, was so severely exploited by U.S. and Cuban capitalists that the condition of the working class eventually became intolerable, the tension being especially sharpened under the tyrant Batista (1952–58); Castro's 26th of July Movement and the Communist Party therefore formed the elite which led the masses towards a coherent realization of their misery and the country towards the "objective conditions" for revolution. Yet this explanation is also inadequate. Cuba, although a poor country in many respects, was certainly among the richer countries of Latin America. Per capita income reached a figure of $341 at its highest level in 1947. The average daily salary about the same time for the best-paid sugar worker was $3.25, which probably would have given him an annual wage (with a six-day week for the five-month sugar harvest) of nearly $500. This is a small wage, but in many countries in Latin America it would be considered high. Wages apart, however, the general availability of consumer goods, the social services per head, the labour laws, the communications system, literacy rates, all normal criteria indicate that Cuba was among the leading nations of Latin America — to be ranked in terms of development below only Argentina and Uruguay, and perhaps on a level with Chile. Certainly, Cuba had had for two generations before the revolution the highest standard of living of any tropical area in the world. It does not therefore seem to be poverty, any more than North American foolishness, that caused the revolution to take the turn it did.

From "The Origins of the Cuban Revolution" by Hugh Thomas, *The World Today*, XIX, October 1963, pp. 448–460, *passim*. Reprinted by permission.

The difficulty of explaining what happened in Cuba in Marxist terms has led some people to another extreme: they have seen the whole series of events as dictated by the whims of one man. The trouble with this argument is that it really credits Castro with greater powers than any man can singly possess. Instead of describing a monster, this argument creates a god.

The origins of the revolution seem more likely to be found in the fact that Cuban society was not so much underdeveloped as stagnant: semideveloped perhaps, with some of the characteristics of advanced countries when they enter decline. Cuba was not a country in the depths of poverty, but one extraordinarily frustrated, where opportunities existed for economic and social progress but where these were wasted — and the fact of the waste was evident. The undoubted advances whetted the imagination of the working class, but did not satisfy it. The case of the well-paid sugar worker symbolizes the situation; getting $3.25 a day for the five months of the harvest, afterwards he could expect to earn nothing. Unused to saving, and perhaps incapable of doing so since he had to pay off debts incurred during the previous dead season, his life collapsed. For half the year he was comparatively well off, able to choose between a quite wide selection of consumer goods; for the rest of the year he lived in resentment, possibly more extreme than if he had been unemployed all the time, as a large fraction (around one-fifth) of his colleagues in the trade were. About 500,000 persons were in this frustrating position, nearly one-third of the total labour force of about 1.7 million. Nearly all of them were in debt throughout their lives — being disposed for that reason alone to hope for a violent upturn in society, which might declare a moratorium on, or even an annulment of, debts. The key to Cuban society before the revolution is, in fact, the sugar industry. . . .

In addition to being the world's largest producer of sugar, Cuba was, for about a century, the major single source of sugar for the United States, and for a time after the Civil War her sole source of sugar. For most of this century up to 1960, Cuba supplied between 40 and 60 per cent of U.S. sugar, with a drop towards 30 per cent and for a time 25 per cent during the 1930's depression. After this unstable period, Cuba secured a part of the U.S. market by a specific quota, allocated annually according to the U.S. Secretary for Agriculture's estimate of U.S. sugar needs. . . . The quota was a great advantage but also a great bondage, and therefore there is a certain logic in the Cuban Revolutionary Government's criticism of its existence in early 1960 and denunciation of its disappearance in August of the same year. The tragedy of the Cuban sugar industry in the years before the revolution is that it was hard to see how, even with the most effective methods of production, it could expand its share of the world market, or its own production. Both U.S. and world markets were quota-controlled and tariff-protected to the point where expansion was almost forbidden.

One should note, however, that a large percentage of Cuban sugar mills were in fact U.S.-owned. . . . Of course, it was natural for Cubans to denounce the high percentage of foreign ownership, throughout this long period, of the staple product of the country, especially when other sections of the commanding heights of industry were also U.S.-owned; these included almost all public utilities in Havana, railways, and banks, which had been largely U.S.-and Canadian-owned since the bank crash in the 1920's. However, there were some advantages in this: foreign ownership could help to keep the door open to new ideas in technology and research; some of the best schools in Cuba seem to have been run by Americans, some being financed as a public obligation, others privately; American firms were also probably less given to tax evasion than Cuban. The overall effect of U.S. ownership of such prosperity as there was in Cuba was that Americans could not avoid being blamed when things went wrong with the economy; and the economy had been in crisis for as long as anyone could remember.

In fact, Cuban sugar before the revolution was going through the classic experience of a great industry in decline. Cuban sugar-growers never sought to make the best use of their ground, the yield per acre, for instance, being far below that of Puerto Rico or Hawaii. Irrigation was not only rare but not apparently even planned, though it was obvious that it gave a higher yield. There was very little research as to the type of cane best suited for Cuban conditions: the agricultural research center at Sagua la Grande was hardly able to carry on, since even the meagre ear-marked funds often "disappeared" before they got there. Further, the industry was hamstrung by bureaucratic control. . . .

The country was also at the mercy of world sugar demand. Changes of a percentage of a cent in the world market price of sugar not only meant the creation or ruin of fortunes in Cuba, but also indicated whether ordinary life was intolerable or acceptable. . . . For example, in 1950 under the impact of post-Korean rearmament, the whole of Cuba's molasses from the 1951 harvest was sold at 20 cents a gallon, instead of 5 cents a gallon a year earlier. . . .

Credit was almost impossible to obtain unless the proposed project was in some way connected with sugar, yet investment in new industries (perhaps making use of sugar by-products) and diversification of agriculture were the only way forward. This blockage could be observed throughout the economy. Education, health, social services of all kinds, public services, commerce, departments of agriculture other than sugar, trade unions, all gave the impression of being not only incapable of development, but also afraid of it. The Cuban educational system had deteriorated between 1925 and 1959. A smaller proportion of school-age children were enrolled in Cuban schools in 1950 than in 1925. . . .

Other Latin American economies were, and are, as unstable and as unbalanced as that of Cuba: and the central cause of the trouble, the monocrop, appears elsewhere. At the same time, none of the countries whose economies are to a lesser or greater extent monocultures actually depends on sugar, whose price has always been highly volatile. . . .

The institutions of Cuba in 1958–59 were amazingly weak. The large middle and upper class had failed to create any effective defence against the demands of what may be taken to be the majority when those demands came at last to be clearly expressed, as they did in January 1959, by a group self-confessedly middle class in origin. Perhaps the first and strongest factor working in favour of the revolution was the absence of any regionally based obstacles. . . .

To the absence of a regional restraining force was added the weakness of two other traditional conservative forces — the Church and the regular army. The Cuban Church has never really found an identity. Churches are few in Cuba. The Church played no part in the development of the Cuban spirit of independence, which instead was nurtured by freemasonry and rationalism. Few priests before 1898 were Cuban born, and even after 1900 the majority continued to come from Spain. Church and State had been separated in the Constitution of 1901, State subsidies also disappearing. Later on, the Church made something of a comeback, a large number of Catholic schools being founded in the 1930's; in 1946 a Catholic university was also founded. In the 1950's this educational emphasis led to the appearance of almost radical Catholic groups which opposed Batista. In Oriente, there was, in the early stages, some degree of relationship between the 26th of July Movement and the Church — chiefly since it was widely known that the intervention of the Archbishop of Santiago had helped save Castro's life after the Moncada attack in 1953. The leading Catholic and conservative newspaper, the *Diario de la Marina*, was, on the other hand, among the first to suggest that the 26th of July Movement was communist.

After Castro got to power, the Church made no serious move to gather middle-class opposition, and it was only in 1960, when it was too late, that a series of sporadic pastoral letters appeared denouncing communism. All church schools and convents were closed by the end of 1961, and most foreign priests and secular clergy (i.e., the majority) were expelled. Since then there has been a surprising calm in the relations between Church and State, presumably by mutual consent; the Church in Cuba has, in short, never been a serious factor in the situation.

The regular army, the second traditional opponent of revolutionary regimes, was even less of an obstacle. By early 1959 it had in fact ceased to exist — not simply due to its demoralization in 1957 and 1958, when fighting Castro in the Sierra, but also to the repeated divisions which had weakened its esprit de corps during preceding years. . . .

The trade unions also could offer no serious opposition to the revolution; yet the revolution destroyed them, or anyway converted them into departments of the Ministry of Labour. Cuban labour began to be effectively organized under the shadow of the depression and the Machado dictatorship. Batista enabled the communists to form and dominate a congress of unions in the late 1930's — in return for communist electoral support for himself. Between 1938 and 1947 the unions were, if not structurally, at least in effect a section of the Ministry of Labour. The rather cynical alliance of Batista and the communists (till 1944) was responsible for some enlightened labour legislation: a minimum wage; minimum vacation of one month; 44-hour week and 48-hour-week pay; nine days of annual sick leave; security of tenure except on proof of one of fourteen specific causes of dismissal, and so on — all admirable measures in themselves, enshrined in the 1940 Constitution, and all in effect till 1959. These measures were in fact so favourable to labour in the 1940's and early 1950's as undeniably to hinder the economic development of Cuba; labour opposition to mechanization, for example, seems to have been a serious handicap. The general impression to be gained from the labour scene just before Batista's second coup was less that of solid benefits won by a progressive working class than of a number of isolated redoubts, held with great difficulty and with continuous casualties, in a predominantly hostile territory. . . .

It was equally hopeless to expect the civil service to be a restraining factor in the revolution, although, with nearly 200,000 employees, it was the second largest source of employment, ranking after the sugar workers. Despite the passage of numerous laws, starting in 1908 under the Magoon administration, no Government was able to depend on a reliable civil service. With the exception of the National Bank, during the short period from its inception in 1949 to the Batista coup, all departments of state were regarded as the legitimate spoils of political victors. Of course, in this Cuba was no different from other countries. But in few countries of a comparable degree of wealth was the absence of an administrative career in government so conspicuous. In some Ministries, employees never seem to have appeared except to collect pay; the absence of responsibility was possibly most marked in the Ministry of Education. Also, since the salary scale was low, there was every incentive for employees of all grades to dip their hands in the government till, as their political masters did. Since governmental and non-governmental pension funds, which were lodged in the Treasury, had been used· by the Grau Government to help pay other lavish but unspecified government expenses, it was very difficult after 1947 to allow any employee to retire. Many people thought that in fact 30,000 to 40,000 government employees were really pensioners. Thus government employment was a kind of social assistance.

The scandal of the old bureaucracy is certainly a reason why, after the victory of the 26th of July Movement in 1959, the idea of a total break with the past seemed so attractive. The word government had been debased for so long; not only the old bureaucracy but the old political parties were widely and with justice regarded as organizations for the private distribution of public funds. Who in 1959, even after seven years of Batista, had really forgotten the scandal of Grau's schoolteachers; or of Grau's Minister of Education, Alemán, who had arrived suddenly one day in Miami with, was it $10 million, or was it $20 million in cash in a suitcase? In what way was Batista's cheating in the State lottery worse than Prío's? It was all very well to return to the Constitution of 1940: but how far had it worked between 1940 and 1952? It had in many instances merely laid down general principles; the subsequent legislation had never been carried out to implement it. . . .

Some of the best-intentioned sections of the Constitution were in fact a little absurd, such as the provision in Article 52 that the annual salary of a primary schoolteacher should never be less than a millionth part of the national budget. At the same time, not many people, even sincere democrats, could summon up enthusiasm for the 1940 Constitution, since it had been established with the backing of Batista and the communists. And at a deeper level, there was a genuine doubt among many in Cuba in 1958–59 about the structure of previous Cuban Constitutions ever since independence. Batista's police were certainly bloody, but the old days of gangsterism under the democratic rule of Grau were hardly better. There was a time, for instance, in 1947, when three separate political gangster groups were fighting each other in the streets of Havana, each being separately backed by different divisions of the police, whose chiefs had been specifically appointed by the President to balance them off.

Although Castro did not come to power with a real party organization, or even a real political plan, he nevertheless did have behind him a real revolutionary tradition, a tradition which was firmly rooted in the previous sixty years of Cuban politics, almost the whole of which had been passed in perpetual crisis. . . . All the time between 1902 and 1959, Cubans were trying to prove themselves worthy of the heroic figures of the War of Independence — Martí, Gómez, or Maceo. Efforts were made, understandably, necessarily perhaps, by Castro to make himself, Camilo Cienfuegos, and others the equals of the past. The men of 1959 were undoubtedly in many cases the real sons of the men who made the revolution in 1933. Castro was to do the things that many people had been talking about before. Many moderately middle-class Cubans suspected, without much economic knowledge, that the only way out of the chronic sugar crisis, the only way to diversify agriculture, was to embark on very radical measures; to nationalize American property and to force a break in commercial relations with the United States.

Amateur Marxism was a strong force on the left wing of the *Ortodoxo* Party in the early 1950's, though it is now proving an illusion to suppose that even Marxist-Leninism can bring a swift diversification of agriculture. One can see how the illusion nevertheless became widespread, how anyone who seemed likely to realize it was certain of backing, regardless of whether he trampled on formal democracy. There can be only one reason why the moderates in the Cuban Cabinet of 1959 — the admirable professional and liberal persons who now perhaps back Manuel Ray and argue that Castro has betrayed the revolution — failed to unite and resist Castro, backed by the considerable strength of the Cuban middle class: the reason is surely that they half felt all the time that, given the betrayal of so many previous revolutions, Castro was right. Many moderates after all did stay in Cuba, and many are still there.

What of the communists? They have never dictated events, but merely profited from opportunities offered to them. . . . The communists got 117,000 votes in the presidential elections of 1944, but they were by that time in a curious position, being less a party of revolution than one which had a great deal to lose, almost conservative in their reactions in fact. Thereafter their influence waned, throughout the intermediate period between then and the Castro civil war, until mid-1958 when, after some difficulty, they established a working alliance with Castro, whom they had previously dismissed as a *putschista*. Since then, they have, of course, come into their own in many respects, if not quite absolutely; but their role in the origins of the Cuban revolution seems to have been small.

To sum up: the origins of the Cuban revolution must be sought in the state of the Cuban sugar industry. Similar conditions may exist in other countries of Latin America, in respect of other crops; these have hitherto been less pronounced. Even though other revolutions in the area may in fact be equally due, they have been hindered by the strength of institutions or regional habits, which in Cuba, for historical reasons, were especially weak. Finally, the Cuban revolution of 1959, far from being an isolated event, was the culmination of a long series of thwarted revolutions.

C. The Dominican Republic During and After Trujillo

5. The High Price of Stability

RAYMOND H. PULLEY

During the late 1930's Franklin D. Roosevelt often voiced an abhorrence for the dictatorial governments of the world which at that time were rising as a threat to free institutions. On Constitution Day 1937 (September 17), the President described dictatorship as a "cold-blooded resolve to hold power," and he asserted that "the people of America are rightly determined to keep that growing menace from our shores." These remarks were obviously directed toward the non-democratic governments of the Old World.

In view of Roosevelt's statements against the Mussolini and Hitler regimes in the years before the outbreak of World War II, it seems inconsistent and almost hypocritical that the United States supported, and in some cases helped to maintain, a dictatorship in the Dominican Republic under Rafael Trujillo which was in every way as repugnant to American institutions as the more famous strongman governments of Europe. This investigation of United States-Dominican relations during the period from 1933 to 1940 attempts to arrive at an explanation for this contradiction in the official American attitude toward dictatorial regimes and to sample the temper of vocal opinion concerning Trujillo in the United States.

Rafael Leonidas Trujillo Molina seized control of the Dominican Republic in May, 1930. He came to power by means of a rigged presidential election in which the number of ballots announced in favor of Trujillo exceeded the number of qualified voters in the country. Through civil intimidation and political assassination, he

From "The United States and the Trujillo Dictatorship, 1933–1940" by Raymond H. Pulley, *Caribbean Studies*, V, October 1965, pp. 22–31. Reprinted by permission.

quickly constructed one of the most cynical and brutal dictatorships of the twentieth century.

Trujillo's climb to supreme power in the Republic may be traced from the United States occupation of that island nation in 1916–1924. During that time the Americans attempted to untangle the confused Dominican foreign debt, constructed many useful public works, and formed a constabulary composed of nationals trained by Marines to police the country. When the United States withdrew in 1924, the Dominicans were left with a national army commanded by Trujillo, a favorite of the Marine staff, and a shaky democratic government under Horacio Vázquez. Moreover, in order to insure that the Dominicans would not fall once more into difficulty with the forces of international finance, a convention was drawn up between the two countries whereby the United States would supervise the collection of Dominican customs and guarantee payments upon the Dominican foreign debt until it could be retired.

The termination of the American intervention was shortly followed by a renewal of a struggle for political power between ambitious factional elements which had characterized Dominican history since the celebration of national independence in 1844. Such conditions of disorder and the relative strength of the army were conducive to the development of a military dictatorship. General Trujillo proved to be an effective arbiter of the political disorder when he presented himself as a candidate for the presidency in 1930 and assured his election by machine-gun suppression of all opposition.

The United States watched Trujillo's seizure of the government with calm detachment, with no thought of repeating the intervention of 1916. In March 1930 the State Department informed its representative in Santo Domingo, Charles B. Curtis, that it expected "to recognize Trujillo or any other person coming into office as a result of the coming elections and will maintain the most friendly relations with him . . . ." Even though the farcical nature of the election was known to the United States, Trujillo was accorded official recognition from America on the day of his inauguration, August 16. President Herbert Hoover sent the following wire:

I extend my cordial congratulations to Your Excellency on this auspicious occasion of your elevation to the high office of President of the Dominican Republic, and best wishes for a most successful term of office and the happiness of the people of the Republic under your wise administration.

When Franklin D. Roosevelt became president in March 1933 he publicized the opening of a new United States policy toward the southern republics — that of "the good neighbor." The President proclaimed that future inter-American relations would be conducted in "an atmosphere of close understanding and cooperation" based upon a respect for "mutual obligations and responsibilities." Roosevelt also repudiated armed intervention as a feature of United States policy in the Caribbean area.

In the case of the Dominican Republic Roosevelt appeared to believe that American supervision of the collection of customs should continue in order "to insure the payment of the external debt." It is interesting to note that in 1928 Roosevelt praised the Dominican intervention, stating: "We accomplished an excellent piece of constructive work, and the world ought to thank us."

There is little evidence available to indicate that the Roosevelt administration disapproved of the Trujillo regime on moral grounds during the period 1933–1940, even though by the mid-1930's the bloody nature of the dictatorship was widely known and criticized in the United States. This is strange since in 1933–1934 the President and Sumner Welles, State Department expert on Latin American affairs, helped topple the infamous Machado dictatorship in Cuba. Active armed intervention was repudiated but Welles was sent to Havana and through persuasive diplomacy brought an end to the days of Machado. Welles stated that "such a condition at the front door of the United States could not be allowed to continue indefinitely." He also declared that the Machado government was based upon "Nazi Gestapo" methods and held power through "governmental murder and clandestine assassination." The Trujillo regime in the Dominican Republic was no more or no less "Nazi Gestapo" than the Machado government in its operation, yet the former won the seeming approbation of the United States, while the latter was condemned and eliminated.

During the early years of the Trujillo rule the dictator seems to have favorably impressed a large segment of the American people. In early 1933 one of the country's leading newspapers editorially rhapsodized that "the outstanding policy of President Trujillo has been a sound financial reorganization." The editor continued that the Dominican people were wholly justified in comparing "President Trujillo with the President of the United States as an economist and reformer." American business also appears to have approved of the Dominican tyrant. Louis M. Vidal, the Latin American representative of Trajewski-Pesant Steel Company, stated: "We have a staunch friend in the Dominican Republic, which makes 76 per cent of all its foreign purchases in the United States."

As reports of the methods employed by Trujillo to maintain himself in power began to be known in the United States, criticism of the "Caesar of the Caribbean" gained wide circulation. One of the first comprehensive statements on the nature of the dictatorship appeared in February 1936 in *Foreign Policy Reports*. Cognizance was taken of the terror and repression of popular opinion which existed under Trujillo, and it was stated that the tyrant's "own force of character, his tactics of ruthless repression, combined with absolute control of all government patronage and appointments have made his influence supreme." Although personally critical of the Dominican regime, the *Report* was sympathetic toward United States relations with Trujillo, stating:

The policy of the United States toward the Dominican dictator provides an illustration of the difficulty involved in attempting both the exercise of humanitarian influence and protection of American and other foreign interests without endangering the general application of the "good neighbor" program.

In June 1936 *Review of Reviews* gave a less restrained commentary on the Dominican situation. Alluding to Trujillo's Mulatto heritage, the dictator was called a "dusky despot" and a "big Negrocrat" who was outshining both "the Iron Duce" and "the Man of Munich" as an autocrat. The *Review* also reflected upon Trujillo's exploitation of the Dominican economy, estimating that "his fortune amounts to some millions of dollars, and his power has grown continually." Finally, the article stated that the dictator's "political opponents have a way of conveniently disappearing."

In July of the same year *The Literary Digest* branded the Dominican strong man a "swarthy autocrat" who for six years had "lorded it over the Dominican Republic as undisputed dictator." The *Digest* reported that Trujillo's enemies claimed that "he is a despot whose iron hand has wiped out opposition, clamped down on all freedom of press and speech and that he has enriched himself by monopolizing the country's key industries." Note was likewise taken of the cult of adulation which attended Trujillo; that his camarilla had "hailed him as a savior of the Republic, generalissimo and peace-maker, [and] they urged that he be cited for the Nobel Peace Prize."

Oswald Garrison Villard, writing from Ciudad Trujillo in March, 1937, compared the Dominican dictator to Adolf Hitler, stating that like Hitler Trujillo had done away with "his political enemies and made his political party the only party." Villard found it difficult to gather information during his visit in the Republic because "nobody knows exactly what is going on behind the scenes, or who is in jail, for the press is as completely censored as that of Russia or Germany." The American journalist conceded that the dictator was "a remarkable man" whose "spirit of virility and vitality has penetrated the whole nation." He complimented Trujillo for leading the Republic down the path of economic development, but lamented that material progress was being wrought at the expense of personal freedom.

In January 1938 Carleton Beals, a frequent analyst of the Latin American scene, penned one of the most critical articles to appear concerning the Trujillo regime during the period 1933–1940. Beals declared that the dictator's "administration has been one of the most frightful tyrannies in the history of the Americas or of the world." This writer believed that "Trujillo, among other things, is a product of gangsterism, banditry, militarism, and our own marine occupation." Beals found those who supported Trujillo to be "waist bending adulators," while his opponents "totaled several thousand dead, among them some of the finest men of Dominican literary and professional life."

Beals appears to have been one of the few American writers to take notice of the real nature of the October 1937 Dominican-Haitian border incident. Trujillo despised Haitians with a consuming passion. On October 3–4 with well-organized efficiency some 12,000 to 20,000 Haitians living or working in the Republic were slaughtered by Dominican soldiers. Many were cut down by machetes to give the appearance that the murders had been committed by Dominican farmers who were supposedly distressed over an alleged influx of Haitian workers into the country. At the time the *New York Times* took little notice of the affair and only reported that "as many as 1,000 Haitians have been killed by Dominican soldiers seeking to eject them from Dominican territory."

Beals, however, gave a more accurate account of the atrocity. He stated: "In view of the magnitude of the crime, it seems incredible that our Caribbean news coverage could be so inadequate." Beals rightly determined that the "crimes were not confined to the frontier areas but were committed simultaneously, during the first week of October, throughout the Dominican Republic."

Trujillo, by means of press censorship and repression, attempted to stifle all news of the crime against Haiti. He even went so far as to subsidize the writing and publication in the United States of highly complimentary biographies which justified his regime in glowing terms. In these works the tyrant was pictured as the great benefactor of the Dominican fatherland and the friend of democratic principles everywhere. Two such pieces of Trujillo-inspired propaganda were Lawrence de Besault's *President Trujillo: His Work and the Dominican Republic* (1936, unpublished), and Sander Ariza's *Trujillo: The Man and His Country* (New York, 1939). In addition, the dictator satisfied his ego by flooding America with a continual stream of puerile biographical sketches and books printed in Ciudad Trujillo.

In July 1939 General Trujillo paid a visit to the United States designed to promote good will between the two sister nations. During the previous year the dictator had "retired" from the presidency, but he retained the title of chief of the Dominican armed forces. It was in the latter official capacity that he was received in the United States. The Generalissimo toured the World's Fair in New York, laid a wreath on the tomb of the unknown soldier in Washington, and on July 11 was greeted at the White House by President and Mrs. Roosevelt. The dictator was attended by a large entourage of American military and diplomatic officials everywhere he went.

The meeting with Roosevelt caused some criticism. Carleton Beals, Chairman of the Committee for Dominican Democracy, asked the President not to receive Trujillo, since the latter was no longer President of the Republic "and therefore was entitled to no special official courtesies at Washington." Beals also offered the interesting speculation: "It would appear that good neighbors in both South and North America would not welcome the unnecessary endorsement of an unfortunately home-grown dictatorship while condemning the European variety." Representative Hamilton Fish of New York, a ranking member of the House Committee on Foreign Affairs, countered with the encomium that Trujillo was "a builder greater than all the Spanish conquistadores together."

The efforts of Trujillo and Hamilton Fish notwithstanding, criticism in unofficial American circles continued to develop. Alfred H. Sinks stated in 1940 that the 1,500,000 people of the Dominican Republic "know no other law, no other government than the will of a single man." He continued:

Here in ten years' time Rafael Leonidas Trujillo has built the most thoroughgoing of all current dictatorships. It is an absolute monocracy with no democratic frills. The darkhued Dominicans have considerably less liberty than Mussolini's or Hitler's subjects; their civil rights are approximately those enjoyed by inmates of a penitentiary under a particularly headstrong and unscrupulous warden.

Sinks also took notice of the fact that the United States "has been the best of Good Neighbors" to Trujillo. He explained tacit support of the Caribbean tyrant by pointing to the influence of American business interests in Latin America which had traditionally favored dealing with strong-man governments. By means of a rigid political and social control Trujillo was able to guarantee American and foreign capital a stable area of investment.

The question arises as to why the United States persisted in supporting a bloody tyrant in the Dominican Republic while condemning similar regimes in Europe and while a large portion of vocal opinion disapproved of Trujillo and his methods. The key to the problem can be found in the basic nature of the Good Neighbor Policy as applied to the Caribbean area. Roosevelt's famed doctrine repudiated armed intervention as a means of protecting United States interests in the area, but the President approved of Trujillo and other strong men who were able to maintain stable regimes, protect foreign interests, and follow general lines of policy set forth in Washington. In other words, the Marines and intervention were replaced by a home-grown dictator who based his power upon a Marine-trained constabulary force as a means of creating stability. During the 1930's in Nicaragua and Haiti, as well as in the Dominican Republic, the balance of political power was held by the commander of a constabulary force which had been created by the United States during the period of the interventions. In return for relative non-interference in internal affairs, strong men such as Trujillo and Anastasio Somoza of Nicaragua pursued external policies regarding debts and foreign affairs which generally conformed to the best interests of the United States. Thus Roosevelt under the Caribbean Good Neighbor Policy could turn his back on Trujillo's tyranny.

These suppositions with regard to Dominican-United States relations are borne out by two important points of controversy which developed between the countries during the 1930's. These problems concern the Dominican Emergency Law of 1931 which suspended payment on the foreign debt and the renegotiation of the Convention of 1924.

When Rafael Trujillo came to power the Republic was encumbered by an external debt of some $16,000,000 which was largely held by United States financial interests in the form of Dominican bonds issued in 1922 and 1926. The situation was complicated by a world depression and a highly destructive hurricane which virtually leveled Santo Domingo in September 1930. To meet the country's growing financial crisis, Trujillo had enacted to the so-called Emergency Law of October 1931 which suspended amortization or sinking-fund payments on the foreign debt. All payment upon the debt with the exception of current interest came to an end. Under the Convention of 1924 the United States had assumed responsibility for amortization and interest payments on the bonds, and the Dominicans for their part had agreed to the establishment of an American Customs Receivership in the Republic for the purpose of collecting funds which would insure payment of the debt. The Emergency Law clearly violated the Convention by defaulting upon the debt and diverting customs revenues designated for payment of the debt to public works expenses.

The Hoover administration reacted by dispatching James E. Dunn as financial advisor to the Republic, but little was done to settle the difficulty until Roosevelt assumed office in 1933. The new president immediately instituted a vigorous program for the protection of American financial interests in the Republic. In June 1933 the State Department dispatched Joseph E. Davies, former Ambassador to Belgium and Russia, as financial advisor to the Republic to replace the apparently ineffective Dunn. Secretary of State Cordell Hull, with characteristic bluntness, instructed Davies that the United States could not "express approval or acquiescence in any action that may have had the effect of varying the bonds." In addition, Roosevelt and Hull effected the formation of a non-governmental agency known as the Foreign Bondholders Protective Council, Inc. to serve as a negotiating body to act in behalf of American holders of foreign securities in a time of world depression. It was through this organization, under the tacit supervision of the State Department, that a settlement of the Dominican bond question was reached. It is significant to note that Davies acted as counsel for the Republic during its negotiations with the Protective Council.

Trujillo quickly came to terms. The dictator was found "to be very amenable to the demands of [the] bondholders." In August 1934 the Protective Council announced that an agreement had been reached. The American Receivership of Customs was re-established in accordance with the Convention of 1924, the Republic was to make payments in full upon the interest of the external debt, and amortization was to be resumed at a reduced rate which provided for maturity of the two bond issues in question in 1962 and 1970 instead of the years originally stipulated, 1940 and 1942. In addition, Trujillo was allowed to divert a greater share of the customs receipts into public expenses, such as maintenance of the army and internal improvements.

The settlement of the Dominican Emergency Law question has several significant features. Trujillo's acceptance of Davies as financial advisor is of primary importance because it illustrates that the dictator was willing to submit to an agreement which was for all practical purposes worked out by the State Department through Davies. Thus Trujillo proved himself to be a proper agent for the Good Neighbor Policy in the Caribbean. In addition, Roosevelt's modification of the terms of the receivership, allowing a larger portion of the customs to the Dominicans, virtually assured Trujillo's continuance in power through the expansion of his army.

Resolution of the 1933–1934 debt question left both the United States and the Dominican Republic in a somewhat embarrassing position insofar as the Convention of 1924 was concerned. As long as the United States receivership existed, the outward appearance of American supervision of Dominican affairs continued. Consistent with the image of the Good Neighbor Policy, Hull in February 1937 informed the Dominican government that the United States "would be glad to give the most favorable consideration to any concrete proposal . . . looking towards a revision of the 1924 Convention." The Secretary of State, however, clearly stated that his government would not consider any arrangement "to abrogate the treaty unless the legitimate rights of the bondholders are fully respected."

Shortly thereafter the Dominican Government presented a draft protocol to replace the Convention. The Republic agreed to respect its external debt, but no exact provisions were spelled out as to how the Dominicans expected to handle the bond payments. Negotiations moved slowly through 1937 and into late 1938 with little sign of progress. Hull repeatedly drove home the point that "the rights of the holders of the bonds of the external loans must be adequately safeguarded."

Trujillo, during his July 1939 sojourn in the United States suggested as a possible solution that a Dominican citizen be appointed as Receiver of Customs. Lawrence Duggan, Chief of the State

Department Division of American Republics, countered that Trujillo's plan did not provide for the bondholders. Duggan suggested that an American bank with an established branch in the Republic, the National City Bank of New York, be designated as a depository for Dominican customs and supervisor of amortization payments on the debt. This proposal, not Trujillo's, served as the basis of the final agreement.

No further developments occurred until August 1940 when Sumner Welles, as acting Secretary of State, dispatched Hugh R. Wilson, former Ambassador to Germany, to Ciudad Trujillo as special representative of the Secretary of State with rank of ambassador. Wilson was given full powers to come to an accord with Trujillo's government. The American arrived in the Dominican capital on August 21, and by September 7 the completion of a draft treaty was announced.

The new treaty provided that:

1. The Convention of 1924 be abrogated, with an abolition of the United States Receivership.
2. The National City Bank of New York was to be designated the sole depository of all revenues and public funds of the Dominican Government.
3. A representative of the Bank was to supervise the payment of the Dominican external debt through the Foreign Bondholders Protective Council, Inc.

After the consummation of the treaty in Washington, Trujillo milked the agreement for full propagandistic purposes. His official publication in the United States declared that "with the abrogation of the 1924 Convention, the Dominican Government brings to an end foreign interference that has infringed upon its sovereignty." One of Trujillo's biographers stated that the treaty established "the complete restoration of our country's unqualified sovereignty in financial matters." Trujillo, for his alleged part in the agreement, was said to have earned "the permanent title of Restorer of our Financial Independence." In a gesture toward the United States, the servile Dominican Congress met in extraordinary session in order to confer upon Roosevelt a vote of "profound and sincere sympathy."

Despite Trujillo's show of independence and braggadocio, the terms of the treaty were worked out in the State Department by Welles and Wilson. In the words of R. Henry Norweb, American Minister to the Dominican Republic, the United States was attempting to preserve as a basic aim of any new agreement "the fiction of Dominican sovereignty over the customs service." Designation of an American banking firm as the depository for Dominican revenues assured continued American influence over the financial affairs of the Republic. To the outside world, however, Trujillo appeared to be master of his own house and the United States once again had repudiated intervention under the Good Neighbor Policy.

The settlement of 1934 and the treaty of 1940 seem to illustrate admirably the reasons behind American toleration of Trujillo's tyranny over the people of the Dominican Republic. The dictator proved to be a willing servant of United States governmental and financial interests. In addition, he provided a stable regime which protected foreign holdings in his country and contributed to the general security of the Caribbean area. Thus Trujillo's brutal regulation of the Republic's domestic affairs could be overlooked by the official councils of Washington. The Roosevelt administration took little notice of the Dominican-Haitian incident of October 1937, except to make the good offices of the United States available for mediation of the dispute. No reprimand for this crime against the Haitian people emanated from Washington.

Popular American deprecation of Trujillo's regime has already been recorded. Roosevelt's unwillingness to condemn the dictator on moral grounds and Trujillo's cooperation with American financial interests have also won widespread disapproval in Latin America. One nationalistic Latin American has stated: "The Trujillo dictatorship . . . is the alliance between the policies and interests of yankee imperialism and the worst reactionary and national forces" in Latin America. He declares that "the responsibility of the United States in sustaining dictatorial and antipopular regimes is a fundamental part" of American policy toward the Republics of the South. A more sober Latin American commentator on American-Dominican relations has stated that "the directing maxim of the foreign policy of the Dominican Republic is to guarantee the orientations that originate in Washington, at times with more enthusiasm and extremism than its progenitors."

The price of security for American interests in the Caribbean was extremely high. By supporting the Trujillo regime the Roosevelt administration pursued a clearly contradictory policy toward world dictatorship. Moreover sanction of the Dominican tyrant can be condemned on moral grounds, since Trujillo maintained a stable government, but only at the expense of personal liberty and freedom of thought. In short, during the period 1933–1940 the Trujillo dictatorship was the complete antithesis of what the United States claimed itself to be — the bastion of democracy.

6. The Issue of Communism Divides
Rather Than Unites the Members
of the Inter-American System

GORDON CONNELL-SMITH

The crisis in the Dominican Republic . . . began on April 24, 1965, when a revolt took place in Santo Domingo against the ruling military junta with the apparent aim of restoring to power the former President Juan Bosch who had been overthrown by a coup in September 1963. On April 28, with the outcome of the revolt still undetermined, President Johnson sent in several hundred marines because, he asserted, United States lives were in danger and the authorities in Santo Domingo were no longer able to guarantee their safety. This action, taken without reference to the Organization of American States, was a clear violation of the OAS Charter, specifically of Articles 15 (forbidding intervention "for any reason whatever") and 17 (forbidding even temporary military occupation "on any grounds whatever"). The United States government attempted to justify its precipitate action with a plea that there had been no time for consultation. But it is noteworthy that, as in the case of Nicaragua nearly forty years earlier, no foreigners were killed in the Dominican Republic until after the arrival of the marines. The whole affair was, in fact, painfully reminiscent of the Roosevelt Corollary and the period of intervention that lasted until the launching of the Good Neighbour policy.

Having taken, unilaterally, what it considered the first necessary step in the Dominican situation, the United States government turned to the inter-American system for its endorsement. The OAS Council agreed on April 30 to convoke the Tenth Meeting of Consultation, under Articles 39 and 40 of the OAS Charter, to consider

From *The Inter-American System* (pp. 336–345, *passim*) by Gordon Connell-Smith, published by Oxford University Press (1966) under the auspices of the Royal Institute of International Affairs.

the "serious situation created by the armed strife in the Dominican Republic." The Council also called for an immediate cease-fire and urged the establishment of an international neutral zone. The Papal Nuncio in Santo Domingo (the dean of the diplomatic corps there) was requested to use his good offices to negotiate the cease-fire. Within the OAS, as well as outside it, there was considerable criticism of the United States intervention. Some delegates argued that such intervention was unjustified under any circumstances; others that it was not justified in what was purely an internal dispute. Mexico and Chile introduced resolutions calling for the withdrawal of United States forces from the Dominican Republic, but they were not voted upon. The OAS Secretary General, Dr. Mora, was authorized to go to Santo Domingo to discuss a cease-fire with the leaders of the opposing forces, the Latin American ambassadors there and the Papal Nuncio.

The Tenth Meeting of Consultation opened at the Pan American Union on May 1. It was composed mainly of "special delegates" representing the foreign ministers. The Meeting appointed a five-man conciliation commission (consisting of representatives of Argentina, Brazil, Colombia, Guatemala, and Panama) to visit the Dominican Republic "to do everything possible to obtain the reestablishment of peace and normal conditions." Dr. Mora was to remain in Santo Domingo to represent the OAS presence and continue to use his good offices with the contending parties. At the Meeting the United States delegate (Ambassador Ellsworth Bunker) defended his country's unilateral action by declaring: "This is not intervention in any sense by the United States in the affairs of the Dominican Republic. United States forces were dispatched purely and solely for humanitarian purposes for the protection of the lives not only of United States citizens but the lives of citizens of other countries as well." This bland assertion carried little conviction even then.

On the following day President Johnson announced what was by now common knowledge: the real reason for his intervention:

The revolutionary movement [in the Dominican Republic] took a tragic turn. Communist leaders, many of them trained in Cuba, seeing a chance to increase disorder, to gain a foothold, joined the revolution. They took increasing control. And what began as a popular democratic revolution, committed to democracy and social justice, very shortly moved and was taken over and really seized and placed into the hands of a band of communist conspirators. . . . The American nations cannot, must not, and will not permit the establishment of another communist government in the Western Hemisphere.

Many more United States forces were sent into the Dominican Republic, until they numbered over 20,000: a show of power designed to demonstrate the Johnson administration's determination that another communist satellite should not be established in the Americas. The United States government subsequently produced a list of over fifty "Communist and Castroist" leaders whom it accused of seizing control of the Dominican uprising. This was greeted with considerable scepticism. Yet, although accusing the rebels of being dominated by communists, the Johnson administration continued to protest that it was not taking sides in the revolt!

Meanwhile, the United Nations had been apprised of the Dominican situation. The Security Council had been informed of both the United States action and the resolutions of the OAS. The Soviet Union called for an urgent meeting of the Security Council on May 1; it was not convened, however, until two days later. Her delegation submitted a draft resolution condemning the United States intervention, and demanding the immediate withdrawal of United States forces from the Dominican Republic. The United States was able to prevent the adoption of this resolution, but a majority of the Security Council was unwilling to have the question virtually left to the OAS as she urged. France was critical of the intervention, and so was Uruguay, one of the two Latin American members of the Council. The Uruguayan delegate declared that the OAS Charter prohibited any intervention, direct or indirect, and that his country did not regard the "Johnson Doctrine," which was "a corollary of the Monroe Doctrine," as compatible with that charter. He urged the Security Council to exert its authority in the situation.

At the Tenth Meeting of Consultation the United States pressed for the creation of an inter-American peace force to be sent to the Dominican Republic. Opponents of this proposal feared it would merely give an OAS label to what was essentially a United States operation; that it would sanction "collective intervention" and create a dangerous precedent. The United States experienced considerable difficulty in securing the necessary two-thirds majority support. Chile, Ecuador, Mexico, Peru, and Uruguay opposed the resolution, while Venezuela abstained from voting. The fourteen affirmative votes included that of the Dominican Republic, the diplomatic authority of whose delegation was, to say the very least, open to question. However, an inter-American peace force was eventually set up, with a Brazilian commander; Brazil furnished a contingent of men, as did Costa Rica, El Salvador, Honduras, and Nicaragua. The United States forces were to be nominally under the Brazilian commander, who had a United States "deputy." With the arrival of small Latin American contingents, some of the marines were withdrawn; but United States troops still constituted an overwhelming majority of the inter-American peace force.

After a secret mission sent by President Johnson to Santo Domingo in the middle of May had met with failure, the United States supported a Brazilian proposal for the creation of a three-man commission to seek a political solution of the crisis. The key figure would be the United States ambassador to the OAS; the other members were from Brazil and El Salvador. Officially the new commission was to collaborate with Dr. Mora in seeking "the establishment of peace and conciliation that would permit the functioning of democratic institutions in the Dominican Republic." It replaced the first, five-man commission. Mexico and Uruguay opposed the creation of the new body, while Argentina, Chile, and Venezuela abstained in the vote. Argentina now had reservations to her earlier support of the United States. Meanwhile, on May 15 the Secretary General of the United Nations announced the appointment of Sr. José Antonio Mayobre (a Venezuelan), Executive Secretary of ECLA, as his special representative in the Dominican Republic.

The United States continued her efforts to secure the formation of an anti-communist government in Santo Domingo. Neither the rebel leader, Colonel Francisco Caamaño, nor former President Bosch was acceptable to her. In spite of her continued protestations that she was neutral in the struggle and wanted only that the Dominican people should have freedom to choose a new government, her very presence denied them such a choice and her actions, whether consciously or inadvertently, favoured the military junta. Rebel forces were frequently in conflict with those of the United States which were gradually encroaching upon the area controlled by Caamaño. Various efforts at mediation broke down, and it appeared that the position of the rebels was gradually weakening. Caamaño not unnaturally denounced both the United States and the OAS, and clearly would have preferred to deal with the United Nations; neither did the junta, believing its victory was now assured, look with favour upon the inter-American peace force. The latter had failed to develop into a truly representative body and remained dominated by United States forces. Only Brazil and a few of the smaller republics actively supported it. And on July 20 both factions in the Dominican struggle, separately and for their different reasons, petitioned the Security Council for its withdrawal. No solution was in prospect. The United States could not withdraw until she had established a government satisfactory to herself; yet any such government was bound to be regarded as her puppet and would require her assistance — even military support — to sustain it in power. The situation in the Dominican Republic remained unpropitious; so, in consequence, did the outlook for the inter-American system.

Meanwhile, the Dominican crisis has highlighted some of the cardinal features of the inter-American system. In the first place, it well illustrates United States domination of the system and the extent to which its fortunes are dependent upon her policies. The vast disparity of power between the "One" and the "Twenty" (or, rather, nineteen with the exclusion of Cuba) is underlined by the ability of the United States to violate the most fundamental principle of the inter-American system and then not merely escape open censure but even receive a substantial measure of endorsement of her action.

Yet, if the Dominican crisis demonstrates United States power, it also shows the limitations within which she can exercise it. In spite of the deployment of considerable military strength, it has so far [as of July, 1965] proved impossible for her to impose a political solution upon the Dominican Republic. She deemed it expedient to turn to the inter-American system for assistance in establishing an acceptable government in Santo Domingo; and in the OAS she was able to obtain only the bare minimum votes necessary for a formal multilateralization of the moves she has been making to gain her objective. She has failed to secure the creation of a truly inter-American peace force.

The Dominican crisis shows also the role the inter-American system plays in United States foreign policy; to support and not replace the unilateral Monroe Doctrine. Some observers have seen in the intervention confirmation that United States Latin American policy has hardened under President Johnson. But it must be recalled that Mr. Kennedy warned the Latin Americans after the abortive invasion of Cuba that should they "fail to meet their commitments against outside Communist penetration" the United States would not hesitate to act unilaterally. Even when failing to make a show of prior consultation, however, the Johnson administration swiftly sought hemispheric support of its policy once this had been put into effect. Indeed, in spite of her cavalier treatment of the inter-American system, the Dominican crisis demonstrates its value to the United States. The "legitimacy of multilateralization" is of great importance in sustaining her self-image; in staving off criticism of her intervention as aggression comparable with that of which she has consistently accused the communists; and in limiting the role of the United Nations in hemispheric affairs.

At the same time, the Dominican crisis has underlined United States dissatisfaction with the inter-American system as an instrument of her anti-communist policy. Although more blatant, her intervention in Santo Domingo is comparable with the overthrow of Arbenz in Guatemala in 1954 and the invasion of Cuba in 1961: occasions when she acted unilaterally after failing to obtain adequate support from the inter-American system. The United States has criticized the OAS for acting too slowly and its machinery as being too cumbersome to meet an urgent crisis.

This criticism is partly justified, but the truth is that the Latin Americans do not regard the inter-American system as an instrument for furnishing swift endorsement of United States policies. Rather they look to it to impose a measure of restraint upon their powerful neighbour: to maintain the principle of non-intervention. Many do not accept the United States position on the Cold War, and reject the idea of the OAS as an anti-communist alliance. They believe, not without justification, that the United States is inclined to view any movement for substantial social reform as communist-inspired, and they are extremely reluctant to give OAS support to what would in practice be action by the United States. They tend to be more afraid of United States policy to meet the Soviet challenge than of any threat from communism itself. The Dominican intervention has confirmed their fear.

A positive indication of their attitude has been the re-emergence of a group of Latin American countries openly refusing to support the United States anti-communist policy. Mexico, isolated after the Ninth Meeting of Consultation, is still able, by virtue of her internal stability, to resist United States pressures; her former associates at Punta del Este, Argentina and Brazil, are too weak internally to do so. Peru, a leading supporter of measures against Castro at the Eighth Meeting of Consultation, but now under a somewhat more progressive government, deplored the United States intervention in Santo Domingo. Venezuela, for some time a main target of communist subversion, also refused to support the United States. Of the others,

Chile's opposition is ominous. The administration of President Eduardo Frei had been hailed as just the type of Latin American government needed to bring about orderly reform and make a success of the Alliance for Progress. But Frei has proved a severe critic of the OAS, and a firm supporter of Latin American unity and closer ties between Latin America and Europe. The case of Chile illustrates the broad truth that unrepresentative governments in Latin America generally have been the most ready to co-operate with the United States; while progressive leaders in the region are coming increasingly to seek to strengthen bonds between the Latin American countries themselves and with other areas of the world. This has important implications for the inter-American system in the long-term.

Some Latin American countries, and notably Mexico, favour United Nations precedence over the OAS as a means of lessening United States domination in hemispheric affairs. The Dominican crisis is not without significance for the relationship between the two international organizations. Although — because of United States influence — the Security Council was not able (at least up to July 1965) substantially to influence events in the Dominican Republic, there was greater reluctance among its members than hitherto to accept her contention that the matter should be left to the regional body. The Security Council insisted upon debating developments in the Dominican Republic; both the Dominican factions — and Cuba as an interested party — were given a hearing; and the United Nations Secretary General sent his representative to the scene of the struggle. One of the Latin American countries represented on the Security Council not only criticized United States intervention, but also strongly supported United Nations concern with the crisis. Ironically, as already noted, both sides in the Dominican conflict appealed to the Security Council for the withdrawal of the inter-American peace force.

Within the inter-American system, the Dominican crisis is significant, above all, in its implications for the principle of non-intervention so clearly violated by United States action. This study has shown something of the difficulties inherent in implementing this principle as well as in reconciling it with other objectives of the inter-American system. It has also shown how Latin American concern to uphold the principle of non-intervention has been mainly responsible for thwarting United States efforts to promote collective action to meet the challenge from international communism. "Non-intervention" has always been directed primarily against the policies of the United States, and it is not surprising she has come to consider it "obsolete" in the present situation. Today the United States opposes strict adherence to the principle of non-intervention as conflicting with the furtherance of the exercise of representative democracy.

But United States concern for representative democracy in Latin America is a facet of her anti-communist policy. There has been no serious question of her intervening in the case of the many right-wing military coups, from which, of course, this policy generally has benefited. It is only when her own concept of democracy, closely identified with private, capitalistic enterprise, is threatened by communism that she has felt impelled to demand collective action to defend it. Specifically, her policy is aimed at the Castro government of Cuba, which she accuses of imposing a totalitarian régime upon its people behind the shield of non-intervention. . . .

The Dominican crisis has re-emphasized what the Cuban problem had already demonstrated: that the issue of communism divides rather than unites the members of the inter-American system. The OAS has been quite unable to agree upon a common policy to meet the communist challenge let alone put it into swift operation. The United States has failed to carry her southern neighbours with her on this issue in spite of all the pressures her power and wealth enable her to bring to bear upon them. At the same time her efforts to do so have encouraged reactions in Latin America which make a long-term answer to the communist challenge much more difficult. She has strengthened the military and those groups opposed to changes which she herself has declared are necessary in Latin America, and has yet further alienated more progressive elements upon whose co-operation the long-term answer depends. For even if she desired to do so, it is beyond the power of the United States to maintain anti-communist but unrepresentative governments in Latin America indefinitely.

The Organization of American States can be strengthened only as a body in which Latin American governments are genuinely consulted on the vital issues of the hemisphere and may hope to have influence on the decisions taken. United States efforts to make it a more effective instrument to combat communism will only weaken it; especially if these efforts take the form of unilateral action designed to force the hands of the other members. The immediate future of the inter-American system depends mainly upon what lessons the United States learns from her current Dominican experience. If she is going to treat all revolts against military juntas or other Latin American dictatorships as "wars of liberation" and part of a world-wide communist conspiracy the prospects for the inter-American system are gloomy indeed.

Section IX

The Age of Getúlio Vargas in Brazil (1930–1954)

The seizure of power by Getúlio Vargas in 1930 marked a watershed in Brazilian history. The economic and social changes which characterize the contemporary period of turmoil in Latin America's largest nation began in the second half of the nineteenth century, but the powerful impetus toward modernity came with Vargas. A consummate politician who well understood the needs of his country, Vargas proved to be a very Brazilian kind of dictator who set up no concentration camps for opponents, and who was always referred to familiarly as Getúlio by foe and friend alike. Although unimpressive physically, with no intellectual pretensions, he managed to ride out the storm of Brazilian politics in the turbulent years 1930 to 1945, during which he put Brazil on the continental and world map as never before. He encouraged the nation's push toward industrialization, which in turn stimulated interstate migration, interregional communication and transportation, and the search for domestic instead of transatlantic markets. He aided the university system to develop rapidly, he brought the urban workers into unions and provided them with a measure of social security, and helped to create a politically and culturally throbbing nation. Yet, when the army told him to leave in 1945 he attempted no resistance. Nor did he flee to the comfortable sanctuary of Miami or Switzerland to enjoy the fruits of a bank account prudently built up in advance, as so many Spanish American dictators have done. He stayed in Brazil, campaigned for the senate and won. And in 1950 he made a real comeback by getting himself elected president. His suicide in 1954, not yet fully explained, closed the career of the greatest Brazilian since the nineteenth-century emperor, Pedro II. The careful study of his life and achievements has just begun. Only a tentative assessment is possible today.

Horace B. Davis, a United States sociologist who had taught in São Paulo, described and analyzed the difficult conditions prevailing in the early years of Vargas' rule (Reading IX.1). Karl Loewenstein, an experienced European political scientist and a member of the Amherst College faculty, shrewdly estimated the sources and extent of the dictator's strength (Reading IX.2). Loewenstein believed that he maintained a reasonable objectivity during his study in Brazil, being "neither corrupted by the courtesy of the government in Brazil nor prejudiced by the protestations of the opponents."

The winds of strong and conflicting European political movements blew in Brazil in the late 1930's and early 1940's. Bailey W. Diffie, a City College of New York historian and long-time student of Brazil, explains why the Nazi and Fascist drive for influence in Brazil ultimately failed (Reading IX.3).

The dictator's archives have not yet been made fully open to scholars, though some documents and interpretations are beginning to appear. While awaiting monographs and more complete documentation, some preliminary descriptions of the many complicated events and developments of this remarkable period in Brazilian history are useful for an understanding of the period. John W. F. Dulles of the University of Texas gives a picture of how Vargas won the presidential election of 1950 (Reading IX.4). Dictators of such dimensions and complexity as Juan Perón of Argentina and Vargas invite comparison, and George Pendle, a British specialist in Latin American affairs, successfully attempted this task at the time that Vargas began his final and disastrous experience as president (Reading IX.5).

Corruption and crisis, no new phenomena in Brazilian politics, marked these final years of his rule, as the Brazilian historian José Maria Bello states (Reading IX.6), and the final act is his death in 1954, a dramatic event which shook the nation. The origin and purpose of the suicide note (Reading IX.7) continue to be the subject of controversy.

A. The Early Years

1. Brazil's Political and Economic Condition
When Vargas Seized Power

HORACE B. DAVIS

When the domination of São Paulo in Brazil's affairs was abruptly terminated in 1930 and Getulio Vargas of Rio Grande do Sul was installed as dictator in October of that year, it looked as if a new chapter might open in Brazilian history. American observers were curious to see whether the 1930 "revolution" was merely a case of the "outs" coming "in," or whether the new government would proceed to a fundamental reorganization of governmental practices and of the Brazilian social system. A number of Americans have a practical as well as a theoretical interest in Brazil's internal affairs. Brazil takes between 1 and 2 per cent of the total exports of the United States. American capital invested in Brazil totals over half a billion dollars, and has been increasing rapidly in the post-war period. Brazil, moreover, ships a billion pounds of coffee per year to the United States, which is its best customer.

The group which seized the government in 1930 did not represent a new or different social class. Few of its promises of democratic reform have been fulfilled. The government's attention has been occupied with measures, only partly successful, to stave off the effects of the world economic depression and to weather a series of political crises both within and without the Vargas group.

Brazil is primarily an agricultural country. Most of its products and nearly all of its exports come from its plantations, orchards, and ranches. Over 70 per cent of the occupied males listed in the last federal census (1920) were engaged in agriculture.

Manufacturing has developed rapidly in the fifteen years since the 1920 census was taken. In 1920 the men engaged in industry,

From "Brazil's Political and Economic Problems" by Horace B. Davis, *Foreign Policy Reports*, XI, No. 1 (March 13, 1935), pp. 2–12, *passim*. Reprinted by permission.

mining and transport were 13.8 per cent of the total; the proportion is higher now, but Brazil has no heavy industry. Its light industry exists only by virtue of a protective tariff. The standard of living of the urban proletariat is distinctly lower than in northern Europe; wretched as it is, however, it contrasts favorably with the miserable degradation which characterizes the bulk of the rural population.

The agricultural regions of Brazil are for the most part organized in large tracts (*latifundia*) controlled by a family or a single individual. These big ranchers and planters constitute the old Brazilian aristocracy. Their tenants are for the most part illiterate. Getulio Vargas told the Constituent Assembly in 1933 that "out of 1,000 Brazilians who should properly receive elementary school education, 513 do not enter school, and of the remaining 487, some 110 register but do not come to classes; 178 attend the first year without learning to read well; 85 finish the second year and become superficially literate; 84 go a little further but do not manage to conclude their studies; and barely 30 get the full common elementary instruction, which is of very unequal value and admittedly deficient as to the thoroughness of the teaching, and which usually does not extend over more than three years, with all the pedagogical gaps which characterize the great majority of the schools in the interior." Since those who have opportunities for education outside of school are few, the children of the new generation are growing up only 37.7 per cent "literate." The diet of the rural workers is poor and inadequate, their clothing cheap and scanty, their health appallingly bad. Referring primarily to the rural population, Director of Public Health Bélisario Penna declared not long ago: "Thirty million human beings without any earthly possessions are dying slowly in Brazil from hunger, syphilis and malarial diseases." Brazil's outstanding problem is to rescue these agricultural workers, the mass of the population, from their misery, and furnish them with a decent livelihood — a task which the excellent natural resources of the country render by no means impossible.

Monoculture and Its Effects. Brazil's agricultural system at present retards the development of higher living standards. Monoculture, or concentration on a single money-crop, characterizes the richest agricultural districts. Brazil's most important product is coffee, which constitutes 70 per cent of its exports. Two-thirds of the coffee comes from the state of São Paulo, where whole counties are devoted exclusively to this product. Other zones of monoculture are the sugar zone in Pernambuco, the cacao zone in Bahía, the herva matte

(Paraná tea) zone in Paraná, the banana zone on the coast north and south of Santos, and the rubber zone in the interior of Pará.

Monoculture exhausts the soil and degrades labor. To monoculture is largely attributable the monotonous and unhealthful diet of the rural population. Landlords competing on a world market find it necessary to cut labor costs to a minimum and are confronted by the problem of obtaining and holding on their large estates a sufficient force of workers to harvest the crop. This problem was solved in the early history of the country by slavery, which lasted until 1889. Since then peonage has developed on a large scale.

Monoculture has been favored by foreign interests, which have considered the production of crops saleable on the world market the only adequate safeguard for their loans to Brazilian planters, and the means by which government borrowings might be repaid. Yet monoculture exposes the finances of both planters and government to the effects of uncontrolled and uncontrollable fluctuations in prices.

The economic crisis has focused attention on these defects in Brazil's traditional system. Sir Otto Niemeyer, British banker who headed an advisory mission to Brazil in 1931, strongly advised the country to terminate its exclusive dependence on coffee. The great drop in the price of coffee after 1929 caused many old coffee plantations to be turned over to different forms of agriculture. This "rush to polyculture" was hailed by informed Brazilian opinion as a progressive step.

In São Paulo, especially in the old coffee zone, a class of small farmers had begun to develop. But even there, it is estimated that the *latifundia* (mostly coffee plantations) still make up half of the cultivated area.

Brazil's social system is unstable. Neither the rural workers nor the urban workers, many of whom are class-conscious European emigrants, have any strong interest in maintaining it. The army is proletarian in origin and has not always sided with the ruling class in a crisis. The minor officers in the army, of the rank of lieutenant and below, have a standing grievance in that the higher ranks are in effect reserved to sons of the ruling class. The famous bandit Lampeão (The Lantern), whose roaming bands have for years defied the police from Bahía to Maranhão and have sacked many a large estate, could hardly have maintained himself so long without a considerable measure of popular support, and the phenomenon which he typifies is a kind of inchoate social revolt.

Influence of Foreign Imperialism. Brazil has never ceased to depend on foreign capitalists for new capital and other services. The intervention of foreign capitalists in Brazil's political life has been exercised sometimes directly, through the grant and withdrawal of favors and the consequent exercise of influence on individual politicians; and sometimes indirectly through the diplomatic intervention of foreign governments.

Foreign capitalists are interested in Brazil for five principal reasons: shippers who serve its ports and other middlemen are interested in developing Brazilian trade; importers of goods produced in Brazil are interested in the country as a source of supplies; foreign exporters are interested in Brazil as a market; investors attempt to place capital in remunerative enterprises or safe securities and then endeavor to protect their investments; bankers are interested in the commissions they receive for handling Brazil's financial transactions.

During the nineteenth century Great Britain exercised a preponderant influence on Brazilian affairs, and British influence is still strong. British ships handle nearly twice as much Brazilian tonnage as the ships of any other non-Brazilian nation; 19.2 per cent of Brazil's imports come from Great Britain and 7 per cent of its exports go to that country; British investments in Brazil far overshadow those of the nationals of any other country; and Brazilian federal and state governments usually approach some London banking house first when they wish to float an important loan.

The only two countries which are at all comparable with Great Britain in the importance of their economic relations with Brazil are France and the United States. Until the World War, French capital invested in Brazil nearly equalled British; and France is somewhat more important than Britain as a market for Brazil's exports, although Brazil imports comparatively little from France. A number of Brazilian government loans have been floated in Paris.

Americans have always been great consumers of coffee; per capita consumption is greater only in the Scandinavian countries. The United States is consequently Brazil's best customer; in 1932, 45.8 per cent of all Brazil's exports went to this country. The United States also supplies 30.2 per cent of Brazil's imports, or half as much again as Britain, the nearest competitor for Brazil's trade. The coffee export trade in Brazil is dominated by two or three American firms. Even before the war New York shared with London and Paris the business of floating Brazilian loans, and since 1918 the importance of the United States as a capital market has greatly increased. It is in the field of investment that economic ties between Brazil and the United States have been most strengthened during the last fifteen years. In 1918 investments by United States capitalists in Brazil amounted to barely $50,000,000; by the end of 1930 the total had grown to $557 million. At that time the United States investment in Brazil was probably greater than investment by any other country except Great Britain, and was growing at a more rapid rate than British investment. Italians, Portuguese and Germans have important investments in Brazil. Japanese capitalists, supported by their government, have recently invested heavily in São Paulo state and in Amazonas. Japanese manufacturers are making vigorous efforts to expand their South American markets.

While there are certain areas where American, or alternatively British, French or Japanese, influence is particularly strong, it would be a mistake to speak of "spheres of influence" in Brazil, as for example in China. But struggles between groups of capitalists from different foreign countries have sometimes shaped the course of Brazilian history, and are assuming ever greater proportions.

Brazil's public finance and currency history has been influenced by the country's continued dependence on foreign capital markets. The budgets of the national government and of the states, and even of some of the larger counties, have been chronically unbalanced, and the difference has been made up by a succession of government loans contracted abroad. At the same time the real budgetary position has been concealed by an involved system of government bookkeeping. From time to time internal inflation, both open and concealed, has resulted in a depreciating foreign exchange. Government funds raised internally have come for the most part from the middle and working classes, through a system of indirect taxes. The wealthier classes have largely escaped taxation. Sir Otto Niemeyer recommended that Brazil terminate its dependence on foreign capital, diversify its agriculture, revise its budgetary system, make greater use of the neglected income and inheritance taxes, and emit paper money only through one central bank of issue.

Dependence on foreigners for services in floating loans has proved expensive for Brazil. The foreign bankers have received large commissions. But, further, their practices have on occasion imposed additional burdens on Brazil. For example, early in 1926 the state of São Paulo negotiated a loan of £10,000,000 in Britain. It was arranged that payments on this loan might be received in Brazil, although the holders of the bonds were in England. The British

bankers through whom the loan had been floated — Lazard Brothers
& Co. — foresaw that a transfer problem might arise if foreign exchange should run short, as it did in the fall of 1931. By ingenious
manipulation, they succeeded in shifting to the state government the
burden of transferring to England a large part of the principal and
interest payments. The government had to resort to the illegal or
"black." exchange market, and thereby lost some hundreds of thousands of dollars.

It should be pointed out that, despite the extensive foreign interests in Brazil, much domestic Brazilian capital has also been invested in trade, industry and agriculture. The most important single
financial interest in Brazil is believed to be the Matarazzo chain of
factories, comprising something like eighty-five establishments.

The ruling group in each of the Brazilian states is a coalition of
the large landowners with the upper urban bourgeoisie, supported
sometimes by foreign capitalists. Since there are no large national
parties, the ruling groups in the several states form alliances to
govern Brazil as a whole.

Political Revolts, 1922–1932 — From 1889 to 1930 there had been
no successful revolt against this domination, although the so-called
Copacabana revolt in 1922 and especially the more extended uprising of 1924 were symptomatic of growing unrest. Some troops
which participated in the 1924 uprising continued in opposition to
the government for two years before it was finally forced across the
border and disbanded. This group was headed by Colonel Luiz
Carlos Prestes, and became known as the "Prestes Column." Its program included the breaking up of the large estates, democratization
of the electoral machinery, and opposition to foreign imperialist
rule. It continued in existence as a political force even after its military resistance had ceased.

The "Revolution" of 1930. The uprising of 1930 represented a
revolt against São Paulo's domination of the national government.
Ever since the 1880's, when the great expansion of coffee planting in
São Paulo began, coffee production had perennially tended to outrun
consumption. On three occasions — in 1906, in 1917, and in 1921 —
the government had intervened to acquire surpluses or regulate new
production, or both. The first intervention had been crowned with
success, and the second had proved vastly profitable. Since 1921 the
government has made a continuous effort to regulate coffee production. At first the policy was merely to market the crop evenly, but

it soon became an effort to maintain artificially high prices. In 1929 this program could no longer be continued and the price of coffee dropped from its high point.

The federal presidency was then in the hands of a Paulista, Washington Luis. It had become customary for the presidency to be rotated, no state holding the office for more than one consecutive four-year term. When Washington Luis supported another Paulista, Julio Prestes, for the presidency, politicians from other states took the view that the Paulistas had determined to dip deeply into the federal treasury in order to save again Paulista coffee-growers from threatened bankruptcy. The *Alliança Liberal* was formed for the purpose of forestalling this possibility. The platform of the *Alliança* did not propose the withdrawal of all government support from the coffee industry — coffee was far too important an element in the national economy for such action — but it did include a plank promising "aid to agriculture, not only to coffee." Other planks called for greater independence of the judiciary and democratization of the electoral machinery. The working class was promised social legislation.

The Prestes Column supported the *Alliança Liberal* in the elections of 1930. After the elections, Prestes himself broke with the *Alliança*. He has since joined the Communist party. However, a number of other exiled leaders of the Column — including João Alberto, Miguel Costa, Juarez Tavora and Isidoro Lopez — continued to support the *Alliança,* and returned from exile in order to participate in the military uprising in October 1930. The support lent by these democratic leaders gave to the successful revolt of 1930 the appearance of a semi-popular uprising. The controlling group in the *Alliança* centered around Flores de Cunha, Oswaldo Aranha, General Goes Monteiro and Getulio Vargas, all of Rio Grande do Sul, supported by political leaders in Minas Geraes, Rio de Janeiro and other states.

The São Paulo Revolt of 1932. On first assuming office as dictator, Getulio Vargas offered the task of organizing a government in São Paulo to the Democratic party. This party, founded in São Paulo only a short time before the 1930 revolt by the venerable Antonio Prado, was the official opposition to the *Partido Republicano Paulista* (PRP) which had held the power for many years in both state and nation. The Democratic party declined the assignment and soon after disappeared. Vargas then turned to the leaders of the Prestes Column. But these, after eighteen turbulent months, proved unable to reconcile the conflicting interests in the state. On June 9, 1932 an insurgent movement enlisted the support even of the federal interventor, and the whole of the state of São Paulo, together with parts of the neighboring states of Minas Geraes and Matto Grosso, fell immediately into the hands of the rebels.

The underlying causes of this revolt were economic. They may be summarized as follows:

1. The Paulistas hoped to have the federal government and the other states carry a larger share of the burden involved in the coffee control program.

2. The coffee growers of São Paulo sought greater assistance in the crisis from the Bank of Brazil which, they pointed out, was granting credits to the cattle-raisers of Rio Grande do Sul.

3. The manufacturers of São Paulo feared a return of lower protective duties.

4. The São Paulo state government depended largely on the coffee export tax. Paulistas feared that the federal government would assume the right to tax exports.

5. The powerful and influential British interests in São Paulo feared the growing rapprochement between the Vargas government and the United States of America. They pointed to the conversations held at a crucial period of the 1930 revolt between Paul V. McKee, president of the American-controlled *Emprezas Electricas Brasileiras,* and leaders of the *Alliança Liberal,* and demanded to know what favors were to be granted American concessionaires.

The Paulista leaders were almost certainly misled as to the amount of support they could expect from the other states. In Rio Grande do Sul, Flores da Cunha had just gone into opposition to the Vargas government. Vargas made his peace with Flores da Cunha, however, and the only help the Paulista constitutionalists received from their *gaucho* allies was an expression of good-will.

Fifty to sixty thousand men were in arms in São Paulo, and about as many took the field for the federal government. The civil war which ensued was the most extensive, though not the longest, that the country had ever known. The casualties, dead and wounded, have been estimated at 15,000.

The Paulistas had inadequate access to modern implements of warfare. They did succeed in obtaining ten Curtiss-Wright airplanes, which reached them from Chile by way of Paraguay, but the machines arrived too late to influence the outcome. Hostilities ended on September 29, 1932. The Paulista defeat was due, according to one of their officers, to "absolute lack of artillery and aviation, as well as a deficiency of automatic arms."

By the peace terms, the Vargas government permitted the leaders of the revolt to leave for Europe, agreed to grant São Paulo greater independence in its own affairs, and promised to reconsider the coffee question. It even underwrote the expenses of the revolt by guaranteeing the 400,000 contos of bonds which the state government had issued — this in spite of the fact that the federal government was engaged in an unsuccessful effort to balance its own budget. Such generosity surprised even the Paulistas. Finally, the Vargas government set about at once to summon a constituent assembly.

It is sometimes said that the leaders of the São Paulo revolt of 1932 desired complete independence from the rest of Brazil, which would have meant independence also for other states and the disappearance of Brazil as a nation. This opinion is contradicted both by all public utterances of the responsible leaders and by the logic of the situation. Most of the inflammatory propaganda against the federal government which circulated during and after the 1932 movement advocated confederation. Separation has been favored by only a few of the minor leaders.

2. Brazil Made Tremendous Advances

KARL LOEWENSTEIN

Change of Profile — Perhaps one way to evaluate the impact of the Vargas regime on the Brazilian people is the dialectic process; that is, to compare the general profile of the country as it presents itself now, with what it was before the regime took over. All observers — those actuated by hostility to the Vargas government no less than its supporters — are unanimously agreed that Brazil since 1930 has made tremendous strides forward. Shedding its nineteenth-century attire the country became modernized — as some old-timers say ruefully — beyond recognition. Under the onslaught of pick and shovel much of the "Austrian" charm has fallen a victim of stream-

lining. Rio's delightful feudal mansions and aristocratic gardens are
rapidly giving way to pretentious skyscrapers and hyper-modern
apartment houses. The old-world atmosphere of the streets and
squares will be lost in a few years. Regulations for the protection
of artistically valuable national patrimony exist, but they are no
match for the soaring prices of real estate. Downtown Rio will soon
be as dully monumentalized as the business districts of our newer
cities. São Paulo, busily sacrificing old quarters for wide new
boulevards, vast park developments, and bold bridges swinging over
the asphalt canyons, is in the throes of a large-scale transformation,
outdoing Chicago. The building boom in Brazil, more often than not
on a brittle financial basis, spreads to the remote sections of the
land. To many it appears as a heavy mortgage on a high-living
standard which is not attainable in the near future. Town planning
has become almost an obsession. But judged by Belo Horizonte,
which succeeded Ouro Preto in 1891 as the capital of Minas Geraes,
the Brazilians know the business of modernizing their cities. It was
planned on the blueprint to the last stone and the last tree before
the first stone was set and the first tree was planted. It is one of the
most fortunate examples of rational urbanization.

Economic Factors — Such outward changes, striking as they are,
may mean very little. They may not even be symptomatic. Moreover, to credit them exclusively to the regime is probably more than
unfair to the past. Nor can economic progress in general since 1930
be ascribed to the policies of the Vargas regime alone. Similarly, as
the technical capacity of the Hitler machine is indebted to a large
extent to the groundwork laid by the republic which overhauled
Germany's industrial equipment, in many respects the Vargas regime
has harvested what has been sown economically by the liberal era.
Industrialization was bound to come to a country which scarcely
one generation ago had begun to emerge from semifeudalism
grounded in agriculture and slave work, once it had become conscious of the riches of its land and the abundance in subsoil wealth
and minerals. Vargas rode into power on the crest of the depression
wave of 1929–1930 which had depleted the purchasing and consuming power of Brazil's European market. Nonetheless imports of
finished goods soared in inordinate proportion as compared with
the export of raw materials. Brazil was compelled to bridge the gap
in its balance of trade by increasing the purchasing power of the
masses at home as well as by building up its own industrial capacity.

Here lie the intrinsic reasons for the rapid industrialization of a heretofore mainly agricultural economy. Factories were created mainly in São Paulo, in the Federal District and in Rio Grande do Sul for manufacturing consumption goods otherwise imported from Europe. With British trade declining and the American imports restricted to capital goods and high-class specialties, Brazil's economy became for some time hooked to that of Nazi Germany. Since Hitler's economists twisted the bartering noose around his neck at will, the Brazilian merchant and businessman was none too happy about the rapidly rising figures of exports to and imports from Germany.

The second push forward to a better integrated economic equilibrium between agriculture and industry came with the second World War when European trade was sharply reduced by the British blockade and the lack of shipping room. We in the United States began to realize that the Good Neighbor Policy is reciprocal. Brazil turned to the United States for goods no longer obtainable from Europe, with some reluctance because American business methods are less elastic than those of the German, Italian, Czech, and Swiss manufacturer and less adapted to the individualized tastes of the Brazilian bourgeois classes. By 1941 the United States had forged ahead to the first place (about 60 per cent) of Brazilian imports and exports. Simultaneously the industrialization drive was intensified, this time, however, with more Brazilian than foreign capital, and it began to extend also to the production of capital goods. During 1941 the establishment of a steel industry on a vast scale got under way, centered on the largest single high-grade iron ore deposit in the world, the Itabira "mountain" in Minas Geraes. . . .

Whatever may be the merits of the Vargas government in promoting national economic life — and at times the policies adopted amounted to a rough handling of the foreign creditors — the facts and figures imply that Brazil has moved into the position of the ranking economic power south of the Rio Grande and that it is about to pass Argentina, in the past South America's recognized political and economic leader. In the last decade Brazilian mineral production has increased at least eight times even without considering the potentialities of the Itabira development. The industrial capacity has tripled, the textile output has risen threefold. The value of industrial production surpasses that of agriculture by 20 per cent and thus another predominantly agrarian country is being converted into an industrialized economy. Agriculture — although at present not more than 3 per cent of the arable land is cultivated — gives the world's largest supply of coffee, the second largest crop of cocoa, the third largest crop of corn; Brazil is fifth in cotton and in sugar, seventh in meat, and ninth in rice; and all this, if one believes the experts, is only the beginning. For a protracted war Brazilian mineral and agricultural resources may become invaluable to the United Nations; while these same riches, in addition to Brazil's strategical position, might tempt the Axis to invasion and conquest.

The Attitude of the Various Social Classes toward the Regime — A detailed description of the economic situation under the regime is beyond the scope of this study. The preceding remarks — based rather upon a field of observation than upon the strength of statistics (government-made statistics anyway) — are to serve only as the background for attempting to present this writer's impression as to how the various social classes react toward the regime. After all, it is the attitude of the people who live under a political society their contentedness or dissatisfaction, which establishes the record and, in the long run, decides the fate of a government. No objective device to measure the happiness of the people exists. What conclusions are submitted here are at best reasoned generalizations.

The regime has pursued successfully two seemingly conflicting or overlapping policies. One is the vigorous encouragement of national capitalization and the promotion of national enterprises, unfettered by state regimentation. The other is the fortunate co-ordination of the free play of private capitalism, with a progressive paternalism in social policies for the benefit of the laboring classes. To present these achievements in a nutshell: the economically most important groups, capital and labor, are, on the whole, satisfied with the existing social and political order; they are not desirous of any fundamental change. This is no mean accomplishment of a government in this period of violent social transformation.

The Regime and the Wealthy: The Businessman and the Entrepreneur — During its first years the Vargas regime was inclined to steer a more anticapitalistic course; but soon the wise policy was adopted of leaving business alone and not harassing it with nationalization or collectivization schemes. The hands-off attitude contributed to reconciling the economically most potent state of São Paulo to the regime more than might have been expected after the bitterness left by the defeat of 1932. Vargas himself is said to understand little of economics and personally he is not committed to any specific economic doctrine. What the well-oiled editorials of some papers write about a "directed economy" is ideological window dressing. The businessman can work in peace. The government does what capital and business — not altogether identical because of wealth derived from landed property — want it to do, provided the policies do not run counter to that other prominent trend of the regime, solicitude for the laboring masses. In spite of much speculation about eventual "nationalization" relatively little large-scale experimentation in government ownership of national resources or their utilization by the government has materialized to date. There is also much less talk about "corporativism" than is habitual in other authoritarian states which use "corporative" ideologies as soporifics for the discarded political rights of the people. The manifold boards, councils, committees, commissions can scarcely be considered as significant demonstrations of an incipient corporative trend in economic life; their functions are mainly advisory and only to a small extent regulatory. The Brazilians are realists who do not believe in the mirage of state capitalism camouflaged as corporativism. Brazil under Vargas is one of the few lands remaining on the globe where a genuinely liberal climate of economic life prevails. The profit margin in both industrial and agricultural production is relatively large, partly because of the still very cheap living conditions, partly because of the deterioration of the currency which began with the National Revolution and showed no sign of abatement until very recently. Businessmen like to complain about the costs of the social services, which amount to about 10 per cent of the annual employees wage sheet. But evidently they are bearable because of the profits in exports derived from the currency depreciation and because of the slowly rising purchasing power of the masses of consumers at home. The other complaint frequently ventilated in no uncertain terms refers to the appalling amount of bureaucratization and government control — "fiscalization" — through which a greedy state squeezes money from various and sundry victims. But the Administrative State whose advent in Brazil is so loudly heralded sails in the wake of an inflation in government personnel. The hordes of technically superfluous petty officials are a sort of substitute for the lacking government party; the more people the government keeps on its pay roll the more have a stake in the perpetuation of the existing political and social order.

Traditionally, the wealthy class of Brazil derives its income from agricultural sources. There are still huge *latifundia*, not unlike semifeudal duchies in size and administration; particularly in the less opened spaces of the vast country the owner of the *fazenda* is a political as well as a social and economic power. But the coffee and cotton aristocracy invested their profits in industry, and the men successful in business — the Crespi, Mattarazzo, Guinle, Simonsen — control today large tracts of land managed on a rationalized basis like industrial enterprises. The old landed nobility and the new aristocracy of entrepreneurs have merged. In spite of the battering which landed wealth took in a predominantly one-crop economy, the landowners still form a disproportionately large group in the governing class; and they see to it that the regime abstains from taxing away the foundations of their power as has happened in Britain. They are part and parcel of the regime; Vargas has nothing to fear from them.

By economic liberalism prevailing within, Brazil benefits also foreign capital. But foreign business is not favored by the government. Under the nationalization drive its position has become more and more precarious. Economic nationalism under the slogan "Brazil for the Brazilians" is very popular among all classes. But for the time being it is tempered by political expediency because Brazil still needs foreign capital and foreign technical experience. The resentment is directed mainly against British capital — unjustified as these complaints about British economic dominance are, because the British helped greatly to develop the country and, on the whole, did not draw inordinately high returns from their enterprise and investment. Today it is American capital which flows freely into Brazil in the form of official and private loans. The interdependence of Brazilian and American economic interests will prevent, at least as long as we are copartners against the Axis, an intensification of the nationalization efforts. Had war not come, the restriction of foreign economic activity might, in the end, not be distinguishable from outright expropriation.

The Regime and the Masses: Labor and Farmer

The Urgency of Social Reform. As a rule it is none too difficult for an authoritarian regime to find support among the well-to-do classes by protecting their vested property rights. Mussolini, Franco, and even Hitler in his early years of rule are cases in point. A much more arduous task is that of winning the sympathy of the nameless masses of the toilers in the workshops and on the farms. For this reason all modern dictators enter the stage as the friends of the forgotten man, as the protector of the underdog. Perhaps the most striking feature of present-day Brazil — and one that is universally admitted — is that Vargas personally and the regime in general are extremely popular among the laboring masses. Vargas has won the soul of the common man. Himself stemming politically from the liberal left and not belonging to the old ruling class, he succeeded in squaring the circle by keeping the wealthy in good humor and improving the lot of the poor. He accomplished this task not by *circenses* alone; the Brazilians are too realistic and he is far from being a spectacular showman. He offered them *panis*. Already in the early thirties a vast program of social reform was inaugurated; it was carried on, without the impediments of a bourgeois-minded parliament, after the inception of the *Estado Novo*. Responsible observers doubt whether Brazil, having scarcely emerged from a semifeudal economy, is ripe for the advanced social services which are uniformly superimposed upon an unevenly developed economic structure. The labor standards proclaimed by the regime are decidedly too high for the actual social level of the laboring masses. For the time being the garment of social paternalism is much too wide for the undersized body economic. Frequently, progressive social policies and economic liberalism seem incongruous. Be that as it may Vargas, by anticipating a situation in which private capitalism would have to yield to increasing pressure from the masses, took the wind out of the sails of a potential Communist movement and forestalled an eventual social revolution.

The trend toward social — or, some observers say, socialistic — reform is in line with what one observer aptly describes as "an easy receptivity on the part of law students who represent the majority of the governing class of the country, for all modern laws observed in more advanced world centers." One may add that such an ambitious eclecticism, emanating from the reform-minded ministerial bureaucracy, is discernible also in other fields of governmental activities, with a resultant cleavage between the professed aims of official policy and their inadequate realization in daily life. Any casual visitor who, strolling away from the marble hotels, casinos, glittering show windows and race courses, chances into the appalling quarters of the poor on the hills in Rio de Janeiro or into the slums of São Paulo, will encounter such misery that not even the tropical sun can romanticize it for him, let alone for the people who have to live in tin-can shacks and mud hovels. Living conditions in the interior are so primitive that the foreigner, with the glamor of the sophisticated residential sections of the big cities on the sea-shore still before his eyes, is prone to saddle the governing class of the present no less than of the past regimes with the gross neglect of the masses of a fine and decent people. In the rural districts shoes are commonly not available for the families of the agricultural laborer; clothes are of the cheapest cotton; dirt floors in the roughly made houses, nonexistent sanitary commodities, the scantiest and poorest furniture (if it is more than some pots and pans, wooden dishes, and a few pieces of miserable bedding), demonstrate that the most advanced social legislation, enacted in the faraway capital by well-meaning officials, is utterly unable to raise the living standard of the poor. Brazil is about to embark on a drugstore civilization. What is needed, however, is one which is firmly grounded in the little red schoolhouse. . . .

Those Who Are Discontented. A generalizing statement on the adhesion of the people to the regime is at best hazardous. Yet presumptuous as it may be on the part of a foreigner whose personal knowledge and powers of observation are necessarily limited, he cannot but come to the conclusion that the bulk of the people are in favor of the regime. Perhaps by way of a modification one may say that obviously no class as a whole is basically averse to it. Most of all the common people feel little if any political pressure. They live on as before, their personal life is affected by the government only in that they have a little more money to earn and to spend, that somewhat better opportunities for educating their children exist, that they partake of tangible social advances. That Brazil under Vargas does not live up to the postulate of government by the people does not cause them deep grief. During the liberal era his participation in politics through the polls and otherwise, meager as it was, did not help much the man in the street personally. Now he is told to keep out of politics and he does not seem to miss them. Support of the regime is wholly unemotional; its existence, achievements, and failures are accepted as a matter of fact and with a good deal of common sense. There is no state mysticism as in Germany or in the early days of Fascism in Italy. Nor can it be said that, considering the general climate of optimism which prevails anyway in Brazil, the regime has noticeably galvanized the mind and soul of its people. Fanaticism does not go well with Brazilian irony and tolerance. To sum up: the regime rests on a broad, a very broad basis of popular acceptance, perhaps as broad as in most democracies where the opposition is bitter against the group in power for the sake of opposition. Brazil under Vargas is indeed Vargas's Brazil.

Yet there is ample evidence of dissatisfaction, of unspecified grumbling as well as of very definite complaints. There is no use denying that a political malaise is widespread among many intellectuals and in the bourgeois layers. Exception is taken to specific measures of the regime and to its atmosphere in general. Such complaints when vented by businessmen refer to the overbureaucratization and to certain economic policies; others rail against nepotism, current inefficiency, and venality of government personnel. Discontent is most outspoken in São Paulo, traditional stronghold of liberal constitutionalism, but it is encountered also in Minas Geraes and notably in the south. In general the popularity of the regime decreases in proportion to the distance from the capital. Dissatisfaction with general political conditions is latent even among otherwise loyal officials and members of the governing class. In fact most of them are at heart liberal and democratic. An authoritarian regime which disdains rigid regimentation of public opinion leaves room for dialectics. The terms "disciplined democracy" and "Administrative State" so much in use by official propaganda, are a dialectic camouflage of the profoundly liberal current underneath. The nostalgic desire for the return to genuinely democratic forms of government persists. This applies to internal as well as to foreign policy. Deeply affected by the fall of France, the intellectuals and the bourgeoisie were unswervingly faithful to the cause of the Democracies, even in the dark days of one-sided neutrality in 1940 and 1941 when the pro-Axis wing of the government strove hard to line up Brazil with the Axis.

What the liberals complain of is that they cannot partake in their government except on conditions set by the regime. They resent the self-ordained infallibility of the governing group whose shortcomings are a public secret. They object to being barred from their legitimate share in the responsibility if not in the spoils. To many independent minds even a benevolent dictatorship is a *capitis diminutio,* undignified for a country so proud of its unbroken tradition of constitutionalism in the past. As one informant, a prominent man in the service of the regime and thoroughly loyal to it, phrased it neatly, "We have won order and tranquillity but we have lost liberty." Few are those who, by changing the sequence of values in this phrase, prefer the former to the latter. What weighs heavily on the minds of the responsible people is the unpredictability of a political order not firmly grounded in the rule of law. The oblique notion of the "interest of the state" as interpreted by an irresponsible bureaucracy casts its dark shadow over the entire realm of the "Administrative State." For a liberal lawyer — and Brazil is sociologically a lawyer's land as our civilization is typified by the businessman — the manner in which the regime deals with the courts and molds the law in accordance with political expediency is frankly exasperating. All this does not imply hostility let alone active opposition to the regime. But it contributes to the climate of political uneasiness which one cannot fail to encounter once the thin veneer of "All quiet on the internal front" has been rubbed off. Perhaps Oswaldo Aranha — himself a *ci-devant* liberal and a genuine democrat — gave an apt estimate of the situation to this writer when he declared that nations today are confronted by the choice between liberty and equality, and that the regime has chosen equality. Equality the regime has successfully striven to achieve. Among the Brazilians personality and human values count for more than money or social distinction, and the regime has given a chance of collaboration to everybody who is willing to do so. To a foreigner this sounds rather cryptic considering that Brazil is after all still an oligarchy though one rooted in a solidly democratic foundation. The gist of it is that the dictatorship cannot obliterate liberal tradition. In view of a future world order it is comforting to know that a nation which in the past has enjoyed liberal constitutionalism will not easily forget it. . . .

Portrait of a Leader. It may sound a truism, but the greatest asset of the regime is Getulio Vargas himself. The decisive impression the foreign visitor gains in Brazil is how unequivocally well-disposed the Brazilians in all layers of the population are toward the man who Atlaslike carries the regime on his shoulders. As in most South American states, the dictatorship is personalistic in character. In that, it is altogether different from the European totalitarian pattern. No government party protects it, no coercive ideology supports it. The regime rests on no visible props, except the army; it is based on the popularity of one man alone.

It is true that the armed forces helped him into the saddle. Nor could he hold power without their continued support. Brazil is a Latin-American state in which *pronunciamentos* and military juntas flourish. He did all in his power to keep the army and navy leaders in good humor, by increased salaries for the officers and men, by heaping prestige on the military establishment, and by acceding to the political influence it was able to exact. Much more than in other South American states the Brazilian army is a separate caste, not dissimilar to the position of the military in France. It is a sort of professional nobility which jealously guards its privileged position and does not easily brook interference even by the powerful head of the government. Frequently enough the generals took matters into their own hands, at times forcing his hand. But after what probably was the most difficult task of his career, Vargas overcame the political ascendancy of the armed forces. When he appointed, in January, 1941, a civilian, J. P. Salgado Filho, to head the newly established Ministry of Air, it was the symbol of the victory of civilian government over the military caste. But the armed forces are anything but democratic. They are certainly ardent patriots — at least many of them; but military success holds an understandable spell for them and military successes of the Axis close to Brazil might well spell Vargas's doom. When, at the Rio de Janeiro Conference, he cast Brazil's lot with the United Nations, it was a leap in the dark. Nobody can foretell what the hidden totalitarians among the generals will do in case of a successful landing of the Axis on Brazilian soil; it is perhaps better not to harbor too many illusions about the loyalty of some of the Brazilian leaders to the cause of democracy, who may pay lip service now but do not feel the beat of the heart for it.

On Vargas's personal vocation as a leader not a single dissenting voice can be heard. Knowing Latin-American habits one need not make much of the fact that everybody calls him by his first name. The members of the opposition no less than the horde on the bandwagon praise his quickly grasping intelligence, his common sense in evaluating realities, his administrative ability — he is a hard working bureaucrat with extremely methodical organizing habits. They admire his silent tenacity, his devotion to and knowledge of administrative technique; for these are rare qualities among modern statesmen, and in no wise conform to the melodramatic pattern of the present-day dictator. It was the great Swiss prophet of the coming cataclysm, Jakob Burckhardt, who predicted two generations ago the age of the *"simplificateurs terribles."* Vargas is not one of them: his formulas are no emotional simplification and he realizes that visionary speculation never can supplant the honest devotion to administrative routine. That he is the shrewdest of politicians, with a

Machiavellian touch, goes without saying. It is the heritage of his Latin descent and environment. His favorite technique consists in quietly letting conflicting opinions come to a deadlock and then solving it by an unchallengeable decision. He is an opportunist, equally remote from preconceived doctrinairism and from nebulous political ideologies. The regime has no theory except that of eclectic realism. This explains sufficiently why some interviewers — with whom this writer does not agree — call him enigmatic; an opportunist does not readily commit himself.

Vargas does not evoke strong emotional responses in his people. He has little mystical appeal or _"charisma."_ He has given ample proof of cold-blooded personal courage. But Vargas and the Brazilian people do not lend themselves to heroworship. Vargas is neither a vegetarian mystic with voices nor a cynical _braggadocio_ with vices; he is a bourgeois person with bourgeois tastes and some very human failings which are no secret to many people. The personalist dictatorship in South America has few if any irrational ingredients. As is customary in authoritarian states he has been made an object of lionization by the official propaganda. It is not known whether he enjoys it much; at least he does not show it and it evidently has not gone to his head. But adulation has its definite limits. He refrains from posing as a superman. For the man on horseback he has scarcely the stature. He knows the intellectual irony of his Brazilians and especially the sharp tongues of the _Cariocans_ too well to allow the propaganda machine to play up his personality into something mystical or heroic. He knows that ridicule has killed many a man.

Vargas's living habits are inoffensive and conform to bourgeois standards. He is a good father of his family; he likes horseback riding and golf, he is fanatically devoted to everything which has to do with airplanes. He has no spectacular literary or artistic tastes, which is fortunate for the intellectual life of Brazil. Of his cultural propensities nothing is known from which the inference can be drawn that they are at best average. He has a sense of humor — a rare quality among dictators — and he knows a good joke when he hears it, even one which victimizes him. He shares intellectual irony with his people.

There is another point which those knowing the atmosphere in European dictatorships cannot fail to notice. Perhaps it is too much to say that Vargas has no personal enemies. No man at the helm of the state can avoid making enemies. But there are not many who either fear or hate him. It is inconceivable that he should evoke that devouring hatred and that abject fear which European dictators instil into opponents or into their subjects. Many times he has shown his tolerance and a complete absence of political vindictiveness. His popularity today — as he has sided with public opinion against the Axis and with the United Nations — is perhaps greater than at any time in his career. This is no mean achievement for a man who has wielded power for more than a decade with practically no constitutional limitations. For once power has not corrupted a man.

With reference to Napoleon it has been said that the essential qualities of the great statesman are idealism and moderation. Vargas certainly has moderation, but he seems devoid of idealism. If idealism is equivalent to vision some concepts of the future of his country may underlie the rank opportunism of his conduct of government. However later historians may judge him as a statesman, one thing can already be stated with certainty after more than ten years of uncontested rule: in the history of Brazil he can claim a rank next to Dom Pedro. No higher praise can be bestowed on a Brazilian.

3. Foreign Influences at the Outbreak of World War II

BAILEY W. DIFFIE

During the years 1933–39 much was said and written about foreign dangers to Brazil. Solemn and ofttimes vivid warnings tended to awaken in the people of the United States a feeling of possible peril to themselves and to their neighbors from foreign penetration in the Americas. It is difficult to evaluate these warnings accurately in view of the fact that an indeterminate portion was instigated by propaganda groups at the service of special interests. While one school of thought in the United States foresaw a dark future for Brazil, another minimized the foreign danger on the grounds that it was deliberately exaggerated. The latter maintained that the Germans emphasized the threats to the American nations inherent in communism and democracy, while in the United States the danger from Nazism and Fascism was accentuated out of proportion to the

From "Some Foreign Influences in Contemporary Brazilian Politics" by Bailey W. Diffie, *Hispanic American Historical Review*, XX, August 1940, pp. 402–429, *passim*. Reprinted by permission.

real strength of these two movements. The over-accentuation was true particularly of that group which, under Russian inspiration, hailed itself as the defender of democracy. That this view might be well taken was demonstrated by the fact that the signing of the non-aggression pact between Germany and Russia in August, 1939, silenced the anti-Nazi, anti-Fascist propaganda of the Communist group. The school of belittlers thus shrugged off the question of foreign danger.

The problem is not quite so simple however. Whatever the causes, many of the American nations did become alarmed over foreign penetration. The object of the present article is to examine the situation in Brazil. Since quite obviously it would be impossible here to study all foreign influences in Brazil, this discussion is limited to those nations whence immigration into Brazil occurred in sufficient numbers to create a body of nationals significant in proportion to the total population.

More than 4,600,000 immigrants entered Brazil between 1820 and 1937 inclusive. Of these, 880,000 entered before 1890, and 3,722,000 from 1890 through 1937. The chief contributors to this immigration were:

Italy	1,502,958	(32.6 per cent of the total)
Portugal	1,394,156	(30.3 " " " " ")
Spain	595,022	(12.9 " " " " ")
Germany	222,951	(4.9 " " " " ")
Japan	180,359	(3.9 " " " " ")

It is difficult to determine the proportion to the total population of the elements descended from the main body of immigrants listed above. With the total population of Brazil placed at approximately 42,000,000 in 1939, the following figures are as near an accurate estimate as it is possible to get at the present time:

Of unmixed Portuguese descent	5,000,000
Of Italian or half Italian descent	3,500,000
Of German or half German descent	900,000
Of Spanish, Slavic, Turkish, Syrian, etc., descent	2,600,000
Of Japanese descent	300,000
Total	12,300,000

Eliminating the Portuguese, we have 7,300,000 people of foreign descent, an element amounting to approximately one fifth of the total population. Moreover, a large proportion of this element is concentrated in the southern part of Brazil, in the states of Rio de Janeiro, Minas Gerais, São Paulo, Paraná, Santa Catarina, and Rio Grande do Sul, where the total population is approximately half that of the entire nation. In this area, therefore, those of foreign descent constituted about one third of the population. The proportion was even greater in São Paulo and the three southern states which had received the brunt of the immigrants. The tendency of the Brazilian population to shift to the south made the concentration of the non-Portuguese element still more significant. The following table of regional population percentages shows this:

Region	1872 %	1890 %	1920 %
Extreme North	3.3	3.3	4.7
Northeast	46.5	41.9	36.7
South	48.0	52.6	56.1
Center (Goyaz and Mato Grosso)	2.2	2.2	2.5

As used here "South" means Espírito Santo, Rio de Janeiro, Minas Gerais, São Paulo, and the southern states.

Brazil welcomed the immigrant. She was proud of her immense unoccupied spaces and wished to fill them with people. Brazilians admired the hard-working newcomer and lavished praise on the industrious Germans, Italians, Poles, and Japanese. High hopes were entertained that Brazil was to eclipse the United States as a refuge for downtrodden mankind. . . .

Brazil had one of the requisites most important for such a paradise of ethnic fusion, almost complete freedom from racial prejudice. The color of the skin was not a factor in Brazil. As Alfredo Ellis, a Brazilian descended from those Southerners who fled the South after the Civil War, remarked: "We [Brazilians] never had, like the North Americans, this tortuous tendency for racial antagonism and hundred per centism." . . .

Despite such olympian conceptions of a super melting pot, Brazil had difficulties with her immigrants and had not yet found the alchemical formula to transform the base metal of human fiber into the twenty-four carat *homo sapiens*. Time had not been able to wipe out entirely the biological boundaries that separated the Mongoloid from the Negroid, nor these from the Caucasian. In addition, Brazil was beset with comparatively minor differences that separated the Luso-Brazilians from those whose forbears came from Italy, Germany, or elsewhere. . . .

Whether the failure of Brazil to assimilate the immigrants constituted a political danger, is a question that cannot be answered
without examination of such conditioning factors as the political
machinery, the influence that could be exerted by foreign powers,
industrialization, and the Brazilian armed forces.

The outlines of the political system are well known. Brazil has
had no national political parties. Instead she has had state parties
dominated by rival *chefes*, or *coroneis*. As Pedro Calmon pointed
out, these coroneis were a revised version of the *capitães-móres* of
colonial times; they were still "latifundarios," which made them "as
much feudal lords as the *donatarios* of olden times." Their function
was to win elections, and their strength was decisive in political
matters. In 1843 the Minister Araujo Viana remarked that "it is
accepted unquestionably that when the local electoral boards are
named, the representatives of the nation have already been elected."
Changes occurred after 1843, of course, but the political chefe remained important. Significant to our discussion is the fact that the
political chefes were on the whole members of the old Luso-
Brazilian stock. This system made it very difficult for the immigrant
to become a power in politics without first becoming a chefe. Although some did achieve this position, on the whole only a small
percentage of those of non-Lusitanian origin gained key places in
Brazil's political life before becoming thoroughly Brazilianized. . . .

The political danger to Brazil lay in the weakness, indifference,
and self-interest of those who ruled. While the old parliamentarian-
ism persisted with its contempt for the masses, its electoral corruption, its rule of the oligarchs, its occasional resort to violence for the
attainment of power, the extremists of the left and right appealed
directly to the people, who were unprepared to choose wisely. A
situation resulted wherein it might be possible for a determined
minority to seize power. Brazilians apparently accepted the concept
of government by the élite, rather than government by the people.
Moreover, to many the idea of force was not entirely unwelcome.
Thus was created a situation which was in many ways favorable to
Fascism. . . .

If the old political oligarchy should lose its power suddenly, however, the most likely heir to its position would be the army, still
predominantly Luso-Brazilian in its officer staff. Officers formed a
privileged class. They considered themselves a nobility. In order to
protect their position they participated in politics. The army was
perhaps the chief support of the Vargas regime. It is no exaggeration

to say that in the eyes of the officers the nation was the servant of the armed forces. Again it is important to note that the officers were drawn almost exclusively from the upper-class Luso-Brazilians. The entrance of immigrants into this group may not have been impossible, but it was, to say the least, difficult. And while it was true that many officers had shown themselves sympathetic to Fascism and Nazism, the proportion was not alarming by 1939. Army dominance was a guarantee that foreigners could participate in politics only to a limited extent.

Let us now see how the foreign elements listed at the beginning of this study might under the conditions just specified constitute important sources of danger.

Italy, Portugal, Spain, Germany, and Japan furnished about eighty-five per cent of the immigrants entering Brazil between 1820 and 1937. Immigrants came also from Syria, Yugoslavia, England, Lithuania, Rumania, France, Poland, Turkey, Austria, Russia, and other nations, but I have found no evidence to indicate that Brazil considered them as political problems. While their cultural assimilation was by no means complete in all cases, their political influence, if any, was not of a nature to cause alarm. Moreover of the five principal foreign elements neither the Portuguese nor the Spanish constituted a problem. The former caused trouble in the period following independence but by 1939 their assimilation was so thorough and so rapid that they were practically native Brazilians. The Spanish had likewise been assimilated rapidly. The Japanese, Italians, and Germans, however, have given rise to misgivings.

Japanese immigration began in 1908; before 1938 about 180,000 had entered the country. The attitude of the Brazilians toward the Japanese varied greatly from time to time. A great deal depended on whether the Japanese immigrant was considered as the advance guard of an army out to rule the world, or as excess population which Japan was glad to ship from her overcrowded shores. . . .

The Japanese invasion of Manchuria in 1931 and the attack on China in 1937 affected the Brazilian attitude toward Japanese immigration. In the Constitutional Convention of 1934, Xavier de Oliveira, advocating a ban on the Japanese, received strong support. His speeches, published in book form in 1937, helped create a Japanese alarm of the first order. . . .

The Italians were the most numerous of all the immigrants. Approximately one third of all who entered after 1820 came from Italy. About thirty-eight per cent of the people of the state of São Paulo in 1939 were of Italian origin. Little alarm was felt concerning them until after 1922. The Italians were considered the best example of the fusibility of the immigrant. Alfredo Ellis in his study of the people of São Paulo had little but praise for them. "Everywhere," he noted, "one sees children of the Italians perfectly assimilated. . . . Even in our legislative bodies . . . there are descendants of Italians in perfect homogeneous mixture with 'hundred per cent' Paulistas, sharing the spirit of São Paulo in a harmony and unanimity that is truly impressive." . . .

This was true of the pre-war immigration. Of the post-war immigration Ellis remarked:

Those of today are the exact antithesis. . . . They have their national mentality now strongly rigid. . . . They form a circle around the old Italians who are enriched and incompletely assimilated, and they make of the consulate something of a central sun of Italianism, from which they attempt to radiate the propaganda enjoined on them by the bombastic speeches of Mussolini. These are deep-dyed Italians and are the least stable of the foreigners who come to us. They are unassimilable. No love retains them here, no single tie binds them to us. It is an element that is even undesirable and pernicious because it attempts to arouse the extinct spirit of Italianism in the old Italian group, retarding the assimilation of latest arrivals who are not deeply impregnated with the spirit of São Paulo. These people came late, however. The true wave of Italian immigration is already ours.

Pandiá Calogeras in 1926 warned of what the consequences might be if Italy tried to exert political influence in Brazil.

To act in a way that might disturb [the existing] atmosphere would be the gravest error that could be committed. And this is what would happen if Fascism should consider applying in foreign countries the processes in force in the motherland. And still more if, with the vain intent of maintaining alive and cohesive the national feeling on a foreign soil . . . [Fascism] should attempt to perform acts of sovereignty.

There is considerable evidence to indicate that Italy did not heed this warning by Calogeras. The Italian minister, Grandi, informed the Italian Parliament in 1927 that "the Italian colonies in foreign countries should be small fatherlands, and the person designated to represent the sovereignty should, in this sense, carry out his part faithfully. The former 'Commissariat of Emigration' is transformed into a 'Directory of Italians in Foreign Countries.' Emigration has become a political function." . . .

In line with this policy, the embassy and consulates of Italy in

Brazil were made Fascist propaganda and organization centers. At the time Calogeras was warning Italy about the "gravest error that could be committed," Italy was already embarked on a campaign calculated to maintain the allegiance of the Italo-Brazilians to Italy. . . .

It is very doubtful, however, whether the results obtained were commensurate with the efforts expended. As Ellis observed, the weight of evidence makes it appear that the bulk of the Italo-Brazilians remained loyal to Brazil.

The German element caused greater alarm than did the Italian although by 1938 only 222,951 Germans had entered the country as against 1,502,958 Italians. The alarm resulted from the marked failure of the assimilation process, evidenced by the use of schools, churches, clubs, and political parties as a means to maintain the German spirit.

Germans were encouraged to come in the nineteenth century and permitted to come freely during the twentieth. They settled principally in Rio Grande do Sul and Santa Catarina, but also in Paraná and São Paulo. Their prosperity in these regions was undeniable, and the Brazilians had little but praise for their qualities as individuals.

The degree of German assimilation is difficult to determine. The official statistics do not specify the origins of Brazilians who marry. Thus a marriage between people apparently Brazilians might be in fact the marriage of people of German origin, living in a German region where German only is spoken. Oliveira Vianna in his work *Raça e Assimilação* concludes that, while the Germans were fusing, the process was slow. Alfredo Ellis remarks concerning the Germans of São Paulo: "Even before Germany became a unified Empire . . . the Germanic element resisted letting itself be absorbed easily. . . . If [the Germans] were more numerous among us, the German spirit would be maintained with much greater persistence. Is this not what is seen in Santa Catarina?" He found that in São Paulo the Germans showed less tendency to intermarry than did the Italians, the Portuguese, or the Spaniards, and even less than the Syrians.

German activity after 1933 steadily increased Brazil's apprehension. As one writer who acknowledges his close attachment to the concept of Germanism says, there was no distinction between Germans and German-Brazilians before 1933, but

after 1933 the German citizens of Brazil — as everywhere else — formed National-Socialist associations to express their solidarity with the fatherland. The primary principle, to which every member pledged himself, was non-interference in the political affairs of the country in which he was living, and strict obedience to her laws. The German-Brazilians were purposely excluded from the associations of German citizens in order that there should be no conflict with their civil obligations as citizens of Brazil.

These Nazi organizations alarmed many Brazilians. They failed to comprehend what manner of men these were who had to form clubs in order to obey the law! According to the German author whom we have just cited, the clubs had no political significance, "the German fatherland had merely exercised a cultural guidance over descendants of its emigrated subjects, but had refrained from the slightest political paternalization." This last statement was generally disbelieved in Brazil. As early as the spring of 1933 the Nazis began discriminating against Germans and German-Brazilians in business who refused to adhere to the Nazi movement. It is from this same date that the intensified effort to use the schools, churches, clubs, and political parties for Nazi purposes was most noticeable. . . .

The most direct form of German activity was political. This work was carried on by Germans sent from Germany, and by German-Brazilians who cooperated with them. Dr. Heinrich Hunsche, one of the National Socialist organizers, indicated the nature of his objectives when he complained of the absorption of many of the German-Brazilians in business, to the exclusion of political interests, and called for their participation in Brazilian life in a manner that would "have a decisive influence in Brazilian political affairs." In line with German purposes a National Socialist Party was organized in Brazil, and Hans von Cossel was made its leader. This organization gained such influence among the Germans that some Germans were known to go to the Party agents rather than to the German consuls when they needed aid, and Germans obeyed the Party at considerable personal sacrifice. In 1937 Herr Friedrich Thiss went to Brazil as the personal representative of Hitler with the object of controlling the Germans of South Brazil, including those of the third and fourth generation born in Brazil. The National Socialists were strong enough in Blumenau, Santa Catarina, to censor the mail there, and the German colonies of the interior of Brazil were kept in an almost permanent state of agitation by the activities of the Nazis and their opponents who were anti-Nazi. . . .

It is undeniable that the Germans were active in Brazil; the success of their efforts is subject to debate. While it is evident that certain members of both Protestant and Catholic churches cooperated with the Nazis, it is equally clear that there were important sections of both churches that did not adhere to Nazism.

The younger elements, whether born in Germany or Brazil, were conspicuous in the Germanism movement, but here again a universal statement is unfounded. Perhaps as many as half or even more of the estimated five hundred thousand of German descent in Rio Grande do Sul were anti-Nazi. Against this must be balanced the fact that some people of German descent played a part in the politics of South Brazil. . . . There also arises the question of the degree of Germanization among the urban and rural Germans respectively. The bulk of the evidence would seem to indicate that allegiance to Germanization was in direct ratio to isolation, the rural Germans remaining German longer than those who lived in the towns. Some of the cities that were almost purely German in population would be exceptions to this statement.

There are other factors that bear on the degree of Germanization. . . . While it is difficult for a people to change national characteristics because of the weight of tradition, custom, family, literature, folklore, inertia, schools, and other factors, it is equally difficult to retain characteristics unadulterated when environment is changed radically, as in the case of the Germans (and other immigrants) who moved to Brazil. However much they might have wished to remain Germans, however much encouragement they received from the homeland, the new country to which they went tended to negative the desired result. This factor was one that raised important obstacles in the path of Hitler (or in the case of other nationalities, of Mussolini or the Japanese).

One further point is pertinent. The immigrants in Brazil were not persecuted or segregated. They were welcomed. This made it exceedingly difficult for "liberation" or "minority" agitation to have much effect. Without stimulus from the homeland the immigrant tended to acclimate himself fairly quickly to his new country, and if the stimulus for retaining allegiance to a homeland was applied from the outside, the opposition of the Brazilians was aroused to the implied dangers.

These are but a few of the considerations that made the Nazi, and Fascist, efforts in Brazil only partly successful. While there is no doubt that a great many of the newly arrived Germans were Nazis, as were many of the older settlers, there was much opposition to Nazism among both the older and newer arrivals. The reaction of the older German-Brazilians to the Nazis was frequently: "If you don't like this country, go back to where you came from." Still another difficulty of the Nazis was the fact that many of the German immigrants were Jews, although this point was never advertised by Messrs. Rosenberg and Streicher. Most of the Jews were assimilated, but they nevertheless offered resistance to Nazi propaganda. Dr. Blumenau himself, founder of the city of Blumenau, was a Jew.

Both Nazism and Fascism attempted to influence Brazil through the medium of the *Integralista* Party. This party was organized along national, rather than state, lines, and was indeed the first nation-wide party in Brazilian history. To accentuate its claims of being the only national (and nationalistic) party, it tried to identify itself with everything Brazilian. Although it was a "shirt" movement, thereby qualifying for membership in the "Textile Internationale," its adoption of green as its color identified it with the predominant color of the Brazilian flag. It reached into the Greek alphabet and transformed the hitherto neutral *Sigma* into a political symbol, using it as Hitler uses the swastika. It also plucked from a Guarani-Indian dictionary the word *Anaué* for salute, although many enthusiastic Integralists preferred the honest confession of *Heil Hitler*.

Moreover, its program was borrowed unblushingly from Fascism and Nazism, and the motherlands of these political movements were frankly favorable to Integralism. The numerous resemblances to Nazism and Fascism serve as a part of the evidence of the close tie between them. For example, although Integralism could hardly adopt a thorough-going racialism with Brazil as the environment of its action, it was violently anti-Semitic, publishing the anti-Semitic propaganda emanating from Germany. It also attacked capitalism, communism, liberalism, the French Revolution, protestantism, England, France, Japan, the United States, and Russia. As an example one may cite the work of Affonso de Carvalho, an Integralist. The author vigorously attacks England, France, the United States, and Russia, and condemns every liberal movement since the French Revolution. He discourses bitterly on the foreign peril but never once does he mention a German or Italian danger. All others he attacks; for the Germans and Italians he has naught but praise.

Although the Integralists insisted that their movement had no direct tie with Germany and Italy, there was nevertheless a close connection between the activities of Integralists, Nazis, and Fascists. Active Nazi and Fascist propaganda was carried on among the Germans and Italians, and many of the leaders of the Integralist Party were German- and Italo-Brazilians, although [Integralist leaders] Plinio Salgado and Gustavo Barroso were both Luso-Brazilians. Reinhard Maack insists that fifty-five per cent of the Integralist leaders in Rio Grande do Sul were German-Brazilians. Many others were Italo-Brazilians. The two elements thus constituted the preponderant influence in the Integralist movement. The alarming results which this influence might have were accentuated by the fact, mentioned earlier in this paper, that many German- and Italo-Brazilians, although born in Brazil, considered themselves citizens of Germany or Italy. Here, as elsewhere, lack of unity lessened the danger to Brazil. Many of the Nazis, for example, considered Integralism as a rival and not as an ally. The race concepts were direct opposites, the Nazis preaching race purity and the Integralists advocating assimilation. The objectives of the two coincided in the most important particular — they both intended to seize the country.

Nazism and Fascism used Integralism as an instrument for their own propaganda. While no central coordinating body for the three existed, Nazis and Fascists encouraged the Integralists. In Rio Grande do Sul the Nazi chieftain, Walter Hornig, although he had no open connection with Integralism, was on friendly terms with its leaders and gave his informal support. Some individuals were, however, members of both the Nazi and Integralist organizations. One of the official Integralist handbooks by Miguel Reale, *A.B.C. do Integralismo*, was issued also in German. . . .

The Integralists floated a bond issue of six thousand contos in 1937, to be paid off when they took over the State. Some of the bonds were discounted in the German Transatlantic Bank of Rio de Janeiro. They also received indirect financial aid from the German and Italian governments. The connection between the Integralists and Vargas before (and for a time after) the coup d'état of November 10, 1937, was close. Vargas was in constant touch with them, receiving Plinio Salgado at the Catete Palace and reviewing Integralist parades. The Integralists received financial aid from the government, coöperated with Vargas in the November 10 coup d'état, were offered a position in the *Estado Novo*, and expected to be treated as an exception in the decrees abolishing political parties. Vargas later turned on the Integralists probably because he regarded their demands for power as excessive, because he decided against aligning Brazil with the Rome-Berlin-Tokyo Axis, and because he found that the Integralists were not as strong as they had represented themselves.

The Integralists were outlawed as a political party along with the other parties in December, 1937, but did not disband. Although they continued ostensibly as a cultural society, in reality they were still a political organization. They promoted uprisings in March and again on May 11, 1938. After the second attempt a number of their leaders were arrested, among those accused being several Germans known to be connected with the Nazi movement in Brazil. The party ceased to exist in 1938, at least as a legal movement.

The cumulative effect of the various activities outlined above created a considerable alarm which was reflected in the political life of the country. Before the Integralist revolt of May 11, 1938, the German ambassador on the grounds that the decree applied to domestic parties only protested against inclusion of foreign political groups in the banning of political parties. The attempt to secure special privileges for foreign political parties, activities of which were directed against the government, when domestic parties had been abolished, further increased the uneasiness of many Brazilians. This demand on the part of the German ambassador, Dr. Karl von Ritter, created a situation where the ambassador became *persona non grata* to the Brazilian government. He was given to understand that no Nazi activities would be countenanced.

At about the same time the Nazi agent, Ernst Dorsch, was arrested and the government continued its campaign against Nazis and Fascists, inspired largely by the alarm felt by the Brazilian army. This alarm was heightened by the knowledge that some German-Brazilians in the south were discussing the possibility of setting up an Integralist-Nazi-Fascist state in southern Brazil, the three southernmost states, Rio Grande do Sul, Santa Catarina, and Paraná to be turned over to German domination and São Paulo to Italian control. It is not possible at this time to verify whether any such plans were being fostered by Germany and Italy, but it is possible to say that high officials in both the national and state governments of Brazil thought so, and their political actions were based on the belief that the reports were true. A decree was issued on April 18, 1938, which forbade political activity by foreign associations. The government indicated by its arrest of Germans in connection with the May 11 revolt of the Integralists that it did not believe this decree was being observed. As late as 1939 there was still uneasiness in Brazilian government circles over foreign activity.

Brazilians have become increasingly worried over the doctrine that vacant land is the patrimony of mankind and should not be allowed to remain idle while millions of humans live on a low standard because of lack of sufficient land. The aggression of Japan, Germany, Italy, and Russia accentuated such fears. The millions of acres of absolutely unused lands in Brazil, the failure to develop the rich deposits of iron, manganese, and other minerals caused a natural uneasiness, a recognition that weak nations have always been absorbed by strong ones, that as Bismarck once remarked, natural riches in the hands of those who do not know how to develop them, nor care to do so, are a permanent danger to the possessor. Brazil wondered if she could defend herself.

One result of the alarm over the activities of foreigners was a series of decrees limiting the privileges of foreigners and naturalized Brazilians. These affected the lives of thousands of the immigrants. They were intended to protect Brazil against undue political influence by her immigrant elements, but they went beyond this, placing distinct curbs on the personal and economic rights of immigrants, including those who had become Brazilian citizens. . . .

As 1939 ended Brazil was making a drive to assimilate her foreigners. The National Security Council was given the duty of proposing methods. The Ministries of Justice and Interior, and Education and Health were cooperating. Schools were to be established to teach the Portuguese language and the history of Brazil to children in foreign-language areas. Teachers were to be trained, and cultural societies formed to foster Brazilianization. The Ministry of Labor, Industry, and Commerce was to see that the legal minimum of Brazilians were employed in agriculture, commerce and industry, and credit organizations. (This minimum is two thirds of the employees.) The Immigration and Colonization Council sought to avoid the concentration of immigrants, prevent foreign companies from acquiring large landed estates, and keep foreigners from absorbing Brazilian properties in colonial regions. Schools, with certain exceptions, might not be run by foreigners. Use of foreign languages was forbidden in public offices, barracks, and during military service. In order to effect more rapid assimilation Brazilians were to be settled in the centers of foreign population.

The evidence as to the efforts made by foreign nations, especially Germany and Italy, to use their own nationals and Brazilians to influence Brazilian political affairs is so strong as to be beyond doubt. But the efforts should be distinguished rigorously from the results obtained. To all appearances the foreign drive was a failure as affairs stood at the end of 1939. Of the many reasons for this result, three would seem to predominate: the Brazilian political system was too complicated, and the hold of the Luso-Brazilians on this system too firm, for foreign elements to influence it substantially; the Brazilian army, though containing elements sympathetic to foreign ideologies, remained faithful to the nation; and, because of the great publicity given to the foreign danger, the Brazilians were aware of the threats to their nation and proved themselves capable of taking adequate measures of defense.

B. The Return of Vargas

4. The Election of 1950

John W. F. Dulles

The elections were scheduled for October 3, 1950, . . .

Getúlio put on a strenuous and effective campaign. From the moment he left Rio for the north in mid-August until he returned to São Borja on the last day of September, he had no rest from speaking engagements, jostlings, and travel. There were the small planes, in the likes of which two gubernatorial candidates lost their lives; there were the poorly lit airfields and the many bad roads. State capitals and remote towns heard Getúlio stand on his record, criticize the Dutra regime, and pledge himself, with the help of the people, to carry on the program he had begun in 1930.

São Paulo, which he visited briefly in the first part of August and for a week in September, was filled with Vargas propaganda before he appeared. But the facade of São Paulo University was draped with black crepe and the University flag flown at half mast. The *Estado de S. Paulo* refused to use Vargas' name, instead referring always to "the Former Dictator."

The Vargas campaign was backed by an abundance of volunteer workers: typists, propagandists, and people who offered automobiles

From *Vargas of Brazil: A Political Biography* by John W. F. Dulles (Austin: University of Texas Press, 1967), pp. 294–299, *passim*. Reprinted by permission.

and space in homes and offices. Scores of old associates, such as Luís Simões Lopes and Lourival Fontes, worked for Vargas' return to power. It being necessary for candidates to print their own ballots, one supporter had 200 million Vargas *cédulas* printed, and pilots were persuaded to carry stacks of them to far-away places. Anticipating several million votes, the Vargas people were also anticipating a prevalent trick of destroying opponents' ballots.

The Peronista press in Argentina had been busy attacking the pro-United States Dutra regime. As was probably inevitable, the Brazilian press accused the Argentine press of reflecting Vargas' "political affinity with Perón" and mixing into Brazilian politics in favor of Vargas. Although Vargas never met Perón, Jango Goulart was on warm terms with the Argentine ruler and had sold him Brazilian lumber.

When Dutra's chief military aide affirmed that foreign financial assistance was being received by Brazilian candidates, the Argentines reacted. Dutra's side then denied having said that such contributions came from Perón. But Buenos Aires' *Democracia*, principal organ of Peronism, accused Dutra's aide of "irresponsible insolence" and declared his rectification "no less offensive than his original assertion." Although the Argentine ambassador in Rio officially denied that the government of Argentina was involved in the Brazilian political campaign, Getúlio's enemies kept this issue alive.

The Communists learned from Prestes that the principal candidates were "reactionaries." Vargas was a "tyrant landowner," [PSD candidate Cristian] Machado a "banker-agent of Yankee imperialism," and [UDN candidate Eduardo] Gomes the "instrument of the most reactionary high clergy and the puppet of rich landowners." Good Communists, Prestes said, should cast blank ballots. He went into hiding, accused of sedition, after issuing his August 1950 manifesto calling for a violent agrarian revolution and the confiscation of key enterprises, especially foreign corporations.

Their party outlawed, Communists inscribed their names as candidates of legal parties. When the Superior Electoral Tribunal refused to remove the names of suspected Paulista Communists running for local offices on the ticket of the Social Labor Party, Communists hailed the decisions as a "setback for those bandits, Getúlio and Ademar [de Barros]." The Liga Eleitoral Católica (LEC), much more fussy than the Electoral Tribunal, listed 623 objectionable candidates, including Vargas' running mate.

The amiable Machado promised that if elected he would carry on with Dutra's Five-Year Plan, which was to spend $500 million to improve health, transportation, and the supply of energy. He urged the creation of more rural banks to help revive "stunted" agricultural production. The unsmiling *brigadeiro* offered a government in which all groups and parties would collaborate.

Getúlio sympathized with the good Brazilian people, afflicted by "sufferings," "privation," and a living-cost increase which he variously described as 300 per cent and 400 per cent. In the last four years, he said, the printing presses had turned out under Dutra as much new currency as they had turned out under him in fifteen years. But, he added, his own issues had been used for war costs and for creating such assets as the steel and iron-ore companies.

Brazil, Getúlio said, must be rescued from the stagnation and apathy in which she was foundering. Offering to renew what he called an interrupted upsurge in progress and production, Vargas kept reiterating that he was not a man of empty promises. Pointing to his record, he told Santa Catarina's workers that under his regime coal had come to be produced "properly and methodically." For the Northeast there had been roads and dams; also the Alcohol and Sugar Institute. The Paulo Afonso hydro-electric project he described as "one of the few things initiated by my Government which the new Government did not discontinue." In the course of fulfilling the pledges made when he campaigned in 1930 he had created the Labor Ministry and given the working man up-to-date labor legislation.

"My adversaries," Getúlio declared in Recife, "call me Father of the Poor, and Father of the Rich. But I never have been factious or an extremist. Above all, I tried to act justly and to realize the common good. Rich and poor are equally Brazilian."

The issue of nationalism he confined to minerals and oil, which, he said, his Government had made a part of the national patrimony. Foreign capital was welcome but it should not be used "to turn our natural resources over to the control of foreign companies." In particular he discussed petroleum, "which my Government proved exists." "Those who turn their petroleum over to others alienate their own independence."

He praised Roosevelt and talked about the FEB. Saying that "my Government got Brazil to participate in the United Nations," he promised to support the world organization. Speaking to audiences which were hearing about the Marshall Plan and the war in Korea, he said that

Brazil must not be asked to collaborate and make sacrifices, with the benefits distributed to others. We have important and urgent problems to solve. Petroleum is one of these. If they want our efficient co-operation, they must first help us find the solution, in accordance with Brazilian interests, which must have preference.

Election day would be the twentieth anniversary of the outbreak of the 1930 revolution. As he went from city to city, reminding his hearers of his previous visits, he evoked the names of local heroes who had helped make the revolution. At Belo Horizonte, whose main square had become a bedlam of loudspeakers and swirling election ballots, Getúlio recalled Antônio Carlos "with his prophetic 'Let us make the revolution before the people make it,'" and Olegário Maciel, "the perfect reflection of the Mineiro's quality of fulfilling his word."

At Ponta Grossa, Paraná, he recalled his arrival twenty years earlier, at the head of the revolutionary forces which had made their headquarters there. The wild acclaim had then made Getúlio certain of victory. And so it did again, with the familiar refrain, "We want, we want, we want Ge-Ge-Getúlio," ringing in his ears. This time, he said, it would be a different type of victory, won by the secret vote, an achievement of the revolution.

The anti-Vargas press suggested that the Former Dictator was uttering his political swan song and would soon be retired for good. But the voters decided otherwise:

For President	
Getúlio Dorneles Vargas	3,849,040
Eduardo Gomes	2,342,384
Cristiano Machado	1,697,193
For Vice-President	
João Café Filho	2,520,790
Odilon Braga	2,344,841
Altino Arantes	1,649,309

. . . The last hurdle was the legal contest brought on when opponents of Vargas maintained that the "majority" mentioned in the 1946 Constitution meant an absolute majority. The Superior Electoral Tribunal in January, 1951, thirteen days before inauguration day, ruled that the Constitution meant a majority over one's closest opponent. Vargas and Café Filho were declared elected.

5. Perón and Vargas in 1951

GEORGE PENDLE

In General Perón and Dr. Vargas, the republics of Argentina and Brazil have produced two statesmen who are not merely outstanding figures but who, also, are truly representative of the civilization of the Atlantic area of South America, as it exists today. Both men were born amidst the wide pasturelands of the Uruguay-Plata river system, and they both still enjoy a return to the country, where they don the baggy cotton trousers traditionally worn by local horsemen. That, obviously, is the proper background for rulers of American nations, whose wealth is in the good earth and whose rural workers, though they be poor and (by present-day western standards) backward, provide the means for the urban populations to increase and prosper. General Perón and Dr. Vargas. are representative South Americans in their outlook, which is optimistic and nationalistic; in their taste for demagogic methods of government; and in their general manner, which is human and engaging. They greatly differ in appearance. Juan D. Perón, aged 56, is tall, dark, handsome, and, as is customary with Argentines of his age, putting on weight. When younger, he was the champion swordsman in the army, and one of its best shots. Getúlio D. Vargas, aged 67, is short, plump, smiling, and wears spectacles. As a youth in southern Brazil he entered the army, but abandoned it for law and politics.

Together, these two men rule some 70 million people, and, so doing, they have adopted programmes and faced problems which are remarkably similar. They have both devised plans for transforming their under-developed, under-populated, under-educated countries into industrialized, self-sufficient nations; and they have both been compelled by internal and external circumstances to curtail those plans. At the present time Argentina and Brazil lack heavy industries and are deficient in the fuel that modern mechanization requires. They are therefore dependent on Europe and the U.S.A. for plant and for many vitally important manufactured articles and raw materials, all of which have to be paid for by exports of local

From "Perón and Vargas" by George Pendle, *The Fortnightly*, New Series, CLXX, November 1951, pp. 723–728. Reprinted by permission.

produce. The progress of industrialization has been retarded in both countries by the difficulty experienced in obtaining those supplies because, first, of the Atlantic nations' rearmament drive and, secondly, of the inadequacy of the exportable surplus of the products of the Argentine and Brazilian soil. In both countries, people are still drifting from the rural districts into the towns, and the production of livestock and crops is not keeping pace with present-day requirements. Two examples will serve to illustrate the disequilibrium between town and country in this vast area of the American continent: Argentina, though it possesses enormous herds of cattle, has been unable to export the quantities that it undertook to ship to several foreign markets in the past year or so. And it is remarkable that this land of cattle produces insufficient milk to satisfy the demand of the population of Buenos Aires. Likewise Brazil, in whose north-eastern regions the world's supply of natural rubber originated, is now actually importing raw rubber for the needs of the local factories and, although recently self-sufficient in automobile tyres, is again obliged to supplement the local output by purchasing tyres abroad.

Each statesman has learned something from the other. Dr. Vargas was the pioneer in creating a new South American brand of social and economic reform which owed much to Mussolini's corporate State and which Perón in 1945 began to adopt, adapt, and "legalize" in Argentina. The main point of similarity — and originality — in the policies of the two men, is that they have both relied chiefly on the support of the working class, instead of on that of the army and the upper middle-class oligarchy, which formerly constituted the foundation of political power in Latin America. Until the coming of Getúlio Vargas and Juan Perón, the working classes of Brazil and Argentina were generally neglected by their rulers. But the social reforms that have been introduced in both countries have so far benefited the organized urban workers rather than the scattered peons who labour in the forests, the plains, and the high mountains, and this is one of the principal defects alike of Getúlio Vargas' *Estado Novo* and Juan Perón's *Justicialismo*.

It is natural that the current social and economic movement should be developing on approximately parallel lines in Brazil and Argentina, and that the results should differ from the European prototypes of Fascism and the welfare State. For generations, the Latin Americans have been accustomed to "paternal" governments. Therefore Dr. Vargas' undemocratic régime of 1930–1945 did not really shock the Brazilian masses, and General Perón's demagogic methods do not displease the majority of Argentines to-day. Times change, however, and General Perón has effectively demonstrated that a Latin American *caudillo* can, and now-a-days should, operate within the law. Dr. Vargas' refusal to allow elections in Brazil, at the end of the last war, was the cause of his temporary eclipse. His uncompromising paternalism clashed with the aims of the then newly victorious United Nations, which included Brazil in their number, and he was obliged to retire to his ranch in the south. It is too early yet to know the shape that the new Vargas régime (which began in January 1951) will take; but it is already evident that the ex-dictator has learned a lesson from his earlier error and from his pupil General Perón's subsequent example. On the first occasion, in 1930, Dr. Vargas seized power by force; but in 1950 he conducted his electoral campaign in accordance with normal practices of democracy. In 1937, he decreed a new constitution of his own making; but Juan Perón has since proved the wisdom of never breaking the law of the land: it is better to arrange for the law to be changed. When the Argentine president wishes to take unconstitutional action, he usually bides his time, first assuring that Congress shall by legal methods alter the constitution according to his requirements. It is of course inevitable that Latin American constitutions shall constantly be altered to satisfy local, present day needs. None of these constitutions was a spontaneous Latin American growth. They were all created in imitation of United States and European models existing at the time of the attainment of independence by the Latin American peoples a hundred or so years ago, and they have rarely been respected by the local populations, who have preferred to give their allegiance to colourful — and, in most cases, unconstitutionally-minded — caudillos. The caudillo is applauded, not for his democratic principles (which, normally, are lacking), but for his human qualities, his personal prowess and charm. It is required, first of all, that he shall be virile and *simpático*. But Latin Americans are convinced that it is their destiny to be in the vanguard of civilization, so nowadays they expect to be granted the opportunity of demonstrating to the world that they are not backward in their observance of democratic etiquette. Democracy, therefore, is gradually becoming a reality in Latin America, though Europeans and North Americans often fail to recognize it in its unorthodox Latin American form.

There are, of course, points of dissimilarity in the conditions prevailing in Argentina and Brazil. One of General Perón's advantages, is that his people live in a land where the climate is mainly temperate. They are not faced with the heart-breaking Brazilian problem of rendering a vast tropical jungle habitable by whites and *mestizos* before its natural wealth can be exploited. The Argentines are usually able to work somewhat harder than the easy-going Brazilians, many of whom still believe that the ideal life is "to gather the fruit without planting the tree." General Perón, moreover, has had the backing of a much larger parliamentary majority than Dr. Vargas, and the support of a much more powerful militant political party, which, until quite recently, was in appearance a united body, in spite of its great size. The Argentine president is also blessed (though it is a mixed blessing) with the enthusiastic and able assistance of a popular consort. Dr. Vargas, on the other hand, can count on receiving much greater financial and technical aid from Washington in exchange for past and future favours. Although Brazil is becoming increasingly nationalistic in temper, no one imagines that the courteous Brazilians are seeking continental hegemony for themselves — a suspicion which has sometimes existed in regard to the more extreme and arrogant Argentine nationalists. Moreover, from the United States point of view Brazil, because of its proximity to the Panama Canal and the west coast of Africa, is of much greater strategic importance than Argentina, and Brazilian raw materials (such as manganese) are particularly valuable in a time of rearmament.

In one significant respect, however, General Perón has benefited from Washington's antagonism: it has stimulated Argentine anti-Americanism, on which he thrives. His contention that foreign "imperialists" are plotting to overthrow his regime is far from meaningless to most of his compatriots, no matter how ridiculous it may seem to North American and British newspaper readers. Many Argentines, indeed, consider that the president's violent treatment of supposedly U.S.-sponsored radicals, socialists, and military insurgents is not only justifiable, but necessary — the notorious events of the last electoral period being fresh in everyone's memory. At that time (1945) the American ambassador at Buenos Aires, Mr. Spruille Braden, delivered a number of public addresses in that city denouncing dictatorships. He avoided openly attacking the Argentine Government (whose most powerful member was Colonel Perón, though he was not yet president); but no one misunderstood the ambassador's intention, which was to emphasize that the U.S.A. disliked the Colonel and his friends and would be pleased if they were displaced. The *Peronistas* made good use of Mr. Braden's indiscretions. Anti-Braden circulars and posters were widely distributed and exhibited, and the forthcoming elections were represented as being in reality a personal contest between Juan D. Perón and Uncle Sam's ambassador. In February 1946, just a few days before the elections, the State Department at Washington issued a blue book, in which certain Argentine citizens were charged with having collaborated with Nazi Germany during the war. In this publication, the outstanding presidential candidate of the day, Juan Perón, was prominently mentioned as having been a collaborationist. This information, derived from the captured papers of the German Foreign Office, was known to have been in the possession of the U.S. Government for some time. Its release on the eve of the Argentine elections was recognized as being a deliberate attempt by Washington to discredit Colonel Perón and ensure his defeat at the polls. The peronistas' riposte was simple and effective: they plastered the walls of Buenos Aires with the slogan: "Perón or Braden." In the February 1946 elections Juan Perón was democratically elected to the presidency and, thereby, in the Argentine view, Mr. Braden was decisively defeated. During the recent electoral campaign President Perón has lost no opportunity of reminding the Argentine people that less than six years ago a North American ambassador and the State Department did everything in their power to secure the rejection of the country's most popular candidate.

It is inflation, however, rather than foreign "imperialism," that constitutes the most serious immediate threat to Peronismo, for the rising cost of living has caused a decline in the workers' gratitude for the benefits accorded to them under the Perón regime. It was doubtless the knowledge of the growth of working-class dissatisfaction that encouraged a group of military officers to attempt the September coup d'état. It is in the tradition of the Argentine army, which has a high regard for the national honour and dignity, periodically to enter the Casa Rosada and eject a president who has been too long in power; but such methods seem out-of-date in a republic wherein the democratically elected (though demagogically minded) president has always professed a high regard for legality. Nevertheless, the crushing of this revolt has neither cured the inflationary disease, nor eliminated current discontent.

Meanwhile in Brazil Dr. Vargas, also, is plagued by inflation, which has compelled him to postpone some of the much-advertised schemes for economic and social development. No one yet knows whether the new Vargas régime, faced by such a grave problem, will require authoritarian powers. A few months ago a speech by the president did contain an ominous threat. On that occasion the ex-dictator not only criticized the Brazilian profiteers whose speculations have certainly contributed to the fabulous rise in the cost of living: he also warned them of "the day when the people will take the law into their own hands." More recently, however, Dr. Vargas' pronouncements have displayed a moderation which has been conspicuously lacking in the utterances of the Argentine president, and it is probable that the time will come when General Perón will be obliged to learn a useful lesson from the Brazilian's example in this respect, just as previously he learned from Dr. Vargas that in modern South America the good will of the working-class was the surest foundation for a caudillo's ambitions. Of course, Dr. Vargas is an older man, and a statesman of much longer experience, than his Argentine opposite number. His new Government does not consist entirely of *Vargistas*, as it might have done, but contains talented men from rival parties. In spite of his habit of appealing directly to the masses in his public speeches, so far during this second term in office he has given no indication that he really intends to override the authority of Congress. At the present time, therefore, the courses followed by these two South American statesmen are tending to diverge in one particular: whereas Dr. Vargas, safely in power, is behaving with unwonted restraint, General Perón, coming to the end of a period of power, is growing increasingly aggressive, under the pressure of adverse circumstances. If he can again convince the public that his opponents have the backing of foreign "imperialists," and if he can prove that the mass of the working-class are behind him, his position — either as a re-elected president, or (after the Nicaraguan model) as the strong man behind a puppet president — should be secure for a long time to come. If he is wise, he will then emulate Dr. Vargas' moderation.

There is one other important similarity in the attitude and methods of the two men. Although both are essentially South American personalities, they are both very "modern." They believe in mechanization, industrialization, propaganda to the masses, social security, motor-roads, air-lines, and so on. And both of them have known how to borrow the latest foreign ideas of government — totalitarian or democratic, capitalist or socialist, according to their immediate needs. It was General Perón — but it might just as well have been Dr. Vargas — who remarked in a recent address to Congress: "We collected all the good ideas that we found on our road to Government House." He says that he does not want monetary reserves (and Dr. Vargas, with certain qualifications, would agree), but equipment, machines, and essential raw materials; hydroelectric plant, diesel engines, tractors, harvesters, aeroplanes, trans-Atlantic ships, television, fuel, atomic energy, chemicals. He is, moreover, "modern" even in some of the more superficial implications of that term. Married to a radio actress of considerable glamour, he realizes the enormous prestige enjoyed by stars and sporting aces to-day. He bestows his personal patronage on local sporting heroes – boxers, motor-car racers, swimmers, and footballers – and thus shares in their vast popularity. Nor is Argentina a negligible competitor in international sport at the present time.

It is evident that something momentous is now occurring in Argentina and Brazil; the immense fertility of those great countries, their local qualities and traditions, and the latest theories, techniques, and conceits of Europe and the U.S.A. are all being stirred (so to say) in a melting-pot, whose final product will surely be a distinctively South American civilization. We can only guess, how long the process will take. Long ago, Montaigne ventured a prophecy. He wrote: "This late-world shall but come to light when ours shall fall into darkness."

6. Crisis and Corruption

José Maria Bello

When Vargas resumed the presidency he publicized the situation that had existed when he was deposed, in order to contrast it with the one he now inherited: budget deficits, one billion cruzeiros; bills payable, two billion; owing to the Treasury by the Banco do Brasil, one billion; paper in circulation, 31 billion; reduction in credits abroad, one billion, and in the gold reserve, 700 million. All this, according to Vargas, was without an increase in production and with continual deficits in the balance of payments. A policy of rigid fi-

Reprinted from *A History of Modern Brazil, 1889–1964* by José Maria Bello, translated from the Portuguese by James L. Taylor, with the permission of the publishers, Stanford University Press. © 1966 by the Trustees of the Leland Stanford Junior University.

nancial housecleaning was therefore imperative as the basis for economic recovery. But that is not what took place. New measures were useless or self-defeating, especially in the area of foreign exchange, when drafts on foreign banks, used to pay for imports, were being sold at auction by the Banco do Brasil. Unrestricted importation of luxury items, and stockpiling on the gratuitous assumption that the Korean War would spread, used up the remainder of the foreign credits. The volume of paper currency rose from 31 billion in 1951 to 50 billion in 1954, equivalent to 1,000 cruzeiros per capita, as compared with 600 in 1950 and 80 in 1930. With spiraling inflation came an uncontrollable increase in prices and in speculation, including foreign exchange. Exchange parity, as determined in international agreements, was maintained, thus increasing the depreciation of the currency on the domestic market, which in turn, among other effects, made it impossible to sell Brazil's traditional export items abroad; they were referred to as *produtos gravosos* [products that are overpriced in foreign money]. The monetary inflation was accompanied by credit inflation, which was brought on mainly by financing schemes, many of them scandalous, underwritten by the Banco do Brasil and the semiautonomous government agencies, such as the Social Security Institute.

Among the official achievements were the expansion of the steel mill at Volta Redonda and of the hydroelectric plant at the Paulo Afonso falls. The restriction on imports, the high premium on foreign exchange, and inflation all combined to stimulate the rapid development of urban industries, which were concentrated around the country's two largest cities [São Paulo and Rio], and were owned or controlled by a few groups and families. The increase in agricultural production was more the result of cultivation of new areas, such as northern Paraná, than of greater yields from those already in use. Domestic transportation, except the airlines, progressed little; the shortage of fuel became chronic. Attraction of foreign capital was made difficult by a rigidly nationalistic mentality, which was typically expressed in the exclusion of foreigners, except as engineers and technicians, from participation in the oil industry or in Petrobrás, the State oil monopoly. Even native-born Brazilians, if married to foreigners, could not own shares in Petrobrás, though they might be fully qualified for the highest public posts, including the presidency itself. The sudden upheavals in the economic structure were reflected ever more sharply in the general tone of Brazilian society, which revealed all the well-known symptoms of social maladjustment that are precipitated by inflation: a prosperity often more apparent than real; a growing disparity between the living standards of the small, wealthy groups and those of the masses and the lower-middle class; the contagious decline in morals; and the universal temptation to indulge in luxury and display. This phenomenon was also manifested in the glaring contrast between the poor regions and the South, especially São Paulo, which contained 80 per cent of the nation's economic and financial resources and produced the same percentage of the national income, now increased by inflation to nearly 400 billion cruzeiros. The old political elite, pushed aside in 1930, had seemed to want to return to public life under the new constitutional regime, but had refrained from doing so because of self-interest, skepticism, an inability to understand or adjust to the changes in the Brazilian social landscape, or an aversion to rampant demagoguery and electoral corruption.

Brazil continued to echo, with the usual lag, the philosophical, literary, and artistic trends of Europe: Bergsonism, Neo-Thomism, Neo-Kantianism, that is, all the different forms of the spiritual reaction that had begun early in the century. The postwar reaction in European thought was not to reach Brazil until later. In the plastic arts early French impressionism had been left behind. Brazilian music, inspired by native folklore, had developed along more original lines, although the nation's most outstanding composer, Heitor Villa-Lobos, was appreciated more abroad than at home. Brazilian architecture, especially in public buildings and skyscrapers, was renowned throughout the world for its imagination and style. Fiction, after living through the experimentation of the "modernists" of the 1920s and 1930s, had achieved better balance. Free verse was in the ascendant. There was a marked trend toward political, sociological, and historical essays. There was an improvement in the makeup of newspapers, and an expansion of publishing houses and bookstores. Brazilian motion pictures devoted to native themes began to attract favorable attention at European film festivals. The first television stations made their appearance. Revisions and reforms of education legislation followed one after another. With Minister Gustavo Capanema's reform of education, new public and private universities sprang into being, some of them on solid ground, but most of them not. Because of her immense territory, potential wealth, and economic evolution, and the continuity of her diplomatic policy, Brazil aroused greater interest in the world. She stopped being a rather unknown and picturesque country, easily confused with the others in

Latin America, and began to acquire her own distinctive personality.

After spending five years on his frontier ranch in Rio Grande do Sul, with no interest in travel and, it appears, almost no social contacts, Getúlio Vargas seemed more withdrawn, more silent, and more weary. He returned to the Catete, therefore, a different man from the one who had entered it in 1930, or even from the one who had left it in 1945. His ouster from power that year had perhaps heightened his prejudice against politicians and his distrust of the military. The nation, however, seemed to take him back tranquilly. Even those who had fought him the hardest seemed to have some confidence in him. By appointing four members of the PSD and one representative of the UDN to his cabinet, Vargas revealed his peacemaking intentions. Afterwards, as General Dutra had done, he reshuffled the cabinet, but merely replaced the PSD ministers with other members of the same party, and retained João Cleofas of the UDN as Minister of Agriculture. The political truce did not last long. As in 1937 and 1945, the suspicion spread that Vargas, relying on the support of the masses, was plotting to perpetuate himself in power. The tone of the opposition in Congress and in the press became more vehement day by day. More and more frequently his administration was accused of corruption, public graft, embezzlement, illicit gains, and indefensible financing by the Banco do Brasil, which was a powerful hybrid machine, sovereign manipulator of the national credit, and virtually under the exclusive control of the Executive. The scandalous mismanagement of the Treasury, which had been all but plundered with complete impunity, could no longer be hidden from the public, especially when the inquiry ordered by Vargas into the conduct of the Banco do Brasil during Dutra's administration proved fruitless. Inconclusive investigations into charges of graft and corruption became the order of the day.

The government's authority was severely impaired by the scandal-filled atmosphere. Much of the opposition campaign was directed against João Goulart, Vargas's protégé and the Vice-President of the PTB, who became Labor Minister in 1953. According to the opposition, Goulart was employing the power and financial resources of his office illegally to convert the labor unions and federations into a vast political machine, in order to establish a syndicalist republic in the image of Perón's justicialismo. Some of his bitterest critics were army officers, who demanded his dismissal in the so-called "Colonels' Manifesto" of February 1954. The officers were provoked by Goulart's proposal to double the minimum wage, which would set off another round of inflation, and, incidentally, raise the income of unskilled workers above that of army sergeants. Under pressure from the army, Goulart was removed from office, but he remained a member of Vargas's political household and his wage bill was enacted into law. There was no letup in the violence of the opposition campaign or in the general unrest.

The final crisis of the Vargas regime began on August 5, 1954, with an attempt to assassinate Carlos Lacerda, a newspaper editor and virulent critic of the government. On that night Lacerda, returning from a political meeting and accompanied by an air force officer, Major Rubem Florentino Vaz, was fired upon as he got out of his car in front of his apartment house in Copacabana. The officer was killed and Lacerda wounded. The crime became known as the "crime da Rua Toneleros." The first clues uncovered pointed suspiciously to President Vargas's own large personal guard. The President permitted the officer corps of the air force to take over the criminal investigation from the police, who were suspect. The clues proved correct, and the chief of the palace guard [one Gregório Fortunato] confessed to being the direct instigator of the crime. The chief was a coarse and arrogant half-breed, and the guards were largely characters with bad police records who peddled their palace influence and exploited the "sea of mud," to use Vargas's own desperate expression.

The public outcry could no longer be quelled. In Congress, in the press, in the military clubs, everywhere, the President's resignation was demanded. Vice-President João Café Filho himself suggested they should both resign. Depending possibly on his War Minister's control of part of the army, Vargas considered resisting at all costs; only when he was convinced that he had no means of resistance was he willing to resign temporarily. A final, dramatic cabinet meeting was held on the night of August 23, 1954. Getúlio Vargas announced, not that he would resign, but that he would temporarily step aside as chief of state. This did not satisfy the military. On the morning of the 24th, in his private quarters, after being informed of the unalterable demand for his unconditional resignation, he killed himself with a bullet in the heart.

There followed a whole day of indefinable anguish in the appalled city and across the nation, like the suffocating atmosphere of an impending storm; but prompt military measures, plus perhaps the stupefaction caused by the unprecedented tragedy, kept the storm from bursting. In political circumstances not unlike those of 1945, the military chiefs called on Vice-President João Café Filho to assume the government, perhaps in the belief, soon to prove wrong, that he could carry out within the constitutional framework the reforms necessary to rectify the former state of affairs.

Getúlio Vargas left two brief suicide messages that quickly became known as his "political testament." Here he attributed to unspecified foreign and domestic "interests" the pressures that forced him to take his own life, and described his suicide as a sacrifice to free the Brazilian people from bondage. His name was to be their battle flag and his blood the price of their ransom. Only in time can the full psychological content and meaning of his testament be calmly interpreted and its long-range effects assessed. But if, as seems likely, it was intended to provoke an immediate popular reaction against his enemies, it failed miserably in its purpose. The common people, to whom he addressed his message, did not respond. There were even some who doubted its authenticity. Thus, it was on a note of apparent futility that Vargas, to use his final words, should "depart from life to enter history."

7. Suicide Note

GETÚLIO VARGAS

Once more, the forces and interests which work against the people have organized themselves afresh and break out against me.

They do not accuse me, they insult me; they do not fight me, they vilify and do not allow me the right to defend myself. They must silence my voice and impede my actions so that I shall not continue to defend, as I have always defended, the people and especially the humble. I follow my destiny. After decades of domination and plunder on the part of international economic and financial groups, I placed myself at the head of a revolution and won. I began the work of liberation and I installed a regime of social freedom. I had to resign. I returned to the government on the arms of the people. The underground campaign of international groups joined that of the national groups which were working against the regime of as-

From *Vargas of Brazil: A Political Biography* by John W. F. Dulles (Austin: University of Texas Press, 1967), pp. 334–335, *passim*. Reprinted by permission.

suring employment. The excess-profits law was held up by Congress. Hatreds were unleashed against the just revision of minimum wages. I wished to bring about national freedom in the utilization of our resources by means of Petrobrás; this had hardly begun to operate when the wave of agitation swelled. Electrobrás was obstructed to the point of despair. They do not want the worker to be free. They do not want the people to be independent.

I assumed the government in the midst of an inflationary spiral which was destroying the rewards of work. Profits of foreign companies were reaching as much as 500 per cent per annum. In declarations of import values, frauds of more than $100 million per year were proved. Came the coffee crisis and the value of our main product rose. We tried to defend its price and the reply was such violent pressure on our economy that we were forced to give in.

I have fought month after month, day after day, hour after hour, resisting constant, incessant pressure, suffering everything in silence, forgetting everything, giving myself in order to defend the people who now are left deserted. There is nothing more I can give you except my blood. If the birds of prey want someone's blood, if they want to go on draining the Brazilian people, I offer my life as a holocaust. I choose this means of being always with you. When they humiliate you, you will feel my soul suffering at your side. When hunger knocks at your door, you will feel in your breast the energy to struggle for yourselves and your children. When you are scorned, my memory will give you the strength to react. My sacrifice will keep you united and my name will be your battle standard.

Each drop of my blood will be an immortal flame in your conscience and will uphold the sacred will to resist. To hatred, I answer with pardon. And to those who think they have defeated me, I reply with my victory. I was a slave of the people, and today I am freeing myself for eternal life. But this people whose slave I was will no longer be slave to anyone. My sacrifice will remain forever in their souls and my blood will be the price of their ransom.

I fought against the spoliation of Brazil. I fought against the spoliation of the people. I have fought with my whole heart. Hatred, infamy, and slander have not conquered my spirit. I have given you my life. Now I offer you my death. I fear nothing. Serenely I take my first step toward eternity and leave life to enter history.

Section X

Historians and Historical Controversies

When North Americans go to Latin America they are often surprised to find the past so much alive there and so much a part of the present as to be discussed on the front pages of newspapers. The discovery in Mexico of the bones of Cortez or the alleged bones of Cuauhtémoc, the last Aztec emperor, became prime news and led to passionate arguments on the nature of the Spanish conquest.[1] Taxi drivers may engage their fares in argument over this and other historical problems, and the foreigner soon learns how vigorously some controversies of the past are debated today at several levels of society. History remains very much alive in Latin America because of the widespread conviction there that history is very important. Even more than in some other parts of the world, history writing in Latin America has always been a popular activity, by no means only an academic exercise performed by professors in universities.

The wars for independence which began in 1810 produced an especially abundant historical literature, patriotic in tone and nationalistic in purpose. Concentration on the heroes of this period has sometimes influenced powerfully the scope and attitude of the writers who have concerned themselves with the struggles to throw off the political yoke of the mother countries and the attempts of the new nations to establish their independent lives. In Venezuela, for example, historians have long been, and still are, expected to write about the life and exploits of the Liberator Simón Bolívar, and Argentine historians often devote their greatest attention to General

[1] Lewis Hanke, "The Bones of Cuauhtémoc," *Encounter*, XXV (Sept., 1965), No. 3, pp. 79–85.

José San Martín and other heroes of their nation's early years. So strongly have Latin American historians concentrated on their colonial period and the nineteenth century that many United States historians who are studying the recent past of Latin America are dismayed to find so little concern with this subject in Latin America itself. Indeed, the history of twentieth-century Latin America has only recently begun to be written.

As the Latin American nations developed in the nineteenth century, the question of how the history of America ought to be written was posed in a number of countries. The Brazilian Historical and Geographical Institute held an open competition, shortly after its establishment in 1838, which called forth a remarkable essay by Karl Friedrich von Martius on "How the History of Brazil Should Be Written."[2] The Argentine educator and statesman, Domingo Faustino Sarmiento, delivered a ringing affirmation of faith in the New World when he was appointed Director of History of the Atheneum of La Plata. In his inaugural speech on October 11, 1858, on "The Spirit and Conditions of History in America," he exulted that a new people could arise in the new continent. The bad days of the colonial regime were over:

> Behold erased from history conquest, inheritance, divine right, arbitrariness, and aristocracy, all the elements that for so many centuries were the stuff of history. Behold the declaration of the human species, one and indivisible, a dogma and a fact that are exclusively American.[3]

Sarmiento's vision of the future of the New World has not been fulfilled, but the past continues to be publicly discussed and privately debated throughout Latin America today. With the passage of time the nature of these discussions has changed somewhat. Although Venezuelan historians no longer find it absolutely necessary to write about Bolívar, and Argentine historians may now assume a more objective attitude toward San Martín than formerly,[4] a kind of cultural nationalism still exists. Edmundo O'Gorman, who has

---

[2] This essay has been printed in *History of Latin American Civilization: Sources and Interpretations*, Vol. I (Boston: Little, Brown, 1967), pp. 500–513.

[3] Domingo Faustino Sarmiento, *Obras*, Vol. XXI (Buenos Aires, 1899), p. 102.

[4] A. J. Pérez Amuchástegui, *La "Carta de Lafond" y la preceptiva historiográfica* (Buenos Aires: Ediciones Siglo XX, 1962). This Argentine historian attacks what he calls the "false patriotism" of some Argentines on the Bolívar-San Martín question. But he took the precaution of getting the Institute of San Martín Studies to declare formally that his work was not disrespectful toward the Argentine revolutionary hero, and a copy of this formal declaration appears as a frontispiece to his book.

done so much to draw attention to the need for a more philosophic orientation among historians, has defended Mexico and Spanish America from the charge of "dilettantism" in historical writing and calls for more, not less, imagination. Mexican historians, he feels, should develop their own cultural heritage and not try to imitate English or North American approaches to history and historical writing.[5]

An important development during the last ten or fifteen years has been Soviet Russia's and East Germany's increasing attention to Latin American history and the growth of the Marxist interpretation of history in Latin America itself. As a result of all these influences, Latin American history is a particularly lively and controversial subject today. The documents selected for this section are intended only as representative samples and by no means constitute a complete coverage.

Historians are notoriously individualistic but they like to get together to ventilate their ideas. At the Second International Congress of Historians of the United States and Mexico, held at the University of Texas in 1958, one session which aroused keen interest was focused on the historian's task. Luis Villoro of the University of Mexico presented the Mexican perspective (Reading X.1), and France V. Scholes of the University of New Mexico spoke in a universal vein on freedom for the historian everywhere (Reading X.2). The Brazilian scholar José Honório Rodrigues added another thought: the true historian cannot hide in an ivory tower; he must assume a more active role by relating the past to the turbulent contemporary world (Reading X.3). How the historian makes this relationship has become one of the principal problems of historians everywhere. Waldo Frank, in the book he wrote giving a favorable view of Castro's Cuba, explained the attitude of Cuban historians toward the United States in these words:

One warning to the venturous reader. If he tackles the historians — as he must to place what Cuba was and what it is — he will frequently feel, even with the most scholarly, that he is listening to a debate or a trial in which the chronicler becomes advocate and defender and the United States, including its historians, becomes an ever-present enemy. The Cubans seem to be incapable of objectivity in their accounts of Cuba. Why this has been, I hope the reader of this book will somewhat understand. It is history itself that has put Cuba's historians on the defensive.

[5] Edmundo O'Gorman, "Cinco años de historia en México," *Filosofía y letras*, X (Mexico, 1945), No. 20, pp. 167–183.

Let the reader recall what happened at the Battle of Santiago as contrasted with American accounts. Or let him remember how in the popular American mind the honor of discovering the cause of yellow fever was spirited away from Cuban Dr. Carlos Finlay, the true revealer, and wrongly given to the heroic team of Dr. Walter Reed, who verified Finlay's exposition and made it official.[6]

The stresses and strains in present-day Latin America of course affect the perspectives of those who write its history, whether in Latin America or elsewhere. One veteran United States historian in this field, J. Fred Rippy, believes that the purpose of those writing Latin American history should be to improve inter-American relations.[7] A Colombian holds that those studying his nation's history should emphasize the positive achievements of its past leaders in order to encourage Colombians today to contribute to the fulfillment of their country's needs today.[8]

Few historians are as frank as Eric Williams, Prime Minister of Trinidad and Tobago, who described the history he prepared for the Independence Day of his nation on August 31, 1962, in this way: "This book is not conceived of as a work of scholarship. It is a manifesto of a subjugated people."[9] Dr. Williams in a later publication emphasized the need emerging nations had for a new history:

A new nation like Trinidad and Tobago, finding its own feet for the first time, achieving by its own efforts a new sense of values, cannot but have some importance for an old, tired, tiresome world, whose historian representatives, adorning the greatest of the metropolitan universities, have sought only to justify the indefensible and to seek support for preconceived and outmoded prejudices. The independence of Trinidad and Tobago cannot be developed on the basis of intellectual concepts and attitudes worked out by metropolitan scholars in an age of colonialism.[10]

Though Dr. Williams' viewpoint may seem extreme to some, few writers today concerned with Latin American history have adopted

---

[6] Waldo Frank, *Cuba: Prophetic Island* (New York: Marzani and Munsell, 1961), p. 188.

[7] J. Fred Rippy, *Hispanic American Historical Review*, XLIV (1964), p. 589.

[8] Manuel José Forero, "La calidad humana en la historia de Colombia," *Boletín cultural y bibliográfico*, V (July, 1962), pp. 802–805.

[9] Eric Williams, *History of the People of Trinidad and Tobago* (Port-of-Spain, Trinidad: P.N.M. Publishing Co., 1962), p. viii.

[10] Eric Williams, *British Historians and the West Indies* (Port-of-Spain, Trinidad: P.N.M. Publishing Co., 1964), pp. vi–vii.

the somewhat Olympian attitude of the outstanding Spanish scholar, the late Jaime Vicens Vives:

> We should accept the results of historical facts and reject every combative attitude toward the past. Belligerency in the face of history should be reserved for the politician and the saint. As a scientist the historian should not try to alter historical events, but to understand them in their totality.[11]

Today as never before the attitudes, methods, and prejudices of those who record and interpret the past are recognized as often determining the way in which the history of Latin America is written. The selections (Readings X.1–3) from the Mexican Villoro, the North American Scholes, and the Brazilian Rodrigues open up a debate on the nature of history which is likely to continue for a long time because they embody fundamental attitudes toward some of the basic problems of history.

Students of Latin American history in the next generation will probably have to learn Russian as the quantity and quality of Soviet writing in this field continue to increase. J. Gregory Oswald of the University of Arizona has for some years paid particular attention to the work of Soviet historians and has analyzed their methods and conclusions (Reading X.4).

Many exchanges on history and historical controversies are never formally recorded. Gunnar Mendoza, who is Director of the National Library and Archive of Bolivia, and the editor of this volume of readings fell into the habit of exchanging views on a wide range of historical problems while they were preparing a joint edition of an eighteenth-century manuscript on the history of Potosí in Bolivia. They continued to correspond on the nature of history after this work had been published. One of these conversations by mail forms the basis of the "Dialogue on How the History of Latin American Civilization Should be Taught in the United States" (Readings X.5–6).

[11] As quoted by A. J. Pérez Amuchástegui, *Mentalidades Argentinas, 1860–1930* (Buenos Aires: Eudeba, 1965), p. 212.

A. The Historian's Task

1. The Mexican Idea of History

Luis Villoro

In Mexico historiography was not born as the fruit of a merely contemplative action. The first works of real American history were the response to a decisive deed that radically altered the life of its protagonists: the discovery and conquest of the New World. This was a crucial happening that upset habitual concepts and revealed an unsuspected dimension in the life of the men who participated in it. For them this great event was no matter for erudite studies: it was a situation for action, and they spent themselves, their very lives, in discovering its meaning. On the one hand, the conquerors had to enter their deeds in the history of Christianity, integrate them into the scheme of historical categories that they knew and mastered; the official chroniclers had to place them with relation to the interests and ends of the state; the jurists had to determine by the light of their principles unforeseen situations. To accomplish this, one and all had to present the meaning of the New World, that is, show *what its significance was* for the Spanish state and for the general history of Christianity (which they identified with the universal history of man). On the other hand, missionaries and theologians saw themselves obliged to clarify the nature and supernatural condition of the Indian and his society, *to point out his meaning* for the divine economy; that is, to manifest the true being of those peoples by the light of Providence. Only after that operation could they know what to rely on amid such strange realities. American historiography shares in the general perplexity resulting from the sudden realization

From "The Historian's Task: The Mexican Perspective" by Luis Villoro, *The New World Looks at Its History: Proceedings of the Second International Congress of Historians of the United States and Mexico*, eds. Archibald R. Lewis and Thomas F. McGann (Austin: University of Texas Press, 1963), pp. 173–183. Reprinted by permission.

of the existence of something that did not easily fit into the world as known up to that time; it consisted of the job of transforming the unaccustomed into the understandable, of turning the inhospitable and strange into the familiar. For man was incapable of resisting the naked presence of a reality of whose human nature and significance he was ignorant, and he saw himself obliged to provide for it immediately a meaning within his world.

Thus, historiography was presented in America invested with two basic traits. First, it consisted not only of the description of things never before seen and of the narration of epic deeds, though it *also* consisted of those things. Second, it was principally an attempt to *reveal* the natural and supernatural *meaning* of such things and deeds: to reveal their meaning in a double sense of the word—to grant them a meaning within the world at that time and to indicate the future world that they augured and indicated. The conquest and the discovery were not merely deeds among other similar ones; they were a decisive overturning that indicated what all previous deeds truly consisted of and what future ones were to be like; they were events that placed all deeds in a true light, that manifested the authentic nature of all happenings. Thus, as the conversion to a new faith or a new state of life throws a distinct light on earlier and later stages, so that the convert only then discovers what his life really consisted of and what the real meaning of his acts was, so also the encounter with a new world manifested the true essence and meaning of the peoples they confronted. American historiography surged forth to acquire an awareness of it. It will suffice to recall three outstanding examples.

From the time of the letters of Cortés, in the work of many conquerors and chroniclers it is clear that the conquest of America showed the ecumenical destiny of Spain, and at the same time, gave birth to a new land, welcoming it for the first time into the course of Christian history. The historian wished to broaden the significance of actions; he began to understand the past only at the moment in which the gest became integrated into a process directed toward universal ends and the New World showed the value it held for Christianity. In Sahagún, as in other evangelists, the discovery permitted the American reality, concealed by divine will for so many centuries, to be exposed finally with its true face; it offered then the figure of a fallen and demoniac world. The word of the Scripture made patent the new reality and pointed out its role in the divine designs. Nor were the deeds themselves as important here as the sign, holy or infamous. In Las Casas, finally, the conquest showed in Spain an instrument of Providence and the tide of a singular mission; on the other hand, the destruction of the Indies sealed the future fate of the same treacherous people that Providence had assigned it. In all cases, the historian sought to give to the deeds an intentional structure, when he interpreted their meaning.

Second: A significant structure is not closed and consumed; on the contrary, it encompasses the present moment of the historian and his people, so decisively that the present life becomes transformed by its impact. The past is not seen as distant and split away (from the present); it constitutes a dimension that affects present life. Because the direction we discover in it gives a proper value and consistency to our lives and places a *decision* before us. If the past were reduced to unadorned, "objective" events, stripped of vital significance for the present, our liberty would move in nothingness; *events* that have taken place, as soon as they have taken place, do not at all affect other events that are in the process of happening, for between them no physical causality fits. Only if deeds have a *significant* dimension by which they announce, postulate, demand something that has not been realized in them yet, only then does the past aspire to fulfill itself in us; only then does it convert itself into life that obliges affirmation or rejection. We must answer for it; our own life is bound up in it. That explains the *practical* character of the first American historiography. It tried to transform, to solve, to convince in order to force a decision. From Gómara to Bernal Díaz, the chroniclers were animated by "selfish" objectives; the past they spoke of concerned them personally for it pointed out to each his rights and deserts. The indigenous writers sought in the past noble titles that might grant some worth to their lives and permit them to place themselves in the conqueror's society. The missionaries wrote only to detect where sin and grace were found, with the object of transforming souls. Las Casas, as a good prophet, took up his pen to break through hard hearts and oblige them to be converted. The historian had to fulfill a practical mission. Not because he conceived history as a propaganda organ at the service of the changing objectives of the moment; no. What happened was that, when the *sense* of the past was clarified, former times did not appear as a gathering together of things that "were," but as a still unfinished human structure that demanded our decisions in order to be fulfilled.

Thus history was born in America as a vital knowledge. It had a precise role in the community: it was the revealer of life's meaning, the director of action, the announcer of ends. Thanks to it, the daily happenings of the people were illumined. The historian's task is not a thing of archives or museums; it is the business of life itself.

III — This idea seems to have permanently stamped later historiography in Mexico. Well into the eighteenth century its task continues to be the demonstration of the meaning of the past in order to clarify present life. It is not surprising that a Clavijero, for example, should search in the remote indigenous past for a classical tradition to oppose to that of Europe, in order to emancipate us from our spiritual subjection; nor that he should write with the purpose of attaining a new attitude for the *criollo* (creole) face to face with himself. Clavijero gives importance to the past, dresses it up with the finery of tradition and exemplary qualities in order to kindle better the criollo's pride and awaken his confidence in his own possibilities.

With the political historians of the first half of the nineteenth century the practical character of history is revived. Conservatives and liberals incite their readers to take up an attitude. They see how the past changes according to one's design. The historical attitude that one has will explain the particular meaning that is given to the past. Given the attitude of the liberals, the past urges a radical conversion; its significance consists in leading to the moment of emancipation, in approaching a decision which the people determine freely. It reveals a negative being: it is there to be rejected and to permit the appearance of the act of liberty. But, though denied, that past integrates our own life, for it poses the demand of a liberating conversion. In the conservatives' attitude, on the other hand, the sense of the past consists of a slow vegetal transformation. Little by little the new society is being formed, without conversions or violence. The conservative historian also poses the necessity of a decision: that of being faithful to the evolutionary rhythm of history. In both cases, the past is not an accumulation of "objective" facts that we may contemplate impartially; it is, on the contrary, a call to each "type" to accede to a particular attitude. In both cases, the historian reveals the meaning and direction of human life and demands, therefore, a personal decision.

IV — But if the historian's task consists of showing, from his unique perspective, the significance that events have for life; if this depends on the attitude of the historian; if, in short, our present situation obliges us to emphasize one or another meaning of the past, will not the facts of the past result as dependent on the perspective of the one considering them and will not history in its entirety be dependent on the historian's subjectivity? Will not events lose their character of *invariable* facts and, therefore, their "objectivity"? To answer those and other similar questions, scientific positivist historiography was born, as is well known. In our country it was dominant beginning with the era of positivism and still exists in numerous writers.

The positivist historian thought that he could let the facts talk for themselves, eliminate all personal perspective and reduce all judgments to asseverations that were verifiable; in this way only, he thought, would history accede to the objectivity proper to all positive science. With it he succeeded, undoubtedly, in setting aside the discord of the different historical considerations, born of the circumstantial choices of the historian, and in purging — forever, we hope — scientific history of the capricious play of our subjective whims. Its fight against the arbitrary interjection of the spectator in its object, its demand for objectivity and rigor in historical method will remain as definitive gains; we cannot do without these if we are to constitute historiography as a science.

But, at the same time, converted into a mere object like natural objects, the past definitely seemed remote from present life. Facts, lined up and classified, became as alien and indifferent to present human life as a physical phenomenon. Because we can see in an event only something that concerns us, if we awaken in it a significance that transcends it and points to the present. Mere "objective" facts lack, as such, significant structures; the historian's activity is necessary to give them life. The positivist historian gave to the past a quality of invariability, forgetting its most essential characteristic: that historical facts are but the substratum of *human meanings,* which are not facts but rather intentions that bind the facts together. By considering the object of history to be mere objective verification of data, as physical objectivity is constituted, the positivist historian subtracted his own dimension of meaning from history. At the same time he realized the most radical divorce between his science and his life. The historian no longer had a vital function in which it was incumbent on him to give directives to present life or to clarify its significance.

V — Now, the present moment in Mexican historiography gives signs that the idea of history is in full crisis. The symptoms are many and known to most of you. I shall only point out some of them with the purpose of emphasizing the task that the present situation of the discipline of history imposes upon the American historian.

The first who forcefully pointed to the fundamental crisis of historiography was, among us, an historian whose work deserves, we believe, more attention than it has been given — Edmundo O'Gorman. His criticism led him to reject, as unauthentic, the attempt to convert historiography into a science of bare events, "objectives" after the fashion of the facts of nature. The historian's task would consist, on the contrary, in the creation of the intelligibility of human happenings, using the raw material of facts as a point of departure; a task in which man gives existence to the past and converts it into his own past. In his works is posed the question of the existence of a historical process, America, which would not predate historiographic labor, but would be, in a certain way, its result.

Another symptomatic current is the one usually called in Mexico, with a name that is too restrictive, "the history of ideas," in which the work of Leopoldo Zea is prominent. This type of history had its birth in a question apparently alien to the field of historiography: "What is the Mexican?" that is to say: "What are the traits of our circumstances that, setting us apart, might point out to us our own task?" This question, though born of a philosophic reflection, could only be answered by referring to the process in which our circumstances are formed. The question becomes authentically historic because it asks about a temporal structure animated with meaning: the living circumstances. Here the historian's task would consist of pointing out spiritual directions, collective projects and ideas which order according to purposes the historical process of a nation and admit our moment into an event directed rationally. The historian thus converts yesterday into a rational structure capable of explaining the present.

For our part, in connection with the trends mentioned, we have essayed in a couple of works the application of a new criterion and historiographic method. In accord with them the object of historiography would not be properly the series of "objective" events, but the collective human attitudes that, at each moment, grant them a meaning. While the task of the natural scientist begins by stripping the object of all the "human" notes that cover it, the historian's task begins precisely when he manifests the human meanings that animate the facts; his labor consists of recuperating the human, "interior" dimension of his object.

However different may be the ideas that inspire the trends described above, however greatly they may diverge from each other, they seem to coincide on the two following points: they attempt new ways of access to the past in order to discover in it what constitutes one's own object of historical knowledge; and they share the conviction that the historian's task should be the clarification of significant structures that transcend the sum of the bare facts.

But not only in these trends can symptoms of crisis be observed. Also among the historians who maintain with the greatest vigor the "scientific objective" character of their knowledge, with the legitimate anxiety of not wanting to compromise the universal value of their discoveries, we find signs of a certain concern for recovering the vital dimension of the historical task. José Miranda has expounded in lectures the need for historiography as a help in the solution of theoretical problems in specialized knowledge and has upheld the idea that history should respond always to the practical requirements that community life poses. The historical task would have a social function, present at all times. And in the most ambitious and promising attempt of recent years, *The Modern History of Mexico*, undertaken by a group of historians directed by Daniel Cosío Villegas, we seem to perceive a certain ambiguity: on one side, the expressed attempt to maintain the "impartiality" of history, radically eliminating the historian's subjectivity, reducing his labor to the rational classification and orderly relation of facts; on the other, an implicit attempt to utilize those facts as practical teaching. Questions are asked about those "responsible" for a situation, human causes of failure are sought, with the objective, perhaps, of establishing a diagnosis of the immediate past that might clarify the significance of the present moment. If this is what they are aiming at, under a layer of dispassionate objectivity, it would again point out the vital and practical roots of history. But *The Modern History of Mexico* is not yet concluded and we must still reserve judgment.

VI — The symptoms described above tell us something of the crisis of historiography, and more still of its perpetual dignity. For the crisis comes from the fact that the historian does not resign himself to forget the distinguished human range of his science. Indeed, history possesses a unique dignity among all the "spiritual sciences." While all the others have to do with some kind of human *products* or some region of culture considered objectively, history should not stop at any cultural product, but rather ask about the very *producing activity*. It should not treat properly of all the things left by men, but rather of human life and of its component process in the world. Therefore one must not consider cultural documents and remains as finished things, whose sense would be contained completely in themselves, but rather as vestiges, as indices of the creative life of the spirit. The documents that man leaves in his passage, the testimonies of his external deeds, the sum of his products, should be only signs to be interpreted, ciphers that give to active life its meaning.

But its dignity does not stop there. The historian must respond to the question that man poses to himself about his temporal condition. His science permits him to say a great deal about the human condition and its fugitive destiny. When he unveils the past the historian must discover characteristic attitudes and processes in which we participate by the mere fact of being men. When he asks himself about the meaning of life that extends ours toward the past, he must manifest the intentional vectors and indices of processes that are fulfilled in us. Thus, history teaches us, not because we ingenuously ask for remedies for the solution of our present problems, but because, in regaining the human meanings of the past, it clarifies a dimension of our own situation and grants a new significance to each one of our actions. Because of it, historiography cannot be a theoretical science in the same sense that other sciences are; it has, essentially, a practical function to fulfill, which derives directly from its theoretical labor.

But to fulfill that task, it is necessary to have a clear idea of its object and its methods of work. If present historiography seems to us, often, divorced from life, occupied as it is in the hunting for data whose deep dimension it pretends to be unaware of; if at times we fear that it has sold its humanist range for "objective verification," it is doubtless because it has become confused about the true object.

Dilthey and his school on one side, Windelband and Rickert on the other, pointed out with precision the difference between the object and method of history and the object and method of the natural sciences. To continue to confuse these categories, as many historians in America do, without having at times a full awareness of that confusion, results in historiography moving away from its vital and human function. We cannot renounce, of course, the scientific character of history, nor do without, therefore, the invariability and transcendence of its objects, nor the rigor of its methods. But all science must adapt its methods to the specific character of the object it treats. If that of historiography consists of human meanings, which animate the past without being confused with it, the methods leading to its knowledge should be procedures destined to show, by the vestiges of that past, the activity giving it meaning, and cannot be at all like the methods of the positivist natural sciences.

We believe that American historians need to consider more seriously the problem of the object and methods of their science. We do not ask them to write philosophy. Whoever thinks this shows that he has a poor idea of the historian, reducing him to the role of simple technician or ingenuous narrator. The historian must reflect on the human bases and ends of his science. Only he can formulate new hypotheses of work and apply them in concrete procedures; until this is done all the philosophic theories about history are empty speculations. Therefore, the great reforms of historiography were never the result of the philosophers of history as such, but of the historians. Only if the historian acquires a complete awareness of the specific character of his object and rediscovers in it the creative life of man in all its richness, only if he considers the dignity of its human function, will he regain the leading role in society which was his of yore.

2. The Historian Must Be Free

FRANCE V. SCHOLES

When I was invited to participate in this session of the Congress I had some misgiving about the topic for discussion. For I felt that surely the essential and basic tasks of the historian are the same in our two countries; that they could not — and should not — be de-

From "Freedom for the Historian" by France V. Scholes, *The New World Looks at Its History: Proceedings of the Second International Congress of Historians of the United States and Mexico*, eds. Archibald R. Lewis and Thomas F. McGann (Austin: University of Texas Press, 1963), pp. 173–183. Reprinted by permission.

scribed in local terms; that the role and functions of the historian and the ideals of his profession transcend national definitions and dimensions.

I was pleased and gratified, therefore, on reading the papers of Sr. Villoro and Mr. Whitaker, to find that they cover a considerable measure of common ground, although they approach the question of the historian's task in different ways and with different emphases. Sr. Villoro describes the crisis in historiography in Mexico. Mr. Whitaker's remarks reflect unrest in the field of historical studies in this country. Both of the speakers have discussed, in somewhat different terms or frames of reference, basic problems of methodology and interpretation, the proper range and purpose of historical investigation and historical writing, and other current issues of debate which beset and plague all of us. And having found that they summon as witnesses or examples so many great names, past and present, I could only ask myself: what can I add to the subject in ten minutes?

I have two things to say. First, to applaud the remarks of Mr. Whitaker concerning the role and essential dignity of the individual historian. I hope that this Congress recognizes and will assert the right of the individual historian to pursue his labors in his own way and according to his own lights; the right freely to choose his own subject for investigation; the right not to be placed under pressure, direct or indirect, by any agency, private or governmental (including universities); the right to channel his investigations along lines for which funds may be available, without sacrificing research projects of his own preference or choice. I can only deplore the policies of some agencies which sometimes seem to profess more wisdom than the individual scholar in regard to what should be studied or what merits long-range investigation; and in particular, I wish to register protest against the current emphasis upon and preference for projects which deal with contemporary problems or the contemporary scene. Historians have an obligation, without any doubt, to use their knowledge and talents for the public service. But historians also know, better than others perhaps, that what may seem to be "hot stuff" today may be "cold turkey" tomorrow. And I have serious doubt that very many studies undertaken as a public service at the request or behest of the money-dispensing agencies will be ranked as historical classics.

I also hope that this Congress will recognize the right of the individual historian to resist current trends and emphases in historiography if he wishes to do so, and especially with reference to the insistent demand for interpretations of one kind or another, as that based on that vague and nebulous thing called philosophy of history. In this connection I find great comfort in Sr. Villoro's concluding statement that the great reforms of historiography have not been made by the philosophers of history as such but by the historians themselves. And I assume that this statement refers to classics of historiography, past and present, written by scholars who claimed the right to perform their tasks in their own way.

So let us lift up our hearts in praise of the fact that the individual historian has been — and should be — the master of his craft. Long may he reign.

And now my second point. I share Sr. Villoro's view — do not all of us? — that complete objectivity is an illusion. But I also have more faith in the ability of the historian to seek out and establish "objective facts" than have many of our contemporary theorists, some of whom seem to view almost with disdain traditional norms of methodology, including sincere and patient preoccupation with documentary sources. Let us not forget that the master of a craft can be no better than his tools and the materials which he fashions, with love, honesty, and integrity, into a finished product. A revered friend once told me that I spend my time dusting off the "documentary cadavers of the past." Perhaps! But I do believe and know that these "documentary cadavers" often have more life and vitality in them than some of the arid conceptualizations that are sometimes palmed off as history.

It is for these reasons that I wish to question the validity of Mr. Whitaker's remark that facts in and for themselves do not deserve freedom of speech. I doubt that the physicist would agree, and I hope that most historians do not agree. For who has the right to decide what are useless or useful facts? Much of the debate about "facts," "objective history," and the need for vital interpretations reflects, in my opinion, a certain lack of confidence in the ability of the individual historian to make value judgments. We all know that the historical investigator must select those "facts" which he believes deserve emphasis or have significant value, that by this very act he gives interpretation to his data. But again, I plead for recognition of his right to fashion his product as he chooses.

The papers of Sr. Villoro and Mr. Whitaker have demonstrated again the obvious and rather time-worn fact that fashions in historiography are constantly changing, and that what may seem to be new is not so new after all. Mr. Whitaker has quoted Conyers Read's statement that the first prerequisite of a historian is "a sound social philosophy," because he follows the evolution of society with reference to his "concept of what is socially desirable," and consequently his view of the past "inevitably projects itself into the future." If this be a valid measure of what a historian is or should be, then I submit that the "decision" school of Mexican historians described by Sr. Villoro fits this requirement, for they doubtless believed that they had a sound social philosophy, on the basis of which they viewed the past and the future. The same would be true of Mr. Whitaker's "for" and "against" characterization of some United States historians. Moreover, most of the current theories of history reflect "for" or "against" attitudes. Even the "objectivist" or "positivist" school of historiography was not completely devoid of conscious purpose and value judgments. The writing of history has always reflected a vital and human element, if only that of the individual laborer in the vineyard.

So, in closing, let me plead once more for his right to seek out, select, and record his data in his own way and with as much sincerity and integrity as he can summon for his task.

3. History Belongs to Our Own Generation

José Honório Rodrigues

Theodore Mommsen wrote that we live in the present but do not understand it and that History begins only when life itself is stilled. The relationship between the historical process — the indivisible unity of the past, present, and future — and historiography does not seem well defined by this statement, for the latter is always a reflection of the former. It is up to each generation to provide a meaningful vision of the world, either as Nature or as History. . . .

The relationship between History as a vital socio-cultural process and historical writing as the understanding of the life and changeability of the forms of this same process, whether already lived or still living, is so intimate that only a perversion of its purposes per-

From "La historiografía brasileña y el actual proceso histórico" by José Honório Rodrigues, *Anuario de Estudios Americanos*, XIV, 1957, pp. 63–85, *passim*. Reprinted by permission.

mitted the abandonment of descriptions "in statu nascendi" in favor
of "post mortem" reconstructions. It is not necessary to wait until
an event reaches its point of rest — transitory or eternal — before
historical writing about it can be conceptualized. History is not a
macabre anthology of the death of creativity, nor a museum of
antiquities; it is the balcony from which the virtues and sins of the
human race are most forcefully hidden or displayed.

History belongs, not to the dead, but to the living, as a present
reality which the conscience must heed. For this reason it is not alien
to life. But unfortunately the idea of History for its own sake . . .
dominates historical writing and has led to a crisis in historical
thought. This crisis is due not only to specialization, which digs
ever deeper into the dark well of the particularity and singularity of
events, but also to the fact that the audience is increasingly being
limited to professional historians.   . . .

But in Brazil the central point of the crisis lies not only in increasing specialization, which is characteristic of few historians, but
above all in the failure to relate the historical process to historiographical thought. It is not a question of the non-existence of contemporary history, the study of which we leave to French, American,
and Soviet historians, but a lack of historiographical response to the
demands of current history. Scholarly specialization may have
limited the audience of the European or American historian, but he
did not cease to illuminate the contemporary scene with his monographs; in Brazil, however — and I believe in all the underdeveloped
world — neither specialization nor the few existing syntheses dared
to face the problems and themes being proposed by the historical
process.   . . .

[In Brazil] we continue playing out of tune because we continue
to write history through history — that is, problems and themes of
our historiography, with a few exceptions, have been the same since
it freed itself, with Varnhagen, from the tutelage of Portuguese
historiography and fell into the domineering embrace of French
thought. . . . There is little authentic and profound investigation
that might serve as a basis for generalizing and accessible syntheses.
There is still a lack of an adequate correspondence between historical times, especially those most meaningful for an understanding of
the present and the consequent illumination of the past.   . . .

The revolution of 1930, the modifications of the economic and
social structure, the struggle for power of the middle class produced
a formidable feeling of national self-consciousness. At no time in

our historiography did history seek to serve the present as much as it did just before and after the 1930 revolution. Special collections of Brazilian studies were founded, such as the *Brasiliana* in 1931 and *Documentos Brasileiros* in 1936. . . .

Collections of this type should have stimulated a more pragmatic thought in which the present, with its problems and themes, would become the screen on which the light of the past would be projected. The silent voice of History had to become a national voice that would be heard and pondered by all. But this did not happen. "Historian's" history, purely descriptive history, classical history . . . overwhelmed the collections, which ended largely in debating the same problems and theses. . . . The collections became descriptive, specialized, and erudite, thereby defeating their original purposes. . . .

One of the ways in which historiography can serve the nation is by studying current themes and problems in the light of history. This does not mean that we ought to study more contemporary history, which should not be confused with the study of historical themes relevant to the present. To clarify the historical origins of the present and to study "current" history are two different things, and both ought to be present in such collections and in the concerns of contemporary historiography. But in truth this occurs only in exceptional cases, and this condition is the source of the dissonance between the present historical period and contemporary historiography, between the present historical process and historical thought. It is also the source of the disenchantment and mistrust that characterizes the attitude of innumerable scholars with respect to the results of modern Brazilian historiography. . . .

The enthusiasm of the 1930's, which attracted generous spirits to history who have now left it or cultivate it only occasionally, was replaced by skepticism because of the practical results obtained. . . . Brazilian historiography was unable to continue renewing itself, that is, to pursue its studies along classical lines and at the same time to progress by heeding the call of the new problems and themes of a new Brazil, of which the political movement of 1930 was one of the first signs. Brazilian historiography was unable to proceed as did that of the United States, for example, which established a strict relationship between the historical process and historiography after Turner in 1893 sought to free it from European hypotheses and revealed the peculiarity of its history in the light of environmental conditions and the historical process itself. Since then American historiography

. . . has faced the complexities of the present by studying the problems and themes created by the present. And at the same time that it freed itself from European hypotheses, it isolated itself until the moment that its national interests placed these same problems in a scene of global significance. . . .

The revolutionary movement of 1930 stirred a great attempt at self-knowledge on the part of Brazil and the Brazilians, which was in part weakened by scholarly specialization and by the lack of harmony between the questions of the present and the answers of the past. Nevertheless, the new historical process, which began in 1945 . . . , has not met with the slightest initiative on the part of Brazilian historiography. It is not a question of wanting to transform history into a pragmatic discipline, nor of eliminating objective investigation, and much less of writing contemporary history, which we also need. It is a question of answering the concrete questions that the historical process raises, for each generation has to write its own history, and this is the main reason why it is written.

To respond to the present does not mean to write about the present but about those themes which concern the present, because if the historians who are painstaking, wise, and well-trained do not do it, those who are unscrupulous and unqualified will. Alexander and Caesar are much more contemporary than Demosthenes or Cicero. The study of 1822 and the Independence years teach more than the first years of civilian government during the First Republic, which are as dead as Lloyd George or Bismarck. . . .

A historiography that wishes to be of service to its generation ought to restore, as Geoffrey Barraclough said, the connection between the past and the present. For this reason it must face the complexities of the day, studying new themes or reviewing old ones, not only by examining them in relation to different interpretive theories but especially by revealing content significant to present generations. Might not the system of *capitanias* and land distribution offer a historical perspective for agrarian reform? How many economic, social, and political themes might not be viewed or reviewed in the light of this idea of turning history into a living force? . . .

Even though serving the present does not mean writing contemporary history, it is necessary to remember that the latter must be written by Brazilian historians, who ought not to leave it in the hands of chroniclers and newspaper columnists. Alongside them there can and ought to be a history of the present written with the same methods as "post mortem" history, though it may present greater difficulties. . . .

The belief that contemporary history differs from any kind of historical knowledge is based, according to Barraclough, on a false concept of historical knowledge. Only in one point does the position of the historian of the present differ from that of other historians: in the reaction that his opinion may provoke. No one will have difficulty in accepting the opinion of a historian on the ministries of the Marquess of Parana or of the Viscount Rio Branco, but anyone will feel free to criticize or examine the opinion that he might make on the Vargas government or of the movements of General Teixeira Lott. The reason is not that the historian is better informed about the former than the latter or that he approaches them in different manners. . . . His attitude as a historian will be basically the same in both cases; he will be a partisan perhaps, but a partisan in both cases, for there is as much reason for a historian to be a partisan of the Viscount Rio Branco as of General Teixeira Lott. The difference shall not be in the historian's attitude but in the attitude of the public, and for three reasons: (1) The public read newspaper accounts about Vargas and formed its own opinion, but it did not read newspaper accounts about the Viscount Rio Branco and therefore does not feel competent to judge him; (2) The public feels, though its sentiment may be ingenuous or self-deceiving, that the actions of Lott may be relevant to the practical questions of the moment on which it ought to take a stand. And finally, the public lived and is still living the tensions and debates of 1945 and 1955; they are part of its own direct experience, and consequently it is still directly involved in them. Therefore, it is not surprising that the verdict of history, no matter how veracious it may be, may buffet the emotions of the public and even its sense of dignity. . . .

Since the historian does not expect to comfort anyone with the hopes of tomorrow as the politicians do, he always arouses bitter disappointment. If the historian of contemporary life is doing his job properly, he ought to expect to make great enemies, for he shall not be on the side of the Government or of the Opposition. In any form the writing of contemporary history would present great advantages: it would avoid the errors and lies of official literature and irresponsible reporting; it would present a picture of the problems and historical situation of the nation; and it would contribute to the re-fashioning of history by future historians, serving as an authentic primary source. . . . For this reason Soviet historians are right

when they say, like Siderov, that investigations of contemporary
history ought to be focussed not on superficial events and facts or on
chance happenings . . . but on the basic problems which determine
the development of society. . . .

It is necessary to avoid the fossilization, the ultraconservatism,
the foolishness of certain public institutions, official and non-official,
that transform history into a tomb, for there are those who would
make use of them to cultivate a sterile traditionalism, sterile and
passive, which constitutes a useless weight in this hour when the
new Brazil is conquering the old Brazil. . . .

It is necessary to reform the teaching of history on the university
level, for we cannot ignore the new non-European forces in the
world — China, India, the Near and Far East, Africa — nor be content with a superficial knowledge of world powers like the United
States and the Soviet Union, the first of which ought to be the subject of an autonomous discipline in the university alongside the
special study of Spanish America. What will become the future of
Brazilian generations — and young people of school and university
age constitute the majority of the nation — if they remain danger-
ously ignorant of the actual distribution of power and the forces that
really operate in the world in which we live? The present short-
sighted division of history into ancient, medieval, modern, contemporary, and American history is of no benefit to youth and
inculcates a false sense of continuity, as well as an erroneous vision
of the preponderance of Europe, a continent whose destiny is today
forged outside of its borders.

Just as the future of Europe will be more closely linked with the
most highly Europeanized peoples — and among these the whole of
America stands out — so the future of the peoples once dominated
by Europe depends in large part on the two new giants of power,
the United States and the Soviet Union. Our dependence imposes a
historico-universal vision, for we produce national history and consume world history.

B. The Soviet Image of Latin America

4. Contemporary Soviet Research on Latin America

J. GREGORY OSWALD

Soviet historians, economists, and anthropologists have explored Latin American history from the pre-Columbian epoch to the present, but in the period since World War II one finds the greatest depth of materials and the most sophisticated application of Marxist dialectics. For this reason, the translated readings in *The Soviet Image of Latin America, 1945–1965: A Documentary History* are limited to the contemporary period.

The book will contain four parts, which, except for the last, are arranged topically into theoretical, socio-political, and economic categories. Soviet Communist Party documents and policy decisions included in Part One reveal the purpose of Soviet research on Latin America — namely, to evaluate its economy, political and ideological traditions, social structure, and international relations in order to determine the appropriate tactics for promoting national liberation movements. The second and third parts demonstrate how rapidly Soviet scholars have responded to academic programs recommended by the Communist Party. Proceeding from the extreme left to the extreme right, Part Two will contain chapters devoted to political movements and the classes generally associated with these movements, while Part Three probes Latin America's basic economic problems. A final section will include historical essays on Cuba, Mexico, Brazil, Argentina, and Chile.

Inasmuch as the ultimate purpose of Soviet Latin American research as reflected in Part One is to promote socialist revolution, it is appropriate to begin Part Two with a chapter devoted specifically to the national liberation movement. Introductory articles in this

From "Contemporary Soviet Research on Latin America" by J. Gregory Oswald, *Latin American Research Review*, I, Spring 1966, pp. 80–87, *passim*. Reprinted by permission.

chapter describe the basic causes and significant aspects of the national liberation movement while others detail the role of the nationalist and petty bourgeoisie, students, intelligentsia, proletariat, and peasants in fomenting Marxist revolutions. A study of the Cuban revolution measures its impact upon Latin American national liberation movements and demonstrates how its leaders manipulated middle and lower classes to overthrow the Batista regime. A leading Soviet historian surmised that the Cuban revolution succeeded because all forms of political struggle were flexibly applied with the appropriate action dependent upon the exigencies of each particular situation.

Revolutionaries who advocate armed rebellion as the only means of achieving national liberation receive criticism for maintaining erroneous and dogmatic positions and are labeled "petty bourgeois ultra-leftists." A study of peasant warfare in Colombia substantiates the more pragmatic Soviet approach which eschews unnecessary or abortive armed confrontations. Despite intermittent guerrilla warfare in parts of Tolima and Cundinamarca, the Colombian peasant rebellion seems to have been premature, for "the overwhelming majority of the peasants still believed in the illusions sown in their minds by the liberals."

Although economic and social inequities have inspired national liberation movements in Latin America, Soviet writers emphasize that motivation alone cannot attain revolutionary changes without the cooperation of all political organizations, labor unions, and social classes which oppose American imperialism. One article explains how the Communist Party can unify these groups and why it must maintain or obtain control of revolutionary movements. In harmony with this popular-front concept, a labor analyst criticizes the petty sectarianism which has divided Latin American socialists and communists and lauds their recent cooperative efforts in Chile and Uruguay.

To promote wars of national liberation in Latin America, it has been necessary for Soviet scholars to analyze the middle classes and social democratic reform movements. Many of these studies, which are included in the succeeding chapter, establish definite categories within the middle classes in order to ascertain precisely "which of the local bourgeois strata are capable of participating in the anti-imperialist struggle, and to what degree." Earlier categorizations solely based on wealth and social status were revised in order to reclassify the middle classes according to their attitude toward national capital and foreign imperialism.

The middle-class groups which cooperate closely with foreign interests and which actively oppose national liberation movements are the pro-imperialist and wealthy conciliatory bourgeoisie. Traditionally, the commercial bourgeoisie participating exclusively in international trade were epitomized as the principal pawn of foreign interests. Since the second world war, however, Soviet writers have expanded the pro-imperialist category to include foreign business representatives and officials of national or mixed companies which are partially owned or financed by foreign capital. Members of the wealthy conciliatory bourgeoisie depend financially on the maintenance or development of the state sector. Although the latter's emphasis upon economic protection and state planning separates it from the pro-imperialists, both benefit by aid from capitalist nations.

The national bourgeoisie, encompassing the majority of the small and medium-scale merchants, and the petty bourgeoisie, which include most salaried workers, merit careful scrutiny by Soviet scholars. Their significance lies both in their considerable ideological influence upon the working class and in their anti-imperialistic potentialities. Selections which analyze the national bourgeoisie reflect equivocal attitudes. While the national bourgeoisie are antagonized by American economic imperialism, they accept Soviet support not to embrace socialism but to counter imperialism and thereby enhance the growth of national capital. Some sectors of the petty bourgeoisie, particularly students and professors, form the vanguard of national liberation movements; yet a significant sector supports social democratic reformist parties which solicit foreign investment and cooperate with the United States. Separate interpretive accounts of APRA, the MNR, and Acción Democrática clarify the Soviet view of these social democratic parties.

Transcending class distinctions and their allied political movements is a chapter which examines the social doctrine of the Roman Catholic Church and the Christian Democratic Movement. An initial selection predictably portrays the church in Latin America as the bulwark of conservatism and anti-communism. More recent articles, however, reflect Soviet anxiety over the increasing flexibility of the Church toward social and economic reforms and its deliberate efforts to disassociate itself from unpopular political regimes. Catholic labor organizations have flaunted their opposition to faltering dictatorships. Even the Church hierarchy favored workers' demands in arbitrating labor disputes in order to mislead the masses and gain their favor. Thus the Church no longer anesthetizes the masses' class consciousness by extolling Christian humility and self-sacrifice, but instead allies itself with popular demands in order to pacify the masses and avoid a radical atheistic revolution.

Having identified the cunning of the Church's expedient measures, Soviet historians anticipated the growing ascendancy of the Christian Democratic Movement in certain Latin American countries. For many years a minor political group of Catholic progressives, it has been embraced recently by part of the conservative hierarchy as a political antidote to reformist and national liberation movements. The Christian Democrats, like the national bourgeoisie, seek a third position independent of the capitalist and socialist blocs in international affairs and advocate social reforms to mitigate class conflicts at home. While questioning the sincerity of their most radical proposals, Soviet writers assert that the communists "are seeking unity with those Catholics who, regardless of their approach to the problem of basic goals or methods of achieving them, are ready to work jointly for the good of the working class."

Materials in the succeeding chapter on the forces of conservatism expose the interrelationships among the Latin American "triad of reaction": the rural oligarchy; the wealthy bourgeoisie; and U.S. imperialism. Since World War II, the landed elite began investing heavily in banking and light industries. Simultaneously, the wealthy bourgeoisie, unable to compete with American and West European heavy industries, have used their investment to acquire land. American corporations complete the conservative combination by establishing joint companies with the rural and urban elite and by collaborating in the suppression of labor unions and social reforms.

Several selections analyze post-war dictatorships in general and the Pérez Jiménez, Rojas Pinilla, and Laureano Gómez dictatorships in particular. According to Soviet writers, U.S. companies tried to check the impressive proliferation of Latin American competitors established during World War II by supporting these dictators. Thus, the timing of the post-military coups was not coincidental but "represented in actuality an attempt at the forcible resolution of this conflict in favor of the American monopolies and domestic reaction."

A comprehensive section on international problems could easily circumscribe the entire book because U.S. imperialism and other foreign influences play vital roles in almost every Soviet discussion of Latin America. To counterbalance this obsession and to avoid excessive repetition, only Soviet analyses of the Pan Americanism, Pan Hispanism, *Latinidad*, Third Force Movements, and of Latin

America's relations with the socialist bloc countries and the United Nations are evaluated in the chapter on international forces.

Pan Americanism, the most objectionable of the international forces, was initiated under the guise of American spiritual and democratic unity. The United States deceitfully twisted these lofty ideals to bolster dictatorial puppets who embraced American economic interests and discriminated against their European competitors. During Franklin D. Roosevelt's administration, the United States broadened the social base of Pan Americanism to include sectors of the nationalist and petty bourgeoisie, "but it could in no case succeed in creating any kind of unity between American capitalists and the Latin American working class." Roosevelt's policy was quickly erased by John Foster Dulles. Rejecting the concept of liberty, equality, and brotherhood, Dulles stressed the belief in the spiritual realm as the common bond of Pan Americanism, thus shifting to a slogan more congenial with his reactionary-clerical allies in Latin America.

The idea of maintaining a third position in international affairs is less objectionable but more dangerous to the fruition of the national liberation movement. It stimulates an intermediate posture between the "two imperialisms – that of the United States and the 'imperialism' of the Soviet Union" – and is promoted by a number of bourgeois nationalists as a method to uphold Latin America's political and economic sovereignty. France and other Latin-European nations have exploited this idea to promote Latinidad, a concept of cultural unity with Latin America which "is a convenient screen to cover up their sharp competition with the more important partner [the United States]." The Cuban revolution supposedly demonstrates the impracticality of the third force position, for "the machinations of U.S. imperialistic elements aimed at strangling Cuba called for immediate brotherly solidarity. . . ." This vital support was not given to Cuba by nations espousing a third force but "by the Soviet Union and by all the other countries of the socialist camp. . . ." It therefore follows that independence from the United States can only be upheld through alignment with the socialist camp and that Cuba, in spite of the missile debacle, is presumably an independent nation.

Part Three, concerned with economic problems, opens with a chapter on the urban working class and organized labor. Soviet economists trace the growth of the proletariat, its altered role in an increasingly industrial society, and its problems which are aggravated by automation and the great migration of rural workers to the city. One persistent issue is wage discrimination against women,

Indians, Negroes, and Latin Americans in contrast to the lucrative positions held by U.S. and European employees. American companies frequently hold salaries below legal minimums by a system of permanent apprenticeship whereby an employee works at a reduced salary and is dismissed when he qualifies as a journeyman.

Labor abuses are endured by the working class because it remains divided by bourgeois-inspired trade unions. Soviet writers assert that the leaders of the Organización Regional Interamericana de Trabajadores (ORIT), which is controlled by its major affiliate, the AFL-CIO, collaborate with foreign and domestic business interests by opposing the national liberation movement and deliberately creating labor disunity. Other labor organizations which eschew class struggle and are allied with bourgeois political groups such as the Apristas, Peronistas, and Christian Democrats, are also analyzed and criticized. Despite these obstacles to labor unity, the communists are consoled by the cooperation of socialist-communist trade unions in Chile and are confident that the rank and file of bourgeois-oriented unions will overthrow their leaders as the condition of the working class deteriorates.

Two articles which categorize the rural classes and analyze the principal methods of exploiting the peasantry provide a fundamental background to the themes outlined in a succeeding chapter on agricultural and agrarian problems. Soviet scholars maintain that the landed elite and the wealthy, or kulak, farmers continually expand their properties at the expense of small and middle landholders. Not only do they receive lower transportation rates from commercial middle-men and lower interest rates from state banks but frequently they control private banks and commercial organizations which charge small farmers exorbitant interest rates. The system of issuing government credits to wealthy landholders who in turn grant usurious loans to small farmers is detailed in an article about Brazilian agriculture.

With the capitalization of agriculture and the concentration of financial and commercial sources in the hands of the rural elite, there has been a marked decrease in the number of small and middle farmers. Many of them either migrate to urban centers or join the semi-proletariat class which must work part-time as peons, sharecroppers, or tenant farmers in order to retain their symbolic parcel of land. Their plight is brought into sharp focus in a study of the forms of land rent in Argentina.

Although sectors of the national and petty bourgeoisie are seeking solutions to agrarian problems, a Soviet analyst explains why their measures are inadequate. Rather than confiscate *latifundias,* the bourgeois reformists merely distribute public lands or unused private property. He predicts that wealthy agricultural capitalists with their financial and commercial resources intact will continue to extend their holdings at the expense of the new colonists. Selections on the status of Mexican agriculture during the Alemán administration and the failure of the Bolivian revolution indicate why even radical bourgeois reforms have been inadequate.

Not unaware of the importance of agricultural development, Soviet economists nevertheless write more extensively on industrialization and Latin America's primary industrial problem, economic imperialism. An initial selection describes the stimulus to the growth of national industries in Latin America provided by the second world war with its shortages of manufactured products and consequent surplus of foreign exchange.

Succeeding articles describe the various techniques employed by the U.S. government and American corporations to undermine the expansion of national industries. One method was to extend U.S. foreign aid to only those Latin American nations which lowered import tariffs and abolished import licensing and multiple currencies. While this effectively removed the protective shield from Latin America's infant industries, the Export-Import Bank subsidized American exporters and foreign subsidiaries. U.S. foreign aid also insulated American power companies from the wrath of Latin American nationalists who were angered by power shortages and the consequent retardation of national industrial development. When nationalization of these companies appeared imminent, the United States granted new credits conditional to the extension or renegotiation of favorable contracts with American utilities.

When the national bourgeoisie realized their inability to withstand the encroachment of the foreign interests, they turned to the state. The Soviet attitude toward this expedient, as reflected in an article on Latin America's state petroleum companies, is strongly affirmative. Yet nationalization is not extensively employed by bourgeois ruling circles, and Soviet economists are dissatisfied with many characteristics of state capitalism in Latin America. The system has revived revisionist groups in the labor movement which shun class struggle and advocate a peaceful transition to socialism through state monopolies. Having grasped the implications of state capitalism, American corporations are now forming mixed companies with state entities in order to merge their interests with those of the national bourgeoisie. The Alliance for Progress, discussed at length in two articles, further increased U.S. rapport with the national and petty bourgeoisie, thereby partially fulfilling its purpose — the alienation of these sectors from the national liberation movement.

The Latin American and Central American common markets are more recent manifestations of the national bourgeoisie's determination to expand local industry and forge a hemispheric market protected from foreign competition. Contrary to the spurious reasoning of bourgeois economists, however, "Latin American integration is by no means regarded by U.S. monopolistic capital as an economic threat." Very few national industries command the capital resources necessary to compete in a common market with U.S. affiliates in Latin America. Moreover, the lowering of customs barriers inevitably intensifies competition, necessitates the reduction of production costs through cutting wages, and consequently increases the misery of the lower classes. Instead of a common market of mutually competitive Latin American nations, Soviet economists recommend the expansion of trade with socialist bloc nations, whose economies complement those of Latin America.

In contrast to the preceding sections of the book, the readings in Part Four present the history and specific problems of individual nations. The chapters on Cuba, Mexico, Brazil, Argentina, and Chile are not exhaustive surveys but sketches revealing Soviet thought on the fundamental issues of contemporary historiography.

No other event in Latin American history has been so well documented in Soviet writing as the Cuban revolution. An introductory selection accentuates the abuses of the Batista dictatorship and its intimate ties with American business and governmental coteries. A detailed study of the revolution emphasizes the infinite variety of revolutionary techniques and exhaustive use of anti-imperialistic forces which were indispensable factors in achieving national liberation. Succeeding selections analyze the results of Cuban agrarian, industrial, and educational reforms and conclude with a treatise on political reorganization and the creation of a new party.

Soviet writers interpret with qualified approval the Mexican revolution as it has evolved during the Cárdenas administration. They view the reforms of the latter as preliminary steps characteristic of the radical wing of the national bourgeoisie. An historical account of Pemex stresses its achievements and the subtle methods employed by American petroleum companies to continue harassing it. While retaining most of the state capitalist institutions founded by Cárdenas, the Ávila Camacho and Alemán administrations initiated legislation which subverted the intentions of the Mexican revolution and placed its control firmly in the hands of the wealthy bourgeoisie. Articles on Mexican state capitalism and Mexican labor also reflect the deterioration of revolutionary principles at the expense of the working classes.

The history of contemporary Brazil is focused largely upon one man, Getúlio Vargas. Soviet writers label his dictatorship as fascistic, demagogic, and reactionary. His pro-allied foreign policy reflected geographical pragmatism rather than the rejection of nazism. The Soviet view of his post-war administration is equivocal, but his growing opposition to American foreign interests seems to have redeemed his former shortcomings. Although Vargas initiated many inflationary measures, Soviet economists reserve their strongest criticism for Kubitschek's policy of inflationary expansion. Ultimately the working classes paid dearly for this expansion as pay raises invariably lagged behind the soaring cost of living. The Quadros and Goulart governments are viewed as the most progressive in Brazilian history, yet their fate, like that of Vargas, was sealed by the disunity and consequent inability of anti-imperialist forces to withstand the inevitable attack of Brazilian reactionaries.

One figure, Juan D. Perón, dominates the contemporary history of Argentina to an even greater extent than does Vargas in Brazil. Soviet historians vilify the Perón dictatorship and detail the insidious manner in which he gained control of the working classes and ultimately subordinated their interests to those of the national bourgeoisie. Nevertheless, they respect his perception of popular needs and attempt to reduce the Anglo-American stranglehold upon Argentine industries, utilities, and transportation media. Moreover, Soviet writers praise members of the left wing of the present Peronista Party and express confidence that they will overthrow their demagogic leaders, who, like Perón, give only lip service to the workers' demands.

Unlike that of Brazil and Argentina, the Chilean working class is united, and the nation is on the threshold of revolutionary reforms. While Soviet analysts express confidence in the ultimate electoral victory of the Frente de Acción Popular, they recognize the challenge and appeal of Christian Democratic propaganda. An article on the Christian Democratic Party questions the sincerity of its

conservative members who, though currently passive, could block
the basic reform legislation advocated by the Party's more progressive leaders.

C. Dialogue on How to Teach Latin American History in the United States

5. Unthinkable Thoughts

LEWIS HANKE

Though it may seem to some that doubts concerning the health
of our Latin American studies today are treason or worse, I am
convinced that teaching will largely determine whether a sound and
steady growth will be achieved in the long run for the United States.
Of course research cannot be entirely separated from teaching, but
the future depends to a considerable extent, in my opinion, on how
we teach and where we teach about Latin America. Though this
applies to some extent to all Latin American subjects, I shall confine
my remarks to history teaching, as it is the one most familiar to me
and is probably the field in which most of our students take courses.

Our future also depends on our conception of the place of Latin
American history in the educational structure of the United States.
Let me warn you that I have been thinking what Senator J. W.
Fulbright calls "unthinkable thoughts." They may be summarized as
follows:

1. The study and teaching of Latin American history should not
aim at inculcating "Panamericanism" or to promote the "Good
Neighbor" concept, or to defend any particular political action or
economic policy of the United States in Latin America, not even to
fight Communism there! Nor to define, as one historian has described

From "Studying Latin America: The Views of an 'Old Christian'" by Lewis
Hanke, *Journal of Inter-American Studies*, IX, 1967, pp. 43–64, *passim*. Reprinted by permission.

his interests, the "cultural and institutional imperatives of the past which shape contemporary process."

2. Latin American history will have an important place in our educational system only if it is recognized as a subject worth studying as a significant segment of world history, which will throw light on another culture than our own.

3. To achieve this object, Latin American history must be taught as the development of a civilization similar to ours but also different in some respects, and it must be taught at the high school as well as the college level. The primary purpose must be to produce better educated citizens, and not specialists.

Each of these "unthinkable thoughts" requires some explanation.

The influence of cultural nationalism has never been stated more clearly than by Herodotus, the Father of History. Herodotus, after visiting the Egyptians, concluded that they were a puzzling people. Women went to market in Egypt while the men remained at home to weave. Just the opposite occurred in Greece. And, most strange, the Egyptians wrote from right to left. He noted, however, the surprise of the Egyptians at his observations concerning their writing habits. It was not they who were strange, the Egyptians maintained, who wrote from right to left, but the Greeks, who wrote from left to right. This kind of ethnocentrism thus has existed for a long time and one should not be surprised to find it a powerful force today from Maine to Patagonia. All students, therefore, need to have "windows on the world" opened up for them to allow them to learn about other people, other cultures, and other points of view. Howard Mumford Jones in a recent provocative report on "Uses of the Past in General Education" describes this situation as a need for what he calls "de-education" and "re-education." As he explains it: "By de-education I mean the ability to get outside one's own cultural pattern, and by re-education I mean cultivating the capacity to accept some simpler culture at its face value, not to look down on it."

Of course it doesn't have to be necessarily a simpler culture; one might very well study a sophisticated culture. The possibilities are numerous — Russian culture, Chinese culture, African culture, Arabic culture, etc. There are many "windows on the world" for our students to look through. Our twentieth-century American — thanks to the growth of area studies since World War II — has a wealth of material to draw upon. Moreover, the spirit of our age seems to be more favorable than any time since the sixteenth century toward the study of other cultures. For the interest of a people, of a nation, in the culture of other peoples is a relatively recent phenomenon and far from universal even today. So far as I know it was the Spanish missionaries who went to America in the wake of Columbus who first displayed a lively interest in another culture than their own. Medieval travellers did report on the strange customs they encountered, but with the Spanish missionaries there was an organized effort for specific objectives. A priest who accompanied Columbus on his second voyage first studied the Indian languages he found on the island of Hispaniola, and soon there developed a remarkable drive among the early friars to learn to speak the many languages of America, in order to convert the Indians. But some Spaniards studied Indian cultures partly because their curiosity was aroused, such as the Franciscan Bernardino de Sahagún, the first anthropologist in America.

In the years since the Spaniards first studied Indian cultures, however, studies of other cultures were sporadic everywhere until recently. In the United States, the American Council of Learned Societies in the 1930's began its important pioneer work. Then World War II boomed all language study and some cultural studies for strategic purposes. Area studies development since the end of World War II has been notable. In years to come it is likely that historians will consider our present age as a remarkable one, not only for its achievements in outer space but also because the United States has devoted so much attention to the study of many languages and many cultures, some of them quite removed from our own culture. The United States has indeed made astonishing progress during the last twenty years in African, Arabic, Chinese, Japanese, Russian, and other studies and this development will surely mean a greater and greater enrichment of the educational offerings of our high schools and colleges, and thus of the understanding by our students of other cultures.

But Latin American history has certain obvious advantages which make it an unusually valuable, and available, "window on the world." Spanish and Portuguese are relatively easy languages — at least in comparison with the languages just mentioned — and Spanish is more widely taught in our colleges today than any other. To study a culture, a knowledge of the language is certainly highly desirable; thus Latin American history enjoys the advantage of offering no great linguistic barrier to students. Again, many Latin Americans live in the United States and their presence — increasingly felt in cities far beyond New York — also helps to make possible learning about their culture. Moreover, Latin America as a travel area is open — except for Cuba — and 1.5 million American tourists visit Mexico every year, which helps powerfully to explain her economic stability. Thus students who read about Latin American history in class may also know a Latin American, or visit some part of that large and varied area which includes primitive tribes, sophisticated urbanites, ancient archaeological sites, exciting modern architecture, painting, music, and literature. Therefore if we are agreed that American high school and college students would benefit from an exposure to another culture as part of their fundamental education, the study of Latin American history offers many advantages for both the students and the professors, who will have to learn how to teach Latin American history. Nor does one visit suffice. Many of us have favorite aunts or uncles who made the grand tour of Europe back around the time of Theodore Roosevelt and who ever afterwards considered themselves experts on the state of Europe generally. But the world does not stand still, and the changes which are occurring in Latin America and elsewhere require periodic visits of our professors if they are to be adequately prepared for the classroom. The Scarborough Report in Britain some twenty years ago stated that a specialist should revisit his area at least every three years and few would deny the reasonableness of this recommendation.

This brings me to my next point. How can the history of more than 200 million people to the south of the Rio Grande be presented most effectively to our students?

My answer is a simple one. Latin American history should be looked upon not as a "crisis" subject, but as the unfolding story of a culture, a civilization both interesting and worthy of study. It is natural that the coming of Castro, the Bay of Pigs fiasco, the missile crisis, and United States intervention in the Dominican Republic should stir our students to an increased awareness of Latin American affairs, but a "current events" approach in which attention focuses on transitory dictators, military juntas, economic crises will not, I am convinced, provide the kind of course required by the nature of the world in which we live and by the place of the United States in the present and foreseeable world.

What should be included in a course — perhaps to be called "a History of Latin American Civilization"? Much more on the art, literature, and philosophy of the people of Latin America from pre-

Columbian times to the present; much less on the rather dull political events that clutter up many of our presentations. For, contrary to the newspaper presentation of Latin America, this vast area is much more than a festering mass of economic discontent and political turmoil. One need not be a pollyanna to see that much more is to be found there. This may shock some who feel that the only true history is "contemporary" history and that anything that happened before 1900 should be studied today only if it can be shown that today's problems had their roots in that far-off age. As Howard Mumford Jones wrote:

> The past is not the present. On the contrary, the past is significantly different from the present — that is why it can be useful to us, and that is why it has meaning and imaginative charm. General education is impoverished when we neglect this central truth in an anxiety to prepare everybody for today's world . . . difference enriches: likeness palls.

The presentation of a course on Latin American civilization is much more possible of achievement now because many of our younger scholars have been able to live and work in Latin America, thanks to fellowship grants from the government and foundations. Even though there is altogether too much emphasis on recent events — as though the last few weeks or months or years were always the most significant — and on studying revolutions, still the fellowship holders learn a lot about Latin American life that is not usually included in their doctoral dissertations. On their return, these well-prepared younger scholars are bound to try to incorporate in their teaching and in their research what they have absorbed in Latin America. They are finding out how relatively backward we are in teaching about Latin America at any level, when compared with the teaching of United States history or European history; one need only look at the materials available for instruction. Maps, paperbacks, textbooks, collections of readings, "problems" books — none of the instruments for teaching Latin American history seem to me to be comparable in quality or in variety to what students take for granted in United States or European history. Part of this cultural lag is undoubtedly due to the fact that more students take these other courses so that a much larger market exists than for teaching materials on Latin America. But it is also true that we simply have not devoted enough energy or imagination to the task.

One obvious way to present a course on Latin American civilization in such a way as to challenge and interest our students would be to use the comparative approach. I do not mean comparison with Africa, Asia, or any other underdeveloped area outside the hemisphere, though such an approach might be useful under some circumstances. But the American hemisphere has been and still is a great laboratory in which experiments have been tried out in many fields, and we should be willing to use this experience for educational purposes. For Frenchmen, Englishmen, Spaniards, Portuguese, and many other peoples have participated in the exploration and colonization in the Americas but we have not yet adequately incorporated this historical experience into our teaching of history at any level. Our students learn about Columbus and his brave companions in the first chapter of all the textbooks on United States history, and then the textbook usually turns to discuss the Pilgrims and the first Thanksgiving. If any additional information is given, it is likely to be a reference to the destruction of the noble Indians by the cruel Spaniards. Why could not our courses on Latin American Civilization incorporate some material comparing what went on in the Spanish and Portuguese empires with what occurred under British and French rule? I am not proposing a history of the Americas — though separate courses with this orientation might be developed for advanced students in colleges — but rather the recognition of the fact that different types of colonial cultures developed in the Americas, and that most students would already have some knowledge about the British and French experience in the New World to serve them as background. In unrolling the history of Latin American Civilization, we should make use of this knowledge by drawing comparisons — when possible and when appropriate — with Spanish and Portuguese experience in such fields as Economics, Education, Land, Religion, Science, and Slavery. . . .

Whether the present state of affluence lasts or not, if we use our tremendous resources wisely enough, Latin American studies will be more varied, more interesting, and more significant in our national education than ever before.

6. Social Injustice: A Constant
in Latin American History (1492–   )

GUNNAR MENDOZA

1. You state that the present boom in Latin American studies in the United States may not lead to sound and healthy growth unless we stop to consider what should be the place of Latin American history in the educational structure of the United States.

I think that some significant background facts should not be overlooked, as they usually are, in this connection. The historian of Latin America in the United States not only "teaches" or "writes" Latin American history but inevitably "makes" history by contributing to the formation of collective ideas and attitudes in his own country toward Latin America. The fact that students are the first living material with which the historian has to deal in the fulfillment of his task of "making" history, and that the students are supposed to become the historians of tomorrow and be engaged in the same task, is a primary factor to be considered. Thus the historian has a very heavy responsibility with respect to the dilemma before him: either to follow a course determined outside the field of history — a situation which I believe is becoming increasingly more common among North American scholars — or to decide for himself which should be the correct or the incorrect aims: correct or incorrect for the good of the inevitable and permanent (that is, not only immediate but also future) relationship between Latin America and the United States.

Accordingly, in order to determine the place that Latin American history should occupy in the educational structure of the United States, it would seem that the historian should begin by defining his own attitude toward past, present, and future relations between both areas. This definition in turn presupposes an understanding of the realities of the United States and Latin America. Such an understanding should at least be historical, that is, free of any considerations other than those suggested by the historical facts them-

Prepared especially for this volume by the author and published with his permission.

selves; otherwise, we would have to apply the adage: "Physician, heal thyself." (The equivalent Spanish proverb: "En casa de herrero, cuchillo de palo.")

Regardless of whether Latin American history is recognized as a significant part of universal history and its teaching aimed at producing well-educated citizens, or whether it is considered as a means to other ends, the indispensable ethical and technical premises for the Latin Americanist's task would appear to be an understanding of the realities of Latin America and the United States and the definition of his attitude toward past, present, and future relations between both peoples. Only in this way, I believe, will he be in a position not only to teach and write history but also to help make history, as he should. Otherwise, the historian may become merely a transmitter of facts, a propagandist, or at best only a scholar.

2. Even such means as the inculcation of Panamericanism, the promotion of the Good Neighbor concept, and the opposition to Communism, which you reject, may become adequate and permanent, provided that they are based on a complete understanding and evaluation of Latin American reality.

3. It is your opinion that the primary purpose of the teaching of Latin American history should not be the production of specialists but of better citizens. However, it seems inevitable that the present content of relations between both civilizations will serve to create specialists as well. What is to be desired is that teaching should contribute to the formation of specialists who are not only trained in a purely mechanical sense but who also possess a sound historical orientation. Can this be achieved if the Latin Americanist himself does not understand Latin America? Such an understanding is replete with difficulties.

A dramatic example of these difficulties is the great difference between the concept of revolution — a word that is currently fashionable in both North and South America, though it was taboo twenty-five years ago — as it is understood in the United States and in Latin America. According to the Latin American concept, there can be no true revolution if it does not begin by eliminating the privileged class — insofar as it is privileged — of Latin America, that archaic social group which still clings in spirit to the colony. Such a process of elimination is indispensable and urgent — indeed, it cannot be delayed — because this class, under different names and through its control of the government, business, the army, and the clergy, and, in fact, all the structure of the state, considered only its own interests and has always believed and still believes that the masses exist only to make sacrifices, like the *mitayos* of the colony. And since this class has the desire and means with which to resist its elimination — an eventuality that would mean the perpetuation of the injustice and backwardness of the people of Latin America — this process will have to be effected, as the motto of Chile's national emblem puts it, if not with reason, then with force. The true revolution for independence has still not been completed in Latin America because there can be no true independence so long as the privileged class and the social structure it created in the Latin American countries endure. The United States and France have carried out their revolutions, which today constitute exemplary episodes in human history. Is it too much to expect that Latin America will also make its own revolution — with reason or with force?

Meanwhile, in the United States the Latin American revolution is conceived of as a change that will be orderly (very orderly), gradual (very gradual), peaceful (very peaceful), without class conflict, and — what is more impossible because it is anti-historical — carried out by the privileged class itself. In the United States Latin American public figures of the type of Belaúnde Terry are usually considered revolutionary, but so far as the interests of the masses are concerned they are not even reformist. Peru is one of the countries that most needs a profound and prompt agrarian reform, but the reforms being preached there now leave the entire feudal structure of the land system intact — at a time when even the experts of the United Nations have realized that there can be no agrarian reform in Latin America without a radical and rapid change in the system of landownership. No doubt there are exceptions among the historians of the United States, but they are the exceptions that confirm the rule. The tendency is to envision a very smooth change, one which at best might be accomplished in 500 years and at worst perhaps never.

After 150 years of "independence," the Indians of vast Latin American areas, who make up the great majority of the population, are living in conditions practically the same or worse than those of the sixteenth century. And what is said about the Indian is true of the non-privileged class as a whole, which constitutes the enormous majority of the population of the Latin American countries. After 450 years of oppression of millions of human beings by a few hundred others, the time for waiting has passed; it is time for those millions of human beings to lose patience and to shake the pillars of the temple, saying with Samson, "Let me die with the Philistines." Social cataclysms are usually the direct consequence of social oppression and repression.

In this case, the historian's dilemma is not different from the politician's although the motivations and aims of each are obviously different: to be in favor of oppression or against it, to be in favor of injustice or against it. No middle course is possible. The Latin Americanist cannot refuse to face and to make his choice before this dilemma, and I believe that the choice he makes will help to determine the future of the Western Hemisphere.

4. As you say, all students need to have "windows on the world" opened to them so that they may learn about other peoples and other cultures. Nevertheless, the Latin American nations are not simply "other peoples." They are peoples who occupy the same continent as the United States, and their respective dwelling-places are not isolated from each other, but are contiguous and actively and intimately related. This inevitable contiguity and inter-relationship between the United States and Latin America demonstrate the necessity of understanding and evaluating Latin American reality historically. It is even more imperative if one recalls that despite the similarities between both peoples, the historical differences are perhaps greater and deeper.

One may mention here another example corresponding to the character stamped on human relations in each of the two civilizations. In the United States there was, from the beginning, a deliberate and consistent effort to establish an egalitarian society; and although the exploitation of man by man was accepted while slavery existed, the slaves and their descendants represented, and still represent, only a minority in the society as a whole; and even so, the problem of this minority is without doubt one of the most serious in the historical reality of the United States. In Latin America, on the other hand, from the first day of the Conquest, society was established, again deliberately and consistently, on the basis of man's exploitation by man, the exploited being as 900 and the exploiters as ten.

The type of society that Spain and Portugal built in the New World and which, independent of the secession of colonies and their metropolis, persists today, is then, a society based, *sine qua non,* on the premise of the exploitation of a vast majority of people by a small minority. This has not been discovered by the communists, for Las Casas, who had no opportunity to be a communist, and the entire series of "critical" historians of the colonial period, were already familiar with such a condition to the Ibero-American colonial and social structure, and thanks to their efforts on behalf of historical truth, the essence of the social history of the colonial period is also familiar to us now.

This historical fact — a society based upon injustice — has been and continues to be the principal fact of Latin American reality. It permeates this reality just as water permeates the pores of a sponge, so that when one studies Latin American history, the fact of social injustice always emerges, as water drips when the sponge is squeezed. There have been, to be sure, great efforts in Latin America to check injustice . . . but the tragic fate of Latin American history to date seems to be that, to paraphrase the words of the Marquis of Varinas regarding the Indians in the seventeenth century, even efforts on behalf of justice have resulted and still result in even greater injustice.

Regardless of the chapter of Latin American history that one studies — economy, politics, religion, philosophy, literature, music, painting — the reality of injustice will always be what is most characteristic of Latin America. There are no neutral colors on the Latin American canvas. If a neutral color emerges anywhere, it is a foreign reflection, alien to Latin American reality. And since we are speaking of colors, painting offers an excellent illustration of this truth in relation to historical reality. Is there any connection between Latin America and the abstract paintings done in Latin America, which are identical to those done in Paris, Copenhagen, or Florence — in contrast to the paintings of Portinari, Sabogal, Ribera, or Guayasamín, in which the first thing that one sees is the social reality of Latin America?

5. You remind us that American students of history may also know a Latin American, or visit some Latin American area which includes different and sometimes contradictory features. Perhaps the first and most obvious feature of Latin America for the traveller, even if he is only flying over an area, is a nature that man has been able to dominate only partially so far, and the past, present, and future significance of this Latin American characteristic should be a matter of concern for historians. From the insufficient control of nature has resulted the dependence on monoproduction which is one of the most serious causes for the so-called underdevelopment of Latin American countries. The privileged class of Latin America

and the interests of the more developed countries, which usually act in agreement with that class, have been concerned only with the production in Latin America of what was easy and lucrative for their immediate profit. As a result, there are Latin American countries today which are already confronted with the consequences of the "demographic explosion" whereas, in the very same countries, enormous and potentially rich territories still remain underpopulated or have not even been explored. The paradox is more dramatic if we consider that for this "demographic explosion" of underdeveloped countries the same remedy is recommended today as that which is currently used as a solution for the demographic problems of more developed countries, i.e., birth control. Simultaneously, true agrarian reform is slowed down in Latin America. We are on the eve of resolving the social problem of that part of the world with pills. How have our societies come to face such an odd situation? Latin Americanists should also include this kind of topic in their studies on Latin America.

6. You also point at "grave economic and political problems" as a subject of concern for the student of Latin American peoples. What in Latin America itself is called, par excellence, the "social problem" should be considered too. The economic problem which the Spanish and Portuguese conquerors and colonists had to face and solve was mainly the obtaining of a labor force. They solved it by virtually enslaving the entire aboriginal population, and, in the areas where the aboriginal population was exterminated as a result of the hard conditions of work, or where there were not enough Indians, by bringing large quantities of Negro slaves from Africa. Thus, they only solved their *own* economic problem, and created the Latin American social problem, which, through successive and unceasing oppressions and repressions, became one of the most serious facts in the world today. The political Latin American problem, which consists of the exclusion by the privileged class of the vast majority of the people from the decision of national affairs, was an obvious consequence of the social and economic problems. This shows again to what extent that whenever the historical Latin American sponge is squeezed, what pours from it is social injustice.

7. You assert that Latin American history should be looked upon "as the unfolding story of a culture, a civilization both interesting and worthy of attention in itself" and not "as a 'crisis' subject." The same statement might just as easily be made about Egyptian civilization, but for us, this civilization is at best an object of arche-

ological curiosity; no matter how well-intentioned we may be, the
fortunes of the fellahs do not affect our sensibilities except in a very
fleeting fashion. In other words, the Latin Americanist in the United
States cannot, without distorting his mission, consider Latin American history as an instrument for mental gymnastics or spiritual improvement in order to perfect his students' conception of the world.
I believe that for him Latin American history has a more personal
and immediate reality, one toward which he cannot adopt the
attitude of a spectator watching a film or a listener hearing a concert
in a comfortable chair. Ever since the United States and Latin
America found themselves on the stage of the human drama, their
histories became inevitably linked.

As a result, Latin American history is today in part the history
of the United States, just as the history of the United States is in
part Latin American history. The North American historian who
studies Latin American history is in reality studying his own history.
And the question of whether Latin American history is a "crisis"
subject is not a matter to be determined according to the inclinations
or opinions of the historian. If the facts reveal crisis, the historian
must accept them in that light. He can, of course, separate the facts
that are critical — such as the social problem — from those that are
not, and forget the critical facts. But in so doing, he contradicts himself as a historian. And by "crisis" we mean not what Latin America
may represent in the United States' struggle for universal hegemony
but the essential significance of Latin American history insofar as it
constitutes a continuous social crisis characterized by the exploitation of the majority by the minority, in all its chapters and
paragraphs, in all of its periods, places, and themes. In appearance
stone and brick have little to do with crisis, but no study of Latin
American architecture, for example, would be complete if it were
limited to the classification of styles, the fixing of dates, the identification of architects, and the investigation of influences. Reduced to
these elements, the history of Latin American architecture says little
or nothing. But it is also the inevitable reflection of social conditions,
and the dates, skills, styles, and influences take on meaning when
they are related to the social structure of the time: a building wholly
founded on the rock of social injustice. Our largest and most beautiful monuments laid one upon the other would form Egyptian
pyramids, and our *naborías, yanaconas, mitayos, mingas,* and slaves
are another chosen people subject to the yoke of oppression for
nearly half a millennium — with the difference that the Israelites

finally reached Canaan, while for the wretched ones of Latin America it would appear that Moses has not been born and the promised land has not even been glimpsed. The masses of Latin America are still building pyramids.

In sum, it seems that the mission of the historian of Latin America in the United States is daily becoming more difficult and complex. Since Prescott's pioneer work — an excellent example of the free enterprise system applied to historical production — the possibilities regarding selection, understanding, and decision have become surrounded by greater uncertainties. The need to propagate Panamericanism and the Good Neighbor concept may have represented a loss of autonomy for the historian, but the increasing absorption of scholars in economic, political, and strategic programs related to the search for "national security" gives the current scene an appearance that had not been suspected fifteen years ago. If Latin American history is a "crisis" subject, its study in the United States is also facing a period of serious crisis.

Bibliographic Suggestions

SECTION I

A. General

1. Griffin, Charles C. *Los temas sociales y económicos en la época de la independencia* (Caracas: Publicación de la Fundación John Boulton y la Fundación Eugenio Mendoza, 1962), pp. 75–88. See also his "Aspectos económico-sociales de la época de la emancipación hispanoamericana: una bibliografía selecta de la historiografía reciente, 1949–1959," Academia Nacional de la Historia (Caracas), *El movimiento emancipador de Hispanoamérica, Actas y Ponencias de la Mesa Redonda de la Comisión de Historia del Instituto Panamericano de Geografía e Historia* (Caracas, 1961), Tomo I, pp. 349–360.
2. Humphreys, R. A. "The Historiography of the Spanish American Revolutions," *Hispanic American Historical Review*, XXXVI (1956), pp. 81–93.
3. Jones, Tom B., Elizabeth Ann Warburton, and Anne Kingsley, eds. *A Bibliography on South American Economic Affairs: Articles in Nineteenth-Century Periodicals* (Minneapolis: University of Minnesota Press, 1955).

B. Brazil

4. Armitage, John. *The History of Brazil from the Period of the Arrival of the Braganza Family in 1808 to the Abdication of Dom Pedro the First in 1831*, 2 vols. (London, 1836).
5. Heaton, Herbert. "When a Whole Royal Family Came to America," *Annual Report of the Canadian Historical Association* (1939), pp. 48–60.
6. ———. "A Merchant Adventurer in Brazil," *Journal of Economic History*, VI (1946), pp. 1–23. On John Luccock.

7. Manchester, Alan K. *British Preëminence in Brazil* (New York: Octagon Books, 1964).
8. Street, John. "Lord Strangford and Río de la Plata, 1808–1815," *Hispanic American Historical Review*, XXXIII (1953), pp. 477–510.
9. Tarquínio de Souza, Octávio. "Independencia, Primeiro Reinado, Regencia," in Rubens Borba de Morais and William Berrien, eds., *Manual bibliográfico de estudos brasileiros* (Rio de Janeiro: Gráfica Editora Souza, 1949), pp. 408–423.

C. *Economic*

10. Burgin, Miron. *Economic Aspects of Argentine Federalism, 1820–1852* (Cambridge, Mass.: Harvard University Press, 1946). See pp. 7–17 for economic conditions before and during independence in Argentina.
11. Carrera Damas, Germán. *Materiales para el estudio de la cuestión agraria en Venezuela 1800–1830* (Caracas: Consejo de Desarrollo Científico y Humanístico de la Universidad Central de Venezuela, 1964). A notable collection of documents, preceded by a revisionist monograph on José Tomás Boves in which it is demonstrated that this caudillo was not an agrarian reformer who disregarded private property. Useful bibliography, pp. clix–clxiv.
12. Ferns, H. S. "The Establishment of the British Investment in Argentina," *Inter-American Economic Affairs*, V, No. 2 (1951), pp. 67–89.
13. Gilmore, N. Ray. "The Condition of the Poor in Mexico, 1834," *Hispanic American Historical Review*, XXXVII (1957), pp. 213–226. An unusual document, based on replies by the British Minister to a questionnaire which originated in the Home Office, which was then engaged in amending the English Poor Laws and sought information on social conditions in Mexico.
14. Humphreys, R. A. "Economic Aspects of the Fall of the Spanish American Empire," *Revista de Historia de América*, No. 30 (Mexico, 1950), pp. 1–7.
15. ———. "British Merchants and South American Independence," *The Proceedings of the British Academy*, LI (1966), pp. 151–174
16. Potash, Robert A. *El banco de avío en Mexico. El fomento de la industria, 1821–1846* (Mexico: Fondo de Cultura Económica, 1959). For a succinct statement on economic conditions on the eve of independence, see "La herencia colonial" (pp. 11–26).
17. Rippy, J. Fred. "Latin America and the British Investment 'Boom' of the 1820's," *Journal of Modern History*, XIX (1947), pp. 122–129.

18. Tanner, Earl C. "Caribbean Ports in the Foreign Commerce of Providence, 1790–1830," *Rhode Island History,* XIV–XV (1955–1956).

19. ———. "South American Ports in the Foreign Commerce of Providence, 1800–1830," *ibid.,* XVI (1957), pp. 65–78. Based on manuscript material at Harvard and in Providence, these studies indicate the influence of Yankee traders in developing commerce. "Where high profits were to be made, commerce found a way."

D. *Other Topics*

20. Arnade, Charles W. *The Emergence of the Republic of Bolivia* (Gainesville: University of Florida Press, 1957).

21. Baumgartner, Louis E. "The Myth of Central American Independence," *Bucknell Review,* XIV (March, 1966), No. 1, pp. 95–102. The "fathers of independence" broke the bonds with Spain to protect their own interests.

22. Benson, Nettie Lee, ed. *Mexico and the Spanish Cortes, 1810–1822* (Austin: University of Texas Press, 1966). Eight essays on the influence of the Spanish Parliament in establishing an electoral system, and in introducing reforms in the Church, the economy, the military, and the press.

23. Browning, W. E. "Joseph Lancaster, James Thomson, and the Lancasterian System of Mutual Instruction, with Special Reference to Hispanic America," *Hispanic American Historical Review,* IV (1921), pp. 49–98.

23a. Cuenca, Humberto. "Caracter y sentido de la revolución y la guerra de independencia," *Anales del Instituto Pedagógico Nacional* (Caracas, 1944), no. 2, pp. 319–340. Emphasizes political character of the Venezuelan independence movement. The author holds that it was not social or economic.

24. Gray, William H. "The Social Reforms of San Martín," *The Americas,* VII (July, 1950), pp. 3–11.

25. Humphreys, R. A. *Liberation in South America, 1806–1827; The Career of James Paroissien* (London: The Athlone Press, 1952). The emphasis is on Paroissien, but the volume also gives a valuable general picture.

26. King, James F. "A Royalist View of the Colored Castes in the Venezuela War of Independence," *Hispanic American Historical Review,* XXXIII (1953), pp. 526–537.

27. ———. "The Colored Castes and the American Representation in the Cortes of Cádiz," *ibid.,* XXXIII (1953), pp. 33–64.

28. Lombardi, John V. "Los esclavos en la legislación republicana de Venezuela," *Boletín Histórico* (Caracas: January, 1967), No. 13, pp. 3–28.

29. Parker, Franklin D. "José Cecilio del Valle: Scholar and Patriot," *Hispanic American Historical Review*, XXXII (1952), pp. 516–539.
30. Rodríguez, Simón. *Escritos de Simón Rodríguez*, 3 vols. Pedro Grases, ed. (Caracas: Sociedad Bolivariana de Venezuela, 1954–1958). The educational theories and practices of Rodríguez, the mentor of Bolívar, merit much more attention in the English-speaking world than they have received to date. See also the volume edited by Pedro Grases, *Simón Rodríguez, escritos sobre su vida y su obra* (Caracas: Concejo Municipal de Caracas, 1954).
31. Salcedo Bastardo, J. L. *Visión y revisión de Bolívar*, Third ed. (Caracas: privately printed, 1957). Emphasis on the Liberator's anti-slavery efforts, his strong interest in education, administrative reform, and financial questions.
32. Villoro, Luis. *La revolución de independencia. Ensayo de interpretación histórica* (Mexico: Universidad Nacional Autónoma de Mexico, 1953). An interpretation of the struggle between Order and Liberty during the revolt and the Iturbide Empire.
33. Watters, Mary. "Bolívar and the Church," *The Catholic Historical Review*, XXI (1935), pp. 299–310.
34. ———. "A Venezuelan Educator: Don Feliciano Montenegro Colón," *The Americas*, III (1947), pp. 277–294.
35. Young, John L. "Bolivar's Program for Elementary Education," Andrew W. Cordier, ed. *Columbia Essays in International Affairs: The Dean's Papers, 1965* (New York, 1966), pp. 390–323.

SECTION II

A. *General*

1. Angelis, Pedro de. *Acusación y defensa de Rosas*, Rodolfo Trostiné, ed. (Buenos Aires: Ed. La Facultad, 1945). A compilation of writings by Rosas' official propagandist, plus a study by Enrique de Gandía on "Las ideas políticas de Pedro de Angelis."
2. Cady, John F. *Foreign Intervention in the Río de la Plata, 1838–50* (Philadelphia: University of Pennsylvania Press, 1929).
3. Carro Martínez, Antonio. "El caudillismo americano," *Revista de Estudios Políticos*, 93 (1957), pp. 139–163. Argues that caudillismo often is appropriate to the need.
4. Chapman, Charles E. "The Age of Caudillos: A Chapter in Hispanic-American History," *Hispanic American Historical Review*, XII (1932), pp. 281–300.

5. ————. "List of Books Referring to Caudillos in Hispanic America," *ibid.*, XIII (1933), pp. 143–146.
5a. Cotner, Robert C. "The Intellectual Opposition to Juan Manuel de Rosas," *The Historian*, XI (Autumn, 1948), no. 1, pp. 73–94.
6. García Calderón, Francisco. *Latin America: Its Rise and Progress* (London, 1913). An older interpretation, but still valuable.
7. Hamill, Hugh M., ed. *Dictatorship in Spanish America* (New York: Alfred A. Knopf, 1965). See pp. 235–242 for an up-to-date and extensive bibliography.
8. Humphreys, R. A. "Latin America. The Caudillo Tradition," in Michael Howard, ed., *Soldiers and Governments: Nine Studies in Civil-Military Relations* (London: Eyre and Spottiswoode, 1957).
9. Johnson, John J. "Foreign Factors in Latin American Dictatorship," *Pacific Historical Review*, XX (1951), pp. 127–141.
10. Kroeber, Clifton B. "Rosas and the Revision of Argentine History, 1880–1955," *Inter-American Review of Bibliography*, X (1960), pp. 3–25.
10a. Lafuente Machaín, Ricardo de. *Enrique Lafuente, 1815–1850* (Buenos Aires: Sebastián de Amorrortue hijos, 1947. Excellent description of Buenos Aires, city and society, during the Rosas period.
10b. Magariños de Mello, Mateo J. *La misión de Florencio Varela a Londres, 1843–1844* (Montevideo: Ed. C. García, 1944). European intervention in the countries of the Río de la Plata in the time of Rosas.
11. Rippy, J. Fred. "Dictatorship in Spanish America," in *Dictatorship in the Modern World*, Guy Stanton Ford, ed. (Minneapolis: University of Minnesota Press, 1936).
12. Sarmiento, Domingo F. *Life in the Argentine Republic in the Days of the Tyrants; or Civilization and Barbarism*, Tr. by Mrs. Horace Mann (New York: Collier, 1961).
13. Vallenilla Lanz, Laureano. *Cesarismo democrático* (Caracas, 1929).
14. Wilgus, Alva Curtis, ed. *South American Dictators During the First Century of Independence*, Second ed. (New York: Russell and Russell, 1963).

B. *For Comparative Purposes*

(See also Section VI, Bibliographic Suggestions)

15. Blanksten, George I. *Perón's Argentina* (Chicago: University of Chicago Press, 1953).
16. Callcott, Wilfred H. *Santa Anna: The Story of an Enigma Who*

Once Was Mexico (Norman: University of Oklahoma Press, 1936).
17. Cunninghame Graham, R. B. *José Antonio Páez* (London, 1929).
18. Jones, Chester Lloyd. "If I Were Dictator," in his *Guatemala Past and Present* (Minneapolis: University of Minnesota Press, 1940), pp. 339–356.
19. Lavin, John. *A Halo for Gómez* (New York, 1954).
20. Nava, Julian. "The Illustrious American: The Development of Nationalism in Venezuela under Antonio Guzmán Blanco," *Hispanic American Historical Review*, XLV (1965), pp. 527–543.
21. Rourke, Thomas [pseud. for D. J. Clinton]. *Gómez, Tyrant of the Andes* (New York, 1956).
22. Smith, Peter H. "Image of a Dictator: Gabriel García Moreno," *Hispanic American Historical Review*, XLV (1965), pp. 1–24.
23. Stribling, T. S. *Fombombo* (New York: The Century Co., 1923). A literary account of a dictator in Venezuela.
24. White, Edward Lucas. *El Supremo: A Romance of the Great Dictator of Paraguay* (New York: Dutton, 1967). Excellent re-creation of the life and times of Francia, dictator of Paraguay.
25. Wise, George S. *Caudillo: A Portrait of Antonio Guzmán Blanco* (New York: Columbia University Press, 1951).

SECTION III

1. Allen, Cyril. "Félix Belly: Nicaraguan Canal Promoter," *Hispanic American Historical Review*, XXXVII (1957), pp. 46–59.
2. Bazant, Jan. "Evolución de la industria textil poblana (1554–1845)," *Historia Mexicana*, XIII (1964), No. 4, pp. 473–516.
3. ———. "Industria algodonera poblana de 1800–1843 en números," *ibid.*, XIV (1964), No. 1, pp. 131–143.
4. *Economic Literature of Latin America: a Tentative Bibliography*. Compiled by the staff of the Bureau for Economic Research in Latin America, Harvard University, 2 vols. (Cambridge, Mass.: Harvard University Press, 1935–1936). Now out of date, but still to be consulted.
5. Gilmore, Robert Louis. "Nueva Granada's Socialist Mirage," *Hispanic American Historical Review*, XXXVI (1956), pp. 190–210.
6. ———, and John Parker Harrison. "Juan Bernardo Elbers and the Introduction of Steam Navigation on the Magdalena River," *ibid.*, XXVII (1948), pp. 336–359.
7. Graham, Richard. "Change and the Stranger: Britain and the

Onset of Modernization in Brazil" (in press, Cambridge University Press, 1968).

8. Gray, W. H. "Steamboat Transportation on the Orinoco," *Hispanic American Historical Review,* XXV (1945), pp. 455–469.

9. Harrison, John P. "Science and Politics: Origins and Objectives of Mid-Nineteenth Century Government Expeditions to Latin America," *ibid.,* XXXV (1955), pp. 175–202.

10. Johnson, John J. *Pioneer Telegraphy in Chile, 1852–1876* (Palo Alto: Stanford University Press, 1948).

11. Johnson, V. L. "Edward A. Hopkins and the Development of Argentine Transportation and Communication," *Hispanic American Historical Review,* XXVI (1946), pp. 19–37.

12. Levin, Jonathan V. "Peru in the Guano Age," in *The Export Economies: Their Pattern of Development in Historical Perspective* (Cambridge, Mass.: Harvard University Press, 1960), pp. 27–123.

13. Manchester, Alan K. *British Preëminence in Brazil* (New York: Octagon Books, 1964).

14. Marchant, Anyda. "A New Portrait of Mauá the Banker: A Man of Business in Nineteenth-Century Brazil," *Hispanic American Historical Review,* XXX (1950), pp. 411–431, *passim.* See also Miss Marchant's subsequently published full-length study, *Viscount Mauá and the Empire of Brazil: A Biography of Irenêo Evangelista de Souza (1813–1889)* (Berkeley: University of California Press, 1965).

14a. Mosk, Sanford. "Latin America and the World Economy, 1850–1914," *Inter-American Economic Affairs,* II (Winter, 1948), pp. 53–82.

15. Peterson, Harold. "Edward A. Hopkins: A Pioneer Promoter in Paraguay," *Hispanic American Historical Review,* XXII (1942), pp. 245–261.

16. Pletcher, David M. *Rails, Mines and Progress: Seven American Promoters in Mexico, 1867–1911* (Ithaca: Cornell University Press, 1958).

17. ———. "Prospecting Expedition across Central America, 1856–1857," *Pacific Historical Review,* XXI (1952), pp. 21–41.

18. Potash, Robert. *El banco de avío en Mexico. El fomento de la industria, 1821–1846* (Mexico: Fondo de Cultura Económica, 1959).

19. Randall, Robert William. "Anatomy of a Failure: The Real del Monte Mining Company in Mexico, 1824–1949" (Doctoral Dissertation, Harvard University, 1965).

20. Rippy, J. Fred. *Latin America and the Industrial Age* (New York: Putnam, 1947).

21. Scheips, P. J., and Ambrose W. Thompson. "Neglected Isthmian Promoters," *Hispanic American Historical Review,* XXXVI (1956) pp. 211–218.
22. Williams, J. J. *The Isthmus of Tehuantepec* (New York, 1852). Describes plans for a railroad to connect the Atlantic and Pacific oceans.
23. Ynsfran, Pablo Max. "Sam Ward's Bargain with President López of Paraguay," *Hispanic American Historical Review,* XXXIV (1954), pp. 313–331. How a New York bon vivant with many financial schemes "won the confidence of President Carlos Antonio López of Paraguay, a distrustful and difficult character."

SECTION IV

The available travelers' accounts form a remarkably rich and interesting literature on Brazilian history, and provide valuable readings for special reports and term papers. The literature is so vast that only a selection can be given here.

A. *General*

1. Berger, Paulo, *Bibliografia do Rio de Janeiro, 1500–1900* (Rio de Janeiro: São Jose, 1965).
2. Burns, E. Bradford. "A Working Bibliography for the Study of Brazilian History," *The Americas,* XXII (1965), pp. 54–88.
3. ———, ed. *A Documentary History of Brazil* (New York: Alfred A. Knopf, 1966).
4. Cardozo, Manoel. "Slavery in Brazil as Described by Americans, 1822–1888," *The Americas,* XVIII (1961), pp. 241–260.
5. Freyre, Gilberto. *Vida social no Brasil nos meados de século XIX* (Recife, 1964). Expanded and updated version of his Master's essay at Columbia University, originally published as "Social Life in Brazil in the Middle of the Nineteenth Century," *Hispanic American Historical Review,* V (1922), pp. 597–628.
6. Garraux, A. L. *Bibliographie brésilienne. Catalogue des ouvrages français et latins relatifs au Brésil, 1500–1898,* Second ed. (Rio de Janeiro, 1962).
7. Hamilton, Charles. "English Speaking Travellers in Brazil, 1851–1887," *Hispanic American Historical Review,* XL (1960), pp. 533–547.
8. Harris, Marvin. *Patterns of Race in the Americas* (New York: Walker, 1964). Challenges the Freyre-Tannenbaum thesis of relatively mild slavery in Brazil.

9. Klein, Herbert S. *Slavery in the Americas: A Comparative Study of Virginia and Cuba* (Chicago: University of Chicago Press, 1967).

10. Matos, Odilon Nogueira de. "Viajantes estrangeiros que percoreram o Brasil durante o século XIX," *Boletim Paulista de Geografia*, XXXVIII (1961), pp. 57–73. Limited to those travelers whose works have been translated into Portuguese.

11. Mello, Leitão Cándido de. *Visitantes de Primeiro Imperio* (São Paulo, 1934).

12. Moraes, Rubens Borba de and William Berrien, eds. *Manual bibliográfico de estudos brasileiros* (Rio de Janeiro: Gráfica Souza, 1949). Still the best volume on Brazilian bibliography.

13. Nelson, Margaret W. "The Negro in Brazil as Seen Through the Chronicles of Travellers, 1800–1868," *Journal of Negro History*, XXX (1945), pp. 203–218.

14. Palop, Josefina, "El Brasil visto por los viajeros alemanes," *Revista de Indias*, año XXI (1961), pp. 107–127. Most of these travelers' accounts are still in the original German.

15. Pierson, Donald. *Survey of the Literature on Brazil of Sociological Significance Published up to 1940* (Cambridge, Mass.: Harvard University Press, 1945).

16. Williams, Mary W. "The Treatment of Negro Slaves in the Brazilian Empire: a Comparison with the United States of America," *Journal of Negro History*, XV (1930), pp. 315–336.

B. *Individual Travel Accounts*

17. Adelbert, Prince of Prussia. *Travels in the South of Europe and Brazil*, tr. by Sir R. H. Schomburgh and J. E. Taylor (London, 1849). This German prince went to Brazil for adventure in 1842–1843, and gave a sombre picture of the lives of Negroes, who were regarded by their owners as an intermediate step between beast and man.

18. Agassiz, Professor and Mrs. Louis. *A Journey in Brazil* (Boston, 1868). The famous Swiss-American scientist spent most of his time in the Amazon. Young William James accompanied the expedition.

19. Callcott, Maria Graham. *Journal of a Voyage to Brazil and Residence There, During Part of the Years 1821, 1822, 1823* (London, 1824). Maria Graham, subsequently Lady Callcott (1785–1842), spent about a year in Brazil during her two visits there between 1821 and 1823. She was a talented writer and illustrator.

20. Christie, William D. *Notes on Brazilian Questions* (London, 1865). Christie was a former British Minister to Brazil, for whom

the "Christie Affair" was named. Valuable for British policy. He denied the myth of the mildness of slavery in Brazil.

21. Couty, Louis. *L'esclavage au Brésil* (Paris, 1881). A French professor of medicine at the Polytechnic School in Rio in the 1870's and 1880's. Considered slave labor decidedly inferior to that of free men and argued that Brazil was being retarded economically by slavery, since it favored monoculture because slaves could not adapt to new methods and work routines.

22. Davatz, Thomas. *Memórias de um colono no Brasil* (São Paulo, 1941). A Swiss colonist who was in Brazil from 1855 to 1857.

23. Dunn, Ballard S. *Brazil, the Home for Southerners* (New York, 1866). A Southerner who advocated Confederate migration to Brazil.

24. Ewbank, Thomas. *Life in Brazil* (New York, 1856). An American who was in Brazil in 1846. Described slave markets.

25. Leclerc, Max. *Cartas do Brasil*, Tr. by Sérgio Milliet (São Paulo, 1942). By a Frenchman who reported on conditions in 1889–1890.

26. Luccock, John. *Notes on Rio de Janeiro and the Southern Parts of Brazil Taken During a Residence of Ten Years . . . 1808 to 1818* (London, 1820). A British merchant who traveled widely. A careful observer, particularly on slavery. Emphasizes the unfortunate effects slavery had on white women, who grew lazy and fat because they were surrounded by slaves who did all the work. See the article by Herbert Heaton, "A Merchant Adventurer in Brazil," *Journal of Economic History*, VI (1946), pp. 1–23.

27. Mawe, John. *Travels in the Interior of Brazil*, Second ed. (London, 1821). A British merchant who describes gold and diamond washing in 1808–1810. Slaves had extremely arduous lives as miners.

28. Ribeyrolles, Charles. *Brasil pitoresco*, Tr. by G. Penalva (São Paulo, 1941). A French exile of 1848, he went to Brazil in 1858–1860. Detailed view of the work routine of slaves, whose lives he considered much more dehumanized than that of the European proletariat. Slaves were kept locked up, were denied a family life, and were subject to any punishment their master desired.

29. Rugendas, João Mauricio. *Viagem pitoresco atraves do Brasil*, Tr. by Sérgio Milliet (São Paulo, 1940). A German artist who saw Rio and southern Brazil in the mid-1830's. He found slavery there less harsh than in other countries.

30. Saint Hilaire, Augustin. *Voyage dans les provinces de Rio de Janeiro et de Minas Gerais*, 4 vols. (Paris, 1830–1851). A French botanist, who traveled extensively during 1816 and 1822. An

excellent, detailed account of the history, government, economic and spiritual life, geography, and customs.

31. Spix, Johann Baptist von and Karl Friedrich Philip von Martius, *Travels in Brazil, in the Years 1817–1820*, 2 vols. (London, 1824). Report by Bavarian scientists, who included much material on life in Brazil as they observed it during the years 1817–1820. The English translation has about half of the original German text.

SECTION V

1. Basadre, Jorge. *Chile, Perú y Bolivia independientes* (Barcelona: Salvat, 1949). A splendid synthesis by a Peruvian historian.
2. Burr, Robert N. "The Balance of Power in Nineteenth-Century South America: An Exploratory Essay," *Hispanic American Historical Review*, XXXV (1955), pp. 37–60; *By Reason or Force: Chile and the Balancing of Power in South America, 1830–1905* (Berkeley: University of California Press, 1965).
3. Drosdoff, Daniel A. "The Changing Significance of José Manuel Balmaceda (1891–1963): A Historiographical Essay" (Master's Essay, Columbia University, 1965).
4. Espinosa, Julio Bañados. *The Chilean Revolution and the Balmaceda Administration. Speech Delivered at the Chilean House of Representatives on the 28th of April, 1891* (Washington, D.C., 1891), pp. 12–31.
5. Galdames, Luis. *History of Chile*, Tr. by I. J. Cox. (Chapel Hill: University of North Carolina Press, 1941).
6. Hardy, Osgood. "Was Patrick Egan a Blundering Minister?" *Hispanic American Historical Review*, VIII (1928), pp. 65–81. An examination of the charge that the United States supported Balmaceda.
7. ———. "British Nitrates and the Balmaceda Revolution," *Pacific Historical Review*, XVII (1948), pp. 165–180.
8. ———. "The Itata Incident," *Hispanic American Historical Review*, V (1922), pp. 195–226.
9. Hervey, Maurice H. *Dark Days in Chile: An Account of the Revolution of 1891* (London, 1891–1892).
10. Montt, Pedro. *Exposition of the Illegal Acts of Ex-President Balmaceda, Which Caused the Civil War in Chile* (Washington, D.C., 1891), pp. 13–18, 22–23.
11. Nabuco, Joaquim. *Balmaceda* (Rio de Janeiro, 1894). One of the

few books by a Brazilian on Chile. Here the Brazilian statesman supports the revolutionists against Balmaceda.

12. Pike, Fredrick B. *Chile and the United States, 1880–1962* (Notre Dame: University of Notre Dame Press, 1963). A challenging volume, with an excellent bibliography.

13. ———. "Aspects of Class Relations in Chile, 1850–1960," *Hispanic American Historical Review*, XLIII (1963), pp. 14–33.

SECTION VI

A. *General*

1. Bulnes, Francisco. *The Whole Truth about Mexico* (New York: M. Bulnes Book Co., 1916). Aimed to "destroy the theories and enthusiasms of those who have approved and applauded the overthrow of the long-lived Mexican tyrant."

2. Bancroft, Hubert Howe. *Porfirio Díaz: Su biografía* (San Francisco: n.d.). Laudatory.

3. Beals, Carleton. *Porfirio Díaz: Dictator of Mexico* (Philadelphia: Lippincott, 1932).

4. Cosío Villegas, Daniel, ed. *Historia moderna de México*, 7 vols. (Mexico: Editorial Hermes, 1955–1966). Monumental and indispensable.

5. ———. "El porfiriato: su historiografía o arte histórico," *Extremos de América* (Mexico: Tezontle, 1949), pp. 113–182. Copious bibliography.

6. Flandrau, Charles M. *Viva Mexico!*, C. Harvey Gardner, ed. (Urbana: University of Illinois Press, 1964). Paperback reprint of this classic account of life on a coffee plantation in eastern Mexico during the later period of the Porfiriato, as seen by a young American.

7. Gruening, Ernest. *Mexico and Its Heritage* (New York: Century, 1928). A rich mine of information and interpretation.

8. Molina Enríques, Andrés. *Los grandes problemas nacionales* (Mexico, 1909). See Chapter 5 on "El secreto de la paz porfiriana."

9. Potash, Robert A. "The Historiography of Mexico Since 1821," *Hispanic American Historical Review*, XL (1960), pp. 383–424.

B. *Special Topics*

10. Breymann, Walter N. "The Científicos: Critics of the Díaz Regime, 1892–1903," *Proceedings, Arkansas Academy of Science,*

VII (1955), pp. 91–97. Opposes the view that the científicos were always willing partners-in-crime to all the vices and excesses of the Porfiriato.

10a. Brown, Lyle C. "The Mexican Liberals and Their Struggle Against the Díaz Dictatorship, 1900–1906," *Antología MCC, 1956* (Mexico: Mexico City College Press, 1956), pp. 317–362.

11. Brushwood, James S. "La novela mexicana frente al porfirismo," *Historia Mexicana*, VII, No. 3 (1958), pp. 368–405.

12. Callcott, W. H. *Liberalism in Mexico, 1857–1929* (Stanford: Stanford University Press, 1931).

13. Cañizares, Leandro J. *Don Porfirio, el gobernante de mente lúcida, corazón de patriota y mano de hierro* (Habana: Lex, 1947). A defense, by a Cuban.

14. Caso, Alfonso, et al. *Conferencias del Ateneo de la Juventud,* Juan Hernández Luna, ed. (Mexico: Universidad Nacional Autónoma de México, 1961). Lectures by Caso, Alfonso Reyes, José Vasconcelos, and other members of the famous Ateneo which flourished during the last years of the Porfiriato.

15. Cosío Villegas, Daniel. "El Norte de Porfirio Díaz," *Anuario de Historia*, I (Mexico, 1961), pp. 13–57.

16. ———. "Lección de la barbarie. Comentario sobre *México bárbaro*," in *Problemas agrícolas e industriales de México*, VII (1955), No. 2, pp. 187–193.

17. ———. *The United States Versus Porfirio Díaz*, Tr. by Nettie Lee Benson (Austin: University of Texas Press, 1966). A study of the tension between Mexico and the United States during the years 1876–1880.

18. Cumberland, Charles C. "Precursors of the Mexican Revolution of 1910," *Hispanic American Historical Review*, XXII (1942), pp. 344–356.

19. González Navarro, Moisés. "Las huelgas textiles en el Porfiriato," *Historia Mexicana*, VI, No. 2 (1956).

20. López Portilla y Rojas, José. *La parcela, novela*, Antonio Castro Leal, ed. (Mexico: Porrúa, 1946). An 1898 novel, which describes the conflict of land tillers with land owners during the Porfiriato.

21. Pletcher, David M. *Rails, Mines and Progress: Seven American Promoters in Mexico, 1867–1911* (Ithaca: Cornell University Press, 1958).

22. Roehl, Charlotte. "Porfirio Díaz in the Press of the United States." (Dissertation, University of Chicago, 1953).

23. Schiff, Warren. "The Germans in Mexican Trade and Industry During the Díaz Period," *The Americas*, XXIII (1967), No. 3, pp. 279–296. Mexico favored German businessmen in order to counteract United States influence. German businessmen and

industrialists, though few in number, had great success due to their perseverance, good judgment, competence, and identification with Mexican life.

24. Schmitt, Karl M. "Catholic Adjustment to the Secular State: The Case of Mexico, 1867–1911," *The Catholic Historical Review*, XLVIII, No. 2 (1962), pp. 182–204. On the accommodation between Porfirio Díaz and the Church, and on the minority who never reconciled themselves to the new, largely secularized state.

25. ————. "The Díaz Conciliation Policy on State and Local Levels, 1876–1911," *Hispanic American Historical Review*, XL (1960), pp. 513–532.

25a. ————. "The Mexican Positivists and the Church-State Question, 1876–1911," *Journal of Church and State* (Spring, 1966).

26. Sierra, Justo. "Discourse at the Inauguration of the National University," in José Luis Martínez, ed. *The Modern Mexican Essay*. Tr. by H. W. Holborn (Toronto: University of Toronto Press, 1965), pp. 32–53. The most important address of the outstanding intellectual who was Díaz's Minister of Education.

27. Stabb, Martin S. "Indianism and Racism in Mexican Thought, 1857–1911," *Journal of Inter-American Studies*, I (1959), pp. 405–423. Concern for the Indian and indigenismo was present under the Díaz regime.

28. Tischendorf, Alfred. *Great Britain and Mexico in the Era of Porfirio Díaz* (Durham, N.C.: Duke University Press, 1961).

SECTION VII

A. *General*

1. Blanquel, Eduardo. "Dos ideas sobre América: Edmundo O'Gorman y Leopoldo Zea," *Anuario de Historia*, I (Mexico, 1961), pp. 143–159.

2. Chapman, Arnold. *The Reception of United States Fiction in Latin America, 1920–1940* (Berkeley: University of California Press, 1966).

3. Crawford, William Rex. *A Century of Latin American Thought*, Rev. ed. (Cambridge, Mass.: Harvard University Press, 1961).

4. Del Río, Ángel. *The Clash and Attraction of Two Cultures: The Hispanic and Anglo-Saxon Worlds in America*, Tr. and ed. by James F. Shearer (Baton Rouge: Louisiana State University Press, 1965).

5. Frondizi, Risieri. "Is There an Ibero-American Philosophy?"

Philosophy and Phenomenological Research, IX (1950), pp. 345–355.

6. ———. "On the Unity of the Philosophies of the Two Americas." *Review of Metaphysics,* IV (1951), pp. 617–622. Is there a "Pan American philosophy? Is this a piece of political propaganda, a legitimate aspiration, or an actual fact?"

7. Henríquez Ureña, Pedro. *Literary Currents in Hispanic America* (Cambridge, Mass.: Harvard University Press, 1945). A basic study for cultural history.

8. Onís, Jose de. *The United States as Seen by Spanish American Writers, 1776–1890* (New York: Hispanic Institute in the United States, 1952). The writers selected focus on these questions: Should Spanish American nations look toward the United States as their model? Did the United States represent a menace to them?

9. Ugarte, Manuel. *The Destiny of a Continent,* J. Fred Rippy, ed. (New York, 1925). A famous anti-American volume.

10. Unión Panamericana. *Conocimiento y desconocimiento de América,* Second ed. (Washington, D.C., 1961). Report on a round table discussion.

11. Zea, Leopoldo. *The Latin American Mind,* Tr. by James H. Abbott and Lowell Dunham (Norman, Okla.: University of Oklahoma Press, 1963).

B. *Rodó*

12. Berrien, William Joseph. "Rodó: Biografía y estudio crítico" (Doctoral dissertation, University of California, Berkeley, 1937). Considers Rodó and his influence in Latin America *passé.*

13. Esquenazi-Mayo, Roberto. "Revalorización de Rodó," *Actas del Primer Congreso Internacional de Hispanistas* (Oxford: The Dolphin Book Co., 1964). Rodó should be considered as a modern prose writer, not a prophet.

14. Gálvez, Manuel. *El diario de Gabriel Quiroga: opiniones sobre la vida argentina* (Buenos Aires, 1910). An Argentine traditionalist who accused his countrymen of exhibiting Caliban-like characteristics.

15. Rodríguez Monegal, Emir. "Imagen documental de José Enrique Rodó," *Cuadernos Americanos,* año 7, Vol. 41, No. 5 (1949), pp. 214–226.

C. *On Mexico*

16. Brushwood, John S. *Mexico in Its Novel: A Nation's Search for Identity* (Austin: University of Texas Press, 1966).

17. Paz, Octavio. *The Labyrinth of Solitude: Life and Thought in Mexico*, Tr. by Lysander Kemp (New York: Evergreen, 1961).
18. Phelan, John Leddy. "México y lo Mexicano," *Hispanic American Historical Review*, XXXVI (1956), pp. 309–318.
19. Romanell, Patrick. *Making of the Mexican Mind* (Lincoln, Nebraska: University of Nebraska Press, 1952).

D. *Other Topics*

20. Aldridge, Alfred Owen. "The Character of a North American as Drawn in Chile, 1818," *Hispania*, XLIX (1966), No. 3, pp. 489–494. Shows that there was "a highly critical view of North American materialism three quarters of a century before the concept of Yankee imperialism became widespread in South America."
21. Boehrer, George C. A. "José Carlos Rodrigues and O Novo Mundo, 1870–1879," *Journal of Inter-American Studies*, IX (1967), No. 1, pp. 127–144. Rodrigues edited a popular magazine in Portuguese, in New York, and "accepted as a fact that the U.S. was materialistic."

SECTION VIII

1. Álvarez Tabío, Fernando. *Pan-Americanism, Imperialism, and Non-Intervention* (no place, no date). A polemic by the Head of the School of Political Sciences, University of Havana, who is also Assistant Director, Institute of International Affairs, Ministry of Foreign Relations. The OAS is named "the monstrous abortion of Panamericanism."
2. Ameringer, Charles D. "Philippe Bunau-Varilla: New Light on the Panama Canal Treaty," *Hispanic American Historical Review*, XLVI (1966), pp. 28–52.
3. Blanshard, Paul. *Democracy and Empire in the Caribbean* (New York: Macmillan, 1947).
4. Buell, Raymond Leslie. "The American Occupation of Haiti," *Foreign Policy Association Information Service*, V (1929), Nos. 19–20, pp. 341–392.
5. Dean, Arthur H. *William Nelson Cromwell, 1854–1948* (New York: Ad Press, Ltd., 1957). Chapter 7 is a defense of Cromwell's connection with Panama Canal negotiations.
6. Feis, Herbert. *The Diplomacy of the Dollar: First Era, 1919–1932* (Stamford, Conn.: Archon Books, 1965).
7. Friedlander, R. A. "A Reassessment of Roosevelt's Role in the

Panamanian Revolution of 1903," *Western Political Quarterly* (June, 1966).

8. Gatell, Frank O. "The Canal in Retrospect: Some Panamanian and Colombian Views," *The Americas*, XV (1958), pp. 23–36.

9. Hanke, Lewis, *Mexico and the Caribbean*, Rev. ed. (Princeton: Van Nostrand, 1967). General account emphasizing twentieth-century developments, plus documents.

10. Healy, David F. *The United States in Cuba, 1898–1902: Generals, Politicians, and the Search for Policy* (Madison: University of Wisconsin Press, 1963).

11. Hill, Roscoe R. "American Marines in Nicaragua, 1912–1925," *Hispanic American Essays: A Memorial to James Alexander Robertson*, A. Curtis Wilgus, ed. (Chapel Hill: University of North Carolina Press, 1942), pp. 341–360.

12. Krehm, William. *Democracia y tiranías en el Caribe* (Mexico: Unión Democrática Centroamericana, 1950). A former *Time* reporter attacks nonintervention as a "cruel fraud" because it permits the existence of dictatorial regimes.

12a. Livermore, Seward W. "Battleship Diplomacy in South America, 1905–1925," *Journal of Modern History*, XVI, no. 1 (March 1944), pp. 31–48.

13. McCrocklin, James H. *Garde D'Haiti, 1915–1934: Twenty Years of Organization and Training by the United States Marine Corps* (Annapolis: The United States Naval Institute, 1956).

14. Mecham, J. Lloyd. *The United States and Inter-American Security, 1889–1960* (Austin: University of Texas Press, 1961).

15. Millspaugh, Arthur C. *Haiti Under American Control, 1915–1930* (Boston: World Peace Foundation, 1931).

15a. Plank, John N. "The Caribbean: Intervention, When and How," *Foreign Affairs*, XLIV (Oct., 1965), no. 1, pp. 37–48.

15b. Platt, D. C. M. "The Allied Coercion of Venezuela, 1902–03. A Reassessment," *Inter-American Economic Affairs*, XV, no. 4 (Spring, 1962).

16. Poppino, Rollie. *International Communism in Latin America: A History of the Movement, 1917–1963* (New York: The Free Press of Glencoe, 1964).

16a. Posner, Walter H. "American Marines in Haiti, 1915–1922," *The Americas*, XX (January, 1964), no. 3, pp. 231–266.

17. Reuter, Frank T. *Catholic Influence on American Colonial Policies, 1898–1904* (Austin: University of Texas Press, 1967).

18. Rey, Julio Adolfo. "Revolution and Liberation: A Review of Recent Literature on the Guatemala Situation," *Hispanic American Historical Review*, XXXVIII (1958), pp. 239–255. A useful review of the copious literature on the 1954 overthrow of Arbenz.

19. Smith, Robert F. *Background to Revolution: The Development of Modern Cuba* (New York: Alfred A. Knopf, 1966).
20. Stansifer, Charles L. "Application of the Tobar Doctrine to Central America," *The Americas*, XXIII (1967), No. 3, pp. 251–272. Carlos Tobar, one-time foreign minister of Ecuador, proposed that governments coming into power through "revolution against the constitutional order" be denied recognition.
21. Wilson, Charles Morrow. *Empire in Green and Gold: The Story of the American Banana Trade* (New York: Henry Holt, 1948).

SECTION IX

A. *General*

1. Bello, José Maria. *A History of Modern Brazil, 1889–1964*. Tr. James L. Taylor (Stanford: Stanford University Press, 1966).
2. Burns, E. Bradford. *Documentary History of Brazil* (New York: Alfred A. Knopf, 1966).
3. Cruz Costa, João. *A History of Ideas in Brazil: The Development of Philosophy in Brazil and the Evolution of National History.* Tr. Suzette Macedo (Berkeley: University of California Press, 1964).
4. Dulles, John W. F. *Vargas of Brazil: A Political Biography* (Austin: University of Texas Press, 1967).
5. Furtado, Celso. *The Economic Growth of Brazil: A Survey from Colonial to Modern Times* (Berkeley: University of California Press, 1963).
6. Peixoto, Alzira Vargas do Amaral. *Getúlio Vargas, meu pai* (Rio de Janeiro: Editôra Globo, 1960).
7. Silva, Hélio. *O ciclo de Vargas* (Rio de Janeiro: Editôra Civilização Brasileira, 1964–   ). A large work now in progress. Five volumes had appeared by early 1967.
8. Skidmore, Thomas E. *Politics in Brazil, 1930–1964: An Experiment in Democracy* (New York: Oxford University Press, 1967).
9. Smith, Carleton Sprague, ed. "Perspective on Brazil," *Atlantic Monthly* (1956). A supplement devoted largely to Brazilian Culture.
10. Wagley, Charles. "The Brazilian Revolution: Social Change in Brazil since 1930," in Lyman Bryson, ed., *Social Change in Latin America Today: The Implication for United States Policy* (New York: Vintage Press, 1960).

B. *Special Topics*

11. Alexander, Robert. *Communism in Latin America* (New Brunswick, N.J.: Rutgers University Press, 1957). See Chap. VII (pp. 93–134) on "Prestes and the Partido Comunista do Brasil."

12. Dulles, John W. F. "Farewell Messages of Getúlio Vargas," *Hispanic American Historical Review*, XLIV (1964), pp. 551–553.

13. Havighurst, Robert, and J. Roberto Moreira. *Society and Education in Brazil* (Pittsburgh: University of Pittsburgh Press, 1965).

14. Freitas, Marcondes, J. V. "Social Legislation in Brazil," in *Brazil: Portrait of Half a Continent*, eds. T. Lynn Smith and Alexander Marchant (New York: The Dryden Press, 1951), pp. 385–399.

15. Hambloch, Ernest. *His Majesty the President of Brazil* (New York: Dutton, 1935). A frank but incomplete picture of politics in the pre-Vargas period by a former British commercial attaché in Rio. He underestimates Vargas and also denounces the republican politicians. His ideal is Pedro II's empire, which he believes was a halcyon era.

16. Haring, C. H. "Vargas Returns to Brazil," *Foreign Affairs*, XXIX (1951), pp. 308–314. On Vargas' election victory in October, 1950.

17. Jaguaribe, Hélio. "The Dynamics of Brazilian Nationalism," *Obstacles to Change in Latin America*, Claudio Veliz, ed. (London: Oxford University Press, 1965), pp. 170–172.

18. Leite, Aureliano. "Causas e objetivos de revolução de 1932," *Revista de História*, XIII (São Paulo, 1962), pp. 139–144.

19. Leite Linhares, Maria Yedda. "Vargas: A tomada do poder," *Tempo Brasileiro*, año IV (1966), No. 8, pp. 39–55. Introduction to a book in preparation on *Getúlio Vargas e a revolução de 1930*.

20. Lipson, Leslie. "Government in Contemporary Brazil," *The Canadian Journal of Economics and Political Science*, XXII (May, 1956), pp. 183–198.

21. Putnam, Samuel. "The Vargas Dictatorship in Brazil," *Science and Society*, V (1941), pp. 97–116. A condemnation of the Vargas regime as fascism, in large part established and supported by the United States.

22. Saunders, John V. D. "A Revolution of Agreement among Friends: The End of the Vargas Era," *Hispanic American Historical Review*, XLIV (1964), pp. 197–213.

23. Skidmore, Thomas E. *Politics in Brazil, 1930–1964: An Experiment in Democracy* (New York: Oxford University Press, 1967), pp. 3–47.

24. Wirth, John D. "Tenentismo in the Brazilian Revolution of

1930," *Hispanic American Historical Review*, XLIV (1964), pp. 161–179.
25. Young, Jordan M. *The Brazilian Revolution of 1930 and the Aftermath* (New Brunswick, N.J.: Rutgers University Press, 1967).

SECTION X

A. *General*

1. Cline, Howard F., ed. *Latin American History: Essays in Its Study and Teaching*, 2 vols. (Austin: University of Texas Press, 1967). An anthology illustrating the development of the field.
2. Fetter, Frank W. "A South American Myth: The Christ of the Andes Inscription," *Hispanic American Historical Review*, XII (1932), pp. 87–92.
3. Gandía, Enrique de. *Nueva historia de América. Las épocas de libertad y antilibertad desde la independencia*. (Buenos Aires: Editorial Claridad, 1946). One section is entitled "Interpretaciones de la historia de América" and presents the views of eminent historians of various countries.
4. Simmons, Merle E. "Una polémica sobre la independencia de Hispano-America," *Boletín de la Academia Nacional de Historia*, XXX (Caracas, 1948), No. 117, pp. 82–125. A polemic between Blanco White and Servando Mier in 1811.

B. *On Individual Historians or Countries*

5. Bosch García, Carlos. *Historia de las relaciones entre México y los Estados Unidos, 1819–1848* (Mexico: Escuela Nacional de Ciencias Políticas y Sociales, 1961). The bibliography is organized according to the objectivity or patriotism of the writers included.
6. Briceño Iragorry, Mario. *Introducción y defensa de nuestra historia* (Caracas, 1952).
7. Bronner, Fred. "Jose de la Riva-Agüero, Peruvian Historian," *Hispanic American Historical Review*, XXXVI (1956), pp. 490–502.
8. Burns, E. Bradford, ed. *Perspectives on Brazilian History* (New York: Columbia University Press, 1967). Translation of some basic studies on Brazilian history, plus an essay by the editor on Brazilian historiography.
9. Campos, Pedro Moacyr de. "Esboço da historiografia brasileira

dos séculos XIX e XX," in Jean Glénisson, *Iniciação aos estudos históricos* (São Paulo: Diffusão Européia do Livro, 1961), pp. 250–293.

10. Carbia, Rómulo D. *Historia crítica de la historiografía argentina (desde sus orígenes en el siglo XVI)* (Buenos Aires: Universidad de la Plata, 1939).

11. Carrera Damas, Germán. *Tres temas de historia* (Caracas: Imprenta Universitaria, 1961). Analyzes the social measures of the Second Patriot Republic (1813–1814), Mario Briceño-Iragorry's novel, *Los Riberas* (Caracas-Madrid, 1957) as a source for the rise of the Venezuelan "burguesía," and the state of history as a university discipline in the universities of Venezuela.

12. ———. *Historia de la historiografía venezolana. Textos para su estudio* (Caracas: Universidad Central de Venezuela, 1961). An impressive collection of documents and studies.

13. ———. *Historiografía marxista venezolana y otros temas* (Caracas: Universidad Central de Venezuela, 1967).

14. Corbitt, Duvon C. "Cuban Revisionist Interpretations of Cuba's Struggle for Independence," *Hispanic American Historical Review*, XLII (1963), pp. 395–404.

15. ———. "Historical Publications of the Oficina del Historiador de la Ciudad de la Habana," *ibid.*, XXXV (1955), pp. 492–497. Detailed commentary on the work of Emilio Roig de Leuchsenring, one of the most vigorous critics of United States policy.

16. Delpar, Helen. "Las ideas históricas de Jorge Basadre," *Revista Chilena de Historia y Geografía*, No. 131 (1963), pp. 225–248.

17. Gandía, Enrique de. *La revisión de la historia argentina* (Buenos Aires: Ediciones Antonio Zamora, 1952). Philosophies, interpretations, and techniques of Argentine historians.

18. Hilton, Stanley E. "Argentine Neutrality, Sept., 1930–June, 1940: A Reexamination," *The Americas* (1966), pp. 227–257. Argues that Argentina was willing to aid in the struggle against Nazism prior to the fall of France.

19. Lecuna, Vicente. "La obra de Madariaga sobre Bolívar," *Revista Nacional de Cultura*, año 12, No. 87–88 (Caracas, 1951), pp. 9–32. Criticism by the leading Venezuelan Bolivarist.

20. McGann, Thomas F. "The Assassination of Sucre and Its Significance in Colombian History, 1828–1848," *Hispanic American Historical Review*, XXX (1950), pp. 259–289. The author convicts Obando of the crime. See also Luis Martínez-Delgado and Thomas F. McGann, "The Assassination of Sucre: Communications to the Editor," *ibid.*, XXXI (1951), pp. 520–529.

21. Pereyra, Carlos. *México falsificado*, 2 vols. (Mexico: Polis, 1950). Aims to correct the "falsehoods" and exaggerations originating in the "Revolutionist" version of Mexican history.

22. Smith, Robert Freeman. "Twentieth-Century Cuban Historiography," *Hispanic American Historical Review*, XLIV (1964), pp. 44–73.
23. Tobar Donoso, Julio. "González Suárez, defensor por excelencia en el Ecuador de la Libertad de la iglesia," *Boletín de la Academia Nacional de Historia*, XXIV (Quito, 1945), pp. 147–200. On this outstanding Ecuadorian historian, see also Nicolás Jiménez, *Biografía del ilustrísimo Federico González Suárez* (Quito: Publicaciones del Archivo Municipal, 1937).
24. Warren, Harris Gaylord. "The Paraguayan Image of the War of the Triple Alliance," *The Americas*, XIX (1962), pp. 3–20. A revisionist interpretation of a subject that merits more investigation. The popular thesis that the war was precipitated by the ambitions of the imperialistic dictator of Paraguay, Francisco Solano López, is now challenged by the thesis that the true causes were the dictator's fears of Brazilian advances upsetting the equilibrium of the Plata region and his fear of the reassertion of Porteño claims to the old viceroyalty of Río de la Plata.

C. *On Soviet Interpretations*

25. Lavretskii, I. R. "A Survey of the Hispanic American Historical Review, 1956–1958," *Hispanic American Historical Review*, XL (1960), pp. 340–360. A critical analysis by a Soviet historian. See also the remarks by J. Gregory Oswald, "A Soviet Criticism of the Hispanic American Historical Review," *ibid.*, XL (1960), pp. 337–339.
26. Mendel, Arthur P. "Current Soviet Theory of History: New Trends or Old?", *American Historical Review*, LXXII (1966), pp. 50–73. On recent changes in Soviet thinking on historical theory. Apparently a modest "thaw" is in progress.
27. Ortega y Medina, Juan A. *Historiografía soviética ibero-americanista (1945–1960)* (Mexico: Universidad Nacional Autónoma de México, 1961).
28. Richards, Edward B. "Marxism and Marxist Movements in Latin America in Recent Soviet Historical Writing," *Hispanic American Historical Review*, XLV (1965), pp. 577–590.

GENERAL BIBLIOGRAPHIC SUGGESTIONS

Knowledge of where to look for material is particularly important for Latin American history, because its publications appear in many countries and without guidance one may spend much time without visible result. Moreover, great strides have been made in this field during the last decade or so; the quantity and quality of historical publications have sharply increased, which makes the problem of finding pertinent items more serious than ever before. Great improvement may be expected a few years hence when Charles C. Griffin completes the *Guide to the Historical Literature on Latin America* he is preparing, with the assistance of a number of specialists, under the sponsorship of the Conference on Latin American History of the American Historical Association. Another basic volume now in preparation is the third edition of the standard C. K. Jones, *A Bibliography of Latin American Bibliographies*.

Everyone eventually discovers for himself his own bibliographic and reference tools based on his experience and his needs. Some basic works exist, however, and the following list, as well as the preceding "Bibliographic Suggestions," is intended to save the time of students by indicating a few of the most useful works.

I. *General*

1. *Handbook of Latin American Studies.* Harvard University Press published this annual bibliography from 1936 through 1939, and since 1940 the University of Florida Press has issued it. Prepared by the Hispanic Foundation of the Library of Congress, the *Handbook* has become an indispensable reference work. An index to the first 25 volumes will soon appear.
2. *Hispanic American Historical Review.* A quarterly, published by Duke University Press, whose volume 50 will appear in 1970. Two useful guides have been prepared: Ruth Lapham Butler, ed., *Guide to the Hispanic American Historical Review, 1918–1945* (Durham: Duke University Press, 1950); and Charles Gibson

and E. V. Niemeyer, *Guide to the Hispanic American Historical Review, 1946–1955* (Durham: Duke University Press, 1958).

The *Hispanic American Historical Review* has made an important contribution to the study of Latin America in the modern age by publishing in recent years a number of historiographic articles. Some are listed in the "Bibliographic Suggestions" in this volume. Other useful guides are:

a. Arnade, Charles W. "The Historiography of Colonial and Modern Bolivia," XLII (1962), pp. 333–384.

b. Barager, Joseph R. "The Historiography of the Río de la Plata Area Since 1830," XXXIX (1959), pp. 588–642.

c. Griffith, William J. "The Historiography of Central America since 1830," XL (1960), pp. 548–569.

d. Hoffmann, Fritz L. "Perón and After," XXXVI (1956), pp. 510–528; XXXIX (1959), 212–233.

e. Stein, Stanley J. "The Historiography of Brazil, 1808–1889," XL (1960), pp. 234–278.

f. ———. "The Tasks Ahead for Latin American Historians," XLI (1961), pp. 424–433.

g. Szászdi, Adam. "The Historiography of the Republic of Ecuador," XLIV (1964), pp. 503–550.

3. Humphreys, R. A. *Latin American History: A Guide to the Literature in English* (London: Oxford University Press, 1958). Though now somewhat out of date, this little volume brings together in an organized way reliable information on the large amount of material available in English on Latin America.

II. *Portugal and Brazil*

4. Burns, E. Bradford. "A Working Bibliography for the Study of Brazilian History," *The Americas*, XXII (1965), pp. 54–88. The most useful list for general purposes.

5. Stein, Stanley J. "The Historiography of Brazil, 1808–1889," *Hispanic American Historical Review*, XL (1960), pp. 234–278.

6. Welsh, Doris. *A Catalog of the William B. Greenlee Collection of Portuguese History and Literature and the Portuguese Materials in the Newberry Library* (Chicago: The Newberry Library, 1953). A fundamental work based upon the rich collection in the Newberry Library.

III. *Spain and Spanish America*

7. *Índice Histórico Español.* Editorial Teide, Barcelona. Established in 1953 by the late Jaime Vicens Vives, the distinguished Catalan

scholar, this annotated bibliography immediately became the best source of information on current publications relating to all periods of Spanish and Spanish American history. Despite the death of the founder in 1960, the *Índice* continues to appear.

8. Sánchez Alonso, Benito. *Fuentes de la historia española e hispanoamericana,* Third ed., 3 vols. (Madrid: Consejo Superior de Investigaciones Científicas, 1952).